APR 2 0 1999

W9-BEW-794

THIS IS NO LONGER THE PROPERTY OF THE SEATTLE PUBLIC LIBRARY

Netherlands, Belgium, Luxembourg

The complete guide, thoroughly up-to-date

Packed with details that will make your trip

The must-see sights, off and on the beaten path

What to see, what to skip

Mix-and-match vacation itineraries

City strolls, countryside adventures

Smart lodging and dining options

Essential local do's and taboos

Transportation tips, distances and directions

Key contacts, savvy travel tips

When to go, what to pack

Clear, accurate, easy-to-use maps

Books to read, videos to watch

Fodor's Travel Publications, Inc.
New York • Toronto • London • Sydney • Auckland
www.fodors.com

Fodor's The Netherlands, Belgium, Luxembourg

EDITOR: Nancy van Itallie

Editorial Contributors: Jennifer Abramsohn, David Brown, Linda Burnham, Nancy Coons, Matthew Davis, Brent Gregston, Andrew May, Helayne Schiff, M. T. Schwartzman (Gold Guide editor), Eric Sjogren, Clare Thomson.

Editorial Production: Linda K. Schmidt

Maps: David Lindroth, *cartographer*; Steven Amsterdam and Bob Blake, *map editors*

Design: Fabrizio La Rocca, *creative director*; Guido Caroti, *associate art director*; Jolie Novak, *photo editor*

Production/Manufacturing: Robert B. Shields

Cover Photograph: Peter Guttman

Copyright

Copyright © 1999 by Fodor's Travel Publications, Inc.

Fodor's is a registered trademark of Random House, Inc.

All rights reserved under International and Pan-American Copyright Conventions. Published in the United States by Fodor's Travel Publications, Inc., a subsidiary of Random House, Inc., New York, and simultaneously in Canada by Random House of Canada, Limited, Toronto. Distributed by Random House, Inc., of New York.

No maps, illustrations, or other portions of this book may be reproduced in any form without written permission from the publisher.

Fourth Edition

ISBN 0–679–00060–7

Special Sales

Fodor's Travel Publications are available at special discounts for bulk purchases for sales promotions or premiums. Special editions, including personalized covers, excerpts of existing guides, and corporate imprints, can be created in large quantities for special needs. For more information, contact your local bookseller or write to Special Markets, Fodor's Travel Publications, 201 East 50th Street, New York, NY 10022. Inquiries from Canada should be directed to your local Canadian bookseller or sent to Random House of Canada, Ltd., Marketing Department, 2775 Matheson Boulevard East, Mississauga, Ontario L4W 4P7. Inquiries from the United Kingdom should be sent to Fodor's Travel Publications, 20 Vauxhall Bridge Road, London SW1V 2SA, England.

PRINTED IN THE UNITED STATES OF AMERICA

10 9 8 7 6 5 4 3 2 1

CONTENTS

Maps

ON THE ROAD WITH FODOR'S

WHEN I PLAN A VACATION, the first thing I do is cast around among my friends and colleagues to find someone who's just been where I'm going. That's because there's no substitute for a recommendation from a good friend who knows your tastes, your budget, and your circumstances, someone who's just been there. Unfortunately, such friends are few and far between. So it's nice to know that there's *Fodor's The Netherlands, Belgium, Luxembourg.*

In the first place, this book won't stay home when you hit the road. It will accompany you every step of the way, steering you away from wrong turns and wrong choices and never expecting a thing in return. Most important of all, it's written and assiduously updated by the kind of people you *would* hit up for travel tips if you knew them. They're as choosy as your pickiest friend, except they've probably seen a lot more of the Netherlands, Belgium, and Luxembourg. In these pages, they don't send you chasing down every town and sight in these countries but have instead selected the best ones, the ones that are worthy of your time and money. To make it easy for you to put it all together in the time you have, they've created short, medium, and long itineraries and, in cities, neighborhood walks that you can mix and match in a snap. Will this be the vacation of your dreams? We hope so.

About Our Writers

Our success in helping to make your trip the best of all possible vacations is a credit to the hard work of our extraordinary writers and editors.

Jennifer Abramsohn, now based in Cologne, Germany, has written for *The Wall Street Journal* and writes for other newspapers as well as magazines and on-line publications. Her frequent visits to nearby Luxembourg enabled her to update the chapter on that country for Fodor's this year.

Linda Burnham, who wrote the Netherlands chapter, began her love affair with Amsterdam—and travel—perched on a settee in the lobby of the Amstel Hotel at the beginning of a post-college Eurail tour. Six years on staff with KLM later turned Holland into more than a destination: It became a second home. Her Dutch friends say she knows their country better than they do. She has co-authored several books about the Netherlands, the Caribbean, and the United States, and has written for *Travel & Leisure, Harper's Bazaar, Modern Bride,* and *Condé Nast Traveler.*

Having grown up in Michigan and worked as a writer and editor in New York, Chicago, and Little Rock, **Nancy Coons,** who wrote the introduction, the Luxembourg chapter and parts of the Belgium chapter, and two portrait essays, moved to Europe in 1987. She contributes regularly to Fodor's publications and has written features on European topics for *The Wall Street Journal, Opera News,* and *National Geographic Traveler.*

Born on New Year's Eve in London's East End and adopted on April Fool's Day, **Matthew Davis** is happy to go where fortune leads him. Most recently, it's been Belgium, where he works as production editor for *The Bulletin,* Europe's top English-language magazine. An expert on the country's cultural life, he's written for several magazines, including *Screen International,* and revised the Belgium chapter in collaboration with Clare Thomson. "Belgium is one of Europe's most switched-on countries," he says. "The dance and music scenes are thriving, and the cafe culture is second to none."

Brent Gregston, who revised the Gold Guide and parts of the Netherlands chapter, lives in Amsterdam. After studying philosophy in Freiburg, Germany, he has worked as a translator for the U.S. State Department and later as an editor for an on-line travel site.

Andrew May was born and raised in northeast England. At first he put his training in violin, piano, musicology, and marketing to work as a classical music reviewer. Moving to Amsterdam in 1992, he diversified into translation, wrote his own travel guide, and started contributing to Fodor's guidebooks, including revising parts of the Netherlands chapter. Despite an unshakeable British accent when using their language, he hopes never to cease surprising the Dutch with more knowledge of the Netherlands than they usually expect to amass in a lifetime.

After 25 years in Belgium, **Eric Sjogren**, who wrote parts of the Belgium chapter, knows most of its nooks and crannies. He has lived in Stockholm, New York, London, and Frankfurt, but Brussels to him is "the most liveable city I know." Eric is a contributor to the *New York Times* Travel Section and writes on travel, food, business, and the arts for magazines in Scandinavia and the United States.

Clare Thomson, who updated the Belgium chapter in collaboration with Matthew Davis, was brought up in London and studied at Cambridge University. After two years in Paris as researcher and dog-handler for *The New Yorker*'s European correspondent, Thomson went in search of her mother's Baltic roots, a journey that resulted in her first book, *The Singing Revolution.* Staff writer for Brussels's English-language magazine *The Bulletin* since 1991, Thomson has filed news and travel reports for leading British newspapers and London's *Time Out.* "Brussels," says Thomson, still smarting from the glitzy arrogance of the French capital, "is a relaxed, hospitable, and endlessly surprising city."

Connections

We're pleased that the American Society of Travel Agents continues to endorse Fodor's as its guidebook of choice. ASTA is the world's largest and most influential travel trade association, operating in more than 170 countries, with 27,000 members pledged to adhere to a strict code of ethics reflecting the Society's motto, "Integrity in Travel." ASTA shares Fodor's devotion to providing smart, honest travel information and advice to travelers, and we've long recommended that our readers—even those who have guidebooks and traveling friends—consult ASTA member agents for the experience and professionalism they bring to your vacation planning.

On Fodor's Web site (www.fodors.com), check out the new Resource Center, an online companion to the Gold Guide section of this book, complete with useful hot links to related sites. In our forums, you can also get lively advice from other travelers and more great tips from Fodor's experts worldwide.

How to Use This Book

Organization

Up front is the **Gold Guide,** an easy-to-use section arranged alphabetically by topic. Under each listing you'll find tips and information that will help you accomplish what you need to in The Netherlands, Belgium, and Luxembourg. You'll also find addresses and telephone numbers of organizations and companies that offer destination-related services and detailed information and publications.

The first chapter in the guide, Destination: The Netherlands, Belgium, and Luxembourg, helps get you in the mood for your trip. New and Noteworthy cues you in on trends and happenings, What's Where gets you oriented, Pleasures and Pastimes describes the activities and sights that make these countries unique, Great Itineraries lays out a selection of complete trips, Fodor's Choice showcases our top picks, and Festivals and Seasonal Events alerts you to special events you'll want to seek out.

Chapters in *Fodor's The Netherlands, Belgium, Luxembourg* focus on the countries' main cities and the most interesting provinces within each country. The sections on the cities begin with exploring the sights, subdivided by neighborhood; after an introductory overview, each subsection recommends a walking tour then lists the top sights in alphabetical order. This allows you to find must-sees in a snap and helps chart a personalized itinerary. Following the exploring highlights of each main city are sections on dining, lodging, nightlife and the arts, outdoor activities and sports, and shopping. Regional sections are divided by geographical area and each kicks off with a suggested itinerary; within each area, towns are covered in logical geographical order, and attractive stretches of road and minor points of interest between them are indicated by the designation *En Route.* Throughout, Off the Beaten Path sights appear after the places from which they are most easily accessible. And within town sections, all restaurants and lodgings are grouped together.

To help you decide what to visit in the time you have, all chapters begin with our recommended itineraries. The A to Z section that ends each country chapter covers getting there, getting around, and basic information about the country such as currency, telephones, and holidays. It also provides helpful contacts and resources.

At the end of the book you'll find Portraits, including followed by suggestions for pretrip research, from recommended reading to movies on tape that use these countries as a backdrop.

Icons and Symbols

Our special recommendations

✕	Restaurant
🏨	Lodging establishment
✕🏨	Lodging establishment whose restaurant warrants a special trip
☺	Good for kids (rubber duck)
☞	Sends you to another section of the guide for more information
⊠	Address
☎	Telephone number
☉	Opening and closing times
💷	Admission prices (those we give apply only to adults; substantially reduced fees are almost always available for children, students, and senior citizens)

Numbers in white and black circles ③ ❸ that appear on the maps, in the margins, and within the tours correspond to one another.

Dining and Lodging

The restaurants and lodgings we list are the cream of the crop in each price range. Price charts appear near the beginning of each chapter in our country-wide overviews in the Pleasures and Pastimes section of each country chapter.

Hotel Facilities

We always list the facilities that are available—but we don't specify whether they cost extra: When pricing accommodations, always ask what's included. Assume that hotels operate on the **European Plan** (EP, with no meals) unless we specify that they use the **Continental Plan** (CP, with a Continental breakfast daily) or that they require full- or half-board arrangements.

Restaurant Reservations and Dress Codes

Reservations are always a good idea; we note only when they're essential or when they are not accepted. Book as far ahead as you can, and reconfirm as soon as you arrive. Unless otherwise noted, the restaurants listed are open daily for lunch and dinner. We mention dress only when men are required to wear a jacket or a jacket and tie.

Credit Cards

The following abbreviations are used: **AE**, American Express; **DC**, Diners Club; **MC**, MasterCard; and **V**, Visa.

Don't Forget to Write

You can use this book in the confidence that all prices and opening times are based on information supplied to us at press time; Fodor's cannot accept responsibility for any errors. Time inevitably brings changes, so always confirm information when it matters—especially if you're making a detour to visit a specific place.

Were the restaurants we recommended as described? Did our hotel picks exceed your expectations? Did you find a museum we recommended a waste of time? Keeping a travel guide fresh and up-to-date is a big job, and we welcome your feedback, positive *and* negative. If you have complaints, we'll look into them and revise our entries when the facts warrant it. If you've discovered a special place that we haven't included, we'll pass the information along to our correspondents and have them check it out. So send your thoughts via e-mail at editors@fodors.com (specifying the name of the book on the subject line) or on paper in care of the editor at Fodor's, 201 East 50th Street, New York, New York 10022. In the meantime, have a wonderful trip!

Karen Cure

Karen Cure
Editorial Director

The Netherlands, Belgium, and Luxembourg

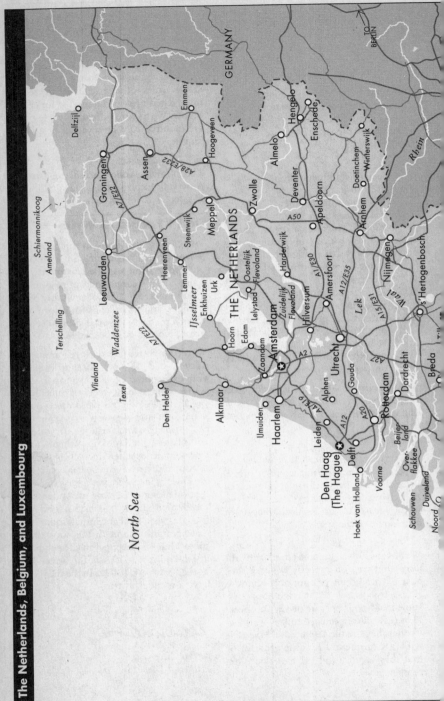

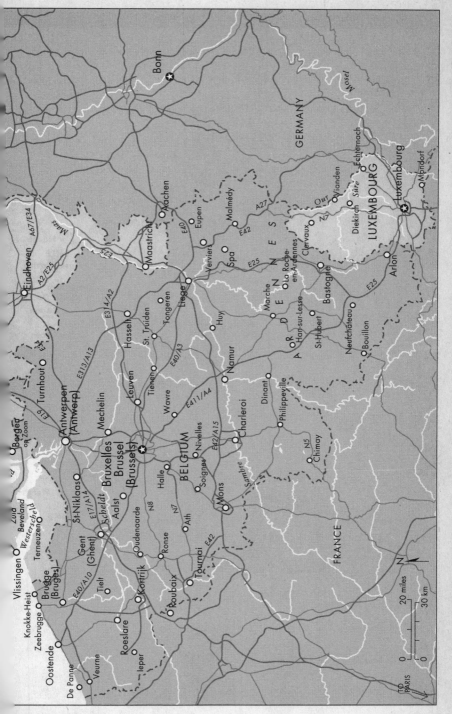

Europe

Reykjavík
ICELAND

NORWAY
Bergen

NORTHERN
IRELAND

SCOTLAND

Edinburgh

North
Sea

Skagerr

Belfast

Irish
Sea

DENMARK

IRELAND

Dublin

UNITED
KINGDOM

Hamburg

WALES

ENGLAND

NETHERLANDS

Cardiff

The Hague

Amsterdam

London

Rotterdam

GER

ATLANTIC
OCEAN

English Channel

Brussels

Bonn

BELGIUM

Frankfurt

Paris

LUXEMBOURG

FRANCE

Zürich

Mun

Bern

SWITZERLAND

Lyon

LIECHTENST

Milan

Ve

PORTUGAL

Madrid

ANDORRA

Marseille

Nice

Monte
Carlo

Florence

MONACO

Lisbon

Barcelona

Corsica

SPAIN

Seville

Granada

Balearic
Islands

Sardinia

Tyrrhe

Gibraltar

Mediterranean Sea

MOROCCO

ALGERIA

0   400 miles

0   600 km

TUNISIA

SMART TRAVEL TIPS A TO Z

Basic Information on Traveling in the Low Countries, Savvy Tips to Make Your Trip a Breeze, and Companies and Organizations to Contact

THE GOLD GUIDE / SMART TRAVEL TIPS

AIR TRAVEL

BOOKING YOUR FLIGHT

Price is just one factor to consider when booking a flight: frequency of service and even a carrier's safety record are often just as important. Major airlines offer the greatest number of departures. Smaller airlines—including regional and no-frills airlines—usually have a limited number of flights daily. On the other hand, so-called low-cost airlines usually are cheaper, and their fares impose fewer restrictions, such as advance-purchase requirements. Safety-wise, low-cost carriers as a group have a good history—about equal to that of major carriers.

When you book, **look for nonstop flights** and **remember that "direct" flights stop at least once.** Try to **avoid connecting flights,** which require a change of plane. Two airlines may jointly operate a connecting flight, so ask if your airline operates every segment—you may find that your preferred carrier flies you only part of the way. International flights on a country's flag carrier are almost always nonstop; U.S. airlines often fly direct.

Ask your airline if it offers electronic ticketing, which eliminates all paperwork. There's no ticket to pick up or misplace. You go directly to the gate and give the agent your confirmation number instead of waiting in line at the counter while precious minutes tick by.

CARRIERS

When flying internationally, you must usually choose between a domestic carrier, the national flag carrier of the country you are visiting, and a foreign carrier from a third country. You may, for example, choose to fly KLM Royal Dutch to the Netherlands or Sabena to Belgium. National flag carriers have the greatest number of nonstops. Domestic carriers may have

better connections to your home town and serve a greater number of gateway cities. Third-party carriers may have a price advantage.

Both **KLM** and **Sabena** airlines have flights between Amsterdam and Brussels, KLM has flights from Amsterdam to Luxembourg, and Sabena has flights from Brussels to Luxembourg. While the Netherlands has domestic air service, Belgium and Luxembourg do not.

➤MAJOR AIRLINES: **Air Canada** (☎ 800/776–3000). **American** (☎ 800/433–7300). **British Airways** (☎ 800/247–9297 to the Netherlands only). **Delta** (☎ 800/221–1212). **KLM Royal Dutch** (☎ 800/777–5553). **Martinair** (☎ 800/366–4655). **Sabena** (☎ 800/955–2000). **TWA** (☎ 800/892–4141). **United** (☎ 800/241–6522).

CONSOLIDATORS

Consolidators buy tickets for scheduled international flights at reduced rates from the airlines, then sell them at prices that beat the best fare available directly from the airlines, usually without restrictions. Sometimes you can even get your money back if you need to return the ticket. Carefully read the fine print detailing penalties for changes and cancellations, and **confirm your consolidator reservation with the airline.**

➤CONSOLIDATORS: **Cheap Tickets** (☎ 800/377–1000). **Discount Travel Network** (☎ 800/576–1600). **Unitravel** (☎ 800/325–2222). **Up & Away Travel** (☎ 212/889–2345). **World Travel Network** (☎ 800/409–6753).

CUTTING COSTS

The least-expensive airfares to the Netherlands, Belgium, and Luxembourg are priced for round-trip travel and usually must be purchased in advance. It's smart to **call a number of airlines, and when you are quoted a good price, book it on the spot**—the same fare may not be available the next day. Airlines generally allow you to change your return date for a fee. If you don't use your ticket, you can apply the cost toward the purchase of a new ticket, again for a small charge. However, most low-fare tickets are nonrefundable. To get the lowest airfare, **check different routings.** Compare prices of flights to and from different airports if your destination or home city has more than one gateway. Also price off-peak flights, which may be significantly less expensive.

Travel agents, especially those who specialize in finding the lowest fares (☞ Discounts & Deals, *below*), can be especially helpful when booking a plane ticket. When you're quoted a price, **ask your agent if the price is likely to drop any lower.** Good agents know the seasonal fluctuations of airfares and can usually anticipate a sale or fare war. However, waiting can be risky: The fare could go *up* as seats become scarce, and you may wait so long that your preferred flight sells out. A wait-and-see strategy works best if your plans are flexible. If you must arrive and depart on certain dates, don't delay.

CHECK IN & BOARDING

Airlines routinely overbook planes, assuming that not everyone with a ticket will show up, but sometimes everyone does. When that happens, airlines ask for volunteers to give up their seats. In return these volunteers usually get a certificate for a free flight and are rebooked on the next flight out. If there are not enough volunteers, the airline must choose who will be denied boarding. The first to be bumped are passengers who checked in late and those flying on discounted tickets, so **get to the gate and check in as early as possible,** especially during peak periods.

Although the trend on international flights is to drop reconfirmation requirements, many airlines still ask you to reconfirm each leg of your international itinerary. Failure to do so may result in your reservation's being canceled.

Always **bring a government-issued photo ID to the airport.** You may be asked to show it before you are allowed to check in.

ENJOYING THE FLIGHT

For more legroom, **request an emergency-aisle seat.** Don't sit in the row in front of the emergency aisle or in front of a bulkhead, where seats may not recline.

If you don't like airline food, **ask for special meals when booking.** These can be vegetarian, low-cholesterol, or kosher, for example.

When flying internationally, try to maintain a normal routine, to help fight jet-lag. At night, **get some sleep.** By day, **eat light meals, drink water (not alcohol), and move around the cabin** to stretch your legs.

Many carriers have prohibited smoking on all of their international flights; others allow smoking only on certain routes or certain departures, so **contact your carrier regarding its smoking policy.**

FLYING TIMES

Flying time to the Netherlands and Belgium is about seven hours from New York and 10½ hours from Los Angeles (there are no nonstop flights to Luxembourg).

HOW TO COMPLAIN

If your baggage goes astray or your flight arrangements go awry, complain right away. Most carriers require that you **file a claim immediately.**

➤AIRLINE COMPLAINTS: U.S. Department of Transportation **Aviation Consumer Protection Division** (✉ C-75, Room 4107, Washington, DC 20590, ☎ 202/366–2220). **Federal Aviation Administration Consumer Hotline** (☎ 800/322–7873).

AIRPORTS

The major airports are **Schiphol Airport** in Amsterdam, **Brussels National Airport** at Zaventem, and **Findel Airport** in Luxembourg-Ville.

➤AIRPORT INFORMATION: **Schiphol Airport** (☎ 31/20/601–9111). **Brussels National Airport** (☎ 32/2/753–2111). **Findel Airport** (☎ 352/47981).

BIKE TRAVEL

BIKES IN FLIGHT

Most airlines will accommodate bikes as luggage, provided they are dismantled and put into a box. Call to see if your airline sells bike boxes (about $5; bike bags are at least $100) although you can often pick them up free at bike shops. On international flights you can sometimes substitute a bike for a piece of checked luggage for free; otherwise, it will cost about $100. Domestic and Canadian airlines charge a $25–$50 fee.

BOAT & FERRY TRAVEL

➤FROM THE U.K.: Hoverspeed LTD (☎ 01843/595522) has services between Dover and Oostende with up to eight daily round trips. **P&O North Sea Ferries** (✉ King George Dock, Hedon Rd., Hull HU9 5QA, UK, ☎ 01482/377177) operates overnight ferry services from Hull to Zeebrugge and Rotterdam, and **Stena Line** (✉ Charter House, Park St., Ashford, Kent TN24 BEXUK, ☎ 01233/647047) operates the car ferry service between Harwich in Essex and Hoek van Holland.

BUS TRAVEL

Bus service among the Benelux countries is minimal. *See* individual country chapters for specific availability.

➤FROM THE U.K.: You can travel from London and between Brussels and Amsterdam (but not between cities in the same country) on **Eurolines** (✉ 4 Cardiff Rd., Luton, Bedfordshire, LU11PP, UK, ☎ 0990/143219; ☎ 540/298–1395 in U.S.).

DISCOUNT PASSES

If you're planning to travel extensively in Europe, it may make sense to invest in a **Eurolines Pass** for unlimited travel between 29 major cities including Amsterdam and Brussels. **Point-to-Point** tickets between 400 cities in Europe are good value for fewer stops.

➤PASSES & INFORMATION: **Eurolines** (☎ 0171/730–8235).

BUSINESS HOURS

See A to Z sections in individual country chapters.

CAMERAS & COMPUTERS

EQUIPMENT PRECAUTIONS

Always **keep your film, tape, or computer disks out of the sun.** Carry an extra supply of batteries, and **be prepared to turn on your camera, camcorder, or laptop** to prove to security personnel that the device is real. Always **ask for hand inspection of film**, which becomes clouded after successive exposure to airport X-ray machines, and **keep videotapes and computer disks away from metal detectors.**

➤PHOTO HELP: Kodak Information Center (☎ 800/242–2424). *Kodak Guide to Shooting Great Travel Pictures,* available in bookstores or from Fodor's Travel Publications (☎ 800/533–6478; $16.50 plus $4 shipping).

CAR RENTAL

The major car rental firms have booths at the airports. This is convenient, but the airports charge rental companies a fee that is passed on to customers, so you may want to wait until you arrive at the downtown locations of rental firms. Consider also whether you want to get off a transatlantic flight and into an unfamiliar car in an unfamiliar city.

Rates in the Netherlands, Belgium, and Luxembourg vary from company to company; daily rates for budget companies start at approximately $40 for an economy car including collision insurance. This does not include mileage, airport fee, and 17.5% VAT tax. Weekly rates often include unlimited mileage.

➤MAJOR AGENCIES: **Alamo** (☎ 800/522–9696, 0800/272–2000 in the U.K.). **Avis** (☎ 800/331–1084, 800/879–2847 in Canada, 008/225–533 in Australia). **Budget** (☎ 800/527–0700, 0800/181181 in the U.K.). **Dollar** (☎ 800/800–4000; 0990/565656 in the U.K., where it is known as Eurodollar). **Hertz** (☎ 800/654–3001, 800/263–0600 in Canada, 0345/555888 in the U.K., 03/9222–2523 in Australia, 03/358–6777 in New Zealand). **National InterRent** (☎ 800/227–3876; 0345/222525 in the U.K., where it is known as Europcar InterRent).

CUTTING COSTS

To get the best deal, **book through a travel agent who is willing to shop around.**

Also **ask your travel agent about a company's customer-service record.** How has the company responded to late plane arrivals and vehicle mishaps? Are there often lines at the rental counter? If you're traveling during a holiday period, does a confirmed reservation guarantee you a car?

Be sure to **look into wholesalers,** companies that do not own fleets but rent in bulk from those that do and often offer better rates than traditional car-rental operations. Prices are best during off-peak periods. Rentals booked through wholesalers must be paid for before you leave the United States.

➤RENTAL WHOLESALERS: **Auto Europe** (☎ 207/842–2000 or 800/223–5555, FAX 800–235–6321). **DER Travel Services** (✉ ☎ 800/782–2424, FAX 800/282–7474 for information or 800/860–9944 for brochures). **Europe by Car** (☎ 212/581–3040 or 800/223–1516, FAX 212/246–1458). **Kemwel Holiday Autos** (☎ 914/835–5555 or 800/678–0678, FAX 914/835–5126).

INSURANCE

When driving a rented car you are generally responsible for any damage to or loss of the vehicle. Before you rent, **see what coverage you already have** under the terms of your personal auto-insurance policy and credit cards.

Collision policies that car-rental companies sell for European rentals typically do not cover stolen vehicles. Before you buy additional coverage for theft, check with your credit-card company and personal auto insurance—you may already be covered.

REQUIREMENTS

In the Netherlands, Belgium, and Luxembourg your own driver's license is acceptable. An International Driver's Permit is a good idea; it's available from the American or Canadian automobile association, and, in the United Kingdom, from the Automobile Association or Royal Automobile Club. These international permits are universally recognized, and having one in your wallet may save you a problem with the local authorities.

SURCHARGES

Before you pick up a car in one city and leave it in another, **ask about drop-off charges or one-way service fees,** which can be substantial. Note, too, that some rental agencies charge extra if you return the car before the time specified in your contract. To avoid a hefty refueling fee, **fill the tank just before you turn in the car,** but be aware that gas stations near the rental outlet may overcharge.

CAR TRAVEL

A network of well-maintained superhighways and other roads covers the three countries, making car travel convenient. Traffic can be heavy around the major cities, especially on the roads to southern Europe in late June and late July, when many Belgians begin their vacations, and on those approaching the North Sea beaches on summer weekends.

AUTO CLUBS

➤IN AUSTRALIA: **Australian Automobile Association** (☎ 06/247–7311).

➤IN CANADA: **Canadian Automobile Association** (CAA, ☎ 613/247–0117).

➤IN NEW ZEALAND: **New Zealand Automobile Association** (☎ 09/377–4660).

➤IN THE U.K.: **Automobile Association** (AA, ☎ 0990/500–600), **Royal Automobile Club** (RAC, ☎ 0990/722–722 for membership, 0345/121–345 for insurance).

➤IN THE U.S.: **American Automobile Association** (☎ 800/564–6222).

FROM THE U.K.

From Calais, you can choose to drive along the coast in the direction of Oostende or via Lille and Tournai toward Ghent, Antwerp, and Amsterdam; or toward Mons and Brussels; or toward Namur and Luxembourg.

ROAD MAPS

Michelin maps are regularly updated and are the best countrywide maps;

they offer the advantage of being consistent with Michelin maps of other countries you may visit. They are available at newsdealers and bookshops. Free city maps are generally available at tourist offices, and more complete city guides can be bought in bookshops. Gas stations near borders generally sell a variety of more detailed maps.

RULES OF THE ROAD

Be sure to observe speed limits. In the Netherlands, the speed limit is 120 kph (74 mph) on superhighways, 100 kph (60 mph) on urban-area highways, and 50 kph (30 mph) on suburban roads. On motorways in Belgium, the speed limit is 120 kph (74 mph), but the cruising speed is mostly about 140 kph (about 87 mph). In Luxembourg, the speed limit on motorways is 120 kph (74 mph), but most drivers seem to treat that as a minimum!

For safe driving, go with the flow, stay in the slow lane unless you want to overtake, and make way for faster cars wanting to pass you. In cities and towns, approach crossings with care; local drivers may exercise the principle of priority for traffic from the right with some abandon.

THE CHANNEL TUNNEL

Short of flying, the "Chunnel" is the fastest way to cross the English Channel: 35 minutes from Folkestone to Calais, 60 minutes from motorway to motorway, or 3 hours from London's Waterloo Station to Paris's Gare du Nord.

➤CAR TRANSPORT: Le Shuttle (☎ 0990/353535 in the U.K.).

➤PASSENGER SERVICE: In the U.K., Eurostar (☎ 0345/881881), InterCity Europe (✉ Victoria Station, London, ☎ 0171/834–2345, 0171/828–0892 for credit-card bookings). In the U.S., BritRail Travel (☎ 800/677–8585), Rail Europe (☎ 800/942–4866).

CHILDREN & TRAVEL

CHILDREN IN THE NETHERLANDS, BELGIUM, AND LUXEMBOURG

Be sure to plan ahead and **involve your youngsters** as you outline your trip. When packing, include things to keep them busy en route. On sightseeing days try to schedule activities of special interest to your children. If you are renting a car don't forget to **arrange for a car seat** when you reserve.

➤LOCAL INFORMATION: In Luxembourg, the **National Tourist Office** (☞ Visitor Information, *below*) publishes a free pamphlet listing available holiday apartments and houses and all their facilities. There's also a new brochure for "Rural Holidays" listing a number of farms that take in visitors.

FLYING

If your children are two or older, **ask about children's airfares.** As a general rule, infants under two not occupying a seat fly at greatly reduced fares or even for free.

The adult baggage allowance usually applies to children paying half or more of the adult fare. When booking, **ask about carry-on allowances for those traveling with infants.** In general, for babies charged 10% of the adult fare you are allowed one carry-on bag and a collapsible stroller, which may have to be checked; you may be limited to less if the flight is full.

Experts agree that it's a good idea to use safety seats aloft for children weighing less than 40 pounds. Airlines, however, can set their own policies: U.S. carriers allow FAA-approved models but usually require that you buy a ticket, even if your child would otherwise ride free, as the seats must be strapped into regular seats. Airline rules vary, so it's important to **check your airline's policy about using safety seats during take-off and landing.** Safety seats cannot obstruct the movement of other passengers in the row, so get an appropriate seat assignment as early as possible.

When making your reservation, **request children's meals or a free-standing bassinet** if you need them; the latter are available only to those seated at the bulkhead, where there's enough legroom. Remember, however, that bulkhead seats may not have their own overhead bins, and there's no storage space in front of you—a major inconvenience.

GROUP TRAVEL

When planning to take your kids on a tour, look for companies that specialize in family travel.

➤FAMILY-FRIENDLY TOUR OPERATORS: **Families Welcome!** (✉ 92 N. Main St., Ashland, OR 97520, ☎ 541/482–6121 or 800/326–0724, FAX 541/482–0660).

Grandtravel (✉ 6900 Wisconsin Ave., Suite 706, Chevy Chase, MD 20815, ☎ 301/986–0790 or 800/247–7651) for people traveling with grandchildren ages 7–17.

HOTELS

Most hotels in the Netherlands, Belgium, and Luxembourg allow children under a certain age to stay in their parents' room at no extra charge, but others charge them as extra adults; be sure to **ask about the cutoff age for children's discounts.**

➤BEST CHOICES: At the **Best Western** hotels (☎ 800/528–1234) in Brussels, Oostende, and Brugge in Belgium; Luxembourg-Ville; and more than 40 cities in the Netherlands, children under 12 may stay free when sharing a room with two paying adults. A maximum of five persons is allowed per room. The **Intercontinental** hotels (☎ 800/327–0200) in Amsterdam, The Hague, and Luxembourg allow one child of any age to stay free in his or her parents' room. **Hilton** hotels (☎ 800/445–8667) in Amsterdam, Rotterdam, Antwerp, and Brussels also allow one child of any age to stay free in his or her parents' room. Many hotels throughout the region have family rooms.

CONSUMER PROTECTION

Whenever possible, **pay with a major credit card** so you can cancel payment or be reimbursed if there's a problem, provided that you can supply documentation. This is the best way to pay, whether you're buying travel arrangements before your trip or shopping at your destination.

If you're doing business with a particular company for the first time, **contact your local Better Business Bureau and the attorney general's offices** in your state and the company's home state, as well. Have any complaints been filed?

Finally, if you're buying a package or tour, always **consider travel insurance** that includes default coverage (☞ Insurance, *below*).

➤LOCAL BBBs: **Council of Better Business Bureaus** (✉ 4200 Wilson Blvd., Suite 800, Arlington, VA 22203, ☎ 703/276–0100, FAX 703/525–8277).

CUSTOMS & DUTIES

When shopping, **keep receipts** for all of your purchases. Upon reentering the country, **be ready to show customs officials what you've bought.** If you feel a duty is incorrect, appeal the assessment. If you object to the way your clearance was handled, get the inspector's badge number. In either case, first ask to see a supervisor, then write to the appropriate authorities, beginning with the port director at your point of entry.

IN THE NETHERLANDS, BELGIUM, AND LUXEMBOURG

For specific regulations in the Netherlands, Belgium, and Luxembourg, *see* individual chapters.

IN AUSTRALIA

Australia residents who are 18 or older may bring back $A400 worth of souvenirs and gifts (including jewelry), 250 cigarettes or 250 grams of tobacco, and 1,125 ml of alcohol (including wine, beer, and spirits). Residents under 18 may bring back $A200 worth of goods.

➤INFORMATION: **Australian Customs Service** (Regional Director, ✉ Box 8, Sydney, NSW 2001, ☎ 02/9213–2000, FAX 02/9213–4000).

IN CANADA

Canadian residents who have been out of Canada for at least 7 days may bring in C$500 worth of goods duty-free. If you've been away less than 7 days but more than 48 hours, the duty-free allowance drops to C$200; if your trip lasts 24–48 hours, the allowance is C$50. You may not pool allowances with family members. Goods claimed under the C$500

THE GOLD GUIDE / SMART TRAVEL TIPS

exemption may follow you by mail; those claimed under the lesser exemptions must accompany you. Alcohol and tobacco products may be included in the 7-day and 48-hour exemptions but not in the 24-hour exemption. If you meet the age requirements of the province or territory through which you reenter Canada, you may bring in, duty-free, 1.14 liters (40 imperial ounces) of wine or liquor *or* 24 12-ounce cans or bottles of beer or ale. If you are 16 or older you may bring in, duty-free, 200 cigarettes and 50 cigars.

You may send an unlimited number of gifts worth up to C$60 each duty-free to Canada. Label the package UNSOLICITED GIFT—VALUE UNDER $60. Alcohol and tobacco are excluded.

➤INFORMATION: **Revenue Canada** (⊠ 2265 St. Laurent Blvd. S, Ottawa, Ontario K1G 4K3, ☎ 613/993–0534, 800/461–9999 in Canada).

IN NEW ZEALAND

Although greeted with a "Haere Mai" ("Welcome to New Zealand"), homeward-bound residents with goods to declare must present themselves for inspection. If you're 17 or older, you may bring back $700 worth of souvenirs and gifts. Your duty-free allowance also includes 4.5 liters of wine or beer; one 1,125-ml bottle of spirits; and either 200 cigarettes, 250 grams of tobacco, 50 cigars, or a combo of all three up to 250 grams.

➤INFORMATION: **New Zealand Customs** (⊠ Custom House, 50 Anzac Ave., Box 29, Auckland, ☎ 09/359–6655, ☎ 09/309–2978).

IN THE U.K.

If you are a U.K. resident and your journey was wholly within the European Union (EU), you won't have to pass through customs when you return to the United Kingdom. If you plan to bring back large quantities of alcohol or tobacco, check EU limits beforehand.

➤INFORMATION: **HM Customs and Excise** (⊠ Dorset House, Stamford St., London SE1 9NG, ☎ 0171/202–4227).

IN THE U.S.

U.S. residents may bring home $400 worth of foreign goods duty-free if they've been out of the country for at least 48 hours (and if they haven't used the $400 allowance or any part of it in the past 30 days).

U.S. residents 21 and older may bring back 1 liter of alcohol duty-free. In addition, regardless of your age, you are allowed 200 cigarettes and 100 non-Cuban cigars. Antiques, which the U.S. Customs Service defines as objects more than 100 years old, enter duty-free, as do original works of art done entirely by hand, including paintings, drawings, and sculptures.

You may also send packages home duty-free: up to $200 worth of goods for personal use, with a limit of one parcel per addressee per day (and no alcohol or tobacco products or perfume worth more than $5); label the package PERSONAL USE, and attach a list of its contents and their retail value. Do not label the package UNSOLICITED GIFT, or your duty-free exemption will drop to $100. Mailed items do not affect your duty-free allowance on your return.

➤INFORMATION: **U.S. Customs Service** (Inquiries, ⊠ Box 7407, Washington, DC 20044, ☎ 202/927–6724; complaints, Office of Regulations and Rulings, ⊠ 1301 Constitution Ave. NW, Washington, DC 20229; registration of equipment, Resource Management, ⊠ 1301 Constitution Ave. NW, Washington DC 20229, ☎ 202/927–0540).

DISABILITIES & ACCESSIBILITY

ACCESS IN THE NETHERLANDS, BELGIUM, AND LUXEMBOURG

The Netherlands leads the world in providing facilities for people with disabilities. Train and bus stations are equipped with special telephones, elevators, and toilets. Visitors can obtain special passes to ensure free escort service on Dutch trains (☎ 030/230–5566). For general assistance at railway stations, contact the **NS/Nederlandse Spoorwegen** before 2 PM at least one day in advance, or by 2 PM Friday for travel on Saturday,

Sunday, Monday, or public holidays. Modern intercity train carriages have wheelchair-accessible compartments, and many have a free Red Cross wheelchair available. Train timetables are available in Braille, and some restaurants have menus in Braille. Some tourist sites also have special gardens for visitors with vision impairments. For information on accessibility in the Netherlands, and for general information relevant to travelers with disabilities, contact the national organization **De Gehandicaptenraad**.

Each year the **Netherlands Board of Tourism** (☞ Visitor Information, *below*) publishes a booklet listing hotels, restaurants, hostels and campsites, museums, and tourist attractions, as well as gas/petrol stations with 24-hour services and boat firms, with adapted facilities. For travelers with visual impairments, all Dutch paper currency is embossed with different symbols for each denomination. For information on tours and exchanges for travelers with disabilities, contact **Mobility International Nederland**.

In Belgium and Luxembourg, hotels with facilities to receive guests with disabilities are identified in guides published by national and local tourist offices. Awareness of the sensitivities of people with disabilities is generally high but has not yet impacted on the language; the words handicapé (French) and gehandicapt (Dutch) are still commonly used. Visitors with disabilities should be aware that many streets in the Benelux countries are cobblestone.

For information on facilities in Belgium, contact the **Association socialiste des personnes handicapées** or **Vlaamse Federatie voor Gehandicapten**. Two holiday complexes have facilities built especially for people with disabilities: **De Ceder** in Flanders and **Les Riezes et les Sarts** in the Ardennes.

The **Luxembourg Ministry of Health** handles provisions for people with disabilities. Most trains and buses have special seats for riders with disabilities, and parking lots have spaces reserved for people with disabilities. Contact **Info–Handicap**.

►LOCAL RESOURCES: **NS/Nederlandse Spoorwegen** (⊠ Netherlands Railways, ☎ 030/230–5566 weekdays 8–4). **De Gehandicaptenraad** (⊠ Postbus 19152, 3501 DD Utrecht, ☎ 030/230–6603 or 030/231–3454). **Mobility International Nederland** (⊠ Postbus 41, 9244 ZN Beetsterswaag, ☎ 0512/382–5586). **Info–Handicap** (⊠ Box 33, 5801 Luxembourg, ☎ 0352/366466).

LODGING

The following hotels in Brussels (listed from most expensive to least) have rooms for guests with disabilities: Conrad, Hilton, Jolly Hotel Grand Sablon, Meridien, Radisson SAS, Renaissance, Sodehotel La Woluwe, Bristol Stephanie, Sheraton Brussels, Sheraton Brussels Airport, Arctia, Four Points, Métropole, Holiday Inn Brussels Airport, Jolly Atlanta, Mercure, Novotel Brussels (off Grand'Place), Novotel Airport, Aris, Atlas, Palace, Albert Premier, Astrid, Capital, Green Park, Fimotel Airport, Fimotel Expo, Ibis (Brussels Centre, Sainte-Catherine, and Airport), Balladins, Orion, Campanile, Comfort Inn, Gerfaut, France.

The same applies for a number of hotels outside Brussels, including the Ramada Hotel in Liège, the Switel and Hilton hotels in Antwerp, Hotel Pullman in Brugge, and Hotel des Ardennes in Spa-Balmoral.

►CONTACTS 8: Accessible rooms are available at the **Hilton hotels** (☎ 800/531–5900) in Brussels, Amsterdam, and Rotterdam. The **Intercontinental Hotel** (☎ 800/327–0200) in Luxembourg has two wheelchair-accessible rooms. The **Ramada Inns** (☎ 800/228–2828) in Liège and Amsterdam have rooms for guests with disabilities.

MAKING RESERVATIONS

When discussing accessibility with an operator or reservations agent, **ask hard questions.** Are there any stairs, inside *or* out? Are there grab bars next to the toilet *and* in the shower/tub? How wide is the doorway to the room? To the bathroom? For the most extensive facilities meeting the latest legal specifications, **opt for newer accommodations,** which are more likely to have been designed with access in mind. Older buildings or ships may have more limited facilities. Be sure to **discuss your needs before booking.**

TRANSPORTATION

►COMPLAINTS: **Disability Rights Section** (✉ U.S. Department of Justice, Civil Rights Division, Box 66738, Washington, DC 20035–6738, ☎ 202/514–0301 or 800/514–0301, TTY 202/514–0383 or 800/514–0383, FAX 202/307–1198) for general complaints. **Aviation Consumer Protection Division** (☞ Air Travel, *above*) for airline-related problems.

TRAVEL AGENCIES & TOUR OPERATORS

As a whole, the travel industry has become more aware of the needs of travelers with disabilities. In the United States, the Americans with Disabilities Act requires that travel firms serve the needs of all travelers. Note, though, that some agencies and operators specialize in making travel arrangements for individuals and groups with disabilities.

►TRAVELERS WITH MOBILITY PROBLEMS: **Access Adventures** (✉ 206 Chestnut Ridge Rd., Rochester, NY 14624, ☎ 716/889–9096), run by a former physical-rehabilitation counselor. **Accessible Journeys** (✉ 35 W. Sellers Ave., Ridley Park, PA 19078, ☎ 610/521–0339 or 800/846–4537, FAX 610/521–6959), for escorted tours exclusively for travelers with mobility impairments. **Flying Wheels Travel** (✉ 143 W. Bridge St., Box 382, Owatonna, MN 55060, ☎ 507/451–5005 or 800/535–6790, FAX 507/451–1685), a travel agency specializing in customized tours and itineraries worldwide. **Hinsdale Travel Service** (✉ 201 E. Ogden Ave., Suite 100, Hinsdale, IL 60521, ☎ 630/325–1335), a travel agency that benefits from the advice of wheelchair traveler Janice Perkins.

►TRAVELERS WITH DEVELOPMENTAL DISABILITIES: **Sprout** (✉ 893 Amsterdam Ave., New York, NY 10025, ☎ 212/222–9575 or 888/222–9575, FAX 212/222–9768).

DISCOUNTS & DEALS

Be a smart shopper and **compare all your options** before making any choice. A plane ticket bought with a promotional coupon may not be cheaper than the least expensive fare from a discount ticket agency. For high-price travel purchases, such as packages or tours, keep in mind that what you get is just as important as what you save. Just because something is cheap doesn't mean it's a bargain.

CLUBS & COUPONS

Many companies sell discounts in the form of travel clubs and coupon books, but these cost money. You must use participating advertisers to get a deal, and only after you recoup the initial membership cost or book price do you begin to save. If you plan to use the club or coupons frequently, you may save considerably. Before signing up, find out what discounts you get for free.

►DISCOUNT CLUBS: **Entertainment Travel Editions** (✉ 2125 Butterfield Rd., Troy, MI 48084, ☎ 800/445–4137; $20–$51, depending on destination). **Great American Traveler** (✉ Box 27965, Salt Lake City, UT 84127, ☎ 801/974–3033 or 800/548–2812; $49.95 per year). **Moment's Notice Discount Travel Club** (✉ 7301 New Utrecht Ave., Brooklyn, NY 11204, ☎ 718/234–6295; $25 per year, single or family). **Privilege Card International** (✉ 237 E. Front St., Youngstown, OH 44503, ☎ 330/746–5211 or 800/236–9732; $74.95 per year). **Sears's Mature Outlook** (✉ Box 9390, Des Moines, IA 50306, ☎ 800/336–6330; $19.95 per year). **Travelers Advantage** (✉ CUC Travel Service, 3033 S. Parker Rd., Suite 1000, Aurora, CO 80014, ☎ 800/548–1116 or 800/648–4037; $59.95 per year, single or family). **Worldwide Discount Travel Club** (✉ 1674 Meridian Ave., Miami Beach, FL 33139, ☎ 305/534–2082; $50 per year family, $40 single).

CREDIT-CARD BENEFITS

When you use your credit card to make travel purchases you may receive free travel-accident insurance, collision-damage insurance, and medical or legal assistance, depending on the card and the bank that issued it. American Express, MasterCard, and Visa provide one or more of these services, so **look at a copy of your credit card's travel-benefits policy.** If you are a member of an auto club, always **ask hotel and car-rental reservations agents about auto-club discounts.** Some clubs offer additional discounts on tours, cruises, and admission to attractions.

DISCOUNT RESERVATIONS

To save money, **look into discount-reservations services** with toll-free numbers, which use their buying power to get a better price on hotels, airline tickets, even car rentals. When booking a room, always **call the hotel's local toll-free number** (if one is available) rather than the central reservations number—you'll often get a better price. Always ask about special packages or corporate rates.

When shopping for the best deal on hotels and car rentals, **look for guaranteed exchange rates.** With your rate locked in, you won't pay more, even if the price goes up in the local currency.

➤AIRLINE TICKETS: ☎ **800/359–4537** (Fly 4 Less).

➤HOTEL ROOMS: **Hotels Plus** (☎ 800/ 235–0909). **International Marketing & Travel Concepts** (☎ 800/790– 4682). **Steigenberger Reservation Service** (☎ 800/223–5652). **Travel Interlink** (☎ 800/888–5898).

PACKAGE DEALS

Packages and guided tours can save you money, but don't confuse the two. When you buy a package, your travel remains independent, just as though you had planned and booked the trip yourself. Fly/drive packages, which combine airfare and car rental, are often a good deal. If you **buy a rail/drive pass,** you'll save on train tickets and car rentals. All Eurail- and Europass holders get a discount on Eurostar fares through the Channel Tunnel.

ELECTRICITY

To use your U.S.-purchased electric-powered equipment, **bring a converter and adapter.** The electrical current in the Netherlands, Belgium, and Luxembourg is 220 volts, 50 cycles alternating current (AC); wall outlets take Continental-type plugs, with two round prongs.

If your appliances are dual-voltage, you'll need only an adapter. Don't use 110-volt outlets, marked FOR SHAVERS ONLY, for high-wattage appliances such as blow-dryers. Most laptops operate equally well on 110 and 220 volts and so require only an adapter.

EMERGENCIES

➤EMERGENCIES: In Belgium, dial 101 for **police;** dial 100 for **accidents and ambulance.** In Luxembourg, dial 113 for **police;** dial 112 for **ambulance, doctor, and dentist.** In the Netherlands, dial 112 for **police, ambulance and fire.**

GAY & LESBIAN TRAVEL

The Netherlands is one of the most liberal countries in the world in its social and legal attitude toward gays and lesbians. The age of consent is 16, there are stringent anti-discrimination laws, and gay couples registered as living together have some of the same rights as heterosexual couples. At press time legislation was before parliament to fully legalize same-sex marriage.

Social attitudes in Belgium toward gays and lesbians are about the same as in the Netherlands, especially in bigger cities, but there's no equally far-reaching legislation. Luxembourg is the most conservative of the three countries, but in Luxembourg City attitudes similar to those in the other two countries apply.

➤LOCAL RESOURCES: There are several gay and lesbian organizations in Brussels, including the **English-Speaking Gay Group** (EGG; ✉ B.P. 198, 1060 Brussels, Belgium, email: 100522.30@compuserve.com) and **Shalhomo** (✉ Av. Besme 127, 1190 Brussels, Belgium), for Jewish gays and lesbians.

FOR RELATED INFO ON THE WEB VISIT **WWW.FODORS.COM/RESOURCE**

THE GOLD GUIDE / SMART TRAVEL TIPS

Helpful gay and lesbian organizations in the Netherlands include the COC Nederland (⊠ Nieuwezijds Voorburgwal 68/70, 1012 SE Amsterdam, Netherlands, ☎ 020/623–4596), the national gay organization; Gay & Lesbian Switchboard (☎ 020/623–6565); and the SAD Schorerstichting (⊠ P.C. Hooftstraat 5, 1071 BL Amsterdam, Netherlands, ☎ 020/662–4206), for general information and HIV advice.

▶GAY- AND LESBIAN-FRIENDLY TRAVEL AGENCIES: Corniche Travel (⊠ 8721 Sunset Blvd., Suite 200, West Hollywood, CA 90069, ☎ 310/854–6000 or 800/429–8747, FAX 310/659–7441). Islanders Kennedy Travel (⊠ 183 W. 10th St., New York, NY 10014, ☎ 212/242–3222 or 800/988–1181, FAX 212/929–8530). Now Voyager (⊠ 4406 18th St., San Francisco, CA 94114, ☎ 415/626–1169 or 800/255–6951, FAX 415/626–8626). Yellowbrick Road (⊠ 1500 W. Balmoral Ave., Chicago, IL 60640, ☎ 773/561–1800 or 800/642–2488, FAX 773/561–4497). Skylink Travel and Tour (⊠ 3577 Moorland Ave., Santa Rosa, CA 95407, ☎ 707/585–8355 or 800/225–5759, FAX 707/584–5637), serving lesbian travelers.

HEALTH

MEDICAL PLANS

No one plans to fall ill while traveling, but it happens, so **consider signing up with a medical-assistance company.** Members receive doctor referrals, emergency evacuation or repatriation, 24-hour telephone hot lines for medical consultation, cash for emergencies, and other personal and legal assistance. Coverage varies by plan, so **review the benefits of each carefully.**

▶MEDICAL-ASSISTANCE COMPANIES: International SOS Assistance (⊠ 8 Neshaminy Interplex, Suite 207, Trevose, PA 19053, ☎ 215/245–4707 or 800/523–6586, FAX 215/244–9617; ⊠ 12 Chemin Riantbosson, 1217 Meyrin 1, Geneva, Switzerland, ☎ 4122/785–6464, FAX 4122/785–6424; ⊠ 10 Anson Rd., 14-07/08 International Plaza, Singapore, 079903, ☎ 65/226–3936, FAX 65/226–3937).

INSURANCE

Travel insurance is the best way to **protect yourself against financial loss.** The most useful plan is a comprehensive policy that includes coverage for trip cancellation and interruption, default, trip delay, and medical expenses (with a waiver for preexisting conditions).

Without insurance, you will lose all or most of your money if you cancel your trip, regardless of the reason. Default insurance covers you if your tour operator, airline, or cruise line goes out of business. Trip-delay covers unforeseen expenses that you may incur due to bad weather or mechanical delays. It's important to compare the fine print regarding trip-delay coverage when comparing policies.

For overseas travel, one of the most important components of travel insurance is its medical coverage. Supplemental health insurance will pick up the cost of your medical bills should you become sick or be injured while traveling. U.S. residents should note that Medicare generally does not cover health-care costs outside the United States, nor do many privately issued policies. Residents of the United Kingdom can buy an annual travel-insurance policy valid for most vacations taken during the year in which the coverage is purchased. If you are pregnant or have a pre-existing condition, make sure you're covered. British citizens should buy extra medical coverage when traveling overseas, according to the Association of British Insurers. Australian travelers should buy travel insurance, including extra medical coverage, whenever they go abroad, according to the Insurance Council of Australia.

Always **buy travel insurance directly from the insurance company;** if you buy it from a cruise line, airline, or tour operator that goes out of business you probably will not be covered for the agency or operator's default, a major risk. Before you make any purchase, **review your existing health and home-owner's policies** to find out whether they cover expenses incurred while traveling.

➤TRAVEL INSURERS: In the U.S., Access **America** (✉ 6600 W. Broad St., Richmond, VA 23230, ☎ 804/285–3300 or 800/284–8300). **Travel Guard International** (✉ 1145 Clark St., Stevens Point, WI 54481, ☎ 715/345–0505 or 800/826–1300). In Canada, **Mutual of Omaha** (✉ Travel Division, 500 University Ave., Toronto, Ontario M5G 1V8, ☎ 416/598–4083, 800/268–8825 in Canada).

➤INSURANCE INFORMATION: In the U.K., **Association of British Insurers** (✉ 51 Gresham St., London EC2V 7HQ, ☎ 0171/600–3333). In Australia, the **Insurance Council of Australia** (☎ 613/9614–1077, FAX 613/9614–7924).

LANGUAGE

Belgium has three official languages: Dutch, French, and German (spoken by a small minority). In Luxembourg the official language is French, but German is a compulsory subject in schools, and everybody speaks Luxembourgish, the native tongue (a language descended from an ancient dialect of the Franks); most people also know a fair amount of English. In the Netherlands, Dutch is the official language, but almost everybody knows at least some English and many speak it very well.

LANGUAGES FOR TRAVELERS

➤PHRASE BOOKS AND LANGUAGE-TAPE SETS: *Fodor's French for Travelers*, *Fodor's German for Travelers* ($16.95 each; phone orders, ☎ 800/533–6478).

LODGING

All three countries offer a range of choices, from the major international hotel chains and small, modern local hotels to family-run restored inns and historic houses, to elegant country châteaux and resorts. Prices in metropolitan areas are significantly higher than those in outlying towns and the countryside.

Most hotels that cater to business travelers will grant substantial weekend rebates. These discounted rates are often available during the week as well as in July and early August, when business travelers are thin on

the ground. Moreover, you can often qualify for a "corporate rate" when hotel occupancy is low. The moral is, always ask what's the best rate a hotel can offer before you book. No hotelier was ever born who will give a lower rate unless you ask for it.

➤RESERVATIONS: If you're making your own travel arrangements, you can have hotel reservations in Belgium made for you free of charge by writing or faxing **Belgian Tourist Reservations** (BTR; ✉ Bd. Anspach 111, 1000 Brussels,, ☎ 02/513–7484, FAX 02/513–9277). For self-catering accommodations and B&Bs in Wallonia, contact **Belsud Réservation** (✉ R. Marché-aux-Herbes 61, 1000 Brussels, ☎ 02/504–0280, FAX 02/514–5335). For hotel as well as B&B reservations in Antwerp, contact the **Tourist Board** (✉ Grote Markt 15, 2000 Antwerp, ☎ 03/232–0103, FAX 03/231–1937).

APARTMENT & VILLA RENTALS

If you want a home base that's roomy enough for a family and comes with cooking facilities, **consider a furnished rental.** These can save you money, especially if you're traveling with a large group of people. Home-exchange directories list rentals (often second homes owned by prospective house swappers), and some services search for a house or apartment for you (even a castle if that's your fancy) and handle the paperwork. Some send an illustrated catalog; others send photographs only of specific properties, sometimes at a charge. Up-front registration fees may apply.

➤RENTAL AGENTS: **Europa-Let/Tropical Inn-Let** (✉ 92 N. Main St., Ashland, OR 97520, ☎ 541/482–5806 or 800/462–4486, FAX 541/482–0660). **Interhome** (✉ 124 Little Falls Rd., Fairfield, NJ 07004, ☎ 973/882–6864 or 800/882–6864, FAX 973/808–1742). **Property Rentals International** (✉ 1008 Mansfield Crossing Rd., Richmond, VA 23236, ☎ 804/378–6054 or 800/220–3332, FAX 804/379–2073). **Rent-a-Home International** (✉ 7200 34th Ave. NW, Seattle, WA 98117, ☎ 206/789–9377 or 800/488–7368, FAX 206/789–9379). **Vacation Home Rentals Worldwide** (✉ 235 Kensington Ave.,

Norwood, NJ 07648, ☎ 201/767–9393 or 800/633–3284, FAX 201/767–5510). **Hideaways International** (✉ 767 Islington St., Portsmouth, NH 03801, ☎ 603/430–4433 or 800/843–4433, FAX 603/430–4444; membership $99) is a club for travelers who arrange rentals among themselves.

HOSTELS

No matter what your age, you can **save on lodging costs by staying at hostels.** In some 5,000 locations in more than 70 countries around the world, Hostelling International (HI), the umbrella group for a number of national youth hostel associations, offers single-sex, dorm-style beds and, at many hostels, "couples" rooms and family accommodations. Membership in any HI national hostel association, open to travelers of all ages, allows you to stay in HI-affiliated hostels at member rates (one-year membership is about $25 for adults; hostels run about $10–$25 per night). Members also have priority if the hostel is full; they're eligible for discounts around the world, even on rail and bus travel in some countries.

➤HOSTEL ORGANIZATIONS: **Hostelling International—American Youth Hostels** (✉ 733 15th St. NW, Suite 840, Washington, DC 20005, ☎ 202/783–6161, FAX 202/783–6171). **Hostelling International—Canada** (✉ 400-205 Catherine St., Ottawa, Ontario K2P 1C3, ☎ 613/237–7884, FAX 613/237–7868). **Youth Hostel Association of England and Wales** (✉ Trevelyan House, 8 St. Stephen's Hill, St. Albans, Hertfordshire AL1 2DY, ☎ 01727/855215 or 01727/845047, FAX 01727/844126); membership in the U.S. $25, in Canada C$26.75, in the U.K. £9.30).

MAIL

See individual country chapters.

MONEY

COSTS

See individual country chapters.

CREDIT & DEBIT CARDS

Should you use a credit card or a debit card when traveling? Both have benefits. A credit card allows you to delay payment and gives you certain rights as a consumer (☞ Consumer Protection, *above*). A debit card, also known as a check card, deducts funds directly from your checking account and helps you stay within your budget. When you want to rent a car, though, you may still need an old-fashioned credit card. Although you can always *pay* for your car with a debit card, some agencies will not allow you to *reserve* a car with a debit card.

Otherwise, the two types of plastic are virtually the same. Both will get you cash advances at ATMs worldwide if your card is properly programmed with your personal identification number (PIN). (For use in the Netherlands, Belgium, and Luxembourg, your PIN must be four digits long.) Both offer excellent, wholesale exchange rates. And both protect you against unauthorized use if the card is lost or stolen. Your liability is limited to $50, as long as you report the card missing.

➤ATM LOCATIONS: **Cirrus** (☎ 800/424–7787). **Plus** (☎ 800/843–7587) for locations in the United States and Canada, or visit your local bank.

➤REPORTING LOST CARDS: To report lost or stolen credit cards, call the following toll-free numbers: **American Express** (☎ 800/327–2177); **Diners Club** (☎ 800/234–6377); **Master Card** (☎ 800/307–7309); and **Visa** (☎ 800/847–2911).

CURRENCY

The monetary unit in Belgium is the Belgian franc (BF); in Luxembourg, the Luxembourg franc (Flux), which is interchangeable with the Belgian franc; and in the Netherlands, the guilder (Fl). The currency exchange rates quoted in the following chapters fluctuate daily, so check them at the time of your departure.

EXCHANGING MONEY

For the most favorable rates, **change money through banks.** Although fees charged for ATM transactions may be higher abroad than at home, Cirrus and Plus exchange rates are excellent, because they are based on wholesale rates offered only by major banks. You won't do as well at exchange booths in airports or rail and bus stations, in hotels, in restaurants, or in stores, although you may find their hours more convenient. To avoid lines at airport exchange booths, **get a bit of local currency before you leave home.**

➤EXCHANGE SERVICES: Chase *Currency To Go* (☎ 800/935–9935; 935–9935 in NY, NJ, and CT). **International Currency Express** (☎ 888/842–0880 on the East Coast, 888/278–6628 on the West Coast). **Thomas Cook Currency Services** (☎ 800/287–7362 for telephone orders and retail locations).

TRAVELER'S CHECKS

Do you need traveler's checks? It depends on where you're headed. If you're going to rural areas and small towns, go with cash; traveler's checks are best used in cities. Lost or stolen checks can usually be replaced within 24 hours. To ensure a speedy refund, buy your own traveler's checks—don't let someone else pay for them: irregularities like this can cause delays. The person who bought the checks should make the call to request a refund.

PACKING

LUGGAGE

How many carry-on bags you can bring with you is up to the airline. Most allow two, but the limit is often reduced to one on certain flights. Gate agents will take excess baggage—including bags they deem oversize—from you as you board and add it to checked luggage. To avoid this situation, make sure that everything you carry aboard will fit under your seat. Also, get to the gate early, and request a seat at the back of the plane; you'll probably board first, while the overhead bins are still empty. Since big, bulky baggage attracts the attention of gate agents and flight attendants on a busy flight, make sure your carry-on is really a carry-on. Finally, a carry-on that's long and narrow is more likely to remain unnoticed than one that's wide and squarish.

If you are flying internationally, note that baggage allowances may be determined not by piece but by weight—generally 88 pounds (40 kilograms) in first class, 66 pounds (30 kilograms) in business class, and 44 pounds (20 kilograms) in economy.

Airline liability for baggage is limited to $1,250 per person on flights within the United States. On international flights it amounts to $9.07 per pound or $20 per kilogram for checked baggage (roughly $640 per 70-pound bag) and $400 per passenger for unchecked baggage. You can buy additional coverage at check-in for about $10 per $1,000 of coverage, but it excludes a rather extensive list of items, shown on your airline ticket.

Before departure, **itemize your bags' contents** and their worth, and label the bags with your name, address, and phone number. (If you use your home address, cover it so that potential thieves can't see it readily.) Inside each bag, **pack a copy of your itinerary.** At check-in, **make sure that each bag is correctly tagged** with the destination airport's three-letter code. If your bags arrive damaged or fail to arrive at all, **file a written report with the airline before leaving the airport.**

PACKING LIST

The best advice for a trip to the Netherlands in any season is to pack light, be flexible, bring an umbrella (and trench coat with a liner in winter), and always have a sweater or jacket available. For daytime wear and casual evenings, turtlenecks and flannel shirts are ideal for winter, alone or under a sweater, and cotton shirts with sleeves are perfect in summer. Blue jeans are popular and are even sometimes worn to the office; sweat suits, however, are never seen outside fitness centers. For women, high heels are nothing but trouble on the cobblestone streets of Amsterdam and other old cities, and sneakers or running shoes are a dead giveaway that you are an American tourist; a better choice is a pair of dark-color walking shoes or low-heeled pumps.

In Belgium and Luxembourg, bring a woolen sweater, even in summer; if you hit a rainy spell, a raincoat and umbrella may prove indispensable. Practical walking shoes are important, whether for rough cobblestones or forest trails. Women here wear skirts more frequently than do women in the United States, especially those over 35. Men would be wise to include a jacket and tie, especially if you're planning to visit one of the upper-echelon restaurants.

In your carry-on luggage **bring an extra pair of eyeglasses or contact lenses** and **enough of any medication you take** to last the entire trip. You may also want your doctor to write a spare prescription using the drug's generic name, since brand names may vary from country to country. **Never put prescription drugs or valuables in luggage to be checked.** To avoid customs delays, carry medications in their original packaging. And don't forget to copy down and carry addresses of offices that handle refunds of lost traveler's checks.

PASSPORTS & VISAS

When traveling internationally, **carry a passport even if you don't need one** (it's always the best form of I.D.), and make **two photocopies of the data page** (one for someone at home and another for you, carried separately from your passport). If you lose your passport, promptly call the nearest embassy or consulate and the local police.

ENTERING THE NETHERLANDS, BELGIUM, AND LUXEMBOURG

All U.S., Canadian, U.K., Australian, Irish, and New Zealand citizens, even infants, need only a valid passport to enter the Netherlands, Belgium, or Luxembourg for stays of up to 90 days.

PASSPORT OFFICES

The best time to apply for a passport or to renew is during the fall and winter. Before any trip, be sure to check your passport's expiration date and, if necessary, renew it as soon as possible. (Some countries won't allow you to enter on a passport that's due to expire in six months or less.)

➤AUSTRALIAN CITIZENS: **Australian Passport Office**, Melbourne (☎ 131–232).

➤CANADIAN CITIZENS: **Passport Office**, Ottawa (☎ 819/994–3500 or 800/567–6868).

➤IRISH CITIZENS: **Passport Office** , Dublin (☎ 671–1633)

➤NEW ZEALAND CITIZENS: **New Zealand Passport Office**, Wellington (☎ 04/494–0700 for information on how to apply, 0800/727–776 for information on applications already submitted).

➤U.K. CITIZENS: **London Passport Office** (☎ 0990/21010), for fees and documentation requirements and to request an emergency passport.

➤U.S. CITIZENS: **National Passport Information Center** (☎ 900/225–5674; calls are charged at 35¢ per minute for automated service, $1.05 per minute for operator service).

SENIOR-CITIZEN TRAVEL

To qualify for age-related discounts, **mention your senior-citizen status up front** when booking hotel reservations (not when checking out) and before you're seated in restaurants (not when paying the bill). Note that discounts may be limited to certain menus, days, or hours. When renting a car, **ask about promotional car-rental discounts,** which can be cheaper than senior-citizen rates.

Radisson SAS hotels in Brussels and Amsterdam offer a 25% reduction off the rack rate to senior citizens over 65. For other hotels, check on the availability of senior rates when you book.

➤EDUCATIONAL PROGRAMS: **Elderhostel** (✉ 75 Federal St., 3rd Floor, Boston, MA 02110, ☎ 617/426–8056). **Interhostel** (✉ University of New Hampshire, 6 Garrison Ave., Durham, NH 03824, ☎ 603/862–1147 or 800/733–9753, FAX 603/862–1113).

STUDENT TRAVEL

TRAVEL AGENCIES

To save money, **look into deals available through student-oriented travel agencies.** To qualify you'll need a bona fide student I.D. card. Members of international student groups are also eligible.

➤STUDENT I.D.s & SERVICES: **Council on International Educational Exchange** (✉ CIEE, 205 E. 42nd St., 14th Floor, New York, NY 10017, ☎ 212/822–2600 or 888/268–6245, FAX 212/822–2699), for mail orders only, in the United States. **Travel Cuts** (✉ 187 College St., Toronto, Ontario M5T 1P7, ☎ 416/979–2406 or 800/667–2887) in Canada.

➤STUDENT TOURS: **AESU Travel** (✉ 2 Hamill Rd., Suite 248, Baltimore, MD 21210-1807, ☎ 410/323–4416 or 800/638–7640, FAX 410/323–4498).

Contiki Holidays (✉ 300 Plaza Alicante, Suite 900, Garden Grove, CA 92840, ☎ 714/740–0808 or 800/266–8454, FAX 714/740–2034).

TAXES

AIRPORT

The Brussels National Airport tax is BF525, levied on all tickets and payable with your ticket purchase.

HOTELS

All hotels in the Netherlands charge a 6% Value Added Tax, which is usually included in the quoted room price. In addition, some local city authorities impose a "tourist tax." This is added to your bill, but usually amounts to just an extra dollar or two a day.

All hotels in Belgium charge a 6% Value Added Tax (TVA), included in the room rate; in Brussels, there is also a 9% city tax.

Hotels in Luxembourg charge a visitor's tax of 5%, included in the room rate.

VALUE-ADDED TAX (V.A.T.)

In the Netherlands a sales tax (BTW/VAT) of 17.5% is added to most purchases, such as clothing, souvenirs, and car fuel. Certain items (books among them) fall into a 6% band, as do hotel tariffs and restaurant meals.

In Belgium, VAT ranges from 6% on food and clothing to 33% on luxury goods. Restaurants are in between; 21% VAT is included in quoted prices.

To get a VAT refund you need to be resident outside the European Union and to have spent Fl 300, BF5,001, or FLUX3,000 or more in the same shop on the same day. Provided that you personally carry the goods out of the country within 30 days, you may claim a refund. Systems for doing this vary. Most leading stores will issue you a "VAT cheque" as proof of purchase (and charge a commission for the service). Then have these tax-refund forms stamped at customs as you leave the final European Union country on your itinerary; send the stamped form back to the store. Alternatively and for a simpler procedure, if you shop at a store that displays a Europe Tax Free Shopping sticker, ask for a refund check at the store, have it validated at customs at the airport, and claim a cash refund (minus 20% handling) at an ETS booth.

TELEPHONES

COUNTRY CODES

The country code for Belgium is 32; for the Netherlands, 31; for Luxembourg, 352. When dialing a Belgian or Dutch number from abroad, drop the initial 0 from the local area code. Luxembourg does not use area codes.

INTERNATIONAL CALLS

AT&T, MCI, and Sprint international access codes make calling the United States relatively convenient, but you may find the local access number blocked in many hotel rooms. First ask the hotel operator to connect you. If the hotel operator balks, ask for an international operator, or dial the international operator yourself. One way to improve your odds of being connected to your long-distance carrier is to travel with more than one company's calling card (a hotel may block Sprint, for example, but not MCI). If all else fails, call from a pay phone in the hotel lobby.

➤ACCESS CODES: **AT&T Direct** (Belgium, ☎ 080010010; Luxembourg, ☎ 08000111; Netherlands,☎ 08000229111; other areas, ☎ 800/435–0812). **MCI WorldPhone** (Belgium, ☎ 080010012; Luxembourg, ☎ 08000112; Netherlands, ☎ 08000229122; other areas, ☎ 800/

THE GOLD GUIDE / SMART TRAVEL TIPS

444–4141). **Sprint International Access** (Belgium, ☎ 080010014; Luxembourg, ☎ 08000115; Netherlands, ☎ 08000229119; other areas, ☎ 800/877–7746).

TIPPING

For specific tipping practices, *see* individual country chapters.

TOUR OPERATORS

Buying a prepackaged tour or independent vacation can make your trip to the Netherlands, Belgium, and Luxembourg less expensive and more hassle-free. Because everything is prearranged, you'll spend less time planning.

Operators that handle several hundred thousand travelers per year can use their purchasing power to give you a good price. Their high volume may also indicate financial stability. But some small companies provide more personalized service; because they tend to specialize, they may also be more knowledgeable about a given area.

BOOKING WITH AN AGENT

Travel agents are excellent resources. In fact, large operators accept bookings made only through travel agents. But it's a good idea to **collect brochures from several agencies,** because some agents' suggestions may be influenced by relationships with tour and package firms that reward them for volume sales. If you have a special interest, **find an agent with expertise in that area**; ASTA (☞ Travel Agencies, *below*) has a database of specialists worldwide.

Make sure your travel agent knows the accommodations and other services. Ask about the hotel's location, room size, beds, and whether it has a pool, room service, or programs for children, if you care about these. Has your agent been there in person or sent others you can contact? **Do some homework on your own,** too: Local tourism boards can provide information about lesser-known and small-niche operators, some of which may sell only direct.

BUYER BEWARE

Each year consumers are stranded or lose their money when tour opera-

tors—even very large ones with excellent reputations—go out of business. So **check out the operator.** Find out how long the company has been in business, and ask several travel agents about its reputation. If the package or tour you are considering is priced lower than in your wildest dreams, **be skeptical.** Try to **book with a company that has a consumer-protection program.** If the operator has such a program, you'll find information about it in the company's brochure. If the operator you are considering does not offer some kind of consumer protection, then ask for references from satisfied customers.

In the United States, members of the National Tour Association and United States Tour Operators Association are required to set aside funds to cover your payments and travel arrangements in case the company defaults. It's also a good idea to choose a company that participates in the American Society of Travel Agents' Tour Operator Program (TOP). This gives you a forum if there are any disputes between you and your tour operator; ASTA will act as mediator.

▶TOUR-OPERATOR RECOMMENDATIONS: **American Society of Travel Agents** (☞ Travel Agencies, *below*). **National Tour Association** (✉ NTA, 546 E. Main St., Lexington, KY 40508, ☎ 606/226–4444 or 800/755–8687). **United States Tour Operators Association** (✉ USTOA, 342 Madison Ave., Suite 1522, New York, NY 10173, ☎ 212/599–6599 or 800/468–7862, ℻ 212/599–6744).

COSTS

The more your package or tour includes, the better you can predict the ultimate cost of your vacation. Make sure you know exactly what is covered, and **beware of hidden costs.** Are taxes, tips, and service charges included? Transfers and baggage handling? Entertainment and excursions? These can add up.

Prices for packages and tours are usually quoted per person, based on two sharing a room. If traveling solo, you may be required to pay the full

double-occupancy rate. Some operators eliminate this surcharge if you
agree to be matched with a roommate
of the same sex, even if one is not
found by departure time.

GROUP TOURS

Among companies that sell tours to
the Netherlands, Belgium, and Luxembourg, the following are nationally
known, have a proven reputation, and
offer plenty of options. The classifica-
tions used below represent different
price categories, and you'll probably
encounter these terms when talking to
a travel agent or tour operator. The
key difference is usually in accommodations, which run from budget to
better, and better-yet to best.

➤SUPER-DELUXE: **Abercrombie &
Kent** (✉ 1520 Kensington Rd., Oak
Brook, IL 60521-2141, ☎ 630/954-
2944 or 800/323-7308, FAX 630/
954-3324). **Travcoa** (✉ Box 2630,
2350 S.E. Bristol St., Newport Beach,
CA 92660, ☎ 949/476-2800 or 800/
992-2003, FAX 949/476-2538).

➤DELUXE: **Globus** (✉ 5301 S. Federal
Circle, Littleton, CO 80123-2980, ☎
303/797-2800 or 800/221-0090, FAX
303/347-2080). **Maupintour** (✉
1515 St. Andrews Dr., Lawrence, KS
66047, ☎ 785/843-1211 or 800/
255-4266, FAX 785/843-8351).
Tauck Tours (✉ Box 5027, 276 Post
Rd. W, Westport, CT 06881-5027, ☎
203/226-6911 or 800/468-2825, FAX
203/221-6866).

➤FIRST-CLASS: **Brendan Tours** (✉
15137 Califa St., Van Nuys, CA
91411, ☎ 818/785-9696 or 800/
421-8446, FAX 818/902-9876).
Caravan Tours (✉ 401 N. Michigan
Ave., Chicago, IL 60611, ☎ 312/
321-9800 or 800/227-2826, FAX
312/321-9845). **Central Holidays**
(✉ 206 Central Ave., Jersey City, NJ
07307, ☎ 201/798-5777 or 800/
935-5000). **Insight International
Tours** (✉ 745 Atlantic Ave., #720,
Boston, MA 02111, ☎ 617/482-
2000 or 800/582-8380, FAX 617/
482-2884 or 800/622-5015). **Trafalgar Tours** (✉ 11 E. 26th St., New
York, NY 10010, ☎ 212/689-8977
or 800/854-0103, FAX 800/457-6644).

➤BUDGET: **Cosmos** (☞ Globus,
above). **Trafalgar Tours** (☞ *above*).

PACKAGES

Independent vacation packages are
available from major tour operators
and airlines. The companies listed
below offer vacation packages.

➤AIR/HOTEL: **Central Holidays** (☞
Group Tours, *above*). **Delta Vacations**
(☎ 800/872-7786). **DER Tours** (✉
9501 W. Devon St., Rosemont, IL
60018, ☎ 800/937-1235, FAX 847/
692-4141 or 800/282-7474, 800/
860-9944 for brochures). **TWA
Getaway Vacations** (☎ 800/438-
2929). **US Airways Vacations** (☎
800/455-0123).

➤FROM THE U.K.: **British Airways
Holidays** (Astral Towers, Betts Way,
London Rd., Crawley, West Sussex
RH10 2XA, ☎ 01293/722-727, FAX
01293/722-624). **Cosmos** (✉
Tourama House, 17 Homesdale Rd.,
Bromley, Kent BR2 9LX, , ☎ 0181/
464-3444 or 0161/480-5799).
Travelscene (✉ Travelscene House,
11-15 St. Ann's Rd., Harrow, Mid-
dlesex HA1 1AS, , ☎ 0181/427-
8800).

THEME TRIPS

➤ART AND ARCHITECTURE: **Endless
Beginnings Tours** (✉ 9825 Dowdy
Dr., #105, San Diego, CA 92126, ☎
619/566-4166 or 800/822-7855, FAX
619/549-9655).

➤BARGE/RIVER CRUISES: **Etoile de
Champagne** (✉ 88 Broad St., Boston,
MA 02110, ☎ 800/280-1492, FAX
617/426-4689). **European Water-
ways** (✉ 140 E. 56th St., Suite 4C,
New York, NY 10022, ☎ 212/688-
9489 or 800/217-4447, FAX 212/
688-3778 or 800/296-4554). **KD
River Cruises of Europe** (✉ 2500
Westchester Ave., Purchase, NY
10577, ☎ 914/696-3600 or 800/
346-6525, FAX 914/696-0833).
Kemwel's Premier Selections (✉ 106
Calvert St., Harrison, NY 10528,
☎ 914/835-5555 or 800/234-4000,
FAX 914/835-5449). **Le Boat** (✉ 10 S.
Franklin Turnpike, #204B, Ramsey,
NJ 07446, ☎ 201/236-2333 or 800/
922-0291).

➤BEER: **MIR Corporation** (✉ 85 S.
Washington St., #210, Seattle, WA
98104, ☎ 206/624-7289 or 800/
424-7289, FAX 206/624-7360).

►BICYCLING: **Euro-Bike Tours** (✉ Box 990, De Kalb, IL 60115, ☎ 800/321–6060, FAX 815/758–8851). **Uniquely Europe** (✉ 2819 1st Ave., Suite 280, Seattle, WA 98121-1113, ☎ 206/441–8682 or 800/426–3615, FAX 206/441–8862). **Vermont Bicycle Touring** (✉ Box 711, Bristol, VT, 05443-0711, ☎ 802/453–4811 or 800/245–3868, FAX 802/453–4806).

►GARDENS: **Coopersmith's England** (✉ Box 900, Inverness, CA 94937, ☎ 415/669–1914, FAX 415/669–1942). **Expo Garden Tours** (✉ 70 Great Oak, Redding, CT 06896, ☎ 203/938–0410 or 800/448–2685, FAX 203/938–0427).

►MOTORCYCLE: **Edelweiss Bike Travel** (✉ Hartford Holidays Travel, 129 Hillside Ave., Williston Park, NY 11596, ☎ 516/746–6761 or 800/877–2784, FAX 516/746–6690).

TRAIN TRAVEL

Rail travel in Europe, even first-class including supplements, is consistently 60%–75% cheaper than the lowest available one-way airline fare.

Eurostar operates high-speed passenger-only trains, which whisk riders between new stations in London and Brussels (Midi) in 3¼ hours. At press time, fares were $230 for a one-way, first-class ticket and $111 for an economy fare. A number of promotional return fares are available.

On the new Thalys high-speed trains, a one-way ticket from Brussels to Paris costs $90 in first class and $60 in economy.

DISCOUNT PASSES

To save money, **look into rail passes.** But be aware that if you don't plan to cover many miles, you may come out ahead by buying individual tickets.

The Netherlands, Belgium, and Luxembourg are among the 17 countries in which you can **use EurailPasses,** which provide unlimited first-class rail travel, in all of the participating countries, for the duration of the pass. If you plan to rack up the miles, get a standard pass. These are available for 15 days ($538), 21 days ($698), one month ($864), two months ($1,224), and three months ($1,512). If your plans call for only limited train travel, **look into a Europass,** which costs less money than a EurailPass. Unlike with Eurailpasses, however, you get a limited number of travel days, in a limited number of countries, during a specified time period. For example, a two-month pass ($386) that includes the Netherlands, Belgium, and Luxembourg allows between 5 and 15 days of rail travel but costs $150 less than the least expensive EurailPass. Keep in mind, however, that the Europass is also good only in France, Germany, Italy, Spain, and Switzerland.

In addition to standard Eurailpasses, **ask about special rail-pass plans.** Among these are the Eurail Youthpass (for people under age 26), the Eurail Saverpass (which gives a discount for two or more people traveling together), a Eurail Flexipass (which allows a certain number of travel days within a set period), the Euraildrive Pass and the Europass Drive (which combines travel by train and rental car). Whichever pass you choose, remember that you must **purchase your pass before you leave** for Europe.

Many travelers assume that rail passes guarantee them seats on the trains they wish to ride. Not so. You need to **book seats ahead even if you are using a rail pass**; seat reservations are required on some European trains, particularly high-speed trains, and are a good idea on trains that may be crowded—particularly in summer on popular routes. You will also need a reservation if you purchase sleeping accommodations.

►INFORMATION AND PASSES: **CIT Tours Corp.** (✉ 15 W. 44th St., 10th Floor, New York, NY 10036, ☎ 212/730–2400 or 800/248–7245 in the U.S., 800/387–0711 or 800/361–7799 in Canada). **DER Travel Services** (✉ 9501 W. Devon Ave., Rosemont, IL 60018, ☎ 800/782–2424, FAX 800/282–7474 for information or 800/860–9944 for brochures). **Rail Europe** (✉ 500 Mamaroneck Ave., Harrison, NY 10528, ☎ 914/682–5172 or 800/438–7245, FAX 800/432–1329; ✉ 2087 Dundas E, Suite 106, Mississauga, Ontario L4X 1M2, ☎ 800/361–7245, FAX 905/602–4198).

TRAVEL AGENCIES

A good travel agent puts your needs first. Look for an agency that has been in business at least five years, emphasizes customer service, and has someone on staff who specializes in your destination. In addition, **make sure the agency belongs to a professional trade organization,** such as ASTA in the United States. If your travel agency is also acting as your tour operator, *see* Buyer Beware in Tour Operators, *above*).

➤LOCAL AGENT REFERRALS: **American Society of Travel Agents** (ASTA, ☎ 800/965–2782 24-hr hot line, FAX 703/684–8319). **Association of British Travel Agents** (✉ 55–57 Newman St., London W1P 4AH, ☎ 0171/637–2444, FAX 0171/637–0713). **Association of Canadian Travel Agents** (✉ 1729 Bank St., Suite 201, Ottawa, Ontario K1V 7Z5, ☎ 613/521–0474, FAX 613/521–0805). **Australian Federation of Travel Agents** (☎ 02/9264–3299). **Travel Agents' Association of New Zealand** (☎ 04/499–0104).

TRAVEL GEAR

Travel catalogs specialize in useful items, such as compact alarm clocks and travel irons, that can **save space when packing.** They also offer dual-voltage appliances, currency converters, and foreign-language phrase books.

➤CATALOGS: **Magellan's** (☎ 800/962–4943, FAX 805/568–5406). **Orvis Travel** (☎ 800/541–3541, FAX 540/343–7053). **TravelSmith** (☎ 800/950–1600, FAX 800/950–1656).

U.S. GOVERNMENT

Government agencies can be an excellent source of inexpensive travel information. When planning your trip, **find out what government materials are available.**

➤ADVISORIES: **U.S. Department of State** (✉ Overseas Citizens Services Office, Room 4811 N.S., Washington, DC 20520; ☎ 202/647–5225 or FAX 202/647–3000 for interactive hot line; ☎ 301/946–4400 for computer bulletin board); enclose a self-addressed, stamped, business-size envelope.

➤PAMPHLETS: **Consumer Information Center** (✉ Consumer Information Catalogue, Pueblo, CO 81009, ☎ 719/948–3334 or 888/878–3256) for a free catalog that includes travel titles.

VISITOR INFORMATION

TOURIST INFORMATION

➤BELGIAN NATIONAL TOURIST OFFICE: In the U.S.: ✉ 780 3rd Ave., New York, NY 10017, ☎ 212/758–8130, FAX 212/355–7675. Canada: ✉ Box 760 NDG, Montréal, Québec H4A 3S2, ☎ 514/484–3594, FAX 514/489–8965. U.K.: ✉ 29 Princes St., London W1R 7RG, ☎ 0171/629–0230, FAX 0171/629–0454.

➤LUXEMBOURG NATIONAL TOURIST OFFICE: In the U.S.: ✉ 17 Beekman Pl., New York, NY 10022, ☎ 212/935–8888, FAX 212/935–5896. U.K.: ✉ 122 Regent St., London W1R 5FE, ☎ 0171/434–2800.

➤NETHERLANDS BOARD OF TOURISM: In the U.S.: ✉ 225 N. Michigan Ave., Suite 1854, Chicago, IL 60601, ☎ 312/819–1500, FAX 312/819–1740; for brochures, ☎ 888/464–6552. Canada: ✉ 25 Adelaide St. E, Suite 710, Toronto, Ontario M5C 1Y2; mailing address only. U.K.: ✉ 25–28 Buckingham Gate, London SW1E 6LD, ☎ 0171/828–7900.

WEB SITES

For useful information, including links to hotel reservation services, try the following Web sites: www.visitbelgium.com, www.goholland.com, and www.visitluxembourg.com.

WHEN TO GO

The best times to visit these three countries are late spring—when the northern European days are long and the summer crowds have not yet filled the beaches, the highways, or the museums—and in fall.

Because **Belgians** take vacations in July and August, these months are not ideal for visiting the coast or the Ardennes, but summer is a very good time to be in Brussels, Antwerp, or Liège. In summer you will also be able to get a break on hotel prices; on the other hand, this is also vacation time for many restaurants. For touring

THE GOLD GUIDE / SMART TRAVEL TIPS

the country and visiting much-frequented tourist attractions such as Brugge, the best times are April–June and September–October.

Luxembourg is a northern country—parallel in latitude to Newfoundland, Canada—with the same seasonal extremes in the amount of daylight. In late spring, summer, and early fall, you have daylight until 10 PM; in winter, however, be prepared for dusk closing in before 4 PM. There's rarely a long spell of heavy snow, but winters tend to be dank and rainy. Many attractions, especially outside the city, maintain shortened visiting hours (or close altogether) from late fall to Pentecost (late spring), except for a brief time around Easter. Summer is the principal tourist season, when Luxembourg polishes up its sightseeing train and restaurants set out terrace tables under the sycamores; gardens are in full bloom and weather can be comfortably hot. Spring and early fall are attractive as well.

The Netherlands' high season begins in late March to late April, when the tulips come up, and runs through October, when the Dutch celebrate their Autumn Holiday. June, July, and August are the most popular months with both international visitors and the Dutch themselves—it can be difficult to obtain reservations, particularly in beach towns on the North Sea coast and at campgrounds, during mid-summer. The cultural season lasts from September to June, but there are special cultural festivals and events scheduled in summer months.

The Netherlands has a mild maritime climate, with bright, clear summers and damp, overcast winters. The driest months are from February through May; the sunniest, May through August. In the eastern and southeastern provinces, winters are colder and summers warmer than along the North Sea coast.

CLIMATE

What follows are average daily maximum and minimum temperatures in the major cities of the Netherlands, Belgium, and Luxembourg.

➤FORECASTS: **Weather Channel Connection** (☎ 900/932–8437), 95¢ per minute from a Touch-Tone phone.

AMSTERDAM

Month	°F	°C	Month	°F	°C	Month	°F	°C
Jan.	40F	4C	May	61F	16C	Sept.	65F	18C
	34	1		50	10		56	13
Feb.	41F	5C	June	65F	18C	Oct.	56F	13C
	34	1		56	13		49	9
Mar.	47F	8C	July	70F	21C	Nov.	47F	8C
	38	3		59	15		41	5
Apr.	52F	11C	Aug.	68F	20C	Dec.	41F	5C
	43	6		59	15		36	2

BRUSSELS

Month	°F	°C	Month	°F	°C	Month	°F	°C
Jan.	40F	4C	May	65F	18C	Sept.	70F	21C
	31	-1		47	8		52	11
Feb.	45F	7C	June	72F	22C	Oct.	59F	15C
	32	0		52	11		45	7
Mar.	50F	10C	July	74F	23C	Nov.	49F	9C
	36	2		54	12		38	3
Apr.	58F	14C	Aug.	72F	22C	Dec.	43F	6C
	41	5		54	12		34	1

LUXEMBOURG

Month	°F	°C	Month	°F	°C	Month	°F	°C
Jan.	38F	3C	May	65F	18C	Sept.	67F	19C
	31	-1		47	8		50	10
Feb.	40F	4C	June	70F	21C	Oct.	56F	13C
	31	-1		52	11		43	6
Mar.	50F	10C	July	74F	23C	Nov.	45F	7C
	34	1		56	13		38	3
Apr.	58F	14C	Aug.	72F	22C	Dec.	40F	4C

1 Destination: The Netherlands, Belgium, and Luxembourg

REFLECTIONS IN A PEWTER BOWL

SLATE-COLOR SKIES CURVE like a pewter bowl over an undulating landscape, the long, low horizon punctuated by blunt steeples and a scattering of deep-roofed farmhouses that seem to enfold the land like a mother goose spreading wings over her brood. Inky crows wheel over spindle-fingered pollards; jackdaws pepper the ocher grainfields; and a magpie, flashing black and white, drags a long, iridescent tail through the damp air. These are the 16th-century landscapes of Pieter Bruegel the Elder—stained-glass planes in sepia tones, leaded by black branches, crooked spires, dark-frozen streams.

And these, too, are the 20th-century landscapes of Belgium, the Netherlands, and Luxembourg—a wedge of northern Europe squeezed between the massive and ancient kingdoms of France and Germany, bounded by the harsh North Sea to the northwest, defined by the rough, high forests of the Ardennes to the southeast. No wonder so much of their appeal, past and present, is interior—bountiful, sensual still lifes, the glowing chambers of Vermeer, the inner radiance in the portraits of Rembrandt: Their weather-beaten cultures have turned inward over the centuries, toward the hearth. Indoors, Bruegel's otherwise sepia scenes warm subtly with color—earthy browns, berry reds, loden greens, muted indigos, coral cheeks. So it is today: The Netherlanders gather in gold-lit, smoke-burnished "brown cafés," old bentwood chairs scraping across weathered stone floors; the Flemish nurse goblets of mahogany beer by candlelight in dark-beamed halls, a scarlet splash of paisley runner thrown over the pine tabletop; red-vested Walloons—French-speaking Belgians—read the newspaper in high-back oak banquettes polished blue-black by generations of rough tweed. In Luxembourg, the glass of light beer and *drüp* of eau-de-vie go down behind the candy-color leaded glass of spare, bright-lit *stuff,* or pubs, where village life finds its social focus, day in, day out. In each of these small northern lands, so often lashed by rain, soaked by drizzle, wrapped in fog, with winter dark closing in at 4 PM and winter daylight dawdling until 9 AM, the people live out the rich-hued interior scenes of the Old Masters.

Yet the skies do clear, come spring, and at last the light lingers until well after 10 at night. Then the real pleasure begins—an intense appreciation that residents of moderate climates would be hard-put to understand. As if the people's gratitude took physical form, it manifests itself in flowers, a frenzy of color spilling from every windowsill, spreading like ocean waves across tulip fields, over rose trellises, through wisteria-woven archways. Fruit trees explode like fireworks, and whole orchards shimmer pink. Chestnut branches sag under the weight of their leaves and the heavy, grapelike clusters of blossom that thrust upward, defying gravity. In the midst of this orgy of scent and color, Dutch university students bicycle along canals in loose batik-print cotton; Flemish farmers in blue overalls open their half-doors and bask; the international bankers of Luxembourg swing their Versace suit coats over their shoulders and head for the benches in the green Petrusse Valley.

Then café society, and home life with it, moves lock, stock, and barrel outdoors, to bask, lizardlike, in the rare warmth. Terrace cafés on the Grote Markts and Grand'-Places rival any piazza in Italy. And when there's no café around, the family simply sets out a cluster of folding chairs, perhaps a checkered-cloth-covered card table, whether smack on the sidewalk or behind the barn door, to make the most of fine weather. A suntan remains (as it does in sun-starved North Germany) the most sought-after of status symbols—doubly prestigious if flaunted in midwinter, as northerners, once pale and prune-skinned, return from the ski slopes of the Alps or the beaches of the Canary Islands. The extremes of their climate, from inexorable gray to luxurious sun, may form a common bond, but the three countries of the Netherlands, Belgium, and Luxembourg sustain sharply different cultures, languages, and terrain.

The Netherlands is a tangle of inner conflicts—Catholic versus Protestant (they lean 60–40 toward the latter, that 60% still functioning as one of Europe's Reformation strongholds); puritanical versus prurient (though you can't buy liquor on Sunday in some areas, in others prostitutes sit, whalebone-stayed, in display windows like so much grade-A beef). In fact, in narrow, low row houses up and down town streets, whole blocks-full of ordinary people live without curtains, their evening lives and possessions open to viewing by passersby. Each summer the Netherlanders turn their backs on the beach, load up their trailers, and migrate south; though they're leaving behind the most heavily populated land on the Continent, they flock together in crowded trailer parks wherever they go, rank on cozy rank decked with lace curtains and black-and-yellow Dutch license plates.

The Belgian situation goes beyond mere contradiction: It is a country torn in half, split by two tongues and two distinct cultures. The division between Wallonie and Flanders traces back to Merovingian times, and the Walloon patois and Belgian French represent the last northward wave of the Roman empire and its lingual residue. Twice in this century Flemish citizens (and possibly a king) were known to collaborate with German invaders, allying themselves against what they saw as French-speaking domination. In turn, francophone Belgians, made powerful by their region's blossoming heavy industry, looked down upon their Flemish countrymen: The country's constitution was not translated into Dutch until 1961. Today the bickering over bilingual rights, which leaves Brussels a no-man's-land, extra-wide enamel signs naming every street and alley in two tongues, is especially acute. Many intellectuals believe politicians on both sides are whipping up national sentiment, when they should be looking at urgent matters like reform of the police and justice system.

The cultures are as different as their languages: The Flemish are proud and tidy, their homes filled with the exterior light that pours in through tall, multipaned windows; a spare, avant-garde current in fashion, film, and literature shows their Dutch leanings. The Walloons, on the other hand, remain more laissez-faire, their homes often dark, cozy, and cluttered with knickknacks and lace. A women's clothing shop in Ghent is likely to include progressive, trendy, severe clothing, while the equivalent in Liège will show cardigans, A-line skirts, and fussy floral prints. These two separate worlds share a Catholic culture that, beyond the spiritual realm, finds expression in a shared appreciation of the good things in life, such as the pleasures of the table.

If Belgium and the Netherlands show inner conflict, the natives of little Luxembourg present a solid front to the outside, interacting in French, German, or English, but maintaining their private world in their own native *Lëtzebuergesch* (Luxembourgish). Thus, having survived centuries of conquest and occupation, they can open their country to European Union "Eurocrats" and more than a hundred international banks, and still keep to themselves. Luxembourg sustains two parallel cultures, with some cafés catering to trendy, international, or tourist crowds and others reserved for the loden-coated locals, who may greet an aberrant visitor with stunned silence as thick as the cigarette smoke that fills the air.

The Netherlands, Belgium, and Luxembourg—as diverse within themselves as they are to one another. And yet all this diversity has been thrown together by the dominant cultures pressing in at the borders—France and Germany. Having been conquered and economically dwarfed for generations, the three little countries felt compelled, in 1958, to form an alliance, an economic union that served as a foundation for the European Union. Since then, "Benelux" has become a convenient abbreviation for a small, independent wedge of northern Europe where even fruit juice is labeled in French and in Dutch.

But, of course, Benelux is considerably more than an arbitrary economic unit. It is a rich and varied region, laced with canals, sprinkled with orchards, its cities burnished with age, where museums display the landscapes of Bruegel and Van Ruysdael and the interiors of Van Eyck, Vermeer, and Rembrandt, while their inspiration—the magnificent, brooding countryside and time-polished interiors—remains much unchanged.

—Nancy Coons

WHAT'S WHERE

The Netherlands

"God made the world," say the citizens of Holland, "but the Dutch made the Netherlands." Nearly half of this democratic monarchy's 15,450 square mi has been reclaimed from the sea, and the doughty inhabitants have been working for generations to keep it from slipping back. Hence the special look of the Dutch landscape, the subject of some of the most beautiful Old Master paintings ever created. In scenery and structure, the country's north and south regions differ little, for both have the same North Sea beach-line on the northwestern side, the same sand dunes and bulb-fields in the center, and the same type of rivers on their land borders. Yet each of the country's five main regions—Amsterdam, the Randstad, the Green Heart, the Border Provinces, and the North—possesses its own distinct flavor. The capital, Amsterdam, is one of the most amazing cities in Europe and the Netherlands' Shop Window. South of the capital is the Randstad (Ridge City), comprising four adjacent urban centers—Leiden, The Hague, Rotterdam, and Utrecht; together they make up the true cultural and economic heart of the nation. To the east of the Randstad is the "Green Heart," with vast national parks studded with lovely museums and palaces. Near the Belgian and German borders are the Border Provinces and Maastricht—where billiard-table flatness gives way to gentle hills and a more cosmopolitan and convivial way of life. The Northern provinces are hemmed in by the North Sea and, to the east, Germany. The unique province of Friesland has only been part of the Netherlands for the last 500 years, and some of its residents, many of whom still speak a separate language, might even dispute that to this day. Everywhere, of course, the Dutch people are at one and the same time *deftig* (dignified, respectable, and decorous) and *gezellig* (cozy, comfortable, and enjoying themselves).

In most areas, the biggest slopes are those leading up to the canal bridges; the tallest objects are the windmills with their white cloth sails stretched to pick up the slightest breeze. Everywhere stand cozy villages—the kind painted by Hobbema—and shining, immaculate cities (the whole country looks as though it has been scrubbed with Dutch cleanser). In the end, although it is one of Europe's smallest countries, the Netherlands manages to pack within its borders as many pleasures and treasures as countries five times its size.

Amsterdam

One of the great historic cities of the world, Amsterdam has also embraced modernity with a passion. Although called the City of Canals—it has more than a thousand of them—Amsterdam is no Venice, content to live on gondolas, moonlight serenades, and its former glory. It is one of the most forward-looking, cosmopolitan, and bustling cities around; on every street the delicious dichotomies of old and new stand side by side. Built on a latticework of concentric canals arching from the IJ River like a great aquatic rainbow, Amsterdam is held together by the linchpins of its great public squares—the Dam, the Rembrandtplein, the Munt, and the Leidseplein. The Dam, an open square overlooked by the Royal Dam Palace, is a godsend to visitors as a landmark, for even the worst student of foreign languages can easily obtain help if lost by asking for the "Dam." This is a city you have to get to know from the water in order to be properly introduced; glass-roof canal boats make that possible.

The city's major sites include the **Royal Dam Palace**; the **Schreierstoren,** from which Henry Hudson set sail in the *Half Moon* in 1609 to discover New York; **Rembrandt's House**; the fascinating attic **church of the Amstelkring**; the **Begijnhof**—the most peaceful courtyard in the city; the **Gouden Bocht** (Golden Bend), replete with stately burghers' mansions bearing stepped gables and Daniel Marot doorways; and, of course, the incomparable **Rijksmuseum** and the **Vincent van Gogh Museum.** With 22 Rembrandts, including the great *Night Watch,* and more than 200 Van Goghs, Amsterdam is a prime art repository. Diamonds galore fill the shops and factories of the historic **Jewish Quarter** east of the Zwanenburgwal. The **Anne Frank house** is a wrenching reminder of the horrors of war. In one of the thousands of *bruine kroegjes* (brown cafés) *koffie* is the drink of choice. Offering the Netherlands' hottest nightlife, impressive concerts, and fine restaurants, Amsterdam reinvents itself with every sunset. West of the city the

"Bloemen Route" (Flower Road) leads from Aalsmeer—the greatest floral village in Europe—to the gorgeous **Keukenhof** Gardens and the town of Lisse. This is the Holland of tulips, hyacinths, and narcissi, ablaze with the colors of Easter in the spring and generally a rainbow of color year-round. Just north of Amsterdam, the windmill-filled **Zaanse Schans** region demonstrates the many uses of windmill-produced power throughout the Netherlands.

Metropolitan Holland and the Hague

Like filings around the end of a magnet, six major urban centers cluster in an arc just to the south of Amsterdam. While the capital remains a world-class city, these six cities offer a truer look at Dutch culture and society. It is a short step from the ocean of annual color of "Die Bloemen Route" to a haven of perennial color—the city of **Haarlem,** the earliest center of Dutch art, which gave rise to one of the most important schools of landscape painting in the 17th century. Here are the excellent Frans Hals and Teylers museums and St. Bavo's Cathedral. **Leiden,** the birthplace of Rembrandt and site of a great university, remains a charming town where windmills rise over the cityscape. Here also is the Pieterskerk, church of the Pilgrim Fathers who worshiped in it for 10 years before setting sail for America in 1620. **The Hague,** called 's-Gravenhage or Den Haag by the Dutch (and "the Largest Village in Europe" by residents), is a royal and regal city—filled with patrician mansions and gracious parks, and home to Queen Beatrix and the International Court of Justice. At the city's Mauritshuis (much more intimate than the Rijksmuseum) the canvases on display are uniformly excellent—Vermeer's *View of Delft* and *Girl with the Pearl* are just two.

The windswept beach resort of **Scheveningen** offers some of the best herring in the world. The tree-lined canals, humpbacked bridges, and step-gabled houses of **Delft** preserve the atmosphere of the 16th and 17th centuries better than any other city in the country, captured unforgettably in the canvases of Vermeer and Pieter de Hoogh. Delft, of course, colored the world with its unique blue, best found in its famous blue-and-white Delftware china.

Rotterdam, a true phoenix of a city, rose from the ashes of World War II to become one of the busiest ports in Europe. In **Utrecht**'s history-soaked town center not far from the Oude Gracht (Old Canal) stands the 338-ft tower of "the Cathedral that is Missing." This city is the centerpiece of a region that is considered by many Dutch to be the most beautiful in the country: The landscape fairly bursts with lovely old trees (a rarity in the polders, or countryside reclaimed from the sea) and storybook castle-châteaux.

The Border Provinces and Maastricht

In most Dutch provinces the sea presses in to the land, constantly striving to win a foothold; Zeeland to the contrary pushes out into the water, invading the invader's territory and looking for trouble. On strips of land, like thumbs of a right hand, pointing westward toward the North Sea, Zeeland remains an ancient and romantic place. **Zierikzee** is a yachting port and **Veere** relentlessly picturesque; **Middelburg, Breda,** and **'s-Hertogenbosch** all have historic significance. To the south, past Limbourg province, lies **Maastricht,** the oldest city in the Netherlands. Wedged somewhat hesitatingly between Belgium and Germany, the town remains an intoxicating mixture of three languages, times, currencies, and customs. There are imposing Romanesque and Gothic churches, hundreds of historic gable-stone houses, and fabulous French food (where else can you enjoy breakfast with champagne in the Netherlands?). Each March, the European Fine Art Fair—some say this is the best art fair in Europe—draws in such high-rollers as Baron Thyssen-Bornemisza, Prince Bernhard, and J. Paul Getty, Jr.

The Green Heart: From Apeldoorn to Arnhem

Although as steeped in history as any other Dutch region, Gelderland seems to put the emphasis on the beauties of outdoor life, for it is a province studded with national parks and Edenic forests. Glorying in the title "The Largest Garden City in the Netherlands," **Apeldoorn** is so lavishly endowed with trees, natives challenge visitors to find the place! Thousands do every year, mostly to visit the **Palace Het Loo**—the Dutch Baroque castle and hunting lodge that was home to William and

Mary (who went on to become king and queen of England). Set within **De Hoge Veluwe,** the nation's largest natural preserve, is the world-class **Kröller-Müller Museum,** which has extraordinary paintings of the post-Impressionists as well as a multitude of works by Van Gogh, including his *Sunflowers* and *Potato Eaters.* This region is, above all, a walking and bicycling paradise, and hikes through lush woods and moors can often delightfully end at grand country mansions, such as Het Wezenveld, Bruggenbosch, and Hunderen, outside Apeldoorn. The major towns of the region—**Zwolle, Deventer, Zutphen**—all have historic churches or town squares. The capital of the region is **Arnhem,** best known for "the bridge too far" of World War II. Its chief attractions are the battlefields, memorials, and war cemeteries that have become sacred places of pilgrimages, set in a region rich in scenic beauty.

The North

Leeuwarden is the capital of Friesland and birthplace of Saskia, Rembrandt's wife, and of the mysterious Mata Hari. Crafts are a highlight here: the fine Netherlands Ceramic Museum, and the Fries Museum is a great introduction to the cultural heritage of the province. Along the IJsselmeer coastline, now protected from the ravages of the sea and tides, there are plenty of quaint, though defunct, fishing villages. Out on a promontory, the former port of **Hindeloopen** seems to have been lost in time. In nearby **Makkum** is Tichelaar's Royal Makkum Pottery and Tile Factory. Flotillas of yachts tack across the myriad interconnected lakes around **Sloten** and **Sneek,** where the province's connection with the sea and water is most evident. The **Wadden Islands,** just a short ferry ride from the mainland, are also home to seafarers. The largest of these five islands, **Texel,** is easy to reach from Amsterdam through less-visited **North-Holland** and **West-Friesland** to the port of Den Helder. The other islands are more remote, though the roadway across the **Afsluitdijk** (Enclosing Dike) at the northern end of the IJsselmeer reduces journey times considerably. **Terschelling** is the most popular island, with bustling terraces during the high season and the extraordinary theatrical events of the Oerol Festival in June. Like its neighbor, **Ameland,** the island is primarily a nature reserve. The more exclusive,

secluded, car-free islands of **Vlieland** and **Schiermonnikoog,** oases of unspoiled nature on bird migration routes, are favorite weekend getaways for the Dutch. Farther east is **Groningen,** a sophisticated university town, filled with architectural delights, pretty canals, and the magnificent gardens of the Prinsenhoftuin, where 250 years of topiary, lawn-making, and hedge-growing have produced a masterpiece on nature's canvas. Here and there, distinctive storks' nests mounted atop wheels perch high upon poles—a fitting icon for this lovely, verdant agricultural region.

Belgium

Stamp-size Belgium has visitor attractions out of all proportion to its magnitude. Old World charm, a great cuisine, golden beaches, and the scenic forest of the Ardennes: these are but a few. The rest is art, to which Belgium, at the cultural crossroads of Europe, has been one of the supreme contributors. Jan van Eyck, said to have invented oil painting, heads a distinguished list of Flemish artists that includes Rogier Van der Weyden, Dirck Bouts, Hugo Van der Goes, Hans Memling, Quentin Matsys, the Pieters Bruegel (elder and younger), Pieter Paul Rubens, and Anthony Van Dyck. Their work still shines with the mystic aura of the 15th century, the rich humanism of the Renaissance, the decorative exuberance of the Baroque. You can still find the people and the landscapes of Flanders almost unchanged since Pieter Bruegel the Elder brought his extraordinary powers of observation to focus on scenes of Flemish peasant life.

The top two cities are Brussels (Bruxelles, Brussel), a lively capital, a great shopping center, and the site of several fine museums, and Antwerp, a bustling port that is also a notable museum city. The so-called picture-book towns, Ghent (Gand, Gent) and Brugge (Bruges), are gems of medieval reminiscence. If you are interested in military history, or appalled by the suffering that war has caused, Belgium offers you a chance to marvel or remember: from Kortrijk (Courtrai), where Flemish peasant soldiers defeated French horsemen in 1302; to Waterloo, where Wellington confronted Napoléon; to Ieper (Ypres), site of the bloodiest stalemates of World War I; and Bastogne, where Hitler's armies fought their rearguard. Among the numerous other cities of historic and artistic interest are Liège, Leuven (Louvain), Namur (Namen), Mechelen (Malines), and Tournai (Doornik). The ancestor of all health resorts is Spa. On the seacoast, Oostende and Knokke-Heist are the two main lures. Away from the busy life of Belgium's cities lie the rolling hills, dark woods, and green fields of the Ardennes and Belgium's greatest natural curiosity, the grottoes of Han-sur-Lesse and of neighboring Rochefort.

Brussels

In Belgium, all roads lead to Brussels—and this goes for the railroads and airlines, too. Brussels is now the capital of the European Union, the boomtown home of international businesspeople, Eurocrats, and lobbyists with their legendary expense accounts. However, side by side with the European institutions lies the old traditional capital, the ancient heart of the Brabant. In many respects, it is a thoroughly modern city, with shining steel-and-glass office blocks jostling Gothic spires and Art Nouveau town houses.

Victor Hugo once called the city's **Grand'-Place** "the most beautiful square in the world." Flanked by flamboyantly decorated 17th-century guild houses, many of whose ground floors harbor superb cafés, it's dominated by the newly resplendent Hôtel de Ville (town hall), which is in regal Brabant Gothic style. In summertime, the square is spectacularly floodlit at night. Three blocks behind the town hall stands Belgium's "oldest inhabitant," the charming *Manneken Pis*—many amusing legends surround this statue of a peeing boy. The city's superlatives include: magnificent Rubenses and Bruegels at the **Musée d'Art Ancien,** the grand **Cathédrale de St. Michel et Ste. Gudule,** the delightful museum devoted to the art of comic strips, the fashionable square of the **Grand Sablon** (great antiques, pastry shops, and restaurants), the opulent **Théâtre de la Monnaie** for the best concerts and ballet, and the haunting Magritte and Delvaux paintings on view at the **Musée d'Art Moderne.** The **Victor Horta house,** the finest Art Nouveau building on the continent, is now a museum, and other treasures of both Art Nouveau and Art Deco lie in the residential areas to the south and southeast of the city center. Brussels also serves some of Europe's finest cuisine: from *biftec et frites* (steak and fries) in a bistro to *waterzooi* (an elegant chicken stew) in a brasserie to *gaufres* (waffles) or death-by-chocolate pralines on the sidewalk.

Outside the Capital: From Waterloo to Hainaut

The countryside around Brussels has a delightful atmosphere of historic interest and rural calm. Wellington's Headquarters stand near the battlefield at **Waterloo,** most of which remains as it was that fateful day in 1815. In **Mechelen** (Malines in French), once famed as Margaret of Austria's court city, Saint Rombout's Cathedral's great carillon reawakened modern worldwide interest in this art. The town of **Leuven** (Louvain) is home to the great university where Erasmus taught. In **Gaasbeek** one of Belgium's most beautiful châteaux is set within a landscape that inspired the great Bruegel.

Ghent, Brugge, and the Coast

"The Art Cities of Flanders" is a phrase that conjures up images of proud Ghent, now calm but in the past often torn by civil strife, and medieval Brugge (Bruges), contemplating its weathered beauty in the dark mirror of its peaceful canals. In the 15th century, these were among the richest cities in Europe, and the aura of that golden age still seems to emanate from their cloth halls, opulent merchants' homes, and cathedrals. **Ghent** is a city—one of Belgium's largest—not an inanimate museum, as is often said of Brugge. While much is medieval in this city, every stone is, in fact, part of 20th-century life. On a summer evening, viewed from Sint-Michielsbrug (St. Michael's Bridge), Ghent's noble medieval buildings assume a fairy-tale quality under the floodlights. One of the three great medieval spires is that of **St. Bavo's Cathedral,** home of that world-wonder, the 15th-century *Adoration of the Mystic Lamb* altarpiece, which Jan van Eyck must have painted with a magnifying glass, so miraculous is its detail. Among the town's other sights are the Gravensteen, the grand castle of the counts of Flanders; the imposing Town Hall; the proud Belfort (Belfry); and many fine centuries-old buildings.

If it were not for people in modern clothes (and the fact that certain portions of the city are modern business districts), it would be difficult to realize you are living in the 20th century in **Brugge.** Scarcely a facade on any street or canal fails to conjure up visions of the past. Like a northern Venice, it is laced with tranquil canals and quaint bridges (Brugge, indeed, means bridges). This town is most famed as the birthplace of Flemish painting, and in the **Groeninge Museum** on the Dijver hang some of the finest masterpieces of Jan van Eyck (his magnificent *Madonna with Canon Van der Paele*), Van der Goes, Memling, Gerard David, and Hieronymus Bosch. Nearby stands the **Memling Museum** (with just six paintings—but they are six of the greatest Memlings in the world) within the walls of the 12th-century St. John's Hospice. Nothing remains of the castle that gave the **Burg** its name, but even so this is an extraordinary square, with its Gothic town hall and Romanesque chapel. The highways south from Brugge and Ghent point to Flanders Fields—there are countless military cemeteries in the area surrounding **Ieper** (Ypres), risen from the ashes of World War I. The **North Sea Coast** has more than 20 resorts, the James Ensor Museum in **Oostende,** and some of the best seafood in the country.

Antwerp

If you like to combine atmosphere and history with urban excitement, trendy Antwerp may fit the bill even better than Brussels. While the city has grown and modernized apace—today it is a mighty port and diamond mecca (handling 70% of the world's diamonds)—it preserves a great deal of yesterday's glories. In Antwerp's greatest period, the late 17th century, three painters—Pieter Paul Rubens, Jacob Jordaens, and Anthony van Dyck—made the city into a standard bearer of style second only to Rome. At the **Cathedral,** three great Rubens altarpieces dazzle the eye. Off the Meir, **Rubenshuis,** the house occupied by the artist from 1610 for the last quarter century of his life, is a truly patrician palace, marked by a large Flamboyant Baroque portico and a lovely garden. Nearby is the **Mayer van den Bergh Museum,** a connoisseur's delight, with several masterpieces on view, including Bruegel's unforgettable *Dulle Griet* (Mad Meg). Two other august houses are a few blocks away: the **Rockoxhuis,** home of Rubens's patron, and the **Plantin-Moretus Museum,** once the home and

print shop of Europe's most noted 17th-century publisher. Here too are a **Diamond District,** opulent churches, Renaissance guild halls, and the **Koninklijk Museum voor Schone Kunsten,** with its noted Rubens masterworks and four centuries of Dutch and Flemish art on view. East of Antwerp lies the province of **Limbourg** with its prosperous farms and orchards, dotted with ancient towns.

The Ardennes and the Black Country

Perhaps more than any other part of historic Belgium, the **Meuse Valley** is marked by humans' centuries of efforts to survive and protect themselves. Here, side by side, are the graves of Stone-Age hunters and neatly lined crosses for the countless casualties of this century's wars. Next to each town are hilltop forts that sought to hold up invaders, French as well as German. Signs of the great Belgian craft of metalwork are everywhere, especially in **Dinant,** squeezed between the river and the cliffside; in 17th-century **Namur,** at the confluence of the Meuse and the Sambre; and in **Huy,** "the epitome of romantic towns." The symbol of Walloon independence and pride is **Liège,** hard hit by the international steel crisis but still an important industrial center (Val-St-Lambert crystal is made here). Its old city is riddled with secret courtyards, narrow medieval lanes, steeply stepped streets, and *cafés chantants,* where everyone bursts into song.

The Ardennes is a rolling forest region, full of fast-flowing streams and wooded glens, one of Belgium's most favored vacationlands. The enchanted Forest of Arden of Shakespeare's *As You Like It* offers the double charm of quaint villages and a beautiful landscape. The Ardennes forms an arc through the Belgian provinces of Namur, Liège, and Luxembourg, and on to the neighboring Grand Duchy. It remains one of the finest places in Europe to fill your lungs with fresh mountain air.

To the west, ancient **Tournai** beckons, with its great museum of tapestries, fabulous five-tower cathedral, and the **château of Beloeil,** Belgium's greatest garden. Nearby, too, is **the Borinage,** the area south of Mons, where Vincent van Gogh went as a preacher to the poor in 1878, and **Chimay,** where the lure is Madame Tallien's legendary Chateau de Chimay.

Luxembourg

When you try to locate Luxembourg on a map, look for "Lux." at the heart of Western Europe. Even abbreviated, the name runs over—west into Belgium, east into Germany, south into France—as the country's influence has done for centuries. The Grand Duchy of Luxembourg is a thriving, Rhode Island–size land that offers variety and contrasts out of all proportion to its size. On the northern borders of the country and down along the Our and Súre rivers is a rugged, wildly beautiful highland country studded with castles, rich in history. To the south, rich farmlands lie in the broad, central river valleys, giving way to lush vineyards along the southeastern frontier down the Wine Route through the Moselle Valley. A 20-minute drive north from the French border stands the capital, its ancient fortress towering above the south central plain. Seen through early morning mists, it revives the magic of Camelot. It is the nerve center of a thousand-year-old seat of government, a functional working element of the European Union, a spot where the past still speaks, the present interprets, and the future listens.

There is an old saying that describes the life of the Luxembourgers—or *Luxembourgeois,* if you prefer the more elegant French term: "One Luxembourger, a rose garden; two Luxembourgers, a kaffeeklatsch; three Luxembourgers, a band." This is a country of parades and processions, good cheer, and a hearty capacity for beer and Moselle wine. Everybody here speaks French and German, and English is widely understood, which is fortunate because the official language, Lëtzeburgesch, is like nothing else you ever heard before.

Luxembourg City

The capital of the country looks just like a setting for Franz Lehar's operetta, *The Count of Luxembourg;* yet, despite its medieval aura, this city is a major European Union center. All periods exist together in a kind of helter-skelter harmony, but the place seems ageless: Centuries-old bridges, watchtowers, and ramparts reassert themselves to the exclusion of all incongruities. The city itself is small, a perfect place to explore on foot, recreating the past when this was one of the impregnable citadels of Europe.

Luxembourg's appellation as the "Gibraltar of the North" is due to the thousand-year-old fortress known as the **Bock.** Nearby is the 17th-century **Citadelle du St-Esprit** (Citadel of the Holy Spirit). The historic military **Casemates** (tunnels) run under parts of the city. The **Place d'Armes** is the most welcoming corner of town. Other attractions are the **Grand Ducal Palace,** the **Musée National,** and the **Grand'rue,** the city's leading shopping street, which overflows with luxury boutiques. The beautiful scenic ramparts of **the Corniche** offer magnificent views over the deep valley below.

The Luxembourg Ardennes

The northern part of the country, called the Luxembourg Ardennes, is similar in many ways to its Belgian namesake. Romantic winding valleys of fast rivers, ideal for angling, cut into the plateau of high hills. Here and there are magnificent medieval castles—such as those at **Vianden, Bourscheid, Wiltz,** and **Clervaux.** The last was virtually reduced to rubble (but now amazingly restored) by an event that shook the world just over 50 years ago—the devastating Battle of the Ardennes, or Bulge. In **Diekirch** and **Wiltz** are museums devoted to this heroic battle.

The Petite Suisse and the Moselle

In the region that Luxembourgers regard as their own Switzerland, **Müllerthal** is not exactly the Alps but still a hiker's paradise, with leafy hills, flowering fields, and rushing streams. At **Echternach,** a major center of pilgrimage and the arts, the town's exquisite abbey was once famed for its fine medieval school of illumination. To the south, in the **Moselle Valley,** vines cover every exposed slope. The method of making sparkling Moselle wine is illustrated by local vintners in the most refreshing way—by offering you several glasses of the bubbly stuff!

NEW AND NOTEWORTHY

The Netherlands

The Netherlands' newest **museums** are drawing in the crowds and making use of their expanded facilities to host exceptional exhibitions. In the northern provinces the

Groningen Museum has gained a reputation for excellent modern art shows, while the Fries Museum in Leeuwarden has a whole wing dedicated to the mysterious Mata Hari, the dancer and spy who was born in the city. To **Amsterdam's skyline** has been added the remarkable, ship-shape new Metropolis Science & Technology Center, designed by Renzo Piano, architect of the Pompidou Center in Paris. On the other side of town, the **Museumplein** has received a complete remodeling. It has now been landscaped as a green pedestrian area, a fitting backdrop to the modernistic extensions to the **Van Gogh Museum** and the **Stedelijk Museum for Modern Art** that open in 1999. Summer 1999 sees an extraordinary collection of Dutch still-lifes assembled from around the world at the **Rijksmuseum.** You can take in a unique exhibit of **Rembrandt** self-portraits at the Maurtishuis in The Hague, a show of Rembrandt's art collection at the Rembrandthuis Museum in Amsterdam, and a display of portraits of Rembrandt's mother at the Stedelijk Museum De Lakenhal in Leiden from October 1999 to January 2000.

The **magnificent old buildings** that comprise a good deal of the Netherlands' charm need constant care and renovation; happily, Amsterdam's medieval **Waag** (weigh house) has just been given a new lease on life as a restaurant, café, and center for new media after having been shut for decades.

The celebration of **400 years of Dutch-Japanese Ties** continues in 1999. The Dutch established the first European trading post in Japan in an expedition of 1598. The Rijksmuseum is celebrating this anniversary as well as its own 200th birthday. Fans will gather in Amsterdam or Rotterdam in July 2000 for the finale of the **European Soccer Cup. SAIL 2000** in Amsterdam is the final destination for the World Tall Ships Race, with the splendid three-masters sailing up the North-Sea Canal in a spectacular Parade of Sail on August 24, 2000. Beginning in June 1998, the construction of a replica of a 19th-century three-master that will sail in this event takes place in the harbor behind the Dutch Maritime Museum. The next **Floriade,** the ~~quadrennial~~ world event that
every-10-years

covers the flower-growing region between Amsterdam and the Haarlemmermeer with colorful blooms and landscaped gardens, takes place in 2002.

Belgium

Brussels is one of Europe's nine designated **cities of culture** for 2000: The year's program includes an artistic parade (June), an exhibition of Brussels 15th- and 16th-century altarpieces and tapestries (Apr.–Nov.), and other art shows and events (summer). The anniversary spotlight in 1999 turns upon Oostend eccentric James **Ensor,** who died in 1949. Exhibitions and events in both Brussels and Oostend honor the artist, who devoted himself to satirical portraits of local dignitaries and scathing social commentaries in what was to become the trademark Expressionist style. In 2000 Ghent again hosts *Floralies,* a prestigious flower show mounted every five years. Also in 2000, Ghent, Mechelen and Brussels commemorate the 500th anniversary of the birth of **Charles V** with a wide range of cultural festivities. At Antwerp's **Fine Arts Museum** in 1999, the 400th anniversary of **Van Dyck**'s birth is marked by an encyclopedic display of his life's work. The main auditorium of the Palais des Beaux-Arts in Brussels is closed for restoration starting in June 1999. It reopens in June 2000 with an enormous **Warhol Retrospective.** A new **booking office** (☎ 0800/21221) has opened in Brussels that will provide information and reservations for events all over the country. There is no charge for the service. Payment is by direct debit or (for visitors) major credit card.

Luxembourg

Luxembourg's ever-booming economy, fed by tax-pampered banks and a growing population of well-paid Eurocrats, is bursting at the seams, and it shows more than ever. Flashy new mirrored-glass banks and office buildings are popping up in Luxembourg City and its suburbs, and the infrastructure of highways, bridges, and tunnels get slicker every year. Public works abound on the cultural side, too, with a new national theater (Théâtre National de Luxembourg), a newly nationalized orchestra (Orchestre Philharmonique de

Luxembourg), and a plethora of cutting-edge public sculpture. Construction is in progress on the **Musée Grand Duc Jean**, dedicated to contemporary art and designed by I.M. Pei. It is scheduled to open in 2000. But the old ways aren't gone yet: The fur-coated nouveau-gentry shop at Versace and sip champagne at intermission, while the old guard—in loden green and crocheted cloches—dig loyally into their sausage and sauerkraut.

FODOR'S CHOICE

No two people will agree on what makes a perfect vacation, but it's fun and helpful to know what others think. We hope you'll have a chance to experience some of Fodor's Choices yourself while visiting the Benelux countries. For detailed information about each entry, refer to the appropriate chapters within this guidebook.

The Netherlands

Quintessential Holland

★ **Begijnhof, Amsterdam.** Feel the gentle breeze of history in the solitude of a serene courtyard that has hardly changed since the Pilgrim Fathers worshiped here centuries ago.

★ **Amsterdam canals at night.** Walking along the canals of Amsterdam after dark is one of the simplest, cheapest, and most memorable experiences that Holland has to offer. Pedestrians (and cyclists) rule over traffic, the most beautiful gables are subtly lit up, and the pretty humpbacked bridges are festooned with lights. Alternatively, get up early and stroll out before the city is awake, as the mist gently rises off the water.

★ **Anne Frank House, Amsterdam.** The swinging bookcase that hid the door is still here, as well as the magazine pictures that young Anne pasted on the walls for decoration. It is impossible not to be moved as you wander through the secret apartment where the Frank family hid from the Nazis.

★ **Portuguese Synagogue, Amsterdam.** A gracious survivor of the ravages wrought on the city's Jewish Quarter during World War II, this 17th-century synagogue is suffused with subdued light on sunny days.

★ **Prinsenhof, Delft.** Sit quietly in the courtyard garden, then explore the atmospheric 15th-century convent before strolling off along what is probably the oldest canal in the Netherlands. At times it seems that you are stepping right into Vermeer's *View of Delft.*

★ **Caves of Mount St. Peter, Maastricht.** Wander along some of the 20,000 passages and into the dim, echoing halls of a vast subterranean complex of caves that provided a refuge for the people of Limburg from AD 50 up to the Second World War.

★ **St. John's Cathedral, 's-Hertogenbosch.** Pilgrims set off from here to Santiago de Compostela in Spain, but you can stay behind to see the richly carved pulpit and ornate 17th-century organ.

★ **Dom Tower, Utrecht.** Climb through a puzzling complexity of twisting stairways to find yourself atop the tallest church tower in the Netherlands, with panoramic views across city and countryside.

Where Art Comes First

★ **Rijksmuseum, Amsterdam.** As if the best collection of Dutch Golden Age art in the world were not enough, "the Rijks" also offers a cornucopia of other aesthetic delights. The collection of applied arts is especially comprehensive, from early Oriental Buddhas to 17th-century four-poster beds swathed in tapestry. Rembrandt's enormous *Night Watch* is a hot contender for the title of "the world's most famous painting."

★ **Vincent van Gogh Museum, Amsterdam.** It is difficult to pick a favorite from the more than 200 paintings by this great artist on view here, but *Sunflowers* is among the top choices. None of the versions you may have seen in reproduction can match the lustre of the original, where brilliant blues appear unexpectedly between the bright yellows and greens.

★ **Paleis Het Loo, Apeldoorn.** Stroll through the elegant formal gardens, view the sumptuous Dutch Baroque palace that was home to the Dutch royal family until the 1960s, then pop inside to feast your eyes on the rich furnishings.

★ **Nieuwe Kerk, Delft.** Here, typically Dutch building materials of brick and wood give even soaring Gothic buildings a down-to-earth feel. Inside, however, you'll find the magnificent marble mausoleum of the royal House of Orange.

★ **Groninger Museum, Groningen.** One of the Netherlands' most adventurous contributions to modern architecture stands like a gateway to the city as you leave the train station. Three distinctive pavilions, designed by different architects, are connected by waterways. Exhibitions include local history and an innovative series dedicated to modern fashion designers.

★ **Sint Servaas Basilik, Maastricht.** Restorers have done a wonderful job in bringing back to life the bright colors and delicate floral designs inside this 7th-century basilica, and the treasury brims with jewel-encrusted reliquaries and other precious objects.

★ **Kröller-Müller Museum, Otterloo.** Art collections based on the quirks of one person's taste are often the choicest ones, as is here proved by Hélène Müller's stash of Van Goghs and modern art. Not only is the art world-class, the museum is in the heart of the Netherlands' most beautiful nature reserve.

★ **Rietveld-Schroeder House, Utrecht.** A pinnacle of Dutch modernism awaits you in a suburb of Utrecht. With its white walls, plate-glass windows, and clean straight lines, this villa—designed by Gerrit Rietveld—set the mark for much 20th-century European design.

Great Hotels

★ **The Grand Hotel, Amsterdam.** The Grand's last incarnation was as Amsterdam's City Hall, and it is resplendent with decor by some of the top artists of the 1920s and 1930s. Ask to see the Wedding Room and keep an eye open for the mural by Karel Appel. $$$$

★ **Amstel Inter-Continental, Amsterdam.** The Grand Duchess of Amsterdam hotels is quite at home with royal guests and stands, quietly proud of her most recent face-lift, at a prime spot on the river Amstel. Take the hotel luxury launch for a classy trip on the canals. $$$$

★ **Hotel Derlon, Maastricht.** After you have unpacked your suitcase and admired the original artwork on the walls, go downstairs for a look at the hotel's private museum of antiquities, then saunter outside for a coffee on the most beautiful square in Maastricht. $$$$

★ **Hotel de Ville, Groningen.** Completed in late 1997 and occupying a group of monumental houses in the city center, the hotel has all the trappings of modern style. The brasserie serves original variations on local dishes and even delivers supper to your room. $$$

★ **Auberge Corps de Garde, Groningen.** Small is beautiful in this 17th-century barracks house. The hotel rooms have a homey atmosphere, while the restaurant downstairs ranks with the most elegant in town—a veritable honey pot to the gourmets of the northern provinces. $$

★ **Canal House, Amsterdam.** Experience the gracious life in a genuine Amsterdam canal house, overflowing with antiques. Linger over breakfast beneath a crystal chandelier, and then enjoy the calm of the quiet garden courtyard. $$

★ **Kasteel Elsloo, Elsloo.** Wine, dine, and spend the night in the castle where an erstwhile Prince of Monaco lived with his bride. The next morning take a promenade in the castle park—lovingly landscaped in the picturesque English style. $$

Memorable Restaurants

★ **Excelsior, Amsterdam.** Enjoy a view across the Amstel to the delicate spire of the old Munttoren, as waiters in stiff formal attire glide up to serve you with the very best haute cuisine and *grands vins*. $$$$

★ **Prinses Juliana, Valkenburg aan de Geul.** Various heads of state have feasted here before you, including members of the Dutch royal family. So sit back, enjoy the plush surrounds, and order up the vintage champagne. $$$$

★ **Nolet's Restaurant, Het Reymerswale.** Climb upstairs for a table that has a view over the dike to the very waters that have provided your meal. Oysters and mussels are the specialty here, and the lobster bisque is so popular that Danny Nolet has taken to bottling it for guests to take home. $$–$$$$

★ **Café Américain, Amsterdam.** The painted-glass Art Deco lamps here once cast their light on the cream of Amsterdam's intelligentsia. Today, even though most tables are occupied by tourists, the café-society atmosphere lingers. $$$

★ **De Silveren Spiegel, Amsterdam.** Two tiny rooms in a crooked, 17th-century house offer space for just a handful of diners. The owner lives upstairs and serves at table, his shaggy dog sits (sometimes) obediently in one corner, and the chef works wonders. $$$

★ **Kastel Doorwerth, Arnhem.** Step across the drawbridge of a diminutive stone castle for a fine meal in the onetime stables; then explore the ramparts or go for a walk in the surrounding woods. $$$

★ **Belhamel, Amsterdam.** A stunning Art Deco interior with a fine view down the Herengracht provides a superb setting for a well-prepared and attentively served dinner. In summer you can dine canal-side; in winter the emphasis is on hearty game dishes. $$

★ **Polman's Huis, Utrecht.** Tall windows and an impossibly distant stucco ceiling dwarf the coffee drinkers in this grandest of grand cafés. $$

★ **Haesje Claes, Amsterdam.** The epitome of *gezelligheid* (cozy comfort) is chock-full of solid wooden furniture, adorned with brass trinkets, and renowned for its slap-up meals. This is the place, on a cold day, for pea soup so thick that your spoon stands upright. $

Special Memories

★ **Bikes on dikes (most anywhere).** Trundling along the top of a dike on a sit-up-and-beg Dutch bicycle, with the sea to one side of you, wetlands (alive with bird life) on the other, and the wind in your hair, is transporting in more ways than one. Enhance the delight by stopping over at one of myriad waterside cafés or charming villages along the way.

★ **Carnival, Maastricht.** Medieval Christian pageantry combines with pagan revelry in the last days before Lent. Join the merriment of parades and parties as the ebullient southern Dutch go all out for a jolly good time.

★ **Oosterschelde, Zeeland.** For an awesome insight into how this low-lying country keeps constant battle with water, visit the Delta Storm Barrier, and then stroll in the bracing breeze along the shores of the Oosterschelde before stopping off at a harbor restaurant for oysters fresh from the water's edge.

Belgium

Quintessential Belgium

★ **The canals of Brugge.** If you wake up at dawn to view these canals without people, they will look like three-dimensional Hans Memling paintings. Aboard a boat gliding under humpbacked bridges and past quayside merchant's homes, you get an intimate glimpse of the city—complementing the grand façades that are its public face.

★ **Grand'Place, Brussels.** This jewel box of a square ranks among Europe's great treasures. The soaring lines of the Gothic Town Hall dominate one side, in contrast with the elaborately decorated Baroque guildhalls that surround it.

★ **Sint-Michielsbrug, Ghent.** From this vantage point, the spiritual, mercantile, and military glory that was Ghent is spread out before you. To the east are the three great medieval spires of the gray St. Nicholas Church, the honey-color St. Bavo's Cathedral, and the gilt-encrusted Belfry. To the north, on either side of the River Leie, note the grand old quays of Korenlei and Graslei, with, in the background, the ancient fortress of s'-Gravensteen. At night, under floodlights, the view assumes a fairy-tale quality.

★ **La Roche-en-Ardenne, Ourthe River Valley.** This is the vacation land Belgians dream about. Deep down between wooded hills, the lively river winds a meandering course, carrying kayaks that seem to move now toward you, now away. Families camp on the riverside while children splash in the chilly water. A small village clings to the hillside, its farms and church built of stone and slate. From above, look out over an undulating vista of green hills.

★ **Malmedy, Les Hautes Fagnes.** These "High Fens" are mossy, waterlogged moors—a windswept, desolate landscape punctuated by bushes and copses of beech and oak trees, rich in bird life and mountain vegetation. The frequent mist adds to the mystery, and hikers are urged not to stray from the well-marked paths.

★ **The North Sea Coast.** One long, wide beach, the North Sea Coast often looks like a scene from an Impressionist painting: couples strolling arm-in-arm, riders galloping along the water's edge, kites flying high above, tiny tots digging sand castles to be swallowed by the tide. Out at sea—pleasure craft and fishing vessels. Behind the dike—vacation apartment houses, sand dunes, and cafés serving pancakes and waffles.

Where Art Comes First

⭐ **Museum Mayer Van den Bergh, Antwerp.** If you think of Pieter Bruegel as a painter of jolly village scenes, you're in for a surprise. His *Dulle Griet* (badly translated to "Mad Meg," as if she were some 16th-century bag lady) strides angrily across a landscape of surrealist horrors, a sword in one hand and a cooking pot in the other. Many interpretations have been advanced, but it certainly can be read as a prophetic antiwar statement, as pertinent to the war in Bosnia as to the Thirty Years' War, which in Bruegel's day was just around the corner.

⭐ **St. John's Hospital, Brugge.** The small Memling Museum is installed in this vast hospital, which served Brugge's sick and poor for 800 years. This is the most important collection of the few works by Memling to have survived. The realism of the so-called Flemish Primitives is present in all meticulously rendered details, but just as some of his women's faces are covered by a delicately painted veil, so there is in his work a gossamer veil of mysticism that points up the spirituality of the subject.

⭐ **Modern Art Museum, Brussels.** In conception and structure, the museum is among Europe's most unusual. Snaking into the ground like an upended Guggenheim, its winding passages offer surprises at every turn—the disturbingly altered reality of René Magritte and Giorgio Di Chirico, the naïve eroticism of Paul Delvaux, and the caustic polemics of James Ensor. Wilder modern creations by Pierre Alechinsky and sculptor Pol Bury round out a superb collection.

⭐ **St. Bavo's Cathedral, Ghent.** Van Eyck's *Adoration of the Mystic Lamb,* completed in 1432, inspires all the awe that its creator could have hoped for. This mother of all oil paintings was executed with brilliant, miniaturist realism. Though the brush strokes are microscopic, they are brilliantly held together by a unifying view of the redemption of mankind.

⭐ **St. Bartholomew's Church, Liège.** Under the prince-bishops of Liège in the 11th and 12th centuries there flourished *L'Art Mosan*—one of the most distinctive of all medieval styles. The leader of the school was Renier de Huy, and here you will find his masterpiece, a huge baptismal bronze font decorated with sculpted reliefs. Note, in particular, the high-relief scenes of St. John the Baptist and of the baptism of Christ—sculptures of extraordinary plasticity and emotion.

Lodging and Dining Gems

⭐ **Firean, Antwerp.** Every detail is authentic Art Deco at this small hotel. It is family-owned with family service and wonderful attention to details, including its own-brand toiletries. Just inside the Ring Road, it is well located if you'd rather not negotiate Antwerp's one-way maze, but you have to hop a tram to get to the Old Town from here. $$$

⭐ **Die Swaene, Brugge.** Chandeliers, Louis XV furniture, four-poster beds, Burgundy wallpaper, ancient tapestries, candlelit dinners, open fireplaces, marble nymphs, canalside setting: If romance is what you crave, you'll find it here. The cuisine keeps getting better and now ranks as one of the best in the gourmet heaven that is Brugge. $$$ (hotel), $$$$ (restaurant)

⭐ **Amigo, Brussels.** Even diplomats feel at home here thanks to personalized service (and even bankers appreciate that a junior suite costs no more than a double in the top price category). Although a mere 50 years old, the Amigo blends perfectly into its Old Town surroundings. $$$

⭐ **Welcome/Truite d'Argent, Brussels.** The smallest hotel in Brussels is one of its most charming. It owes its double name to the fact that taxi drivers are more familiar with the name of its 100-year-old restaurant, the Truite d'Argent ($$$). The good news: Michel and Sophie Smeesters are working on expanding from 6 to 10 rooms. Wearing his chef's hat, Michel prepares great seafood specialties, with Sophie in charge of the dining room. $

Taste Treats

⭐ **Ogenblik, Brussels.** Slap in the historic center, in the Galeries Saint-Hubert, this rough-and-ready bistro has been packing them in for more than 20 years. Marble-top tables, green-shade lamps, and superior grub all add up to a delightfully friendly ambience. $$$

★ **Neuze Neuze, Antwerp.** The ever-present, mustachioed Domien Sels has transformed several small 16th-century houses in the shadow of the cathedral into one stylish restaurant that seems to consist exclusively of nooks and crannies. His is a cuisine of surprises: goose liver meunière with caramelized pineapple, sole with a purée of shrimps. And he pulls it off! $$

★ **Chez Léon de Bruxelles, Brussels.** Léon has celebrated its first century by changing its name from plain old Chez Léon; prices have started to edge upward but little else has changed. Most diners opt for the specialty, a heaping bowl of blue-shelled mussels accompanied by lots of super fries, but Léon does a mean *filet américain* (steak tartare) as well. $

Special Memories

★ **Vlaeykensgang, Antwerp.** Linger in the alley that progress forgot—where small whitewashed houses stand shoulder to shoulder along a narrow cobblestone alleyway—and listen to the Monday evening carillon concert from the great cathedral. As you emerge into Pelgrimstraat, you're rewarded by the best possible view of the white cathedral spire, whose Gothic lines sweep upward to an incomparable, openwork summit.

★ **The Ommegang, Brussels.** Once a year, in July, the noble ladies and gentlemen of Belgium revert to the pomp and circumstance of yore, as they reenact the stately procession, with standards flying, that greeted the Holy Roman Emperor Charles V on the self-same Grand'Place in 1549. Horsemen, acrobats, fire-eaters, and stilt-walkers participate with gusto.

★ **The Grottes de Han, Han-sur-Lesse.** As you wander through the dark, cool caves, where Neolithic people found shelter and later generations found a hiding place from marauding armies, you come upon a vast hall under a domelike rock roof 400 ft high. Suddenly, on the guided tour, a single torch-carrier appears, running a slalom-like course down the steeply slanting wall: You feel transported thousands—not hundreds—of years back in time.

★ **The Last Post, Ieper.** Every night at 8, buglers sound the Last Post at the Menin Gate in memory of the 300,000 British soldiers who passed through here to their death in the trenches of "Flanders Fields." For one poignant moment, traffic is stopped, as Ieper remembers.

Luxembourg

Quintessential Luxembourg

★ **Luxembourg City.** The 1,000-year-old fortress city, classified as a World Heritage Monument by the United Nations, was once thought so formidable a stronghold that its mere presence was considered a threat to international peace. Today the vast panorama of medieval stonework and fortified towers guards Luxembourg's considerable wealth as one of the world's leading financial centers and its political clout within the European Union as home to the European Court of Justice.

★ **The Château of Vianden.** This grandiose castle suddenly looms dramatically from the top of a hill as you approach Vianden. It has a special significance to Luxembourgers: It was the ancestral home of the ruling Orange-Nassau dynasty and was the last part of Luxembourg to be liberated by U.S. troops in World War II.

Dining and Lodging Gems

★ **La Bergerie, Geyershof.** A soufflé of brill, flavored with basil, may not be what you expect in the middle of the Luxembourg forest, but that's what father and son team Claude and Thierry Phal have in mind for you in this pastoral hideaway. They don't come any more idyllic than this, and if you wish, they'll whisk you off for an overnight at the villa/hotel of the same name in nearby Echternach. $$ *(hotel)*, $$$$ *(restaurant)*

★ **Clairefontaine, Luxembourg City.** Tony and Margot Tintinger have served one pope, several presidents, and many prime ministers in their swank restaurant, decorated with restrained opulence. It stands on the handsomest square in town, a stone's throw from the ministries that supply much of the clientele, and on fine days tables spill out over the square. The menu begins with five different preparations of *foie gras d'oie* (goose liver), which suggests that this is far from your garden-variety bar-and-grill. $$$$

★ **La Cascade, Luxembourg City.** A splendid, turreted villa from the turn of the century has been converted into this delightful hotel on the banks of the Alzette. An Italian-inspired lunch on the comfortable,

sunny riverside terrace is a special treat.
$$

Special Memories

⭐ **Le Bock, Luxembourg City.** This is Sigefroid's 1,000-year-old castle, protected in its heyday by three rings of defense and 53 forts. As you wander through the casemates—underground corridors tunneled through the rock—stop at an aperture to look out over the valley below, and imagine the thousands of banner-topped tents and campfires of an army laying siege to the impenetrable fortress.

⭐ **Müllerthal.** Spread your picnic of dark bread, pink Ardennes ham, and smoky sausage alongside a twisting brook in Luxembourg's "Little Switzerland." Butterflies flutter over the meadow, swallows dart about in the sky, and the only sounds are the drone of the bees and the rustle of the stream rushing between high bluffs. If you feel drowsy, it's not just because of the Moselle you drank with your meal.

GREAT ITINERARIES

Haute Cuisine and Country Air

The peripatetic gourmet first chooses overnight stops to ensure that each evening meal is a feast. It is a bonus that many of the finest small hotels with outstanding restaurants are in out-of-the-way places that you might not otherwise visit. This kind of travel obviously does not come cheap.

➤ DURATION: 14 days.

➤ GETTING AROUND: **By Car.** In the Netherlands, the drive from Amsterdam to Kerkrade, by way of Oisterwijk, is 380 kilometers (228 miles). In Belgium, highways link Antwerp and Noirefontaine, by way of the coast, for an arc of some 600 kilometers (360 miles). To travel from meal to meal in Luxembourg, a car is indispensable.

By Train. In the Netherlands there are good train connections from Amsterdam, by way of Middelburg and Den Bosch. Trains in Belgium connect, through Brussels, with the main towns on the route; a car is necessary in the Ardennes. In Luxembourg, only Luxembourg City is easily reached by direct rail lines.

➤ THE MAIN ROUTE: **3 Nights: The Netherlands.** From Amsterdam, travel south toward Middelburg; take the Yerseke-Kruiningen exit on the highway toward **Kruiningen.** Restaurant Inter Scaldes sits alone in the countryside, offering fine French cuisine and luxury accommodations. The following day can be a leisurely drive to **Oisterwijk** between Tilburg and 's-Hertogenbosch (Den Bosch), for an overnight stay at Hotel-Restaurant De Swaen in the town square. The following day, travel south through Limburg province to **Kerkrade** for dinner in the castle at Hotel Kasteel Erenstein and overnight in its luxury accommodations across the road, a half-timbered, former Limburg farmstead. A word of advice: Book your overnight stays well in advance.

9 Nights: Belgium. Start the Belgian portion of your trip in **Antwerp,** where 't Fornuis is the top restaurant. The 10 rooms of De Rosier are only minutes away. Make your next stop **Brugge,** to eat at the revered De Karmeliet or the young, imaginative Den Gouden, both within easy walking distance of the aristocratic rooms of De Tuilerieen. From Brugge, head for the coast and **Oostende,** where you can stay and dine at the sumptuous Oostendse Compagnie, overlooking the sea. At the west end of the coast, dine and stay in **De Panne** at the exquisite Le Fox. As you head inland, stop first at Eddy Vandekerckhove's Gastronomic Village just outside **Kortrijk,** where the rooms have views of a tropical garden or the Flemish countryside, and the cuisine will delight you. **Brussels** would be an obvious stop, with its Comme Chez Soi and other renowned restaurants. For something more unusual, stop instead at **Genval,** near Brussels, where the Château du Lac's restaurant, Le Trèfle à Quatre, offers lake views and superb food. Farther east, just west of **Hasselt,** the world-class Scholteshof restaurant provides extraordinary dining and superb accommodations. The Clos Saint-Denis in nearby **Tongeren** runs a close second but offers no lodging. Head south to **Noirefontaine** in Belgian Luxembourg and treat yourself to an overnight stay at the luxurious Moulin Hideux, where you can savor fine, leisurely meals and work off the calories by taking enchanting walks in the woods.

3 Nights: Luxembourg. In **Luxembourg City,** settle for the night in either the traditional Hotel Cravat or the modern luxury of Le Royal. You'll dine in the splendid Clairefontaine on the charming square of the same name. The next day, head south toward the French border for **Frisange,** where Lea Linster will serve a world-class lunch, and dine at super-chef Franky Steichen's L'Agath, south of the city. Next day, explore the castle country of the Ardennes, lunching at Le Châtelain in **Vianden.** Book for the night at the Bergerie in **Echternach.** Take advantage of shuttle service to the idyllic restaurant, also called La Bergerie, in the middle of the woods, where Claude and Thierry Phal's cooking reaches new heights.

Ancient Crafts of the Low Countries

The extraordinary flourishing of decorative crafts in the Low Countries during the Middle Ages was the result of the rulers' insatiable appetite for ornamentation, an appetite shared by local gentry and wealthy burghers. The clothing and jewelry lovingly depicted in 15th-century Flemish paintings indicate the high standards of the artisans of the era, whose traditions continue.

➤ DURATION: 10 days.

➤ GETTING AROUND: **By Car.** Luxembourg City is easy to reach by car. The Villeroy & Boch complex lies just outside the center, on the northwest edge, toward Wiltz. The Belgian section of the itinerary (Luxembourg City to Rotterdam) is about 780 kilometers (468 miles), some 10 hours' driving time. The Dutch section (Antwerp to Delft to Amsterdam to Hindeloopen) is about 290 kilometers (174 miles).

By Train. If you're visiting Luxembourg by train, use city buses to reach the Villeroy & Boch outlet. All Belgian cities on this itinerary are accessible by train, but you'll have to double back from Brugge to Brussels to get to Antwerp. Train travel in the Netherlands is efficient.

➤ THE MAIN ROUTE: **1 Night: Luxembourg.** A weekday stop in Luxembourg will give you a chance to visit the on-site factory outlet store of Villeroy & Boch, whose popular vitro-porcelain sells here at discount prices. Watch for specials on patterns being phased out, and be sure to dig through the bargain bin. The factory

does not ship, so be prepared to schlep. If you can round up a group of 20 visitors, you can take a guided tour of the factory.

1 Night: Liège. Arriving from Luxembourg, start your Belgian crafts tour in Liège. The Val Saint-Lambert glassworks in Seraing, on the outskirts of the city, is one of the finest in the world; you can visit the showroom and watch glassblowers in action. The factory outlet offers great values.

3 Nights: Brussels. Halfway between Brussels and Antwerp, **Mechelen** has the only workshops in Belgium where traditional tapestry weaving is still practiced; Gaspard De Wit's Royal Tapestry Manufacture (open for visits Saturday morning only) is at the Refuge van Tongerlo. In **Brussels,** some of the finest examples of Belgian tapestry, from the 14th to 16th centuries, are on view in the Musées Royaux d'Art et d'Histoire (Royal Museums of Art and History), and lace and needlework are on view in the Musée du Costume et de la Dentelle (Costume and Lace Museum). **Tournai** (southwest of Brussels) is one of the old centers of tapestry; at the new Museum of Tapestry (and Textile Arts) you can see how it is done.

1 Night: Brugge. Brugge is intimately associated with lace-making, and there are a large number of shops selling everything from lace souvenirs to works of art. The best place to get a real understanding of the craft is the Kantcentrum (Lace Center), incorporating a museum and a lace-making school.

1 Night: Antwerp. Diamonds are big business in Antwerp, where the origins and history of diamond cutting are shown at the Provincial Diamond Museum. Diamondland, where you can also see diamond-cutting demonstrations, is probably the most spectacular diamond showroom in the world.

3 Nights: The Netherlands. Begin in **Delft** with a visit to the factory De Porcelyn Fles to watch artists paint the famous blue-and-white ceramic ware known as Delft. Continue to **Amsterdam** for a visit to a diamond factory. Then go north to **Leeuwarden,** Friesland's provincial capital, where the Keramiekmuseum Het Princessehof (Princessehof Ceramics Museum) has a splendid collection of ceramics and tiles from around the world. In the Frisian village of **Makkum** to the west, the prized Dutch multicolor ceramic ware is produced at the Tichelaars Koninklijk Makkumer Aardewerk en Tegelfabriek (Tichelaars Royal Makkum Pottery and Tile Factory). In nearby **Hindeloopen** you can see the traditional brightly painted Frisian furniture in the Museum Hidde Nieland Stichting.

The Ardennes

To experience the Ardennes fully, you must take your time. Explore the hamlets and river valleys off the highway. Stop in the small towns along the way for a meal of hearty Ardennaise fare—smoked ham, cheese and farm bread, crayfish and trout from the rushing streams—enjoy the inns, visit the churches and castles. You'll be amply rewarded!

➤ DURATION: 8 days.

➤ GETTING AROUND: **By Car.** The Belgian portions of the trip add up to about 430 kilometers (258 miles). Much of this is on secondary routes, so expect driving time of about eight hours. To see the best of the Luxembourg Ardennes, you'll need a car for the *routes nationales* and secondary roads that snake through the forests.

By Train. The cities on the itinerary are accessible by train, but not necessarily in the same sequence as they are listed below. Rail connections in Luxembourg are minimal, though a train does run from Luxembourg City to Clervaux, in the north.

➤ THE MAIN ROUTE: **2 Nights: Liège and Malmedy.** From **Liège,** go by way of Eupen toward Malmedy, stopping to explore the high moorland known as the **Hautes Fagnes.**

1 Night: La-Roche-en-Ardenne. Passing Stavelot, continue to La-Roche-en-Ardenne in the heart of the Belgian mountain range. Here, in the valley of the River Ourthe, you will see the finest scenery the Ardennes offers.

2 Nights: Luxembourg. Enter the Grand Duchy of Luxembourg from the north, stopping to visit **Clervaux**'s castle museum before winding through rolling countryside toward **Vianden,** where the spectacular castle dominates the hill village. Then, though it falls just below the Ardennes plateau, drive into **Luxembourg City** for the medieval fortifications, cathedral, and Old Town streets.

3 Nights: Belgium. Driving west from Luxembourg City, follow the Semois River, with a stop to see the romantic ruins of Orval Abbey, and then to **Bouillon** with its mountaintop fort. Through dense woods you reach **Saint-Hubert,** going on to **Han-sur-Lesse,** with its remarkable caves and nature reserve. Follow the Lesse to **Dinant**—part of the way by kayak, if you wish—spectacularly situated on the River Meuse. As you drive along the Meuse, notice the sheer cliffs lining the riverbank on the opposite side. Continuing along the river, with stops in **Huy** and **Modave,** you return to **Liège.**

FESTIVALS AND SEASONAL EVENTS

The top seasonal events of the Netherlands, Belgium, and Luxembourg are listed below, and any one of them could provide the stuff of lasting memories. Contact each country's tourist office for complete information, or call the contact numbers below (The Netherlands' country code is 31, Belgium's is 32, and Luxembourg's is 352; drop the initial 0 if calling from outside the country).

THE NETHERLANDS

WINTER

➤ JAN.–FEB.: **Film Festival Rotterdam** (☎ 0900/403–4065) celebrates international avant-garde cinema.

➤ FEB. (WEEK BEFORE LENT): **Carnaval** (☎ 043/325–2121) dances through the cities of Brabant and Limbourg provinces.

➤ MAR.: The **European Fine Art Fair** (☎ 073/614–5165) gathers artists and works in Maastricht, and international rowing crews compete in Amsterdam's **Head of the River** (☎ 035/525–8169

SPRING

➤ APR.: **Rotterdam Marathon** draws runners from

around the globe, and the **Flower Parade** (☎ 0252/434–710) passes through Lisse to open the **National Floral Exhibition** at Keukenhof gardens (☎ 0252/465–555). **National Museum Weekend** opens 450 museums across the country to visitors free or at a discount. April 30 is the unforgettable **Queen's Day,** the Dutch monarch's official birthday, when Amsterdam erupts with a city-wide, all-day street party and the queen makes a more sedate official visit to a selected town in the provinces.

➤ MAY: **National Bicycle Day** (May 8) races through the Netherlands; an international modern dance festival, **Spring Dance** (☎ 030/232–4125) bounds into Utrecht; and the **Jazz Festival Breda** (☎ 076/581–2090) makes the city jump. The **Eleven Cities Bicycle Tour** (May 24; ☎ 515/573–263) and the five-day **Eleven Cities Walking Tour** (☎ 058/292–5578) circle Friesland.

SUMMER

➤ JUNE: **Holland Festival of the Performing Arts** (☎ 020/530–7110) captures Amsterdam, spilling over to The Hague, Rotterdam, and Utrecht; **Parkpop** (☎ 070/361–8888), a pop music festival, livens up The Hague; **Pinkpop** (☎ 046/475–2500) bursts into Landgraf; and the **Oerol Festival** (☎ 0562/443–000) takes over the island

of Terschelling, attracting thousands of visitors with 10 days of mid-summer outdoor theater and spectacle.

➤ JULY: The Hague hosts the **North Sea Jazz Festival** (☎ 015/214–8900) the **International Organ Competition** (☎ 023/511–5733) brings musicians to Haarlem in even-number years; and the **International Four Days Walking Event** (☎ 070/360–4141) strides through Nijmegen.

➤ JULY/AUG.: *Skutsjeseilen* **Sailing Regattas** skim the lakes in Friesland.

➤ AUG.: Utrecht hosts the internationally renowned **Holland Festival of Early Music;** the Amsterdam **Prinsengracht Concert** brings flotillas of boats for classical music performances on a floating stage on the canal. In 2000 **Sail Amsterdam** (☎) draws tall ships from around the world.

AUTUMN

➤ SEPT.: The **Bloemencorso Floral Parade** (Sept. 4; ☎ 0297/325–100) makes a day-long procession of floats from Aalsmeer to Amsterdam; **Gaudeamus International Music Week** (☎ 020/694–7349) honors contemporary classical music and its young composers in Amsterdam; and the **Opening of Parliament** (☎ 070/356–4000) takes place in The Hague on the third Tuesday—the queen arrives in her golden coach.

➤ Oct.: The **Holland Dance Festival** (☎ 0900/ 340–3505) brings ballet and other dance companies to the Hague.

➤ Nov.: With the **St. Nicolaas Parade** (☎ 0900/ 400–4040) in Amsterdam and in cities throughout the country, the arrival of Sinterklaas launches the Christmas season.

➤ Nov./Dec.: At **Jumping Indoor Maastricht** (☎ 0499/398–115) and **Jumping Amsterdam** (☎ 020/665–4835) international equine competitors display dressage and jumping prowess.

BELGIUM

WINTER

➤ End Jan.: Brussels's **International Film Festival,** which is forcing its way onto the international agenda, takes place across the capital.

➤ Early Feb.: **Carnival** is celebrated with great gusto, especially at Binche with its extravagantly costumed Gilles, and at Malmedy, Oostende, and Eupen.

➤ Mar. 9: In Stavelot, the hilarious Blancs Moussis, with their long red noses, swoop through town during the **mid-Lent carnival.**

SPRING

➤ Late Apr.: One of the world's leading flower shows, the **Floralies** (☎ 09/222–7336), is held every five years in the Flanders Expo Hall in Ghent: next in 2000.

➤ Late Apr.–early May: The **Royal Greenhouses** (☎ 02/513–0770), at Laeken Palace near Brussels, with superb flower and plant arrangements, are open to the public for a limited period.

➤ Early May: On **Ascension Day,** the Procession of the Holy Blood (☎ 050/448664) in Brugge is one of the oldest and most elaborate religious and historical processions in Europe. Early seat reservations are recommended.

➤ May: The **Queen Elisabeth International Music Competition** (☎ 02/513–0099) is one of the most demanding events of its kind. In 1999, the focus is on young pianists; in 2000 on singers.

➤ May: The **KunstenFESTIVALdesArts** (☎ 02/512–7450) in Brussels is a month-long international celebration of contemporary drama, dance, and music.

➤ Late May: The **Brussels Jazz Marathon** (☎ 0900/ 00606) encompasses gigs and informal sessions in more than 50 clubs and pubs, plus outdoor concerts in the Grand'-Place and Grand Sablon headlining leading jazz musicians. One ticket for all events, plus free shuttle between venues and public transport.

➤ Late May: **Trinity Sunday** in Mons features a procession of the Golden Carriage and St. George's battle with Lumeçon and the dragon.

SUMMER

➤ Last weekend in June: The **Folklore and Shrimp Festival** (☎ 058/511189) in Oostduinkerke features shrimp fishermen on horseback, brass bands, floats, and folklore ensembles.

➤ 1st Tues. and Thurs. in July: The **Ommegang** (☎ 02/512–1961) takes over Brussels' Grand'-Place. It's a sumptuous and stately pageant re-enacting a procession that honored Emperor Charles V in 1549. Book early, particularly for the 450th anniversary in 1999.

➤ Mid-July: The **Gentse Feesten** (☎ 091/241555), originally intended to curb summer drinking by workers in Ghent, is a 10-day celebration of indulgence, with music-making, entertainment, and assorted happenings in the streets of the city and a world-class dance music festival until the early hours.

➤ July 21: **Belgium's National Day** is celebrated in Brussels with a military march, followed by a popular feast in the Parc de Bruxelles and brilliant fireworks.

➤ July–Aug.: Among Belgium's most important rock festivals, attracting international acts, are: **Torhout/Werchter,** held in two separate Flemish towns; **Axion Beach Rock,** in the sweltering seaside heat of Zeebrugge; and **Dour,** a cutting-edge event in the heart of rural Wallonia.

➤ MID-AUG.: A **Flower Carpet,** painstakingly laid out, covers and transforms the entire Grand'-Place of Brussels for two days. Even years only; next in 2000.

➤ AUG. 15: The **Outremeuse Festival** in Liège combines religious and folkloric elements in a joyous tide that sweeps through this section of town.

➤ LATE AUG.: In the **Canal Festival** (☎ 050/448686) in Brugge, events from the city's past are re-created alongside the romantic canals. It is celebrated every third year; next in 2001.

AUTUMN

➤ SEPT.–MID-OCT.: The **Festival of Flanders** (✉ Eugeen Flageyplein 18, 1050 Brussels, ☎ 02/640–1525) brings hundreds of concerts to all the old Flemish cities.

➤ SEPT.–DEC.: Every year, **Europalia** (☎ 02/507–8550) honors a different country with exhibitions, concerts, and other events amounting to a thorough inventory of its cultural heritage. In 1999, Hungary takes center-stage in Brussels and in other cities.

➤ 2ND WEEKEND IN SEPT.: On **National Heritage Day** (☎ 02/511–1840) buildings of architectural or historical interest throughout Belgium that are not normally accessible to the public open their doors to all who come.

➤ EARLY OCT.: The **Flanders International Film Festival,** the most important in the Benelux, screens new Belgian talent as well as important international directors.

➤ NOV.: The **European Community Challenge** (☎ 03/326–1010) in Antwerp is a major event on the international tennis circuit, with a diamond-studded racquet worth $1 million available to anyone who wins the event three times in five years.

➤ 2ND WEEKEND IN DEC.: The **European Christmas Market** in the Grand'Place in Brussels welcomes the traditions and products of many different European countries.

LUXEMBOURG

WINTER

➤ FEB. 9–11: **Carnival** Processions and masked balls are especially festive in Vianden, Echternach, Diekirch, and Wormeldange.

➤ EARLY MAR.: On Laetare Sunday, the festival of **Bretzelsonndeg** is dedicated to lovers, and the banks of the Moselle are decorated with folk art displays.

➤ EASTER MON.: At the **E'maischen** fair at Nospelt in old Luxembourg, lovers give each other "whistling" clay birds (*Peckvillchen*) to usher in spring.

SPRING

➤ THIRD SUNDAY AFTER EASTER: In Luxembourg City and in Diekirch, since the 17th century, for two weeks beginning on this Sunday, grateful villagers have walked in the **Octave** procession from their local church to the cathedral, accompanied by chants, incense, and often the community band. The procession commemorates the Holy Mother's rescue of the devout from a raging plague. During Octave, a **fair** holds forth in the Place Guillaume, with arcade games, crafts, and food stands selling the traditional batter-fried *merlan* (whiting). On the final Sunday the royal family participates in a solemn procession.

➤ MAY–JUNE: The **Echternach Music Festival** presents classical music concerts by renowned soloists and groups in the city's basilica.

➤ WHIT TUESDAY (LATE MAY): During Echternach's **Spring Procession** (Dance-Procession), the most famous spring pageant, pilgrims and townspeople dance through the streets, leaping from one foot to the other and chanting prayers to St. Willibrord, each group accompanied by musicians who all play the same haunting melody.

➤ JUNE 23: **Luxembourg's National Day** honors the country's beloved Grand-Duke with parades, ceremonies, and gun salutes; the night before, there's a torchlight military exercise and spectacular fireworks.

➤ JULY: International **Festival of Open-Air Theater and Music** in Wiltz always attracts thousands.

➤ LATE AUG.: The **Schueberfouer** (a former shepherds' market begun in 1340) has become the capital's giant funfair, interspersed with a procession of sheep with colorful ribbons being herded through the city streets.

➤ 2ND WEEKEND IN SEPT.: The three-day **Wine and Grape Festival** in Grevenmacher is a popular September event.

➤ 2ND SUN. IN OCT.: **Walnut Market** is held in Vianden: an outdoor sale of fresh walnuts, walnut cake, walnut candy, and walnut liqueur to the music of popular bands.

2 The Netherlands

The tulip fields and windmills are here
and so are the canals, but there's more
to the Netherlands than just these
delights. Small enough to drive through
in a day, but interesting enough to take
weeks to explore, the Netherlands is
a colorful array of lush countryside,
historic towns, and beach resorts that
have inspired artists from Vermeer
to Van Gogh. Amsterdam, with its
narrow, canal-side houses; The Hague,
center of international justice;
and Rotterdam, with the world's
largest port, are filled with historic
neighborhoods, art museums, and
restaurants and cafés serving everything
from Indonesian "rijsttafel" to seafood
plucked from local waters.

By Linda
Burnham

Updated by
Brent Gregston
and Andrew
May

IF YOU COME TO THE NETHERLANDS expecting to find its residents shod in wooden shoes, you're years too late; if you're looking for windmills at every turn, you're looking in the wrong place. The bucolic images that brought tourism here in the decades after World War II have little to do with the Netherlands of the '90s. Sure, tulips grow in abundance in the bulb district of Noord and Zuid Holland provinces, but today's Netherlands is no backwater operation: This tiny nation has an economic strength and cultural wealth that far surpass its size and population. Sophisticated, modern Netherlands has more art treasures per square mile than any other country on earth, as well as a large number of ingenious, energetic people with a remarkable commitment to quality, style, and innovation.

The Netherlands, at 41,526 square km (15,972 square mi), is almost half the size of the state of Maine, and its population of 16 million is slightly less than that of Texas. Size is no measure of international clout, however. The country is one of the largest investors in the U.S. economy. The Netherlands encourages internal accomplishments as well, particularly of a cultural nature. Within a 120-km (75-mi) radius are 10 major museums of art and several smaller ones that together contain one of the world's richest and most comprehensive collections of art masterpieces from the 15th to the 20th centuries, including the works of Rembrandt and Vincent van Gogh. In the same small area are a half dozen performance halls offering music, dance, and internationally known performing arts festivals.

The marriage of economic power and cultural wealth is nothing new to the Dutch; during the 17th century, for example, money raised through their colonial outposts overseas was used to buy or commission portraits and paintings by young artists such as Rembrandt, Hals, Vermeer, and Van Ruysdael. But it was not only the arts that were encouraged: The Netherlands was home to the philosophers Descartes, Spinoza, and Comenius; the jurist Grotius; the naturalist Van Leeuwenhoek, inventor of the microscope; and other prominent men of science and letters, who flourished in the country's enlightened tolerance. The Netherlands continues to subsidize its artists and performers, and it supports an educational system in which creativity in every field is respected, revered, and given room to express itself.

The Netherlands is the delta of Europe, where the great Rhine and Maas rivers and their tributaries empty into the North Sea. Near the coast, it is a land of flat fields and interconnecting canals; the center of the country is surprisingly wooded, and the far south has rolling hills. The country is too small for there to be vast natural areas, and it's too precariously close to sea level, even at its highest points, for there to be dramatic landscapes. Instead, the Netherlands is what the Dutch jokingly call a big green city. Amsterdam is the focal point of the nation; it also is the beginning and end point of a 50-km (31-mi) circle of cities called the Randstad that includes The Hague (the Dutch seat of government and the world center of international justice), Rotterdam (the industrial center of the Netherlands and the world's largest port), and the historic cities of Haarlem, Leiden, Delft, and Utrecht. The northern and eastern provinces are rural and quiet; the southern provinces that hug the Belgian border are lightly industrialized but enjoy a sophisticated culture and cuisine amid undulating landscapes. The great rivers that cut through the heart of the country provide both geographical and sociological borders. The area "above the great rivers," as the Dutch

The Netherlands

phrase it, is peopled by tough-minded and practical Calvinists; to the south are more ebullient Catholics. A tradition of tolerance pervades this densely populated land; aware that they cannot survive alone, the Dutch are bound by common traits of ingenuity, personal honesty, and a bold sense of humor.

Pleasures and Pastimes

Dining

The Dutch have a dining advantage over other Europeans in the quantity and quality of the fresh ingredients available to them. Their national green thumb produces the Continent's best and greatest variety of vegetables and fruits, and their dairy farms supply a rich store of creams, cheeses, and butter for sauces. In recent years the traditional grass-roots values of organic farming have been making inroads, in sharp contrast to the intensive greenhouse agriculture in which the Dutch excel. The forests yield game and the sea dikes are covered with rare herbs and other vegetation that nourishes their lambs and calves, resulting in exceptionally tasty, tender meats year-round. The waters of the Netherlands, both salt and fresh, are well known for the quality and variety of the fish and shellfish they yield. Today, even in rural areas, imaginative dishes are prepared with the high-quality fresh ingredients so readily available. Many Dutch chefs have also spent time in the kitchens of France and Belgium to learn the techniques of both traditional and nouvelle haute cuisine. The rest of the population also travels far and wide, and this has influenced dining habits in the Netherlands. You find Chinese, Italian, Mexican, and Indian restaurants even in small cities, and Indonesian restaurants are found everywhere because the Dutch, having colonized that country, developed a taste for the multidish Indonesian meal rijsttafel (rice served with several small, spicy meat, poultry, and vegetable dishes). Traditional cooking and regional recipes with seasonal ingredients can still be savored in Old Dutch restaurants, which usually display the NEERLANDS DIS (Dutch dish) soup tureen sign.

In Amsterdam and major cities, dinner is served until 10 PM in most restaurants, though most diners eat between 7 PM and 9 PM; elsewhere, dining hours vary by local custom. In the northern and eastern provinces, people dine from as early as 6, while in the southern provinces, dinner is later: from 8 to 9. However, even in Amsterdam and other large cities, it is difficult to find a place that will serve you after 10.

Fixed-price and pre-theater menus are found at restaurants throughout the country. Vegetarian menus also are available, particularly in university cities.

Like Amsterdam, the cities of the Randstad offer a tantalizing range of establishments and cuisines, from pancakes at canal-side cafés in Delft to hearty meals beside the old harbor in Rotterdam to the haute cuisine of the restaurant in The Hague where Mata Hari, the World War I spy, once dined. Nicknamed "the Widow of Indonesia" for all the former colonials who live here, The Hague is a good place to try a rijsttafel. The coast, from nearby Scheveningen to IJmuiden, is a center of activity when the herring season opens on the last Saturday in May. Out comes the bunting, and fishermen race to see who can bring home the first catch. If you have the stomach for it, you can enjoy the national summer dish: *haring* (herring), eaten raw with onions. Simply hold the fillet by its tail and slip it whole down your throat, followed by a quick glass of *jenever* (Dutch gin).

One of Holland's national dishes, *hutspot*, comes from Leiden. Tradition has it that this stew-and-mash dish was left simmering on the fire by a fleeing Spanish army when William of Orange relieved the siege of Leiden in 1574, and (together with the haring that William brought with him) was much welcomed by the starving citizens.

"South of the rivers" is found some of the best food in the country—from the fat, succulent oysters and mussels of Zeeland to the French-and German-influenced cuisine of Limburg (around Maastricht), such as *Limburg vla*, a delicious custard flan. The mushrooms and asparagus that grow in Limburg are superb and serve as both ingredient and inspiration for those master chefs in their hillside château restaurants.

CATEGORY	AMSTERDAM, THE HAGUE, & ROTTERDAM	METRO CITIES & MAASTRICHT	OTHER CITIES
$$$$	over Fl 85	over Fl 75	over Fl 65
$$$	Fl 60–Fl 85	Fl 55–Fl 75	Fl 45–Fl 65
$$	Fl 35–Fl 60	Fl 35–Fl 55	Fl 30–Fl 45
$	under Fl 35	under Fl 35	under Fl 30

*per person for three- or four-course meal, including service and taxes and excluding drinks

Lodging

Accommodations in the Netherlands range from Old Dutch cozy through modern European cosmopolitan to the splendid and luxurious. There are attractive family-run hotels in canal houses and historic buildings, smart international chain hotels, and historic castles and manor houses that have been converted into sumptuous resorts, many with their own golf courses and gourmet restaurants. Standards are high. Behind a 17th-century facade, the rooms come equipped with all modern conveniences. Even small hotels and family-owned inns may be decorated in trendy colors and have televisions in the guest rooms.

If your taste is for cozy, canal-house accommodations, head for Delft and Leiden. At the other end of the scale, The Hague offers some of the grandest old-style hotels in the country, dripping with crystal chandeliers and redolent with a history of famous guests. Rotterdam is very much a commercial harbor city, with hotels aimed primarily at the business trade, though the Hotel New York, a converted shipping office from the first part of the 20th century, is an atmospheric exception.

CATEGORY	AMSTERDAM, THE HAGUE, & ROTTERDAM	METRO CITIES & MAASTRICHT	OTHER CITIES
$$$$	over Fl 450	over Fl 400	over Fl 300
$$$	Fl 400–Fl 450	Fl 300–Fl 400	Fl 200–Fl 300
$$	Fl 300–Fl 400	Fl 200–Fl 300	Fl 150–Fl 200
$	under Fl 300	under Fl 200	under Fl 150

*for double room, including tax and service

Painters' Prospects

Even the largest cities have corners where time seems to be holding its breath. Visit some of the larger museums, or browse through a book of Dutch art before you come, and have a look at paintings of church interiors by Saenredam and De Witte, and views of Delft (especially those by Vermeer), of Utrecht, or of Haarlem's St. Bavokerk. Store them away in your mind's eye and, sure enough, as you look across a market square from a certain angle, turn a corner of a canal, or wander through a church, the real world will appear to dissolve and, just for a moment, you will have the sensation of stepping into a 17th-century painting.

Porcelain

Centuries ago, when traders brought the first porcelain back from China, Europeans eyed it with envy and amazement—and immediately set about trying to imitate it. The good burghers of Delft were among the first to crack the secret. True to the original inspiration, Delftware appeared first in blue and white, though the designs were westernized. Today, Delft porcelain is acknowledged as among the finest in the world. No visit to Delft is complete without stopping off at the Royal Porcelain Factory to see plates and tulip vases being painted by hand and perhaps picking up a souvenir or two. Whether you opt for ornate urns or tiny pairs of porcelain clogs, always make sure that you are getting the real thing—genuine Delftware has a distinctive mark underneath.

Exploring the Netherlands

Amsterdam, the capital of the Netherlands, combines its extraordinarily rich cultural heritage with an adventurous, cosmopolitan verve. It's known as the youth capital (and the gay capital) of Europe, yet it also has the largest historic city center on the Continent and some of the most august art collections in the world. South of Amsterdam, the borders of a number of cities—Leiden, The Hague, Rotterdam, and Utrecht—run so close to each other that the Dutch have given this conurbation a single name, calling it the Randstad (Ridge City). This metropolitan agglomerate forms the cultural, economic, political, and social heart of the nation; it is also home to the world's largest port (near Rotterdam) and the International Court of Justice (in The Hague).

The region along the Belgian and German borders, south of the Randstad, is, as the Dutch will often remind you, "another country." Northern Calvinists find their southern Catholic cousins (with their softly accented speech and ebullient ways) quite another breed. Even the countryside is different, as billiard-table flatness gives way to gentle hills—many of them adorned with castles and grand manor houses. The paved squares and busy sidewalk cafés of Maastricht are more reminiscent of France than of towns to the north.

To the east of the Randstad is the country's green heart, yet even amid the forests and duneland of vast national parks there are palaces and museums that can take your breath away. Life up north is even more sedate, with old trading ports and fishing villages between prosperous farms. Much of the land in the provinces of Groningen and Friesland was gradually reclaimed from the sea. You can still see farmsteads built on raised mounds that provided safety for livestock and farmers when floods threatened. The sea is now well under control, and the building of the *Afsluitdijk* (enclosing dike) in 1932 turned the tidal Zuider Zee into the calm, freshwater lakes of the Markermeer and the IJsselmeer. The Netherlands finally taper off into the sandy Wadden Islands.

Great Itineraries

The Netherlands is small and has a superb road and rail network. A couple of hours' traveling will take you halfway across the country. But a lot is packed into this compact land. You could happily spend a week just getting to know Amsterdam. Two to three weeks would be ideal for exploring the rest of the country.

Numbers in the text correspond to numbers in the margin and on the maps.

IF YOU HAVE 3 DAYS
After arriving in 🚉 **Amsterdam** and viewing the famous gables from the comfort of a canal boat (tours take from one to two hours), feast your eyes on Rembrandts and Van Goghs in the city's museums. Your

first night is spent in Amsterdam, so there's plenty of time to explore
the back streets of the Jordaan (Amsterdam's version of Greenwich Village) and to find a cozy restaurant. Next morning, check out some of
Amsterdam's quirkier shops—or visit a diamond-cutting factory if
that's more your style. Then set off along the A4 for ⊞ **The Hague** ⑪–
⑳ to visit a palace or two and the Madurodam miniature village in
Scheveningen ㉑. End the day with a rijsttafel in one of The Hague's
excellent Indonesian restaurants. In the morning, take a tram (20 minutes) to nearby **Delft** ㉒, and visit its renowned porcelain factory, then
set off back along the A4 to ⊞ **Leiden** ⑩. If it's springtime, take the
N206 out of town and through the bulb fields to the spectacular
Keukenhof Gardens. Otherwise, spend the afternoon exploring this attractive old university town, for many years home to the Pilgrim Fathers. Leiden is just half an hour from Schiphol Airport, along the A4.

IF YOU HAVE 5 DAYS

Your first night is in ⊞ **Amsterdam.** This gives you a day on either side
for exploring canals, museums, bustling markets, and the Jordaan district. In the afternoon of your second day, head off along the A4 to ⊞
Leiden ⑩. If it's springtime, follow instead the A9 and the N208
through the bulb fields, allowing an hour for visiting the Keukenhof
Gardens on the way. After a morning spent seeing Leiden's 15th-
century church and beautifully restored windmill, continue along the
A4 to ⊞ **The Hague** ⑪–⑳, seat of the government and home to some
excellent art collections. Next day, take a tram to **Delft** ㉒, one of the
most beautifully preserved historic towns in the country, conveniently
situated on the outskirts of The Hague. Then take the A12 to ⊞
Utrecht ㉗, where you can climb the Gothic Domtoren, the highest church
tower in the Netherlands, for a panoramic view of the countryside. Back
on ground level, you can visit a delightful museum of music boxes, player
pianos, and barrel organs. On the fifth day take the A28, then the A1,
out to the Hoge Veluwe national park, near **Apeldoorn** ㊺, where you
can spend time walking in the forest or visiting the Kröller-Müller Museum with its world-class collection of Van Goghs and modern art. From
Apeldoorn, you can continue your journey into Germany or take the
A1 back to Amsterdam.

IF YOU HAVE 9 DAYS

Two days and two nights in ⊞ **Amsterdam** give you time for a leisurely
exploration of the city. On the third day, follow the A4 to **Leiden** ⑩
(or take the N208 bulb route if it's springtime), and then travel on to
⊞ **The Hague** ⑪–⑳. Visit the historic center and porcelain factory of
Delft ㉒ on the morning of the fourth day, then head across to ⊞
Utrecht ㉗ on the A12. On the way, stop off in **Gouda** ㉖, famed not
only for its cheeses but also for its medieval city hall and the magnificent stained glass in the St. Janskerk. From Utrecht take the A2 south,
stopping for the night in an ancient Limburg manor house or castle,
such as the medieval Kasteel Wittem near ⊞ **Heerlen** ㊾. Spend day six
in ⊞ **Maastricht** ㊶–㊼ (just a short drive from Wittem on the N278),
which has an abundance of sidewalk cafés and a carefree French air.
Maastricht also boasts the Bonnefantenmuseum, which is well stocked
with superb religious carvings and intriguing contemporary art. Then
travel along the German border to the Hoge Veluwe national park near
Apeldoorn ㊺ (take the A2 out of Maastricht, then turn off onto the
N271 and follow it up to Nijmegen, from where the A325 and the A50
take you into the park). The pretty little town of ⊞ **Zutphen** ㉚, which
has a library of rare and beautiful early manuscripts, makes a good
overnight stop (follow the N345 out of Apeldoorn).There are now two
possibilities in the northern provinces: *1.* On day eight travel north to
⊞ **Leeuwarden** ㉓ (follow the A50 to Zwolle, then the A28 to Mep-

pel, and turn finally onto the A32). After visiting the National Ceramics Museum and viewing some of Leeuwarden's elegant 18th-century facades, you can take the A31 to the **IJsselmeer** coastline. Take the dike road (N31), exploring coastal towns such as the pottery town of **Makkum** ⑥⑤, the former fishing village of **Hindeloopen** ⑥⑦ with its painted traditional furniture, and the port of Harlingen along the way. If you have additional time, you can take the ferry from here to the island of **Terschelling** ⑥⑧. 2. On day eight travel north to 🔝 **Groningen** ⑦⓪ (follow A50 to Zwolle, then A28 to Meppel, and turn finally onto A32). If time allows, spend a night on the restful island of **Schiermonikoog** ⑥⑨ (take N361 northbound to the Lauwersoog ferry terminal).

In both cases, return to Amsterdam on the A7, which takes you over the Afsluitdijk, the long dike that closes off the IJsselmeer from the North Sea. If you are heading straight back to Amsterdam, stay on the A7. The island of **Texel** ⑥–⑧ is only a small detour (take N99 and N250 to the ferry terminal at Den Helder). Return to the A7. The picturesque towns of **Enkhuizen** ⑤ and **Hoorn** ④ (take the N302 turnoff from the A7) are typical of the former fishing ports of West Friesland, and merit an overnight stay or a short visit to their museums.

When to Tour the Netherlands

The Netherlands is at its most beautiful in spring. The bulb fields southwest of Amsterdam burst out in vast blocks of bright color, parks and gardens all over the country display brilliant spreads of blossoms, and there's a flower parade through the town of Lisse in early April to mark the opening of the flower exhibition season at Keukenhof Gardens. Keukenhof and other popular parks are best seen in the dewy early morning, before they are thronged with crowds.

Summertime in the Netherlands is festival time. The Holland Festival in Amsterdam in June attracts a glittering array of international stars in the fields of music, opera, theater, and dance. The North Sea Jazz Festival in The Hague in July is one of the premier jazz events in the world. Rotterdam has a massive street festival in August, Utrecht hosts the Holland Festival of Early Music, and pop festivals sprout up in country areas throughout the season. The long summer evenings are ideally spent sitting outside on café terraces or strolling along the canals (in Amsterdam the facades of the more elegant canal houses are softly lit at night).

In early September there is a massive Flower Parade from Aalsmeer to Amsterdam, and even winter has something to offer. Maastricht holds a lively pre-Lent carnival (February–March), and Rotterdam hosts an International Film Festival (late January–February). The rows of decorative gables of Dutch architecture are much more visible once the trees lining the canals have lost their leaves.

AMSTERDAM

Amsterdam is a city with a split personality: It's a gracious, formal cultural center built on canals, and it's the most offbeat metropolis in the world. There is an incomparable romance about the canals at night, and a depth of cultural heritage in its great art museums; but there is also a houseboat crawling with stray cats permanently parked in front of an elegant gabled canal house, and prostitutes display their wares in the windows facing the city's oldest church. Only in Amsterdam can you marvel at the acoustics of the Concertgebouw one evening and be greeted by a hurdy-gurdy barrel organ pumping out happy tunes on the shopping street the next morning.

Amsterdam's museums are filled with some of the best art in the western world. There are the home-grown Old Masters and Van Gogh in the galleries and art museums, as well as works by artists such as Georg Breitner, who roamed Amsterdam with his friend Vincent van Gogh and produced atmospheric scenes of the city at night and in winter. There's also a wealth of contemporary art. Long an inspiration for generations of artists, the attractive canals and gabled houses are a popular subject for today's Sunday painters.

You can skim the surface of the museums and get a glimpse of the canals in two to three days, but to really savor the city's charm, you need a week or more. The city is best in the spring when the parks and window boxes are filled with flowers and you can get a clear view of the gables between the branches of trees not yet in full leaf. Winters can be icy, with biting winds, but one of the compensations—if the canals freeze over—is ice skating. Amsterdam's best festival is Queen's Day, a street party on April 30 to celebrate the queen's birthday. June sees the star-studded Holland Festival of the Arts, which is part of a longer Amsterdam Arts Adventure, lasting well into the summer.

Exploring Amsterdam

The city is laid out in concentric rings of canals around the old center, crosscut by a network of access roads and alleylike connecting streets; you can easily see most of the city on foot, but there are also trams and water taxis. A walk from the center (Central Station) directly down to the southern edge takes you through the heart of town to the museum district. To the east of the center of town lie the Old Town and the former Jewish Quarter, and to the west you'll find the charming Jordaan. The grandest canals form a semicircle around the entire area.

City of the Arts: From the Dam to the Golden Bend

From inauspicious beginnings as a small fishing settlement built beside a dam in a muddy estuary in the 13th century, Amsterdam had developed, by the 17th century, into one of the richest and most powerful cities in the world. This Golden Age left behind it a tide-mark of magnificent buildings and some of the greatest paintings in western art. Amsterdam's wealth of art—from Golden Age painters through Van Gogh up to the present day—is concentrated on the area around the grassy Museumplein, which also serves as the transition point between the central canal area and the modern residential sections of the city. On the way from the site of the original dam to the museum quarter, you encounter some of the grand mansions built over the ages by Amsterdam's prosperous merchants.

Numbers in the text correspond to numbers in the margin and on the Amsterdam map.

A Good Walk

Begin where Amsterdam began, at the seething hub of the **Dam** ①. On the south side, where Kalverstraat and Rokin meet the square, is **Madame Tussaud Scenerama** ②, a branch of the famous wax museum. For a taste of ancient cultures, take a turn in the **Allard Pierson Museum** ③ farther down Rokin, on the left. From the Dam, follow the busy pedestrian shopping street, Kalverstraat, south to the entrance to the **Amsterdam Historisch Museum** ④ (or get there through the Enge Kapelsteeg alley if you have visited the Allard Pierson Museum). Here you can get an enjoyable, easily accessible lesson on the city's past. Passing through the painting gallery of the Historisch Museum brings you to the entrance of the **Begijnhof** ⑤, a blissfully peaceful courtyard, formerly housing the Beguine lay sisters. Behind the Begijnhof you come to an open square, the Spui, lined with popular sidewalk cafés, and to the Singel, the first of Amsterdam's concentric canals. Cut through the canals by way of the romantic Heisteeg alley and its continuation, the Wijde Heisteeg, turning left down the Herengracht to the corner of Leidsegracht. This is part of the prestigious **Gouden Bocht** ⑥, the grandest stretch of canal in town. Carry on down the Herengracht to the Vijzelstraat and turn right to the next canal, the Keizersgracht. Cross the Keizersgracht and turn left to find the **Museum van Loon** ⑦, an atmospheric canal house, still occupied by the family that has owned it for centuries but open to the public. Turn back down Keizersgracht until you reach Nieuwe Spiegelstraat; take another right and walk toward Museumplein. Rising up in front of you is the redbrick, neo-Gothic splendor of the **Rijksmuseum** ⑧, housing the world's greatest collection of Dutch art and celebrating its second centenary in 1999. When you leave the Rijksmuseum, walk through the covered gallery under the building. Directly ahead is Museumplein itself; to your right is Paulus Potterstraat (look for the diamond factory on the far corner), where you'll find the **Rijksmuseum Vincent van Gogh** ⑨, which contains a unique collection of that tortured artist's work. The wing that is to open in 1999 contains the extensive archive of Van Gogh's drawings and prints. Continuing along Paulus Potterstraat, at the corner of Van Baerlestraat, you reach the **Stedelijk Museum** ⑩, where you can see modern art from Picasso to the present. Just around the corner, facing the back of the Rijksmuseum across Museumplein, is the magnificent 19th-century concert hall, the **Concertgebouw** ⑪. A short walk back up along Van Baerlestraat will bring you to the **Vondelpark** ⑫—acre after acre of parkland alive with people in summer.

TIMING

To see only the buildings, allow about an hour. Expand your allotment depending on your interest in the museums en route. At minimum, each deserves 60–90 minutes. At the Rijksmuseum allow at least that just to see the main Dutch paintings. You could easily pass most of the day there if you want to investigate the entire collection.

The best time to visit the Vondelpark is in late afternoon or evening, especially in summer, as this is when the entertainment starts. In the busy season (July–September), queues at the Vincent van Gogh Museum are long, so it's best to go early or allow for an extra 15 minutes' waiting time.

Sights to See

❸ **Allard Pierson Museum.** The fascinating archaeological collection of the University of Amsterdam is housed here, tracing the early development of Western civilization, from the Egyptians to the Romans, and of the Near Eastern cultures (Anatolia, Persia, Palestine) in a series of well-documented, interestingly presented displays. ⊠ *Oude Turfmarkt 127*, ☎ *020/525–2556.* ☜ *Fl 7.50.* ☉ *Tues.–Fri. 10–5, weekends and holidays 1–5.*

★ ❹ **Amsterdam Historisch Museum** (Amsterdam Historical Museum). Housed in a former orphanage, this museum traces the history of Amsterdam, from its beginnings in the 13th century as a marketplace for farmers and fishermen through the glorious period during the 17th century when Amsterdam was the richest, most powerful trading city in the world. A tall, skylighted gallery is filled with the guild paintings that document that period of power. In one of the building's tower rooms you can have a go on an old church carillon. ⊠ *Kalverstraat 92*, ☎ *020/523–1822.* ☜ *Fl 11.* ☉ *Weekdays 10–5, weekends 11–5.*

★ ❺ **Begijnhof** (Beguine Court). Here, serenity reigns just a block from the screeching of trams stopping next to the bustling **Spui** square. The Begijnhof is the courtyard of a residential hideaway, built in the 14th century as a conventlike residence for unmarried or widowed laywomen. It's typical of many found throughout the Netherlands. The court is on a square where you'll also find No. 34, the oldest house in Amsterdam and one of only two remaining wooden houses in the city center. After a series of disastrous fires, laws were passed in the 15th century forbidding the construction of buildings made entirely from timber. The small **Engelse Kerk** (English Church) in one corner of the square dates from 1400 and was used by the Pilgrim Fathers during their brief stay in Amsterdam in the early 17th century. ✉ *Begijnhof 29,* ☎ *020/623–3565.* 🎫 *Free.* 🕐 *Weekdays 11–4.*

NEED A BREAK? The Spui is an open square that is the focal point of the University of Amsterdam. Several of the pubs and eateries here are good places to take a break, including **Caffe Esprit** (✉ Spui 10, ☎ 020/622-1967), attached to the store of the same name. Try **Broodje van Kootje** (✉ Spui 28, ☎ 020/623-7451) for a classic Amsterdam *broodje* (sandwich). The Spui is at the end of the alley that passes out of the Beguine Court.

⓫ **Concertgebouw** (Concert Building). The Netherlands' premier concert hall, the world-famous Concertgebouw, has been filled since the turn of the century with the music of the Royal Concertgebouw Orchestra, as well as visiting international artists. There are two concert halls in the building, Grote (large) and Kleine (small). The larger hall is one of the most acoustically perfect anywhere. You will recognize the building at once (it is topped with a lyre); enter through the glass extension along the side. There are no tours of the building, so you will need to buy a ticket to a concert to see beyond the broad lobby, or, if you visit on a Wednesday before 12:30 September–June, you can attend a free lunchtime concert. ✉ *Concertgebouwplein 2–6,* ☎ *020/675–4411 (24-hr concert schedule and hot line) or 020/671–8345 (box office).*

NEED A BREAK? **Small Talk** (✉ Van Baerlestraat 52, ☎ 020/671-4864), because of its situation midway between the Concertgebouw and the Sweelinck Music Conservatory, is popular with music students, musicians, and visitors alike, who all pack in for coffee and apple pie or a light meal and a chat.

---

❶ **Dam** (Dam Square). The Dam, the official center of town, traces its roots to the 12th century, when wanderers from central Europe came floating in their canoes down the Amstel River and stopped to build a dam. Soon this muddy mound became the focal point of the small settlement of Aemstelledam and the location of the local weigh house. The Dam is still the official center of town. Once, ships could sail right up to the weigh house, along the Damrak. But in the 19th century the Damrak was filled in to form the street leading to Centraal Station, and King Louis Napoléon had the weigh house demolished in 1808 because it spoiled the view from his bedroom window in the palace across the way. The monument in the center of the square was erected in 1956 to commemorate the liberation of the Netherlands at the end of World War II. ✉ *Follow Damrak south from Central Station; Raadhuisstraat leads from Dam to intersect main canals.*

❻ **Gouden Bocht** (Golden Bend). This stretch of the Herengracht, from the Leidsegracht to the Vijzelstraat, contains some of Amsterdam's most opulent 18th-century architecture. Construction of the main ring of canals, the Prinsengracht (Princes' Canal), the Keizersgracht (Emperors' Canal), and the Herengracht (Gentlemen's Canal), began during the Golden Age. In true Dutch egalitarian style, the most prestigious of the three was the Herengracht. The section of this canal stretching

34

Amsterdam

Het IJ

CENTRAAL
STATION
Front

Centraal
Station

de Ruyterkade

Prins Hendrikkade

Open

Haven

Nieuwendijk

Singel

Spuistr.

Damrak

Beursstraat

Warmoesstraat

Oudebrugsteeg

Zeedijk

Damrak

Oudezijds Kolk

Geldersekade

Prins

Oosterdokskade

Oosterdoksde

Oosterdok

N

Binnen
Waals

kant
eilandsgracht

Binnen
Bantammerstr.

Recht Boomssloot

Oude waal

Oude

Schans

Krom Boomssl.

Oude

Hendrikkade

Rapenburg

Dam

Polin

Damstraat

Ouda

Zijds Voorburgwal

Achter burgwal

St. Antoniesbreestr.

Konings
str.

NIEUW-
MARKT

Nes

Oude

Zijds

Hoogstr.

Nieuwe
Hoogstr.

Nieuwe Uilenburgerstraat

Uilenburgergracht

Valkenburgerstraat

Ropenburgerstraat

Anne Frank str.

Wertheim Park

Plantage Parklaan

Plantage
Kerklaan

Plantage
Middenlaan

Kalverstraat

Oude

Kloveniersburgwal

Raamgr.

Groen

Zuid

Nieuwe Doelenstr.

Staalstraat

nenburgwal

Jodenbreestraat

Mr.
Visser-
plein

Muiderstraat

gracht

Rokin

Nieuwe

Amstel

Amstel

Blauwbrug

WATERLOOPLEIN

Heren

Weesperstraat

Singel

Reguliersdwarsstraat

Rembrandt
plein

Amstelstr.

Nieuwe

Nieuwe

Keizersgracht

Kerkstraat

Heren

gracht

Amstel

Nieuwe

Prinsengracht

Vizelstraat

Keizersgracht

Reguliers

Kerkstraat

Magere Brug

Nieuwe

Nieuwe Achter

gr.

Valckenierstraat

Prinsengracht

Utrechtsestraat

Utrechtse
dwarstraat

Amstel

WEESPERPLEIN

Sarphatistraat

Noorderstr.

Nieuwe Looiersstr.

gracht

Frederiks
plein

Mauritskade

varstr.

Vizelgracht

Wetering
Pl.

Wetering Schans

Den Texstraat

Nicolaas Witsen Kade

Sarphatistraat

Stadhouderskade

F. Bol Straat

KEY

ℹ Tourist Information

Ⓜ Metro Stops

Metro Lines

Tram Lines

Railroad

0   220 yards

0   200 meters

from Nieuwe Spiegelstraat to Leidsestraat is nicknamed the Golden Bend. Built by wealthy merchants, the houses are wide, with elaborate gables and cornices, richly decorated facades, and heavy, centrally placed doors—an imposing architecture that suits the bank headquarters of today as well as it did the grandees of yore. The most notable are numbers 475 (designed by Hans Jacob Husly in 1703); 485 (Jean Coulon, 1739); 493 and 527, both in the Louis XVI style (1770); and 284 (Van Brienen House, 1728), another ornate Louis XVI facade.

② Madame Tussaud Scenerama. A branch of the world-famous wax museum, this Madame Tussaud's—at Dam Square above the P&C department store—includes a life-size, 3-D rendering of a painting by Vermeer—a remarkable vision or a kitschy delight, depending on your sensibility. ⊠ *Dam 20,* ☎ *020/622–9949.* ▭ *Fl 18.50.* ⊙ *Sept.–June, daily 10–5:30; July–Aug., daily 9:30–7:30.*

★ **⑦ Museum van Loon.** The city's best look at life in the canal houses, the Museum van Loon is still a private residence for a descendant of one of Amsterdam's powerful families. Today, the house is filled with portraits, many of them traditional, paired marriage portraits and paintings of children. ⊠ *Keizersgracht 672,* ☎ *020/624–5255.* ▭ *Fl 7.50.* ⊙ *Fri.–Mon. 11–5.*

★ **⑧ Rijksmuseum** (State Museum). Home to Rembrandt's *The Night Watch* and many of the most beloved Vermeer, Hals, and Hobbema paintings extant, this is the Netherlands' greatest museum. When architect P. J. Cuypers came up with the museum's extravagant design in the late 1880s, it shocked Calvinist Holland. Cuypers was persuaded to tone down some of the more ostentatious elements of his neo-Renaissance decoration and to curb the excesses of his soaring neo-Gothic lines—but, while the building was being constructed, he managed to visit the site and reinstate some of his ideas. The result is a magnificent, turreted building that glitters with gold leaf—a fitting palace for the national art collection.

The Rijksmuseum has more than 150 rooms displaying paintings, sculpture, and objects from both the West and Asia, dating from the 9th through the 19th centuries. The primary collection is of 15th- to 17th-century paintings, mostly Dutch (the Rijksmuseum has the largest concentration of these masters in the world); there are also extensive holdings of drawings and prints from the 15th to the 20th centuries.

If your time is limited, then head directly for the Gallery of Honor on the upper floor, in which hangs Rembrandt's *The Night Watch,* as well as a selection of other well-known Rembrandt paintings, and works by Vermeer, Frans Hals, and other great Golden Age artists. A clockwise progression through the rooms of the adjoining East Wing takes you past works by some of the greatest Dutch painters of the 15th to the 17th centuries—meticulous still lifes, jolly tavern scenes, and rich portraits full of character.

The South Wing contains 18th- and 19th-century paintings, costumes and textiles, and the museum's impressive collection of Asian art, which includes some 500 statues of Buddha from all over the Orient.

The Rijksmuseum's collection of drawings and prints is far too vast to be displayed completely, and only a small selection is shown in the Print Room at any one time. Here you might catch a glimpse of Italian Renaissance sketches, Rembrandt engravings, or early-19th-century photographs.

Elsewhere in the museum you can wander through room after room of antique furniture, silverware, and exquisite porcelain, including Delftware. The 17th-century doll's houses—made not as toys but as show-pieces for wealthy merchant families—are especially worth seeing. ⊠ *Stadhouderskade 42,* ☎ *020/673–2121.* 🖃 *Fl 12.50.* ☉ *Daily 10–5.*

★ ⑨ **Rijksmuseum Vincent van Gogh** (Vincent van Gogh Museum). This light-filled building, based on a design by Gerrit Rietveld and opened in 1973, venerates the short but prolific career of the 19th-century Dutch painter after which it is named. The collection of 200 paintings and 500 draw-ings by Van Gogh ranges from the dramatic *Sunflowers* to ear-less self-portraits. The permanent collection also includes other important 19th-century artists, and the temporary exhibitions are always su-perbly presented. The year 1999 marks the 200th anniversary of his birth and the opening of a new museum extension, designed by the Jap-anese architect Kisho Kurokawa. The new annex is a free-standing, mul-tistory, oval structure, built in a bold combination of titanium and gray-brown stone and connected to the main galleries by an underground walkway. It provides permanent exhibition space for the museum's print collection, allowing more room to show the works of Van Gogh him-self. ⊠ *Paulus Potterstraat 7,* ☎ *020/570–5200.* 🖃 *Fl 12.50.* ☉ *Daily 10–5.*

⑩ **Stedelijk Museum** (Municipal Museum). Hot and happening modern art has one of its most respected homes here at the Stedelijk. Works by such trendy contemporary artists as Jeff Koons are displayed along-side a collection of paintings and sculptures by the granddaddies of mod-ernism: Chagall, Cézanne, Picasso, Monet, and others. Major movements that are well documented here are COBRA (Appel, Corneille), Ameri-can pop art (Johns, Oldenburg, Liechtenstein), American action paint-ing (Willem de Kooning, Pollock), and neorealism (De Saint-Phalle, Tinguely). ⊠ *Paulus Potterstraat 13,* ☎ *020/573–2911.* 🖃 *Fl 9.* ☉ *Daily 11–5.*

⑫ **Vondelpark.** Known as the Green Lung of Amsterdam, the Vondelpark was first laid out in 1865 as a 25-acre "Walking and Riding Park." It soon expanded to cover some 120 acres. In the process, it was renamed after Joost van den Vondel, the "Dutch Shakespeare." Landscaped in the informal English style, the park is an irregular patchwork of copses, ponds, and fields linked by winding pathways. In good weather the park buzzes with activity. People come to roller skate and play tennis. Dutch families string up flags between the branches and party under the trees. Lovers stroll through the fragrant formal Rose Garden. Chil-dren sit transfixed by colorful acrobatics in the outdoor theater. Later, the clowns give way to jazz bands and cabaret artists who play well into the night, and the Vondelpark takes on the atmosphere of a giant outdoor café. From June to August free outdoor concerts and plays are performed at the open-air theater from Wednesday through Sunday.

Over the years a range of sculptural and architectural delights have made their appearance in the park. There's an elegant 19th-century band-stand, and the famous **Round Blue Teahouse,** a rare beauty of func-tionalist architecture, built beside the lake in 1937. **Picasso** himself donated a sculpture (which stands in the middle of a field) to com-memorate the park's centenary in 1965. An elegant 19th-century en-tertainment pavilion has been converted into the **Nederlands Filmmuseum** (Netherlands Film Museum). Although there is no per-manent exhibition, the museum has shows every day in its two cine-mas, drawing on material from all over the world as well as from its substantial archive (which includes such gems as hand-tinted silent movies). On summer Saturdays, there are free outdoor screenings. ⊠ *Stadhouderskade. Filmmuseum, Vondelpark 3,* ☎ *020/589–1400.*

Historic Amsterdam: From the Jewish Quarter to Rembrandt's House

From the time in the 15th century when the diamond cutters of Antwerp first arrived to find refuge from the Spanish Inquisition, the area east of the Zwanenburgwal has traditionally been Amsterdam's Jewish Quarter. During the 16th and 17th centuries, Jewish refugees from Spain, Portugal, and Eastern Europe also found a haven in Amsterdam. By 1938, 10% of Amsterdam's population was Jewish, but this community was reduced to about ½th of its former size by the devastation of the Nazi occupation.

The area to the north and northeast of the Jewish Quarter is the oldest part of Amsterdam. This is the site of Amsterdam's original harbor and the core of the Old Town, an area steeped in the history and romance of exotic trade and exploration, much of it conducted under the auspices of the immensely wealthy Dutch East India Company (VOC).

A Good Walk

Start at what was once the heart of Amsterdam's Jewish Quarter, **Waterlooplein** ⑬. Today the square is dominated by the imposing modern **Muziektheater/Stadhuis** ⑭, which is surrounded by a large and lively flea market. East of Waterlooplein, on Jonas Daniël Meijerplein, is the **Joods Historisch Museum** ⑮, skillfully converted out of a number of old synagogues. Just to the east of that, on the corner of Mr. Visserplein and Jonas Daniël Meijerplein is the stately **Portugees Israelitische Synagoge** ⑯. Its interior is simple but awe-inspiring because of its vast size and floods of natural light. From here, you might like to make a short diversion, especially if you have children in tow. Tram 9 or 14 will take you along Plantage Middenlaan to the **Hortus Botanicus** ⑰, to the **Artis** ⑱ zoo (which was attractively laid out in parklike surroundings in the 19th century and has a well-stocked aquarium), and on to the **Tropenmuseum** ⑲, which has riveting displays on tropical cultures and a special children's section. On the way you might want to pop in to the **Verzetsmuseum** ⑳, which explains the Dutch resistance to the occupying forces, passive and active, during the Second World War. Alternatively, you can walk from the synagogue up Jodenbreestraat, where—in the second house from the corner by the Zwanenburgwal—you'll find the **Museum het Rembrandthuis** ㉑, the mansion where Rembrandt lived at the height of his prosperity, which now houses a large collection of his etchings. Cross the bridge to St. Antoniesbreestraat and follow it to the **Zuiderkerk** ㉒, whose rather Asian spire is the neighborhood's chief landmark. Take St. Antoniesbreestraat north to **Nieuwmarkt** ㉓. Take Koningsstraat to the Kromboomssloot and turn left, then right at Rechtboomssloot (both pretty, leafy canals) and follow it through this homey neighborhood, the oldest in Amsterdam, to Montelbaanstraat; turn left and cut through to the broad Oude Waal canal. Follow it right to the **Montelbaanstoren** ㉔, a tower that dates back to the 16th century. Up Kalkmarkt from the tower is Prins Hendrikkade, which runs along the eastern docks. Following Prins Hendrikkade east you enter the 20th century with a bang at the new**Metropolis Science & Technology Center** ㉕. A little farther on is the **Nederlands Scheepvaartmuseum** ㉖ where there is a fascinating replica of an old Dutch East India ship. Across the bridge on Hoogte Kadijk is the **Museumwerf 't Kromhout** ㉗, where wooden sailing boats are still restored and repaired. If, on the other hand, you go west along Prins Hendrikkade to Gelderskade, you can see the **Schreierstoren** ㉘, where legend has it that women used to stand weeping and waiting for their men to return from sea. Follow Oudezijds Kolk, beside the

Schreierstoren, south to the **Zeedijk** ㉙, in the 1980s the seedy haunt of drug dealers but now lined with restaurants, cafés, and galleries that form the heart of Chinatown. From Zeedijk, take Oudezijds Voorburgwal south to **Museum Amstelkring** ㉚, a tiny but atmospheric canal house that has a church hidden in its attic. Continue south on Oudezijds Voorburgwal through part of the red-light district to the **Oude Kerk** ㉛, Amsterdam's oldest church, which grew up haphazardly from the 14th to the 16th centuries. From here you can continue south on Oudezijds Voorburgwal through more of the red-light district to Damstraat and the Dam.

TIMING

To see only the buildings along the main route, block out an hour and a half. Detours to Artis and the Tropenmuseum will need an extra 30 minutes' traveling time; and to the Scheepvaartsmuseum and Museumwerf 't Kromhout, another 45 minutes. Museums along this route need at least a 30-minute visit, though the Museum Amstelkring and the Tropenmuseum deserve a little longer.

Note that the flea market does not operate on Sunday and that the children's section of the Tropenmuseum has very specific visiting times. Although the Zeedijk has been considerably cleaned up of late, it is still advisable to take care when visiting this area and the red-light district. Don't carry too many valuables, and avoid the district late at night.

Sights to See

㉘ **Artis** (The Amsterdam Zoo). Keep young travelers entertained with a visit to Amsterdam's zoo (known officially as the Natura Artis Magistra). Built in the mid-19th century, Artis is a 37-acre park that is home to a natural history museum, a zoo with an aviary, an aquarium, and a planetarium. A special Artis Express canal boat from the central railway station makes getting here fun. ⊠ *Plantage Kerklaan 40,* ☎ *020/523–3400.* ⊞ *Fl 22.* ☉ *Zoo, daily 9–5; planetarium, Mon. 12:30–5, Tues.–Sun. 9–5.*

⑰ **Hortus Botanicus.** The attractive botanical garden was laid out as an herb garden for doctors and pharmacists in 1638. It has since been expanded to incorporate a covered swamp and an ornamental garden, where 6,000 species are represented. ⊠ *Plantage Middenlaan 2,* ☎ *020/625–8411.* ⊞ *Fl 7.50.* ☉ *Apr.–Sept., weekdays 9–5, weekends and holidays 11–5; Oct.–Mar., weekdays 9–4, weekends and holidays 11–4.*

⑮ **Joods Historisch Museum** (Jewish Historical Museum). Four synagogues, dating from the 17th and 18th centuries, have been skillfully combined into one museum for documents, paintings, and objects related to the history of the Jewish people in Amsterdam and the Netherlands. Across from the entrance to the museum is a statue erected after World War II to honor a solidarity strike by Amsterdam's dock workers in protest of the deportation of Amsterdam's Jews during the war. ⊠ *Jonas Daniël Meijerplein 2–4,* ☎ *020/626–9945.* ⊞ *Fl 8.* ☉ *Daily 11–5.*

㉔ **Montelbaanstoren** (Montelbaans Tower). A slightly listing tower dating from 1512, when, perpendicular, it formed part of the city's defenses, the Montelbaanstoren now houses the City Water Office. Since 1878, this department has maintained the water levels in the canals and engineered the nightly flushing of the entire city waterway system, closing and opening the sluices to change the direction of the flow and cleanse the waters. (The canals remain murky green despite the process, due to algae.) The elegant clock tower was added early in the 17th century. ⊠ *Oude Schans 2.*

㉚ **Museum Amstelkring** ("Our Lord in the Attic" Museum). This appears to be just another canal house, and on the lower floors it is, but the attic of this building contains something unique—a small chapel that dates from the Reformation in Amsterdam, when open worship by Catholics was outlawed. ✉ *Oudezijds Voorburgwal 40,* ☎ *020/624–6604.* 🎫 *Fl 10.* ☉ *Mon.–Sat. 10–5, Sun. 1–5.*

★ ㉑ **Museum het Rembrandthuis** (Rembrandt's House). One of Amsterdam's most striking sights, this was the house that Rembrandt, flush with success, bought for his family. He chose a house on what was once the main street of the Jewish Quarter because he felt that he could then experience daily and at firsthand the faces he would use in his religious paintings. Later Rembrandt lost the house to bankruptcy when he fell from popularity following his wife's death. He came under attack by the Amsterdam burghers, who refused to accept his liaison with his housekeeper. The house today is a museum of Rembrandt prints and etchings and includes one of his presses. ✉ *Jodenbreestraat 4–6,* ☎ *020/624–9486.* 🎫 *Fl 7.50.* ☉ *Mon.–Sat. 10–5, Sun. and holidays 1–5.*

㉗ **Museumwerf 't Kromhout** (Museum Wharf The Kromhout). One of Amsterdam's oldest shipyards is still redolent of tar, wood shavings, and varnish. Although the shipyard is run as a museum, old boats are still restored here. There's a whiff of diesel in the air, too. During the first part of the 20th century, 't Kromhout produced the diesel engine used by most Dutch canal boats. Models of old engines are on display. ✉ *Hoogte Kadijk 147,* ☎ *020/627–6777.* 🎫 *Fl 3.50.* ☉ *Weekdays 10–4.*

⑭ **Muziektheater/Stadhuis** (Music Theater/Town Hall). A brick and marble complex known locally as the Stopera (from Stadhuis and opera), this is the cornerstone of the revival of the Jewish Quarter, which was derelict and devastated after World War II. Built as a home for everything from opera performances to welfare applications, it is a multifunctional complex that includes theaters, offices, shops, and even the city's wedding chamber (Dutch marriages all must be performed in the Town Hall, with church weddings optional). Feel free to wander through the lobbies; there is interesting sculpture as well as a display that dramatically illustrates Amsterdam's position below sea level. Tours of the backstage areas are run twice weekly. ✉ *Waterlooplein 22,* ☎ *020/551–8054.* 🎫 *Fl 8.50 for tours.* ☉ *Open daily. Tours Wed. and Sat. at 3.*

㉖ **Nederlands Scheepvaartmuseum** (The Netherlands Maritime Museum). Once the warehouse from which trading vessels were outfitted for their journeys, with everything from cannons to hardtack, the building now incorporates room after room of displays related to the development and power of the Dutch East and West Indies companies, as well as the Dutch fishing industry. Moored alongside the building at the east end of Amsterdam Harbor is a replica of the VOC (Dutch East India Company) ship *Amsterdam.* ✉ *Kattenburgerplein 1,* ☎ *020/523–2222.* 🎫 *Fl 12.50.* ☉ *Tues.–Sat. 10–5, Sun. and holidays noon–5, June–Sept. also Mon. 10–5.*

㉕ **newMetropolis Science & Technology Center.** Opened in early 1997, this is already a landmark, designed by Renzo Piano, the architect of the Pompidou Centre in Paris. The building's colossal, copper-clad volume rises from the harbor waters like the hull of a ship poking up into the skyline above the entrance to the IJ Tunnel in the city's Eastern Docks. Inside is a high-tech, hands-on world of historic, present-day, and futuristic technology. The rooftop café terrace offers a superb panoramic view across the city. ✉ *Oosterdok 2,* ☎ *0900/919–1100, 55¢ per minute.* 🎫 *Fl 23.50.* ☉ *Sun.–Fri. 10–6, Sat. 10–9.*

㉓ Nieuwmarkt (New Market). Dating from the 17th century—when farmers from the province of Noord-Holland began setting up stalls here—the Nieuwmarkt soon became a busy daily market. The **Waag** (Weigh House) in the center of the square was built in 1488 and functioned as a city gate until the early 17th century, when it became the weighing house. One of its towers housed a teaching hospital for the academy of surgeons of the Surgeons' Guild. It was here that Rembrandt came to watch Professor Tulp in action prior to painting *The Anatomy Lesson*. Now the building is occupied by a restaurant. ⊠ *Bounded by Kloveniersburgwal, Geldersekade, and Zeedijk.*

㉛ Oude Kerk (Old Church). Amsterdam's oldest church, the Oude Kerk was built between 1366 and 1566 and restored from 1955 to 1979. It is a pleasing hodgepodge of styles and haphazard side buildings. Rembrandt's wife, Saskia, is buried here. Seminude women display their wares in the windows around the church square and along the surrounding canals—the neighborhood has doubled as a red-light district for nearly six centuries. ⊠ *Oudekerksplein 23,* ☎ *020/625–8284.* 💺 *Fl 5.* ☉ *Apr.–Oct., Mon.–Sat. 11–5, Sun. 1–5; Nov.–Mar., Fri.– Sun. 1–5.*

⑯ Portugees Israelitische Synagoge (Portuguese Israelite Synagogue). A square brick building behind brick courtyard walls, this noted synagogue was built between 1671 and 1675 by the Sephardic Jewish community that had emigrated from Portugal during the preceding two centuries. Its spare, elegantly proportioned wood interior has remained virtually unchanged since it was built and still is lighted by candles in two immense candelabra during services. ⊠ *Mr. Visserplein 3,* ☎ *020/ 624–5351.* 💺 *Fl 5.* ☉ *Apr.–Oct., Sun.–Fri. 10–12:30 and 1–4; Nov.–Mar., Mon.–Thurs. 10–12:30 and 1–4, Fri. 10–12:30 and 1–3, Sun. 10–noon.*

㉘ Schreierstoren. Although today this is a shop for nautical instruments, maps, and books, during the 16th century it was a lookout tower for the women whose men were fishing at sea. This gave rise to the mistaken belief that the name meant "weeper's" or "wailer's" tower. But the word "Schreier" actually comes from an old Dutch word describing the position of the tower astride two canals. A plaque on the side of the building tells you that it was from this location that Henry Hudson set sail on behalf of the Dutch East India Company to find a shorter route to the East Indies, discovering instead Hudson's Bay in Canada and, later, New York harbor and the Hudson River. The Schreierstoren overlooks the old **Oosterdok** (Eastern Dock) of Amsterdam Harbor. ⊠ *Prins Hendrikkade 94-95.*

⑲ Tropenmuseum (Museum of the Tropics). This museum honors the Netherlands' link to Indonesia and the West Indies. It is a magnificent tiered, galleried, and skylighted museum decorated in gilt and marble. Displays and dioramas portray everyday life in the world's tropical environments. Upstairs in the **Kindermuseum** (Children's Museum) children can participate directly in the life of another culture through special programs involving art, dance, song, and sometimes even cookery. Adults may visit the children's section, but only under the supervision of a child age 6–12. ⊠ *Linnaeusstraat 2,* ☎ *020/568–8295.* 💺 *Fl 10; Kindermuseum, Fl 2.50.* ☉ *Mon. and Wed.–Thurs., 10–5, Tues. 10–9:30, weekends and holidays noon–5; Kindermuseum activities Wed. at 2 and 3:30, weekends at 12:30, 2, and 3:30.*

⑳ Verzetsmuseum (Museum of the Dutch Resistance). Here are displays explaining the Dutch resistance to the occupying forces, passive and active, during World War II. The new location, opening in mid–1999, is poignantly close to the former **Schouwburg** theater on Plantage

Middenlaan, which is now a memorial to the Jews who were assembled here before being sent to the concentration camps. ✉ *Plantage Kerklaan 61,* ☎ *020/620–2535.* 🎫 *Fl 8.* ⊘ *Tues.–Fri. 10–5, weekends noon–5.*

⑬ Waterlooplein. The wooden pushcarts that were used when the flea market here began (before World War II) are gone, but the Waterlooplein remains a bustling shopping arena, wrapped around two sides of the Stopera (Music Theater/Town Hall complex). A stroll past the stalls provides a colorful glimpse of Amsterdam entrepreneurship in action, day in and day out, in every sort of weather. ✉ *Waterlooplein.* ⊘ *Weekdays 9–5, Sat. 8:30–5:30.*

NEED A   **Espressobar "Puccini"** (✉ Staalstraat 21, ☎ 020/620–8458. ⊘ Tues.–
BREAK?   Sat. 8:30–8, Sun. 10–6) is a stylish breakfast and lunch venue, just
           across the water from the Waterlooplein flea market and the Muziek-
           theater. You can get a full Continental breakfast or freshly made sand-
           wiches with interesting fillings, while the cakes, some created in the
           superb *chocolaterie* next door, are mouthwatering treats.

㉙ Zeedijk. Once known throughout the country as the black hole of Amsterdam for its concentration of drug traffickers and users, Zeedijk is now the busy heart of the city's Chinatown, and there is even a Buddhist temple. The restored old buildings now house shops, restaurants, and galleries. No. 1 Zeedijk, a café, is one of only two timbered houses left in the city. ✉ *Oudezijds Kolk (near Central Station) to Nieuwmarkt.*

㉒ Zuiderkerk (South Church). Built between 1603 and 1611 by Hendrick de Keyser, one of the most prolific architects of the Golden Age, this church is said to have inspired the great British architect Christopher Wren. The Zuiderkerk was one of the earliest churches built in Amsterdam in the Renaissance style and was the first in the city to be built for the Dutch Reformed Church. The city planning office maintains a display here that offers a look at the future of Amsterdam. ✉ *Zandstraat.* 🎫 *Free.* ⊘ *Tower: June–Oct., Wed. 2–5, Thurs.–Fri. 11–2, Sat. 11–4.*

The Canals: City of 1,001 Bridges

One of Amsterdam's greatest pleasures is also one of its simplest—a stroll along the canals. The grand, crescent-shape waterways of the *grachtengordel* (belt of canals) are lined with splendid buildings and pretty, gabled houses. But you can also wander off the main thoroughfares, along the smaller canals that crisscross them, sampling the charms of such historic city neighborhoods as the Jordaan.

A Good Walk

Begin at the busy **Dam** ①, where the imposing **Het Koninklijk Paleis te Amsterdam** ㉜ fills the western side of the square. The richly decorated marble interiors are open to the public when the queen is not in residence. To the right of the palace looms the Gothic **Nieuwe Kerk** ㉝. Circle around behind the palace, follow the tram tracks into the wide and busy Raadhuisstraat, and continue along it to the Westermarkt. The **Westerkerk** ㉞, on the right, facing the next canal, is another Amsterdam landmark, and Rembrandt's burial place. Make a right past the church and follow the Prinsengracht canal to the **Anne Frankhuis** ㉟, where you can visit the attic hideaway where Anne Frank wrote her diary. Continue north along the Prinsengracht. The neighborhood to your left, across the canal, is the **Jordaan** ㊱, full of curious alleys and pretty canals, intriguing shops and cafés. At the intersection of the Prinsengracht and Brouwersgracht, turn right onto the **Brouwersgracht** ㊲, which many believe is the most beautiful canal in Amsterdam. Cross the canal and follow it back to the Singel. On the other side, follow the tram tracks to the left toward the harbor. Ahead of you is the palatial **Centraal Station** ㊳. From Centraal Station the **Damrak** ㊴ leads past the **Beurs van Berlage** ㊵—the building that is seen as Amsterdam's first significant venture into modern architecture—and back to the Dam.

TIMING

It is difficult to say how long this walk will take as it leads you through areas that invite wandering and the exploration of side streets. At a brisk and determined pace, you can manage the route in about an hour. But you could also easily while away an afternoon in the Jordaan, or take a leisurely stroll along the Prinsengracht. Allow a minimum of half an hour each for the Royal Palace and the Anne Frank House. Waiting in line to get into the Anne Frank House can add another 10–20 minutes (get there early to beat the midday crowds).

The best time for canal walks is in late afternoon and early evening—or early in the morning, when the mists still hang over the water. If you're planning to go shopping in the Jordaan, remember that shops in the Netherlands are closed Monday morning. With its many restaurants and cafés, the Jordaan is also fun to visit at night.

Sights to See

★ ㉟ **Anne Frankhuis** (Anne Frank House). This unimposing canal house where two Jewish families hid from the Nazis for more than two years during World War II is one of the most frequently visited places in the world. The families were eventually discovered and sent to concentration camps, but young Anne's diary survived as a detailed record of their life in hiding. If you have time to see nothing else in Amsterdam, don't miss a visit to this house. The swinging bookcase that hid the door to the secret attic apartment is still there, you can walk through the rooms where Anne and her family lived, and there is also an exhibition on racism and oppression. ⊠ *Prinsengracht 263,* ☎ *020/556–7100.* ▨ *Fl 10.* ☉ *June–Aug., Mon.–Sat. 9–7, Sun. 10–7; Sept.–May, Mon.–Sat. 9–5, Sun. 10–5.*

NEED A
BREAK?   A traditionally Dutch way of keeping eating costs down is pancakes—laden with savory cheese and bacon, or fruit and liqueur if you have a sweet tooth. The **Pancake Bakery** (⊠ Prinsengracht 191, ☎ 020/625–1333) is one of the best places in Amsterdam to try them; the menu offers a choice of more than 30 combinations.

㊵ **Beurs van Berlage** (Berlage's Stock Exchange). Completed in 1903, the Stock Exchange is considered Amsterdam's first modern building. In 1874, when the Amsterdam Stock Exchange building on the Dam showed signs of collapse, the city authorities held a competition for the design of a new one. The architect who won was discovered to have copied the facade of a French town hall, so he was disqualified and the commission was awarded to a local architect, H. P. Berlage. The building that Berlage came up with proved to be an architectural turning point. Gone are all the fripperies and ornamentations of the 19th-century "neo" styles. The new Beurs, with its simple lines, earned Berlage the reputation of being the "Father of Modern Dutch Architecture." Today it serves as a concert and exhibition hall. The small museum has exhibits about the former stock exchange and its architect, as well as access to the tower. ⊠ *Damrak 213–277,* ☎ *020/626–8936.* ▨ *Fl 6.* ☉ *Tue.–Sun. 10–4.*

㊲ **Brouwersgracht** (Brewers Canal). The pretty, tree-lined canal is bordered by residences and former warehouses of the brewers who traded here in earlier centuries. It is blessed with long views down the main canals and plenty of sunlight, all of which makes the Brouwersgracht one of the most photographed spots in town. The canal runs westward from the end of the Singel (a short walk along Prins Hendrikkade from Central Station).

38 Centraal Station (Central Station). Designed by P. J. Cuypers, the architect of Amsterdam's other imposing gateway, the Rijksmuseum, this building is a landmark of Dutch neo-Renaissance style (and does bear a distinct resemblance to the museum on the other side of town). It opened in 1885 and has been the hub of transportation for the Netherlands ever since. From time to time the sumptuous **Koninklijle Wachtkamer** (Royal Waiting Room) on Platform 2 is opened to the public—and is certainly worth a visit. ⊠ *Stationsplein,* ☎ *0900/9292 (public transport information).*

39 Damrak (Dam Port). This busy street leading up to Centraal Station is now lined with a curious assortment of shops, attractions, hotels, and eating places. It was once a harbor bustling with activity, its piers loaded with fish and other cargo on their way to the weigh house at the Dam. During the 19th century it was filled in, and the only water that remains is a patch in front of the station that provides mooring for canal tour boats.

★ **32 Het Koninklijk Paleis te Amsterdam** (Royal Palace, Amsterdam). Built in the mid-17th century as the city's town hall, the Koninklijk Paleis stands solidly on 13,659 pilings sunk deep into the marshy soil of the former riverbed. Designed by Jacob van Campen, one of the most prominent architects of the time, the Stadhuis (City Hall) is a high point of the Dutch Classicist style. Inside and out, the building is adorned with rich carvings. The prosperous burghers of the Golden Age wanted a city hall that could boast of their status to all visitors—and indeed, the Amsterdam Stadhuis became known as "the Eighth Wonder of the World." When you walk into what was originally the public entrance hall, the earth is quite literally at your feet. Two maps inlaid in the marble floor show Amsterdam not just at the center of the world, but of the universe as well.

During the French occupation of the Netherlands, Louis Napoléon, who had been installed as king in 1808, decided that this was the building most suitable for a royal palace. It has been the official residence of the House of Orange ever since. Louis filled his new palace with fashionable French Empire furniture, much of which remains.

Queen Beatrix, like her mother and grandmother before her, prefers to live in the quieter environment of a palace in a park outside The Hague and uses her Amsterdam residence only on the highest of state occasions. So, once again, the former Stadhuis is open to the public. ⊠ *Dam,* ☎ *020/624–8698.* ☜ *Fl 7.* ☉ *Oct.–May, Tues.–Thurs. 1–4; June–Sept., daily 12:30–5; occasionally closed for state events.*

★ **36 Jordaan.** The renovation generation has helped make the Jordaan (pronounced yohr-dahn)—Amsterdam's Greenwich Village—the winner in the revival-of-the-fittest sweepstakes. In the western part of town, it is one of the most charming neighborhoods in a city that defines charm, basking in centuries-old patina and yet address to chic eateries and boutiques. It was originally called *jardin,* French for "garden." During the French occupation of Amsterdam, the vegetable gardens to the west of the city center were developed as a residential area. The new city quarter was referred to as the jardin, and the streets and canals (which follow the lines of the original irrigation ditches) were named for flowers and trees. In the mouths of the local Dutch, *jardin* became Jordaan, the name by which the quarter is known today.

The Jordaan was a working-class area and the scene of odorous industries, such as tanning and brewing. Its inhabitants developed a reputation for rebelliousness, but their strong community spirit also gave them a special identity, rather like London's Cockneys. Until a generation ago, native Jordaaners would call their elders "uncle" or "aunt"— and they still have a reputation for enjoying a rousing sing-a-long.

Since the 1980s, the Jordaan has gone steadily upmarket, and now it is one of the trendiest parts of town. The narrow alleys and leafy canals are lined with quirky specialty shops, good restaurants, and designer boutiques. Students, artists, and the fashionable set fill the cafés. But many of the old Jordaaners are still here—as the sound of jolly singing emanating from some local pubs will testify. The Jordaan is bounded by the Prinsengracht, Looiersgracht, Lijnbaansgracht, and Brouwersgracht canals. After a visit to the Anne Frank House, you could cross the bridge to Egelantiersgracht, the canal that runs through the heart of the Jordaan. Then zigzag through pretty side streets, such as 3e (Derde) Egelantiersdwarsstraat, Tuinstraat, and 1e (Eerste) Tuindwarsstraat, for coffee on the Noordermarkt (Northern Market). Weave back south along alleys you haven't explored yet to the antiques markets on Looiersgracht.

㉝ Nieuwe Kerk (New Church). Begun in the 14th century, the Nieuwe Kerk is a soaring Gothic structure that was never given its spire because the authorities ran out of money. Inside are the graves of the poet Vondel (known as the "Dutch Shakespeare") and Admiral Ruyter, who sailed his invading fleet up the river Medway in England in the 17th century, becoming a naval hero in the process. Dutch monarchs are not crowned but are "inaugurated." This church is where the ceremony has been held for every monarch since 1815. In between times it serves as a venue for special exhibitions, including the annual World Press Photo exhibition. ✉ *Dam,* ☎ *020/626–8168.* ▣ *Admission varies according to exhibition.* ⊙ *Daily 11–5.*

㉞ Westerkerk (Western Church). Built between 1602 and 1631, the Westerkerk has a tower topped by a copy of the crown of the Habsburg emperor, Maximilian I. Maximilian gave Amsterdam the right to use his royal insignia in gratitude for help from the city in his struggle for control of the Low Countries. The tower, with its gaudy yellow crown, is an Amsterdam landmark. Its carillon is the comforting "clock" of the canal area of Amsterdam, and its chimes were often mentioned in the diary of Anne Frank, who was hiding just around the corner. Rembrandt and his son Titus are buried here; the philosopher René Descartes lived on the square facing the church. ✉ *Prinsengracht (corner of Westermarkt),* ☎ *020/624–7766.* ⊙ *Tower: June–Sept., Tues.–Wed. and Fri.–Sat. 2–5.*

Dining

Amsterdammers enjoy good food, particularly when it's shared with good company. In couples or small groups, they seek out the quieter, cozy places or go in search of the new culinary stars of the city; to celebrate or entertain, they return to the institutions that never disappoint them with the quality of their cuisine or service; and in large groups, you invariably find the Dutch trooping into their favorite Indonesian restaurant to share a rijsttafel. The city's more than 700 restaurants span a wide variety of ethnic cuisines; you'll find everything from international fast-food joints to chandeliered, waterfront dining rooms frequented by the royal family. In between are small, chef-owned

46

Amsterdam Dining and Lodging

Het IJ

de Ruyterkade

Centraal
Station

**CENTRAAL
STATION**
Front

Oosterdokskade

Oosterdok

Open
Haven
Front

Prins Hendrikkade

Nieuwendijk

Zeedijk

Oudezijds Kolk

Geldersekade

Prins

Hendrikkade

Oosterdokskade

Damrak

Oudebrugsteeg

Waals

Binnen

kant

Singel

Spuistr.

Nieuwendijk

Damrak

Beursstraat

Warmoesstraat

Zeedijk

Bantammerstr.

Binnenkant

eilandsgracht

Oude waal

Dam

Zijds Voorburgwal

Achter

burgwal

St. Antoniesbreestr.

Konings

Recht Boomssloot

str.

Oude

Schans

**NIEUW-
MARKT**

Rapenburg

Nieuwe Zijds Voorburgwal

Pokin

Damstraat

Oude

Oude
Hoogstr.

Nieuwe
Hoogstr.

Krom Boomssloot

Nieuwe Uilenburgerstraat

Uilenburgergracht

Oude

Anna ... rankstr.

Kalverstraat

Nes

Zijds

Oude

Kloveniersburgwal

Raamgr.

nenburg wal

Jodenbreestraat

Valkenburgerstraat

Rapenburgerstraat

Wertheim Park

Plantage Parklaan

Plantage
Middenlaan

Spui

Nieuwe
Doelenstr.

Groen

burgwal

Staalstraat

Zwa

Amstel

Mr.
Visser-
plein

Muiderstraat

Heren

gracht

Plantage
Middenlaan

Singel

Amstel

Amstel

Blauwbrug

Nieuwe
Amstel

WATERLOOPLEIN

Flower
market

Reguliersdwarsstraat

Rembrandts
plein

Amstelstr.

Nieuwe

Keizersgracht

Kerkstraat

Weesperstraat

Heren

gracht

Nieuwe

Prinsengracht

Vijzelstraat

Keizersgracht

Utrechtsestraat

Amstel

Nieuwe

Reguliers

Kerkstraat Magere Brug

Nieuwe

Nieuwe Achter

Valckenierstraat

Prinsengracht

gracht

Utrechtse dwarsstraat

Nieuwe

WEESPERPLEIN

Sarphatistraat

dwarsgracht

Noorderstr.

Nieuwe Looiersstr.

Amstel

Mauritskade

Wetering
Pl.

Wetering Schans

Frederiks
plein

Sarphatistraat

Den Texstraat

Nicolaas Witsen Kade

F. Bol Straat

str...

Stadhouderskade

KEY

i	Tourist Information
M	Metro Stops
▬▬	Metro Lines
┈┈	Tram Lines
───	Railroad

0   220 yards

0   200 meters

establishments on the canals and their side streets, restaurants that have stood the test of time on the basis of service, ambience, and consistency. For a dining chart that explains the range of price categories, *see* Dining *in* Pleasures and Pastimes at the beginning of this chapter.

$$$$ ✕ **Beddington's.** Near the Concertgebouw and the art museums, Beddington's sits at the junction between the business district and the city's most prestigious modern residential neighborhoods. The decor is ultra–minimal, designed by artist Boris Sipek. The English chef, Jean Beddington, takes an imaginative multicultural approach in the kitchen, mixing Japanese and other East Asian flavors and concepts with those from England, Spain, and the West Indies. The main courses you might encounter here are bisque of clams and lobster or perfectly balanced spring lamb with thyme. ✉ *Roelof Hartstraat 6–8,* ☎ *020/676–5201. Reservations essential. Jacket required. AE, DC, MC, V. Closed Sun., closed lunch Sat.–Mon.*

$$$$ ✕ **De Kersentuin.** The name of this cheerful, high-ceiling restaurant, which means "cherry orchard," signals the color scheme that extends from the dinnerware to the decor. It is a good place for a leisurely meal. Although there are large windows overlooking a residential street, the focal point is the kitchen, open behind glass panels. As you dine, you can watch chef Rudolf Bos and his staff prepare French dishes with a Far Eastern twist, such as perch flavored with coconut and spicy Thai sauce, or calves' sweetbreads marinated in soy sauce and ginger. ✉ *Dijsselhofplantsoen 7,* ☎ *020/664–2121. Reservations essential. Jacket and tie. AE, DC, MC, V. Closed Sun. No lunch.*

$$$$ ✕ **Excelsior.** The Excelsior's view over the Amstel River, to the Munt-
★ plein on one side and the Music Theater on the other, is the best in Amsterdam. The dining room is a gracious, chandeliered hall with plenty of room for diners, waiters, dessert trolleys, preparation carts, towering palms, tall candelabra, and a grand piano. The approach is traditional French with a twist: You might choose a lobster bisque or an adventurous dish such as grilled turbot with shrimp and parmesan risotto. For dessert, try the delicious lemon tart or poached figs. There are five fixed-price menus. ✉ *Hotel de L'Europe, Nieuwe Doelenstraat 2–8,* ☎ *020/531–1777. Jacket and tie. AE, DC, MC, V. No lunch Sat.*

$$$$ ✕ **'t Swarte Schaep.** This cozy upstairs restaurant overlooking the noisy
★ Leidseplein is named for a legendary black sheep that roamed the area in the 17th century. It's a study in traditional Dutch decor, with copper pots hanging from the wooden beams and heavily framed paintings on the walls. Together with this Old Holland atmosphere, the excellent French cuisine—which includes chateaubriand with béarnaise sauce and lobster mousse with asparagus salad—sometimes attracts members of the Dutch royal family during their incognito visits to the capital. Dinner orders are accepted until 11—late even for Amsterdam. ✉ *Korte Leidsedwarsstraat 24,* ☎ *020/622–3021. Reservations essential. AE, DC, MC, V.*

$$$–$$$$ ✕ **Le Garage.** On April 1, 1990, a backstreet garage near the Concertgebouw began a new lease on life. Oil stains and engine parts had given way to mirrored walls, plush seating, and clinking cutlery. Chef Joop Braakhekke, who is famed in the Netherlands as the zany presenter of a TV cooking show, comes up with superb New Dutch cuisine, including a few old family recipes, such as eel stewed with raisins, barley, and herbs. Media stars, politicians, and leading lights in the Dutch art world eat here, making this a hot spot for celebrity-spotters. ✉ *Ruysdaelstraat 54,* ☎ *020/679–7176. Reservations essential. Jacket and tie. AE, DC, MC, V.*

$$$ ✕ **Café Americain.** Though thousands of buildings in Amsterdam are
★ designated as historic monuments, the one that houses this restaurant is the only structure whose interior, an Art Nouveau treasure designed

by Kromhout, is also protected. Opened in 1902 and said to have been the venue for Mata Hari's wedding reception, the Café Americain is a hybrid restaurant-café serving everything from light snacks to full dinners. To one side are formal tables draped with white linens, where traditional entrées such as medallions of beef with béarnaise sauce are served; to the other side are tiny bare-top tables, perfect for a quick coffee and pastry. There is a well-stocked buffet complete with hot dishes, salads, and desserts. ⊠ *American Hotel , Leidsekade 97,* ☎ *020/624–5322. Reservations not accepted. AE, DC, MC, V.*

$$$ ✕ **Christophe.** After Algerian-born Christophe Royer opened his *eet tempel* (eating temple) on a small canal between the Keizersgracht and Prinsengracht in the 1980s, he and his French kitchen staff quickly became recognized for their fine French cuisine with Arabic and African influences. The constantly changing menu may include *crevettes à l'orange* (shrimp with orange sauce) or *pigeon à la marocaine* (pigeon cooked with coriander and other tangy spices); there is also a selection of vegetarian dishes, including a delicious artichoke with cumin. Not only is the menu special, but so are Christophe's welcoming atmosphere and personalized service. ⊠ *Leliegracht 46,* ☎ *020/625–0807. Reservations essential. Jacket advised. AE, DC, MC, V. Closed Sun., Mon., lunch; 1st wk in Jan. and 2 wks in July–Aug.*

$$$ ✕ **De Silveren Spieghel.** This intimate restaurant is in a delightfully
★ crooked 17th-century house. The cuisine is French-influenced but uses the best of local ingredients, including lamb from the island of Texel and the honey of Amsterdam's Vondelpark. The seasonal game dishes are always worth trying, especially those that come with rose-petal sauce, and the fixed-price menus represent excellent value for the money. ⊠ *Kattengat 4–6,* ☎ *020/624–6589. Reservations essential. AE, MC, V. Closed Sun. Lunch by appointment (phone a day ahead).*

$$$ ✕ **D'Vijff Vlieghen.** Dining in a traditional canal-house environment is part of the Amsterdam experience, though you are more likely to find yourself seated among closely packed tables of Swedes and Japanese than among Dutch diners. But don't let that stop you; the "Five Flies" is a charming spot that in the 1950s and 1960s was frequented by the likes of Walt Disney and Orson Welles. Set in five adjoining houses that date from 1627, the restaurant incorporates a series of small, timbered dining rooms, each well adorned with mementoes and bric-a-brac, ranging from music boxes, liqueur kegs, and violin cases to two etchings by Rembrandt. The kitchen, long a bastion of traditional Dutch meat-and-potatoes cooking, is now drawing on fresh local ingredients in such dishes as suckling pig cutlets coated in pastry, and grilled halibut with a mussel ragout. ⊠ *Spuistraat 294–302,* ☎ *020/ 624–8369. Jacket and tie. AE, DC, MC, V.*

$$$ ✕ **Dynasty.** At this trendy, interesting spot, the decor is a fanciful mating of Asian and Art Deco. A mural in red, white, and black encircles the room, and dozens of amber and dove-gray Chinese paper umbrellas hang upended from the ceiling. Chef K.Y. Lee's menu is as fascinating as the decor: The medley of Asian cuisines includes authentically prepared, classic Chinese dishes, such as Three Meats in Harmony, and selections from the cuisines of Thailand, Malaysia, and Vietnam, such as succulent duck and lobster on a bed of watercress. There are two fixed-price menus. ⊠ *Reguliersdwarsstraat 30,* ☎ *020/626–8400. Jacket required. AE, DC, MC, V. No lunch. Closed Tues.*

$$$ ✕ **Tout Court.** Chef John Fagel, who comes from a well-known Dutch
★ family of chefs, has stuck by his intention to serve "good food without a fuss." This comfortable, meticulously appointed restaurant is tucked away on a side street between the canals. The owner-chef mixes generous Dutch helpings with rich sauces: saddle of lamb filled with spinach, guinea fowl stuffed with mushrooms, roast brill with leeks,

and a heavenly bouillabaisse. At dinner there are three set menus, including a seven-course feast. ✉ *Runstraat 13*, ☎ *020/625–8637. AE, DC, MC, V. Closed Sun.–Mon.*

$$–$$$ ✕ **De Belhamel.** A stunning Art Deco interior and a fine view down the Herengracht set the tone for a well-prepared and attentively served dinner. In winter the emphasis is on hearty game dishes such as hart with a red wine and shallot sauce. In summer you can sample lighter fare. ✉ *Brouwersgracht 60*, ☎ *020/622–1095. AE, MC, V. No lunch.*

$$–$$$ ✕ **De Kooning van Siam.** This Thai restaurant, which is favored by the city's Thai residents, sits smack in the middle of the red-light district, but don't let that keep you away. Although the beams and wall panels are still visible in this old canal house, there is nothing Old Dutch about the furniture or the wall decorations. Food choices are somewhat limited: Selections might include very hot stir-fried beef with onion and chili peppers or a milder chicken and Chinese vegetables with coconut, curry, and basil. ✉ *Oude Zijds Voorburgwal 42*, ☎ *020/623–7293. AE, DC, MC, V. Closed Feb.*

$$–$$$ ✕ **De Oesterbar.** "The Oyster Bar" is a local institution. It's the first place to think of when you hanker for a half-dozen oysters fresh from the Oosterschelde or the simply prepared catch of the day. The choices are straightforward: grilled, baked, or fried fish served with tartar sauce, potatoes, and salad. Live lobster is also available in season. The no-nonsense room on the main floor has a small bar at the back, with white tile walls incorporating nautical murals and a long row of eerily lighted fish tanks along one side. In the upstairs dining room, the mood is oddly bordellolike, with elaborately patterned wallpaper and an assortment of innocuous paintings on the walls. ✉ *Leidseplein 10*, ☎ *020/623–2988. Reservations essential. AE, DC, MC, V.*

$$–$$$ ✕ **D' Theeboom.** The menu here offers you a royal choice of mouthwatering and original French haute cuisine for a surprisingly low price. The interior is sparsely but stylishly furnished and the atmosphere is sophisticatedly smart. This is one of the few restaurants where you can linger over a long lunch during the week. ✉ *Singel 210*, ☎ *020/623–8420. Reservations essential. Jacket advised. AE, DC, MC, V. Closed lunch weekends.*

$$–$$$ ✕ **Lonny's.** Lonny Gerungan offers Indonesian cuisine at its best. His
★   family have been cooks on Bali for generations, and the recipes used for the feasts in his restaurant are those that his forefathers used to prepare for royal banquets on the island. Treat yourself to a *Selamatan Puri Gede*, more than 15 succulently spicy dishes served with rice. The waiters wear sarongs, and the restaurant is decorated with silky fabrics and colorful parasols. ✉ *Rozengracht 46–48*, ☎ *020/623–8950. Reservations essential. AE, DC, MC, V. No lunch.*

$$–$$$ ✕ **Lucius.** The plain setting and the simple service belie the fact that this is one of the best fish restaurants in town. On the exclusively marine menu, your choices range from grilled lobster to more adventurous creations such as sea bass with buckwheat noodles and mushrooms. You can also opt to have any fish available cooked to your taste. The wine list includes a good selection from California and even a Dutch wine from Apostlehoeve in Limburg province, the country's only vineyard. ✉ *Spuistraat 247*, ☎ *020/624–1831. Reservations essential. AE, DC, MC, V. No lunch. Closed Sun.*

$$–$$$ ✕ **Pier 10.** This intimate restaurant, perched on the end of a pier behind
★   Centraal Station, was built in the 1930s as a shipping office. Ask for a table in the tiny glass-enclosed room at the far end of the restaurant, where you can see the water lap gently beneath the windows and the harbor lights twinkle in the distance. Owner-chef Steve Muzerie sometimes comes up with odd combinations, such as licorice mousse with a sauce made from *advocaat* (a liqueur made with beaten egg yolks,

sugar, and spirit), but his culinary inventions are usually delicious. Try the goose with wild mushrooms, or a gigantic Caesar salad. ⊠ *De Ruyterkade Steiger 10,* ☎ *020/624–8276. Reservations essential. AE, MC, V.*

$$ ✗ **Bodega Keyzer.** After 85 years spent serving musicians, concert-goers, and residents of the neighborhoods surrounding the art museums and Concertgebouw, this half restaurant, half café-bodega has evolved into something as familiar and comfortable as an old shoe. You can come at almost any hour for a simple drink or a full meal. The interior is paneled with dark wood, the lights are dim, and Oriental rugs cover the tables. The menu is equally traditional—among the meat and fish selections are tournedos, schnitzel, and sole meunière—though it may also include a more adventurous *ris de veau* (veal sweetbreads) with orange and green pepper sauce or fricassee of veal with nut-basil sauce. ⊠ *Van Baerlestraat 96,* ☎ *020/671–1441. AE, DC, MC, V. Closed Sun.*

$$ ✗ **Brasserie van Baerle.** Begun as a neighborhood lunch and Sunday brunch restaurant, this bright, appealing spot with an uncomplicated European modern decor now even draws late diners who come in following performances at the nearby Concertgebouw. The chef's creativity is the main attraction. Imaginative dishes include spicy Asian salads and heavier fare, such as duck in truffle sauce. There is outdoor dining in good weather. ⊠ *Van Baerlestraat 158,* ☎ *020/679–1532. AE, DC, MC, V. Closed Sat. and Dec. 25–Jan. 2.*

$$ ✗ **Japan Inn.** This lively Japanese restaurant is a refreshing contrast to the many tourist-trap outlets around the Leidseplein. You can choose one of various menus or order single portions to create your own dinner. There are yakitori cooked meats and fish, as well as sushi and sashimi, all served with miso soup and salad. ⊠ *Leidsekruisstraat 4,* ☎ *020/620–4989. AE, DC, MC, V. No lunch.*

$$ ✗ **Kantjil en de Tijger.** This lively Indonesian restaurant is a favorite ★ with the locals and close to the bars on the Spui. The menu is based on three different rijsttafel, with a profusion of meat, fish, and vegetable dishes varying in flavor from coconut-milk sweetness to peppery hot. Alternatively you can select separate dishes to create your own feast. ⊠ *Spuistraat 291/293,* ☎ *020/620–0994. AE, DC, MC, V. No lunch.*

$$ ✗ **Rose's Cantina.** A perennial favorite of the sparkling set, this restaurant serves up spicy Tex-Mex food and lethal cocktails. The noise level can be lethal, too. Pop in for a full meal or sundowner. In summer you can sit in the gardens facing the backs of the stately mansions on the Herengracht. ⊠ *Reguliersdwarsstraat 38,* ☎ *020/625–9797. AE, DC, MC, V.*

$$ ✗ **Sama Sebo.** Come to this small, busy, and relaxed neighborhood Indonesian restaurant near the Rijksmuseum and Museumplein for a rijsttafel feast with myriad small dishes, a simple *bami goreng* (spicy fried rice with vegetables), or a lunch of *nasi goreng* (spicy fried noodles with vegetables). The colors are muted tans and browns with rush mats covering the walls. When things are busy, the restaurant can be cramped. ⊠ *P.C. Hoofstraat 27,* ☎ *020/662–8146. AE, DC, MC, V. Closed Sun.*

$$ ✗ **Sluizer.** Sluizer is really two side-by-side restaurants with a bistro-like atmosphere—one serves only meat, the other only fish. Both are simply decorated and unpretentious; both are known for good food that is prepared without a lot of fanfare or creativity; both are reasonably priced; and, not surprisingly, both are crowded every night. ⊠ *Utrechtsestraat 43–45,* ☎ *020/622–6376 (meat) or 020/626–3557 (fish). AE, DC, MC, V.*

$$ ✕ **Toscanini.** This cavernous, noisy Italian restaurant is very popular
★ with local trendies. The food is superb, and all prepared at the last minute.
You'll find pasta with game sauce, subtle fresh fish dishes, such as trout
with fresh basil, and other delights, as well as such familiar favorites
as a varied plate of antipasti, which is scrumptious here. ⊠ *Linden-
gracht 75,* ☎ *020/623–2813. Reservations essential. No credit cards.
Closed Tues. No lunch.*

$$ ✕ **Van Puffelen.** This traditional restaurant and *proeverij* (tasting
house) is on a quiet section of the Prinsengracht, with a terrace if weather
permits. On one side is the proeverij with a large selection of traditional Dutch jenever for you to sample. The bustling popular restaurant has classic late-19th-century fittings and fills up with locals every
night of the week. If it's too noisy you can escape to the more secluded
and intimate mezzanine floor. Starters include goat cheese salad; the
fish or meat main course or daily special, might be braised duck's breast
with passion-fruit sauce. Red meat tends to be done rare, so let them
know if you prefer medium to well-done. Service is alert, and there is
an excellent and reasonably priced wine list. ⊠ *Prinsengracht 375–
377,* ☎ *020/624–6270. Reservations essential. AE, DC, MC, V.*

$ ✕ **Caffe Esprit.** Clean-cut and popular, this restaurant has tall windows
★ that overlook the busy Spui square; the decor is simple black, white,
and gray, with just a handful of small tables and a small counter to
take care of overflow. The menu is contemporary American, with
choices such as Surf Burger garnished with avocado and bacon or Yan-
kee Doodle sandwich (crisp roll with pastrami, mustard, mayonnaise,
and grilled paprika). Salads include Popeye's Favorite Salad—wild
Italian spinach, bacon, croutons, mushrooms, and egg, with warm tarragon vinaigrette. There are also pastas, pizzas, standard sandwiches,
and a children's menu. ⊠ *Spui 10,* ☎ *020/622–1967. Reservations
not accepted. No credit cards. Closed Sun.*

$ ✕ **Het Gasthuys.** In this bustling restaurant near the university you'll
be served handsome portions of traditional Dutch home cooking,
choice cuts of meat with excellent fries, and piles of mixed salad. Sit
at the bar or take a table high up in the rafters at the back. In summer
you can watch the passing boats from an enchanting canal-side terrace. ⊠ *Grimburgwal 7,* ☎ *020/624–8230. No credit cards.*

$ ✕ **The Goodies.** Fresh homemade pastas, healthy salads, and simple
but tasty meat and fish are the secret of this spaghetteria's success. During the day the restaurant is a popular café serving filling sandwiches
on Italian farmer's bread, salads, and deliciously thick fruit shakes. ⊠
Huidenstraat 9, ☎ *020/625–6122. Reservations essential. AE, MC, V.*

Lodging

There are some 270 hotels from which to choose in Amsterdam; most
are small mom-and-pop operations, best described as pensions, found
along and among the canals or in residential neighborhoods beyond
the center. These smaller canal-side hotels, often in historic buildings
with antique furniture, capture the charm and flavor of Amsterdam.
The larger hotels, including the expensive international chains, are clustered around Centraal Station, at Dam Square, and near Leidseplein.
Amsterdam is a busy city; reservations are advised at any time of the
year and are essential in tulip season (late March–June).

Amsterdam is a pedestrian's paradise but a driver's nightmare. Few hotels have parking lots, and cars are best abandoned in one of the city's
multistory lots for the duration of your stay. Within the concentric ring
of canals that surround the downtown area, the quiet museum quarter is a convenient choice, close to both the Rijksmuseum and Vondelpark. Most atmospheric is the historic canal-side neighborhood

with its gabled merchants' houses. Wherever you choose, one thing is certain: Most hotels offer rooms that are spotlessly clean. For price categories, *see* Lodging *in* Pleasures and Pastimes at the beginning of this chapter.

$$$$ ⊞ **Amstel Inter-Continental Hotel.** This grand 125-year-old hotel has an interior designed in 1992 by Pierre Yves Rochon of Paris, who has created a Dutch atmosphere with a European touch. Rooms are the most spacious in the city; the decor resembles that of a gracious home, with Oriental rugs, brocade upholstery, Delft lamps, and a color scheme inspired by the warm tones of Makkum pottery. The generous staff-guest ratio and the top-notch food help to explain the hotel's popularity among royals and celebrities. ⊠ *Professor Tulpplein 1, 1018 GX,* ☎ *020/622–6060,* FAX *020/622–5808. 58 rooms, 21 suites. 2 restaurants, 2 bars, room service, in-room VCRs, indoor pool, spa, health club, laundry service and dry cleaning, business services, convention center, meeting rooms, free parking. AE, DC, MC, V.*

$$$$ ⊞ **The Grand Westin Demeure Amsterdam.** The hotel's city-center site
★ has long been associated with stately lodging: It started in the 14th century as a convent, becoming a *Princenhof* (Prince's Court) in 1578. William of Orange stayed here in 1580 and, a little later, Maria de Medici. The buildings served as the Town Hall of Amsterdam from 1808 to 1988, and even Queen Beatrix's wedding was celebrated here in 1966. Today's incarnation, opened in 1992, is a deluxe hotel; contemporary guests have included Michael Jackson. There are Gobelin tapestries, Jugendstil (Art Nouveau) stained-glass windows, and, in the café, a mural that Karel Appel created early in his career to repay a debt to the city. The rooms, which vary in size, are attractively furnished in deep tones of burgundy damask and bold floral prints; the best of them overlook the garden courtyard. The kitchen of the brasserie-style restaurant, Café Roux, is supervised by the incomparable Albert Roux. ⊠ *Oudezijds Voorburgwal 197, 1012 EX,* ☎ *020/555–3111,* FAX *020/555–3222. 138 rooms, 28 suites, 11 apartments. Restaurant, bar, in-room modem lines, in-room safes, minibars, room service, indoor pool, massage, sauna, Turkish bath, baby-sitting, laundry service and dry cleaning, meeting rooms, car rental, parking (fee). AE, DC, MC, V.*

$$$$ ⊞ **Hotel de l'Europe.** Quiet, gracious, and understated in both decor and service, this hotel overlooks the Amstel River, the Muntplein, and the flower market. The rooms are furnished with reserved, Empire-style elegance: The city-side rooms are full of warm, rich colors; the riverside rooms, decorated in pastel shades and brilliant whites, have French windows to let in floods of light. The marble baths are large and luxurious. A junior suite might be a worthwhile choice here. ⊠ *Nieuwe Doelenstraat 2–8, 1012 CP,* ☎ *020/623–4836,* FAX *020/624–2962. 80 rooms, 20 suites. 2 restaurants, bar, room service, indoor pool, barbershop, beauty salon, hot tub, massage, sauna, exercise room, business services, meeting rooms, free parking. AE, DC, MC, V.*

$$$$ ⊞ **Pulitzer.** Twenty-four 17th- and 18th-century houses were com-
★ bined to create this hotel, which faces both the Prinsengracht and the Keizersgracht canals and is just a short walk from Dam square; the place retains a historic ambience. Most guest rooms have beam ceilings; there are gardens in the middle of the block. Refurbishment begun in 1996, while increasing comfort and convenience, is also gradually replacing modern furnishings with more appropriate antique styles. From here you may hear the hourly chiming of the nearby Westerkerk clock. ⊠ *Prinsengracht 315–331, 1016 GZ,* ☎ *020/523–5235,* FAX *020/627–6753. 218 rooms, 7 suites, 5 apartments. 2 restaurants, bar, in-room safes, room service, pool, sauna, steam room, baby-sitting, laundry service and dry cleaning, business services, convention center, meeting rooms, parking (fee). AE, DC, MC, V.*

$$$ 🏨 **American.** The American, one of the oldest hotels in Amsterdam,
★   is housed in one of the city's most fancifully designed buildings. Directly on Leidseplein, it's in the middle of everything—nightlife, dining, sightseeing, and shopping are all at hand. Rooms are comfortably spacious and furnished in art deco style. ⊠ *Leidseplein 28, 1017 PN,* ☎ *020/624–5322,* FAX *020/625–3236. 178 rooms, 10 suites. Restaurant, bar, room service, exercise room, shop, laundry service and dry cleaning, parking (fee). AE, DC, MC, V.*

$$ 🏨 **Ambassade.** Ten 17th- and 18th-century houses have been joined
★   to create this hotel, which is elegantly decorated with Oriental rugs, chandeliers, and antiques. The canal-side rooms are spacious, with large windows and solid, functional furniture. The rooms at the rear are quieter, but smaller and darker. Service is attentive and friendly and there are two elegant lounges. ⊠ *Herengracht 341, 1016 AZ,* ☎ *020/626– 2333,* FAX *020/624–5321. 46 rooms, 5 suites, 1 apartment. Bar, in-room safes, room service, spa, baby-sitting, laundry service and dry cleaning, business services, meeting rooms, car rental, parking (fee). AE, DC, MC, V.*

$$ 🏨 **Atlas Hotel.** Just a block from Amsterdam's city-center Vondelpark, this hotel, renowned for its personal and friendly atmosphere, blends into a well-to-do residential area. The moderately sized rooms are decorated in art nouveau style. It's within easy walking distance of the museums. *Van Eeghenstraat 64, 1071 GK,* ☎ *020/676–6336,* FAX *020/671–7633. 23 rooms. Restaurant, bar, laundry service and dry cleaning, parking (fee). AE, DC, MC, V.*

$$ 🏨 **Canal House.** This is what you imagine a canal-house hotel to be like: a beautiful old home with high, plaster ceilings, antique furniture, old paintings, and a backyard garden bursting with plants and flowers. Every room is unique in both size and decor, and there isn't a television in sight. The elegant chandeliered breakfast room overlooks the garden, and there is a small bar in the front parlor. The American owners have put a lot of love and style into the Canal House—the result is an intimate hotel for adults. ⊠ *Keizersgracht 148, 1015 CX,* ☎ *020/ 622–5182,* FAX *020/624–1317. 26 rooms. AE, DC, MC, V.*

$$ 🏨 **Jan Luyken.** This small, out-of-the-way place is barely noticeable
★   among the homes and offices of a 19th–century residential neighborhood, yet it is just one block away from the Museumplein and fashionable shopping streets. The personal approach is a relaxing alternative to the large hotels, but it is also well equipped to handle the needs of the business traveler. ⊠ *Jan Luykenstraat 58, 1071 CS,* ☎ *020/573– 0730,* FAX *020/676–3841. 63 rooms. Restaurant, 2 bars, in-room safes, room service, laundry service and dry cleaning, business services, parking (fee). AE, DC, MC, V.*

$–$$ 🏨 **Hotel Winston.** For the young and the young-at-heart, once a crash pad above a notorious bar, the hotel was transformed in 1996; each room has paintings or decor by a contemporary artist. It's right in the center of town, so ask for a quiet room overlooking the inner courtyard if you want to sleep before the early hours. The downstairs bar has quickly regained its reputation as a vibrant venue for live performance and late-night music; the restaurant has daily changing menus with imaginative dishes from all round the world. ⊠ *Warmoesstraat 123, 1012 JA,* ☎ *020/623–1380,* FAX *020/639–2308. 66 rooms. Restaurant, bar. AE, DC, MC, V.*

$–$$ 🏨 **Seven Bridges Hotel.** This homey hotel has idyllic views of the seven canal bridges from which it took its name, but is also within a stone's throw of Rembrandtplein. All rooms are meticulously decorated with Oriental rugs, art deco lamps, and marble sinks. Top-floor rooms are the smallest and priced accordingly; the first-floor room is practically palatial. Breakfast is delivered to your room. Reserve well in advance.

⊠ *Reguliersgracht 31, 1017 LK,* ☎ *020/623–1329. 10 rooms, 6 with shower/bath. AE, MC, V.*

$ 🖬 **Amstel Botel.** This floating hotel, moored near Centraal Station, is an appropriate lodging in watery Amsterdam. The rooms are cabin-like, but the portholes have been replaced by windows that provide fine views of the city across the water. Make sure you don't get a room on the land side of the vessel, or you'll end up staring at an ugly postal sorting office. ⊠ *Oosterdokskade 2, 1011 AE,* ☎ *020/626–4247,* FAX *020/639–1952. 176 rooms. AE, DC, MC, V.*

$ 🖬 **Hotel de Filosoof.** This hotel, on a quiet street near the Vondel Park, attracts artists, thinkers, and people looking for something a little different; bona fide Amsterdam philosophers are regularly to be found in the salon's comfy armchairs. Each room is decorated with a different cultural motif—there's an Aristotle room furnished in Greek style, with passages from the works of Greek philosophers hung on the walls, and a Goethe room adorned with Faustian texts. ⊠ *Anna van den Vondelstraat 6, 1054 GZ,* ☎ *020/683–3013,* FAX *020/685–3750. 29 rooms, 25 with bath. Bar. AE, MC, V.*

$ 🖬 **Hotel Washington.** This small, family-run hotel is just a stone's
★ throw from the Museumplein and often attracts international musicians performing at the nearby Concertgebouw. It is simply decorated in white and pastel shades, with modern prints on the walls. Large windows let in a flood of light. The best rooms have balconies. ⊠ *F. van Mierisstraat 10, 1071 RS,* ☎ *020/679–6754,* FAX *020/673–4435. 24 rooms, 19 with shower. AE, DC, MC.*

Nightlife and the Arts

Amsterdam's theater and music season begins in September and runs through June, when the Holland Festival of Performing Arts is held. *What's On in Amsterdam* is a comprehensive, English-language publication distributed by the tourist office that lists art and performing-arts events around the city. Reserve tickets to performances at the major theaters before your arrival through the **National Reservation Center** (⊠ Postbus 404, 2260 AK Leidschendam, ☎ 3170/320–2500, FAX 070/320–2611). Tickets can also be purchased in person at the tourist information offices through the **VVV Theater Booking Office** (⊠ Stationsplein 10) Monday through Saturday, 10–4; the **AUB Ticketshop** (⊠ Leidseplein, corner Marnixstraat, ☎ 020/621–1211) Monday through Saturday, 9–9; or at theater box offices.

The Arts

FILM

Mainstream cinemas are concentrated near the Leidseplein; the largest is the seven-screen **City 1–7** (⊠ Kleine Gartmanplantsoen 13–25, ☎ 020/623–4579). The four-screen **Alfa 1–4** (⊠ Kleine Gartmanplantsoen 4A, ☎ 020/627–8806) shows art films and movies not on the big-time commercial circuit. Worth visiting, if only for the pleasure of sitting in its magnificent Art Deco auditorium, is the **Tuschinski** (⊠ Reguliersbreestraat 26, ☎ 020/626–2633).

MUSIC

There are two concert halls, large and small, under one roof at the **Concertgebouw** (⊠ Concertgebouwplein 2–6, ☎ 020/671–8345). In the larger one, Amsterdam's critically acclaimed **Koninklijk Concertgebouworkest** (Royal Concert Orchestra) is often joined by international performers. The smaller hall is a venue for chamber music and up-and-coming musicians. There are free lunchtime concerts in the Concertgebouw on Wednesday at 12:30. The **IJsbreker** (⊠ Weesperzijde 23, ☎ 020/668–1805) is at the cutting edge of contemporary music and often hosts festivals of international repute.

OPERA AND BALLET

The grand and elegant **Muziektheater** (✉ Waterlooplein 22, ☎ 020/
551 8911) seats 1,600 people and hosts international opera, ballet, and
orchestra performances throughout the year. The Muziektheater is
home to **De Nederlandse Opera** (The Netherlands National Opera) and
Het Nationale Ballet (The Netherlands National Ballet). Both offer largely
classical repertoires, but the dance company has, in recent years, gained
a large measure of fame throughout Europe for its performances of 20th-
century ballets, and the opera company is gaining international praise
for its imaginative and adventurous stagings.

PUPPETS AND MARIONETTES

The young and the young at heart can enjoy puppet and marionette
shows at **Amsterdam Marionettetheater** (✉ Nieuwe Jonkerstraat 8, ☎
020/620–8027).

THEATER

Amsterdam's municipal theater, the **Stadsschouwburg** (✉ Leidseplein
26, ☎ 020/624–2311), mainly stages theater in Dutch but sometimes
hosts smaller visiting opera companies and is beginning to turn its eye
to the profitable possibilities of multicultural programming. For lavish, large-scale productions, the place to go is **Koninklijk Theater Carre**
(✉ Amstel 115–125, ☎ 020/622–5225), built in the 19th century as
permanent home to a circus. Amsterdam's Off-Broadway–type theaters are centered in an alley leading off the Dam and include **Frascati**
(✉ Nes 63, ☎ 020/623–5723 or 020/623–5724) and **Brakke Grond**
(✉ Nes 45, ☎ 020/626–6866).

Nightlife

Amsterdam nightlife centers mainly on two city squares: Leidseplein,
where the cafés and discos tend to attract young visitors to the city,
and Rembrandtplein, which fills up with a more local crowd. Trendier
nightspots and many of Amsterdam's gay venues are on the streets in
between the two squares; Reguliersdwarsstraat is a particularly happy
hunting ground, while Warmoesstraat and other streets in the red-light
district are the scene of leather-oriented gay bars and throbbing rock
clubs.

BROWN CAFÉS

Coffee and conversation are the two main ingredients of *gezelligheid*
(a good time) for an Amsterdammer, and perhaps a beer or two as the
evening wears on. The best place for these pleasures is a traditional
brown café. Wood paneling, wooden floors, comfortably worn furniture, and walls and ceilings stained with eons' worth of tobacco smoke
give the cafés their name—though today a little carefully applied paint
achieves the same effect. Traditionally, there is no background music,
just the hum of chitchat. You can meet up with friends or sit alone and
undisturbed for hours, enjoying a cup of coffee and a thorough read
of the newspapers and magazines from the pile in the corner.

Once the tasting house of an old family distillery, **De Admiraal** (✉ Herengracht 319, ☎ 020/625–4334) still serves potent liqueurs—many with
obscene names. **De Reiger** (✉ Nieuwe Leliestraat 34, ☎ 020/624–7426)
has a distinctive Jugendstil bar and serves food. If you want to hear
the locals sing folk music on Sunday afternoon, stop by **De Twee
Zwaantjes** (✉ Prinsengracht 114, ☎ 020/625–2729). A busy, jolly
Brown Café, **In de Wildeman** (✉ Kolksteeg 3, ☎ 020/638–2348), attracts a wide range of types and ages. **Nol** (✉ Westerstraat 109, ☎ 020/
624–5380) resonates with lusty-lunged, native Jordaaners having the
time of their lives. **Rooie Nelis** (✉ Laurierstraat 101, ☎ 020/624–4167)
is one of the cafés that have kept their traditional Jordaan atmosphere
despite the area's tendency toward trendiness. The high-ceiling

't Smalle (⊠ Egelantiersgracht 12, ☎ 020/623–9617) has a waterside terrace and is a favorite after-work gathering place.

CABARETS AND CASINO
Boom Chicago (⊠ Leidseplein 12, ☎ 020/530–7306) at the Leidseplein theater belongs to a bunch of zany ex-pat Americans who opened their own restaurant-theater to present improvised comedy inspired by life in Amsterdam; dinner and seating begin at 7, show time is at 8:15. **Kleine Komedie** (⊠ Amstel 56–58, ☎ 020/624–0534) has for many years been the most vibrant venue for cabaret and comedy (mainly in Dutch). One of the best additions to the nightlife scene of Amsterdam in recent years is the **Lido Dinner Show** (⊠ Leidsestraat 105, ☎ 020/626–2106), which offers cabaret and light entertainment while you dine. The **Holland Casino Amsterdam** (⊠ Max Euweplein 62, ☎ 020/620–1006), which is part of the Lido complex near Leidseplein, is one of the largest in Europe (more than 90,000 square ft) and offers everything from your choice of French or American roulette to computerized bingo, as well as the obligatory slot machines to eat up your supply of loose guilders.

COCKTAIL BARS
Ciel Bleu Bar (⊠ Hotel Okura, Ferdinand Bolstraat 333, ☎ 020/678–7111) has a glass-wall lounge 23 stories high, where you can enjoy the sunsets over Amsterdam and watch the night lights twinkle to life. **Le Bar** (⊠ Hotel de l'Europe, Nieuwe Doelenstraat 2–8, ☎ 020/623–4836), cozy and stylish, is a favorite meeting place for businesspeople. Comfy leather chairs and soft lighting give the **Golden Palm Bar** (⊠ Grand Hotel Krasnapolsky, Dam 9, ☎ 020/554–9111) something of the atmosphere of a British gentlemen's club.

DANCE AND ROCK CLUBS
Unabashedly commercial, **Cash** (⊠ Leidseplein 12, ☎ 020/422–0808) attracts Dutch youth from the provinces and reveling tourists. The huge, popular **Escape** (⊠ Rembrandtplein 11–15, ☎ 020/622–1111) can handle 2,500 people dancing to a DJ or live bands; attractions include laser light shows, videos, and shops selling clubwear. **iT** (⊠ Amstelstraat 24, ☎ 020/625–0111), with four bars, special acts and bands, and celebrities, tends toward a gay crowd on Friday and Saturday nights, straight on Thursday and Sunday nights. If you feel like dancing in a gracious old canal house, head for **Odeon** (⊠ Singel 460, ☎ 020/624–9711), where jazz and rock play in various rooms, many of which retain their spectacular painted and stucco ceilings. Converted from an old cinema, **Roxy** (⊠ Singel 465, ☎ 020/620–0354) is the trendiest discotheque in the Netherlands at the moment; unless you are pretty fast-talking or smartly dressed, you may not get past the door; Wednesday is gay night. A group of artists runs **Seymour Likely Too** (⊠ Nieuwezijds Voorburgwal 161, ☎ 020/420–5663), giving vent to their creativity in the decor—such as the Beuys Bar, decorated in the style of Joseph Beuys, a father of the avant-garde; sound is in the capable hands of some of Amsterdam's most popular DJs.

GAY BARS
Major newsstands carry specialized publications that include ads and listings for entertainment possibilities oriented to the interests of gays and lesbians. The gay scene in Amsterdam is concentrated mostly on Warmoesstraat, Reguliersdwarsstraat, Amstelstraat and along the Amstel, and Kerkstraat near Leidseplein. The **Gay & Lesbian Switchboard** (☎ 020/623–6565) can provide information from 10 AM to 10 PM, as can the **COC** action group (⊠ Rozenstraat 14, ☎ 020/626–3087), which also operates as a coffee shop, youth café, and dance club.

Tankards and brass pots hang from the ceiling in the **Amstel Taveerne** (⊠ Amstel 54, ☎ 020/623–4254), and the friendly crowd of Amsterdammers around the bar bursts into song whenever the sound system plays an old favorite. **April's Exit** (⊠ Reguliersdwarsstraat 42, ☎ 020/625–8788) attracts a smart young crowd of gay men. **Downtown** (⊠ Reguliersdwarsstraat 31, ☎ 020/622–9958) is a pleasant daytime coffee bar with a sunny terrace. **Le Montmartre** (⊠ Halvemaansteeg 17, ☎ 020/620–7622) attracts a hip crowd of younger gay men, who stop for a drink before heading out clubbing. Amsterdam's best women-only bar, **Saarein** (⊠ Elandsstraat 119, ☎ 020/623–4901) has a cozy brown-café atmosphere.

JAZZ CLUBS
In the smoky, jam-packed atmosphere of **Alto** (⊠ Korte Leidsedwarsstraat 115, ☎ 020/626–3249), you can hear the pick of local bands. **Bamboo Bar** (⊠ Lange Leidsedwarsstraat 64, ☎ 020/624–3993) has a long bar and cool Latin sounds. At **Bimhuis** (⊠ Oude Schans 73–77, ☎ 020/623–3373), the best-known jazz place in town, you'll find top musicians, including avant-gardists, performing on Friday and Saturday nights, and weeknight jam sessions. **Bourbon Street Jazz & Blues Club** (⊠ Leidsekruisstraat 6–8, ☎ 020/623–3440) presents mainstream blues and jazz to a largely tourist clientele. **Joseph Lam** (⊠ Van Diemenstraat 242, ☎ 020/622–8086) specializes in Dixieland and is open only on Saturday.

MULTICULTURAL PERFORMANCES
Akhnaton (⊠ Nieuwezijdskolk 25, ☎ 020/624–3396) is a multicultural stage and dance club renowned for its world music. African nights are especially good, but there's lots of salsa and jazz, too, and even hip-hop. **De Melkweg** (The Milky Way; ⊠ Lijnbaansgracht 234A, ☎ 020/624–1777 or 020/624–8492) is internationally known as a multicultural center for music, theater, film, and dance, with live music performances at least four nights a week and an innovative programming policy that tends increasingly toward multimedia events. **Paradiso** (⊠ Weteringschans 6, ☎ 020/623–7348), a former church, reverberates nightly to unusual sounds—anything from the latest rock band to a serious contemporary composer. Flexible staging arrangements make this a favorite venue for performance artists and multimedia events.

Outdoor Activities and Sports

Beaches
After their long, dreary winter, Amsterdammers count the days until they can hit the beaches at **Zandvoort,** a beach community directly west of the city, beyond Haarlem, where clean beachfront stretches for miles and many of the dunes are open for walking. The train station is close by, and there are lifeguards on duty. Separate areas of the beach are reserved for nudists, though topless bathing is common practice everywhere in the Netherlands.

Participant Sports
BIKING
The most convenient places to rent a bicycle are **Centraal Station** (⊠ Stationsplein 12, 1012 AB, ☎ 020/624–8391) and **McBike** (⊠ Marnixstraat 220, 1016 TL, ☎ 020/626–6964). Expect to pay from Fl 10 per day, plus a deposit of Fl 50–Fl 200 per bicycle. You'll need a passport or other identification.

GOLF
The new and luxurious **BurgGolf** is outside Amsterdam in Noord Holland province. It is a 27-hole course, comprising a 9-hole course and

a more difficult 18-hole course. ⊠ *Golden Tulip Hotel Purmerend, Westerweg 60, 1445 AD, Purmerend,* ☎ *0299/481–666.* 🖃 *Greens fees: Fl 75 weekdays, Fl 95 weekends.*

HEALTH CLUBS

Several hotels in Amsterdam have fitness facilities for guests, usually including exercise machines, weights, sauna, and whirlpool. The **Holiday Inn Crowne Plaza** (⊠ Nieuwezijds Voorburgwal 5, 1012 RC, ☎ 020/620–0500) has a large indoor swimming pool. Two of the more comprehensive hotel-based fitness facilities are **Barbizon Fit Palace** (⊠ Prins Hendrikkade 59–72, ☎ 020/556–4899) and **Splash Renaissance** (⊠ Kattengat 1, ☎ 020/621–2223), both of which offer personal training, aerobics, weight training, massage, solarium, Turkish bath, sauna, and whirlpool. **Sporting Club Leidseplein** (⊠ Korte Leidsedwarsstraat 18, ☎ 020/620–6631) offers fitness facilities, sauna, and super-fast tanners. Day rates at all of the above are Fl 25, with extra charges for special services.

JOGGING

Sunday morning is about the only time when Amsterdam's city center gets enough of a break from foot, bike, and car traffic to allow for a comfortable jog. Beyond the city near the suburb of Amstelveen, **Amsterdamse Bos** (Amsterdam Woods) is a large, spacious place to run. **Oosterpark** (Eastern Park), behind the Tropenmuseum, and **Vondelpark** (Vondel Park), near the art museums, are the only parks within the city proper.

SQUASH

The **Sporting Club Leidseplein** (⊠ 18 Korte Leidsedwarsstraat, ☎ 020/ 620–6631) is a squash, fitness, and aerobics club. There are five courts; the use of a sauna is included, and you can rent equipment and take lessons. Day cards for all facilities are Fl 25 weekdays until 4 PM; services are priced separately on evenings and weekends.

Spectator Sports

ROWING

Amsterdamse Bos (Amsterdam Woods), a large park south of the city, has monthly rowing events organized by Stedelijk Beheer Sport en Recreatie (☎ 020/643–1414) and canoeing events four times a year. The **Dutch Marine Academy** stages a rowing event (☎ 020/624–7699) on the city's canals in September.

SOCCER

Soccer is a near obsession with the Dutch, and if you want to impress an Amsterdam host, you would best be advised to know the current standing of the local team, Ajax (pronounced *eye*-axe), relative to that of its archrivals, Rotterdam's Feyenoord (pronounced *fia*-naut) and Eindhoven's PSV (Philips Sports Vereninging). The Dutch soccer season runs from August to June, with a short break in midwinter; matches are played at the **Amsterdam ArenA** (⊠ Haaksbergweg 59, ☎ 020/311–1333).

Shopping

The variety of goods available here and the convenience of a shopping district that snakes through the city in a continuous parade of boutiques and department stores are the major joys of shopping in Amsterdam. Be sure to visit the year-round outdoor flea market at Waterlooplein, a holdover from the pushcart days in the Jewish Quarter. Shopping hours in the Netherlands are regulated by law: One night a week is reserved for late shopping. In Amsterdam, department stores and many other shops are closed Monday morning but open Thursday evening. Increasingly, following an easing of legislation governing shopping hours, you'll find main branches of major stores in the center of the city open on Sunday afternoon.

Shopping Districts and Streets

The **Dam** square is home to two of Amsterdam's main department stores. Several popular shopping streets radiate from the square, offering something for nearly all tastes. **Kalverstraat,** the city's main pedestrians-only shopping street, is where Amsterdam does its day-to-day shopping. The imposing new **Kalvertoren** shopping mall (⊠ Kalverstraat, near Munt), offers covered shopping and a rooftop restaurant with magnificent views of the city. **Leidsestraat** offers a range and variety of shopping similar to Kalverstraat's, but with more of an eye to the tourist trade. **Max Euweplein** is a small plaza-style shopping mall surrounding a summer café and adjacent to the Amsterdam Casino. **Nieuwendijk** is a busy pedestrian mall, good for bargain hunters. The **Magna Plaza** shopping center (⊠ Nieuwezijds Voorburgwal 182), built inside the glorious old post office behind the Royal Palace, is *the* place for A-to-Z shopping in a huge variety of stores. The posh and prestigious **P.C. Hooftstraat,** generally known as the P.C. (pronounced "pay-say"), is home to chic designer boutiques; this is where diplomats and politicians buy their glad rags. **Rokin** is the place to go for high-price fashion and jewelry, Old Masters, and expensive antiques. **Utrechtsestraat** offers a variety of opportunities for the trendier shopper. **Van Baerlestraat,** leading to the Concertgebouw, is lined with clothing shops that are smart—but not quite smart enough to have made it to the adjoining P.C. Hooftstraat.

Department Stores

C&A (⊠ Damrak 79, ☎ 020/626–3132) offers discount clothing. **De Bijenkorf** (⊠ Dam 1, ☎ 020/621–8080) is the city's best-known department store and the stomping ground of its monied middle classes. The gracious and conservative **Maison de Bonneterie en Pander** (⊠ Rokin 140–142, ☎ 020/626–2162), all crystal chandeliers and silently gliding shop assistants, stocks an elegant range of clothing and household items. The Amsterdam branch of England's **Marks & Spencer** (⊠ Kalverstraat 66–72, ☎ 020/620–0006) is a good bet for inexpensive clothing and expensive food. **Metz & Company** (⊠ Keizersgracht 455, ☎ 020/624–8810) stocks up on textiles and household goods from **Liberty of London** and adds a range of breathtakingly expensive designer articles from all over the world; at the top-floor café you can get the best bird's-eye view of the city. **Peek & Cloppenburg** (⊠ Dam 20, ☎ 020/622–8837) specializes in durable, middle-of-the-road clothing. **Vroom & Dreesmann** (⊠ Kalverstraat 203, ☎ 020/622–0171), Amsterdam's third smartest department store after De Bijenkorf and Maison de Bonneterie, sells good-quality clothing.

Street Markets

Few markets compare with Amsterdam's **Waterlooplein** flea market. It is a descendant of the haphazard pushcart trade that gave this part of the city its distinct and lively character in the early part of the century. You're unlikely to find anything of value here, but it's a good spot to look for the secondhand clothing young Amsterdammers favor, and it is a gadget lover's paradise. The flea market is open Monday through Saturday 9:30–5. The **Bloemenmarkt** (along the Singel canal, between Koningsplein and Muntplein) is another of Amsterdam's must-see markets, where flowers and plants are sold from permanently moored barges. The market is open Monday through Saturday 9:30–6 (some flower stalls are open Sunday). On Saturday, the Noordermarkt and Nieuwmarkt host an **organic farmers' market,** with specialist stalls selling essential oils and other New Age fare alongside the oats, pulses, and vegetables. **Sunday art markets** are held in good weather from April to October on Thorbeckeplein, and from April through November at Spui. The **Postzegelmarkt** stamp market is held twice a week (Wednesday and Saturday 1–4) on Nieuwezijds Voorburgwal.

Specialty Stores

ANTIQUES

Antiques always have been a staple item of shopping in Amsterdam, and the array of goods available at any time is broad. There are more than 150 antiques shops scattered throughout the central canal area. The greatest concentration of those offering fine antiques and specialty items is in the **Spiegel Quarter.** Nieuwe Spiegelstraat and its continuation, Spiegelgracht, constitute the main thoroughfare of the quarter, with shops on both sides of the street and canal for five blocks, from the Golden Bend of the Herengracht nearly to the Rijksmuseum, including several dealers under one roof in the **Amsterdam Antiques Gallery** (⊠ Nieuwe Spiegelstraat 34, ☎ 020/625–3371). For a broad range of vintage and antique furniture, curios, jewelry, clothing, and household items, try **Kunst- & Antiekmarkt De Looier** (⊠ Elandsgracht 109, ☎ 020/624–9038), an art and antiques market housing more than 50 dealers. Rokin, between Dam and Muntplein, is the location of the Amsterdam branch of **Sotheby's** (⊠ Rokin 102, ☎ 020/550–2200). A number of the sorts of art and antiques stores where museum curators do their shopping, including **Waterman** (⊠ Rokin 116, ☎ 020/623–2958), are on Rokin. Shops on **Rozengracht** and **Prinsengracht,** near the Westerkerk, offer country Dutch furniture and household items; you'll also find antiques and curio shops along the side streets in that part of the city. The indoor flea market, **De Rommelmarkt** (⊠ Looiersgracht 38, ☎ 020/627–4762), is a warren of stalls selling everything from Art Deco lamps to defunct electrical equipment.

There are old maps and prints (including botanicals) in antiques shops all over Amsterdam, but for a broad selection of high quality, visit **A. van der Meer** (⊠ P.C. Hooftstraat 112, ☎ 020/662–1936), a gallery that has specialized in 17th-, 18th-, and 19th-century works for more than 30 years. Daumier etchings, hunt prints, and cityscape engravings can also be found here. **De Haas** (⊠ Kerkstraat 155, ☎ 020/626–5952) specializes in smaller pieces from the beginning of the 20th century. **Galerie Frans Leidelmeyer** (⊠ Nieuwe Spiegelstraat 58, ☎ 020/625–4627) is a good source of top-quality Art Deco and Jugendstil artifacts. **Tangram** (⊠ Herenstraat 9, ☎ 020/624–4286) deals in the Art Deco and Jugendstil items that are so popular in the Netherlands.

ART

Many of the galleries that deal in modern and contemporary art are centered on the **Keizersgracht** and **Spiegel Quarter.** *What's On in Amsterdam,* published by the tourist office, is a good source of information on current exhibitions; another is the Dutch-language publication *Alert,* which has the most comprehensive listings available. Among the dealers specializing in 20th-century art along the Keizersgracht are **D'Art 1970** (⊠ Keizersgracht 516, ☎ 020/622–1511), **Galerie Espace** (⊠ Keizersgracht 548, ☎ 020/624–0802), and **Kunsthandel M.L. De Boer** (⊠ Keizersgracht 542, ☎ 020/623–4060). In the Spiegel Quarter, the leading galleries are: **C.M. Kooring Verwindt** (⊠ Spiegelgracht 14–16, ☎ 020/623–6538), **E. Den Bieman de Haas** (⊠ Nieuwe Spiegelstraat 44, ☎ 020/626–1012), **Galerie Asselijn** (⊠ Lange Leidsedwarsstraat 200, ☎ 020/624–9030), **Galerie Guido de Spa** (⊠ 2e Weteringdwarsstraat 34, ☎ 020/622–1528), **Marie-Louise Woltering** (⊠ Nieuwe Spiegelstraat 53, ☎ 020/622–2240), and **Wetering Galerie** (⊠ Lijnbaansgracht 288, ☎ 020/623–6189).

Couzijn Simon (⊠ Prinsengracht 578, ☎ 020/624–7691) specializes in molting teddies and other vintage toys. **Eurasia Antiques** (⊠ Nieuwe Spiegelstraat 40, ☎ 020/626–1594) is a treasure trove of old paintings, engravings, and Asian art. **Galerie Animation Art** (⊠ Berenstraat 39, ☎ 020/627–7600) offers original Disney and other cartoon sketches.

BOOKS

Allert de Lange (⊠ Damrak 60–62, ☎ 020/624–6744) has a good selection of fiction and books on travel and history. True to its name, the **American Book Center** (⊠ Kalverstraat 185, ☎ 020/625–5537) is strongly oriented to American tastes and expectations. **The English Bookshop** (⊠ Lauriersgracht 71, ☎ 020/626–4230) is a cozy canalside bookshop with a good range of English literature, travel books, and magazines. **Premsela** (⊠ Van Baerlestraat 78, ☎ 020/662–4266) specializes in art books and stocks many luscious, tempting tomes. **Waterstone's** (⊠ Kalverstraat 152, ☎ 020/638–3821) has four floors of English-language books, from children's stories to computer manuals.

CERAMICS AND CRYSTAL

Focke & Meltzer (⊠ P.C. Hooftstraat 65–67, ☎ 020/664–2311; ⊠ Hotel OOkura Shopping Arcade, ☎ 020/678–7111) is the primary source in Amsterdam of authenticated Delft and Makkumware, as well as fine crystal.

CIGARS AND SMOKING

Davidoff (⊠ Van Baerlestraat 84, ☎ 020/671–1042) stocks fine cigars and other smokers' requisites. One of the best places in the world to buy cigars and other smoking materials is **Hajenius** (⊠ Rokin 92, ☎ 020/623–7494), in business since 1826.

COFFEE, TEA, AND SPICES

Jacob Hooy & Co. (⊠ Kloveniersburgwal 12, ☎ 020/624–3041) has been selling herbs, spices, and medicinal potions from the same shop beside the Nieuwmarkt since 1743. Gold-lettered wooden drawers, barrels, and bins contain not just spices and herbs but also a daunting array of *dropjes* (hard candies and medicinal drops) and teas. **S. Levelt's Koffie- en Theehandel N.V.** (⊠ Prinsengracht 180, ☎ 020/624–0823) offers nearly 100 different kinds of tea and more than two dozen coffees.

DIAMONDS AND JEWELRY

The **Amsterdam Diamond Center** (⊠ Rokin 1–5, ☎ 020/624–5787) houses several diamond sellers. **Coster Diamonds** (⊠ Paulus Potterstraat 2–4, ☎ 020/676–2222) not only sells jewelry and loose diamonds but gives free demonstrations of diamond cutting. You can see a replica of the most famous diamond cut in the factory—the Koh-I-Noor, one of the prize gems of the British crown jewels. **Van Moppes Diamonds** (⊠ Albert Cuypstraat 2–6, ☎ 020/676–1242) has an extensive diamond showroom and offers a glimpse of the process of diamond cutting and polishing.

Bonebakker (⊠ Rokin 88/90, ☎ 020/623–2294) is one of the city's oldest and finest jewelers and carries an exceptionally fine range of watches and silverware. **Premsela & Hamburger** (⊠ Rokin 120, ☎ 020/624–9688; closed weekends) has sold fine antique silver and jewelry since 1823. The century-old **Schaap and Citroen** (⊠ Kalverstraat 1, ☎ 020/626–6691) has an affordable range of jewelry and watches.

DUTY-FREE

If you don't have time to shop in Amsterdam, save your guilders for the airport, as **Amsterdam Airport Shopping Centre** (⊠ Amsterdam Schiphol Airport, ☎ 020/601–2497) is bigger, better, and cheaper than almost any other airport duty-free shopping area in the world.

The airport's departure hall looks more like a shopping mall than a transportation facility, and auxiliary shops for the most popular items (liquor, perfume, chocolates) are found in every wing of the terminal.

MEN'S CLOTHING

For high-style apparel and designer togs, head to **Dik** (⊠ P.C. Hooftstraat 35, ☎ 020/662–4328). **The English Hatter** (⊠ Heiligeweg 40, ☎ 020/623–4781) has tweed jackets, deerstalkers, and many other trappings of the English country gentleman. **Gaudi** (⊠ P.C. Hooftstraat 116, ☎ 020/679–9319) is a mecca for the trendy and label conscious. **McGregor and Clan Shop** (⊠ P.C. Hooftstraat 113, ☎ 020/662–7425) has a distinctly Scottish air, with chunky knitwear and the odd flash of tartan. **Meddens** (⊠ Heiligeweg 11–17, ☎ 020/624–0461) stocks a good range of fairly conservative men's casual and formal wear. **Mulberry Company** (⊠ P.C. Hooftstraat 46, ☎ 020/673–8086) sells stylish fashions from England. **Oger** (⊠ P.C. Hooftstraat 81, ☎ 020/676–8695) puts suits on the backs of leading Dutch politicians and TV personalities. **Society Shop** (⊠ Van Baerlestraat 20, ☎ 020/664–9281) stocks good basics for businessmen.

SHOES AND HATS

Bally Shoes (⊠ Leidsestraat 8–10, ☎ 020/622–2888) is a byword for good taste in women's shoes. **Dr. Adams** (⊠ P.C. Hooftstraat 90, ☎ 020/662–3835) sells chunkier, more adventurous styles of shoes for men and women. **Shoebaloo** (⊠ Koningsplein 7, ☎ 020/626–7993) is the place for 8-inch heels, mock leopard-skin boots, and other outrageous footwear. **Smit Bally** (⊠ Leidsestraat 41, ☎ 020/624–8862) sells classically smart shoes for men.

The well-stocked **Hoeden M/V** (⊠ 422 Herengracht, ☎ 020/626–3038), in a canal house, carries Borsalino hats for men and women as well as Dutch and international designer hats.

WOMEN'S CLOTHING

In the **Jordaan** neighborhood, generation after generation of experimental designers have set up shop to show their imaginative creations. Antiques- and used-clothing shops are also in this part of town. Designer shops stand shoulder to shoulder in the **P.C. Hooftstraat: Benetton** (⊠ P.C. Hooftstraat 72, ☎ 020/679–5706), **Edgar Vos** (⊠ P.C. Hooftstraat 134, ☎ 020/662–6336), **Leeser** (⊠ P.C. Hooftstraat 117, ☎ 020/679–5020), and **Max Mara** (⊠ P.C. Hooftstraat 110, ☎ 020/671–7742). **Boetiek Pauw** (⊠ Van Baerlestrasse 66 and 72, ☎ 020/662–6253), which also operates men's and children's shops, is part of a chain that stands out for the quality of both design and craftsmanship of its clothing. The international fashion house **Esprit** (⊠ Spui 1c, ☎ 020/626–3624) has a large branch in central Amsterdam. **Claudia Sträter** (⊠ Beethovenstraat 9, ☎ 020/673–6605; ⊠ Kalverstraat 179–181, ☎ 020/622–0559) is part of a Dutch minichain that sells simply styled, well-made clothes for all occasions.

Side Trip

Even if you are in Amsterdam for just a couple of days, it is easy to sample one of the best-known aspects of quintessential Holland—the bulb fields. The flower-growing area to the west of Amsterdam is a modern-day powerhouse of Dutch production techniques, which mean that you can encounter Dutch flowers all over the world at any time of the year. In spring, the bulb fields blaze with color: Great squares and oblongs of red, yellow, and white look like giant Mondrian paintings laid out on the ground. It is a spectacular sight, whether you travel through the fields by bike or bus, or pass by in the train on your way to Leiden.

Numbers in the margin correspond to points of interest on the Side Trip from Amsterdam and Folkloric Holland map.

En Route   If you are driving from Amsterdam, take the A4 southbound toward Leiden. Take the N207 turning for Lisse. The **Bollenstreek Route** (Bulb District Route) is a special itinerary through the heart of the flower-growing region that was laid out by the Dutch auto club, ANWB. The route is marked with small blue and white signs that read BOLLENSTREEK. It begins in **Oegstgeest**, near Leiden, and circles through **Rijnsburg** (site of one of Holland's three major flower auction houses), where there is a colorful Flower Parade on the first Saturday in August. On the way you pass through **Lisse**, which has a Flower Parade on the last Saturday in April. Lisse is also the site of the Keukenhof Gardens.

①   **Keukenhof** is a 70-acre park and greenhouse complex where nearly 7 million flowers bloom every spring. In the last weeks of April you can catch tulips, daffodils, hyacinths, and narcissi all flowering simultaneously. In addition there are bright floral mosaics and some 50,000 square ft of more exotic blooms under glass. The first tulip bulbs were brought to the Netherlands from Turkey in the mid-16th century. During the 17th century the bulbs became a prized possession and changed hands for extraordinary amounts of money. Today Dutch botanists use Keukenhof as a showcase for their latest hybrids, so black tulips and gaudy frilled varieties also make an appearance. ✉ *N207, Lisse;* ☎ *0252/465–555. Keukenhof Express train via Lovers Rail,* ☎ *020/ 557–7666.* 🎫 *Fl 17.50.* ☉ *Late Mar.–May, daily 8–7:30.*

In the dunes north of **Noordwijk** is a vast, sandy nature reserve, almost as big as the bulb district itself. Small canals and pools of water are dotted about in between the dunes, providing a haven for bird life. In addition to Noordwijk, the Bulb Route (☞ *above*) passes through the beach community of **Katwijk** and through **Sassenheim**, where there is an imposing 13th-century ruined castle.

②   At **Aalsmeer,** about 19 km (12 mi) southwest of Amsterdam near Schiphol Airport, **Bloemenveiling** Aalsmeer (Aalsmeer Flower Auction) is held five days a week from the pre-dawn hours until mid-morning. The largest flower auction in the world, it has three auction halls operating continuously in a building the size of several football fields. You walk on a catwalk above the rolling four-tier carts that wait to move on tracks past the auctioneers. The buying system is what is called a Dutch auction—the price goes down, not up, on a large "clock" on the wall. The buyers sit lecture-style with buzzers on their desks; the first to register a bid gets the bunch. ✉ *Legmeerdijk 313, Aalsmeer,* ☎ *0297/392–185. NZH Bus 172 from stop opposite American Hotel near Amsterdam's Leidseplein.* 🎫 *Fl 7.* ☉ *Weekdays 7:30–11.*

Amsterdam A to Z

Arriving and Departing

BY CAR
Major European highways leading into the city from the borders are E19 from western Belgium; E25 from eastern Belgium; and E22, E30, and E35 from Germany. Follow the signs for *Centrum* to reach center city. Traffic is heavy but not stationary at rush hour.

BY PLANE
Amsterdam Schiphol Airport (☎ 0900/0141) is 25 km (15 mi) southeast of the city and has efficient road and rail links. The comprehensive "Helloport" telephone service, charged at Fl 1 per minute, provides information about flight arrivals and departures as well as all transport and parking facilities.

Side Trip from Amsterdam and Folkloric Holland

De Koog
Texel
Den Burg · Oudeschild
Den Helder

KEY
Rail Lines
Ferry

N99
N9
Noordhollands
N248
E22/A7
N242
N241

Stavoren

IJsselmeer

0   10 miles
0   15 km

Enkhuizen

Alkmaar

Noordoost Polder
Urk

Castricum
N243
Hoorn
Markermeer

N247
Purmerend
Edam
Volendam
Marken
Monnickendam

Oostelijk Flevoland

Zaandam

Haarlem
Zandvoort
Amsterdam
Zuidelijk Flevoland
E232/A8

Noord-wijk
Hillegom
Schiphol Airport
Aalsmeer

Katwijk
Keukenhof
Sassenheim

Leiden
Oude Rijn
A4
Utrecht
Eem
Amersfoort
E30/A1
Apeldoorn

Between the airport and downtown: KLM Shuttle (☎ 020/649–5651) operates a shuttle bus service between Amsterdam Schiphol Airport and major city hotels. The trip takes about half an hour and costs Fl 17.50 one-way. The **Schiphol Rail Link** (☎ 0900/9292) operates between the airport and the city 24 hours a day, with service to the central railway station or to stations in the south of the city. The trip takes about 15 minutes and costs Fl 5.75. There is a **taxi** stand directly in front of the arrival hall at Amsterdam Schiphol Airport. All taxis are metered, and the fare is approximately Fl 60 to central Amsterdam. Service is included, but small additional tips are not unwelcome.

BY TRAIN

The city has several substations, but all major Dutch national, as well as European international trains arrive at and depart from **Centraal Station** (☎ 0900/9292, 75¢ per minute, for local and national service information; 0900/9296, 50¢ per minute, for international). The station also houses the travel information office of **NS/Nederlandse Spoorwagen** (Netherlands Railways) and their international rail office.

Getting Around

Amsterdam is a small city, and most major sites are within its central district. The canal-laced core is surrounded by concentric rings of 15th- to 17th-century canals, built following the pattern of earlier city walls and drainage ditches. Six roads link the city center with the more modern outer neighborhoods. Once you understand the fanlike pattern of Amsterdam's geography, you will have an easier time getting around. All trams and most buses begin and end their journeys at Centraal Station, sightseeing and shopping are focused at Dam square, and the arts and nightlife are centered in the areas of Leidseplein, Rembrandtplein, and Waterlooplein.

Bicycling is the most convenient way to see Amsterdam. There are bike
lanes on all major streets, bike racks in key locations, and special bike
parking indentations in the pavement. For a list of rental shops, *see*
Outdoor Activities and Sports, *above*.

Taxi stands are at the major squares and in front of the large hotels.
You can also call **Taxicentrale** (☎ 020/677–7777), the central taxi dis-
patching office. Fares are Fl 5.60, plus Fl 2.80 per kilometer. A 5-km
(3-mi) ride will cost about Fl 20.

The transit map published by **GVB** (Gemeentelijk Vervoer Bedrijf/City
transport company; main information office: ✉ Prins Hendrikkade 108–
114, ☎ 020/551–4911) is very useful. It's available at the GVB ticket
office across from the central railway station, or at the VVV tourist
information offices next door. It is also reprinted as the center spread
in *What's On in Amsterdam,* the fortnightly guide to activities and shopping published by the tourist office. The map shows the locations of
all major museums, monuments, theaters, and markets, and it tells you
which trams to take to reach them.

Single-ride tickets valid for one hour can be purchased from tram and
bus drivers for Fl 3.25, but it is far more practical to buy a *strippenkaart*
(strip ticket) that includes from 2 to 45 "strips," or ticket units. The
best buy for most visitors is the 15-strip ticket for Fl 11.50. A new service for visitors is the Circle Tram 20, which rides both ways around
a loop that passes close to most of the main sights and offers a hop-
on, hop-off ticket for one–three days. By tradition, Dutch trams and
buses work on the honor system: Upon boarding, punch your ticket
at one of the machines situated in the rear or center section of the tram
or bus. The city is divided into zones, which are indicated on the transit map, and it is important to punch the correct number of zones on
your ticket (one for the basic tariff and one for each additional zone
traveled). Occasional ticket inspections can be expected: A fine of Fl
60 is the price for "forgetting" to stamp your ticket.

A **Water Taxi** (☎ 020/622–2181) provides a novel, if pricey, means of
getting about. Water taxis can be hailed anytime you see one cruising
the canals of the city, or called by telephone. The boats are miniature
versions of the large sightseeing canal boats, and each carries up to eight
passengers. The cost is Fl 90 for a half hour, including pick-up charge,
with a charge of Fl 30 per 15-minute period thereafter. The rate is per
ride, regardless of the number of passengers.

Contacts and Resources

Should you arrive without a room, head for one of three **VVV Lo-
giesservice** (VVV Accommodation Service) offices: Platform 2 at Centraal Station; opposite Centraal Station (✉ Stationsplein 10; ☉ personal
visits, Mon.–Sat. 8–8, Sun. 9–5); and near Leidseplein (✉ Leidsestraat 106, ☉ weekdays 9–8, Sat. 9–7, Sun. 9–5). This is a same-day
hotel booking service that, for a modest charge of Fl 5, can help you
find a room.

Avis (✉ Nassaukade 380, ☎ 020/683–6061). **Budget** (✉ Overtoom
121, ☎ 020/612–6066). **Hertz** (✉ Overtoom 333, ☎ 020/612–2441).

CHANGING MONEY

GWK/Grenswisselkantoren (⊠ Centraal Station, ☎ 020/627–2731) is a nationwide financial organization specializing in foreign currencies, where travelers can exchange cash and traveler's checks, receive cash against major credit cards, and receive Western Union money transfers. There is also a GWK branch at the Leidseplein. Many of the same services are available at banks, and cash can be exchanged at any post office.

CONSULATES

U.S. Consulate (⊠ Museumplein 19, Amsterdam, ☎ 020/664–5661). **British Consulate** (⊠ Koningslaan 44, Amsterdam, ☎ 020/676–4343). **Canadian Embassy** (7 Sophialaan, The Hague, ☎ 070/361–4111). **Australian Embassy** (Carnegielaan 4, 5217 KH, Den Haag, ☎ 070/310–8200). **New Zealand Embassy** (Carnegielaan 10, 5217 KH, Den Haag, ☎ 070/346–9324). **Eire/Republic of Ireland Embassy** (Dr Cuyperstraat 9, 2514 BA, Den Haag, ☎ 070/363–0993).

EMERGENCIES

National Emergency Alarm Number (☎ 112). **Police only** (☎ 622–2222). **City police stations** (⊠ Elandsgracht 117; ⊠ Lijnbaansgracht 219; ⊠ Warmoesstraat 44–46; ⊠ entrance to IJtunnel). **Doctors and Dentists: Referrals** (☎ 020/592–3434); 24-hour service for all medical assistance, including names and opening hours of pharmacists and dentists. **Hospital Emergency Rooms: Academisch Medisch Centrum** (⊠ Meibergdreef 9, ☎ 020/566–9111), **Boven 't IJ Ziekenhuis** (⊠ Statenjachtstraat 1, ☎ 020/634–6346), **Central Medical Service** (☎ 020/592–3434, **Onze Lieve Vrouwe Gasthuis** (⊠ 1e Oosterparkstraat 279, ☎ 020/599–9111), **Slotervaartziekenhuis** (⊠ Louwesweg 6, ☎ 020/512–4113), and **VU Ziekenhuis** (⊠ De Boelelaan 1117, ☎ 020/444–4444).

GUIDED TOURS

Afternoon bus tours of the city operate daily. Itineraries vary, and prices range from Fl 25 to Fl 35. A three-hour city tour that includes a drive through the suburbs is offered by **Key Tours** (⊠ Dam 19, ☎ 020/624–5051). A 3½-hour tour, focusing on the central city and including a canal-boat cruise, is offered by **Lindbergh Excursions** (⊠ Damrak 26, ☎ 020/622–2766). However, it must be said that this city of narrow alleys and canals is not best appreciated from the window of a coach. Also, a number of visitors feel unhappy that part of some tours involves a visit to a diamond factory, where they feel pressured into listening to a sales pitch. The same bus companies operate scenic trips to attractions outside the city.

The quickest, easiest way to get your bearings in Amsterdam is to take a canal-boat cruise. Trips last from 1 to 1½ hours and cover the harbor as well as the main canal district; there is a taped or live commentary available in four languages. There are also dinner and candlelight cruises. Excursion boats leave from piers in various locations in the city every 15 minutes from March to October, and every 30 minutes in winter. Most launches are moored in the inner harbor in front of Centraal Station. Fares are about Fl 12–Fl 15. Operators of canal cruises include **Holland International** (⊠ Prins Hendrikkade, opposite Centraal Station, ☎ 020/622–7788), **Meyers Rondvaarten** (⊠ Damrak, quays 4–5, ☎ 020/623–4208), **Rederij D'Amstel** (⊠ Nicolaas Witsenkade, opposite the Heineken Brewery, ☎ 020/626–5636), **Rederij Lovers** (⊠ Prins Hendrikkade 26, opposite Centraal Station, ☎ 020/622–2181), **Rederij P. Kooij** (⊠ Rokin, near Spui, ☎ 020/623–3810), **Rederij Noord/Zuid** (⊠ Stadhouderskade 25, opposite Parkhotel, ☎ 020/679–1370), and **Rederij Plas** (⊠ Damrak, quays 1–3, ☎ 020/624–5406).

The **VVV** (☞ Visitor Information, *below*) maintains lists of personal guides and guided walking and cycling tours for groups in and around Amsterdam and can advise you on making arrangements. The costs are from Fl 208 for a half day and Fl 333 for a full day. The tourist office also sells brochures outlining easy-to-follow self-guided tours through the central part of the city. Among them are "A Journey of Discovery Through Maritime Amsterdam," "A Walk Through the Jordaan," "Jewish Amsterdam," and "Rembrandt and Amsterdam." **Audio Tours** (✉ Oude Spiegelstraat 9, behind Dam Palace, ☎ 020/421–5580) allows you to wander at your own pace with their 2–3 hour tape cassette-tape tours (with a map in case you lose track) for Fl 15 per tour, plus a Fl 100 returnable deposit. There are three tours available.

Several boat trips to museums are available: **Canalbus** (✉ Nieuwe Weteringschans 24, ☎ 020/623–9886), which makes six stops along two different routes between Centraal Station and the Rijksmuseum, costs Fl 27.75 including a ticket for the Rijksmuseum and reductions for other museums. Following a longer route is **Museumboot Rederij Lovers** (✉ Stationsplein 8, ☎ 020/622–2181), which makes seven stops near 20 different museums. The cost is Fl 22 for a day ticket that entitles you to a 50% discount on admission to the museums.

From April through October, guided three-hour bike trips through the central area of the city are available through **Yellow Bike** (✉ Nieuwezijds Kolk 29, ☎ 020/620–6940). **Let's Go** tours (contact the VVV for further details) takes you out of the city-center by train before introducing you to the safer cycling of the surrounding countryside. Their tours include Edam and Volendam, Naarden and Muiden and, in season, a Tulip Tour.

Walking tours focusing on art and architecture are organized by **Artifex** (✉ Herengracht 342, 1016 CG, ☎ 020/620–8112), **Stichting Arttra** (✉ Staalstraat 28, 1011 JM, ☎ 020/625–9303), and **Archivisie** (✉ Postbus 14603, 1001 LC, ☎ 020/625–8908). For walking tours of the Jewish Quarter, contact **Joods Historisch Museum** (✉ Jonas Daniel Meyerplein 2–4, Postbus 16737, 1001 RE, ☎ 020/626–9945, ℻ 020/624–1721).

TRAVEL AGENCIES
American Express International (✉ Damrak 66, ☎ 020/520–7777). **Thomas Cook** (✉ Damrak 1, ☎ 020/620–3236). **Holland International Travel Group** (✉ Dam 6, ☎ 020/622–2550). **Key Tours** (✉ Dam 19, ☎ 020/623–5051). **Lindbergh Excursions** (✉ Damrak 26, ☎ 020/622–2766). For student travel, **NBBS** (✉ Rokin 38, ☎ 020/624–0989).

VISITOR INFORMATION
The **VVV** (Amsterdam Tourist Office; ✉ Spoor 2/Platform 2, Centraal Station; ✉ Stationsplein 10, opposite Centraal Station; ✉ Leidsestraat 106, near Leidseplein; ✉ Stadionplein; ✉ Schiphol Airport; ☎ 0900/400–4040, Fl 1 per minute, weekdays 9–5, ℻ 020/625–2869).

Folkloric Holland

Amsterdam is actually in the southern part of the province of Noord-Holland. Just across the Noordzee Kanaal (North Sea Canal) behind Amsterdam's Centraal Station as far as the Kop van Holland (the Top of Holland) and the island of Texel, this part of the country offers a taste of unspoiled rural life. Characterful towns, once home to the Dutch fishing fleets and the adventurous captains of the Dutch Golden Age who traveled to the East and West Indies and beyond, are now obsolete because of the *Afsluitdijk* (Enclosing Dike) at the north end of the former Zuider Zee. This extraordinary piece of civil engineering was completed in 1932, protecting the low-lying land from the ravages of the open seas and creating a massive freshwater lake. These ports are now busy harbors for the leisure craft that ply the protected waters.

Numbers in the margin correspond to points of interest on the Side Trip from Amsterdam and Folkloric Holland map.

Zaandam

❸ *16 km (10 mi) northwest of Amsterdam.*

The **Zaanse Schans** is a gem of windmill-studded countryside in the province of Noord Holland. It is just north of Zaandam, where Peter the Great of Russia learned the craft of shipbuilding. The village is filled with classic green wooden houses. Many have been restored as private homes, but a whole cluster is open to the public, including the workshop of a clog maker, the shops of a traditional cheese maker, a bakery museum, and the working windmills themselves. ⊠ *Kraaienest, Zaandam,* ☏ *075/616–8218.* ▨ *Free.* ◷ *Daily 8:30–6.*

Hoorn

❹ *43 km (27 mi) north of Amsterdam.*

The former capital of West-Friesland was an important center for the fleets of the VOC (Dutch East India Company) during the 17th century. Willem Cornelis Schouten, one of the town's sons, was the first sailor to round the southern cape of America (in 1616), and christened it Cape Hoorn. Jan Pieterszoon Coen, whose statue lords over the Rode Steen square, founded the city of Batavia in Java, the present-day Jakarta, and governed it from 1617 until his death in 1629. Hoorn's decline was precipitated by the growing naval power of the British during the 18th century and the opening of the Noord-Holland's canal linking Amsterdam directly to the North Sea.

The **Westfries Museum** (West Frisian Museum) is housed in the provincial government building from 1632, where the delegates from the seven cities of West-Friesland used to meet. The cities are represented by the coats of arms decorating the stunning facade, a testimony to the province's former grandeur. The council chambers are hung with portraits of the region's grandees, and the exhibitions explain the town's maritime history and the exotic finds of its adventurous sailors. ⊠ *Rode Steen 1,* ☏ *0229/280–028.* ▨ *Fl 6.* ◷ *Apr.–Sept., weekdays 11–5, Sat. 2–5, Sun. noon–5; Oct.–Mar., weekdays 11–5, weekends 2–5.*

NEED A
BREAK?
De Waag (The Weigh House; ⊠ Rode Steen 8, ☏ 0229/215–195) is a monumental building dating from 1609, with wooden beams and the antique weighing equipment still intact. It was designed by Hendrick de Keyser. There are soups, salads, and well-filled sandwiches during the day, and at dinner time you can choose from fish specialties or French cuisine. The terrace affords a stunning view of the towering ornamental facade of the Westfries Museum across the square.

❺ Near the former harbor town of **Enkhuizen,** about 19 km (12 mi) east
🖐 of Hoorn, is the **Zuiderzee Museum.** It is one of the Netherlands' most complete outdoor museums, with streets, neighborhoods, and harbors created with historic buildings. There are 130 houses, shops, and workshops where old crafts are still practiced. To reach the museum you have to take a boat from the main entrance, a romantic way to take a step back in time. The children's island takes youngsters back to life in the former fishing village of Marken during the 1930s.

✉ *Wierdijk 12–22, Enkhuizen,* ☎ *0228/351–111.* 🎫 *Fl 17.50; indoor museum only, Fl 7.50.* ⊙ *Indoor museum, daily 10–5; outdoor museum, Apr.–Oct., daily 10–5.*

Texel

85 km (53 mi) north of Amsterdam.

The largest of the Wadden Islands is also the easiest to reach, just over an hour from Amsterdam by road or rail, and only 20 minutes from the mainland by ferry. With an early start you could tour it by bike in a day. Otherwise take a night or two to enjoy the nature, sea breeze, and clear skies. Texel is nicknamed "Holland in miniature" because of the variety of landscape and natural features: woodlands, open meadows, saltwater marshes, dunes, and broad beaches. The many nature reserves make it a paradise for bird-watchers. Water sports are important here, and the island's annual *Ronde om Texel,* a 100-km (60-mi) catamaran race around the island held in mid-June and preceded by a week of other maritime events, has become famous. The island also has an international sea-kayaking school, parachute jumping, and a golf course.

One of Texel's remarkable natural features is **De Hoge Berg** (the High Mountain), the 50-ft high pinnacle of a ridge formed by glacial movement during the last Ice Age and declared a natural monument in 1968. Climbing its grass-covered pathways is hardly a problem, but it offers a stunning overview of the whole island. Throughout the island you can spot the unusual *schapeboet,* sheep shelters that look like truncated barns, some thatched with local reed, with their sloping rumps turned to the westerly winds. The characteristic *tuinwallen* (garden walls) that were used to divide plots of farmland were built up from sods of earth. These have become a habitat for all kinds of plants, animals, and insects.

❻ Den Burg is at the center of the island, geographically, as well as in terms of size, choice of places to eat, and shops. The step-gabled house occupied by the **Oudheidskamer** (Museum of Antiquities) dates from 1599 and gives a sense of local life in times gone by, with exquisitely tiled fireplaces and antique furniture in a homey setting. ✉ *Kogerstraat 1,* ☎ *0222/313–135.* 🎫 *Fl 3.* ⊙ *Apr.–Oct. weekdays 10–noon and 1:30–3:30.*

❼ Oudeschild is the island's historic harbor town, still used as a port by Texel's modern fishing fleet. During the 17th century, VOC (Dutch East India Company) ships would anchor here, awaiting favorable winds to take them off on their adventurous journeys, and smaller boats would bring them provisions. Sports fishing trips and shrimping fleets now set out from here.

The **Maritiem en Jutters Museum** (Maritime and Beachcomber's Museum) contains a bemusing collection of beachcombers' finds and is just next door to the landmark **Traanroier molen** (Tear Rower windmill), which was used for hulling grain. The museum also has exhibitions about the local fishing industry, lifeboats, and marine archaeology, including the finds from a VOC ship that sank in the Wadden Sea in 1640. ✉ *Barentszstraat 21, Oudeschild,* ☎ *0222/314–956.* 🎫 *Fl 8.* ⊙ *Sept.–June, Tues.–Sun. 10–5; July–Aug., daily 10–5.*

One of Texel's oldest constructions is **Fort De Schans.** Built in the 15th century, this fort is surrounded by water-filled moats. It was extended in 1811 on the orders of Napoléon. ✉ *Schansweg, 1 km (½ mi) south of Oudeschild.* 🎫 *Guided tours Fl 10.* ⊙ *Tours: Apr.–Oct., Wed. 10.*

8 **De Koog,** a modern seaside town, is a practical base for exploring the North Sea coastline and its nature reserves. In high season it is subject to hordes of sunseeking tourists. Much of northwestern Texel is new, the result of dikes built early in the 17th century. Sand was deposited on the seaward side of these dikes, forming a second row of dunes that protected the land behind. However, if the sea breaks through the dunes or man-made dikes during a storm, the valleys behind them can become tidal salt marshes. This is how the **De Slufter** and **De Muy** nature reserves were formed, ideal feeding and breeding grounds for birds such as the spoonbill, sandpipers, and even the rare avocet.

The **Ecomare** nature center for the Wadden Sea and the North Sea is a good starting point for discovering the natural wonders of these abundant habitats. There is a seal rehabilitation center, a bird sanctuary, and fieldwork programs for the public. ⊠ *Ruyslaan 92, De Koog,* ☎ *0222/317–741.* ☞ *Fl 12.50.* ☉ *Apr.–Oct., daily 9–5; Nov.–Mar., Mon.–Sat. 9–5.*

Dining and Lodging

Texel's sheep outnumber the human population. The lambs are famous for their succulent pre-salé saltiness, acquired from grazing in meadows sprayed by the salt-laden sea winds. The island is also known for its organic dairy products and vegetables. The salt marshes make it possible to farm unusual vegetables such as sea aster, a leaf that makes a tasty addition to salads. There is plenty of holiday accommodation on Texel, from campsites in the dunes to private villas hidden in woodlands. Contact the VVV (☞ Visitor Information, *below*) for further information; a variety of packages that can reduce hotel costs considerably are available.

$$$$ ✕ **Het Vierspan.** This intimate but sophisticated restaurant serves carefully prepared Continental cuisine emphasizing the famous local products, for example a starter of carpaccio of duck's breast followed by saddle of Texel lamb. The day menu is created using only the very freshest products. ⊠ *Gravenstraat 3, Den Burg,* ☎ *0222/013–176. AE, MC, V. No lunch.*

$$–$$$$ ▥ **Hotel & Villa Opduin.** This establishment tries to uphold the values of the family hotel from which it has developed. Though architecturally the hotel is nothing short of a modern, blocklike monstrosity, the rooms are spacious and filled with light. There are a few luxury top-floor suites with a view of the sea; the hotel's dependance, Villa Opduin, has simple, cheap rooms with shared bathrooms. ⊠ *Ruyslaan 22, 1796 AD, De Koog,* ☎ *0222/317–445,* ☒ *0222/317–777. 59 rooms, 42 suites, 6 apartments. Restaurant, bar, lobby lounge, in-room safes, minibars, indoor pool, sauna, tennis court, bicycles, children's programs, convention center, meeting rooms. AE, MC, V.*

$$ ▥ **Hotel De Lindeboom.** Spacious, light rooms with modern furnishingsare above a popular café-restaurant with a sunny terrace that overlooks an open square in the peaceful center of town. ⊠ *Groeneplaats 14, 1791 CC, Den Burg,* ☎ *0222/312–041,* ☒ *0222/310–517. 22 rooms. Restaurant, bar. No credit cards.*

$ ▥ **Hotel-Restaurant De Zeven Provinciën.** The old-fashioned tavern with simple rooms nestles safely behind the sea dike on the eastern side of the island. The restaurant serves traditional Dutch food throughout the day. ⊠ *De Ruyterstraat 60, 1792 AK, Oudeschild,* ☎ *0222/312–652. 14 rooms. Restaurant, bar. No credit cards.*

Outdoor Activities and Sports

BIKING
Bicycles can be rented from the ferry terminal and all over the island for about Fl 7.50 per day.

Training courses and rentals are available at **Zeilschool De Eilander** (⊠ Paal 33, De Cocksdorp, ☎ 0222/316–500) and **J. Schuringa** (⊠ Westerslag, Paal 15, De Koog, ☎ 0222/314–847).

GOLF
The island's golf course and driving range is **De Texelse** (⊠ Roggeslootweg 3, De Cocksdorp, ☎ 0222/316–539), with a 9-hole links course and a 9-hole practice course.

KAYAKING
Sea and surf excursions and supervised training courses are offered by **Zeekanocentrum Texel** (⊠ Lijnbaan 37, Den Burg, ☎ 0222/315–066) or **SeaMount Tracks** (⊠ Rommelpot 19, Den Hoorn, ☎ 0222/319–393), who offer weeklong certificate courses.

PARACHUTING
Paracentrum Texel (⊠ Vliegveld Texel, ☎ 0222/311–464) offers supervised training and jumps.

Folkloric Holland A to Z

Arriving and Departing

BY CAR
To reach the **Zaanse Schans,** you need to navigate the most confusing part of the country's road system, Amsterdam's A10 ring road, from which you take the exit for A8 toward Zaandam. Take the Zaandam exit, then follow local signs. **Hoorn** is north of Amsterdam just off E22/A7. To reach **Enkhuizen** take the Hoorn exit from E22/A7 and continue eastward on N302. To reach **Texel,** travel north from Amsterdam on N203, N9, and N250 to the port of Den Helder.

BY FERRY
The hourly ferry to the island of Texel runs from 6 AM to 9 PM daily in summer. For more detailed **ferry information** call ☎ 0222/369–600. The **TelekomTaxi** (☎ 322–211, local calls only) minibus service takes you from the ferry terminal to your lodgings anywhere on the island of Texel, and picks you up for the return journey if you call an hour ahead. Buy your taxi tickets in advance (Fl 7 per ride) at the ferry ticket office in Den Helder.

BY TRAIN
Koog-Zaandijk is the station nearest to Zaanse Schans, on the local line from Amsterdam to Alkmaar. The village can be reached on foot in a few minutes. **Local trains** operate once an hour direct from Amsterdam to Hoorn and Enkhuizen. **Intercity trains** run direct to Den Helder every hour, with connecting buses to the ferry terminal. The **Waddenbiljet** all-inclusive return ticket, the easiest and most economical method for getting to Texel, includes bus services on the island itself. For **national train information** call ☎ 0900/9292 (75¢ per minute).

Contacts and Resources

GUIDED TOURS
Contact the local or regional VVV tourist offices (☞ Visitor Information, *below and* Guided Tours *in* Amsterdam, *above*) for information about guided group tours and qualified guides.

VISITOR INFORMATION
VVV Noord Holland (⊠ Oranjekade 41, 2011 VD, Haarlem, ☎ 023/531–9413). **VVV Texel** (⊠ Emmalaan 66, 1790 AA, Den Burg, ☎ 0222/314–741, FAX 0222/310–054). **VVV West-Friesland** (⊠ Veemarkt 4, 1621 JC, Hoorn, ☎ 0900/403–1055, 75¢ per minute; FAX 0229/215–023). **VVV Zaanstreek/Waterland** (⊠ Gedempte Gracht 76, 1506 CJ, Zaandam, ☎ 075/616–2221, FAX 075/670–5381).

METROPOLITAN HOLLAND AND THE HAGUE

The population of the Netherlands clusters in the arc around Amsterdam. More than 25% of the country's 15 million residents live in and around 10 small- to medium-size cities that are within 80 km (50 mi) of the capital. And that doesn't count the tulip growers, vegetable farmers, dairy farmers, and villagers who fill in what little open land remains in this area. The Dutch refer to the circle formed by the four cities of Amsterdam, Den Haag (The Hague in English), Rotterdam, and Utrecht as the Randstad (Ridge City) because the cities lie along the same ridge. The megalopolis also is called "The West" by young Randstad wanna-bes waiting for their opportunity to hit the big time. In addition to harboring the capital of international justice (The Hague) and the world's largest port (Rotterdam), Metropolitan Holland is the political and historic heart of the Dutch nation.

Exploring Metropolitan Holland

A route south of Amsterdam, running near the coast, takes you through the heart of Metropolitan Holland, starting with Haarlem and ending at Rotterdam. Utrecht, the remaining city in the Randstad conurbation, sits inland. The land stretches flat for as far as the eye can see, though the coast west of Haarlem and Leiden undulates with long expanses of dunes, many of which are nature reserves. In spring, the farmland between these two towns is bright with tulips and other blooms.

Each of the cities in the region could detain you for at least a day. If you don't have a week at your disposal, you will have to be disciplined and selective and begin planning a return trip.

Bright fields of flowers make the springtime ideal for a trip around Haarlem and Leiden. If you're into the arts, you might prefer to schedule your trip to catch one of the area's two world-renowned festivals: the Rotterdam Film Festival, in late January and early February, and the North Sea Jazz Festival in The Hague, which blasts away for three days in July.

Numbers in the text correspond to numbers in the margin and on the Metropolitan Holland map.

Haarlem

❾ *20 km (13 mi) west of Amsterdam, 41 km (26 mi) north of The Hague.*

Often eclipsed by Amsterdam, Haarlem is an important small city in its own right. It is home to one of the finest church organs in the world, and its museums contain art that fills in gaps or expands upon the collections of Amsterdam's major museums. The heart of Haarlem lies, as it does with many a Dutch town, in its market square. Surrounding Haarlem's Grote Markt are the medieval town hall and the old fish- and meat-market halls dating from the 17th century and frequently used by the Frans Hals Museum for special exhibitions. In its center is the imposing Grote Kerk, often painted by the masters of the Golden Age.

The late Gothic St. Bavo's Church, more commonly called the **Grote Kerk** (Great Church), was built on the square in the 15th century and is the burial place of Frans Hals—a lamp marks his tombstone behind the brass choir screen. The imposing wooden vault shelters two whimsical historic sights: In the north transept, the Dog Whippers' chapel pays tribute to men who ejected snarling dogs from the sacred premises; a carved capitol on the left-hand arch depicts a man whipping a dog.

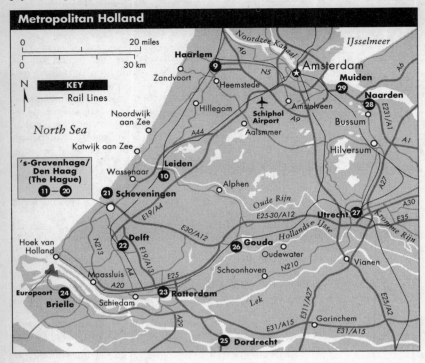

Metropolitan Holland

A pillar in the Brewer's Chapel, now a café, bears the portraits and measurements of Haarlem's tallest 18th-century man (8 ft, 8 inches) and its shortest (2 ft, 9 inches). The church is the home of the Müller Organ, on which both Handel and Mozart played (Mozart at age 10). Installed in 1738, and long considered to be the finest in the world, this gilded and gleaming instrument has been meticulously maintained and restored through the years to protect the sound planned by its creator, the master organ builder Christian Müller. Between May and October the official town organists of Haarlem give free weekly or twice-weekly concerts. ⊠ *Grote Markt,* ☎ *023/533–0877.* ☞ *Fl 2.50.* ⊙ *Apr.–Aug., Mon.–Sat. 10–4; Sept.–Mar., Mon.–Sat. 10–3:30.*

NEED A BREAK?

The spacious **Grand Café Brinkmann** (⊠ Grote Markt 9–13, ☎ 023/532–3111), adorned with cherubic ceiling paintings, offers baguettes, tacos, and other light snacks. Windows edged with Art Deco stained glass overlook the Grote Markt and St. Bavo's Church across the square.

Just off the Grote Markt, tucked into a small gabled town building above a shop, is the **Corrie ten Boom House,** which honors a family of World War II resistance fighters who successfully hid a number of Jewish families before being captured themselves by the Germans in 1944. Most of the ten Boom family members died in the concentration camps, but Corrie survived and returned to Haarlem to tell the story in her book, *The Hiding Place.* The family clock shop is preserved on the street floor, and their living quarters now contain displays, documents, photographs, and memorabilia. Visitors can also see the hiding closet, which the Gestapo never found, although they lived six days in the house hoping to starve out anyone who might be hiding here. ⊠ *Barteljorisstraat 19,* ☎ *023/531–0823.* ☞ *Free.* ⊙ *Apr.–Oct., Tues.–Sat. 10–4; Nov.–Mar., Tues.–Sat. 11–3.*

The **Frans Hals Museum** spreads itself through a series of small houses that, in the 17th century, was an old men's home. The cottages, arranged around an attractive garden courtyard, now form a sequence of galleries for paintings, period furniture, silver, and ceramics. The 17th-century collection of paintings that is the focal point of this museum includes the works of Frans Hals and other masters of the Haarlem School, including Hendrick Goltzius, Judith Leyster, Johannes Verspronck, Pieter Claesz, Willem Heda, Adriaen van Ostade, and Jacob van Ruysdael. The museum has a modern art collection, with the works of Dutch impressionists and expressionists, including sculpture, textiles, and ceramics, as well as paintings and graphics; there are also an 18th-century dollhouse and a re-created 18th-century pharmacy. From the Grote Markt, follow Warmoesstraat and its continuations, Schagchelstraat and Groot Herlig Land, to the museum. ⊠ *Groot Herlig Land 62,* ☎ *023/511–5775.* 🖃 *Fl 8.* ☉ *Mon.–Sat. 11–5, Sun. and public holidays 1–5.*

Ⓒ Having first opened its doors in 1784, the **Teylers Museum** is one of the oddest in the world. The museum itself is a grand old building with mosaic floors and wooden cabinets; its major artistic attraction is the superb collection of master drawings and prints by Michelangelo, Rembrandt, and others, based on a collection that once belonged to Queen Christina of Sweden. Unfortunately, only a few of the drawings are on display at any one time because of their fragility. Among the scientific curiosities are collections of fossils and crystals and examples of early machines and scientific tools. There is also a collection of coins and medals and even a rare 31-tone Fokker organ. In the beautiful oval library you can use brass parabolic mirrors (dating from 1800) to send the soft ticking of a watch right across the room; the Luminescence Cabinet is stocked with fluorescent and phosphorescent rocks and minerals that glow with extraordinary colors in the dark. Follow the canals from the Hals Museum past the Turfmarkt to Spaarne. ⊠ *Spaarne 16,* ☎ *023/531–9010.* 🖃 *Fl 10.* ☉ *Tues.–Sat. 10–5, Sun. and holidays noon–5.*

Dining and Lodging

$$$ ✕ **De Componist.** Easily recognizable by its Art Nouveau facade, the
★ restaurant is just a hundred steps from the Grote Markt. High ceilings, pale yellow walls, and ornamental moldings continue the style inside. Depending on the time of year, the menu offers oysters, seafood salad with sole and octopus, spring lamb with fresh herbs, or wild game. ⊠ *Korte Veerstraat 1,* ☎ *023/532–8853. AE, DC, MC, V.* ☉ *Open daily, dinner only.*

$$$ ✕ **Peter Cuyper.** This small but gracious restaurant has a traditional beamed dining room that is brightened with flowers, crisp linens, and light from an enclosed garden (open in summer) filtering through the windows. Try a fillet of corn-fed hen stuffed with wild mushrooms, or one of the delicious soups. The restaurant is convenient to both the Frans Hals and the Teyler museums. ⊠ *Kleine Houtstraat 70,* ☎ *023/532–0885. Reservations essential. AE, DC, MC, V. Closed Sun.–Mon.*

$$ ✕ **De Lachende Javaan.** Stepping into "The Laughing Javanese" off an Old Haarlem street that hasn't changed in centuries—you are hit with a flash of color and pungent smells. You can sit upstairs at one of the window tables and look out over the sober gabled houses while eating *kambing saté* (skewers of lamb in soy sauce) and *kipkarbonaade met sambal djeroek* (grilled chicken with a fiery Indonesian sauce). ⊠ *Frankestraat 25–27,* ☎ *023/532–8792. AE, DC, V.* ☉ *Dinner only. Closed Mon.*

$$$ 🏨 **Carlton Square Hotel.** This modern high-rise, in a residential district beyond the center, has rooms that are bright and spacious with white, art deco–inspired furniture. ✉ *Baan 7, 2012 DB,* ☎ *023/319–091,* FAX *023/329–853. 106 rooms. Restaurant, bar. AE, DC, MC, V.*

$$–$$$ 🏨 **Golden Tulip Lion d'Or.** This traditional hotel near the railway station has been here since the early 18th century. Thoroughly modernized, it has spacious guest rooms and meeting rooms. A jogging path runs behind the hotel. ✉ *Kruisweg 34–36, 2011 LC,* ☎ *023/532–1750,* FAX *023/532–9543. 36 rooms. Restaurant, business services, parking (fee). AE, DC, MC, V.*

$ 🏨 **Hotel Faber.** Within walking distance of the beaches of Zandvoort, this is a small, family-style hotel with bright, tidy rooms and a summer terrace. ✉ *Kostverlorenstraat 15, 2042 PA, Zandvoort,* ☎ *023/571–2825,* FAX *023/571–6886. 30 rooms with shower or bath. Bar. AE, MC, V.*

Nightlife and the Arts

Haarlem hosts the **International Organ Competition** in even-number years during the first week of July, giving people ample opportunity to hear the renowned Müller organ at full throttle.

Outdoor Activities and Sports

AUTO RACING

One of Europe's best-known auto racing tracks is near Haarlem at **Circuit Park Zandvoort** (✉ Burgemeester van Alphenstraat, ☎ 023/571–6004 or 023/571–8284); the racing season runs from March to October.

BEACHES

Near Haarlem, **Zandvoort** is also the principal beach for Amsterdam. It is busy, but very large, and if you wander south for 10 minutes or so you can find isolated spots among the dunes; after about 20 minutes, you come to the nude, in places gay, sunbathing beach.

BIKING

You can rent bicycles in Haarlem from **Van Bentum** (✉ Stationsplein, ☎ 023/531–7066) and **De Volkenfietser** (✉ Koningstraat 36, ☎ 023/532–5577).

Leiden

🔟 *35 km (22 mi) south of Haarlem, 45 km (28 mi) south of Amsterdam, and 16 km (10 mi) northeast of The Hague.*

Leiden owes its importance to its watery geography—it stands at the junction of two branches of the Rhine—the "Old" and the "New." Birthplace of Rembrandt and site of the nation's oldest and most prestigious university, Leiden has played an important role in Dutch history. In 1574, the city was the object of a major siege at the hands of the Spanish; the story of that siege, and the city's deliverance by the uniquely Dutch tactic of breaching the dikes to flood out an invader, is an important part of national lore. Leiden is also the town that was home to the Pilgrim Fathers for some 12 years, before they set off for the New World. A place where windmills still rise over the cityscape, Leiden derives its charm today from its relaxed and spirited university-town atmosphere.

Following the wide Rapenburg canal from the center of town, you reach Leiden University's **Hortus Botanicus** (botanical garden), the oldest in Europe, which includes extensive beds of flowers, rare plants, and towering trees, as well as an orangery, a Japanese garden, and several greenhouses. ✉ *Rapenburg 73,* ☎ *071/527–5188.* 🎫 *Fl 5.* ☉ *Apr.–Sept., Mon.–Sat. 9–5, Sun. 10–5; Oct.–Mar., weekdays 9–4:30, Sun. 10:30–3.*

Founded in 1575, **Rijksuniversiteit van Leiden** (Leiden University) soon drew the great thinkers and scientists of the 16th and 17th centuries, including the philosopher René Descartes. Today it is still one of the most respected academic establishments in the country, and the students preserve many time-honored traditions. The old university buildings are not open to the public, but in the "Academic Quarter," between the Rapenburg and Singel canals, students give Leiden a lively atmosphere.

Within a stone's throw of the university is **Pieterskerk** (St. Peter's Church), often surrounded by students sunning themselves in the church square. It is the oldest church in the city, dating from 1428. Inside are the graves of the painter Jan Steen and of Rembrandt's parents. A mysterious dried-up mummy was discovered in 1979 in a secret room under the pulpit, exciting tales of murder and illicit lovers. Also on the church square is the **Gravensteen,** which once was the home of the Counts of Holland. ✉ *Pieterskerkhof,* ☎ *071/512–4319.* ✆ *Free.* ⊙ *Daily 1:30–4.*

A few of the houses occupied by the Pilgrim Fathers still stand in the quarter around the Pieterskerk. Among them is the former home of **William Brewster** (✉ Pieterskerkchoorsteeg), spiritual leader of the Pilgrims. At the entrance is a small plaque placed by the Society of Mayflower Descendants.

The **Leiden American Pilgrim Museum** occupies a small 16th-century house furnished to illustrate what the Pilgrims' daily life was like before they left for the New World. Brief texts and 17th-century engravings tell the story of their extraordinary odyssey. ✉ *Beschuitsteeg 9,* ☎ *071/ 512–2413.* ✆ *Fl 3.* ⊙ *Wed.–Sat. 10–5, Sun. noon–5.*

The **Rijksmuseum van Oudheden** (National Museum of Antiquities) has a particularly fine Egyptian and classical collection, as well as Dutch archaeological artifacts. Pass through a soaring gallery in which the Egyptian temple of Taffah has been reconstructed, and continue through two floors of Greek and Roman sculpture, Egyptian tombs, funerary urns, and collections of everyday items from the pre-Christian eras, including glassware, ceramics, jewelry, and weapons. ✉ *Rapenburg 28,* ☎ *071/516–3163.* ✆ *Fl 7.* ⊙ *Tues.–Sat. 10–5, Sun. noon–5.*

NEED A BREAK?	**De Waterlijn** (✉ Prinsessekade, ☎ 071/512–1279) occupies one of the most attractive spots in town. Just past the end of the Rapenburg canal (which is itself lined with gracious buildings), this strikingly modern, glass-walled café on a moored boat offers views of old boats, gabled houses, and a windmill. The Dutch apple tart is good here.

★ **Stedelijk Museum De Lakenhal** (De Lakenhal Museum) contains an impressive collection of paintings, furniture, and silver and pewter pieces, set in the sumptuous surrounds of a 17th-century Cloth Hall. Leiden was once a center of the wool trade, and this is the building where the cloth was inspected and traded, and where the Guild Governors met. The galleries are hung with paintings by Rembrandt, Gerrit Dou, Jan Steen, and Salomon van Ruysdael, as well as a grand collection of the works of Lucas van Leyden, including his triptych, *Last Judgment.* Also of interest here are the reconstructed guild rooms. ✉ *Oude Singel 28–32,* ☎ *071/516–5360.* ✆ *Fl 5.* ⊙ *Tues.–Fri. 10–5, weekends and holidays noon–5.*

★ ⊙ Leiden's **Molenmuseum de Valk** (Windmill Museum de Valk) began grinding grain in 1743. You can wander around the perfectly preserved living quarters on the ground floor, then clamber past the massive millstones and climb seven stories to the top of the mill. On the way up you can pop out onto the "reefing-stage"—the platform than runs around the outside of the mill halfway up its length. This is a wonderful place to get an insider's view of the windmill heritage of the Netherlands. ✉ *2e Binnenvestgracht 1,* ☎ *071/516–5353.* 🎫 *Fl 5.* ☉ *Tues.–Sat. 10–5, Sun. and holidays 1–5.*

Ⓒ Europe's first permanent space exhibition, **Noordwijk Space Expo,** includes real satellites, engines, and space stations, as well as models and pieces of moon rock. ✉ *Keplerlaan 1, Noordwijk, 13 km (8 mi) northwest of Leiden,* ☎ *071/364–6446.* 🎫 *Fl 13.50.* ☉ *Tues.–Sun. 10–5.*

Dining and Lodging

$$$ ✕ **Bistro La Cloche.** This chic, attractive French-Dutch restaurant, just off the Rapenburg canal on the small street leading to St. Peter's Church, is done up in soft pastels, with flowers everywhere. It has a pleasant but small street-side café area and quieter dining upstairs. ✉ *Kloksteeg 3,* ☎ *071/512–3053. Reservations essential. AE, DC, MC, V.*

$$$ ✕ **Oudt Leyden.** This formal Dutch-style restaurant has a traditional menu of simple grilled and sautéed meats and fishes. It shares a kitchen with its neighbor, Pannekoekenhuysje (☞ *below*). ✉ *Steenstraat 51–53,* ☎ *071/513–3144. AE, DC, MC, V. Closed Sun.*

$$ ✕ **Mangerie de Jonge Koekop.** Just a few minutes from the old De Valk Windmill, near the center of old Leiden, this restaurant attracts students and locals. The turn-of-the-century building was gutted and has been refurbished with tasteful but no-frills decor, including cream ceramic-tile floors, apple-green tablecloths, and wicker chairs. The good-value, excellent food includes such mouthwatering dishes as mushrooms with goat cheese and mustard sauce, baked in a fluffy filo pastry case. ✉ *Lange Mare 60,* ☎ *071/514–1937. AE, DC, MC, V.*

$$ ✕ **M'n Broer.** Run by a pair of twins, "My Brother" is a cozy brasserie with a Brown Café atmosphere. The kitchen serves up such hearty meals as seafood pie and roast duck with port sauce; the portions are generous, and the food is good. ✉ *Kloksteeg 7,* ☎ *071/512–5024. Reservations not accepted. No credit cards.*

$–$$ ✕ **Annie's Verjaardag.** This restaurant consists of a low-ceilinged, arched cellar, often full of chatty students, and a water-level canal-side terrace. During the day, there is a modest selection of salads and sandwiches on baguettes, and at least one more-substantial offering. After six you can choose from a fuller menu that includes cheese fondue, grilled trout, and spare ribs. ✉ *Hoogstraat 1a,* ☎ *071/512–5737. Reservations not accepted. No credit cards.*

$ ✕ **Pannekoekenhuysje.** This restaurant, a traditional Dutch pancake house, shares a kitchen with its neighbor, Oudt Leyden (☞ *above*), but it has a totally different menu and environment: red-checked tablecloths and a relaxed mood. ✉ *Steenstraat 51–53,* ☎ *071/513–3144. AE, DC, MC, V. Closed Sun.*

$$$ 🏨 **Holiday Inn Leiden.** Just off the secondary highway between Leiden and The Hague and not far from the beaches at Katwijk, this is more a resort than a hotel. There is a vast interior garden lobby, and the decor of the guest rooms carries out the garden theme with bold colors and floral curtains. ✉ *Haagse Schouwweg 10, 2332 KG,* ☎ *071/535–5555,* FAX *071/535–5553. 200 rooms. Restaurant, bar, pool, sauna, 7 tennis courts, bowling, squash. AE, DC, MC, V.*

$ 🏨 **De Ceder.** This is a small, friendly, and very tidy family-style hotel in a converted home out near the teaching hospital of Leiden University. The garden rooms are particularly desirable, and the breakfast room overlooks the garden. ✉ *Rijnsburgerweg 80, 2333 AD,* ☎ *071/517–5903,* FAX *071/515–7098. 16 rooms, 10 with bath/shower. Bar. AE, DC, MC, V.*

Outdoor Activities and Sports

BEACHES

Leiden's coastal resorts are at **Katwijk** and **Noordwijk,** in the dunes beside the North Sea.

BIKING

The place to rent a bicycle in Leiden is the **Rijwiel Shop** (☎ 071/513–1304), next to the railroad station.

CANOEING

A canoe may be the very best way to get a close view of the bulb fields that fill the countryside between Haarlem and Leiden. The **VVV Leiden Tourist Office** (☎ 071/514–6846) has mapped out four different routes of varying lengths through the Dune and Bulb Area. Ask, too, about the Singel sightseeing route through Leiden's canals and moats. For information on canoe rentals contact **Jac. Veringa** (☎ 071/514–9790).

TENNIS AND SQUASH

You can play tennis and squash at the **Holiday Inn Racket Center** (✉ Haagse Schouwweg 10, ☎ 071/535–5100).

Shopping

Thursday is the night the shops stay open late here. Leiden's street market is held in the city center on the Nieuwe Rijn on Wednesday and Saturday, 9–6, and at Vijf Mei plein on Tuesday, 9–2.

The Hague and Its Environs

16 km (10 mi) southwest of Leiden, 57 km (36 mi) southwest of Amsterdam.

As becomes an aristocrat, Den Haag has several names. The French call it La Haye, whereas the official Dutch name is 's-Gravenhage or, literally, the Count's Hedge, while Den Haag is favored by the Dutch in conversation. In English it is known as The Hague. The hedge recalls the early 13th century when the Counts of Holland had a hunting lodge in a small woodland village called Die Haghe. Then, around 1248, Count Willem II built a larger house; the noted Knights' Hall, or Ridderzaal, was added in 1280; and gradually Den Haag became the focus of more and more government functions. Today, while Amsterdam remains the official capital of the Netherlands, 's-Gravenhage/ Den Haag is the seat of government and home of the reigning monarch, Queen Beatrix. An elegant city dotted with parks and open squares, it exudes a graciousness that Amsterdam lacks and has a formal and traditional lifestyle that befits its role as a diplomatic capital and world center of international peace and justice. Almost seamlessly connected to The Hague is the popular beach and fishing resort of Scheveningen, nicknamed "our national bathing place," and aglitter with all the bright lights and entertainments of a seaside holiday town.

Numbers in the margin correspond to points of interest on The Hague map and the Metropolitan Holland map.

⑪ **Binnenhof** (Inner Court).The governmental heart of the Netherlands is in the very center of The Hague. For many centuries the court of the Counts of Holland, the Binnenhof is now a complex of buildings from a spectrum of different eras. It incorporates the halls used by the First and Second Chambers of the Staten Generaal (States General, equivalent to the U.S. Senate and House of Representatives).

⑱ **Haags Gemeentemuseum** (Hague Municipal Museum). The museum is best known for housing the world's largest collection of works by Piet Mondrian (1872–1944), as well as 50 drawings by Karel Appel. In addition, there are paintings by members of The Hague School and an arts-and-crafts section that displays magnificent local silverware, old glass, earthenware, ceramics, and Dutch and Chinese porcelain. The building, designed by H. P. Berlage and completed in 1935, is regarded as one of the best examples of museum architecture in the 20th century. It has just reopened after an extensive restoration. ⊠ *Stadhouderslaan 41,* ☏ *070/338–1111.* 🎟 *Fl 10.* ⊙ *Tues.–Sun. 11–5.*

⑫ **Hofvijver** (Court Lake). Beside the Binnenhof (☞ *above*) lies a long, rectangular reflecting pool, complete with tall fountains.

★ ⑭ **Mauritshuis.** The small 17th-century palace is tucked into a corner behind the Parliament Complex and overlooking the Court Lake. It contains one of the nation's choicest collections of art, known as the Royal Gallery of Paintings. Among the Dutch masterpieces in it are three Rembrandt self-portraits and his breakthrough painting, *The Anatomy Lesson.* Also here are three highly prized paintings by Vermeer (*Girl with the Pearl, View of Delft, Diana with the Nymphs*); more than a dozen works by Jan Steen, who portrayed daily life and ordinary people in the Netherlands in the 17th century; and paintings by other Dutch and Flemish masters, including Hals, Van Ruysdael, Potter, Rubens, and Van Dyck. ⊠ *Korte Vijverberg 8,* ☏ *070/302–3456.* 🎟 *Fl 12.50.* ⊙ *Tues.–Sat. 10–5, Sun. 11–5.*

👋 ⑲ **Museon.** This museum incorporates science exhibits on the origins of the universe and evolution with three themes: Earth, Our Home; Between Man and the Stars; and Ecos, an environmental show. Special exhibitions are frequent here and are always excitingly presented, with lots of hands-on and interactive displays. Archaeological and intercultural subjects are common themes. The Museon adjoins the Haags Gemeentemuseum (☞ *above*). ⊠ *Stadhouderslaan 41,* ☏ *070/338–1338 and 070/338–1305.* 🎟 *Fl 10.* ⊙ *Tues.–Fri. 10–5, weekends and public holidays noon–5.*

⑯ **Museum Bredius.** Housed in an 18th-century patrician mansion, the collection of traveler and art connoisseur Abraham Bredius illustrates the point that private collections are often the most delightful. It includes works by the likes of Rembrandt and Jan Steen, as well as lesser-known works of the period, all held together by the thread of a personal vision. The house itself, overlooking the Hofvijver (Court Lake), makes a magnificent setting for the paintings. ⊠ *Lange Vijverberg 14,* ☏ *070/362–0729.* 🎟 *Fl 6.50.* ⊙ *Tues.–Sun. noon–5.*

⑳ **Omniversum.** The IMAX theater shows a rotating program of spectacular presentations, including several with natural and futuristic themes, on a film screen that is six stories high. ⊠ *Pres. Kennedylaan 5,* ☏ *070/354–5454.* 🎟 *Fl 17.50.* ⊙ *Tues. and Wed., hourly 11–5, Thurs.–Sun. and holidays, hourly 11–9.*

⑬ **Ridderzaal** (Knight's Hall). The oldest building in the Binnenhof complex (☞ *above*), from the late 13th century, is where the queen comes each fall to address her government at the annual Opening of Parliament (third Tuesday in September). There are guided tours into the legislative chambers (when they are not in session) and the Knight's Hall, with its provincial flags and stained-glass windows displaying the coats of arms of the major Dutch cities. You can also see a special exhibition on the origin of the Dutch governmental system. ⊠ *Binnenhof 8A,* ☏ *070/364–6144. Reservations essential.* 🎟 *Tour Fl 6; Parliament exhibition free.* ⊙ *Mon.–Sat. 10–4; last guided tour at 3:45.*

NEED A   **'t Goude Hooft** (⊠ De Groenmarkt 13, ☏ 070/346-9713) is the oldest
BREAK?   restaurant in The Hague, with both a traditional Dutch dining room and
               a street café looking out on the old Town Hall.

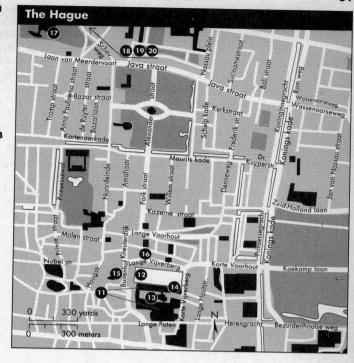

The Hague

⑮ **Schilderijengalerij Prins Willem V** (Prince Willem V Painting Gallery). In 1773, Willem V built a new gallery in his palace and allowed the general public in for a look three days a week, thus earning the reputation of being the Netherlands' first public museum. The small gallery has fine Louis XVI stucco ceilings but keeps an intimate, homey atmosphere. It is rather as if a friend, who happened to have a good collection of 17th-century masters, had invited you over to see them. ⊠ *Buitenhof 35,* ☎ *070/362–4444.* ☜ *Fl 2.50.* ☉ *Tues.–Sun. 11–4.*

⑰ **Vredespaleis** (Peace Palace). Facing the world across a broad lawn, the building houses the International Court of Justice. The court was initiated in 1899 by Czar Nicolas II of Russia, who invited 26 nations to meet in The Hague to set up a permanent world court of arbitration. The present building was constructed in 1903 with a $1.5 million gift from the Scottish-American industrialist Andrew Carnegie. Gifts from each of the participating nations embellish the architecture with examples of their national craftsmanship in the form of statuary, stained-glass windows, gates, doors, clocks, and such. ⊠ *Carnegieplein 2,* ☎ *070/320–4137.* ☜ *Fl 5.* ☉ *May–Oct., weekdays 10–4; Nov.–Apr., weekdays 10–3; guided tours at 10, 11, 2, and 3 (May–Oct. additional tour at 4).*

Westbroek Park. June is the time to visit this park in The Hague, when its 20,000 rosebushes are in magnificent bloom. ⊠ *Kapelweg.* ☜ *Free.* ☉ *Daily 9–1 hr before sunset.*

Dining and Lodging

$$–$$$ ✕ **Le Haricot Vert.** In a 1638 former staff house for the nearby palace, this intimate, candlelit restaurant combines Dutch simplicity and French flair. Succulent meats covered with sauces are served on large white plates with tangles of colorful vegetables. The menu changes seasonally. ⊠ *Molenstraat 9a–11,* ☎ *070/365–2278. AE, MC, V.*

$$ ✕ **Greve.** You sit at long trestle tables, and the waiters arrive with steaming loaves of pumpernickel served on a board. Then come such mouthwatering delights as grilled swordfish with guacamole, or hearty chicken soup, thick with fresh vegetables. Service is quick and friendly, and the atmosphere chatty and informal. Greve has both a restaurant and a café section. ✉ *Torenstraat 138,* ☎ *070/360–3919. Reservations essential. AE, DC, MC, V (restaurant only).*

$$$$ 🏠 **Hotel Des Indes Inter-Continental.** Once a private mansion built principally for grand balls and entertainment, the Des Indes has a grace and graciousness that make it one of the world's very special hotels. It sits on one of The Hague's most prestigious squares. The former inner courtyard is now a towering reception area leading to the restaurant. The rooms are spacious and stylish. One suite, which enjoys a magnificent view over the city toward the beach, is fought over by rock stars who come to perform in nearby Rotterdam. The superlative restaurant pleases everyone. ✉ *Lange Voorhout 54–56, 2514 EG,* ☎ *070/363–2932,* 🖷 *070/345–1721. 70 rooms, 6 suites. Restaurant, bar. AE, DC, MC, V.*

$$$$ 🏠 **Kurhaus Hotel.** Holding the prime position at the center of the beach at Scheveningen, this grand hotel of the old school is fully modernized and bustling. Now engulfed by shops and apartments on the street side, it still has its famous turn-of-the-century profile from the amusement pier, and you still can dine in the magnificent Kurzaal with its fancifully painted, coffered ceiling high overhead. Rooms here are grand and grandly decorated in a variety of modern and traditional styles. ✉ *Gevers Deynootplein 30, 2586 CK, Scheveningen,* ☎ *070/ 416–2636,* 🖷 *070/416–2646. 231 rooms, 10 suites. 2 restaurants, sauna, casino. AE, DC, MC, V.*

$$$ 🏠 **Corona Hotel.** Elegant lodging seems appropriate to an elegant city of diplomacy, and this hotel fits in perfectly. It is conveniently located across from the Parliament Complex, near the Mauritshuis and Museum Bredius at the edge of the shopping district. The rooms are restfully decorated in a muted scheme of white, cream, and dove gray. ✉ *Buitenhof 39–42, 2513 AH,* ☎ *070/363–7930,* 🖷 *070/361–5785. 26 rooms. Restaurant, bar. AE, DC, MC, V.*

$$ 🏠 **Novotel Hotel.** Well located for both the sights and the shopping of The Hague, Novotel is a new and well-appointed full-service hotel with modestly sized rooms; the decor is a bland but tranquilizing beige and white. ✉ *Hofweg 5–7, 2511 AA,* ☎ *070/364–8846,* 🖷 *070/356–2889. 104 rooms, 2 suites. Restaurant, bar. AE, DC, MC, V.*

$–$$ 🏠 **Hotel Petit.** On a residential boulevard between the Peace Palace and The Hague Municipal Museum, this quiet, family-style brick hotel is operated by a young couple. Bright and graciously furnished, it has a pleasant guests-only bar-lounge for relaxing. ✉ *Groot Hertoginnelaan 42, 2517 EH,* ☎ *070/346–5500,* 🖷 *070/346–3257. 20 rooms. Bar. AE, DC, MC, V.*

$–$$ 🏠 **Hotel Sebel.** The friendly owners of this hotel have expanded into two buildings between the city center and the Peace Palace. Tidy and comfortable, the rooms are large and have high ceilings and tall windows for lots of light and air. ✉ *Zoutmanstraat 38, 2518 GR,* ☎ *070/ 345–9200,* 🖷 *070/345–5855. 14 rooms. Bar. AE, DC, MC, V.*

$ 🏠 **City Hotel.** Just off the beach in Scheveningen, this spanking-clean, brightly decorated, and very friendly small family hotel spreads through several houses on a main street leading to the waterfront. ✉ *Renbaanstraat 1–3 and 17–23, 2586 EW, Scheveningen,* ☎ *070/355–7966,* 🖷 *070/354–0503. 20 rooms. Restaurant, bar. AE, DC, MC, V.*

Nightlife and the Arts

For information on cultural events, call the **Uit information** numbers in The Hague (⊠ Uitpost Den Haag, ☎ 070/363–3833). In addition, you can pick up the monthly *Info: Den Haag, Scheveningen en Kijkduin* (Day to Day Tourist Information), which lists (in Dutch) what's going on in major theaters in that area, with English copy describing major events.

THE ARTS

Classical Music. The Hague's **Residentie Orkest** is an excellent orchestra with a worldwide reputation. It performs at Dr. Anton Philipszaal (⊠ Houtmarkt 17, ☎ 070/360–9810) and Nederlands Congresgebouw (⊠ Churchillplein 10, ☎ 070/354–8000).

Dance. The **Nederlands Danstheater** is the national modern dance company of the Netherlands and makes its home at the AT&T Danstheater (⊠ Schedeldoekshaven 60, ☎ 070/360–4930).

Theater and Opera. De Appel company has a lively, experimental approach to theater and performs at its own Appeltheater (⊠ Duinstraat 6–8, ☎ 070/350–2200). Mainstream Dutch theater is presented by the national theater company **Het Nationale Toneel,** which performs at the Royal Schouwburg (⊠ Korte Voorhout 3, ☎ 070/346–9450). **Musicals,** including occasional world tours from Broadway, can be seen at Nederlands Congresgebouw (⊠ Churchillplein 10, ☎ 070/354–8000) or in the adjoining beach resort community of Scheveningen at Circustheater (⊠ Circusstraat 4, ☎ 070/351–1212).

NIGHTLIFE

Cafés. In the beach community of Scheveningen, **Plaza Bar** (⊠ Gevers Deynootplein 118, ☎ 070/351–5426) is a chic and exclusive place that offers all sorts of music, live and recorded.

Dance Clubs. Club Exposure (⊠ Westduinweg 232, ☎ 070/356–1289) in Scheveningen has a trendy clientele and organizes special party and theme nights. The latest local and international bands can be heard at **Het Paard** (⊠ Prinsengracht 12, ☎ 070/360–1618), where you can also dance and watch multimedia shows. The huge **Marathon** (⊠ Wijndaelerweg 3, ☎ 070/368–0324) offers a wide variety of music and attracts a young, energetic crowd. **Thahiti** (⊠ Strandweg 43, ☎ 070/350–2068) in Scheveningen offers live performances as well as hot recorded sounds.

Jazz. One of the festivals for which the Netherlands is well known is the annual **North Sea Jazz Festival** (☎ 015/214–8900), which is the largest of its kind in the world. It is held in The Hague and Scheveningen for four days in July and regularly attracts the greats of jazz as well as thousands of jazz lovers from around the world.

Outdoor Activities and Sports

BEACHES

The beach at **Scheveningen** is one of the most popular in the country and has a boardwalk and amusement pier as well as numerous cafés and sunbathing terraces.

BIKING

You can rent bicycles in The Hague at the **Rijwiel Shop** (⊠ Hollands Spoor, ☎ 070/389–0830; ⊠ Centraal Station ☎ 070/385–3235) and **Garage du Nord** (⊠ Keizerstraat 27, Scheveningen, ☎ 070/355–4060).

HORSE RACING

Near The Hague, **Duindigt Racecourse** (⊠ Waalsdorperlaan 29, Wassenaar, ☎ 070/324–4427) is one of two racetracks in the Netherlands (the other is in Hilversum, between Utrecht and Amsterdam). The racing season runs from mid-March to mid-November and includes both flat and trotting races with betting. Race days are Wednesday and Sunday.

SEA FISHING

Sea fishing is one of the main reasons many people visit Scheveningen. For information and reservations, contact **Sportviscentrum Trip** (⊠ Dr. Lelykade 3, Scheveningen, ☎ 070/354–1122 or 070/354–0887).

Shopping

Late shopping in **The Hague** is on Thursday; in **Scheveningen** on Friday and, during the summer at the Palace Promenade, Monday through Saturday. In **The Hague** there's a Farmers' Market on Wednesday 10–6, and there is an antiques market on Lange Voorhout on summer Thursdays and Sundays.

Side Trip to Scheveningen

㉑ At the seaside resort of **Scheveningen,** next to The Hague, you can enjoy a variety of relaxing pleasures, including a walk on the beach promenade or a swim in a wave pool. The famous and grand old hotel, the **Kurhaus** (☞ Dining and Lodging, *below*), houses a casino as well as several restaurants. There is also shopping seven days a week. Scheveningen is the departure point for deep-sea fishing trips.

🔆 In the **Scheveningen Sea Life Centre** you will encounter hundreds of exotic sea creatures, from starfish to stingrays. The imaginative design of this aquarium includes a transparent tunnel, 30 ft long, where sharks swim above your head. ⊠ *Strandweg 13,* ☎ *070/355–8781.* 🎟 *Fl 15.* ☉ *Sept.–June, daily 10–6; July–Aug., daily 10–8.*

🔆 The miniature village of **Madurodam** comes complete with a collection of small reproductions of typically Dutch buildings set in a sprawling "village" with pathways, tram tracks, and railway stations. All of the most important buildings of the Netherlands have been reproduced. If you are here at sunset you will see the lights come on in the houses. In July and August there is also an after-dark sound-and-light presentation, free to park visitors. ⊠ *George Maduroplein 1,* ☎ *070/ 355–3900.* 🎟 *Fl 19.50.* ☉ *Apr.–Sept., daily 9 AM–10 PM; Oct.–Mar., daily 9–5.*

Delft

★ ㉒ *14 km (9 mi) southeast of The Hague and 71 km (45 mi) southwest of Amsterdam.*

Perhaps more than any other city in the Netherlands, Delft preserves a historic look that is best appreciated by simply wandering along its small canals with their graceful, humpback bridges. In some places, so little has changed that you can recognize the views made famous by the Golden Age painter Johannes Vermeer. Delft rivals Leiden in its importance to the history of the Netherlands; it was here that William of Orange (known as William the Silent), founder of the nation, was assassinated in 1584. The Dutch monarchs that followed him are all buried in the Nieuwe Kerk (New Church), in the shadow of which Vermeer was born and lived. And, of course, Delft is also known around the world for its blue-and-white porcelain.

Delft's **Stadhuis** (Town Hall) stands grandly at one end of the large market square. Above the lavishly embellished building designed by Hendrick de Keyser, one of the most prolific architects of the Golden Age, rises a simpler, more stolid 14th-century tower. Behind the Town Hall is a row of buildings that formerly served as the butter market, the town weigh house, and the guild halls of gold- and silversmiths and pharmacists. ⊠ *Markt 87.*

All but a few of the Dutch monarchs of the House of Orange lie buried in the **Nieuwe Kerk** (New Church), located on the market square. The mausoleum of William the Silent, a massive and ornate structure of black marble and alabaster, dominates the chancel. Nearby in the floor is the stone that covers the entry to the royal crypt, and throughout the church are paintings, stained-glass windows, and memorabilia associated with the Dutch royal family. In summer it is possible to climb the church tower for a view that stretches as far as The Hague and Scheveningen. ⊠ *Markt,* ☎ *015/212–3025.* ☞ *Combination card (Old and New Churches) Fl 4; tower Fl 2.50.* ☉ *Mar.–Oct., Mon.–Sat. 9–6; Nov.–Apr., Mon.–Sat. 11–4.*

Pretty, tree-lined, and with an abundance of historic gabled houses along its banks, the **Oude Delft** takes the honors for being the first canal dug in the city and probably the first city canal to be dug anywhere in the Netherlands. It is located one canal over from the Stadhuis.

NEED A BREAK?	**Kleyweg's Stads-Koffyhuis** (⊠ Oude Delft 133, ☎ 015/212-4625) looks out over the oldest and one of the most beautiful canals in Delft. Inside, you'll find a "stamtafel," a large table laid out with newspapers and magazines, where anyone may sit and chat. There are also smaller individual tables where you can enjoy good coffee and delicious pancakes.

The tower of the **Oude Kerk** (Old Church) manages to lean in four directions at once. But then, this is the oldest church in Delft, having been founded in 1200. It is the final resting place of several important Dutch military and naval heroes, and of Antonie van Leeuwenhoek, the Delft resident who invented the microscope. The tower, which now leans too precariously to be ascended, holds the largest carillon bell in the Netherlands; weighing nearly 20,000 pounds, it now is used only on state occasions. ⊠ *Heilige Geestkerkhof,* ☎ *015/212–3015.* ☞ *Combination card (Old and New Churches) Fl 4.* ☉ *Apr.–Nov., Mon.–Sat. 10–5.*

Delft's most famous sight, **Het Prinsenhof** (Prince's Court), was built as a convent in the early 15th century and is located directly across the Oude Delft from the Oude Kerk. The complex of buildings was taken over by the government of the new Dutch Republic in 1572 and given to William of Orange for his use as a residence. It was here that William was assassinated. The complex now houses a museum devoted to the history of the Dutch Republic; there is also a museum of ethnology and a church. ⊠ *St. Agathaplein 1,* ☎ *015/260–2358.* ☞ *Fl 5.* ☉ *Tues.–Sat. 10–5, Sun. 1–5.*

The **Lambert van Meerten Museum** is in a neo-Renaissance mansion that provides a noble setting for an extensive collection of earthenware and ebony-veneer furniture. Save time for the collection of tiles and its early examples of Delft that seem to depict almost every aspect of Holland's Golden Age, from sea battles to cheese making. ⊠ *Oude Delft 199,* ☎ *015/260–2358.* ☞ *Fl 5.* ☉ *Tues.–Sat. 10–5, Sun. 1–5.*

Delft's former armory, the **Legermuseum** (Netherlands Army Museum), makes an appropriate setting for the country's most important military museum. Despite the gentle images of Dutch life, the origins of the Dutch Republic were violent. It took nothing less than the Eighty Years War (1568–1648) to finally achieve independence from the Spanish crown. All periods of Dutch military history are explored in detail, from Roman times to the German occupation during World

War II. ⊠ *Korte Geer 1,* ☎ *015/15000.* 🎫 *Fl 5.* ☉ *Tues.–Sat. 10–5, Sun. 1–5.*

Dining and Lodging

$$$$ ✕ **De Zwethheul.** Delft's classiest restaurant, in a restored 18th-century building outside the center, actually began as a humble pancake house. In fine weather, you can eat on a beautiful terrace overlooking the Schie river. The sommelier and his wine list are among the best in Holland. Specialties of the house are Bresse chicken ravioli with baked crayfish and trio of lamb in basil sauce. ⊠ *Rotterdamseweg 480,* ☎ *010/470–4166. Reservations essential. AE, DC, MC, V. Closed Mon. No lunch on weekends.*

$$$ ✕ **De Prinsenhof** In the old storerooms of a former convent that now is the Prinsenhof Museum, this restaurant has a sedate, elegant atmosphere. Classic French dishes, such as duck with apple and raisins and a creamy Calvados sauce, are wonderfully prepared and beautifully presented. Entry is by way of a small alley opening onto the Oude Delft canal. ⊠ *Schoolstraat 11,* ☎ *015/212–1860. Reservations essential. AE, DC, MC, V. Closed Sun.*

$$$ ✕ **L'Orage.** The owner-chef of this bright and gracious small French restaurant facing the Old Canal is Jannie Munk, who won the Netherlands' Lady Chef of the Year award in 1994. She creates delicious fish dishes, many based on recipes from her native Denmark. Try the red bass, grilled in its skin and served with risotto and sun-dried tomatoes. ⊠ *Oude Delft 111b,* ☎ *015/212–3629. Reservations required. Jacket and tie. AE, DC, MC, V. Closed Mon.*

$$–$$$ ✕ **Le Vieux Jean.** The tiny, family-run restaurant serves tasty meat-and-potatoes fare as well as good fish dishes such as *kabeljauw* (cod with mustard-sesame sauce). In the adjoining *proeflokaal* (tasting room) you can buy wine and spirits. ⊠ *Heilige Geestkerkhof 3,* ☎ *015/213–0433. Reservations recommended. AE, DC, V. Closed Sun.–Mon.*

$$ 🏨 **Delft Museumhotel & Residence.** This small, elegant hotel has been created within a complex of 11 historic buildings in the prime neighborhood of Delft. Among the choices are small apartments in the adjacent Residence building that opens onto the side alley. ⊠ *Oude Delft 189, 2611 HD,* ☎ *015/214–0930,* 🅵🅰🆇 *015/214–0935. 50 rooms. 2 bars, meeting room. AE, DC, MC, V.*

$–$$ 🏨 **Hotel Leeuwenbrug.** Facing one of Delft's canals, this traditional hotel has an Old Dutch–style canal-side lounge. The rooms are large, airy, and contemporary in decor; those in the annex are particularly appealing. ⊠ *Koornmarkt 16, 2611 EE,* ☎ *015/214–7741,* 🅵🅰🆇 *015/215–9759. 37 rooms with bath or shower. Bar. AE, MC, V.*

$–$$ 🏨 **Les Compagnons.** This is a one-family hospitality package in the heart of Delft. The younger generation operates a small and comfortable hotel on the market square that offers a variety of brightly decorated rooms with a range of amenities that you wouldn't expect in so small a hotel. Dad hosts a restaurant on the next canal, and Mom operates a deli and tearoom in the adjoining store. ⊠ *Markt 61, 2611 GS,* ☎ *015/214–0102,* 🅵🅰🆇 *015/212–0168. 10 rooms. AE, DC, MC, V.*

Outdoor Activities and Sports

BIKING
Bike rentals are available at the **railway station** (☎ 015/214–3033).

SQUASH
Squash courts are available at **Squash Delft** (⊠ Sportring 3, ☎ 015/214–6983).

Shopping

In Delft, market day is Thursday, from 9 to 5, and there is a flea market on the canals in the town center on summer Saturdays.

DELFTWARE

De Porceleyne Fles (⊠ The Royal Delftware Factory, Rotterdamseweg 196, ☎ 015/256−0234) is home to the popular blue-and-white Delft pottery. The galleries here exhibit famous pieces from throughout Delft's history, and regular demonstrations of molding and painting pottery are given by the artisans. The pottery factories of **De Delftse Pauw** (⊠ Delftweg 133, ☎ 015/212−4920 or 015/212−4743), while not as famous as De Porceleyne Fles, produce work of equally high quality. **Atelier de Candelaer** (⊠ Kerkstraat 13, ☎ 015/131−848) makes a convenient stop-off for comparisons of Delftware with other pottery.

Rotterdam

㉓ *12 km (8 mi) southeast of Delft, 77 km (48 mi) south of Amsterdam.*

Were it not for the devastation of World War II, when the city and its port were leveled in the cross fire between Hitler's forces and the Allies, Rotterdam might never have become the dynamic and influential world port it is today. The rebuilding made possible streamlining of the port facilities based on technological advances. A busy harbor since the 17th century, it built bigger facilities in the 19th and early 20th centuries, playing a key role in European trade. Today, its **Europoort** is the world's largest port, a massive complex of piers, warehouses, and refineries stretching for 48 km (30 mi), an awe-inspiring sight from a boat after dark. An imaginative program of postwar building has given Rotterdam an extraordinary concentration of adventurous modern architecture.

As you walk along the Leuvehaven inner harbor past several old ships moored along the quay, you'll come to Rotterdam's noted nautical museum at the head of the harbor. The history of Rotterdam harbor and its important role in world trade come to life in the **Prins Hendrik Maritime Museum.** The museum building contains both changing exhibitions and a permanent collection of models and memorabilia; the warship *De Buffel,* moored alongside the museum, is part of the collection, and several other intriguing old ships are moored along the quay. ⊠ *Leuvehaven 1,* ☎ *010/413−2680.* ▦ *Fl 6.* ☉ *Tues.−Sat. 10−5, Sun. and holidays 11−5.*

In Blaakse Bos, a group of curiously angled, cube-shape apartments that have each been turned to balance on one corner on the top of tall stalks, perhaps the oddest building in this city of bold architecture is the **Kijk-Kubus.** The precarious-looking building, just east of the center of town, is open to the public. ⊠ *Overblaak 70,* ☎ *010/414−2285.* ▦ *Fl 2.50.* ☉ *Tues.−Fri. 10−5, weekends 11−5.*

★ The **Boijmans-van Beuningen Museum** stands shoulder to shoulder with the Rijksmuseum in Amsterdam in the line-up of the Netherlands' exceptional fine-arts museums. Its collection spans the 15th–20th centuries and includes a number of extraordinary early primitives by painters such as Hieronymus Bosch, Sint Jans, and the Van Eycks, as well as Bruegel the Elder and Van Scorel. Later painters, including Rubens and Van Dyck, are also represented. Rembrandt's portrait of his son Titus is part of the collection, as are prints and drawings by Dürer, da Vinci, and later artists such as Cézanne and Picasso. Add to this a remarkable collection of Impressionist, surrealist, and contemporary art, and as the final fillip, a fine assemblage of objects that includes glassware, silverware, and earthenware. ⊠ *Museumpark 18−20,* ☎ *010/441−9445.* ▦ *Fl 7.50.* ☉ *Tues.−Sat. 10−5, Sun. and holidays 11−5.*

Fittingly, for a city of exciting modern architecture, Rotterdam is the site of the **Nederlands Architectuurinstituut** (Netherlands Architectural Institute). The striking glass-and-metal building hosts changing exhibits on architecture and interior design. ⊠ *Museumpark 25,* ☎ *010/440–1200.* ☜ *Fl 7.50.* ⏱ *Tues.–Sat. 10–5, Sun. 11–5.*

The **Kunsthal Rotterdam** (Rotterdam Art Gallery) hosts all manner of major temporary exhibitions—from an Andy Warhol retrospective to rows of compact cars—in a massive, multistory exhibition center, built in 1992. ⊠ *Westzeedijk 341,* ☎ *010/440–0301.* ☜ *Fl 10.* ⏱ *Tues.–Sat. 10–5, Sun. 11–5.*

Delfshaven, the last remaining nook of old Rotterdam, has rows of gabled houses lining the waterfront, and even a windmill. Today Delfshaven is an up-and-coming area of trendy galleries, cafés, and restaurants. ⊠ *Voorhaven. Trams 4 and 6 or metro: Delfshaven.*

The **Euromast** tower, more than 600 ft high, not only affords panoramic views of Rotterdam Harbor but also packs in a number of other attractions. The most exciting is the **Space Cabin** at the tip of the tower, in which you can experience the sensation of a rocket launch. ⊠ *Parkhaven 20,* ☎ *010/436–4811.* ☜ *Fl 14.50.* ⏱ *Apr.–June and Sept., daily 10–7; Oct.–Mar., daily 10–5; July–Aug., Tues.–Sat. 10 AM–10:30 PM, Sun.–Mon. 10–7.*

Dining and Lodging

$$$$ ✕ **Raden Mas of Rotterdam.** At this elegant and exotically decorated Indonesian restaurant, rijsttafel is served both traditional style (from a number of small dishes) and Asian style (all on your plate from the kitchen). Among the traditional elements of a rijsttafel, you will find *sate* (a kebob of chicken or pork in peanut sauce), *gado-gado* (Asian vegetables), and *sambal* (a red-pepper condiment that is very, very hot). ⊠ *Kruiskade 72,* ☎ *010/411–7244. AE, DC, MC, V.*

$$$ ✕ **La Gondola.** In this Italian restaurant there is a photo wall that reads like a history of modern pop music. Directly across from the Rotterdam Hilton, where pop stars tend to stay, it is a relaxing, friendly place with a good selection of traditional Italian specialties. ⊠ *Kruiskade 6,* ☎ *010/411–4284. Reservations essential. Jacket required. AE, DC, MC, V.*

$$–$$$ ✕ **Het Heerenhuys De Heuvel.** Resplendent beside a lake in the city's Maas Park, this airy 19th-century mansion has one of the most attractive locations—and the sunniest terrace—in town. In one wing is a restaurant serving such curiosities as lamb with anchovy butter; in the other is a café offering simpler fare. ⊠ *Baden-Powellaan 12,* ☎ *010/436–4249. AE, DC, MC, V.*

$$$$ ▣ **Rotterdam Hilton.** Don't be surprised if you run into Mick Jagger or Diana Ross if you stay here. This is the hotel of choice for many of the pop and rock performers who bring their tours to Holland; it provides top facilities, a number of suites, a restaurant, and luxury appointments and amenities. It also has one of the best downtown locations in Rotterdam. ⊠ *Weena 10 3012 CM,* ☎ *010/414–4044,* ✍ *010/411–8884. 246 rooms, 8 suites. Restaurant, bar, café, barbershop, beauty salon, dance club, meeting rooms, parking (fee). AE, DC, MC, V.*

$$$–$$$$ ▣ **Park Hotel.** An old town house and a glittering metallic skyscraper are yoked together to form an elegant hotel. The rooms are tastefully furnished in a modern style and most offer panoramic views of the city. It is a few minutes' walk from the Boymans-van Beuningen Museum, and the staff offer the sort of apparently effortless, unobtrusive attention to your every need that makes a stay here a delight. The restaurant nicely balances nouvelle with traditional selections. ⊠ *Westersingel*

70, 3015 LB, ☎ 010/436–3611, FAX 010/436–4212, 189 rooms. Restaurant, bar, lobby lounge, sauna, exercise room, free parking. AE, DC, MC, V.

$$$ 🏨 **Hotel Inntel Rotterdam.** All the rooms in this modern high-rise, built at the opening to the Leuvehaven inner harbor in 1990, have water views, as do the restaurant and the rooftop health club. ⊠ Leuvehaven 80, 3011 EA, ☎ 010/413–4139, FAX 010/413–3222. 150 rooms. Restaurant, café, indoor pool, sauna. AE, DC, MC, V.

$$–$$$ 🏨 **Hotel New York.** The twin towers rising over the water of the Nieuwe Maas, across from the city center, for decades were known to Rotterdammers as the headquarters of the Holland-America Line. In 1993, the old building was renovated and opened as a hotel. Rooms are individually decorated and modern. The enormous restaurant (it seats 400) somehow maintains an intimate, café atmosphere, and the fine, eclectic cuisine attracts Rotterdam's fashionable set. ⊠ Koninginnenhoofd 1, 3072 AD, ☎ 010/439–0500, FAX 010/484–2701. 72 rooms, 1 apt. Restaurant, exercise room, meeting rooms. AE, DC, MC, V.

$ 🏨 **Hotel van Walsum.** On a residential boulevard within walking distance of the Boijmans-van Beuningen Museum, Hotel van Walsum is not far from the Euromast. The gregarious owner proudly restores and re-equips his rooms, floor by floor, on a continuously rotating basis, with the always-modern decor of each floor determined by that year's best buys in furniture, carpeting, and bathroom tiles. There is a bar-lounge and a small restaurant that has a summer garden extension. ⊠ Mathenesserlaan 199–201, 3014 HC, ☎ 010/436–3275, FAX 010/436–4410. 18 rooms, 1 apt. Restaurant, café. AE, DC, MC, V.

Nightlife and the Arts

You can book tickets and find out what's on around town through **Uit Promotie Rotterdam** (☎ 010/413–6540) or **VVV Rotterdam** (☎ 06/3403–4065). The free publication *Inside Out,* available in many cafés, also has listings of what's on.

THE ARTS

Classical Music. In Rotterdam, the concert orchestra is the fine **Rotterdam Philharmonic Orchestra,** which performs at the large concert hall **Concert-en Congresgebouw de Doelen** (⊠ Kruisstraat 2/Schouwburgplein 50, ☎ 010/217–1700).

Dance. Rotterdam's resident modern dance company, **Scapino Ballet,** has the reputation of being one of the most formidably talented troupes in the country. They perform at **Rotterdamse Schouwburg** (⊠ Schouwburgplein 25, ☎ 010/411–8110), which was designed by Dutch architect Wim Quist.

Film. In addition to the annual avant-garde **Film Festival Rotterdam** (☎ 010/413–6540), Rotterdam offers mixed media and film performances at **Lantaren/Venster** (⊠ Gouvernestraat 129–133, ☎ 010/436–1311) and has a special publication for film listings titled *Cargo,* available in bars, cafés, and some shops.

Theater. The leading theater company of Rotterdam is **RO-theatergroup,** which performs (mainly in Dutch) at the new **Rotterdamse Schouwburg** (⊠ Schouwburgplein 25, ☎ 010/411–8110). **Cabaret and musicals** in Rotterdam are performed at **Luxor Theater** (⊠ Kruiskade 10, ☎ 010/413–8326).

NIGHTLIFE

Cafés. Café De Heuvel (⊠ Baden-Powellaan 12, ☎ 010/436–4249), in the middle of Het Park beside the Maas River, has a busy terrace, casual café, and smart restaurant. **Carrera** (⊠ Karel Doormanstraat

10–12, ☎ 010/213–0534) attracts a fashionable young crowd and has an all-night French terrace serving snacks. **De Consul** (✉ Westersingel 28B, ☎ 010/436–3323) offers movies, as well as New Age and pop music. **Hallo** (✉ Stadhuisplein 43, ☎ 010/414–6400) has a well-stocked bar and an intimate dance floor and plays a wide range of music. A big dance floor and great live music make **Nighttown** (✉ West Kruiskade 28, ☎ 010/436–4534) *the* place to be in Rotterdam. There are frequent special party nights.

Gay Bars. Very much part of the late-night scene, **Gay Palace** (✉ Schiedamnsesingel 139, ☎ 010/414–1486) attracts crowds of young gay Rotterdammers to its large dance floor. New on Rotterdam's gay scene is **d'Groove** (✉ Westblaak 81, ☎ 010/414–8796). It plays the latest club music and is already attracting gay Rotterdam celebrities.

Jazz. In August the **Heineken Jazz Festival** (☎ 010/413–3972) fills Rotterdam's streets and cafés with music and bopping youth. **De Twijfelaar** (✉ Mauritsstraat 173, ☎ 010/413–2671) is a cozy, friendly place with jazz sessions on Wednesday. **Dizzy** (✉ 's Gravendijkswal 127A, ☎ 010/477–3014) is a jazz café with a big terrace out back that has performances by Dutch and international musicians every Tuesday and Sunday.

Pop and Rock. When the big stars come to Rotterdam, they perform either at the major soccer stadium, **Feyenoord Stadion** (✉ Van Zandvlietplein 1, ☎ 010/492–9499 or 010/492–9444), or at the **Sportpaleis Ahoy** (✉ Zuiderparkweg 20–30, ☎ 010/410–4204).

Outdoor Activities and Sports

BIKING

You can rent bicycles in Rotterdam from the **Rijwiel Shop** (✉ Stationsplein 1, ☎ 010/412–6220).

MARATHON

Run in late April each year, the **City of Rotterdam Marathon** is the major European running event of the year, where world records are routinely broken.

SOCCER

Rotterdam's Feyenoord team is one of the best in the country and plays at **Feyenoord Stadion** (✉ Van Zandvlietplein 1, ☎ 010/492–9499 or 010/492–9444).

Shopping

Late shopping in Rotterdam is on Friday. An antiques, curiosities, and general **market** (✉ Mariniersweg) is held on Tuesday and Saturday, 9–5. The **stamp, coin, and book market** (✉ Grotekerkplein) is on Tuesday and Saturday, 9:30–4. There is a **Sunday market** (✉ Schiedamsedijk) from April through September, 11–5.

Brielle

㉔ *22 km (14 mi) west of Rotterdam.*

The town of Brielle, established in 1330, prospered throughout the Middle Ages, owing to its location on the Goote river, near the mouth of the Maas river, with direct access to the sea. But the source of its wealth disappeared when the Goote river silted up. Just as Brielle was drifting into obscurity, the provinces of the Netherlands revolted against Spain in 1568, led by Protestant rebels (called *Geuzen*—beggars—by the Spanish), who seized ships from the Spanish and used English ports as a base for pirate attacks on Spanish galleons. On April 1, 1572, the Sea Beggars suddenly appeared before Brielle with 36 boats and 5,000 men. They routed the Spanish garrison and won a victory that inspired the Dutch people to renew their struggle against the Spanish. Every year now, on April 1, the citizens of Brielle turn back the clock, filling the streets with straw and putting up stalls that sell wooden shoes and homespun wool. In the afternoon, locals dressed as Spaniards and Sea Beggars reenact the city's liberation, with historic ships, cannon and musket fire, and hand-to-hand fighting. Inevitably, the Spanish lose and their leaders are paraded through the streets in wooden cages. The day ends in a celebration worthy of the Middle Ages, with the mass consumption of spit-roasted meat and goblets of wine.

Today, Brielle makes a good open-air museum, with its historic monuments, narrow streets, and fortifications. The imposing 15th-century **Katharinakerk** (St. Catherine's Church) has witnessed a substantial part of Dutch royal history. In 1688, Mary Stuart waved good-bye from the church tower to her departing husband William III, who was soon to become king of England. From the top, 318 steps up, you can see the Maas river, expanses of polder, and Rotterdam harbor. ⊠ *St. Catharijneplein,* ☏ *0181/475–475.* ⊡ *Fl 3.* ☉ *Apr.–Oct., weekdays 10–5, weekends 10–4 except during services; Nov.–Mar. weekdays 1–5, weekends 10–4 except during services.*

The **Historisch Museum Den Briel** (Brielle History Museum) is in the former Town Hall. The old town jail is on the third floor; the voice of a "16th-century prisoner" addresses you (in Dutch) from a loudspeaker. Among the other exhibits are paintings by local artists and a re-created medieval marketplace on the ground floor. ⊠ *Markt 1,* ☏ *0181/475–475.* ⊡ *Fl 4.* ☉ *Apr.–Oct., weekdays 10–5, Sat. 10–4, Sun. 1–5; Nov.–Mar., weekdays 1–5, Sat. 10–4.*

Dining

$$ ✕ **Eetsalon Paraplu-Parasol.** In the modern, uncluttered, bright yellow interior of an 18th-century building chef-owner Lamber Stuifbergen excels at dishes such as tournedos Rossini (served with goose-liver paté and Madeira sauce) and venison with chanterelles. ⊠ *Voorstraat 41,* ☏ *0181/415–230. V. Closed Tues.–Wed.*

$$ ✕ **Pablo.** At this Indonesian restaurant the menu changes regularly. Specials of the month, *Pablootjes* (little specials) are always worth trying, as are the core dishes that remain the same. ⊠ *Voorstraat 87–91,* ☏ *0181/412–960. AE. Closed Mon.*

Outdoor Activities and Sports

BEACHES

The area has water sports and the beaches of Rockanje, Oostvoorne, and the shore of the Briellse Meer.

BIKING

Bike rentals are available at the **Camping de Meeuw** (⊠ Batterijweg 1, ☏ 0181/412–777).

CANOEING

Boertje Roeibotenverhuur (⊠ Brielse Veerweg 3, ☏ 0181/412–171) rents rowboats and canoes for Fl 10 an hour, Fl 40 per day.

GOLF

Kleiburg (⊠ Krabbeweg 9, ☏ 0181/413–330), an 18-hole public course, is on the north side of the Brielle Sea.

Dordrecht

㉕ *23 km (15 mi) southeast of Rotterdam.*

The charming old city of **Dordrecht,** at the busiest river junction in Europe, has medieval town gates, a 15th-century church with a leaning tower, and an 18th-century period house museum. The oldest town in Holland, it received its charter in 1220.

Gouda

26 *53 km (33 mi) southwest of Amsterdam; 13 km (8 mi) southeast of Rotterdam*

There is more to Gouda than the rich cheese that made it famous (pronounced "**How**-da" not "**Goo**-da"). A walk through the town is a lesson in Dutch history. A clock on the east side of the Gothic Town Hall tells the story of its founding on July 26, 1272. When the clock strikes, every half-hour, figures representing spectators and standard-bearers emerge from the clock's castle door. After the chimes ring out, a miniature Count Floris appears along with a town official who receives a charter from his hands. Gouda took full advantage of its commercial rights, supplying Holland with beer and clay pipes. It also became a city of stained-glass—illuminated churches, convents, and monasteries, partly in response to the fear inspired by plague in the 15th century. The city's most famous son was the medieval philosopher Erasmus, the offspring of a local priest. Over the centuries, periods of prosperity were followed by economic collapse, particularly under French occupation in the 1790s. By the early 19th century, once-rich Gouda had become synonymous with "beggar." But the industrial revolution restored its fortunes and one of the world's largest multinationals, Unilever, actually got its start making candles and soap here.

The Gothic **Stadhuis** (Town Hall) is the focus of civic life now as it was during the Middle Ages when criminals were hanged from its eastern porch and meat was stored and sold in the cool stone recesses beneath it. The **Trouwzaal** (marriage room) on the first floor is decorated with fine tapestries. The dignified council room is upstairs. ⊠ *Markt 1,* ☎ *0182/588–475.* ⊙ *Weekdays 9–5, Sat. 10–4.*

De Waag (The Weigh House) was built in 1668 by Pieter Post. It is the perfect setting for the **Kaasexposeum** (Cheese Museum), where you can watch people making cheese and sample the local cheeses produced on the thousand-plus farms that surround the city. Upstairs are interactive exhibits about Gouda and the dairy industry as well as a café that serves fresh buttermilk. ⊠ *Markt 35–36,* ☎ *0182/529–996.* ▨ *Fl 5.* ⊙ *Tues.–Fri. 10–5, Sat. 1–5.*

★ **St. Janskerk** (St. John's Church), called the Grote Kerk (Great Church), St. John's is the longest in the Netherlands and has especially memorable stained-glass windows. Most of the building dates from the late 15th century; very little has changed since the tower was finished in 1600. The stained glass dates mostly from the 16th century. Miraculously, the windows survived the Protestant iconoclasts, the French revolutionaries, and World War II. Altogether, the church contains 70 stained-glass windows, some as high as 60 ft. In addition to John the Baptist and Christ, they portray Philip II, King of Spain, and Mary Tudor, the Queen of England. The most recent window was created in 1947 as an expression of joy at the liberation of the Netherlands from German occupation. The magnificent organ dates from the early 18th century and is still played every week between April and September. On Sunday, the church is open only to worshipers. ⊠ *Achter de Kerk 16,* ☎ *01820/12684.* ▨ *Fl 3.50.* ⊙ *Mon.–Sat. 9–5.*

The **Museum Het Catharina Gasthuis** (Catharina Hospital Museum) is housed in the Catharina Hospital, which was founded in 1302. In the 17th century the front was replaced with a classical facade, most probably the work of Pieter Post, who also built the Weigh House. The museum's collections cover nearly every aspect of life in Gouda: 16th-century altarpieces from the church, antique toys, a reconstructed 17th-century pharmacy, kitchen, and classroom; paintings by artists of the Barbizon and Hague schools; a fine work by Jan Steen, *The Quack*; and applied arts from the 16th to the 20th century. A winding staircase leads down from the former chapel to a small room with a display of whips, chains, racks, and wheels used to force confessions or for painful executions. An adjoining room contains an isolation cell that was used for the insane; it is the only one still intact in the Netherlands. ⊠ *Oosthaven 9,* ☎ *0182/588–440.* 🎫 *Fl 4.25.* ⊙ *Mon.–Sat. 10–5, Sun. noon–5.*

The **Stedelijk Museum De Moriaan** (Blackamoor Municipal Museum) houses collections of pottery and clay pipes in a late Gothic building that was originally a sugar refinery and later belonged to a company selling spices and tobacco. The figure above the door with the pipe in its mouth is a "Moriaan" (Blackamoor), which was also the company name. Gouda pottery was famous in the 19th century and the floral earthenware on display represents some of the finest work by Gouda craftsmen, manufactured by companies like the Royal Earthenware Factory, Goedewaagen, and Zenith. Ultimately, cheaper imitations took over the market. ⊠ *Westhaven 29,* ☎ *0182/588–444.* 🎫 *Fl 4.25; free with ticket to Catharina Gasthuis.* ⊙ *Mon.–Sat. 10–5, Sun. noon–5.*

Dining and Lodging

$$$ ✗ **Mallemolen.** Just around the corner from Gouda's last remaining windmill, the "Merry-go-round" has fussy old Dutch charm complete with lacy window curtains. Traditional dishes, with lamb or beef as a centerpiece, taste better here. ⊠ *Oosthaven 72,* ☎ *030/231–3368. Reservations essential. MC, V. Closed Dec. 25.*

$ ✗ **De Goudse Winkeltje.** The perfect place for pancakes is in a cozy 17th-century building that sits on a channel of the Gouwe River across from St. John's Church. ⊠ *Achter de Kerk 9a. No credit cards.*

Shopping

The first thing to buy in Gouda is cheese. In its heyday, Gouda also supplied much of the country with candles, soap, ceramics, brooms, clay pipes, and syrup waffles.

CANDLES

De Vergulde Kaars (The Golden Candle; ⊠ Keizerstraat 42, ☎ 0182/510–825), a small shop and factory in one of the oldest streets in town, sells candles for all occasions.

CHEESE

Gouda is the best-known type of Dutch cheese. The ideal place to buy cheese is the open-air **Kaase Markt** (Cheese Market), held by the town hall on Thursday, June through August, when local farmers bring their cheese into the city. Gouda is usually sold as Jongekaas (unripened cheese), Oudekaas (ripe cheese), or Belegen (middle ripe). While Gouda is the commercial center of the most important cheese region in the Netherlands, the dairies are on the expanses of lush polder that surround it. The **Kaasboerderij Hoogerwaard** (Hoogerwaard Cheese Farm; ⊠ Lageweg 45, ☎ 0180/681–530) shows a video in its 17th-century barn, followed by cheese tasting. You can see cheese made in a traditional way at the **Kaasboerderij Jongenhoeve** (Jongenhoeve Cheese Farm; ⊠ Benedenberg 90, ☎ 0182/351–229), where a farmer's wife leads a tour of her dairy that follows a day in the life of a cheese, from warm milk to brine bath to wooden shelf.

PIPES AND CERAMICS

Adrie Moerings, at **Goudse Pottenbakkerij** (Gouda Pottery Kiln; ✉ Peperstraat 76, ☎ 0182/512–842), is perhaps the last man in the Netherlands who still makes clay pipes professionally. His pottery is on sale at the back of the shop.

Outdoor Activities and Sports

BIKING

Gouda is compact enough to explore on foot but a bicycle makes it easy to tour the rich dairy region that surrounds it. **Rijwielshop Gouda** (✉ Stationsplein 10, ☎ 0182/519–751), next to the train station, rents bikes for Fl 8 a day.

Utrecht

❷ *Utrecht is 58 km (36 mi) northeast of Rotterdam and 40 km (25 mi) southeast of Amsterdam.*

Birthplace of the 16th-century pope Adrian VI, the only Dutch pope, Utrecht has been a powerful bishopric since the 7th century and is still a major religious center. It was here that the Dutch Republic was established in 1579 with the signing of the Union of Utrecht. Although the surrounding city is among the busiest and most modern in the Netherlands, the central core of Utrecht retains a historic character, particularly along its two main canals. If you arrive by train, you might be forgiven for thinking that Utrecht is one enormous covered shopping mall: The railway station is surrounded by the biggest mall in the country.

There are pleasant views up and down the **Oude Gracht** (Old Canal), which winds through the central shopping district. The unique feature of this lively esplanade is that there are upper and lower levels, with shops opening onto the street level, restaurants and cafés opening onto the walkway that is just above water level of the city's unique sunken canals. The best place to begin a tour of the historic city center is from the bridge that connects Lange Viestraat to Potterstraat just beyond Vredenburg Square.

NEED A BREAK? — For a tasty lunch, visit **De Soepterrine** (✉ Zakkendragerssteeg 40, ☎ 030/231–7005), a snug restaurant that serves bowls of steaming home-made soups and hefty salads. Some 10 varieties of soup are made daily, including the traditional Dutch *erwtensoep* (thick pea soup). Soups come with crusty bread and herb butter.

An old church houses one of the most delightful museums in the Netherlands, the **Rijksmuseum van Speelklok tot Pierement** (National Museum from Musical Clock to Street Organ). It is a happy place filled with ticking clocks, music boxes, player pianos, and traditional Dutch barrel organs. To find the museum, follow the Oude Gracht to Steenweg and look for the signs. ✉ *Buurkerkhof 10,* ☎ *030/231–2789.* 🎫 *Fl 9.* ☺ *Tues.–Sat. 10–5, Sun. and public holidays noon–5; guided tours every hr.*

The **Domtoren** (Dom Tower) stands at the Oude Gracht and the Zadel-straat bridge. Climbing the 465 steps of the highest church tower in the Netherlands (367 ft tall) is well worth the effort for the panoramic view of the city and surrounding countryside of Utrecht province. Built in the late 14th century, the stone tower was originally the bell tower of a cathedral that was destroyed in a hurricane late in the 17th century (the outline of its nave can still be seen in the paving squares of the Domplein). Soaring lancet windows add to the impression of majestic height. ✉ *Domplein,* ☎ *030/231–0403.* 🎫 *Fl 4.* ☺ *Apr.–*

Nov., weekdays 10–5, weekends and holidays noon–5; Dec.–Mar., weekends and holidays noon–5. View by tour only; last tour at 4.

Holding its own against the imposing Domtoren across the square, the grand Gothic **Domkerk** (Cathedral) was built during the 13th and 14th centuries and designed after the pattern of the Tournai Cathedral in Belgium. It has five chapels radiating around the ambulatory of the chancel, as well as a number of funerary monuments, including that of a 14th-century bishop. The 15th-century cloister garden adjacent to the Dom Church, the **Pandhof** (House Garden), planted with herbs, offers a peaceful respite. ⊠ *Domplein,* ☎ *030/231–0403.* ✉ *Free; guided tours Fl 4.* ⊘ *May–Sept., weekdays 10–5, Sat. 10–3:30, Sun. 2–4; Oct.–Apr., weekdays 11–4, weekends 2–4.*

Het Catharijneconvent, a vast and comprehensive museum of religious history and sacred art, occupies a former convent near the Nieuwe Gracht (New Canal). There are magnificent altarpieces, ecclesiastical garments, manuscripts, sculptures, paintings, and the country's primary collection of medieval art. ⊠ *Nieuwegracht 63,* ☎ *030/231–7296.* ✉ *Fl 7.* ⊘ *Tues.–Fri. 10–5, weekends and public holidays 11–5.*

Primarily dedicated to painting and the decorative arts, the **Centraal Museum** contains collections of costumes, coins, and medals, as well as an archaeological section. The paintings here include excellent works from the 16th-century Utrecht School, reflecting the strong Italian influence on painters such as Van Scorel, Van Heemskerk, and Terbrugghen. There are also examples of the 20th-century Dutch de Stijl movement, perhaps best known to the rest of the world through the straight black lines and blocks of primary colors seen in the paintings of Mondrian. ⊠ *Agnietenstraat 1,* ☎ *030/236–2362.* ✉ *Fl 6.* ⊘ *Tues.–Sat. 11–5, Sun. and holidays noon–5.*

The **Rietveld–Schroder House** exemplifies several key principles of the De Stijl movement that affected not only art, but modern architecture, furniture design, and even typography in the early part of the 20th century. The house was designed for the Schroder family by Gerrit Rietveld (one of the leading architects of De Stijl), who is best known outside the Netherlands for his design of a brightly painted, angular chair. The open plan, the direct communion with nature from every room, and the use of neutral white or gray on large surfaces, with primary colors to identify linear details, are typical de Stijl characteristics. The house is just a few blocks away from the Centraal Museum. ⊠ *Prins Hendriklaan 50,* ☎ *030/236–2310. Reservations essential.* ✉ *Fl 9 (includes guided tour).* ⊘ *Wed.–Sat. 11–5, Sun. noon–5.*

Dining and Lodging

$$$–$$$$ ✕ **Het Grachtenhuys.** There is the feeling of being in a gracious home at this restaurant in a canal house that overlooks the fashionable New Canal. The young owners offer a choice of four- or five-course menus of French-influenced Dutch cuisine. Tempting selections might include rabbit fillet with a puree of various nuts, or truffle and potato soup with smoked eel. ⊠ *Nieuwegracht 33,* ☎ *030/231–7494. Reservations essential. AE, DC, MC, V. Closed Mon. No lunch.*

$$ ✕ **De Zakkendrager.** Students, concert goers from the nearby Vredenburg Music Center, and fashionable young locals come here for generous grills smothered in scrumptious sauces. The restaurant is cozy, friendly, and informal. Outside, in the tiny walled garden, a 175-year-old beech tree towers over all. ⊠ *Zakkendragerstraat 22–26,* ☎ *030/231–7578. AE, DC, MC, V. Closed Mon.*

$$ ✕ **Polman's Huis.** This grand café of the old school is a Utrecht institution. Its Jugendstil/Art Deco interior is authentic. Other reasons to

find your way to Polman's are its relaxing atmosphere and range of meal choices, from a simple quiche to a steamed fish dinner. ✉ *Keistraat 2,* ☎ *030/231–3368. Reservations not accepted. MC, V. Closed Dec. 25.*

$$ 🏨 **Holiday Inn.** Primarily serving visitors to the convention and exhibition hall next door, this chain hotel (which looks like an office building) makes a convenient choice for other travelers as well. It has the only hotel swimming pool in town. ✉ *Jaarbeursplein 24, 3521 AR,* ☎ *030/297–7977,* FAX *030/297–7999. 275 rooms, 1 suite. Restaurant, bar, exercise room, meeting rooms. AE, DC, MC, V.*

$$ 🏨 **Hotel Smits.** On the main square between the station and the old city center, this medium-size hotel has all the comforts of the larger, business-oriented establishments. The rooms are bright, comfortable, and decorated in soothing plum and burgundy. ✉ *Vredenburg 14, 3511 BA,* ☎ *030/233–1232,* FAX *030/232–8451. 85 rooms, 1 suite. Restaurant, bar, no-smoking rooms. AE, DC, MC, V.*

$–$$ 🏨 **Malie Hotel.** On a quiet residential street in a 19th-century row house, this is a modern and attractive family hotel. Rooms are brightly decorated, though simply furnished. The bar-lounge doubles as a small art gallery. ✉ *Maliestraat 2–4, 3581 SL,* ☎ *030/231–6424,* FAX *030/ 234–0661. 29 rooms. Restaurant, bar. AE, DC, MC, V.*

$ 🏨 **Hotel Ouwi.** A convivial family hotel, it is just off one of the main transit routes to the city center. The rooms are tight and simple in furnishings and decor, but they're very clean and tidy. ✉ *F. C. Dondersstraat 12, 3572 JH,* ☎ *030/271–6303,* FAX *030/271–4619. 21 rooms, 18 with bath/shower; 1 apt. No credit cards.*

Nightlife and the Arts

Contact Utrecht's **VVV tourist information office** (✉ Vredenburg 90, ☎ 06/3403–4085) for both schedules and ticket information. *Uit in Utrecht* is a free publication, available at various venues and cafés, that will let you know what is happening in Utrecht.

THE ARTS

Dance. In Utrecht you will find dance on the programs of **Stadsschouwburg** (✉ Lucas Bolwerk 24, ☎ 030/232–4125), which has a major performance hall as well as the Blauwe Zaal (Blue Room) for small productions.

Music. Utrecht is the site of an exceptionally good **Festival of Early Music** (☎ 030/236–2236) in late summer each year. It also offers a full program of concerts in its fine churches, including the Dom Church (☎ 030/231–0403), St. Peter's Church (☎ 030/231–1485), and St. Catharine's Church (☎ 030/231–4030 or 030/231–8526); and there are programs including both concerts and master classes in the Conservatory of the K&W-gebouw/Arts and Sciences Building (✉ Mariaplaats 27, ☎ 030/231–4044).

Theater and Opera. Visiting opera companies and talented local musicians keep up a high standard at the **Stadsschouwburg** (✉ Lucas Bolwerk 24, ☎ 030/232–4125).

NIGHTLIFE

Cafés. Het Oude Pothuis (✉ Oude Gracht 279, ☎ 030/318–970) has both music and meals six nights a week, plus a stage with instruments available for jam sessions. **Polman's Huis** (✉ Keistraat 2, ☎ 030/231–3368) attracts a lively crowd of students and thirtysomethings.

Disco and Dancing. Fellini (✉ Stadhuisbrug 3, ☎ 030/231–7271) is a popular rock and dancing club in the cellars of the old town hall. **Trianon Union Salsa** (✉ Oudegracht 252, ☎ 030/233–1154) is a hot 'n' jumping salsa club that organizes great weekend parties. On some nights there are salsa classes earlier in the evening before the party starts.

Gay and Lesbian. De Roze Wolk (⊠ Oudegracht 45, ☎ 030/232–2066) is a cozy gay and lesbian bar with a friendly atmosphere and a canal-side dance space in the cellar.

Jazz and Blues. Zeezicht (⊠ Nobelstraat 2, ☎ 030/319–957) is a crowded bar that resonates with jazz and blues on Tuesday.

Outdoor Activities and Sports

BIKING

You can rent a bike from **Rijwiel Shop** (⊠ Centraal Station Utrecht, ☎ 030/311–159) and **Verleun and Co.** (⊠ Van Bijnkershoeklaan 413, ☎ 030/936–368).

SPORTS COMPLEX

The sports center **De Vechtsebanen** (⊠ Mississippidreef 151, ☎ 030/627–878) offers bowling, badminton, volleyball, squash, curling, and a number of other sports; there is a small running track, as well as both indoor and outdoor tennis courts and ice-skating rinks.

Shopping

Late shopping night in Utrecht is Thursday. A **general market** is held at Vredenburg on Wednesday 9–5 and Saturday 8–5; the **antiques market** at the Ossekop (⊠ Voorstraat 19) is Saturday 9–5; **flowers and plants** are sold at Janskerkhof on Saturday 7–4, and by the Old Canal on Saturday 8–5; there is a **health-food market** at Vredenburg on Friday noon–6; and a **flea market** at Waterstraat on Saturday 8–2.

Naarden

 30 km (19 mi) northeast of Utrecht; 20 km (12 mi) southeast of Amsterdam.

The idyllic town of Naarden was the scene of one of the most horrific moments in Dutch history. In 1572, near the beginning of the war for Dutch independence from Spain, Spanish troops massacred the townspeople, as an example to other Dutch rebels, and burned everything but the Gothic church, which is still standing. The event is depicted on a small stone carving above the doorway of the **Spaanse Huys** (Spanish House; ⊠ Turfpoortstraat). In the 17th century, Naarden erected a massive and complex series of fortifications with a double moat, based on the principles of the French military architect Vauban. The new defenses had to take artillery into account so the high stone walls of the Middle Ages became a thing of the past. Instead, low walls were pushed far out into the countryside with arrowhead-shape bastions and moats. Remarkably, these fortifications remained part of Holland's defenses until the World War II. Even today, the only three entrances to Naarden are across a moat.

The three main streets meet at the **Grote Kerk** (Great Church). The highlight of Naarden's late-Gothic church is its painted wooden ceiling, portraying scenes from the Old and New Testaments. The choir screen is one of the finest in Holland. For the best possible view of Naarden and its star-shape ramparts, climb the tower (guided tours on the hour in summer 1–4). ⊠ *Marktstraat,* ☎ *035/694–2836.* 🎟 *Fl 4.50 (includes tour); tower, Fl 4.* ☉ *Mid-May–mid-Sept., daily 2–5.*

The **Stadhuis,** with its double set of step gables, is a classic piece of Holland Renaissance style architecture. It is still in use by the city council and for weddings and cultural events. ⊠ *Marktstraat 22,* ☎ *035/695–7811.* 🎟 *Free.* ☉ *Mon.–Sat. 2–5.*

☺ The **Vestingmuseum** (Fortification Museum) sums up the centuries-long Dutch effort to keep more powerful neighbors at bay. By the 18th century the city's bastions formed the still-visible double-moated star around the town. The museum is located in one of the former bastions. Exhibits and a video tell the story of Naarden and its defenses and a boat takes you out to see them from the water. An exhibition in a second bunker is devoted to Holland's waterlines, which played an important role in the defense of Holland for centuries. The waterlines allowed the flooding of vast stretches of land to discourage invaders; the technique was used until advances in military technology rendered inundation useless. ⊠ *Westwalstraat 6,* ☎ *035/694–5459.* ⌨ *Fl 10 (plus Fl 4 for the boat trip).* ☺ *Mid-Apr.–May and Sept.–Oct., Tues.–Fri. 10:30–5, weekends noon–5; June–Aug., weekdays 10:30–5, weekends noon–5; Nov.–mid-Apr., daily noon–4.*

Dining

$–$$ ✕ **Eetcafé Het Hert.** This cozy little "Eating Cafe" is decorated with copper pots, frilly curtains, and mellow wood paneling. The house specialty is spare ribs that are marinated and then roasted. Fish is always on the menu, too. In summer, you can eat in the garden in the back. ⊠ *Cattenhagestraat 12,* ☎ *035/694–8055. No credit cards.*

Muiden

❷⁹ *12 km (7½ mi) southeast of Amsterdam.*

★   **Rijksmuseum Muiderslot** (Muider Castle Museum). Muider castle on the estuary of the Vecht is Holland's most famous medieval fortress. Count Floris V built the first castle on the spot in 1280 but it was destroyed just 16 years later by a warring bishop from Mechelen. A new castle was built on the remains of the old one in 1370 and has remained in near perfect condition to this day. The castle has served as courthouse, national prison, and residence for the writer and poet P. C. Hooft, who lived here from 1609 to 1674. During his time, the Muiderslot provided a meeting place for some of the best minds in Dutch science and art, collectively known as the the Muiderkring (Muider Circle). The castle has a splendid moat and herb garden, too. Inside, it is furnished and decorated with art and everyday objects from the time of Hooft, which was, of course, much later than that of the castle itself. Visitors must be accompanied by a guide. Guided tours leave on the hour. Call ahead to confirm times for tours in English. ⊠ *Herengracht 1,* ☎ *0294/261–325.* ⌨ *Fl 7.50.* ☺ *Weekdays 10–5, weekends 1–5.*

Metropolitan Holland and The Hague A to Z

Arriving and Departing

BY CAR

N5/A5 goes to **Haarlem** from Amsterdam (from there N208 leads through the bulb district to Leiden); to reach **Leiden, The Hague, Delft,** and **Rotterdam** directly from Amsterdam, take E19 via Amsterdam Schiphol Airport; to continue to **Utrecht** from Rotterdam, take A15 and then the A27, or to reach Utrecht directly from Amsterdam, take E25. Take E30/A12 from The Hague to Utrecht to bypass the congestion of Rotterdam.

BY TRAIN

Getting about by rail is the ideal means of intercity transport in the Metropolitan area. Trains are fast, frequent, clean, and reliable, and stations in all towns are centrally located, usually within walking distance of major sights.

Intercity express trains (☎ 0900/9292) run twice an hour between Amsterdam and Leiden, The Hague, and Rotterdam; and four times an hour between Amsterdam and Haarlem and Utrecht. To get to Delft from Amsterdam, change trains in The Hague. Trains run frequently between The Hague and Rotterdam, The Hague and Utrecht, and Rotterdam and Utrecht.

There are two **railway stations** in The Hague: one in the central business district and the other in the residential area. For reasons that have more to do with politics than practicality, trains from Amsterdam do *not* stop at the central station, which means you must either change trains in Leiden to disembark directly at the central station or take a bus from the high station into the center.

Getting Around

BY BICYCLE

Bicycles can be rented at railway stations or by contacting local rental facilities. In this flat land, a bicycle is an ideal means of getting around, and cities have safe cycle lanes on busy roads.

BY BUS OR TRAM

In combination with trains, the efficient system of buses and trams in the Metropolitan area will easily take care of most of your transportation needs. Bus service is available in all cities in this region, and trams run in The Hague, between Delft and The Hague, in Rotterdam, and in Utrecht; Rotterdam also has an excellent underground metro system with two major lines (east–west and north–south) that extend into the suburbs and cross in the city center for easy transfers from one to the other. For information on public transportation (trains, buses, trams, and ferries) in all major Dutch cities, call 0900/9292 from anywhere in the country.

BY TAXI

Taxis are available at railway stations, at major hotels, and, in larger cities, at taxi stands in key locations. Call to order a **taxi** in Delft (☎ 015/262–0621), Haarlem (☎ 023/515–1515), The Hague (☎ 070/ 390–7722), Leiden (☎ 071/521–2144), Rotterdam (☎ 010/462– 6060 or 010/425–7000), or Utrecht (☎ 030/251–5151 or 030/233– 1122).

Contacts and Resources

EMERGENCIES

National Emergency Alarm Number for police, fire, and ambulance: ☎ 112. **Hospital Emergency Rooms: Delft** (✉ R. De Graafweg 3–11, ☎ 015/260–3060), **Haarlem** (✉ Velserstraat 19, ☎ 023/522–4466), **The Hague** (✉ Bronovolaan 5, ☎ 070/312–4141), **Leiden** (✉ Rijnsburgerweg 10, ☎ 071/526–9111), **Rotterdam** (✉ Dr. Molewaterplein 40, ☎ 010/463–9222), and **Utrecht** (✉ Heidelberglaan 100, ☎ 030/ 250–9111). **Late-Night Pharmacies: Delft** (☎ 015/212–1568), **Haarlem** (☎ 023/531–9148), **The Hague** (☎ 070/345–1000), **Rotterdam** (☎ 010/411–0370), and **Utrecht** (☎ 030/244–1228). Pharmacies stay open late on a rotating basis. Call for addresses on a given night.

GUIDED TOURS

In Leiden, **Jaap Slingerland** (☎ 071/541–3183) runs 3½-hour boat trips, including a windmill cruise, every summer afternoon except Saturday from the *haven* (harbor) across the Braassemer Lake and the Kager Lakes; the fare is Fl 17.50. In July and August there are day trips across Braassemer Lake to visit the bird and recreation center, **Avifauna** (☎ 0172/487–575), in Alphen aan den Rijn; the cost is Fl 7.50, plus admission to the park, Fl 9.50. In The Hague, a **Royal Tour** (☎ 06/340– 35051) that takes in the palaces and administrative buildings associated with Queen Beatrix operates April through September; the cost is Fl 27.50. The **Rotterdam Tourist Hopper** (⊠ Coolsingel, ☎ 0900/4034065 or 010/402–3200) is available twice daily from May through September: Fl 14.50. The best way to see Rotterdam's waterfront is by boat; **Spido Harbor Tours** (⊠ Willemsplein, ☎ 010/413–5400) offers excursions lasting from just over an hour to a full day. In Utrecht, an option is the **Walkman Tour,** available from the tourist office (⊠ Vredenburg 90, ☎ 06/340–34805) for Fl 5.

VISITOR INFORMATION

Stichting Promotie Den Haag/VVV Kantoor Babylon (The Hague Information Office; ⊠ Koningin Julianaplein 30, Babylon shopping center, ☎ 0900/3403505). **VVV Scheveningen** (⊠ Gevers Deynootweg 1134, Palace shopping center Promenade, 2586 BX, ☎ 0900/3403505 or 070/363–5676). **VVV Brielle** (⊠ Markt 1, 3231 AH, ☎ 0181/475–475). **VVV Delft** (⊠ Markt 85, 2611 GS, ☎ 015/212–6100). **VVV Gouda** (⊠ Markt 27, 2801 JJ, ☎ 0182/513–666). **VVV Haarlem** (⊠ Stationsplein 1, 2011 LR, ☎ 0900/6161600 or 023/531–3506, FAX 023/534–0537). **VVV Leiden** (⊠ Stationsplein 210, 2312 AR, ☎ 071/514–6846). **VVV Rotterdam** (⊠ Coolsingel 67, 3012 AC, ☎ 0900/4034065 or 010/402–3200, FAX 010/413–0124). **VVV Utrecht** (⊠ Vredenburg 90, 3511 BD, ☎ 0900/4141414, FAX 030/233–1417).

THE BORDER PROVINCES AND MAASTRICHT

The long border between the Netherlands and Belgium zigzags from the North Sea coast to the German frontier. The shared heritage of religion, architecture, food, and lifestyle makes Brussels as alluring as Amsterdam to the residents of the southern provinces of the Netherlands: These southern Dutch are more gregarious and outspoken than those of the north; they also pursue the good life of food, drink, and conviviality with more gusto, and less guilt, than their Calvinist-influenced countrymen who live "above the Great Rivers." When Amsterdammers want to spend a weekend eating well and being pampered in elegant hotels, they think first of the southern provinces of their own country. The freshness of Zeeland shellfish and the Burgundian lifestyle and French kitchens of the border provinces provide restaurants of exceptional quality, and Limburg's castles often harbor luxurious hotels.

Three provinces hug the Belgian border: Zeeland (Sea Land) is a collection of flat, open, and windswept islands and peninsulas, known for its agriculture and shellfish; Noord Brabant, also known simply as Brabant, is a wooded and water-laced industrial area bordered on both east and north by the river Maas; Limburg is a region of hills and half-timbered farmhouses that extends along the river Maas deep into the south. The capital city of the region, Maastricht, nestles in a peninsula surrounded on one side by Belgium and the other by Germany. This sophisticated small city is a mecca for goods from all over Europe, drawing merchants and shoppers from as far as Amsterdam, Brussels, and Cologne.

Zeeland, in the southwestern part of the Netherlands, is almost entirely taken up by sprawling estuaries. Travel in this area is often circuitous, along many bridges and dikes. As you head eastward, the land begins to undulate until, in Limburg (around Maastricht), the terrain becomes—for the Netherlands at least—quite hilly. The border provinces are spread out, so allow yourself at least a week to really get a feel for the area. Otherwise, concentrate on the eastern and western extremes of the region—Zeeland and Maastricht.

In February, in a last fling of indulgence before Lent, the Catholics of the south throw a Carnival. The villages elect a Prince in November who leads the revels for the four days prior to Ash Wednesday. Most towns have parades (the most spectacular are in Maastricht and Den Bosch) and people in cafés party all night. On the streets, revelers guzzle pancakes and *nonnevotten* (deep-fried dough balls) to ward off the cold. Visitors are made especially welcome, whirled up into the merry-making in no time at all.

The region is at its liveliest at Carnival time (usually in mid-February). Gourmets come in the summer for the asparagus season (early May to June 24). The mussels season (mid-August to April) usually starts off with parties in village squares around Zeeland, where you'll find steaming cauldrons boiling up as many mussels as you can eat.

Numbers in the text correspond to numbers in the margin and on the Border Provinces map.

Zeeland: The Land of the Sea

On the fingerlike peninsulas and islands of the province of Zeeland you are never more than a few miles from a major body of water. You also are never more than a few inches above sea level, if you are above it at all: Floods have put this province almost completely under water on several occasions, most recently in 1953. The province has a lion rising from the sea on its coat of arms and its Latin motto means "I struggle and I survive." Zeeland suffered terribly during World War II. The Germans bombed the capital of Middelburg and nearly destroyed its town hall and 12th-century abbey. At the end of the war, the Allies demolished the Walcheren dikes, flooding most of the island. Today, major dikes, dams, and bridges connect Zeeland's four chief islands and peninsulas, guarding against the possibility of the sea's reclaiming the land again.

Zierikzee

㉚ *67 km (40 mi) southwest of Rotterdam.*

Traveling south from Rotterdam across the islands and frail peninsulas, following A29 to N59, you come to the chief center of Schouwen-Duiveland, the small old city of Zierikzee, a yachting port with an attractive Old Town, cobblestone streets, three historic gateways, and a canal connecting it to the open waters of the Oosterschelde. Zierikzee, founded in 849, is reputed to be the best-preserved town in the Netherlands. Zierikzee's most spectacular attraction is the great tower of the cathedral, **Sint Lievens Monstertoren,** begun in 1454 but never completed (when it reached 199 ft, the townspeople ran out of money).

En Route　From Zierikzee, continue on N59 west to Serooskerke and then turn south onto N57 across the **Oosterscheldekering** dam. This dramatic ride may be restricted in times of high winds; the North Sea to one side, the Oosterschelde bay to the other, and the looming storm-surge barriers beside the road remind you that it requires massive constructions of steel and concrete to resist the forces of the sea.

★ ♻ **㉛** **Waterland Neeltje Jans Delta Expo** offers a firsthand tour of the most important achievement of Dutch hydraulic engineering. The Delta Works, a massive dam and flood barrier, is itself the most impressive thing to look at. There are also exhibits documenting the 2,000-year

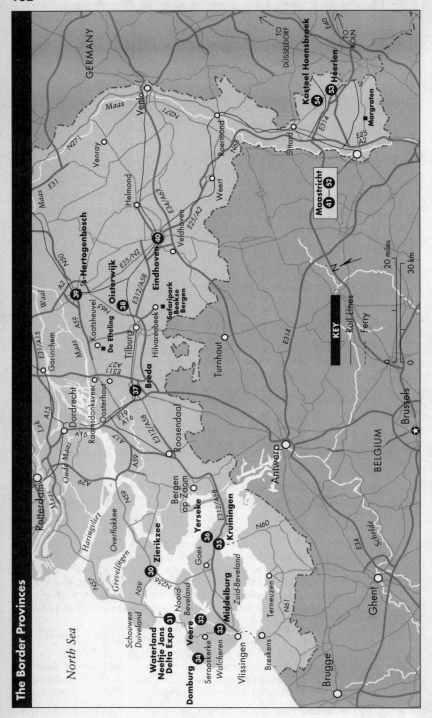

The Border Provinces

history of the Dutch struggle with the sea. Films and slide shows, working scale models, and displays of materials give a comprehensive overview of dikes, dams, and underwater supports. The visit includes a boat trip in good weather, and there is an opportunity to walk inside one of the multistory pilings that make up the support system of the storm-surge barriers. Delta Expo is on Neeltje Jans Island, which was used as a work island during the 20 years it took to build the dam. ⊠ *Eiland Neeltje Jans, Burgh-Haamstede,* ☎ *0111/652–702.* ⊑ *Fl 20.* ☉ *Apr.–Oct., daily 10–5:30; Nov.–Mar., Wed.–Sun. 10–5:30.*

Veere

★ ㉜ *106 km (67 mi) southwest of Rotterdam, 7 km (4 mi) north of Middelburg.*

One of the prettiest small towns in the Netherlands, Veere is well worth a few hours' stopover to explore its quiet streets and admire its elegant architecture. Now the principal sailing port of the Veerse Meer (Veerse Lake), the town was an important seaport during the 16th century, with a busy trade in such items as wool, linen, and salt. Reach Veere by crossing both the Oosterscheldekering and the Veersegatdam dams and then following the dike road.

Veere's fairy-tale Gothic **Stadhuis** (Town Hall), begun in 1474, has a facade that harks back to the town's glory days and seems surprisingly grand for the sleepy village of today. The building has a minaret-style tower, added in 1599. ⊠ *Markt.*

The **Museum De Schotse Huizen** (The Scots' Houses) stands beside 16th-century buildings, facing the town's small inner harbor, that once were the offices and warehouses of Scots wool merchants. Highly ornate, the buildings are named Het Lammetje (The Little Lamb) and De Struys (The Ostrich); you'll know which is which by the facade stones. Inside is a collection of local costumes, porcelain, household items, and paintings. ⊠ *Kaai 25–27, Veere,* ☎ *0118/501–744.* ⊑ *Fl. 5.* ☉ *Mon.–Sat. noon–5, Sun. 1–5.*

Dining and Lodging

$$$ ✕ **'t Waepen van Veere.** The family-run restaurant just a couple of doors from the towering city hall serves fine renditions of Zeeland-style fish soup with rouille, grilled sole, and asparagus when it is in season. ⊠ *Markt 23–27,* ☎ *0118/501–231. Reservations essential. AE, DC, MC, V.*

Outdoor Activities and Sports

SAILING

The lakes and dams of Zeeland are great sailing territory, and there's much fun to be had yachting between the area's attractive small harbors. To arrange a day on the water in Zeeland, contact **Jachtwerf Oostwatering** (⊠ Polredijk 13 B, Veere, ☎ 0118/501–665), **Jachtwerf Wolphaartsdijk** (⊠ Zandkreekweg 5, Wolphaartsdijk, ☎ 0113/581–562), **Marina Veere B.V.** (⊠ Kanaalweg wz 5, Veere, ☎ 0118/501–223), or **WSVW en RYCB** (⊠ Wolphaartsdijk, ☎ 0113/581–565).

Middelburg

㉝ *98 km (62 mi) southwest of Rotterdam, 89 km (56 mi) northwest of Antwerp.*

The ancient capital of the province of Zeeland, Middelburg was an important trading post of the Dutch East and West India companies during the 17th century. Today it is a bustling, friendly town that—despite severe bombing during World War II—preserves many impressive monuments.

A testimony to Middelburg's past grandeur, the elaborately decorated **Stadhuis** (Town Hall) stands resplendent on the market square. Begun in the mid-15th century, it is a showpiece of southern-Dutch Gothic architecture and is adorned with statues of past counts and countesses of Zeeland. Much of the facade, however, is not authentic, having been added as part of an overenthusiastic 19th-century restoration. Inside, the most impressive room is the austere *Vleeshal* (Meat Market), which is now used for exhibitions. To see the rest of the building, you have to join a guided tour. The tours are normally in Dutch and German but, if you ask nicely, most guides will offer some commentary in English, too. ⊠ *Markt,* ☎ *0118/675–450.* ⊡ *Fl 4.* ☉ *Tours Mar.–Oct., Mon.–Sat. 10–5, Sun. noon–5.*

The heart of Middelburg is the 12th-century **Abdij** (Abbey Complex), which incorporates three churches, countless provincial government offices, a major research library (☞ *below*), the provincial cultural and historical museum (☞ *below*), and a tall tower (☞ *below*) that overlooks the city and surrounding countryside. Although it was badly damaged in World War II, the entire complex has been faithfully reconstructed. **Onze Lieve Vrouwe Abdij** (Our Beloved Lady Abbey) was founded in 1150 as a Premonstratensian abbey and served as a monastery until 1574. The **Historama,** a multimedia presentation about the design and history of Middelburg and the abbey, includes a 20-minute video in English. ⊠ *Abdij 9,* ☎ *0118/616–851.* ⊡ *Fl 6.* ☉ *Apr.–Nov., Mon.–Sat. 10–6, Sun. noon–6.*

The **Zeeuws Museum** (Zeeland Museum) is best known for its series of tapestries illustrating the major Dutch sea battles with Spain during the 16th century. The varied collection also includes an Egyptian mummy, votive stelae dating from the Roman period, a collection of rare seashells of the Royal Zeeland Science Association, and a costume hall that is one of the best in the Netherlands. The museum is part of the Abdij complex. ⊠ *Abdij,* ☎ *0118/626–655.* ⊡ *Fl 7.* ☉ *Mon.–Sat. 10–5, Sun. noon–5.*

NEED A BREAK?   **Restaurant De Abdij** (⊠ Abdijplein 5, ☎ 0118/635–022 or 0118/636–196) is a convenient place to stop for lunch. Within the Abbey Complex, next to the Zeeuws Museum, it offers sandwiches, salads, and light meals.

Of particular interest to American visitors to Zeeland is the **Roosevelt Studiecentrum** (Roosevelt Study Center), a library, research center, and exhibition hall. Theodore Roosevelt and Franklin Delano Roosevelt were descendants of a Zeeland family; the purpose of this center is to make known the historical links between the United States and the Netherlands and particularly to publicize the role of the United States in Europe during the 20th century. The study center is part of the Abdij complex. ⊠ *Abdij 9,* ☎ *0118/631–590.* ⊡ *Free.* ☉ *Weekdays 10–12:30 and 1:30–4:30.*

You can climb the 207 steps to the top of the octagonal **"Lange Jan" Abdijtoren** ("Long John" Abbey Tower), which is attached to the Choral Church of the Abbey Complex. The stone tower, 280 ft high, was constructed in the 14th century and is topped with an onion-shape dome from the 18th century. ⊠ *Abdij,* ☎ *0118/682–255.* ⊡ *Fl 3.* ☉ *Apr.–Oct., Mon.–Sat. 10–5, Sun. noon–5.*

Buildings and landmarks typical of the Middelburg region have been duplicated in ½₀th actual size in **Miniatuur Walcheren** (Miniature Walcheren), a miniature city in a garden. The skillfully made models include houses, churches, and windmills, and a reconstruction of Veerse

Lake with motorized boats. Even the trees and plants are in miniature. ⊠ *Koepoortlaan 1, Molenwater,* ☎ *0118/612–525.* 🎫 *Fl 11.* ☉ *Daily 10–5 (July–Aug. until 6).*

☞ The **Ramship de Schorpioen** (Ramship *Scorpion*) is one of only three iron ramming ships of its kind in the world and the oldest surviving Dutch naval vessel. ⊠ *Loskade,* ☎ *0118/639–649.* 🎫 *Fl 5.* ☉ *Apr.– Oct., daily 10–5.*

Dining and Lodging

$$$$ ✕ **Het Groot Paradys.** Facing the market square in a house that dates from the mid-16th century, this intimate restaurant retains a traditional town-house decor. Dishes are made with ingredients from the region, including delicious oysters. Fresh-baked breads are the pride of the kitchen. ⊠ *Damplein 13,* ☎ *0118/626–764. Reservations essential. Jacket required. AE, DC, MC, V. No lunch Sat.*

$$ ✕ **Nummer 7.** Under the same ownership as the more famous Het Groot Paradys, this restaurant has a finesse all its own in a relaxed setting of pale yellow walls and unadorned wooden tables. It is not every day you can eat a three-course meal with generous portions of lentil soup, Zeeland beef with truffle sauce, and creme brulée for Fl. 39.50. ⊠ *Rotterdamsekaai 7,* ☎ *0118/635–679. AE, DC, MC, V.*

$–$$ 🏨 **Le Beau Rivage.** This attractive hotel occupies a gabled, brick, turn-of-the-century canal-side building near the city center. The rooms are comfortable and decorated in pale colors with modern prints on the walls; the management is efficient and friendly. ⊠ *Loskade 19, 4331 HW,* ☎ *0118/638–060,* 📠 *0118/629–673. 9 rooms with shower, 1 suite. Restaurant. AE, MC, V.*

Outdoor Activities and Sports

BEACHES

In the vicinity of Middelburg, you will find the best beaches at **Domburg, Kouderkerke, Oostkapelle, Vrouwenpolder/Serooskerke, Westkapelle,** and **Zoutelande;** all have beach houses to rent, and all but Vrouwenpolder/Serooskerke have beach pavilions.

BIKING

You can rent a bicycle from **L. Petiet** (⊠ Kinderdijk 92, ☎ 0118/624–394) or **Stationsrijwielstalling** (⊠ Kanaalweg 22, ☎ 0118/612–178).

Shopping

Middelburg's **fruit market** is held on Saturday. The **summer antiques and curiosities market** is at the Vismarkt from mid-June through August, Thursday 9–4. Late shopping is on Thursday.

Domburg

❸④ *16 km (10 mi) west of Middelburg.*

Domburg is the oldest seaside resort in Zeeland. During its heyday in the 19th century, Europe's doctors prescribed sea baths as a cure for everything from apathy to thrombosis. Today North Sea winds and water temperatures are still a bracing form of therapy. Unfortunately, the 20th-century beach is near major sea lanes. Swim too far out and you risk colliding with a cargo ship. Beach pavilions offer glass-enclosed sunbathing areas, cafés, and changing rooms that can be rented by the day or half-day. You can also rent a "windscherm," a colored tarp that serves as a wind break.

Outdoor Activities and Sports

At **Westhoeve Nature Reserve** (⊠ Duinvlietweg 8, ☎ 01196/12719), Zeeland's loveliest nature reserve, the forest meets the dunes. You can walk along the sea, behind the dunes, or beneath centuries-old trees.

In spring, keep your eyes open for nesting moorhens and rare flowers like the yellow wood tulip.

Kruiningen

35 *34 km (22 mi) southeast of Middelburg.*

This simple Zeeland farm town is the site of one of the country's outstanding restaurants.

Dining and Lodging

$$$$ ★ ✕ 🏨 **Manoir Inter Scaldes.** In the past 25 years, the owner-chef of this small, gracious country restaurant, Maartje Boudeling, has put Kruiningen on the culinary map. Her imaginative use of the products of her region—seafood, fish, lamb, wild game, and fresh herbs—is unrivaled. Her carpaccio of crayfish, smoked lobster with caviar sauce, and turbot with truffle butter are incomparable. The selection of wines-by-the-glass is remarkable. For diners who want to stay overnight, there is a luxuriously appointed 12-room *manoir* on the premises, in a thatched building on the far side of the restaurant's garden. In the restaurant, reservations are essential, as are jacket and tie. ✉ *Zandweg 2, 4416 NA, Kruiningen,* ☎ *0113/381–753,* FAX *0113/381–763. 12 rooms. Restaurant. AE, DC, MC, V. Closed Mon.–Tues.*

Yerseke

36 *35 km (22 mi) northeast of Middelburg.*

The small fishing port of Yerseke is the oyster nursery of Europe. Lobster boats dock at the piers along the waterfront; the beds that nurture some of the finest, sweetest, and most flavorful oysters and mussels in the world lie in pits below the seawalls. In the small buildings on the docks shellfish are sorted and packed for shipment. In mid-August, Yerseke celebrates with a **Mosseldag** (mussel festival). There are special tours around the oyster beds during the season (Sept.–Apr.), and regular tours of the Oosterschelde departing from Julianahaven.

Dining

Zeeland-style cooking often pairs delicately poached fish with generous portions of rich, wine-based sauce. One way mussels are prepared is by baking them with *Zeeuws spek* (Zeeland grilled bacon) and caramelized onions. Oysters are most often eaten raw.

$$$$ ★ ✕ **Nolet's Restaurant Het Reymerswale.** Yerseke's best and most expensive restaurant is run by the Nolet family, which has two other restaurants as well. The traditional, beamed, second-floor dining room overlooking the water is spacious and graciously decorated. It has a comfortable lounge area with a fireplace and a summer porch in back. The menu's focus is on seafood, classically prepared to finest French standards. Grilled turbot or steamed eels with herbs (in season) are specialties of the house. ✉ *Jachthaven 5,* ☎ *0113/571–642. Reservations essential. AE, DC, MC, V. Closed Feb. and Tues.–Wed.*

$$$$ ✕ **Nolet's Vistro.** The bistro-style annex to Nolet's Restaurant (they share the same kitchen) has a less formal setting and less emphasis on creativity and presentation. The lobsters, crabs, oysters, mussels, and fish are just as fresh. ✉ *Jachthaven 6,* ☎ *0113/572–101. Reservations essential. AE, DC, MC, V.*

$$ ✕ **Nolet.** The simplest and most traditional of Nolet's three restaurants offers crustaceans, bivalves, and fish prepared Zeeland-style, poached, baked, or grilled. ✉ *Lepelstraat 7,* ☎ *0113/571–309. No credit cards.*

Breda

 96 km (60 mi) east of Middelburg, 147 km (93 mi) northwest of Maastricht.

During the 15th and 16th centuries Breda was the seat of the powerful Counts of Nassau, ancestors of the present Dutch royal family. Today, dotted with parks, this small city maintains a quiet medieval charm that is unexpected in a city that is also a major manufacturing center.

The **Stadspark Valkenburg** (Valkenburg Park) dates from 1350 and was originally the castle garden of the counts of Breda. The former castle, **Kasteel van Breda** (Breda Castle), sits majestically beyond the moat; it now houses the KMA (Royal Military Academy) and can be visited only on the city walks organized by the VVV during the summer. It's not far from the railroad station. ⊠ *Kasteelplein.*

The imposing 15th- and 16th-century **Grote Kerk** (Great Church), built in the French-influenced Brabant Gothic style in brick and sandstone, was the family church of the House of Orange-Nassau. William of Orange's first wife and child are buried here, as are several of his ancestors. The church was looted of its brass ornamentation when Napoléon's soldiers used it as a barracks. The splendor of the architecture remains, as does the magnificence of the blue-and-gold-painted 18th-century organ. ⊠ *Kerkplein,* ☎ *076/521–8267.* ☜ *Fl 2.* ⊙ *May–Oct., Mon.–Sat. 10–5, Sun. 1–5; Nov.–Apr., weekdays 10–5.*

Breda's **Stadhuis** (Town Hall), which has pride of place on the market square, counts among its treasures a copy of the celebrated Velázquez painting of the surrender of Breda in 1625. ⊠ *Grote Markt 19.* ⊙ *Wed.–Sat. 10:30–5, Sun. and Tues. 1–5.*

NEED A BREAK? A good selection of restaurants and cafés surrounds the Grote Markt. **Brasserie-Café Beecker & Wetselaar** (⊠ 45–49, ☎ 076/522–1100), next to the Great Church, is a traditional high-ceiling café with a brasserie upstairs.

The entrance to the **Begijnhof** (Beguine Court) is several blocks from the Grote Markt, along Catherinastraat, marked by the austere **Waalse Kerk** (Walloon Church). A home for unmarried or widowed lay women who dedicate their lives to prayer and charitable works, this peaceful and attractive courtyard is one of only two remaining cloisters of this type in the Netherlands (the other is in Amsterdam). A fragrant formal herb garden occupies the center of the court, and in one corner is a sculpture of two Beguines. ⊠ *Catherinastraat 83a,* ☎ *076/541–1303, Walloon Church information.*

OFF THE BEATEN PATH **DE EFTELING** – This fairy-tale park offers a wealth of rides and amusements enhanced by the fanciful and witty depiction of classic fairy tales in dioramas by Dutch artist Anton Pieck. Sleeping Beauty's chest heaves as she breathes, and there are elves and goblins galore. ⊠ *Kaatsheuvel, Brabant,* ☎ *0416/288–111.* ☜ *Fl 35.* ⊙ *Mid-Apr.–late Oct., daily 10–6; July–Aug., 10–10.*

SAFARIPARK BEEKSE BERGEN – This park is home to hundreds of animals living in an open, naturalistic environment. You can ride a safari bus through the park or rent your own safari jeep. There is also a children's farm. ⊠ *Beekse Bergen 1, Hilvarenbeek, Brabant,* ☎ *013/536–0035.* ☜ *Fl 22; Jeep Fl 50 for 1½ hrs.*

Dining and Lodging

$$-$$$ ✕ **Auberge De Arent.** The ceiling murals in this elegant, white, step-gabled 15th-century house, thought to be among the oldest in western Brabant, are of pheasants, rabbits, and snails, all of which are found on the menu in wild season (the fall and winter months). The Arent has a French kitchen, but the adventurous chefs also experiment with piquant sauces and Asian flavors. There is a separate bistro and a wine cellar with a tasting room. ⊠ *Schoolstraat 2,* ☎ *076/514–4601. Jacket and tie. AE, DC, MC, V. No lunch Sat. Closed Sun.*

$$-$$$ ▥ **Hotel Mercure.** Next to the railway station in a building that formerly housed the offices of the telephone company, this member of the French hotel chain is a straightforward business hotel with a no-nonsense approach to decorating. Still, rooms are spacious, and the staff exhibits a certain degree of Gallic charm. ⊠ *Stationsplein 14,* ☎ *076/522–0200,* ℻ *076/521–4967. 36 rooms, 4 suites. Restaurant, bar, meeting rooms. AE, DC, MC, V.*

$$ ▥ **De Klok.** This small hotel is in a busy and friendly part of the lively market square of Breda. There is a café on the street in summer, and a bar and restaurant occupy the lobby. Double rooms are generously sized, and beds have *dekbedden* (comforters) to keep you warm. Baths may have shower or tub; some quads are available. ⊠ *Grote Markt 26–28,* ☎ *076/521–4082,* ℻ *076/514–3463. 28 rooms with bath/shower. Restaurant, bar. AE, DC, MC, V.*

Nightlife

The **Holland Casino Breda** (⊠ Bijster 30, ☎ 076/227–600) is stylish and offers blackjack, roulette, and other favorites.

Outdoor Activities and Sports

BIKING

To rent a bicycle, contact **Rijwielstalling NS** (⊠ Stationsplein 16–20, ☎ 076/521–0501).

CANOEING AND KAYAKING

The **Biesbosch** area near Breda combines small creeks with stretches of open water (busy with powerboats in the summer season). The tiny **Dommel River** meanders through the countryside between 's Hertogenbosch and Eindhoven and beyond. To rent a canoe in the Biesbosch area, contact **Nion Watersport** (⊠ Oosterhoutseweg 20, Raamsdonksveer, ☎ 0162/512–997). Along the Dommel, contact **Adventure Trips** (⊠ Sint Oedenrode, ☎ 0413/477–267), **De Kanovriend** (⊠ Geenhovensedreef 10, Valkenswaard, ☎ 040/201–4632), or **Kanobouw/kanoverhuur Rofra** (⊠ Luikerweg 74, Valkenswaard, ☎ 043/363–8339).

Shopping

Breda has a general market Tuesday through Friday, as well as a secondhand market on Wednesday, at Grote Markt. Late shopping is on Thursday.

Oisterwijk

38 *28 km (18 mi) east of Breda, 39 km (25 mi) northwest of Eindhoven.*

Oisterwijk is a wooded community and resort town that's perfect for a weekend getaway or a quiet day in the country. There's a charming central square planted with lime trees and a bird sanctuary with a number of exotic species.

Dining and Lodging

$$$ ✕▥ **Hotel Restaurant De Swaen.** This French-Victorian town hotel, ★ on a tree-shaded square, has a shallow front porch with rocking chairs that is used as a café terrace in the summer; there is also a patio ter-

race. The crystal-chandeliered restaurant, overlooking the elegant formal garden in back of the hotel, serves excellent French cuisine. There is also a small *auberge* (inn) restaurant, De Jonge Swaen (The Young Swan), that serves simpler, less expensive, traditional Dutch choices. The Swan's hotel rooms are gracious and homey; baths are marble. ⊠ *De Lind 47, 5061 HT,* ☎ *013/521–9006,* FAX *013/528–5860. 18 rooms. Restaurant, bar. AE, DC, MC, V.*

's-Hertogenbosch

39 *45 km (28 mi) east of Breda, and 123 km (77 mi) northwest of Maastricht.*

The name 's-Hertogenbosch means "The Duke's Woods" in Dutch, and while that is the official name of this medieval city, the name you will hear more commonly is Den Bosch (pronounced "den boss"), "The Woods." Not much remains of the woods for which it was named, however: The forests have been replaced by marshes and residential and industrial development.

With spidery Gothic windows and a noble Romanesque tower, the magnificent **St. Janskathedraal** (St. John's Cathedral) stands out as Den Bosch's principal attraction and is the only cathedral in the Netherlands. Built between 1380 and 1520 in the Brabant Gothic style and abundantly decorated with statuary, sculptural details, and grotesques, it is a cruciform, five-aisle basilica with numerous side chapels around the apse. Its nave is supported by double flying buttresses that are unique in the Netherlands. ⊠ *Parade,* ☎ *073/613–9740.* ⊡ *Free.* ⊙ *Mon.– Sat. 10–5, Sun. 1–5.*

NEED A BREAK?	There is a very special sweet treat in store for you in 's-Hertogenbosch: A *Bossche bol* is a ball-shape *choux* (cream puff) pastry, filled with whipped cream, dipped in dark chocolate, and served cool. **Patisserie Jan de Groot** (⊠ Stationsweg 24, ☎ 073/133–830), on the road leading to the railway station, makes the best in town.

Noordbrabants Museum (North Brabant Museum) is the foremost provincial museum in the country. Housed in the imposing former residence of the provincial governor, the museum contains historical, archaeological, and cultural exhibits related to the history of Brabant, as well as an outstanding art collection that includes many 17th- and 18th-century Dutch floral paintings and works by Brabant artists of various periods. ⊠ *Verwersstraat 41; from Parade, follow Lange Putstraat to Verwersstraat and turn left;* ☎ *073/687–7800.* ⊡ *Fl 10.* ⊙ *Tues.–Fri. 10–5, weekends noon–5.*

Dining and Lodging

$$ ✕ **Pilkington's.** In the shadow of the St. Janskerk tower, this informal restaurant has a British touch, with such old-fashioned favorites as shepherd's pie. But there's also duck breast, fresh grilled fish, and all manner of other delights. In good weather the walled garden, covered with climbing roses, is a must. You can also stop off here just for coffee and cake. ⊠ *Torenstraat 5,* ☎ *073/612–2923. AE, DC, MC, V.*

$$$ ✕▨ **Golden Tulip Hotel Central.** More than just a typical full-service business hotel, the Hotel Central has a family-run atmosphere, especially reflected in the warmth of the service. The rooms have a modern, tailored look. The restaurant, De Leeuwenborgh, with a separate entrance on the square, is graciously appointed and intimate. Its mirrors are etched with views of the city's important buildings, and the menu is traditional and French. ⊠ *Markt 51–57, 5211 JW,* ☎ *073/*

692–6926, FAX 073/614–5699. *124 rooms, 3 suites. Restaurant, bar, meeting rooms. AE, DC, MC, V.*

Nightlife and the Arts

Once a week, 's-Hertogenbosch offers back-to-back **carillon recitals** from two sets of bells. The town-hall bells play every Wednesday morning from 10 to 11, followed by another carillon concert from the cathedral from 11:30 to 12:30.

King's Cross (⊠ Vughterstraat 99a, ☎ 073/613–4479) is open late, plays loud music, and attracts a boisterous but good-natured crowd. Sporty types and young businesspeople frequent **Silva Ducis** (⊠ Parade 6–7, ☎ 073/613–0405), an elegant grand café that looks out onto the most attractive square in town. There is a wide range of beer to choose from and jazz or classical music in the background.

Outdoor Activities and Sports

You can rent bicycles at **Cyclepoint** (⊠ Hoek Zuid-Willemsvaart-Hinthamereinde, ☎ 073/613–9020) or **Stationsfietsstalling** (⊠ Stationsplein 22, 5211 AP, ☎ 073/613–4737 or 073/613–4033).

Shopping

There is a large general market every Wednesday and Saturday on the market square. Late shopping is on Thursday.

The shop of the **North Brabant Museum** (⊠ Verwersstraat 41, ☎ 073/687–7800) offers an exceptional collection of art books covering many periods and styles of Dutch and international art.

Eindhoven

40 *38 km (24 mi) south of 's-Hertogenbosch, 125 km (79 mi) north of Maastricht.*

A bustling, modern city, Einhoven has no traditional, historic center to explore, thanks to heavy bombing in World War II, but there are remarkable examples of contemporary architecture throughout the city (even the bus shelters are designed by well-known architects), and there is an exceptional museum of modern art.

The **Stedelijk van Abbemuseum** (Municipal van Abbe Museum) began in 1936 as the simple wish of a local cigar maker, Henri van Abbe, to visit a museum in his own town. Today it has one of Europe's richest collections of contemporary art and owns more works than can be displayed at one time. The galleries and exhibitions are rotated and rearranged continually. There are examples here of every major trend of the last 100 years, including cubism, constructivism, de Stijl, German expressionism, minimalism, and American pop. At press time, the building that houses the old museum was undergoing extensive and lengthy renovations. In the meantime, only a small portion of the collection is on view. ⊠ *Vonderweg 1,* ☎ *040/275–5275.* ⊡ *Fl 6.* ☉ *Tues.–Sun. 11–5.*

NEED A BREAK? **Grand Cafe Berlage** (⊠ Kleine Berg 16, ☎ 040/245–7481) is a spacious Art Deco brasserie with a street-side terrace that serves standard Dutch café fare, such as spareribs, salads, and *uitsmijters* (fried eggs on toast with a variety of accompaniments, including tomatoes, ham, bacon, and cheese).

Dining and Lodging

$$ ✕ **Ravensdonck.** The Ravensdonck is in a large and elegant house with tall windows. The dining room, on the second floor, with windows all around, serves a variety of simple but tasty grilled dishes. A café with

a friendly atmosphere occupies the first floor. There is an amusing touch here, in that you can buy boxes of chocolates in the shape of light bulbs. Why not? It was a light-bulb factory that transformed Eindhoven from a sleepy village at the turn of the century into an international business mecca. ✉ *Ten Hagestraat 2,* ☎ *040/244–3142. Reservations essential. AE, DC, MC, V. No lunch weekends.*

$$$ 🔝 **The Mandarin Hotel.** The Mandarin is unique in that it was designed to meet East Asian standards of service. Its Asian decor includes small bridges spanning water gardens, used as footpaths through the lobby. The restaurants are all Asian in theme and cuisine: One serves fine Chinese specialties, another offers a range of Indonesian and Asian dishes, and the third is a Japanese steak house; there also is a Parisian coffee shop. ✉ *Geldropseweg 17, 5611 SC,* ☎ *040/212–5055,* 🖷 *040/212–1555. 102 rooms, 6 suites. 3 restaurants, indoor pool, saunas, nosmoking rooms, meeting rooms, free parking. AE, DC, MC, V.*

Outdoor Activities and Sports

Eindhoven's soccer team, **PSV** (Philips Sport Vereniging), is one of the top three in the country and plays from September through May at **PSV-stadion Eindhoven** (✉ Frederiklaan 101A, ☎ 040/250–5505).

En Route   As you travel south toward Maastricht, the small town of **Thorn** is well worth a detour. It is known as the "white village" because of its abundance of 18th-century houses and buildings painted white. Visit the 10th-century abbey church, which has an outstanding Baroque altar and three choirs (for canons, princesses, and noblewomen); there also is a small museum.

Maastricht: Capital of Limburg

★ *207 km (130 mi) southeast of Amsterdam, 25 km (16 mi) west of Aachen (Germany).*

The oldest city in the Netherlands, established by the Romans more than 2,500 years ago, Maastricht has enjoyed a long history as a crossroads between Germanic and Latin cultures. As such, it was an appropriate venue for the signing of the latest major treaty regulating the affairs of the European Union. Wedged somewhat hesitantly between Belgium and Germany, this town is an intriguing mixture of three languages, times, currencies, and customs. It is a miracle that it has remained Dutch—probably because the dignity of being the capital of Limburg Province has weighed heavily upon its hoary head. Small, but quintessentially European, Maastricht offers a lighthearted lifestyle, meticulous attention to service, and exceptionally fine, French-influenced cuisine. Every March, jet-setters and millionaires arrive to buy Jordans drawings and Gothic tapestries at its sumptuous European Fine Art Fair, one of Europe's very best. It straddles the river Maas: The old city is on the river's western bank, and its newer neighborhoods and the railway station are on the eastern side.

★ ⑤ **Bonnefantenmuseum** (Bonnefanten Museum). Diversity is the keyword at the excellent provincial museum of Limburg. Not only are there displays on the archaeological history of the province, but there is an art collection with gems from 13th- to 15th-century Romanesque and Gothic Mosan sculpture of the Meuse region; 14th- to 16th-century Italian painting; and 16th- to 18th-century paintings of the South Netherlands, including works by Jan Bruegel and Pieter Bruegel the Younger. An intriguing and intelligently selected exhibition of contemporary art includes work by many important Dutch painters of the late 20th century, several of them from Limburg. ✉ *Av. Ceramique 250,* ☎ *043/329–0190.* 🎫 *Fl 10.* ☉ *Tues.–Sun. 11–5.*

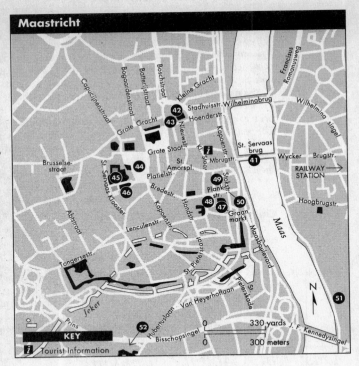

Maastricht

52 Grotten St. Pieter (Caves of St. Peter). These man-made corridors carved deep into the limestone hills have yielded buidling stone since Roman times. There are approximately 200 km (124 mi) of chambers and passageways here. In some areas the mining was so extensive that the ceiling height now is nearly 40 ft; this means that graffiti left by the Romans are now far above your head, while the signatures of such visitors as Napoléon can still be seen. The caves are complex and can be visited only with a guide; they are also chilly and damp, so bring a sweater. ⊠ *Grotten Noord (Northern System), Luikerweg 71; Zonneberg Caves, Slavante 1 (near Enci Cement Works);* ☎ *043/325–2121 for tour times and for English-speaking guide.* 🎫 *Fl 5.50.* ⊙ *Hrs vary; call ahead.*

43 Moosewief (Greengrocer's Wife). The jolly statue of a roly-poly woman carrying a basket of vegetables stands on one side of the **Grote Markt** (market square). Wednesday and Friday are market days in Maastricht, and the square is chockablock with stalls and stands offering fruits, vegetables, meats, and household items. Business here is conducted in three currencies (Dutch, Belgian, and German) and four languages (Dutch, French, German, and English).

47 Onze Lieve Vrouwebasiliek (Our Beloved Lady Basilica). Recent excavations around the church indicate that it may have replaced a Roman temple. The Westwork, a massive flat facade in Romanesque style that is topped with two round turrets, is the oldest part of the structure, dating from the 11th and 12th centuries. Inside is a two-story apse with a double row of columns and a half-domed roof. ⊠ *Onze Lieve Vrouweplein,* ☎ *043/325–1851.* 🎫 *Church free; treasure chamber Fl 3.50.* ⊙ *Easter–Oct., Mon.–Sat. 11–5, Sun. 1–5.*

48 Onze Lieve Vrouweplein (Our Beloved Lady Square). The basilica of the same name (☞ *above*) opens out onto this tree-shaded, intimate square.

49 Op de Thermen. This small residential square, discovered in 1840, was the site of a Roman villa and baths. It hints at the Roman heritage that lies deep beneath the surface of Maastricht. Recently laid paving stones indicate the outline of the ancient buildings—red for a 1st-century house with underfloor heating, gray for a 2nd-century bathhouse, and white for a 4th-century bathhouse. ⊠ *Between Luikerweg and Stokstraat.*

46 St. Janskerk (St. John's Church). The 14th-century Gothic church has a stark white interior and a tall, red tower that offers panoramic views of the city. ⊠ *Vrijthof (enter Henric van Veldekeplein)*, ☎ *043/347–8880.* 🎟 *Free; donation appreciated from tower-climbers.* ☉ *Easter–Oct., Mon.–Sat. 11–4.*

45 St. Servaasbasiliek (St. Servatius Basilica). Beneath the magnificent and historic 7th-century church lie the bones of its namesake, the 4th-century saint whose choice of Maastricht for his see stimulated the development of the city following the departure of the Romans in 402. The basilica's 1993 restoration included a fresh paint job using the bright colors of the original interior design. The focal points of the church are the richly carved 13th-century **Berg Portal,** and the **Schatkamer van Sint Servaas** (Treasure Chamber of St. Servatius) in the 12th-century chapel. This extraordinary collection of treasures dates from 827 and contains religious relics (some of them donated by Charlemagne) and exquisitely wrought liturgical objects. The most important item in the collection is the 12th-century Noodkist, an elaborately decorated, gold-plated oak chest, adorned with gold and silver figures and containing the bones and relics of St. Servatius and other local bishops. ⊠ *Vrijthof,* ☎ *043/325–2121.* 🎟 *Fl 3.50.* ☉ *Dec.–Mar., daily 10–4; Apr.–June and Sept.–Nov., daily 10–5; July–Aug., daily 10–6.*

41 St. Servaasbrug (St. Servatius Bridge). The span crosses the Maas between the old and new parts of town and offers the best views of the old city. Built solidly of gray Namur stone in the late 13th century to replace an even earlier wooden bridge, it is one of the oldest bridges in the Netherlands. ⊠ *Maasboulevard, Wycker Brugstraat.*

42 Stadhuis (Town Hall). Maastricht's civic building stands imposingly at one end of the large market square. Built in 1662 as a proud statement of burgher prosperity, it is filled with fine tapestries, stucco, and paintings. The sumptuous entrance hall is open to the public. ⊠ *Markt 78,* ☎ *043/350–4000.* 🎟 *Free.* ☉ *Weekdays 8:30–12:30 and 2–5:30.*

50 Stokstraat, now a fashionable street lined with galleries and boutiques, was the heart of the original Roman settlement of Maastricht.

44 Vrijthof. Each February, the enormous square explodes with the festivities of Carnival. Ringed with restaurants, grand cafés, dance clubs, and traditional pubs, it is the major public gathering place of Maastricht, year-round.

NEED A BREAK?	A cheerful place to stop any time of day is the plant-filled **Cafe Britannique** (⊠ Vrijthof 6, ☎ 043/321-8691). It serves breakfast (with champagne if you like) as well as simple, light meals throughout the day and drinks, including a house beer, until midnight.

Dining and Lodging

$$$$
★ ✗ **Toine Hermsen.** Despite receiving significant culinary honors, Toine is not a pretentious place. A menu might begin with carpaccio of salmon with lemon-dill sauce and move on to Bresse duck with tomato confit, bell peppers, and potatoes in Provençale sauce; for dessert perhaps almond filo pastry with cherry filling with vanilla ice cream and

champagne sauce. There are fixed price menus for three, four, and five courses. ⊠ *Sint Bernardusstraat 2–4,* ☎ *043/325–8400.* *Reservations essential. Jacket and tie. AE, DC, MC, V. Closed Sun., Mon.*

$$$ ✕ **Old Hickory.** Named after the American regiment that liberated Maastricht in 1944, this spacious restaurant is focused around a large central fireplace. The emphasis is on traditional French gastronomy, and the quality is supreme. Fish and shellfish are the basis for many dishes, and game is served in season—sometimes the product of chef John Kuzelj's own hunting expeditions. John sometimes invites guests to visit his extensive, climate-controlled wine cellar. ⊠ *Meerssenerweg 372,* ☎ *043/362–0548. AE, DC, MC, V. Closed Sun.*

$$–$$$ ✕ **'t Hegske.** This romantic spot is near St. Amorsplein off Vrijthof. Window boxes full of flowering plants decorate the street side, and there is a bubbling fountain in the interior courtyard. The warmth of half-timbered walls, hanging baskets, and antique collectibles here and there add to the intimacy. The kitchen is open, the cuisine classic French. ⊠ *Heggenstraat 3a,* ☎ *043/325–1762. Reservations essential. AE, DC, MC, V. No lunch.*

$$ ✕ **De Blindgender.** Not far from Onze Lieve Vrouweplein, De Blindgender is a particularly warm and cheerful eating pub with large windows looking onto the street. The tables are plain and unadorned, the service is relaxed, and the menu has a good selection of fish dishes, including salmon cooked with sesame seeds. ⊠ *Koestraat 3,* ☎ *043/325–0619. Reservations not accepted. AE, DC, MC, V.*

$$ ✕ **La Ville.** During the day you can take your pick of delicious salads and light meals. In the evening the friendly and enthusiastic staff serve up hearty, French-influenced cuisine, such as filet mignon with shallots and red wine sauce. The restaurant is on Maastricht's prettiest square and has tables under the trees in good weather. ⊠ *Onze Lieve Vrouweplein 28,* ☎ *043/321–9889. AE, DC, MC. No lunch. Closed Tues. Nov.–Apr..*

$$$ ✕🏨 **Kasteel Elsloo.** This 16th-century manor house, with its own park and botanical garden, was once the property of one of Limburg's leading families and the scene of many glittering occasions, including the wedding of a daughter of the family to the Prince of Monaco in the 19th century. Rooms are spacious and restfully decorated. The restaurant, too, has a manor-house ambience; the kitchen is traditional French, serving such dishes as beef with onion confit and port sauce. ⊠ *Maasberg 1, 6181 GV Elsloo, 10 km (6 mi) northeast of Maastricht,* ☎ *046/437–7666,* 𝖥𝖠𝖷 *046/437–7570. 26 rooms, 1 suite. Restaurant, bar. AE, DC, MC, V.*

$$$$ 🏨 **Golden Tulip Hotel Derlon.** The relaxed and quiet elegance of Onze Lieve Vrouweplein is perfectly reflected in this small luxury hotel. Guest rooms are graciously sized and decorated in relaxing, sand-and-seashell tones, and each has its own work of art, most often a contemporary painting; they face either the medieval side street or, if you are particularly fortunate, the tree-filled square. A unique feature of this hotel is a private museum in the cellar, with exhibits ranging from the 1st century BC to the 15th century AD. There is a personal quality to the service, especially in the elegant restaurant. ⊠ *Onze Lieve Vrouweplein 6, 6211 HD,* ☎ *043/321–6770,* 𝖥𝖠𝖷 *043/325–1933. 44 rooms, 1 suite. Restaurant, shops, meeting room. AE, DC, MC, V.*

$$ 🏨 **Hotel Du Casque.** Smack-dab in the center of old Maastricht, this hotel has a tradition that dates back to a 15th-century inn, although today's building is a modern postwar structure. Some rooms overlook the Vrijthof square, and there's direct access to a steak house with a terrace on the square. ⊠ *Helmstraat 14, 6211 TA,* ☎ *043/321–4343,* 𝖥𝖠𝖷 *043/325–5155. 38 rooms with bath/shower. Parking (fee). AE, DC, MC, V.*

$–$$ ⊞ **Hotel Bergere.** The family-owned Bergere occupies an elegant 19th-century building not far from the railway station. There's an elevator, a grand café with a separate entrance, and comfortable, well-appointed rooms. The color scheme is light and fresh in pinks, grays, and beiges. ⊠ *Stationsstraat 40,* ☎ *043/325–1651,* FAX *043/325–5498. 40 rooms with bath/shower, 1 suite. Restaurant, parking. AE, MC, V.*

$ ⊞ **De Poshoorn.** Conveniently situated between the railway station and the Old Town, the Poshoorn has smallish rooms, but they are spotlessly clean and brightly decorated. The hotel is above a café with a friendly clientele, and service is attentive and efficient. ⊠ *Stationsstraat 47,* ☎ *043/321–7334,* FAX *043/321–0747. 9 rooms with bath/shower, 1 suite. Restaurant. AE, DC, MC, V.*

Nightlife and the Arts

For information on what is going on during your visit, check *Maandagenda,* a monthly calendar you will find around town, or *Uit in Maastricht,* published biweekly by the VVV tourist office.

THE ARTS

Carillon Concerts. In summer the air rings with a series of evening concerts played by carillonneurs on various church bells of the city; and throughout the year there are midday concerts every Friday from 11:30 to 12:30 from the cheerful 43-bell carillon atop the town hall in the market square.

Carnival. The Catholic heritage of the southern provinces of the Netherlands is most dramatically felt during the days preceding Ash Wednesday. The public celebration of Carnival survives in its full bloom of conviviality and relative recklessness in Maastricht, with parades, parties, and fancy dress.

Classical Music. In Maastricht, the **Limburgse Symfonie Orkest** (Limburg Symphony Orchestra), the leading regional orchestra, performs at the Theater aan Het Vrijthof (⊠ Vrijthof 47, ☎ 043/321–0380); the box office is open Monday through Saturday 11–4. Maastricht has a thriving and talented **student and amateur** music scene. Performances are at both the Conservatoire Concert Hall (⊠ Bonnefanten 15, ☎ 043/346–6680) and the Kumulus Auditorium (⊠ St. Maartenspoort 2, ☎ 043/329–3141).

Theater. The main theater of Maastricht, the **Theater aan Het Vrijthof** (Theater at Vrijthof; ⊠ Vrijthof 47, ☎ 043/321–0380) has a reputation for exciting programming that extends beyond the city limits. Top-quality national and international companies all play here. In addition, there is a small theater hall, **Podium** (⊠ Het Generaalshuis, Vrijthof 47, ☎ 043/321–0380), and next door, **Het Vervolg Theater** (⊠ Vrijthof 47a, ☎ 043/325–5333), which stage more experimental and esoteric work.

NIGHTLIFE

Cafés. In the heart of the city, with a terrace that hums with life on summer evenings, **De Lanteern** (⊠ Onze Lieve Vrouweplein 26, ☎ 043/321–4326) attracts everyone from tourists to the corner shopkeeper. A special pub to visit is the very old **In den Ouden Vogelstruys** (⊠ Vrijthof 15, ☎ 043/321–4888), first mentioned in town records of the 13th century. It has remained virtually unchanged since 1730 (except, of course, for the modern conveniences of electricity and beer on tap). Named for a type of pot-bellied gin bottle, **Sjinkerij De Bóbbel** (⊠ Wolfstraat 32, ☎ 043/321–7413) is a traditional Maastricht pub, where there's a buzz of conversation rather than background music. It has sand on the floor, simple wooden chairs, and marble-top tables—and a good choice of beers.

Casino. The **Holland Casino Valkenburg** (⊠ Odapark, ☎ 076/525–1100), not far from Maastricht, offers blackjack, roulette, and Punto Banco in chic surrounds.

Dance Clubs. Momus (⊠ Vrijthof 8, ☎ 043/321–1937) is a big, Top-40 discotheque with neoclassical decor of marble and statues. Patronized by students and young arty types, **Satyricon** (⊠ St. Bernardusstraat 16, ☎ 043/321–0321) is a mellow, jazz-oriented "dance-café" that sometimes lets rip with funkier sounds and live concerts.

Gay Bars. La Ferme (⊠ Rechtestraat 29, ☎ 043/321–8928), with a light show and the latest music, is a vortex of South Netherlands gay life. Near the railway station, and decorated with Dutch Rail flotsam and jetsam, **La Gare** (⊠ Spoorweglaan 6, ☎ 043/325–9090) has a long bar, a tiny dance floor, and chatty customers.

Outdoor Activities and Sports

BIKING
Rent bicycles at the **Railway Station** (⊠ Stationsplein, ☎ 043/321–1100).

CANOEING AND KAYAKING
Kayaking is especially pleasant on the river Maas, through the gently hilly countryside. Contact **Kayak Tours Limburg** (⊠ Grote Dries 8, 6223 AE, Borgharen, ☎ 043/363–8339) for rentals.

TENNIS AND SQUASH
To play tennis or squash in Maastricht, visit **Squash Centre Erik van der Pluijm** (⊠ Brusselsestraat 74a, ☎ 043/321–6387) or **Sportpark Mulder** (⊠ Mockstraat 36–38, ☎ 043/363–7295). Rates are about Fl 20 per hour of court time during the day, Fl 40 after 5.

Shopping

Shopping in Maastricht is concentrated in the pedestrian cross streets that connect and surround the three main squares of the city. **Maastrichter Brugstraat** takes you into the network of shopping streets from the St. Servaasbrug. **Maastrichter Smedenstraat** and **Plankstraat** are lined with exclusive shops, with Wolfstraat and the exceptionally fashionable Stokstraat intersecting both of them. In the other direction, Kleine Staat and Grote Staat lead to **Vrijthof,** with a mixed bag of shopping opportunities. Off Grote Staat is a trio of small shopping streets—Spilstraat, Nieuwestraat, and Muntstraat—that end at the Markt. Off Helmstraat is a shopping square, **W. C. Entre Deux.** Late-night shopping is on Thursday.

Maastricht has a tri-country general market in front of the Town Hall on Wednesday and Friday mornings, and a flea market opposite the railway station on Saturday.

Each year Maastricht's MECC Congress and Exhibition Hall is the site of the **European Fine Art Fair** (⊠ European Fine Art Foundation, Box 1035, 5200 BA, 's-Hertogenbosch, ☎ 073/614–5165), for a week beginning in mid-March. Major dealers in antiques and fine art from all over Europe participate, showing paintings, drawings, and prints (traditional and contemporary); furniture and objects; textiles; tapestries; and rugs; there also are music programs and lectures.

En Route   On the way out of Maastricht toward the German border, near the town of Margraten, is the entrance to the 65-acre **Netherlands American Cemetery and Memorial.** The only American military cemetery in the Netherlands, it is the final resting place of more than 8,000 Americans killed in World War II. ⊠ *Rijksweg 2, 10 km (6 mi) east of Maastricht,* ☎ *043/458–1208.* ☞ *Free.* ☉ *May–Oct., daily 9–6; Nov.–Apr., daily 9–5.*

Heerlen

❸ *23 km (14 mi) east of Maastricht.*

Heerlen is the second of the Roman cities in this part of the Netherlands. The discovery in 1940 of the foundations of a large and elaborate Roman bathhouse was proof of the importance of Heerlen as a meeting place for the Roman troops stationed in this northern outpost.

Now enclosed in a large, glass-encircled building, the **Thermenmuseum** (Thermae Museum) has catwalks over a perfectly preserved Roman bath complex. The *thermae* (baths) incorporated open-air sports fields, a large swimming pool, shops, restaurants, and the enclosed bathhouse complex, which included a large dressing room, the hot-air sweating room, and a series of baths (warm, lukewarm, cold, and immersion). ⊠ *Coriovallumstraat 9,* ☎ *045/560–4581.* ☐ *Fl 3.* ☉ *Tues.–Fri. 10–5, weekends and holidays 2–5.*

❺ From the 14th to the 20th century, **Kasteel Hoensbroek** (Hoensbroek Castle) belonged to the same family, who added on bits here and there as the years went by. Nowadays, it is open to the public as the largest and best preserved of the castles in South Limburg. You can see sections dating from the 14th century and products of various architectural styles, including Baroque and Maasland-Renaissance. There are several sparsely but appropriately furnished rooms and various small galleries that show temporary exhibitions. ⊠ *Klinkertstraat 118, 5 km (3 mi) northwest of Heerlen city center,* ☎ *045/522–7272.* ☐ *Fl 6.* ☉ *Daily 10–5:30.*

Dining and Lodging

$$$$ ✕ **De Boterbloem.** An ambitious young couple, Leon and Bianca Winthagen, run this restaurant gem with only eight tables. Specialties include bouillon with mussels and Provençale-style leg of lamb. There are three- and five-course fixed-price menus. ⊠ *Laanderstraat 27,* ☎ *045/571–4241. Reservations essential. AE, DC, MC, V. Closed Sun., Tues., 2 weeks in Feb., and 2 weeks in Aug.*

$$$$ ✕▥ **Prinses Juliana.** The classic French haute cuisine served here has been recognized internationally for more than 10 years. Members of the Dutch royal family and such foreign dignitaries as German chancellor Helmut Kohl have stopped off for a meal. The decor is elegant in an unadorned way so you can pay attention to the food. If you want to stay overnight, the suite-style rooms are bright and spacious. ⊠ *Broekhem 11, Postbus 812, 6300 AV, Valkenburg a/d Geul, 11 km (7 mi) east of Maastricht, 12 km (8 mi) west of Heerlen,* ☎ *043/601–2244,* ☐ *043/601–4405. 23 rooms. Restaurant. AE, DC, MC, V.*

$$$ ▥ **Hotel Kasteel Erenstein.** A 14th-century moated château houses the restaurant, whose menu and wine cellar are French. Across the road, a traditional whitewashed Limburg farmstead houses the luxury hotel. Many of the rooms have beamed ceilings, and some are bilevel and skylighted; others have rooftop balconies. ⊠ *Oud Erensteinerweg 6, 8 km (5 mi) east of Heerlen,* ☎ *045/546–1333,* ☐ *045/546–0748. 44 rooms. Restaurant, bar, massage, sauna, exercise room. AE, DC, MC, V.*

$$$ ▥ **Kasteel Wittem.** This fairy-tale castle hotel, with its duck-filled
★ moat, spindle-roof tower, and series of peekaboo dormers dotting the roof, is human in scale. The family that has owned it for more than 25 years welcomes you to a comfortable environment of vintage Dutch furnishings. The intimate dining room, where the cuisine is French, has towering windows open to views of gardens and fields. There is a summer terrace beside the moat. ⊠ *Wittemer Allee 3, 6286 AA, Wittem/Limburg, 15 km (9 mi) east of Maastricht, 14 km (9 mi) south of*

Heerlen, ☎ 043/450–1208, ℻ 043/450–1260. 12 rooms. Restaurant.
AE, DC, MC, V.

$$$ 🏰 **Kasteel Geulzicht.** Built in the 19th century, this Disneylike hotel is
set in gentle hills. Despite its grand appearance and sumptuous period
entrance hall, the hotel has a cozy, family-run atmosphere. The rooms
are stylishly furnished, often with antiques; some rooms occupy the
castle turrets. The flagstone garden terrace is open only to hotel guests.
⊠ Vogelzangweg 2, 6325 PN, Berg en Terblijt, 6 km (4 mi) east of
Maastricht, 3 km (2 mi) from Thermae 2000 Spa, ☎ 043/604–0432,
℻ 043/604–2011. 11 rooms with bath/shower, 1 suite. Restaurant,
bar. AE, DC, MC, V.

Spa

One of the special treats of South Limburg is **Thermae 2000,** a luxu-
rious hill spa that offers a complete range of services, including indoor
and outdoor spring-fed pools, sauna, steam bath, yoga/meditation, hydro-
gymnastics, aerobics, sports massage, herbal and mud baths, and more.
⊠ Cauberg 27, Valkenburg aan de Geul, Valkenburg, ☎ 043/601–
9419. ⊙ Daily 9 AM–11 PM.

The Border Provinces and Maastricht A to Z

Arriving and Departing

BY CAR

To reach **Zeeland** take E19 from Amsterdam to Rotterdam and pick
up A29 south; connect with N59 west to Zierikzee and N256 across
the Zeelandbrug bridge to Goes, where you can pick up E312/A58 west
to Middelburg, capital of Zeeland province.

To reach the provinces of **Brabant** and **Limburg,** take E25/A2 from Am-
sterdam south through Utrecht. Pick up A27 south to Breda, or stay
on E25 through Den Bosch to reach Eindhoven and other points south.
To travel from Zeeland across to Maastricht, it is far quicker to travel
via Antwerp (in Belgium), taking the A4 and then the E313.

BY PLANE

There are airports in Eindhoven and Maastricht. In addition to regu-
lar flights to both cities from Amsterdam, **KLM City Hopper** (☎ 020/
474–7747) operates service direct from London Gatwick to Maastricht
and from London Heathrow to Eindhoven. Additional services to
Eindhoven from the United Kingdom are scheduled by **Base Business
Airlines** (☎ 061/489–2988) from Birmingham and Manchester.

BY TRAIN

There are frequent **Intercity express trains** (☎ 0900/9292) from Am-
sterdam direct to 's-Hertogenbosch, Eindhoven, Middelburg, or Maas-
tricht. To reach Breda by train, it is necessary to connect either in
Roosendaal or 's-Hertogenbosch.

Getting Around

BY BUS

Local and regional buses leave from and return to the Dutch railway
stations, but bus travel can be slow. The **Public transportation number**
for the entire country is 0900/9292. Operators can also give you in-
formation about local bus routes.

BY TRAIN

As always in the Netherlands, traveling by train between cities is fast
and efficient. There is an **Intercity** train line (☎ 0900/9292) that crosses
the country, west to east within the Border Provinces, twice each hour.
From Breda there also is frequent service direct to Eindhoven, for con-
nections to Maastricht.

BY TAXI

If you are not traveling under your own steam, you will need to hire a taxi to get to some of the more distant castles. To summon a **taxi**, call Breda (☎ 076/522–2111), Eindhoven (☎ 040/252–5252), 's-Hertogenbosch (☎ 073/631–2900), Maastricht (☎ 043/347–7777), or Middelburg (☎ 0118/412–600).

Contacts and Resources

EMERGENCIES

National Emergency Alarm Number for police, fire, or ambulance: ☎ 112. **Hospitals: Breda** (☎ 076/525–8000), **Eindhoven** (☎ 040/233–5933), **'s-Hertogenbosch** (☎ 073/686–9111), **Maastricht** (☎ 043/387–6543), and **Middelburg** (☎ 0118/425–000).

GUIDED TOURS

The **Maastricht Tourist Office** (⊠ Kleine Staat 1, ☎ 043/325–2121) offers a 1–1½-hour guided tour of the city for Fl 5.25. For cruises on the river Maas, contact **Stiphout Cruises** (⊠ Maaspromenade 27, 6211 HS, Maastricht, ☎ 043/325–4151). Fares start at Fl 8.75.

The **Middelburg Tourist Office** (⊠ Markt 65a, ☎ 0118/659–944) occasionally offers guided walking tours (1¼ hrs, daily Apr.–Oct.) for Fl 6.50 per person. Tours of the province are available through **Carlier Tours** (⊠ Elektraweg 9, ☎ 0118/615–015), **Holland International Reisbureau** (⊠ Langeviele 7, ☎ 0118/627–855), and **Holland International Reisbureau Van Fraassen** (⊠ Londensekaai 19, ☎ 0118/627–758).

VISITOR INFORMATION

VVV Breda (⊠ Willemstraat 17–19, 4811 AJ, ☎ 076/522–2444). **VVV Eindhoven** (⊠ Stationsplein 17, 5611 AC, ☎ 0900/1122363 or 040/297–9100). **VVV 's-Hertogenbosch** (⊠ Markt 77, 5211 JX, ☎ 0900/1122334 or 073/613–9624). **VVV Maastricht** (⊠ Het Dinghuis, Kleine Staat 1, 6211 ED, ☎ 043/325–2121, FAX 043/321–3746). **VVV Middelburg** (⊠ Nieuwe Burg 40, 4331 AS, ☎ 0118/416–851). **VVV Veere-Vrouwenpolder** (⊠ Oudestraat 28, 4351 AV, ☎ 0118/501–365). **VVV Yerseke** (⊠ Kerkplein 1, ☎ 0113/571– 864).

THE GREEN HEART

Like a mystery package that opens in a series of ever smaller, ever more intriguing boxes, the wooded heart of the Netherlands is an unfolding treasure. The national park is the wrappings; its ultimate and most precious gift is a museum of art that is buried deep in the forest; another of its surprises is a small palace. The Royal Game Reserve in the north and the fruit- and vegetable-growing region to the east provide the restaurants of the Green Heart with abundant, high-quality ingredients. The forests of the Green Heart teem with game, much of which ends up in local cooking pots. The main game season is in the fall, though clever restaurateurs manage to find something for almost every month; some even go hunting themselves. Braised hare is a specialty, and local boar and venison are delicious, as is the pheasant. Whether cooked as a family-style stew in a simple restaurant or as the creation of one of the area's top chefs, sampling local game is a must.

The Green Heart is great for getting away from it all. The area is well supplied with hotels of all sizes and types, small resorts, and country inns in the woods. Rather than staying in a town, head for one of the village hotels—some are simple, others have a country-house atmosphere, but all have a special charm and relaxing sense of isolation.

Seven hundred years before the European Common Market or the European Union, there was an association of northern European trading cities called the Hanseatic League. It began as a pact among itinerant merchants to travel together for mutual safety, but in time it became an alliance of more than 80 cities scattered over the Continent, including major ports, such as London, Lübeck, Bremen, Hamburg, Cologne, Danzig, Stockholm, Novgorod, and Bergen, as well ~~~ cities on the rivers and coastline of what is now the Netherlands. T~~~~ e was to consult with one another on matters of trading ro~~~~ uniformity of regulations governing trade. Three of th~~~ that were important members of that league are in the ~~~ along the river IJssel, which connects the Rhine with the ~~~ of water known today as IJsselmeer, an open sea (the Zu~~~ the 13th century. After the national park and its captiva~~~ seum, these Hansa towns make an interesting stopover.

Exploring the Green Heart

The Hoge Veluwe National Park and the Royal Forest li~~~ of the Netherlands. Farther east, arranged in an arc t~~~ from north to south are the historic Hanseatic towns an~~~ visit to the Hoge Veluwe National Park and Kröller-Mü~~~ can easily fill an entire day. Allow another day to explore ~~~ of the park and at least another two days to get the mo~~~ Hanseatic towns.

Fall is the ideal time to visit this region. Not only do th~~~ offer all sorts of delicious game dishes, but De Hoge Ve~~~ tacular at this time of year; stretches of the park were espe~~~ with trees that make a mosaic of reds, oranges, and brow~~~

Numbers in the text correspond to numbers in the marg~~~ Green Heart map.

Apeldoorn

55 *89 km (56 mi) east of Amsterdam.*

Though not much of an attraction in itself, the small city ~~~ is the gateway to the Royal Forest and other delights of the~~~ When heiress Hélène Müller married industrialist Anton ~~~ turn of the century, their combined wealth and complen~~~ were destined to give pleasure for generations to come. T~~~ wander through the vast forests of the Hoge Veluwe N~~~ land bought up by Anton, and see the descendants of ~~~ and deer with which he stocked the estate. Or you can ~~~ seum in the middle of the park, established by Hélène a~~~ one of the best collections of Van Goghs in the world, ~~~ excellent selection of late-19th-century and modern art. ~~~ caper about the extensive sculpture garden, and the wh~~~ pick up one of the free bikes that are available in the p~~~ dle off down wooded lanes.

Built in 1685 on the site of a 14th- and 15th-century ca~~~ ing lodge, and serving as a country residence for Willi~~~ wife Mary Stuart (daughter of James II of England), **Pale~~~** Loo Palace) expanded into a full-blown royal palace wh~~~ became king and queen of England. Mary's quarters w~~~ wing and William's to the west. Constructed of brick and ~~~ what are said to be the world's first sash windows, the p~~~ Baroque and has formal French gardens. An avenue of ta~~~ to the central courtyard, where you enter through a high~~~

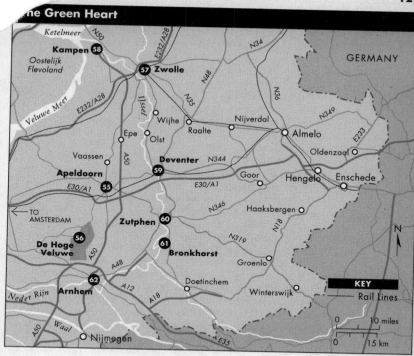

Exhibits fill some of the rooms, and there is a video that documents the building's history and restoration prior to its opening to the public in 1984. Many other rooms are furnished as they had been for William and Mary, but rooms are also maintained in the manner in which they were used by later Dutch monarchs, including Queen Wilhelmina, who was the grandmother of the current queen. Wilhelmina was the last regent to make this her home and died here in 1962. Queen Mary's kitchen, where she made jam, is particularly appealing for the sense of homeyness it gives to the palace. The four gardens, meticulously and formally planted, are decorated with statues and fountains, and lined with tall trees. There are separate King's and Queen's Gardens; the King's is dominated by plantings in blue and orange, the colors of the Dutch royal family. Don't miss the stable; it is full of old royal carriages, including the toy car used by the current crown prince of the Netherlands when he was a child. ⊠ *Amersfoortseweg 1,* ☎ *055/577–2409.* ◻ *Fl 12.50.* ☉ *Tues.–Sun. 10–5.*

⑤⑥ The **De Hoge Veluwe** public nature reserve covers more than 13,000 acres of forest and rolling grassland. The traditional hunting grounds of the Dutch royal family, it is populated with deer, boar, and many birds; it is also filled with towering pines and hardwood trees (oak, beech, and birch), dotted with small villages (**Hoge Soeren**, near Apeldoorn, is particularly charming), and laced with paths for cars, bicycles, and walkers. There is a landlocked, always shifting sand dune to marvel at; the world's first museum of all things that live (or have lived) underground; plus an old hunting lodge, beside a dam, that provides a nice stopping place. You'll find racks of bikes here and there in the park, available free of charge; just be sure to return the bike to any bike rack when you are finished using it. The visitors center contains exhibits on the park and an observation point for animal-watching. ⊠ *Entrances at Hoenderloo, Otterloo, and Schaarsbergen,* ☎ *0318/*

591–627. ☏ *Fl 8; cars Fl 8.* ⏲ *Oct.–Mar., daily 9–6; Apr.–May, daily 8–8; June–Aug., daily 8–10; Sept., daily 9–8.*

The **Kröller-Müller Museum** ranks as the third most important museum of art in the Netherlands, after the Rijksmuseum and the Vincent van Gogh Museum in Amsterdam. Opened in 1938, it is the repository of a remarkable private collection of late-19th-century and early-20th-century paintings, including 278 works by Van Gogh that, when combined with the collection in the Amsterdam museum, constitutes nearly his entire oeuvre. Hélène Kröller, née Müller, the wife of a prosperous industrialist, had a remarkable eye for talent and a sixth sense about which painters and paintings would be important. Her first purchase was Van Gogh's *Sunflowers.* Among his other well-known paintings in her collection are *Potato Eaters, The Bridge at Arles,* and *L'Arlesienne,* copied from a drawing by Gauguin. But Hélène Kröller-Müller was not myopic in her appreciation and perception. She augmented her collection of Van Goghs with works by Seurat, Picasso, Redon, Braque, and Mondrian. The museum also contains 16th- and 17th-century Dutch paintings, ceramics, Chinese and Japanese porcelain, and contemporary sculpture. The building itself, which was designed by Henry van de Velde, artfully brings nature into the galleries through its broad windows, glass walkways, and patios. The gardens and woods around the museum form an open-air gallery, with a collection of 20th-century sculptures by Aristide Maillol, Jean Dubuffet, Richard Serra, and Claes Oldenburg; works by Barbara Hepworth and Alberto Giacometti are under in a special pavilion added in 1953. ✉ *Houtkampweg 6, in National Park De Hoge Veluwe,* ☎ *0318/591–041.* 🎫 *Park and museum Fl 14.* ⏲ *Park and museum Tues.–Sun. 10–5; sculpture garden Tues.–Sun. 10–4:30.*

More than 350 monkeys, apes, chimpanzees, and gorillas wander free in the woods at **Apenheul** park. Some saunter right up to visitors, and there are also bright flocks of tropical birds. When the weather is cold, the animals disappear into snug nooks in the forest. Watch your bags—some of the apes are adept pickpockets. ✉ *JC Wilslaan 21, Park Berg en Bos, 7313 HK,* ☎ *055/357–5757.* 🎫 *Fl 17.50.* ⏲ *Apr.–June, daily 9:30–5; July–Aug., daily 9:30–6, Sept.–Oct., daily 10–5.*

Dining and Lodging

$$$ ★ ✕ **Echoput.** Not far from Het Loo Palace, Echoput is a much-honored and gracious country restaurant. The large fireplace in the lounge is welcoming in winter, the terrace in summer. With the royal hunting grounds nearby, the restaurant is able to offer fine game dishes nearly year-round. ✉ *Amersfoortseweg 86,* ☎ *055/519–1248. Reservations essential. AE, DC, MC, V. Closed Mon.*

$$$ **De Keizerskroon Bilderberg.** A nice cross between a business hotel and a country inn, it is within easy walking distance of Het Loo Palace. Renovations over the past 25 years have obliterated all traces of traditional architecture; in its place is a stylish hotel, with rooms decorated in pastels and furniture that, like the hotel, is a blend of business practical and weekend comfortable. ✉ *Koningstraat 7, 7315 HR,* ☎ *055/521–7744,* FAX *055/521–4737. 101 rooms, 7 suites. Exercise room, pool, sauna, meeting rooms. AE, DC, MC, V.*

$$ **Hotel Oranjeoord.** In a small woodland village that seems to be right out of a Grimm's fairy tale, the Oranjeoord is a relaxed country hotel with garden rooms, terraces, and a sunny dining room. It is a pleasant choice for a country weekend. ✉ *Hoog Soeren 134, 7346 AH, 5 km (3 mi) west of Apeldoorn,* ☎ *055/519–1227,* FAX *055/519–1451. 27 rooms with bath, 1 apt. Restaurant, meeting rooms. No credit cards.*

$ ⊞ **Astra.** On a quiet residential side street, Astra is a small pension-style family hotel that is comfortably furnished in the manner of a Dutch home. Rooms are large for this type of accommodation. There is a pleasant garden terrace behind the house. ⊠ *Bas Backerlaan 12–14, 7316 DZ,* ☏ *055/522–3022,* ℻ *055/522–3021. 28 rooms. Exercise room. AE, DC, MC, V.*

$ ⊞ **De Pomphul.** Owners Mr. and Mrs. Lochem are welcoming hosts at their pension in the tranquil village of Hoog Soeren, near the spring that provides water to Het Loo Palace. It makes an ideal base for exploring the Hoge Veluwe nature reserve on foot or by bicycle. The rooms, though basic, are impeccably clean and comfortable. ⊠ *Hoog Soeren 18, 7346 AH, 5 km (3 mi) west of Apeldoorn,* ☏ *055/519–1136,* ℻ *055/519–1136. 15 rooms with bath. Restaurant. No credit cards.*

Nightlife and the Arts

Incomparable for atmosphere are the concerts on the last Friday of every month at the beautiful **Paleis Het Loo** (⊠ Koninklijk Park 1, ☏ 055/521–2244).

Outdoor Activities and Sports

BIKING

In De Hoge Veluwe national park there are *free* bicycles (a total of 400 vehicles) for use on the 42 km (26 mi) of bicycle paths as well as special cycles for people with disabilities.

TENNIS AND SQUASH

Facilities in the region include **De Maten Sports** (⊠ Ambachtsveld 2, ☏ 055/542–5044).

Shopping

Market days in Apeldoorn are Monday and Wednesday mornings and Saturday at Marktplein in the city center. The late shopping nights are Thursday in the city center, Friday in the suburbs.

Zwolle

57 *41 km (26 mi) north of Apeldoorn, 103 km (65 mi) east of Amsterdam.*

Zwolle was an important depot for trade between the Netherlands and Germany during the time of the Hanseatic League, located as it is between the IJssel and another important Dutch river, the Vecht. Founded in 800, it officially became a town in the 12th century. An important Latin school was in Zwolle, and the religious philosopher Thomas à Kempis lived here in the early 1400s, when he wrote his influential work *Imitation of Christ.* Today Zwolle is an important center of cattle trading, grain processing, coffee roasting, and linen manufacturing.

The brick- and stone-embellished **Sassenpoort,** the only one of the original town gates of 1406 left standing, was for centuries a prison. Nowadays only exhibits and photographs on the theme of Zwolle's history are confined within its towers. ⊠ *Sassenstraat,* ☏ *no phone.* ▦ *Free.* ☉ *Weekdays 10–5, weekends noon–5.*

The **Grote Kerkplein** is the main square of Zwolle and the site of the Gothic Stadhuis (Town Hall). There is also a charming shop, **Zwolse Balletjes Huis** (⊠ Grote Kerkplein 13, ☏ 038/421–8815), that sells the local sweet specialty, *Zwollse balletjes* (fruit-and-spice-flavored hard candies).

The Gothic **St. Michaelskerk** dates from 1446 and contains a magnificent 18th-century organ made by the Schnitger brothers from Hamburg. The church is the final resting place of the 17th-century genre painter Gerard Terborch, who was born in Zwolle. ⊠ *Grote Kerkplein,* ☏ *06/911–22375. ☉ Limited visiting hrs.*

The **Stedelijk Museum Zwolle** (Zwolle Municipal Museum) is housed in a building that dates from the mid-16th century. Its principal display is the wainscoted living-dining Blokzil Room, which came from a house in the north part of the province and exemplifies the lifestyle of a prosperous 17th-century family. ⊠ *Broerenkerkplein 15,* ☎ *038/ 421–4650.* 🎫 *Fl 5.* ☉ *Tues.–Sat. 10–5, Sun. 1–5.*

Dining and Lodging

$$$ ✕ **De Librije.** Housed in the former library of a 15th-century monastery,
★   this atmospheric restaurant is known far afield for the excellence of its cuisine. Try the delicious *polderduif,* wild pigeon from the surrounding waterlands, served with a sauce of local berries. ⊠ *Broerenkerkplein 13,* ☎ *038/423–2329. Reservations essential. Jacket required. AE, DC, MC, V. No lunch Sat. Closed Sun.*

$$$ 🏨 **Bilderberg Grand Hotel Wientjes.** Convenient to both the railway station and the city center, this hotel occupies a stately old building. Most rooms are in the modern wings and are both spacious and brightly decorated. It also has theme rooms, including one styled in Old Dutch and a Chinese-style bridal suite with a lacquered four-poster bed and a two-person bubble bath. ⊠ *Stationsweg 7, 8011 CZ,* ☎ *038/425–4254,* 📠 *038/425–4260. 56 rooms, 1 suite. Restaurant, meeting rooms, no-smoking rooms. AE, DC, MC, V.*

Nightlife

Every Friday is Mellow Night at **Café 't Zonnetje** (⊠ Luttekestraat 6, ☎ 038/423–5293), but other nights explode with live music as people knock back cut-price cocktails. **JC Hedon** (⊠ Papenstraat 5, ☎ 038/ 423–1423) is the hottest, hippest dance club in town, though at press time it was keeping an eye open for new premises.

Outdoor Activities and Sports

CANOEING

In summer it's possible, and highly pleasurable, to canoe on the waterways in and around Zwolle. **Vadesto Kanocentrum** (⊠ Veenrand 5, 8051 DW, Hattem, ☎ 038/444–5428) at the Potgietersingel rents canoes. The **VVV** (Zwolle tourist information office; ☞ Visitor Information *in* The Green Heart A to Z, *below*) sells canoeing maps.

FISHING

Fishing in the streams of Overijssel province near Zwolle is easy and pleasurable. The VVV Zwolle tourist information office (☞ Visitor Information *in* The Green Heart A to Z, *below*) sells one-day fishing licenses for Fl 5. The license includes a list of fishing sites. The tourist office also has a helpful map of the area.

JOGGING

There is a training circuit in Zwolle at the **Haersterveerweg.** Near the center of town are two places suitable for jogging, **Park De Weezenlanden** and **Park 't Engelse Werk.**

TENNIS AND SQUASH

There are good tennis and squash facilities at **Sportpark de Marslanden** (⊠ Marsweg, ☎ 038/421–7189), **Sportpark Wilhelmina** (⊠ Wilhelminastraat, ☎ 038/421–4826), **Squash Zwolle** (⊠ Near Winkelcentrum Aalanden, ☎ 038/454–8485), and **Tenniscentrum Zwolle** (⊠ Palestrinalaan, ☎ 038/454–5100).

Shopping

Market days in Zwolle are Friday morning and Saturday. On Friday, especially, the farmers come to town, and stalls spread through Melkmarkt, Sassenstraat, Grote Markt, Nieuwe Markt, and Grote Kerkplein. On Thursday morning there's an **organically grown produce market** on Grote Kerkplein. Late shopping is on Thursday.

OFF THE
BEATEN PATH South of Zwolle, follow signs for Wijhe-Olst for a scenic drive along the IJssel River, passing rich marshes filled with wildlife and lush plants. This region, between the river and the German border, is known as the **Salland**. A quiet farming area, with its own dialect, it produces asparagus and offers food specialties such as kruitmoes (hot porridge with raisins).

Kampen

58 *14 km (9 mi) northwest of Zwolle, 115 km (71 mi) northeast of Amsterdam.*

Kampen was a wealthy town and a member of the Hanseatic League when its harbor silted up near the end of the Middle Ages. The best view of the ancient skyline is from the **Oude IJsselbrug** (old bridge) across the river. From the bridge, you can take a medieval circuit past the defensive city gates: stroll down the waterfront to the **Koornmarktpoort** (Grain Market Gate) on IJsselkade, recognizable by its two 14th-century towers. Peek into the **Sint Nikolaskerk** (St. Nicholas church) on the Koornmarkt, then cross over to the old moat and Ebbingstraat where **Cellebroederspoort** (Cellebroeders Gate) still stands; farther north on Ebbingstraat is the **Broederpoort** (Broeder Gate). The 14th-century **Oude Raadhuis** is only one of many gabled houses on Oude Straat. The statues on its facade depict Charlemagne, Alexander the Great, and less martial figures representing Moderation, Fidelity, Justice, and Love. Inside, the *Schepenzaal* (Magistrates' Hall) is an excellent example of a medieval courtroom. ⊠ *Oudestraat 133,* ☎ *038/ 339–2999.* 🎫 *Fl 2.* ⊙ *Weekdays 10–4, Sat. 2–4.*

The **Stedelijk Museum Kampen** (Kampen Municipal Museum), occupies a perfectly preserved merchant's house. Its exhibits focus on local history and industry, such as eel-fishing and cigar-making. ⊠ *Oudestr 158,* ☎ *038/331–7361.* 🎫 *Fl 3.* ⊙ *Tues.–Sat. 11–5, Sun. 1–5.*

Deventer

59 *35 km (22 mi) south of Zwolle, 18 km (11 mi) east of Apeldoorn, 107 km (67 mi) east of Amsterdam.*

Founded late in the 8th century by an English cleric named Lubuinus, whose mission in life was to convert the Saxons to Christianity, Deventer was a prosperous port and a powerful bishopric by the 9th century; the town center still reflects this medieval heritage. A center of learning as well, it had a printing industry to disseminate the thoughts of its scholars. It was home at various times to Thomas à Kempis; Pope Adrian VI; Erasmus; and, in the 17th century, French philosopher René Descartes. Deventer has won prizes for the meticulous renovation of its historic houses and public buildings.

Deventer's late Gothic **Waag** (Weigh House), begun in 1528, is a stately testament to the city's Hanseatic past. Inside, an exhibition on town history, from prehistoric times to the present day, includes the Netherlands' oldest bicycle, the spindly *Vélociède,* built in 1870. ⊠ *Brink 56,* ☎ *0570/693–780.* ⊙ *Tues.–Sat. 10–5, Sun. 2–5.*

Two huge medieval houses barely contain the **Speelgoed-en Blikmuseum** (Toys and Tin Museum), an enchanting collection of toys dating from the Middle Ages to the 20th century. There are dolls, puppets, and tin soldiers galore and an exceptional collection of mechanical toys and electric trains. In the museum's darkroom you can see a 17th-century magic lantern and a host of other optical playthings. ⊠ *Brink 47,* ☎ *0570/693–786.* 🎫 *Fl 5.* ⊙ *Tues.–Sat. 10–5, Sun. 2–5.*

The 13th-century Romanesque Gothic **Bergkerk** (Church of the Berg Quarter) sits high on a square with pleasing views down medieval side streets (Bergstraat and Roggestraat are particularly appealing). ⊠ *Bergkerkplein.* 🎫 *Free.* ⊙ *Tues.–Fri. 11–5, weekends 1–5.*

NEED A BREAK?	**Chez Antoinette** (⊠ Roggestraat 10–12, ☎ 0570/016–630) is a restaurant-pub whose menu honors the owners' fascination with everything Portuguese. The building dates from 1303, and the pub (open for lunch and snacks) is the oldest in the city (from 1881).

The **Lubuinuskerk** (St. Lubuinus's Church), a huge stone cross basilica that was built in the 10th century on the site of Lubuinus's small wooden church, has some fine 16th-century murals and a 700-year-old paved floor. Hanging in the 15th-century tower is the oldest extant carillon made by the Hemony brothers, who in the 17th century were the most celebrated bell makers in the world. The tower can be climbed in the summer months for a wide view of the town; the carillon is played at least twice a week. ⊠ *Grote Kerkhof.* 🎫 *Free.* ⊙ *Weekdays 10–5, Sat. 1:30–5.*

Nightlife

De Waagschaal (⊠ Brink 77, ☎ 0570/617–190) is one of the most popular of the concentration of brown cafés on Deventer's main square. A bicycle and other eccentric decor hang on the wall at **Lightenhill's Pub** (⊠ Brink 50–51, ☎ 0570/619–889), which has a range of British beers, such curiously named snacks as Ma Baker's Bitterballs, and occasional live bands.

Outdoor Activities and Sports

Energetic locals in Deventer head for the **Tennis en Squashcentrum** (⊠ Bremenweg 29, ☎ 0570/622–107).

Shopping

Friday and Saturday are market days in Deventer, when the Brink is crowded with fresh-produce stalls and a few antiques dealers. On the first Sunday in August the largest **book market** in the Netherlands stretches for 3 km (2 mi) along the IJssel.

Zutphen

🏠 *15 km (9 mi) south of Deventer, 22 km (14 mi) southeast of Apeldoorn, 107 km (67 mi) east of Amsterdam.*

Known as the Tower City for the many spires that rise above its center, Zutphen is on a small hill at the juncture of the rivers IJssel and Berkel. It was one of the region's wealthiest towns during the 14th and 15th centuries. Today, the charming, once-walled town is a patchwork of medieval houses and courtyards, churches and towers, and the remnants of old city gates.

The small **Henriette Polak Museum** offers changing exhibitions from its substantial collection of 20th-century Dutch figurative art. Climb the stairs to the attic to see the tiny room used in the 17th century as a *schuilkerk*, a secret Roman Catholic church. ⊠ *Zaadmarkt 88,* ☎ *0575/516–878.* 🎫 *Fl 5.* ⊙ *Tues.–Fri. 11–5, weekends 1:30–5.*

NEED A BREAK?	**De Pelikaan** (⊠ Pelikaanstraat 6, ☎ 0575/512–024), a coffee and tea emporium dating from the late 1880s, is filled with heady aromas. In the adjacent tearoom you can take your pick from a long list of tea and coffee blends.

St. Walburgskerk (St. Walburgis Church) was begun in the 12th century in Romanesque style and enlarged in the 16th century in Gothic style. It is busy with roofs and a wide variety of building materials. Within, the side walls and vaults are ornamented with 14th- and 15th-century frescoes; the richly decorated organ loft contains a Baeder organ. The **Librije** (library), in a side chapel, is where you'll find the true treasures of Zutphen: This library dates from 1561, and under its white, vaulted ceilings are rare and beautiful early manuscripts and incunabula, chained to rows of reading stands. ⊠ *Kerkhof 3,* ☎ *0575/514–178.* 🎫 *Fl 3.50; combined with walking tour Fl 5.* ☉ *May–Sept., tours Mon. at 2 and 3, Tues.–Sat. at 11, 2, and 3.*

Dining and Lodging

$ ✕🍴 **Berkhotel.** With a stream running by outside and rooms decorated in English country style (with pastels and floral prints), this hotel doesn't seem to be almost in the heart of town. The restaurant has a grand ambience, with chandeliers, live piano music, palms, and candlelight; the cuisine is strictly vegetarian, prepared with an Asian touch. ⊠ *Marspoortstraat 19, 7201 JA,* ☎ *0575/511–135,* 🖷 *0575/541–950. 19 rooms, 10 with bath/shower, 1 suite. Restaurant, bar, lounge. AE, MC, V.*

Nightlife

Café 't Winkeltje (⊠ Groenmarkt 34, ☎ 0575/511–804) is a welcoming brown café with a mixed crowd, rock and golden oldies over the sound system, and a good assortment of specialty beers.

Shopping

On Thursday morning there's a busy market in the center of town. Late shopping is on Friday.

Bronkhorst

㊛ *9 km (5 mi) south of Zutphen.*

Bronkhorst, the tiniest town in the Netherlands, has a population of just 160. The entire hamlet is protected by the national historic preservation program. There are curious little museums and shops here, as well as an exceptionally good restaurant. The 14th-century chapel is particularly attractive and peaceful.

Dining and Lodging

$$$ ✕🍴 **Herberg de Gouden Leeuw.** This is a peaceful country inn that happens to have an excellent restaurant, with formal and informal dining areas and a fireplace in the lounge. On Saturday night, diners are entertained with piano music. The cuisine is traditional Continental, with such choices as beef bourguignonne and veal cordon bleu. Game, asparagus, and lobster are served in season. Special three- to six-course menus are available. The guest rooms are simple and are inexpensively priced. ⊠ *Bovenstraat 2, 7226 LM,* ☎ *0575/451–231,* 🖷 *0575/452–566. 12 rooms, 2 with shower, 1 suite. Restaurant. AE, DC, MC, V.*

Arnhem

㊷ *25 km (16 mi) south of Apeldoorn, 92 km (58 mi) southeast of Amsterdam.*

Arnhem is best known as the "bridge too far." Near the end of World War II the Allies followed up the invasion of Normandy by seeking to cut off the German army entrenched in the eastern Netherlands. The battle involved the largest airborne operation of the war, and 3,000 British, American, and Canadian lives were lost in three weeks of fighting that left the Allies short of their goal, which was finally achieved seven months later.

The **Airborne Museum** includes a large scale model of the Arnhem region and incorporates memorabilia, weapons, and equipment to depict the crucial battle that took place here during World War II. Tanks and guns sit on the lawn, and an audiovisual presentation describes the progress of the battle. ⊠ *Utrechtseweg 232, Oosterbeek,* ☎ *026/ 333–7710.* ▒ *Fl 6.* ☾ *Mon.–Sat. 11–5, Sun. and holidays noon–5.*

Much of Arnhem was destroyed during World War II, but around the **Korenmarkt** old warehouses have become pubs, cafés, restaurants, and dance clubs, preserving a sense of the old town in a cozy entertainment area. A weekly market is held in the shadows of Arnhem's **Grote Kerk** (Great Church), a three-aisle cross-basilica that dates back to the 15th century. The church is also the site of traveling exhibitions. Among Arnhem's chief attractions are its trolley buses (unique in the Netherlands) and its extensive surrounding parkland, including the 185-acre **Sonsbeek Park.**

The **Nederlands Openlucht Museum** (Open Air Museum), in a 44-acre park, re-creates Dutch country life through farm buildings typical of their regions, transported to the site from every province of the Netherlands. Here you can see furnished farmhouses, outbuildings, windmills, and crafts shops in a setting that reflects the varied nature of the Dutch landscape. The museum is on the northern outskirts of town. ⊠ *Schelmseweg 89,* ☎ *026/357–6111.* ▒ *Fl 17.* ☾ *Apr.–Jan., daily 10–5.*

☙ More than 3,000 animals inhabit **Burgers' Zoo** in Arnhem. Established in 1913 on the principle that there should be as few barriers as possible between human beings and animals, this zoo includes a large safari park with roaming lions, zebras, giraffes, and rhinos, plus a tropical rain forest and a subtropical desert. ⊠ *Schelmseweg 85,* ☎ *026/ 442–4534 or 026/445–0373.* ▒ *Fl 23.50.* ☾ *May–Oct. 9–7, last safari at 5; Nov.–Apr. 9–sunset, last safari at 4.*

Dining and Lodging

$$$ ✕ **Kasteel Doorwerth.** This restaurant offers a rare experience: dining in a moated castle near the Rhine, 8 km (5 mi) from Arnhem. The timbered dining room, once the castle's coach house, is furnished with antiques, and the cuisine is in the new, French-inspired Dutch mode; vegetables and herbs come from the castle gardens. ⊠ *Fonteinallee 4, Doorwerth,* ☎ *026/333–3420. Reservations essential. AE, DC, MC, V. Closed Tues.*

$$–$$$ ✕ **Belvedere.** This noted place to dine is actually in the neighboring town of Nijmegen. Housed in a tall tower high on a hill in the middle of Belvedere Park, overlooking a wide bend in the river Waal, it has possibly the best river view in the Netherlands. In the beamed dining room are only a handful of tables; the menu is new Dutch cooking, including choices such as duck breast in an envelope of goose liver. ⊠ *Kelfkensbos 60, Nijmegen,* ☎ *024/322–6861. Reservations essential. AE, DC, MC, V. No lunch Sat., Mon. Closed Sun.*

$$$ ☗ **Hotel de Bilderberg.** In a wooded setting in the suburb of Oosterbeek, de Bilderberg caters to business travelers as well as weekenders. The rooms are spacious and bright, with comfortable modern furnishings. ⊠ *Utrechtseweg 261, 6862 AK, Oosterbeek,* ☎ *026/334–0843,* ℻ *026/333–4651. 144 rooms. Restaurant, bar, indoor pool, sauna, exercise room, tennis court, meeting room. AE, DC, MC, V.*

$ ☗ **Hotel Blanc.** This small hotel is not far from the railway station in central Arnhem. In a turn-of-the-century town house, the Blanc offers bright and comfortable rooms and a friendly café for guests. ⊠ *Coehoornstraat 4, 6811 LA,* ☎ *026/442–8072,* ℻ *026/443–4749. 22 rooms, 18 with shower, 1 suite. Restaurant, bar, lounge. AE, DC, MC, V.*

$ 🖼 **Hotel Molendal.** In an Art Deco–era house in a residential neighborhood near Sonsbeek Park, the hotel has spacious and high-ceilinged rooms. Decorative elements in public spaces carry out the Art Deco heritage of the building, while the bedrooms have a more modern design. ✉ *Cronjestraat 15, 6814 AG,* ☎ *026/442–4858,* FAX *026/443–6614. 12 rooms with shower, 1 suite. Bar, lounge. AE, DC, MC, V.*

Shopping

Market days in Arnhem are Friday morning and Saturday at Kerkplein. Late shopping is on Thursday.

OFF THE
BEATEN PATH

The pre-Roman city of **Nijmegen** lies strategically near the junction of the Maas–Waalkanal and the river Waal. The river is the main branch of the Rhine and the second of the great rivers of the Netherlands that lead to the North Sea. Nijmegen is a lively university town and shopping center for the region, as well as gateway to the southern provinces. The city's **Belvedere Park** offers a splendid view of the river below and a restaurant in a tower (☞ *above*). Nearby is the **Waalkade** riverfront esplanade, lined with restaurants, shops, and a casino, a pleasant place to stroll.

The Green Heart A to Z

Arriving and Departing

BY CAR

From Amsterdam, take A1 to Apeldoorn and Deventer or Zutphen; A2 and A12 to Arnhem; or A1 and A28 to Zwolle. Nijmegen is easily reached from Arnhem by A325.

BY TRAIN

Frequent **express Intercity trains** (☎ 0900/9292) link Amsterdam with Apeldoorn, Deventer, Zwolle, Arnhem, and Nijmegen. To reach Zutphen by train, change in either Arnhem or Zwolle.

Getting Around

BY BICYCLE

Free bicycles are provided for visitors in the national park De Hoge Veluwe. In the cities of this region, you can also **rent a bicycle** at railway stations or in Apeldoorn from **Blakborn** (✉ Soerenseweg 3, ☎ 055/521–5679), **Harleman** (✉ Arnhemseweg 28, ☎ 055/533–4346), and **M. Janssen** (✉ Koninginnelaan 54, ☎ 055/521–2582); in Arnhem from **Mantel** (✉ 95 Lawick van Pabststraat, ☎ 026/442–0624), **H. Matser** (✉ 784 Kemperbergweg, ☎ 026/442–3172), and **R.W. Roelofs** (✉ 1 G.A. van Nispenstraat, ☎ 026/442–6014); and in Zwolle from **Scholten** (✉ Luttekestraat 7, ☎ 038/421–7378).

BY BUS

There is a comprehensive network of local and regional **bus services** in the Green Heart. They provide a useful supplement to the train service (for information, ☎ 0900/9292).

BY TAXI

Taxis wait at city railway stations; additional stands may be available in central shopping and hotel districts. To call a **taxi:** Apeldoorn (☎ 055/541–3413), Arnhem (☎ 026/445–0000), Deventer (☎ 0570/626–200 or 0570/622–537), Nijmegen (☎ 024/322–6000 or 024/323–3000), Zutphen (☎ 0575/525–345 or 05755/512–935), or Zwolle (☎ 038/455–1133).

Contacts and Resources

EMERGENCIES

National Emergency Alarm Number for police, fire, and ambulance: ☎ 112. **Hospitals: Apeldoorn** (☎ 055/581–8181), **Arnhem** (☎ 026/

321–0000), **Deventer** (☎ 0570/646–666), **Zutphen** (☎ 0575/592–592), and **Zwolle** (☎ 038/429–9911 or 038/426–2222).

The tourist offices (☞ Visitor Information, *below*) in most cities in the region organize walking tours in the summer months. Inquire for times, minimum group size, and whether or not English translation is offered or can be arranged.

In summer (late June–late Aug.) the **VVV Apeldoorn** (☎ 0900/1681636 or 055/578–8884) offers a variety of tours through the surrounding nature parks, including a three-hour combined bus tour and evening walk through parts of the Royal Forest not usually open to the public (Fl 12.50).

VVV Apeldoorn (⊠ Stationstraat 72, 7311 MH, ☎ 0900/1681636 or 055/578–8884, ℻ 055/521–1290). **VVV Arnhem Region** (⊠ Stationsplein 45, 6811 KL, ☎ 0900/2024075 or 026/442–6767, ℻ 026/442–2644). **VVV Deventer** (⊠ Keizerstraat 22, 7411 HH, ☎ 0570/613–100, ℻ 0570/643–338). **VVV Zutphen** (⊠ Groenmarkt 40, 7201 HZ, ☎ 0575/519–355, ℻ 0575/517–928). **VVV Zwolle** (⊠ Grote-Kerkplein 14, 8011 PK, ☎ 0900/122375, ℻ 038/422–2679).

THE NORTH

In the northern provinces of the Netherlands, life is more peaceful; there are quiet streams and a chain of sparkling lakes to tempt you to sample the outdoor life. For the most part, museums are small and quiet but have surprisingly rich displays, and there are luxury resorts hidden in small wooded villages that rival the attractions of the more cosmopolitan parts of the country. The people of Friesland are proud of their ancient culture. Their language, Fries, is very different from Dutch and spoken even among young people. Street signs are often in both languages.

Along the northwestern perimeter of the Netherlands, a short distance across the tidal mudflats of the Wadden Sea, lies the Wadden Islands chain. A large section of these islands is protected nature reserve, ecological sanctuaries of interest to bird-watchers and nature lovers. Visitors are not even allowed to take cars onto two of the islands. The islands are the perfect environment for cycling and walking. Regular ferry services provide easy access throughout the year.

The local pea soup, *snert,* is the ideal culinary weapon against icy Frisian winters. It has the consistency of thick porridge and often has bits of bacon or sausage floating in it. Fill up those extra corners with a slice of *karnemelkbrood* (buttermilk bread), and wash it down with warm milk, flavored with aniseed, or a mug of Frisian tea—served extra sweet.

Most of the main cities of the north are disappointing when it comes to finding interesting accommodations. If you're looking for something other than a standard, business-type hotel, turn your attention to smaller villages or to hotels converted from gracious old country houses, such as De Klinze at Oudkerk, or Landgoed Lauswolt at Beetsterzwaag.

Friesland has an unusual array of sporting activities, including sailing regattas, bike races, long-distance walks, a local version of pole-vaulting, and the *wadlopen,* or "horizontal mountain climbing," as the locals jokingly call it—wading thigh-deep across the mudflats to the Wadden Islands. It is exhausting work, but done with tremendous good cheer. After much laughing, shrieking, and sweating, the group finally arrives at its destination, and everyone dives into a good Frisian feast.

Each winter, as the weather worsens, a frisson of tension ripples through the country. Will this be a year for the *Elfstedentocht,* the "Eleven-Cities Tour"? This important skating race—between 11 Frisian towns—is only possible during severe freezes. The last one was in 1996, but prior to that, no Elfstedentocht had been held for 10 years. The origin of the race goes back hundreds of years, though it was only in 1909 that the present 200-km (120-mi) course was agreed upon. As well as the official race, which attracts participants from all over the world, there is an unofficial *Elfstedentocht* enjoyed by thousands. Spectators line the route, and wayside stalls sell copious amounts of warm food and drink. Whether you're up to such a grueling ordeal or not, the race can be great fun, and no one says you have to finish it. This picturesque route has also become a summertime favorite for cyclists.

You can get a good taste of the area by beginning in Leeuwarden, the capital of Friesland, then looping through the Frisian countryside and heading eastward to the thriving city of Groningen. From Harlingen there are ferries and a hydrofoil to the islands of Terschelling and Vlieland. Ameland can be reached from the port of Holwerd, while Schiermonikoog, the smallest of the islands, can be reached from the port of Lauwersoog.

Summer is the time to come if you like watersports and dislike cold weather. The Wadden Islands enjoy more sunlight per year than the rest of the Netherlands, but they are also slightly more abreeze with westerly winds. Mud-walking to the islands is only possible from May to September. But to get a true feel of the north, why not brave the winter, take your chances in the Elfstedentocht, and experience the delicious warmth of snert working its way throughout your body?

Numbers in the text correspond to numbers in the margin and on The North map.

Leeuwarden

⁶³ *132 km (83 mi) north of Amsterdam.*

An odd mixture of distinctions identifies the small provincial capital of Leeuwarden. On one hand, it was the official residence of the first hereditary *stadhouder* (king) of the Netherlands; on the other, it is believed to have been the birthplace of the notorious dancer-spy, Mata Hari. The *stadhouders* left a legacy of elegant architecture; the town's most infamous citizen is honored by a small statuette beside the canal.

Leeuwarden is the focal point of the Dutch dairy industry and site of one of the largest cattle markets in Europe. It also is home to one of the world's finest collections of Asian ceramics. The 200-km (124-mi) Elfenstedentocht (☞ *above*) ice-skating race departs from Leeuwarden when—or if—there is ice on the canals connecting the capital with 10 other cities of the province (including Harlingen, Franeker, Workum, Hindeloopen, Stavoren, and Sloten).

The **Nederlands Keramiekmuseum Het Princessehof** (The Netherlands Ceramics Museum–The Princess's Palace) takes pride of place in Leeuwarden. The former residence of Marie-Louise of Hesse-Kassell, the widow of the first prince of Orange, is a grand neoclassical monument. Her gracious dining room has been preserved. The Netherlands Ceramic Museum documents the history of fine ceramics, ancient and modern, Asian and European. The remarkable collection of Chinese

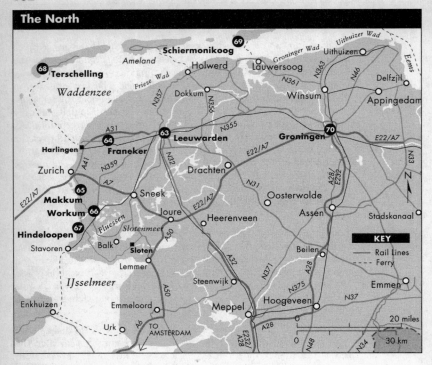

stoneware and porcelain dates from the third millennium BC through the 20th century. Look closely at the plates and tiles commissioned in China by the VOC (Dutch East India Company); you'll notice decidedly Asian features on Dutch-costumed merchants and their female companions. ⊠ *Grote Kerkstraat 11, from railway station, follow wide street across Nieuwestade canal, then jog left to next bridge and continue along Kleine Kerkstraat*, ☎ *058/212−7438*. ☒ *Fl 6.50*. ☽ *Tue.−Sat. 10−5, Sun. and holidays 2−5.*

Standing in a blissfully peaceful square, the 13th-century **Grotekerk** (Great Church), a Jacobin church, has been reconstructed and restored over the centuries, most recently in 1978; it is the traditional burial place of the Nassau line, ancestors of the royal family. ⊠ *Jacobinerkerkhof*, ☎ *058/215−1203*. ☒ *Free*. ☽ *June−Aug., Tues.−Fri. 2−4.*

The **Fries Museum en Verzetsmuseum** (Frisian Museum and Museum of the Resistance) occupies the **Kanselarij** (Chancellery), the ornate Renaissance building that was the residence of George of Saxony when he governed the region in the 16th century. The buildings across the road are linked to the main entrance lobby by an underground tunnel. Inside is a varied collection and period rooms documenting the history and culture of Friesland. Among its treasures is a portrait by Rembrandt of his wife, Saskia; she was the daughter of the mayor of Leeuwarden. The couple married in 1634 in the nearby village of St. Annaparochie. Mata Hari, that other famed daughter of Leeuwarden, has an exhibition to herself in the new wing with a permanent multimedia display about her mysterious life. ⊠ *Turfmarkt 11*, ☎ *058/212−3001*. ☒ *Fl 7.50*. ☽ *Mon.−Sat. 11−5, Sun. 1−5.*

Facing one another across the leafy **Hofplein** are Leeuwarden's **Stadhuis** (Town Hall) and **Hof**, which was the former residence of the Frisian stadhouders. In the center of the square is a statue of Willem Louis, the first stadhouder, locally known as *Us Heit* (Our Father).

The **Waagplein** has been the commercial hub of Leeuwarden for many centuries. Stretching along both sides of a canal, it is dominated by the redbrick **Waag** (Weigh House), decorated with heraldic lions. Built at the end of the 16th century, it was used as a weigh house for butter and cheese until the late 19th century; it now houses a bank and a restaurant.

NEED A BREAK?	In an old wooden Dutch sailing boat, you can enjoy a variety of traditional Dutch pancakes, both sweet and savory. The **Pannekoekschip** (Pancake Ship; ✉ Willemskade 69, ☎ 058/212-0903) is moored midway between the railway station and the center of town.

The weekly **Veemarkt** (cow market) is held in Leeuwarden on Friday morning at the Frieslandhal on the perimeter of town. It is one of the largest in Europe and offers a look into what this part of the Netherlands is really all about. ✉ *Helikonweg*, ☎ *058/294-1500.*

Dining and Lodging

$$$ ✗ **Van Essen.** Tucked away on a pedestrian street, this stylishly modern restaurant has quickly gained a reputation. The chef combines subtle Oriental influences with honest European ingredients. You might be offered a starter of sushi followed by a traditional roast duck or marinated peppers with anchovies and olives. ✉ *Oude Oosterstraat 7,* ☎ *058/212-9393. Reservations essential. AE, DC, MC, V. Closed Mon.–Tues; no lunch weekends.*

$ ✗ **Spinoza.** Three rooms, a cellar bar, and the shady garden courtyard of an 18th-century city mansion make up this popular restaurant. It is one of those cavernous spaces that, through the patina of age and subtle lighting, manages also to be intimate. The cuisine is a mixture of Frisian and Indonesian, so you can follow vegetable-and-cheese soup with chicken in a spicy peanut sauce. There is also a grill-room and a theater-restaurant for live performances. ✉ *Eewal 50–52,* ☎ *058/212-9393. AE, DC, MC, V.*

$$$$ ▥ **Landgoed De Klinze.** In a wooded town not far from Leeuwarden, De Klinze is a semi-resort created from a 17th-century country estate. The roomy suites in the manor house are decorated with vintage furniture and antiques; the bright and spacious guest rooms, decorated in a cheerful lemon-yellow and white, are in a separate, modern wing that also includes the spa. Dinner is in the former parlors, with views of the woods. The cuisine is French. ✉ *Van Sminiaweg 32–36, 9064 KC, Oudkerk, 10 km (6 mi) northeast of Leeuwarden,* ☎ *058/256-1050,* 🖷 *058/256-1060. 22 rooms, 5 suites. Restaurant, indoor pool, beauty salon, spa, bicycles, meeting rooms. AE, DC, MC, V.*

$$$ ✗▥ **Hotel Restaurant Van den Berg State.** A mere 328 yards from the city center, this stately mansion is surrounded by its own landscaped gardens. The rooms are exclusively luxurious, all with spacious bathrooms, and decorated with antiques and stylish soft furnishings. The fine restaurant serves traditional French haute cuisine. There are full-board gourmet midweek and weekend packages. ✉ *Verlengde Schrans 87, 8932 NL,* ☎ *058/280-0584,* 🖷 *058/288-3422. 6 rooms. Restaurant, bar, parking. Closed Christmas–New Year. AE, DC, MC, V.*

$$$ ▥ **Oranjehotel.** Primarily a business hotel, Oranjehotel is directly across from the railway station. The rooms are comfortable; the hotel is a local gathering place and has substantial conference facilities. There is a busy pub and a fine restaurant serving traditional Continental cuisine. ✉ *Stationsweg 4, 8911 AG,* ☎ *058/212-6241,* 🖷 *058/212-1441, 78 rooms. 2 restaurants, bar, in-room modem lines, laun-*

dry service and dry cleaning, business services, convention center, parking. AE, DC, MC, V.

$ ⚏ **Hotel de Pauw.** Across from the railway station, De Pauw has a Victorian feel, with heavy furniture in the lobby's café/bar. Rooms are simple but comfortable and the hosts are welcoming and friendly. ⊠ *Stationsweg 4, 8911 AH,* ☎ *058/212–3651,* ℻ *058/216–0793. 33 rooms. Restaurant, bar, parking. MC, V.*

Nightlife

Café Mukkes (⊠ Grote Hoogstraat 26, ☎ 058/215–9800) brings a rousing selection of local bands to a crowd of enthusiastic young fans. The generally tame nightlife scene in Leeuwarden is enlivened by **De Brouwershoeck** (⊠ Poststraat 21, ☎ 058/215–2916), a music café that offers live jazz, blues, and funk.

Outdoor Activities and Sports

Leeuwarden is a great base from which to set out to enjoy the area's many water sports and quirky indigenous activities or the island of Terschelling (☞ *below*).

CANOEING

Friesland offers a wealth of canoeing opportunities, along quiet countryside waterways and following canals through attractive towns. Canoeing routes have been laid out and special maps have been printed. Check with the respective tourist offices. Three of the largest canoe renting facilities in Friesland are **De Ulepanne/Balk** (⊠ Tsjamkedijkje 1, 8561 HA, Balk, ☎ 0514/602–982), **Makkumerstrand** (⊠ Suderseewei 19, 5784 GK, Makkum, ☎ 0515/232–285), and **Watersportbedrijf De Drijfveer** (⊠ U. Twijnstrawei 31, 8491 CJ, Akkrum, ☎ 0566/652–789).

KAATSEN

During the summer months, you will find local matches of the Frisian ball game *kaatsen* (similar to baseball) being played in villages throughout Friesland; major tournaments are held in August. For details of matches, contact the Koninklijke Nederlandse Kaatsbond (Royal Dutch Kaats Association; ☎ 0517/397–300).

FIERLJEPPEN

Another uniquely Frisian sport is *fierljeppen,* called *polsstokverspringen* in Dutch, which involves pole-vaulting over canals. It originates from farmers having to negotiate the drainage ditches between their fields. The main competition is held in Winsum in August. Further information about spectator events and organized participation is available from the Fierljeppenbond (☎ 0515/542–961).

SAILING AND BOATING

Friesland is bordered by the large and windswept IJsselmeer (Lake IJssel). The province is also cut with a swath of lakes, canals, and small rivers that offer sailing or boating opportunities. Throughout the summer you will find weekend racing on the Frisian lakes. The summer's main event is the two-week series of **Skûtjesilen Races** (late July) using the uniquely Dutch vessels, *skûtjes,* which are wide-bottom sailing barges built to navigate the shallow waters.

More than 150 companies throughout Friesland rent boats and sailboats, including **A.E. Wester en Zn., 'De Blieken'** (⊠ Garde Jagersweg 4–5, Postbus 51, 9001 ZB, Grou, ☎ 0566/621–335), **Botenverhuurbedrijf Grou** (⊠ Wilhelminastraat, 9001 KE, Grou, ☎ 0566/623–810), **Jachtwerf Frisia** (⊠ Oude Oppenhuizerweg 79, 8606 JC, Sneek, ☎ 0515/412–814), **Top En Twel Zeilcentrum** (⊠ It Ges 6, 8606 JK, Sneek, ☎ 0515/419–192), **Watersportbedrijf Anja** (⊠ Meersweg 9a, 9001 BG, Grou, ☎ 0566/621–373), and **Watersportcamping Heeg** (⊠ De Burd 25a, 8621 JX, Heeg, ☎ 0515/442–328).

WINDSURFING
Where there's water and a breeze there are windsurfers. In Friesland the following firms rent both equipment and wet suits: **De Ulepanne/Balk** (⊠ Tsjamkedykje 1, 8571 MS, Balk, ☎ 0514/602–982), **Jeugdherberg Oer 't Hout** (⊠ Raadhuisstraat 18, 9001 AG, Grou, ☎ 0566/621–528), and **Top En Twel Zeilcentrum** (⊠ It Ges 6, 8606 JT, Sneek, ☎ 0515/419–192).

Shopping
Leeuwarden's market days are Monday afternoon at Wilhelminaplein, Wednesday morning at Akkerstraat, Friday (until 3:30) at the Veemarkt. Late shopping is on Thursday.

Franeker

64 *17 km (11 mi) west of Leeuwarden.*

In the Middle Ages, Franeker was a leading academic town. Although there is no university here today, there are Renaissance gables aplenty, pretty canals, and one or two unusual museums.

The **Eise Eisinga Planetarium** is one man's attempt to demonstrate why the planets do not collide. In the late 18th century a local clergyman convinced the inhabitants that the end of the world was imminent, due to a collision of the planets. When his dire prediction failed to materialize, a local scoffer set out to help his neighbors understand why. One wonders what his wife must have thought, for Eise spent years turning his living-room ceiling into a continuously moving display of interplanetary action, and his home's closets and attic into storage for the workings needed to carry out his unusual experiment in education and home decoration. ⊠ *Eise Eisingastraat 3,* ☎ *0517/393–070.* 🖙 *Fl 5.* ☉ *Mid-Sept.–mid-Apr., Tues.–Sat. 10–5; mid-Apr.–mid-Sept., Tues.–Sat. 10–5, Sun.–Mon. 1–5.*

En Route Just a short drive through the flat Frisian waterlands brings you to the small port city of **Harlingen,** where the ferry leaves for the Wadden Island of Terschelling. A walk along its main canal will remind you of Amsterdam in that several homes are copies of canal houses in the capital. After Harlingen, avoid the N31 main road and take the smaller (unnumbered but signposted) road along the dike toward Zurich and Makkum. On one side sprawls farmland and waterlands rich in bird life. On the other, if you stop and climb the dike, you can look out across the Wadden Sea.

NEED A BREAK? Facing the main canal in Harlingen is the pleasant, small hotel-restaurant **Anna Casparii** (⊠ Noorderhaven 69, ☎ 0517/412–065, FAX 0517/414–540), where you can make an overnight stopover, have lunch or dinner, or just a coffee while overlooking the canal.

Makkum

65 *20 km (13 mi) south of Franeker, 37 km (23 mi) southwest of Leeuwarden.*

If you are a lover of fine pottery, you will know that multicolored Makkumware is as important and treasured in Dutch homes as the better-known blue-and-white Delftware. This tiny Frisian town, where it is produced, has some fine old buildings and a sleepy, country atmosphere.

Tichelaars Koninklijke Makkumer Aardewerk en Tegelfabriek (Tichelaar's Royal Makkum Pottery and Tile Factory), a small, family-owned concern that has made Makkumware under license from the royal family for 10 generations, invites you to watch the craftspeople at work; there is also a shop where you can buy the products of the sole supplier of Makkumware to the world. ⊠ *Turfmarkt 63,* ☎ *0515/ 231–341.* 🖃 *Fl 4.* ☉ *Tours Mon.–Thurs. 10–11:30 and 1–4; Fri. 10– 11:30 and 1–3; factory showrooms weekdays 9–5:30, Sat. 10–5.*

The **Fries Aardewerkmuseum De Waag** (Frisian Pottery Museum) is located in a late-17th-century weigh house and displays a small collection of ceramic tiles and other pottery that includes many contributions by the Tichelaar family. ⊠ *Waaggebouw, Pruikmakershoek 2,* ☎ *0515/231–422.* 🖃 *Fl 3.* ☉ *Apr.–Oct., Mon.–Sat. 10–5, Sun. 1:30–5; Nov.–Mar., weekdays 10–noon and 1–4.*

Workum

66 *10 km (6 mi) south of Makkum, 38 km (24 mi) southwest of Leeuwar-den.*

The small seaside town of Workum was once an important trading center and harbor. Today, all that hints of its past prosperity are a few streets of elegant 16th- and 17th-century architecture. But Workum is also home to one of the most-visited museums in Friesland.

One man's art fills the **Jopie Huisman Museum** and attracts 100,000 visitors a year to Workum. Jopie Huisman was born in Workum and lives here still in a house by an eel stream where he fishes every night. What is unusual about the man, and his art, is that he has been a junk man all his life, sketching and painting every chance he had. Without benefit of formal instruction, he produced an abundance of fine canvases and drawings, many reminiscent of the careful duplication of fabric and texture in the work of the early Dutch masters. Jopie Huisman, however, has made haunting compositions of the rags, worn shoes, and discarded dolls he collected in his travels. ⊠ *Noard 6,* ☎ *0515/543– 131.* 🖃 *Fl 5.* ☉ *Mar. and Nov., daily 1–5; Apr.–Oct., Mon.–Sat. 10– 5, Sun. 1–5.*

Hindeloopen

67 *6 km (4 mi) south of Workum, 44 km (28 mi) southwest of Leeuwar-den.*

On a slip of land projecting into the IJsselmeer, Hindeloopen is surrounded on three sides by water, crisscrossed by canals, and virtually stitched together by wooden bridges. Centuries ago, Hindeloopen was a spot favored by sea captains as a home base, and many old houses remain here. The town is also known for its colorful local costume and for its traditional painted furniture.

Museum Hidde Nijland Stichting is in a building that served as town hall from 1683 to 1919 and is brimming with the brightly painted 18th-century wooden furniture that is Hindeloopen's specialty. Finely decorated period rooms give you an idea of how more prosperous mariners lived in past centuries; the walls are covered in decorative 18th-century Frisian tiles. ⊠ *Dijkweg 1,* ☎ *0514/521–420.* 🖃 *Fl 3.50.* ☉ *Mar.– Oct., Mon.–Sat. 10–5, Sun. 1:30–5.*

En Route   From Hindeloopen you are within easy driving distance of the **Frisian Lakes,** which lure Dutch and international sailors and boating enthusiasts every summer. The N359, just outside Hindeloopen or Workum, takes you across the countryside and across the connecting land between one of the largest lakes and its outlet. The small fortified towns of **Sloten** and **Balk** are focal points in this water-dominated area of south-western Friesland, known as **Gaasterland.**

En Route   **Aldfaers Erf** (Our Forefathers' Heritage) is a route that weaves through the Frisian countryside in a small area bounded by the towns of Makkum, Bolsward, and Workum, stopping at 12 restored buildings and workshops. In Exmorra you can visit the agricultural museum, a village grocery, and a schoolroom; in Allingawier, a farm, church, painter's workshop, forge, bakery, and two residences; in Piaam, an ornithological museum; and in Ferwoude, a carpenter's workshop. You can follow the route by car or by bike throughout the year, but all of the stops on the way are open only from April through October. ⊠ *Information: Postbus 176, Bolsward,* ☎ *0515/575–681.* ☉ *Apr.– Oct., daily 10–5.*

Terschelling

🔀 *28 km (17 mi) west of Leeuwarden, 115 km (71 mi) north of Amsterdam.*

With just over 5,000 permanent residents, this 4,000-hectare (10,000-acre) member of the Wadden Island chain experiences a population explosion during high season. It is a favorite Dutch vacation spot, with 30 km (19 mi) of beautiful dunes and endless beaches only 1½ hours by ferry from Harlingen. Originally, the island's main industry was fishing and whaling. The **Oerol Festival** (for information, contact the VVV, ☞ Visitor Information *in* The North A to Z, *below*) started in 1986 as the brainchild of a local landlord. Held during the second and third weeks of June, using the whole island as the set for theatrical productions, it appropriately ends on midsummer night. It has grown into an international event attracting thousands of visitors.

West-Terschelling is the island's main port, surrounding the only natural coastal bay in the whole of the Netherlands. **De Brandaris** lighthouse has kept sailors safe for the last 400 years and towers 150 ft high.The island retains its natural beauty and interest partly because most of the eastern end is a world nature reserve, the **Boschplaat Vogelreservaat** (Boschplaat Bird Sanctuary)—off-limits to wingless visitors from mid-March to mid-August.

Museum 't Behouden Huys (Keeper's House Museum) explains the cultural-historical background of the island and its people. It occupies the former homes of two naval captains dating from 1668; the rooms are richly decorated with tiles and ornate wooden furniture. Also on display are local traditional costumes and tools. ⊠ *Commandeurstraat 30–32,* ☎ *0562/442–389.* 🎫 *Fl 5.* ☉ *Apr.–Oct., weekdays 10–5; mid-June–Aug. also Sat. 1–5, July–Aug. also Sun. 1–5.*

The **Centrum voor Natuur en Landschap** (Center for Nature and Countryside) incorporates an enormous aquarium for marine life from the North Sea and Wadden Sea. ⊠ *Burgemeester Reedekkerstraat 11,* ☎ *0562/442–390.* 🎫 *Fl 7.50.* ☉ *Apr.–Oct. weekdays 9–5, weekends and holidays 2–5.*

Dining and Lodging

As well as the many independent restaurants and hotel restaurants in the main town of West-Terschelling, there are convenient places for lunch and dinner even in the smallest settlements scattered about the island.

$$ ✕ **De Brandaris.** This tavern restaurant—on one of the town's busy and popular streets filled with other bars and restaurants—serves Dutch and Continental cuisine alongside local fish specialties. ⊠ *Boomstraat 3, West-Terschelling,* ☎ *0562/442–554. AE, DC, MC, V.*

$$$ ⊞ **Golden Tulip Hotel Schylge.** This modern hotel overlooking the harbor has all the conveniences you might ever need if the weather isn't clement. The rooms are standard but practical for a beach holiday. Ask about weekend and midweek rates. ⊠ *Burg. Van Heusdenweg 37, 8881 ED, West-Terschelling,* ☎ *0562/442−111,* ℻ *0562/442−800. 85 rooms, 3 suites, 10 apartments. 2 restaurants, 2 bars, brasserie, indoor pool, beauty salon, spa, meeting rooms, parking. AE, DC, MC, V.*

$ ⊞ **Hotel Oepkes.** This family hotel on the quiet outskirts of town is only two minutes from the ferry terminal. The rooms are simple and clean. ⊠ *De Ruyterstraat 3, 8881 AM, West-Terschelling,* ☎ *0562/ 442−005,* ℻ *0562/443−345. 40 rooms. Restaurant, bar, bicycles. AE, DC, MC, V.*

Schiermonikoog

69   *42 km (26 mi) west of Leeuwarden, 42 km (26 mi) north of Groningen, 181 km (112 mi) northeast of Amsterdam.*

This car-free Wadden island, just 16 km (10 mi) long and 4 km (2½ mi) wide, has only 1,000 permanent residents. It takes about ¾ hour by passenger ferry to reach it from the mainland port of Lauwersoog, where you can safely leave your car. The island owes its name to the Cistercian monks who had a monastery here until it was dissolved and appropriated during the Reformation. For a time it was privately owned, at one point by a German count. It returned to the Dutch after World War II. In 1989, nearly the whole island became a National Park; it is a particularly important stop-off for migratory birds heading south in the autumn.

The village, the only residential center, was started circa 1720. Here you can savor the relaxing pace of life on broad, peaceful terraces. Many of the older private houses are protected monuments. **Bezoekerscentrum (De Oude Centrale) Schiermonikoog** (Schiermonikoog Visitors Center) has the only information about the island, concentrating on the wildlife. It organizes guided tours. ⊠ *Torenstreek 20,* ☎ *0519/531− 6419.* ⊡ *Fl 5.* ☉ *Mid-Mar.−Oct., Mon.−Sat. 10−noon and 1:30−5:30; Nov.−mid-Mar., Sat. 1:30−5:30.*

Dining and Lodging

$$ ✕ **Steakhouse Brakzand.** As an alternative to the rather pricey food at the hotel restaurants, daily specials at this dormered house in the middle of the village include typical Dutch dishes or an extensive selection of fresh local fish such as sole fillet. ⊠ *Langestreek 66,* ☎ *0519/ 531−382. MC, V.*

$$ ⊞ **Hotel-Restaurant Van der Werff.** Renowned as the preferred residence of the royal family when they visit, and a hotel since 1726, the Van der Werff has a characterful but fusty atmosphere. The grandly spacious restaurant also serves as the breakfast room, and the lounge is maturely comfortable. Full pension is available. From the ferry you can take the complimentary bus, which must be a good 30 years old. ⊠ *Reeweg 2, 9166 PX,* ☎ *0519/531−203,* ℻ *0519/531−748. 55 rooms. Restaurant, bar, lobby lounge, tennis court, meeting rooms. DC, MC, V.*

Groningen

70   *141 km (89 mi) east of Leeuwarden, 184 km (116 mi) northeast of Amsterdam.*

Groningen is a university town as well as a major commercial center of the northern provinces of the Netherlands. A member of the Hanseatic League in medieval times, it enjoyed six centuries of prosperity as a grain market. The province still leads Western Europe in the production of sugar beets; another of its riches is a large supply of natural gas. Street life is busy in the city, and the region offers pleasant drives in the countryside.

Groningen's **Grote Markt,** the market square in front of the modern Stadhuis (Town Hall), is the scene of one of the biggest daily markets in the Netherlands, selling everything from vegetables to vintage clothing. The **Martinikerk,** which dates from 1230 and was begun as a Romanesque-Gothic cruciform basilica, dominates the Grote Markt. Finished in the 15th century, it has an organ that was installed in 1470, as well as splendid murals from that period; the stained-glass windows date from the late 18th century. ⊠ *Martinikerkhof,* ☎ *050/318–3636.* ☞ *Fl 1.* ☉ *June–Sept., Tues.–Sat. noon–5.*

The peaceful **Prinsenhoftuin** herb and rose garden has an 18th-century sundial in its gate and hedges cut in the shapes of the letters *A* and *W,* after the first names of former governors of Friesland and Groningen provinces. The garden is tucked away behind the Martinikerk. ⊠ *Turfsingel.* ☞ *Free.* ☉ *Apr.–mid-Oct., daily dawn to sunset.*

The **university quarter** invites exploration and carefree wandering. Founded in 1614, the **Universiteit van Groningen** (University of Groningen) was chosen by Descartes in 1645 to arbitrate his conflicts with Dutch theologians. Today it is one of the largest in the Netherlands. The main university building is neo-Renaissance in style, built in 1909. Allegorical figures of Science, History, Prudence, and Mathematics adorn the gable. In the surrounding streets are a number of fashionable houses built by prominent 18th-century citizens and, on the corner of the Broerstraat, a medieval stone house that is one of the oldest in town. ⊠ *Oude Boteringestraat.*

NEED A BREAK? The high ceilings, wall paintings, and stained glass of a stylish 18th-century mansion give **De Librije** (⊠ Oude Boteringestraat 9, ☎ 050/318–3535) a *grand café* atmosphere. Here you can take tea and English scones as you page through magazines and eavesdrop on student gossip.

The **StadsmarkeringProjekt** (City Identification Project) was conceived by the Municipal Physical Planning Department to restore the identity that the city once derived from its medieval city gates. Two architects, three artists, a historian, a philosopher, a choreographer, a playwright, and an economist were each commissioned to design an "identification feature" to stand on 10 of the city's main access roads. Each was given an identifying letter spelling out *Cruoningae,* an ancient name for the city. The resulting sculptures and structures circle the city clockwise from the south and carry such mystifying titles as *Earth, Water, and Gas Flames; A Steel Book on Posts;* and *The Missing Factor X.*

Groninger Museum, opened in 1994, has quickly become a Groningen landmark that confronts you as you leave the railway station. The zanily designed, brightly colored complex consists of three pavilions connected by walkways below water level. It was conceived by Italian designer and architect Alessandro Mendini and includes flashy mosaics and rooms with trapezoid doors. It was made even more irreverent by additions from several "guest architects." You'll find exhibits on Groningen history, art and crafts (including a good collection of Asian porcelain), and visual art from the 16th century to the present. ⊠ *Museumeiland 1,* ☎ *050/366–6555.* ☞ *Fl 10.* ☉ *Tues.–Sun. 10–5.*

☕ At **Abraham's Mosterdmakerij,** a museum-restaurant in the village of Eenrum/Pieterburen, the congenial manager invites diners and visitors into the mustard factory to see how mustard (a local specialty) and vinegar are made. ⊠ *Molenstraat 5, Eenrum/Pieterburen, 20 km (12 mi)* *north of Groningen,* ☎ *0595/491–600.* ✉ *Fl 2.50.* ☉ *Restaurant, daily 10–9; museum, daily noon–6.*

Dining and Lodging

$$$$ ✕ **Muller.** This classic restaurant has a softly lit and sumptuous interior with Louis XVI mirrors above the fireplaces. The six-course menu
★ is a culinary delight, especially the imaginative vegetarian option. The wine list and service are excellent. ✉ *Grote Kromme Elleboog 13,* ☎ *050/318–3208. Reservations essential. Jacket required. AE, DC, MC, V. No lunch, closed Sun.–Mon.*

$$$ ✕ **De Pauw.** This chic, highly styled restaurant, done in cream and soft yellows, has a sophisticated and imaginative menu influenced by the cuisines of Provence and other sunny climes. Dishes include delicate white asparagus shoots (in season), lobster with pesto, and a royal selection of desserts from the trolley. Art decorates the walls, and the vases are filled with peacock feathers. ✉ *Gelkingestraat 52,* ☎ *050/318–1332. Reservations essential. Jacket required. AE, DC, MC, V. No lunch.*

$ ✕ **Het Binnenhof.** In a courtyard setting just around the corner from the hubbub of the Grote Markt, this restaurant is ideal for a quiet meal. Dishes *du jour* include imaginative veggie options. Now part of a theater and arts complex, it was formerly a grand ballroom. ✉ *Oosterstraat 7A,* ☎ *050/312–3697. MC, V.*

$$ ✕⌑ **Auberge Corps de Garde.** This small family-owned hotel is in a gracious 17th-century barracks house facing the city center's encircling canal. Partially furnished with antiques, it is a congenial place with pleasant, spacious rooms that are brightly decorated in tones of green and rose. The restaurant (reservations essential, jacket required) serves excellent new Dutch cuisine, such as quail stuffed with sweetbreads. ✉ *Oude Boteringestraat 74, 9712 GN,* ☎ *050/314–5437,* 𝖥𝖠𝖷 *050/313–6320. 25 rooms. Restaurant, lobby lounge. AE, DC, MC, V.*

$$$$ ⌑ **Landgoed Lauswolt.** This golf and spa resort with a sprawling manor-house hotel sits behind a sweeping lawn in a quiet wooded village. The fine restaurant is a member of the Alliance Gourmandise Néerlandaise. The rooms are large, and suites have separate living rooms. Special golf, spa, and gastronomic packages are available. ✉ *Van Harinxmaweg 10, 9244 CJ, Beetsterzwaag, 40 km (25 mi) southwest of Groningen,* ☎ *0512/381–245,* 𝖥𝖠𝖷 *0512/381–496. 58 rooms. Restaurant, pool, beauty salon, sauna, 9-hole golf course, 2 tennis courts. AE, DC, MC, V.*

$$$ ⌑ **Hotel De Ville.** Opened in late 1997, this hotel occupies a group of gracious houses once used by the university. Proprietor Jacques Muller, who has already proved his acumen with his restaurant, has now created a gem of a hotel, mixing classic features with contemporary styling and comfort in the public spaces and in the individual rooms. ✉ *Oude Boteringestraat 43, 9712 GD,* ☎ *050/318–1222,* 𝖥𝖠𝖷 *050/318–1777. 41 rooms, 3 suites. Restaurant, bar, lobby lounge, in-room safe, minibars, no-smoking floor, room service, parking. AE, DC, MC, V.*

$$ ⌑ **Schimmelpenninck Huys.** The history of this grand old patrician mansion stretches back to the 11th century. It was the scene of revolutionary plotting in the 18th century and was requisitioned as an officers' barracks during the Eighty Years' War. It was also home to Groningen's first dentist. In 1988 the building was rescued from occupation by squatters and lovingly restored. The decor reflects its checkered history. There's a vaulted 14th-century wine-cellar that serves as the bar, the Baroque Room, an Empire Dining Room, and a Jugendstil Grand Café—though the bedrooms are mostly decorated in a tasteful modern style. ✉ *Oosterstraat 53, 9711 NR,* ☎ *050/318–9502,* 𝖥𝖠𝖷 *050/318–3164. 26 rooms, 6 suites. Restaurant, bar, meeting rooms. AE, DC, MC, V.*

Nightlife

CASINO

Holland Casino (⊠ Gedempte Kattendiep 150, ☎ 050/312–3400), the only casino in the northern half of the Netherlands, is in Groningen.

DANCING AND LIVE MUSIC

The most vibrant nightspots in Groningen are on or around **Peperstraat,** near the Grote Markt. The influence of 20,000 university students in town ensures that there is plenty of dancing to the latest music. Up-to-the-minute DJs and a long happy hour attract hordes of students and other young Groningers to **De Blauwe Engel** (⊠ Grote Markt 39, ☎ 050/313–7679). **Jazz Café De Spieghel** (⊠ Peperstraat 11, ☎ 050/312–6300) swings nightly to mainstream jazz, with live bands over the weekends. If your taste is for salsa and other Latin rhythms, then head for the lively **Troubadour** (⊠ Peperstraat 19, ☎ 050/313–2690). **Warhol** (⊠ Peperstraat 7, ☎ 050/312–1350) is dark and cavernous and throbs with heavy rock.

GAY BARS

Groningen's largest and most popular gay disco, **De Golden Arm** (⊠ Hardewickerstraat 7, ☎ 050/313–1676), has two dance floors and three bars and is popular with students during the week. With a terrace on a busy shopping street, **El Rubio** (⊠ Zwanenstraat 26, ☎ 050/314–0039) is a camp way to start an evening among a mixed crowd of gay men and lesbians.

Outdoor Activities and Sports

Although less blessed with open water than neighboring Friesland, the province of Groningen offers opportunities for sailing and boating as well, particularly on the Schildmeer from the boating center at Steendam; contact **Hinrichs Watersport** (⊠ Damsterweg 32, 9629 PD, Schildmeer, ☎ 0596/629–137) for information on boat rentals.

Canoeing through the waterways of the province of Groningen can be great fun. Special canoeing routes have been laid out and maps have been printed. To rent canoes, contact: **De Zijlsterhoeve** (⊠ Zijlsterweg 7, 9892 TE, Aduarderzijl, ☎ 0594/621–423), **Hinrichs Watersport** (⊠ Damsterweg 32, 9629 PD, Schildmeer, ☎ 0596/629–137), or **Horizon** (⊠ Witherenweg 26, 9977 SB, Kleine Huisjes, ☎ 0595/481–980).

Shopping

In Groningen the market is held on the Grote Markt, Tuesday through Saturday; there also is a Sunday flea market between June and mid-October in Groningen on the Grote Markt. Late shopping night is Thursday.

A number of general antiques shops are clustered on the broad shopping street, **Gedempte Zuiderdiep.** Antique book dealers are especially thick in this university city. **De Groninger Boekverkoper** (⊠ Oude Kijk-in-'t-Jatstraat 60, ☎ 050/313–5858) has a good selection of old Dutch prints, as well as books on Groningen. **Isis Antiquarian Bookshop** (⊠ Folkingestraat 20, ☎ 050/318–4233) specializes in Asian studies, as well as translated and Dutch literature.

The North A to Z

Arriving and Departing

BY CAR

To reach the northern provinces from Amsterdam, you can take E22 through Noord Holland province and across the 35-km (22-mi) Afsluitdijk (Enclosing Dike) that divides the IJsselmeer from the North Sea; from the end of the Enclosing Dike, continue on E22 to Groningen or take A31 to Leeuwarden. You also take A31 if you are heading to the Wadden Islands, but stop at Harlingen, where there are ferries to Terschelling. The ferry for Schiermonikoog leaves from Lauwersoog: take N361 from Groningen or N355 then N361 from Leeuwarden. Alternatively, if you are heading straight for Groningen or Leeuwarden, you can follow A6 across the province of Flevoland to Joure and then take the E22 for Groningen or turn north on A32 for Leeuwarden. A third option is to drive to Enkhuizen and take the car ferry to Urk (☞ By Ferry, *below*). From Urk, take N351 to A6 and continue as above.

BY FERRY

Two ferry lines cross the IJsselmeer from May to September to connect the town of Enkhuizen with the northern provinces of Friesland and Flevoland. Both lines are operated by **Rederij Naco** (✉ De Ruyterkade, Steiger 7, Amsterdam, ☎ 020/626–2466), and both accept bicycles but not cars. One goes to Stavoren, where there is a direct train connection to Leeuwarden; the ferry operates three times a day from May to September, and twice daily (except Monday) from October through April; reservations are unnecessary; the fare is Fl 10.50 one-way, Fl 16 round-trip. The other goes to Urk in Flevoland province June through September, Monday through Saturday, twice daily; the fare is Fl 12 one way, Fl 18 round-trip. For ferry services to the Wadden Islands see (☞ Getting Around, By Ferry, *below*).

BY TRAIN

Intercity express trains (☎ 0900/9292, costs 75¢ per minute) operate once an hour direct from Amsterdam to both Leeuwarden and Groningen; there is an additional hourly Intercity service to both cities that requires a connection in Amersfoort. Be sure you are in the right car; trains split en route, so there are separate cars for each destination in both classes of service. If you intend to tour the region by train and you will be including a visit to one of the Wadden Islands, it is worth considering a *Waddenbiljet,* an all-inclusive return ticket including all connecting services and ferries. It is easy and economical, with the added bonus that you can break your outward and return journeys as desired.

Getting Around

BY BUS

To reach the Lauwersoog ferry (☞ By Ferry, *below*) by public transport you have to take bus 63 from Groningen or bus 50 from Leeuwarden. For **bus information** call 0900/9292; costs 75¢ per minute.

BY CAR

Roads are excellent throughout the northern provinces of Friesland and Groningen. In Friesland signs are in two languages, however, with the town names shown in Frisian as well as in Dutch. For example, the provincial capital Leeuwarden is also shown on signs by its Frisian name, Ljouwert.

BY FERRY

Wagenborg Ferries (☎ 0519/349–050) operate passenger ferries to the island of Schiermonikoog about six times each day. The journey takes about one hour. The island of Terschelling is served by **Rederij Doeksen** (☎ 0562/442–141), with ferry (1¾ hours) and superfast hydrofoil (45 minutes) departures from Harlingen at least three times daily, and more often during the summer.

BY TAXI

Taxis wait at the railway stations in both Leeuwarden and Groningen. For a **taxi** in Leeuwarden, call 058/212–2222 or 058/212–3333; in Groningen, call 050/312–8044.

BY TRAIN

In addition to the national rail lines connecting Leeuwarden and Groningen with the south, local trains link up Leeuwarden with the Enkhuizen–Stavoren ferry service; another line connects Leeuwarden with Harlingen (departure point for ferry and hydrofoil services to the Wadden Islands) every half hour; and another links Leeuwarden with Groningen and continues to the German border. A small local train in Groningen province connects Groningen with Winsum (a canoeing center), Uithuizen (departure for guided walks to the Wadden Islands at low tide), and the port of Eemshaven. For **local train information** call ☎ 0900/9292 (costs 75¢ per minute).

Contacts and Resources

CAMPING

With more than 100 campgrounds in the province of Friesland alone, the North offers plenty of opportunity for camping. Unfortunately, there is no national central reservation service for campsites, so you have to contact sites individually. For camping in Leeuwarden, **De Kleine Wielen** (✉ De Groene Ster 14, 8926 XE, ☎ 0511/431–660), open April–October, has sites for 350 tents and touring caravans, as well as places for hikers. In Groningen **Camping Stadspark** (✉ Campinglaan 6, 9727 KH, ☎ 050/525–1624), open March–October, has 200 sites; it also has accommodation for hikers.

EMERGENCIES

National Emergency Alarm Number for police, fire, and ambulance: ☎ 112. **Groningen Police** (☎ 050/599–5995). **Leeuwarden Police** (☎ 058/213–2423). **Schiermonikoog Police** (☎ 0519/531–555). **Terschelling Police** (☎ 0562/442–280). **Hospital Emergency Rooms: Groningen** (☎ 050/361–9111 or 050/524–5245) and **Leeuwarden** (☎ 058/293–3333). The **Wegenwacht** national breakdown and towing service (☎ 06/0888).

GUIDED TOURS

Canal cruise trips are available in summer; in Leeuwarden, contact **Party Cruise Prinsenhof** (✉ Spanjaardstraat 29, ☎ 058/215–3737); in Groningen, **Rederij Kool** (✉ Stationsweg 1012, ☎ 050/312–2713 or 050/312–8379).

Another guided option, as much sport as sightseeing, is to join a Wadlopen excursion for a walk across the sand at low tide from the mainland to the Wadden Islands. Permissible *only* with a guide who knows well the timing of the tidal waters on the Wadden Sea, these walks are available from May through September. Don't even think about attempting this on your own; the tides are very, very tricky. The tourist offices can give you information and recommend qualified guides, or you can contact **De Stichting Wadlooppcentruem Pieterburen** (✉ Postbus 1, Pieterburen, ☎ 0595/528–300, FAX 0595/528–318).

VISITOR INFORMATION

VVV Groningen (✉ Gedempte Kattendiep 6, 9711 PN, ☎ 0900/2023050, Fl 1 per minute, FAX 050/311–0258). **VVV Leeuwarden-Friesland** (✉ Stationsplein 1, 8911 AC, ☎ 0900/32024060, costs 75¢ per minute, FAX 058/213–6555). **VVV Schiermonikoog** (✉ Reeweg 5, 9166 ZP, ☎ 0519/531–233, FAX 0529/531–325). **VVV Terschelling** (✉ Reeweg 5, 9166 ZP, ☎ 0519/531–233, FAX 0529/531–325).

THE NETHERLANDS A TO Z

Arriving and Departing

From North America by Plane

AIRPORTS AND AIRLINES

Amsterdam Schiphol Airport (☎ 0900/0141, costs 75¢ per minute), 25 km (15 mi) southeast of Amsterdam, is linked by rail to every part of the country.

KLM Royal Dutch Airlines (☎ 800/374–7747 in the U.S.) is the national carrier of the Netherlands. Other airlines serving the country include **Delta** (☎ 800/241–4141), **Northwest** (☎ 800/225–2525), **TWA** (☎ 800/221–2000), and **United** (☎ 800/241–6522).

DISCOUNT FLIGHTS

Martinair (☎ 800/627–8462) offers reduced-fare flights to Amsterdam seasonally from Los Angeles, Miami, Newark, Oakland, Orlando, Tampa, Toronto, Vancouver, and Winnipeg.

FLYING TIME

Flying time to Amsterdam from New York is just over seven hours; from Chicago, closer to eight hours; and from Los Angeles, 10½ hours.

From the United Kingdom

BY BUS

Bus/ferry combination service between the United Kingdom and the Netherlands is operated from London to Amsterdam by **Eurolines** (☎ 0990/143–219 in the U.K., 020/560–8787 in the Netherlands).

BY CAR

The **Channel Tunnel** provides the fastest route across the Channel—35 minutes from Folkestone to Calais, or 60 minutes from motorway to motorway. **Le Shuttle** (☎ 0990/353535 in the U.K.), a special car, bus, and truck train, departs frequently throughout the day and night. No reservations are necessary, although tickets may be purchased in advance from travel agents.

The Tunnel is reached from exit 11a of the M20/A20. Drivers purchase tickets from toll booths, then pass through frontier control before loading onto the next available train. Unloading at Calais takes eight minutes. Five-day round-trip for a small car with passengers starts at £95 (low season, night travel); high-season day travel is £135.

BY FERRY

Ferries and super-fast hydrofoils are run between Harwich and Hook of Holland twice daily by **Stena Line** (☎ 0990/707–070 in the U.K.), and overnight between Hull and Rotterdam by **P&O North Sea Ferries** (☎ 01482/377–177 in the U.K.). The trip takes 3 to 12 hours, depending on the route.

BY PLANE

Airlines that serve the Netherlands from the United Kingdom include **Aer Lingus** (☎ 0181/899–4747 in the U.K.), **British Airways** (☎ 0181/897–4000 in the U.K.), and **KLM** (☎ 0990/750–9000 in the U.K.). Flying time to Amsterdam from London is one hour; from Belfast, 1½ hours.

BY TRAIN

British Rail International (☎ 0171/834–2345 or 0171/828–0892 in the U.K.; BritRail Travel, ☎ 800/677–8585 in the U.S., 800/555–2748 in Canada) runs three trains a day from London to Amsterdam.

Eurostar (☎ 0345/881881 in the U.K., 800/942–4866 in the U.S., 800/361–7245 in Canada) high-speed train service whisks riders through the Chunnel between stations in Paris (Gare du Nord) and London (Waterloo) in three hours, and between London and Brussels (Midi) in 3¼ hours. There are eight connecting services a day, including the highspeed **Thalys** (☎ 0900/9228 in the Netherlands), from Amsterdam Centraal Station to the Eurostar. Tickets for these services are available from international ticket counters at Dutch railway stations. Eurostar and Thalys tickets are available in the United Kingdom through **British Rail International** (London/Victoria Station, ☎ 0171/834–2345 or 0171/828–0892 for credit-card bookings) and in North America through **Rail Europe** (☎ 800/942–4866 in the U.S., 800/555–2748 in Canada) and **BritRail Travel** (☎ 800/677–8585 in the U.S., 800/555–2748 in Canada).

Car Rentals

Major international car rental companies, including **Alamo, Avis, Hertz, Eurodollar/Dollar,** and **Europcar/National,** operate desks at Amsterdam Schiphol Airport and have rental offices in Amsterdam and other key cities throughout the Netherlands. In addition, the Dutch firm **Van Wijk Amsterdam** (Amsterdam Schiphol Airport, ☎ 020/601–5277) operates at the airport and other locations.

Customs and Duties

On Arrival
There are no limits on goods (such as perfume, cigarettes, or alcohol) brought into the Netherlands from another EU country, provided that they are bought duty-paid (i.e., not in a duty-free shop) and are for personal use. If you enter from a non-EU country, or have purchased goods duty-free, you may bring in 200 cigarettes or 50 cigars or 100 small cigars or 250 grams of tobacco; 1 liter of alcohol (more than 22%) or 2 liters (less than 22%) of other liquid refreshments, 50 grams of perfume and .25 liter cologne, 500 grams of coffee, 100 grams of tea, and other goods with a total value of up to Fl 125.

There are no restrictions regarding the import or export of currency.

On Departure
To export Dutch flower bulbs, a health certificate issued by the Nederlandse Planteziektenkundige Dienst (Dutch Phytopathological Service) is required; these are provided with packages you buy from specialized flower bulb companies.

Guided Tours

General-Interest Tours
Abercrombie & Kent (✉ 1520 Kensington Rd., Suite 212, Oak Brook, IL 60523, ☎ 630/954–2944 or 800/323–7308) runs six-night barge cruises through the waterways of Holland in the early spring. **Holland Approach, Inc.** (✉ 550 Mountain Ave., Gillette, NJ 07933, ☎ 908/580–9200 or 800/776–4655 outside NJ) offers two-day tours. **Maupintour** (✉ 1515 St. Andrews Dr., Lawrence, KS 66047, ☎ 785/843–1211 or 800/255–4266) offers eight-day tulip-time excursions through Holland.

Special-Interest Tours
The **Netherlands Board of Tourism** (✉ Postbus 458, 2260 MG, Leidschendam, The Netherlands) office maintains a data bank for special-interest travel that includes specialized tours for senior citizens, gays, and travelers with disabilities; information is continually updated, and printouts are available. For offices in North America *see* Visitor Information, *below.*

ARCHITECTURE

Art Horizons International (⊠ 330 W. 58th St., Suite 608, New York, NY 10019, ☎ 212/969–9410, FAX 212/969–9416).

ARTS, CULTURE, AND MUSIC

Ciao! Travel (⊠ 2707 Congress St., Suite 1F, San Diego, CA 92110, ☎ 619/297–8112 or 800/942–2426, FAX 619/297–8114). **International Education** (⊠ Box 10, Merrimac, WI 53561, ☎ 608/493–2296 or 800/558–0215, FAX 608/493–2092). **Travel Time** (⊠ 203 N. Wabash Ave., Chicago, IL 60601, ☎ 312/726–7197 or 800/621–4725, FAX 312/726–0718). **Witte Travel** (⊠ 3250 28th St. SE, Grand Rapids, MI 49512, ☎ 616/957–8113 or 800/469–4883, FAX 616/957–9716).

BARGE AND RIVER CRUISING

The Barge Lady (⊠ 101 W. Grand Ave., Suite 200, Chicago, IL 60610, ☎ 312/245–0900 or 800/880–0071). **European Waterways** (⊠ 140 E. 56th St., New York, NY 10022, ☎ 212/688–9467 or 800/438–4748). **SeaAir Holidays Ltd.** (⊠ 733 Summer St., Stamford, CT 06901, ☎ 203/356–9033 or 800/732–6247).

BIKING

Brooks Country Cycling Tours (⊠ 140 W. 83rd St., New York, NY 10024, ☎ 212/874–5151 or 800/284–8954, FAX 212/874–5286). **International Bicycle Tours** (⊠ Box 754, Essex, CT 06426, ☎ 860/767–7005, FAX 860/767–3090). **Revatours** (⊠ 1450 City Councillors St., Suite 520, Montréal, Québec H3A 2E6, ☎ 514/842–9016 or 800/363–6339 in Canada, FAX 514/842–9015) arrange cycling vacations.

PACKAGE DEALS FOR INDEPENDENT TRAVELERS

Call your travel agent or any of the following operators. **Jet Vacations** (⊠ 880 Apollo St., Suite 241, El Segundo, CA 90245, ☎ 310/640–6800 or 800/538–0999) offers packages that include a choice of hotels, car rentals, and sightseeing in Amsterdam. **Northwest WorldVacations** (⊠ 5130 County Rd. 101, Minnetonka, MN 55345, ☎ 800/727–3005) provides visitors to Amsterdam with hotel, car rental, and tour options for a minimum of two nights.

Language

Dutch is the official language of the Netherlands, although Frisian is spoken in Friesland and there is a strong local dialect in Limburg province. Many city residents speak good English, but in rural areas you may need a phrase book, at least until the residents overcome their shyness about using the English they know.

Lodging

Netherlands Reservation Center (NRC, Postbus 404, 2260 AK, Leidschendam, ☎ 070/320–2500, FAX 070/320–2611) handles bookings for most lodgings in the Netherlands.

Camping

Prices at the country's numerous camping locations range from Fl 25 to Fl 75 per site per night. There is no central reservation bureau for campsites, but you can get general information in Amsterdam from the **ANWB** (Royal Dutch Touring Club; ⊠ Museumplein 5, ☎ 020/673–0844).

Mail

Postal Rates

Airmail letters up to 20 grams (⅔ ounce) cost Fl 1.60 to the United States or Canada, Fl 1 to the United Kingdom; postcards to the United States or Canada cost Fl 1, to the United Kingdom 80¢. Aerograms cost Fl 1.30.

Money and Expenses

Currency

The official monetary unit of the Netherlands is the guilder, which may be abbreviated as Dfl, Fl, F, Hfl, and NLG. There are 100 cents in a guilder; coins are minted in denominations of 5, 10, and 25 cents, and 1, 2½, and 5 guilders. Bank notes are printed in amounts of 10, 25, 50, 100, 250, and 1,000 guilders, with the denominations embossed in raised symbols on each bill. Bank notes in denominations of more than Fl 100 are seldom seen, and some shops refuse to accept Fl 1,000 notes. In winter 1999 the exchange rate was about 1.90 guilders to the dollar, 1.24 to the Canadian dollar, 3.14 to the pound sterling, 1.20 to the Australian dollar, 1.03 to the New Zealand dollar, and 2.80 to the Irish punt.

What It Will Cost

Prices in the Netherlands include a 17.5% BTW/VAT (value added tax). Residents of countries outside the European Union (EU) are entitled to a refund of the BTW on purchases over Fl 300 at one particular shop that are personally carried out of the country within 30 days of purchase. Shops have different systems for granting refunds: Some shops will credit your credit card account, but most require you to present some form of proof of purchase at the customs desk at Schiphol Airport on your way home. Some stores will give you a special "cheque" that may be cashed at the airport; otherwise, you'll receive your refund in the mail. The amount of the refund varies (some organizations deduct a commission), but a refund of 10%–15% is standard.

SAMPLE COSTS

Cup of coffee, Fl 3; glass of beer, Fl 3.50; glass of wine, Fl 4.50; soda or juice, Fl 3–Fl 4; a sandwich, Fl 4–Fl 10; a pastry or dessert, Fl 4–Fl 8.

Opening and Closing Times

Banks are open weekdays from 8 or 9 to 4 or 5; post offices are open weekdays from 8:30 to 5 and often on Saturday from 8:30 to noon. Most national **museums** are closed on Monday, though the larger Amsterdam museums are open daily. **Pharmacies** are open weekdays from 8 or 9 to 5:30, with a rotating schedule in each city to cover nights and weekends. **Shops'** hours, regulated by the government, are Monday from 1 to 6, Tuesday through Friday from 9 to 6, and Saturday from 9 to 5; each city may designate one night a week as a late shopping night, when stores are open until 9. Certain shops now have permission to open from noon to 5 on Sunday. This is administered at a local level and varies from city to city. Some branches of supermarkets now stay open until 7 or 8 on weekdays.

Outdoor Activities and Sports

Boating and Sailing

ANWB (Royal Dutch Touring Club) stores in Amsterdam (✉ Museumplein 5, ☎ 020/673–0844) sells very good nautical maps.

Canoeing

For detailed information on canoeing in the Netherlands, contact the **Dutch Canoe Union** (✉ Postbus 1160, 3800 BD, Amersfoort, ☎ 033/462–2341).

Golf
De Nederlandse Golf Federatie (✉ Postbus 221, 3454 ZL, De Meern,
☎ 030/662–1888) can provide information on golfing around the
country.

Rail Passes

If you plan to travel by train throughout the Netherlands, consider buying one of the following passes. The **Benelux Tourrail** gives you unlimited
travel throughout Holland, Belgium, and Luxembourg on any five days
within one month (U.S. $217/C$299 first class, U.S. $155/C$213 second class). A **Holland Rail Pass** allows unlimited travel throughout Holland for 3, 5, or 10 days within any 30-day period (first class: 3-day
U.S. $97.50/C$139.25; 5-day U.S. $150/C$214.25; 10-day U.S.
$262.50/C$375; second class: 3-day U.S. $65/C$93; 5-day U.S. $100/
C$143; 10-day U.S. $175/C$250). For an additional fee, the **Holland
Rail Pass Transport Link** offers free travel on public transportation as
well (3 days U.S. $9/C$13; 5 days U.S. $15/C$21.50; 10 days U.S.
$23.50/C$33.50). Once in the Netherlands, you can purchase a **Holland Domino** rail pass, valid for 3 days (Fl 90, Fl 65 under 26), 5 days
(Fl 140, Fl 99 under 26), or 10 days (Fl 250, Fl 165 under 26) of unlimited travel within a month. For an extra Fl 5 per day you can get a
pass to travel on all public transport. A **Dagkaart** (day ticket) is available only in the Netherlands and entitles you to unlimited travel within
Holland for one day (first class Fl 99, second class Fl 66), but it's nearly
impossible to travel enough in one day to make them worth the investment. Between June and the end of August, a **Zomertoer** (summer
tour) ticket entitles you to three days of unlimited travel within any
10-day period (second class, Fl 99 for one person, Fl 129 for two; first
class, Fl 155 for one, Fl 199 for two). The NBT offices have information on train services, as do overseas offices of the Netherlands railways. You may need your passport to purchase these passes.

Student and Youth Travel

In addition to the YHA hostels, young visitors to Holland can stay at
a youth hotel, or "sleep-in," which provides basic, inexpensive accommodations for young people. A list of these is available from the
NBT (☎ 212/370–7360 in New York). In summer (and in some cases
year-round), the **Institute for Nature Protection Education** (✉ IVN,
Postbus 20123, 1000 HC, Amsterdam, ☎ 020/622–8115) organizes
work camps in scenic locations, popular among English-speaking visitors age 15–30. Another organization to consider for volunteer work
in Holland is **S/W, International Volunteer Projects** (✉ Willemstraat
7, 3511 RJ, Utrecht, ☎ 030/231–7721).

Telephones

The country code for the Netherlands is 31. Numbers with 0800 or
0900 codes are generally information numbers; the former free, the latter a charged service.

The area code for Amsterdam is 020 (or 20 if you are calling from outside the Netherlands), and it is used only when you call from other parts
of the Netherlands to Amsterdam. Within the immediate environs of
any municipality you do not need to use an area code.

Local Calls
Coin-operated telephones are becoming a rarity in the Netherlands,
except in bars and cafés; most public phones take KPN (Dutch telephone company) phone cards, available from Fl 10, and credit cards.

International Calls

To call outside the Netherlands, dial 00 followed by the country code (1 for the United States and Canada, 44 for the United Kingdom), area code, and number. Dial 0800/022–9111 to reach an **AT&T USA Direct** operator in the United States; 0800/022–9122 to reach an **MCI Call USA** operator; 0800/022–9119 for **Sprint**; or 0800/0410 for an international operator.

Operators and Information

Dial 0900/8008 for **directory enquiries** within the Netherlands, 0900/8418 for numbers elsewhere. Both services cost about Fl 1 per minute. Operators speak English.

Tipping

Service is included in the prices you pay in the Netherlands, though it is customary to round up to the nearest guilder or two on small bills, and up to the nearest 5, 10, or even 25 guilders for good service on large bills.

Transportation

By Car

The Dutch superhighway system is extensive and very well maintained; there are European, national, provincial, and local roads designated as E, A, N, and S, respectively. The **ANWB (Royal Dutch Touring Club)** operates telephone road information services in Dutch only (☎ 0900/9622, costs 75¢ per minute) and has a 24-hour fleet of bright yellow cars and trucks equipped to handle routine repairs free of charge for members of AAA, CAA, or any affiliate of Alliance International du Tourisme (☎ 06/0888). The speed limit on highways in the Netherlands is 120 km (75 mi) per hour, and driving is on the right. A valid driver's license from your home country is all that is required to operate a vehicle in the Netherlands.

By Ferry

An extensive ferry system serves the Netherlands. In **Friesland** province ferries run from Lauwersoog (☎ 0519/349–050 or 0519/349–079), Harlingen (☎ 0562/442–969 or 0562/442–770), and Holwerd (☎ 0519/542–001) to the Frisian Islands. Ferries cross the **Ijsselmeer** from Enkhuizen to Stavoren (☎ 020/626–2466; no cars) or Urk (☎ 0527/683–407). Ferries run from Den Helder (☎ 0222/369–600) in **Noord Holland** province to the Frisian Islands. Ferries in **Zeeland** province operate from Breskens (☎ 0117/381–663), Vlissingen (☎ 0118/465–905), and Perkpolder (☎ 0114/681–234).

By Plane

KLM City Hopper (☎ 020/474–7747) provides regular service between Amsterdam Schiphol Airport and Rotterdam, Eindhoven, and Maastricht, though air travel in a country this small is really unnecessary.

By Train

NS/Nederlandse Spoorwegen (Netherlands Railways; ☎ 0900/9292, costs 75¢ per minute) operates a minimum of one train per hour throughout its system, and major cities are connected by three or more trains each hour. Nearly every corner of the country is covered, supplemented by local and regional bus services. The modern, clean trains have first- and second-class coaches and no-smoking and smoking cars. Rail fares are based upon distance; there are one-way fares, day-return fares for same-day round-trip travel, and multiday fares; bicycles may be carried aboard for a nominal fee. Children under 3 travel free and children under 11 are charged Fl 1 if they are accompanied by an adult.

When you purchase your rail ticket at a station ticket office, you can buy a "train-taxi" ticket for Fl 6 per person. Special "train-taxis" will take you from a special stand outside the station to anywhere within a certain area (usually defined by the town boundaries). Taxis are shared, but waiting time is guaranteed to be no longer than 10 minutes. The scheme also operates for journeys back to the station. Although not available in the large cities, "train-taxis" are ideal for getting to sights on the outskirts of smaller towns, such as Paleis Het Loo outside Apeldoorn.

Visitor Information

In the United States
Netherlands Board of Tourism (✉ 355 Lexington Ave., 21st floor, New York, NY 10017, ☎ 212/370–7360 or 888/464–6552, FAX 212/370–9507, www.goholland.com; ✉ 225 N. Michigan Ave., Suite 1854, Chicago, IL 60601, ☎ 312/819–1636, FAX 312/819–1740; ✉ 9841 Airport Blvd., Suite 710, Los Angeles, CA 90045, ☎ 310/348–9339, FAX 310/348–9344).

In Canada
Netherlands Board of Tourism (✉ 25 Adelaide St. E, Suite 710, Toronto, Ontario M5C 1Y2, ☎ 416/363–1577, FAX 416/363–1470).

In the United Kingdom
Netherlands Board of Tourism (✉ 18 Buckingham Gate, London SW1E 6LB, ☎ 0171/828–7900 or 0891/717–777 from UK).

3 Belgium

This small country packs a scenic and cultural wallop with its historic towns, sophisticated cuisine, and museums filled with works of the great Flemish artists. Brussels, its capital, and Antwerp, an important European port city, are both art and shopping centers, while Gent and Brugge are gems of well-preserved medieval architecture. The battlefields of Waterloo and Bastogne are landmarks of military history; the hills and green fields of the Ardennes offer the glories of nature; and the beach resorts of Oostende and Knokke-Le Zoute and the sulphur waters of Spa, the mother of modern health resorts, are pleasure spots.

BELGIUM IS A COUNTRY FOR CONNOISSEURS: This is the land of Van Eyck, Bruegel, and Rubens, and this is where their greatest work can be seen. The spirit of the Middle Ages lives on in cities of great renown, such as Brugge and Gent, and in others that are waiting to be discovered, such as Mechelen and Lier. The art of living well has been cultivated in Belgium since the days of the great Burgundian wedding feasts that celebrated dynastic marriages. Today, the country has an astonishing number of gourmet restaurants, including some of the world's finest.

Updated by
Clare Thomson
and Matthew
Davis

Belgium fits just over 5 million Dutch-speaking Flemings and almost as many French-speaking Walloons into a country only slightly larger than the state of Vermont and 1½ times the size of Wales. The presence of two language cultures inevitably creates tension, but it also enriches. A diverse geography also enhances the country's attractions. The Belgian landscape ranges from the beaches and dunes of the coast and the tree-lined, placid canals of the "platte land" (flatland), to the sheer cliffs of Ardennes river valleys and the dense forests of the south.

A staunch, unapologetic middle-class culture thrives in Belgium. Dukes, counts, and lesser lords have built many a feudal castle on Belgian land, and abbots and cardinals have constructed towering religious edifices, but it was the merchants who built the cities and commissioned the works of art we admire today. The endless variations of Art Nouveau in the town houses of the Belle Epoque are another manifestation of middle-class individualism, as are the comfortable proportions of today's private homes and public spaces.

Until recently, the Belgians had no common history. Their fate was determined by marriages through which princely families sought to extend their influence and perpetuate their power. Marriage brought the possessions of the dukes of Flanders into the hands of the dukes of Burgundy in the 14th century and then to the Hapsburg family in 1477. A scion of that family, born in Gent, became Emperor Charles V in 1519 when he inherited the Holy Roman Empire from his father and Spain from his mother. This was the beginning of 200 years of Spanish rule. When the Austrian branch of the Habsburg family eventually gained the upper hand, the only real difference for Belgium was that it came to be ruled from Vienna instead of Madrid.

After the fall of Napoléon in 1815, the victorious powers tried to settle matters by awarding the Belgian provinces to the Netherlands. But a cultural divide had opened up between the Low Countries to the north and those to the south, and the staunchly Roman Catholic southerners did not get along with the adamantly Protestant northerners. In military terms, Belgium's 1830 war of independence did not amount to more than a few skirmishes, but the purpose was served and a new nation was formed. It included the former principality of Liège, which under elected prince-bishops had maintained its independence for 800 years.

Colonialism, too, was thrust upon the Belgians. The Congo was the personal fiefdom of King Leopold II (son of Leopold I, first king of independent Belgium), who bequeathed it to the nation in 1908 shortly before his death. The Belgians may have reaped the rewards, but they also had to pay the consequences when colonialism came to a painful end and the independent Congo was born 52 years later.

When Belgian forces put up unexpected resistance against the Germans in 1914, the country became known, a little patronizingly, as "brave

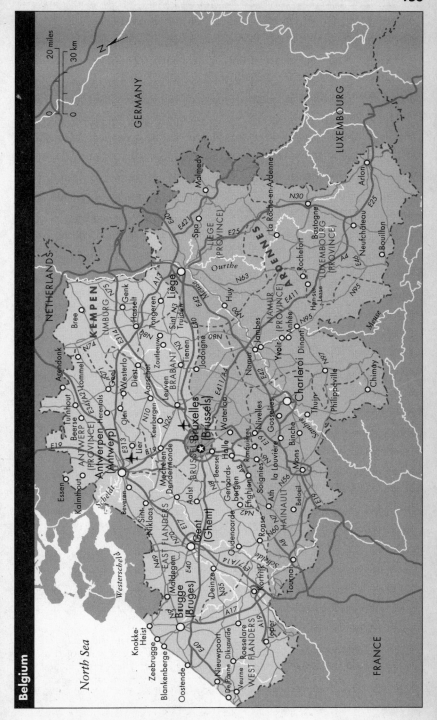

GERMANY

LUXEMBOURG

20 miles
30 km

NETHERLANDS

KEMPEN

LIMBURG N75

Bree

Arendonk

Essen

Kalmthout

Turnhout

Beerse

Geel

Herentals

Westerlo

Diest

Aarschot

Olen

Keerbergen

Lier

Mechelen

Dendermonde

Beveren

Sint-
Niklaas

Aalst

Antwerpen
(Antwerp)

ANTWERP
(PROVINCE)

Scheldt

Hasselt

Genk

Tongeren

Sint
Truiden

Zoutleeuw

Tienen

Jodoigne

Leuven

Waterloo

Halle

Beersel

Gerards-
bergen

Enghien

Soignies

Oudenaarde

EAST
FLANDERS

Gent
(Ghent)

Deinze

Maldegem

Brugge
(Bruges)

Knokke-
Heist

Zeebrugge

Blankenberge

Oostende

De Panne

Veurne

Nieuwpoort

Diksmuide

Roeselare

Ieper

WEST
FLANDERS

Kortrijk

Tournai

Ronse

Ath

Mons

Beloeil

Binche

la Louvière

Thuin

Philippeville

Chimay

Charleroi

Dinant

Namur

NAMUR
(PROVINCE)

Jambes

Huy

Liège

LIEGE
(PROVINCE)

Spa

Malmedy

Ourthe

Meuse

Rochefort

la Roche-en-Ardenne

ARDENNES

Bastogne

LUXEMBOURG
(PROVINCE)

Arlon

Neufchâteau

Bouillon

North Sea

Westerschelde

FRANCE

Bruxelles
(Brussels)

BRUSSEL

BRABANT

Nivelles

Gosselies

Viroin

Lesse

Meuse

Semois

A17

A19

A8

E40

E19

E17

E25

N30

N63

N95

N97

little Belgium." In 1940, during the Second World War, Belgium again was ravaged.

This is perhaps why Belgium is one of the strongest supporters of the European Union (EU). Brussels is the home of the European Commission, where most decisions affecting the EU are initiated. Writers and politicians tend to refer to "Brussels" as a synonym for the Commission, and this can be a mixed blessing. While being the capital of Europe is a heady sensation, it is of secondary importance to forging a commonality of interests. The EU will survive only if it is successful in fashioning unity out of diversity. Exactly the same thing applies to the Kingdom of Belgium.

Pleasures and Pastimes

Architecture

Art Nouveau flourished in Brussels as nowhere else. You'll find many a splendid town house in this fanciful style, with bay windows, turrets, and curlicues of all kinds, by Victor Horta, Paul Hankar, and their pupils, especially in the communes of St-Gilles and Ixelles to the south and southeast of the city center.

Outside the capital, Tournai's Cathédrale Notre-Dame became the prototype for a distinctive style of church building that spread along the Scheldt River during the 12th century. The medieval castles that dot the Belgian countryside evoke the spirit of past ages in the midst of the modern world.

Art

The art of oil painting was invented in Flanders in the 15th century, and there are those who feel that it has not been bettered since the days of Jan Van Eyck, Hans Memling, and their friends and followers. Although much of their output was pilfered by Spanish and Austrian overlords, a treasure trove remains in Flanders's museums and churches. Modern masters, such as James Ensor and Paul Delvaux, lived and worked here as well.

Bicycling

The towpaths of the poplar-lined canals of western Belgium seem to have been built for bicycle riders. In this country, there is no obstacle other than the wind. You can rent mountain bikes and join organized tours, and there's a network of cabins especially for two-wheel travelers. The French-speaking Belgians are less organized about it.

Dining

The Belgians, by and large, take dining seriously and are discerning about fresh produce and innovative recipes. Because they put a high value on the pleasures of the table, they are prepared to pay a steep price for fine meals. Wherever you go, even in the most expensive restaurants, you will almost always find families or groups of friends sharing a celebratory meal.

In Belgium, as in France, the introduction of nouvelle cuisine meant a liberation of creative spirits. Now the trend is back to regional and traditional dishes, but with a modern twist. These may include such hearty dishes as waterzooi, *faisan à la brabançonne* (pheasant with braised chicory), *lapin à la bière* (rabbit cooked in beer), or *carbonnade* (chunky beef stew with beer).

The quintessential Belgian vegetable is not brussels sprout but endive, also known as chicory (witloof or *chicon* in French). We owe endive to an act of serendipity. During one of the many wars in Belgium, a farmer near Mechelen had to abandon the chicory roots (used to produce a coffee substitute) that he had just harvested. When he returned, he found they had sprouted leaves; he tried them, liked them, and thus, endive was born. You'll find it in many guises—braised, au gratin, or in salads, always with a slightly bitter edge. Many other good foods come from Belgium: superb asparagus, smoked ham and sausages, crayfish, and trout. But the mussels the Belgians eat with such gusto and proclaim as their own actually come from Holland.

Belgians also swear by the humble *frites*—chips or fries. They are served in every restaurant and home; you can also get them on street corners and at roadside stands. Also known as *fritures* or *frituur,* they are served with mayonnaise, catsup, or, catering to more advanced tastes, béarnaise or curry sauce. You're not likely to encounter a cheaper or more typical Belgian dish.

Most hotels serve breakfast until 10. Belgians usually eat lunch between 1 and 3, but restaurants open at noon. The two-hour lunch is generally expense-account related. The main meal of the day is dinner, generally eaten between 8 and 10. Peak dining time used to be about 8 but seems to be getting later, and reservations are readily accepted for 9 or 9:30.

Belgians are becoming less formal, and conservative dress is now de rigueur only in the most expensive restaurants. The younger generation, in particular, favors stylish but casual dress when dining out.

Price categories for Belgium are as follows:

CATEGORY	BRUSSELS*	BELGIUM EXCEPT BRUSSELS*
$$$$	over BF3,500	over BF3,000
$$$	BF2,500–BF3,500	BF2,000–BF3,000
$$	BF1,500–BF2,500	BF1,000–BF2,000
$	under BF1,500	under BF1,000

per person for a three-course meal, including service, taxes, but not beverages

Lodging

You can trust Belgian hotels, almost without exception, to be clean and of a high standard. Modern hotels catering to business travelers, especially in Brussels, can be very expensive, but there is also a wide range of perfectly acceptable and reasonably priced hotels, where the only difference is the size of the room and number of amenities. Hotel prices in the rest of the country are considerably lower than in the capital. Taxes and service charges are always included in the quoted price. Hotel lists are available from local tourist offices.

Pensions offer a double room with bath or shower and full board from BF2,500 to BF3,500 in Brussels, about BF500 less elsewhere. There's often a minimum-stay requirement of two to three days. B&B accommodations are available for BF700 and up. For information, check the local tourist office. Youth hostels are also popular, and Belgium is well supplied with camping and trailer sites.

CATEGORY	BRUSSELS*	BELGIUM EXCEPT BRUSSELS*
$$$$	over BF9,000	over BF7,500
$$$	BF6,500–BF9,000	BF5,500–BF7,500
$$	BF3,500–BF6,500	BF2,500–BF5,500
$	under BF3,500	under BF2,500

for two persons sharing double room, including service and tax

Exploring Belgium

One of the great joys of Belgium is manageability—from Brussels, you can reach most parts of the country by road or rail within two hours, and Brugge, Antwerp, Gent, Namur, and Liège are all within an hour's journey. Although its road tunnels are notoriously confusing for first-time users, the capital compensates with an excellent public transport system; given the difficulty of parking in the town center, you'd be well-advised to make full use of it. In Flemish cities, especially Gent and Hasselt, town center pedestrianization is becoming increasingly commonplace, with cycling encouraged as the principal mode of transport (there was even a scheme to introduce student-pulled rickshaws, though these seem not to have caught on).

Highways are of a generally high standard, but the coastal routes in particular tend to become gridlocked in summer as Brussels's denizens make the most of the sunshine. In fact, the only places you may have trouble getting around are the northeast Kempen district, which is prime cycling country, or the woody hills of the Ardennes, where bracing walks are the order of the day.

Numbers in the text correspond to numbers in the margin and on the maps.

Great Itineraries

IF YOU HAVE 3 DAYS

Start in ⊞ **Brussels,** making a beeline for the Grand'Place and, if you must, join the snapping hordes around the Manneken Pis. Then stroll to the neoclassical Place Royale and take in the treasures of Renaissance and 20th-century art in the nearby museums. Or, if fin de siècle opulence is more your thing, visit the stunning Art Nouveau Horta Museum, popping in to see Bruegel's *Fall of Icarus* at the Van Buuren Museum beforehand. On day two, rise with the lark and head for **Brugge** ㉓–㊴, allowing time to enjoy the Flemish Primitive art in the Groeninge and Memling museums and for a whirlwind tour round the historic center. Stay in the equally medieval ⊞ **Gent** ⑭–⑳, one of the world's most agreeable sites for an evening stroll, and better value for money in food and lodging terms. For a memorable last day, visit **Antwerp** and savor the combination of heritage, economic dynamism, and civic pride that has made the city Europe's most fashionable. Then back to the airport via **Lier** ㊸ for a romantic riverfront farewell.

IF YOU HAVE 7 DAYS

Make ⊞ **Brussels** your headquarters, spending two days exploring the magnificent Grand'Place and its historic surroundings, then the district of the neoclassical Place Royale and the museums, whose collections range from Bruegel and Rubens to Delvaux and Magritte. From Brussels, make several one-day excursions: to medieval **Brugge** ㉓–㊴ with its romantic canals, the city where oil painting was invented and where some of the greatest masterpieces of 15th-century art have been preserved; to **Gent** ⑭–⑳ to see Van Eyck's masterpiece, the *Adoration of the Mystic Lamb,* and the splendid towers and enchanting riverfronts; to **Antwerp,** the great port city, whose luminous cathedral contains Rubens's finest works; to Waterloo's brooding battlefield, where the history of Europe was forever changed; and to **Han-sur-Lesse** ㊽ in the Ardennes, whose vast caves seem to echo prehistoric memories.

IF YOU HAVE 10 DAYS

Plan on three days in ⊞ **Brussels,** adding the third day in the capital to see the Horta Museum, arguably the world's finest example of Art Nouveau, and the Comic Strip Museum, housed in another Horta building, honoring another Belgian art form whose best-known heroes are Tintin and Lucky Luke. From Brussels, take day trips to Waterloo and **Antwerp.** Then move on to ⊡ **Brugge** ㉓–㊴ for three days, with excursions to **Gent** ⑭–⑳, the World War I battlefields around **Ieper** ㊷, and the North Sea Coast. Wind up your visit to Belgium with two days in the Ardennes, where, based in ⊡ **Namur** ㉔, you can explore the caves in **Han-sur-Lesse** ㉒ and see the dramatic Meuse River valley; take a day-long drive over forest-clad hills and green plateaus to visit **La Roche-en-Ardenne** ㉑ and the meandering river Ourthe; to **Bastogne** ㉒ of Battle of the Bulge fame; and north past **Stavelot** ㉘ and **Malmédy** ㉗ to the Hautes Fagnes (High Fens) nature reserve and **Liège** ㉖.

When to Tour Belgium

Belgium looks entirely different bathed in bright sunlight than it does during a dank drizzle. While summer is never guaranteed in Belgium, the best time to visit is between April and late September. Throughout the summer, the capital's historic Grand'Place hosts cultural and traditional events, including the Ommegang pageant at the start of July; the 1999 event is doubly remarkable because it marks the 450th anniversary of Charles V's arrival in Brussels, the occasion on which the pageant is modeled.

For a skiing trip in the Ardennes, late December and January are the months to come. To enjoy the splendors of Brugge without the accompanying tourist invasion, then chance the weather and visit in March or October.

If you love mussels, be in Brussels on July 15, when the season officially starts; open-air stalls in the normally overpriced Petite Rue des Bouchers are the place to consume the meaty mollusks with a glass of white wine or a coupe de champagne. The game season begins in September, so to reach authentic culinary heaven, visit the Ardennes around then.

BRUSSELS

Brussels (Bruxelles in French, Brussel in Flemish) is a provincial city at heart, even though it has assumed a new identity as capital of the European Union (EU). Within Belgium, Brussels has equal status with Flanders and Wallonia as an autonomous region. It is a bilingual enclave just north of the language border that divides the country into Flemish- and French-speaking parts. Historically, it is also the capital of Flanders.

At the end of the 19th century, Brussels was one of the liveliest cities in Europe, known for its splendid cafés and graceful Art Nouveau architecture. That gaiety was stamped out by German occupation during the two world wars. The comeback of Brussels on the international scene was heralded by the World's Fair and the Universal Exposition of 1958.

As a by-product of Europe's increasing integration, international business has invaded the city in a big way since the 1960s, resulting in blocks full of steel-and-glass office buildings only a few steps from the cobbled streets and forgotten spots where the city's eventful past is plainly visible. Over the centuries, Brussels has been shaped by the different cultures of the foreign powers that have ruled it. It has learned the art of accommodating them and, in the process, prepared itself for the role of political capital of Europe.

Exploring Brussels

Around the 1,000-year-old historic center of Brussels, a group of ring roads form concentric circles. Crossing them is like traveling back and forth across the centuries. Brussels once had a river, the Senne, but it was buried in the 19th century after becoming clogged with sewage; the absence of left and right river banks can make orientation in the city a bit difficult.

The center, sitting in a bowl, is sometimes known as the Pentagon, from the shape of the oldest ring road, which roughly follows the ancient ramparts; all that's left of them is one of the gates, the Porte de Hal, the Tour Noire (Black Tower) on Place Ste-Catherine, and a small patch of wall next to a bowling alley near Place de la Chapelle. On either side of the 19th-century ring road you can see the cupolas of the Palais de Justice and the Basilique, and in the center, the slender belfry of the Hôtel de Ville rises like a beacon.

Brussels is small enough that you can get a superficial impression of it from a car window in a single day. For more substantial appreciation, you need one day for the historic city heart, another for the uptown squares and museums, and additional days for museums outside the center and excursions to the periphery. There are many attractive nooks and crannies to explore.

Lower Town: The Heart of Brussels

During the latter half of the 10th century, a village began to emerge on the site of present-day Brussels. A population of craftspeople and traders settled gradually around the castle of the counts of Leuven, who were later succeeded by the dukes of Brabant.

Philip the Good, Duke of Burgundy, took possession of Brussels, then known as Brabant, in 1430. Under him, Brussels became a center for the production of tapestry, lace, and other luxury goods. By 1555, when Charles V abdicated in favor of his son, Philip II of Spain, the Protestant Reformation was spreading through the Low Countries. Philip, a devout Catholic, dealt ruthlessly with advocates of the Reformation. His governor, the Duke of Alva, had the leaders of the revolt, the Counts of Egmont and Hoorn, executed on the Grand'Place. A monument to them stands in the square of the Petit Sablon.

In 1695, on the orders of French King Louis XIV, Marshal Villeroy bombarded the city with red-hot cannonballs. The ensuing fires destroyed 4,000 houses, 16 churches, and all of the Grand'Place, with the exception of the Town Hall. The buildings around the square were immediately rebuilt, in the splendor that we see today.

In 1713, the Spanish Netherlands came under the rule of the Austrian Habsburgs. Despite the influence of Enlightenment theories on the province's governors, nationalist feeling had set in among large sections of the populace, which was not stamped out by the repressive armies of Napoléon or the post-Waterloo incorporation of Belgium into a new Kingdom of the Netherlands. On August 25, 1830, a rousing duet from an Auber opera being performed at La Monnaie inflamed patriots in the audience, who burst onto the streets and raised the flag of Brabant. With support from Britain and France, independence came swiftly.

Since then, Brussels has undergone image upheavals almost as significant as the impact of this century's two world wars. At the turn of the century, the wide boulevards and sumptuous Art Nouveau buildings symbolized a city as bustling and metropolitan as Paris; from the

'50s onwards, Brussels became a byword for boring: a gray, faceless city of bureaucrats where cavalier neglect of urban planning created a new word—bruxellization—for the destruction of architectural heritage. Now the pace of European integration (and the wonders of the city's food and drink) has helped to restore the city's international reputation—but internal tensions between Flemings and French-speakers still threaten to tear it apart.

Numbers in the text correspond to numbers in the margin and on the Brussels map.

A Good Walk

Start at **Manneken Pis** ①, at Rues de l'Etuve and du Chêne, a bronze statue of a small boy urinating that symbolizes the insouciant spirit of the *Bruxellois*. Thousands of copies are on sale in the souvenir shops along the three blocks of Rue de l'Etuve leading to the **Grand'Place** ②, the magnificent square surrounded by the Hôtel de Ville (Town Hall) and ornate guild houses. The alley next to the Maison du Roi (opposite the Town Hall) leads into the restaurant-lined Petite Rue des Bouchers with the highly original puppet theater, **Théâtre Toone** ③, in the **Quartier de l'Ilôt Sacré** ④. Turn right at the top of the street to reach the **Galeries St-Hubert** ⑤, an impressively engineered and decorated shopping gallery from 1847.

At the exit from the gallery, turn right on Rue d'Arenberg and cross the uninspiring Boulevard de Berlaymont, heading for the twin Gothic towers of the **Cathédrale St-Michel et Ste-Gudule** ⑥, a 13th-century edifice with outstanding stained-glass windows. Walk back down the hill and turn right on Boulevard de Berlaymont. Take the second flight of stairs on the left, down to the Rue des Sables and the **Centre Belge de la Bande Dessinée** ⑦, or Belgian Comic Strip Center, as engrossing to adults as it is enchanting to kids. A left and a right take you into Rue du Persil and the **Place des Martyrs** ⑧, currently under reconstruction. The pedestrian shopping street, Rue Neuve, half a block away, is filled with bargain-seeking shoppers in the daytime, but deserted at night. It leads to the **Place de la Monnaie** ⑨ and the Théâtre de la Monnaie, one of Europe's leading opera stages.

As you cross the busy Boulevard Anspach onto the Rue des Augustins, the remnants of the **Tour Noire** ⑩ are on your left. To the right, the short Rue des Cyprès leads to the Flemish Baroque **Eglise St-Jean-du-Béguinage** ⑪. Walk down the block-long Rue du Peuplier, and you're in the old Fish Market area, although the canal has been replaced by ponds, and every house is now a seafood restaurant. Turn left toward the blackened church of Ste-Catherine and you'll find a busy market in front of it on the **Place Ste-Catherine** ⑫. Take the first right, Rue de Flandre. Halfway up the block is the gateway to the **Maison de la Bellone** ⑬ with its fine Baroque facade, now a theater museum. Returning to the Place Ste-Catherine, cross the square and take the second street right. This is **Rue Antoine Dansaert** ⑭, the heart of the city's fashionable quarter. You are now facing the grandiose stock exchange, the **Bourse** ⑮. Next to it is Bruxella 1238, an in-situ archaeological museum, and the small **Eglise St-Nicolas** ⑯, hemmed in by tiny houses. You are now on Rue au Beurre, half a block from the Grand'Place.

TIMING

Walking the route will take you about two hours (and the cobblestone streets call for good walking shoes). The Grand'Place requires half an hour (more if you linger in one of its cafés). Stops in churches and museums may add another hour and a half. With a break for lunch, this is a comfortable, one-day program any day of the week, especially Mon-

160

Brussels

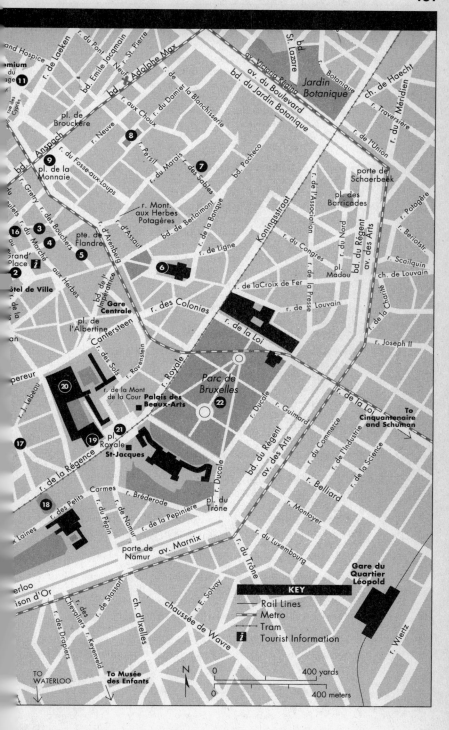

day, when museums are closed (most of the city's must-see museums are in the Upper Town or farther outside the center).

Sights to See

⑮ Bourse (Stock Exchange). The decorative frieze of allegorical statues in various stages of nudity, some of them by Rodin, forms a sort of idealization of the common man. Step inside if you feel like placing a bet on Belgian stocks. Right next to the Bourse lies an in-situ archaeological museum, **Bruxella 1238**, where you can inspect the excavation of a 13th-century church. ⊠ *R. de la Bourse,* ☎ *02/279–4355.* ⊡ *BF100.* ☉ *Guided visits from Town Hall, Wed. 10:15, 11:15, 1:45, 2:30, 3:15.*

⑥ Cathédrale St-Michel et Ste-Gudule. Next to nothing is known about St. Gudule, the daughter of a 7th-century Carolingian nobleman, but this is where her relics have been preserved for the past thousand years. Construction of the cathedral began in 1226. Its twin Gothic towers are gleaming white again after the removal of centuries of grime, and restoration of the interior is under way. Because of the restoration, the choir will not be accessible until 2000, but the remains of an earlier, 11th-century Romanesque church that was on the site can be glimpsed through glass apertures set into the floor. Among the windows in the cathedral, designed by various artists, those by Bernard van Orley, a 16th-century court painter, are outstanding. The window of *The Last Judgment,* at the bottom of the nave, is illuminated from within in the evening. ⊠ *Parvis Ste-Gudule,* ☎ *02/217–8345.* ☉ *Nov.–Mar., daily 7–6; Apr.–Oct., Mon.–Sat. 7–7, Sun. 2–7.*

★ ㋛ ⑦ Centre Belge de la Bande Dessinée (Belgian Comic Strip Center). It fell to the land of Tintin, a cherished cartoon character, to create the world's first museum dedicated to the art of the comic strip. It is an art that, despite its primary appeal to children, has been taken seriously in Belgium for many years, and in this museum it is wedded to another strongly Belgian art form, Art Nouveau. The building was designed by Victor Horta in 1903 for a textile wholesaler, and the lighting and stairs, always important to Horta, are impressive. They serve the purposes of the new owner equally well. Tintin, the creation of the late, great Hergé, became a worldwide favorite cartoon character, and his albums have sold an estimated 80 million copies. But many other artists have followed in Hergé's footsteps, some of them even more innovative. The collection includes more than 400 original plates by Hergé and his successors and 25,000 cartoon works; those not exhibited can be viewed in the archive. There's also a large comic strip shop, a library, and an attractive Art Nouveau brasserie. ⊠ *R. des Sables 20,* ☎ *02/219–1980.* ⊡ *BF200.* ☉ *Tues.–Sun. 10–6.*

⑪ Eglise St-Jean-du-Béguinage. Originally, this elegant, Flemish Baroque church served as the center for the *béguines* (lay sisters) who lived in houses clustered around it. The interior has preserved its Gothic style, with soaring vaults. The surprisingly different architectural styles combine to make this one of the most attractive churches in Brussels. A number of streets converge on the small, serene, circular square, which is surrounded by buildings that help create a harmonious architectural whole. ⊠ *Pl. du Béguinage.* ☉ *Tues.–Fri. 10–5.*

NEED A BREAK?

A la Mort Subite (⊠ R. Montagne-aux-Herbes-Potagères 7, ☎ 02/513–1318) is a Brussels institution named after a card game called "Sudden Death." This café, unaltered for 75 years, serves Mort Subite lambic beers on tap, in a wide range of fruit flavors.

⑯ Eglise St-Nicolas. This small church, surrounded by tiny houses that seem to huddle under it, is almost 1,000 years old. Little remains of the original structure, but a cannonball fired by the French in 1695 is still lodged in one of the pillars. ⊠ *R. au Beurre 1,* ☎ *02/513–8022.* ⊗ *Daily 8–6:30, except during mass; mass in English, Sun. at 10* AM.

Cirio (⊠ R. de la Bourse 18–20) is a peaceful café with outstanding Art Nouveau decor that hasn't changed for generations; nor, apparently, has some of the clientele.

❺ Galeries St-Hubert. A visit to this arcade is like going shopping with your great-grandparents. There are three parts to it: *de la Reine, du Roi,* and *du Prince* (of the queen, the king, and the prince). They were built in 1847 as the world's first covered shopping galleries, thanks to new engineering techniques that allowed architects to use iron girders to design soaring constructions of glass. Neoclassical gods and heroes look down from their sculpted niches on the crowded scene below; flags of many nations billow ever so slightly; and the buskers play classical music, while diffused daylight penetrates the gallery from the glassed arches. The shops are interspersed with cafés, restaurants, a theater, and a cinema. ⊠ *Access from R. des Bouchers or Carrefour de l'Europe.*

★ ❷ Grand'Place. This jewel box of a square is arguably Europe's most ornate and most theatrical. It is close to the hearts of all the people of the city, and all ages come here from time to time. At night the burnished facades of the guild houses and their gilded statuary look especially dramatic: From April to September, the square is floodlit after sundown with waves of changing colors, accompanied by music. Try to be here for the *Ommegang,* a magnificent historical pageant re-creating Emperor Charles V's reception in the city in 1549 (the first Tuesday and Thursday in July). There is a daily flower market in the Grand'-Place; frequent jazz and classical concerts; and in December, under the majestic Christmas tree, a life-size crèche with sheep grazing around it. ⊠ *Intersection of R. des Chapeliers, R. Buls, R. de la Tête d'Or, R. au Beurre, R. Chair et Pain, R. des Harengs, and R. de la Colline.*

Guild Houses of the Grand'Place. Built in ornate Baroque style soon after the 1695 bombardment, the guild houses have a striking architectural coherence. Among the buildings on the north side of the square, No. 1–2, **Le Roy d'Espagne,** belonged to the bakers' guild. It is surmounted by a cupola on which the figure of Fame is perched. **Le Sac,** No. 4, commissioned by the guild of joiners and coopers, and No. 6, **Le Cornet,** built for the boatmen, were both designed by Antoon Pastorana, a gifted furniture maker. **Le Renard,** No. 7, was designed for the guild of haberdashers and peddlers; a sculpture of St. Christopher, their patron, stands on top of the gable. **Le Cygne,** No. 9, was formerly a butchers' guild. Today, it is an elegant restaurant (☞ Maison du Cygne *in* Dining and Lodging, *below*), but before that it was a popular tavern often frequented by Karl Marx. ⊠ *Grand'Place.*

Hôtel de Ville (Town Hall). This Gothic building, which dates from the early 15th century, dominates the Grand'Place (☞ *above*). Nearly 300 years older than the guild houses, which were rebuilt after the French bombardment of 1695, it was renovated most recently in 1997. The left wing was begun in 1402 but was soon found to be too small. Charles the Bold laid the first stone for the extension in 1444, and it was completed four years later. The extension left the slender belfry off center; it has now been fully restored. The belfry is topped by a bronze statue of St. Michael crushing the devil beneath his feet. Over the gateway are statues of the prophets, female figures representing lofty virtues, and effigies of long-gone dukes and duchesses. Inside the Town Hall are a number of excellent Brussels and Mechelen tapestries, some of them in the Gothic Hall, where recitals and chamber-music concerts are held frequently. ✉ *Grand'Place,* ☎ *02/279–4365.* 🎫 *BF75.* ☉ *English-speaking tours, Tues. 11:30 and 3:15, Wed. 3:15, Sun. 12:15.*

NEED A BREAK?   There are plenty of cafés to choose from on Grand'Place. On the ground floor of No. 1, the vast and popular **Le Roy d'Espagne** has an open fire and solid wooden furniture.

⑬ Maison de la Bellonne. This patrician 18th-century building was named for the Roman goddess of war, whose effigy decorates the Baroque facade. It houses a **Theater Museum** and often hosts concerts and dance performances. ✉ *R. de Flandre 46,* ☎ *02/513–3333.* ☉ *Tues.–Fri. 10–6.*

Maison de la Brasserie. On the same side of the Grand'Place (☞ *above*) as the Town Hall, this was once the brewers' guild. Today it houses a modest **Brewery Museum,** appropriate enough in a country that still brews 400 different beers. ✉ *Grand'Place 10,* ☎ *02/511– 4987.* 🎫 *BF100.* ☉ *Daily 10–5.*

Maison du Roi (House of the King). Although no king ever lived in this house—a showplace on the Grand'Place (☞ *above*)—it was named for its grandeur. Today, it houses the **Musée Communal,** which has some fine tapestries, altarpieces, and paintings, notably the *Marriage Procession,* by Pieter Bruegel the Elder. On the top floor you can see the extravagant wardrobe of costumes donated to clothe the little statue of *Manneken Pis* (☞ *below*) on festive occasions. ✉ *Grand'Place,* ☎ *02/279–4355.* 🎫 *BF100.* ☉ *Mon.–Thurs. 10–12:30 and 1:30–4 (Apr.–Sept. until 5), weekends 10–1.*

❶ Manneken Pis. For centuries, the small bronze statue of a chubby boy urinating into a fountain has drawn visitors from near and far. (A rarely remarked-upon fact is that he is left-handed.) The first mention of him dates from 1377. Sometimes called "Brussels's Oldest Citizen," he has also been said to symbolize what Belgians think of the authorities, especially those of occupying forces. The present version was commissioned from sculptor Jerome Duquesnoy in 1619. It is a copy; the original was seized by French soldiers in 1747. In restitution, King Louis XV of France was the first to present *Manneken Pis* with a gold-embroidered suit. The statue now has 517 other costumes for ceremonial occasions, an ever-increasing collection whose recent benefactors include John Malkovich and Dennis Hopper. Thousands of copies, in various materials and sizes, are sold as souvenirs every year. A female version, the Jeanneke Pis, can be found at the Petit Sablon (☞ *below*). ✉ *Corner R. de l'Etuve and R. du Chêne.*

❾ Place de la Monnaie. It was here, during a performance of Auber's *La Muette de Portici* in the **Théâtre de la Monnaie** (✉ Pl. de la Monnaie, ☎ 02/218–1202) on August 25, 1830, that some members of the audience became so inflamed by the duet "Amour sacré de la patrie" that they stormed out and started a riot that let to independence. The pleasing hall is among Europe's leading opera stages. ✉ *Between De Brouckere and Fossé aux Loups at Rue Neuve and Rue des Fripiers.*

❽ Place des Martyrs. This square is dedicated to the 445 patriots who died in the brief 1830 war of independence against the Dutch. The shrine to the patriots is underneath the square. The square itself is a neoclassical architectural ensemble built in 1795 in the cool style favored by the Austrian Habsburgs. This noble square has also been a martyr to local political and real estate interests, notably squabbling between the two linguistic administrations, which have hampered much-needed renovations. ✉ *R. du Persil.*

⑫ Place Ste-Catherine. If you find the Grand'Place overrun by tourists, come to this market square, which is devoid of tourists. This is a working market every weekday from 7 to 5, where people come to shop for necessities and banter with fishmongers. There's a stall where you can down a few oysters, accompanied by a glass of ice-cold muscadet. In the evening the action moves to the old **Vismet** (Fish Market), which branches off from the (forgettable) Eglise de Ste-Catherine. All that remains of the old canal is a couple of elongated ponds, but both sides are lined with seafood restaurants, some excellent, many overpriced. In good weather, there's outdoor waterside dining. ⊠ *Intersection of R. Ste-Catherine, R. du Vieux Marché aux Grains, R. de Flandre, Quai aux Briques, Quai au Bois à Bruler, Pl. du Samedi, R. Plateau, and R. Melsens.*

★ ❹ **Quartier de l'Ilôt Sacré.** Pickpockets, flimflam artists, and jewelry vendors mingle with the crowds in the narrow Rue des Bouchers and even narrower Petite Rue des Bouchers. Still, except for the pickpockets, it's all good-natured fun in the liveliest area in Brussels, where restaurants and cafés stand cheek by jowl, their tables spilling out onto the sidewalks. One local street person makes a specialty of picking up a heaped plate and emptying it into his bag. The waiters laugh and bring another plate. The restaurants make strenuous efforts to pull you in with huge displays of seafood and game. The quality, alas, is a different matter (for some outstanding exceptions, *see* Dining, *below*).

⓮ **Rue Antoine Dansaert.** Bordering the city center and the rundown "little Chicago" district, this is the flagship street of Brussels's fashionable quarter, which extends south to the Place St-Géry. Avant-garde boutiques sell Belgian-designed men's and women's fashions along with more familiar high fashion names. There are also inexpensive restaurants, cozy bars and cafés, avant-garde galleries, and stylish furniture shops.

❸ **Théâtre Toone.** An old puppet theater, now run by José Geal, a seventh-generation member of the Toone family, who's known as Toone VII, this theater has a repertory of 33 plays, including some by Shakespeare. The plays are performed in a local dialect (*vloms*). You won't understand a word, but it's fun anyway. There's a puppet museum (only accessible during the shows) and a bar with great, old-fashioned ambience. ⊠ *Impasse Schuddeveld, off Petite R. des Bouchers,* ☎ *02/511–7137 or 02/513–7486.* ☒ *Performance BF400; entrance to museum free with show.* ☉ *Performance most evenings at 8:30.*

⓾ **Tour Noire** (Black Tower). Part of the 12th-century fortifications, the tower is now regrettably being assimilated into the structure of a chain hotel. ⊠ *Pl. Ste-Catherine.*

Upper Town: Royal Brussels

Uptown Brussels bears the hallmarks of two rulers, Austrian Charles of Lorraine and Leopold II, Belgium's empire builder. The 1713 Treaty of Utrecht, which distributed bits of Europe like pieces in a jigsaw puzzle at the end of one of Europe's many wars, handed the Low Countries to Austria. Fortunately for the Belgians, the man Austria sent here as governor was a tolerant visionary who oversaw the construction of a new palace, the neoclassical Place Royale, and other buildings that transformed the Upper Town.

The next large-scale rebuilding of Brussels was initiated by Leopold II, the second king of independent Belgium, in the latter part of the 19th century. Cousin of Queen Victoria and the Kaiser, he annexed the Congo for Belgium and applied some of the profits to grand urban projects. Present-day Brussels is indebted to him for its wide avenues and thoroughfares.

A Good Walk

Start at the **Place du Grand Sablon** ⑰, window-shopping at its over-priced antiques shops and often unadventurous galleries. Cross the Rue de la Régence into its sister square, the peaceful **Place du Petit Sablon** ⑱, whose formal garden is filled with, and surrounded by, statuary. Turn right on the Rue de la Régence to the **Musée d'Art Ancien** ⑲, which holds many Old Masters, and the spectacular **Musée d'Art Moderne** ⑳, which burrows underground for space to show its modern and contemporary art.

You're now on the gleaming white **Place Royale** ㉑, a pearl of 18th-century neoclassicism, with the Eglise de St-Jacques. Walk down the Rue de la Montagne du Cour; on the left is the elegant courtyard of the Palace of Charles de Lorraine. Continue along the Rue Ravenstein around Victor Horta's **Palais des Beaux-Arts**, the city's principal concert venue, and up the handsome steps to the formal **Parc de Bruxelles** ㉒. At its end, on the right, stands Leopold II's vast, hulking **Palais du Roi**.

Returning to Place Royale, pass through the gateway on the corner next to the church, and up the Rue de Namur to the Porte de Namur. You have now reached the city's most expensive shopping area. As you walk right on the Boulevard de Waterloo, you will pass the same high-fashion names that you find in Paris, London, and New York. The focus of the shopping district is the **Place Louise** ㉓, with the avenue and galerie of the same name.

For a fitting finale, walk down the short Rue des Quatre Bras toward the looming, oppressive **Palais de Justice** ㉔. The balustrade facing the old town has a panoramic view of the city, from the cupola of the Koekelberg Basilica, the world's fifth-largest church, on the left, to the Atomium, the replica of a vastly enlarged molecule, on the right. Walk down the steps to explore the colorful neighborhood of **Les Marolles** ㉕, where many of Brussels's immigrants have settled.

TIMING

Walking time, without stopping, is about an hour and a half. For stops in the art museums (closed Monday) add another couple of hours, plus one hour for window shopping in the Grand Sablon and Place Louise areas.

Sights to See

㉕ **Les Marolles.** If the Grand'Place stands for old money, the Marolles neighborhood stands for old—and current—poverty. Walk down the steps in front of the Palais de Justice and you have arrived. This was home to the workers who produced the luxury goods for which Brussels was famous. There may not be many left who still speak the old Brussels dialect, mixing French and Flemish with a bit of Spanish thrown in, but the area still has raffish charm, although gentrification has begun to set in. The Marolles has welcomed many waves of immigrants, the most recent from Spain, North Africa, and Turkey. Many come to the daily **Flea Market** at the Place du Jeu de Balle, where old clothes are sold along with every kind of bric-a-brac, plain junk, and the occasional gem. ⊠ *Center: R. Haute and R. Blaes. Bordered by Bd. du Midi, Bd. de Waterloo heading southwest from Palais de Justice, and imaginary line running west from Pl. de la Chapelle to Bd. Maurice Lemonnier.*

★ ⑲ **Musée d'Art Ancien** (Fine Arts Museum). In the first of the interconnected art museums, special attention is paid to the great, so-called Flemish Primitives of the 15th century, who invented the art of painting with oil. The Spanish and the Austrians pilfered some of the finest works, but there's plenty left by the likes of Memling, Petrus Christus, and

Rogier Van der Weyden. The collection of works by Pieter Bruegel the Elder is outstanding; it includes *The Fall of Icarus,* in which the figure of the mythological hero disappearing in the sea is but one detail of a scene in which people continue to go about their business. A century later Rubens, Van Dyck, and Jordaens dominated the art scene; their works are on the floor above. The 19th-century collection on the ground floor includes the melodramatic *Death of Marat* by Jacques-Louis David, who, like many other French artists and writers, spent years of exile in Belgium. ⊠ *R. de la Régence 3,* ☎ *02/508–3211.* 🎫 *BF150.* ⊘ *Tues.–Sun. 10–noon and 1–5.*

★ ⓴ **Musée d'Art Moderne** (Modern Art Museum). Rather like New York's Guggenheim Museum in reverse, this modern museum burrows underground and circles downward eight floors. You can reach it by an underground passage from the Fine Arts Museum or you can enter it from the house on Place Royale where Alexandre Dumas (*père*) once lived and wrote. The collection is strong on Belgian and French art of the past 100 years, including Belgian artists who have acquired international prominence, such as the Expressionist James Ensor and the Surrealists Paul Delvaux and René Magritte, as well as sculptor Pol Bury and Pierre Alechinsky. Note that lunch hours at this and the Fine Arts Museum (☞ *above*) are staggered so as not to inconvenience visitors. ⊠ *Pl. Royale 1,* ☎ *02/508–3211.* 🎫 *BF150.* ⊘ *Tues.–Sun. 10–1 and 2–5.*

ⓔ **Palais de Justice.** Many a nasty comment—"the ugliest building in Europe," for instance—has been made about Leopold II's giant late-19th-century Law Courts, on the site of the old Gallows Hill, but, unlike the country's celebratedly inept law enforcers, the pompous edifice does strike fear into the heart of the malefactor. Much of the Marolles district was pulled down to make way for the monstrosity, leaving thousands homeless. ⊠ *Pl. Poelaert.* 🎫 *Entrance hall free.* ⊘ *Weekdays 9–5.*

ⓔ **Parc de Bruxelles.** This was once a game park, but in the late 18th century it was tamed into rigid symmetry and laid out in the design of Masonic symbols. The huge **Palais du Roi** occupies the entire south side of the park. It was built by Leopold II at the beginning of this century on a scale corresponding to his megalomaniacal ambitions. The present monarch, King Albert II, comes here for state occasions, although he lives at the more private Laeken Palace on the outskirts of Brussels. ⊠ *Pl. des Palais, R. Royale, adjacent to Pl. Royale.* 🎫 *Palais du Roi free.* ⊘ *July 22–early Sept., Tues.–Sun. 10–4.*

★ ⓱ **Place du Grand Sablon.** Here's where the people of Brussels come to see and be seen. Once, as the name implies, it was nothing more than a sandy hill. Today, it is an elegant square, surrounded by numerous restaurants, cafés, and antiques shops, some in intriguing alleys and arcades. Every Saturday and Sunday morning a lively antiques market of more than 100 stands takes over the upper end of the square. It's not for bargain hunters, however. Downhill from the square stands the **Eglise de la Chapelle,** dating from 1134. Inside, there's a memorial to Pieter Bruegel the Elder, who was married in this church and buried here just a few years later. At the eastern end of the square stands the **Eglise Notre-Dame du Sablon,** a Flamboyant-Gothic church founded in 1304 by the guild of crossbowmen (the original purpose of the square was crossbow practice) and rebuilt in the 15th century. It's one of Brussels's most beautiful churches, and at night the stained-glass windows are illuminated from within. ⊠ *Intersection of R. de Rollebeek, R. Lebeau, R. de la Paille, R. Ste-Anne, R. Boedenbroeck, R. des Sablons, Petite Rue des Minimes, R. des Minimes, and R. Joseph Stevens.*

NEED A
BREAK?
Wittamer, the best of Brussels's many excellent pastry shops (✉ Grand
Sablon 12, ☎ 02/512-3742), has an attractive upstairs tearoom,
which also serves breakfast and light lunches, accompanied by Wit-
tamer's unbeatable pastries.

⑱ Place du Petit Sablon. Opposite the Grand Sablon (☞ *above*), this square
is surrounded by a magnificent wrought-iron fence, topped by 48
small bronze statues representing the city's guilds. Inside the peaceful
garden stands a double statue of the Flemish patriots, Counts Egmont
and Hoorn, on their way to the Spaniards' scaffold in 1568. Also on
the square is the **Musée Instrumental** (Musical Instruments Museum).
With more than 4,000 instruments, it should be among the largest museums of its kind in the world, but the cramped building which now
houses it does scant justice to the collection. Its scheduled transfer to
the larger, Art Nouveau Old England building near Place Royale—de-
layed by a string of funding and administrative problems—should
now take place in 2000. ✉ *Square: Off R. de la Régence; R. aux Laines,
R. des Petits Carmes. Museum: Place du Petit Sablon 17. ☞ Free. ☉
Tues., Thurs., Sat. 2:30–4:30, Wed. 4–6, Sun. 10:30–12:30.*

㉓ Place Louise. There's a certain type of young Belgian matron—tall, blond,
bejeweled, and freshly tanned whatever the season—whose natural urban
habitat is around Place Louise. The most expensive shops are along
Boulevard Waterloo. Prices are somewhat lower on the other side of
the street, on Avenue de la Toison d'Or, which means the Golden
Fleece. Additional shops and boutiques line both sides of Avenue
Louise and the Galerie Louise, which burrows through the block to
link Avenue de la Toison d'Or with Place Stéphanie. This is an area
for browsing, window-shopping, movie-going, and café-sitting, but don't
go expecting a bargain. ✉ *Av. Louise and Bd. de Waterloo.*

NEED A
BREAK?
Nemrod (✉ Bd. de Waterloo 61, ☎ 02/511-1127) is an expensive
but handily placed café-pub garishly dressed up as a hunting lodge with
a blazing fire. It's very popular for a shopping break or before a show.

★ ㉑ Place Royale. Although the Royal Square was built in the French style
by Austrian overlords, it is distinctly Belgian. White and elegantly
proportioned, it is the centerpiece of the Upper Town, which became
the center of power during the 18th century. The equestrian statue in
its center, representing Godefroid de Bouillon, crusader and King of
Jerusalem, is a romantic afterthought. The buildings are being restored
one by one, leaving the facades intact. Place Royale was built on the
ruins of the Palace of the Dukes of Brabant, which had burned down.
The site has been excavated, and it is possible to see the underground
digs and the main hall, Aula Magna, where Charles V was crowned
Holy Roman Emperor in 1519 and where, 37 years later, he abdicated
to retire to a monastery. The church on the square, **St-Jacques-sur-
Coudenberg,** was originally designed to look like a Greek temple.
After the French Revolution reached Belgium, it briefly served as a "Tem-
ple of Reason." The Art Nouveau building on the northwest corner is
the former Old England department store, soon to house the Musical
Instruments Museum when it moves from cramped quarters in the Petit
Sablon (☞ *above*).

On or near Place Royale are the neoclassical courtyard of the **Palace
of Charles of Lorraine** (✉ Coudenberg); the **Hôtel Ravenstein** (✉ 3
R. Ravenstein), built in the 15th century and the only surviving aristocratic house from that period; and the **Palais des Beaux-Arts** (✉ 23
R. Ravenstein), an Art Deco concert hall, designed in the 1920s by Vic-

tor Horta and remarkable more for the ingenuity with which he over-
came its tricky location than for its aesthetic appeal.

OFF THE
BEATEN PATH

ATOMIUM–Built for the 1958 World's Fair, the model of an iron
molecule enlarged 165 billion times is one of Brussels's landmarks.
Normally, you can take an express elevator to the top, 400 ft up, for
panoramic views of Brussels, but the structure is closed throughout 1999
for some desperately needed renovations. ⊠ *Bd. du Centenaire,* ☎ *02/
474–8904. Metro: Heysel.*

MINI-EUROPE–In a 5-acre park next to the Atomium (☞ *above*) stands
an impressive collection of 1:25 scale models of more than 300 famous
buildings from the 15 European Union countries. ⊠ *Bd. du Centenaire
20,* ☎ *02/478-0550.* ☒ *BF395.* ⊙ *Daily 9:30–5 (July–Aug. until 8).*

OCEADE–Attractions at this water park include water slides, a Jacuzzi,
and a wave pool. ⊠ *Bruparck, near Atomium and next to Mini-Europe,*
☎ *02/478-4944.* ☒ *BF460.* ⊙ *Tues.–Thurs. 10-6; Fri., weekends,
and holidays 10–10.*

Museums and the EU: Cinquantenaire and Schuman

East of the center at the end of Rue de la Loi, Ronde-Point Robert Schuman is the focus of the buildings that house the European institutions.
A number of vast museums flank Brussels's version of the Arc de Triomphe, known as *Cinquantenaire,* planned by Leopold II for the 50th
anniversary of Belgian independence in 1880. Leopold's inability to
coax funding from a reluctant government meant it was not completed
until 25 years later.

A Good Walk

Start at Rond-Point Schuman, where among the buildings of the **European Institutions** you can see the **Justus Lipsius building**, named for
the Renaissance humanist and friend of Rubens and home to the se-
cretive Council of Ministers. You can also see the **Berlaymont**, a star-
shape building normally home to the European Commission, although
it's currently wrapped in plastic sheeting after an asbestos scare. Walk
east toward the colossal, crescent-shape buildings in the distance,
crossing Avenue de la Joyeuse Entrée and entering the Parc du Cinquantenaire. Continue along Avenue John F. Kennedy until you reach
the Cinquantenaire Museum (**Musée Royal de l'Armée et de l'Histoire
Militaire** and the **Musées Royaux d'Art et de l'Histoire**) and **Autoworld.**
From there, walk down the Avenue de Tervuren, a broad, straight road
created by Leopold II at the end of the 19th century to link the Cinquantenaire arch with Tervuren. When you reach Place Montgomery,
take a 44 tram to Tervuren and the **Koninklijk Museum voor Midden
Afrika/Musée Royal de l'Afrique Centrale.**

TIMING

From Rond-Point Schuman, it's about 20 minutes to the Cinquantenaire Museum and Autoworld. To walk to Square Montgomery, allow
around 30 minutes. The tram to Tervuren takes about 20 minutes.

Sights to See

Autoworld. Here, under the high glass roof of the south hall in the Parc
de Cinquantenaire, is arrayed one of the best collections of vintage cars—
more than 450—in the world. ⊠ *Parc du Cinquantenaire 11,* ☎ *02/
736–4165.* ☒ *BF200.* ⊙ *Daily 10–6. Subway: Mérode.*

European Institutions. The European Commission and related institutions have had a significant impact on Brussels. Entire neighborhoods
east of the center have been razed to make room for steel-and-glass

buildings. What remains of the old blocks has also seen an influx of ethnic restaurants catering to the tastes of lower-level Eurocrats; the grandees eat in splendid isolation in their own dining rooms. The landmark, star-shape Berlaymont building was closed in 1991 for asbestos removal. Its white wrappings are due to be removed in sometime in 1999, to the great relief of locals tired of hearing visitors ask if it was done by Christo. During the work, the **European Commission** (⊠ R. de Trèves 120) and the **European Council of Ministers** (⊠ R. de la Loi 170) are occupying temporary headquarters. The controversial **European Parliament** building (⊠ R. Wiertz 43)—France still insists on regular Parliament meetings in Strasbourg—is named Les Caprices des Dieux. Its central element, a rounded glass summit, looms behind the Gare de Luxembourg. ⊠ *Rond-Point R. Schuman. Subway: from Ste-Cathérine via De Brouckère to Schuman.*

Koninklijk Museum voor Midden Afrika/Musée Royal de l'Afrique Centrale (Africa Museum). This is part of King Leopold II's legacy to Belgium, an incredible collection of 250,000 objects, including masks, sculpture, and memorabilia of the journeys of the explorers of Africa. The museum stands in the middle of a beautifully landscaped park. ⊠ *Leuvensesteenweg 13,* ☎ *02/767–5401.* 🎟 *BF50.* ☉ *Mid-Mar.–mid-Oct., Tues.–Sun. 9–5:30; mid-Oct.–mid-Mar., Tues.–Sun. 10–4:30. Subway: to Pl. Montgomery, then Tram 44 to Tervuren.*

Musée Royal de l'Armée et de l'Histoire Militaire (Royal Museum of Arms and Military History). The highlight of this vast collection, part of the Cinquantenaire Museum, is the hall filled with 130 aircraft from World War I to the Gulf War. ⊠ *Parc du Cinquantenaire 3,* ☎ *02/733–4493.* 🎟 *Free.* ☉ *Tues.–Sun. 9–noon and 1–4:30.*

★ **Musées Royaux d'Art et de l'Histoire** (Royal Museums of Art and History). The museum's 140 rooms contain important antiquities and ethnographic collections. The most significant sections are devoted to Belgian archaeology and to the immense tapestries for which Brussels once was famous. Renovations in the late 1990s have brought to the museum a new treasure room, plenty of temporary exhibitions, and a more dynamic approach, as well as a new name, joining it with the Musée Royal de l'Armée et de l'Histoire Militaire as the Cinquantenaire Museum. ⊠ *Parc du Cinquantenaire 10,* ☎ *02/741–7211.* 🎟 *BF100.* ☉ *Tues.–Fri. 9:30–5, weekends 10–5.*

West of the Center

A Good Walk

From the **Kermesse du Midi** ㉖ fair (in July or August only), it's a short walk westward from Boulevard du Midi to the **Gueuze Museum.** Take Rue Crickx or Rue Brogniez to Rue Gheude, then walk north to the end of the street. From the Museum, take a taxi or the 47 tram on Chaussée de Mons to Place de la Vaillance. Rue du Chapître, with the **Anderlecht Béguinage** and the **Maison d'Erasme,** is on your right.

TIMING

It's a 5- to 10-minute walk from the Kermesse to Gueuze. The tram ride takes about 10 minutes.

Sights to See

Anderlecht Béguinage. The Beguines, lay sisters and mostly widows of Crusaders, lived here in a collection of small houses, built between 1252 and the 17th century, grouped around a garden. Now it's open to the public, sharing a common administrative office with the Erasmushuis (☞ Maison d'Erasme, *below*). ⊠ *R. du Chapître 8.*

Gueuze Museum. At this living museum of the noble art of brewing you can see Lambic being produced the old way. The quintessential Brussels beer, created through spontaneous fermentation, is brewed nowhere else and is the basic ingredient in other popular Belgian beers, such as Gueuze, cherry-flavored Kriek, and raspberry-flavored Framboise. Sadly, many of the commercially brewed Lambics bear scant resemblance to the real thing. ⊠ *R. Gheude 56,* ☎ *02/521–4928.* ☞ *BF100.* ☉ *Weekdays 8:30–5, Sat. 10–7 (mid-Oct.–May, until 6). Metro: Gare du Midi.*

🖑 ❷ **Kermesse du Midi.** From mid-July until the end of August, all of Belgium's carnival barkers and showmen and their carousels, ghost trains, Ferris wheels, shooting galleries, rides, swings, and merry-go-rounds congregate along the Boulevard du Midi for this giant and hugely popular funfair. It extends for blocks and blocks. ⊠ *Both sides of Bd. du Midi, from Pl. de la Constitution to Porte d'Anderlecht.* ☞ *Each attraction separately priced.* ☉ *Morning–late night.*

Maison d'Erasme/Erasmushuis (Erasmus House). In the middle of a commonplace neighborhood in the commune of Anderlecht stands this remarkable redbrick building, which has been restored to its condition in 1521, the year the great humanist came to Brussels for the fresh air. First editions of *In Praise of Folly,* and other books by Erasmus, can be inspected, and there are some extraordinary works of art: prints by Albrecht Dürer and oils by Holbein and Hieronymus Bosch. Erasmus was out of tune with the ecclesiastical authorities of his day, and some of the pages on view show where the censors stepped in to protect the faithful. ⊠ *R. du Chapître 31,* ☎ *02/521–1383.* ☞ *BF50.* ☉ *Wed.– Thurs. and Sat.–Mon. 10–noon and 2–5. Subway: Ste-Catherine to St-Guidon station in Anderlecht commune.*

South of the Center: Art Deco and Art Nouveau

A Good Walk

Start at the Art Deco **Musée David-et-Alice-Van-Buuren,** off the commune of Uccle's Rond-Point Churchill; then return to the circle and head left along the affluent Avenue Winston Churchill until you reach Place Vanderkindere. From here, turn right and head down Avenue Brugmann, past a remarkable assortment of Art Nouveau houses. Look particularly for Brunfaut's Hôtel Hannon, at the intersection of Brugmann and Avenue de la Jonction, and the charming redbrick Les Hiboux next door. Cross Chaussée de Waterloo and head up Chaussée de Charleroi, then head right onto Rue Américaine to the **Musée Horta.** Next follow Rue Américaine until you reach Chaussée de Vleurgat, then head along Rue Van Eyck. Take a left onto Rue De Craeyer, cross the roundabout and take Rue de la Monastère. Pick up Avenue Bernier, cross Avenue de la Hippodrome, and you're on Rue du Bourmestre. The **Musée des Enfants** is on the left.

TIMING

Allow two or three hours for this walk, including time in the museums, the 20-minute walk from the Van Buuren to the Horta Museum, and the 15 or so minutes to the Musée des Enfants.

Sights to See

Musée David-et-Alice-Van-Buuren. A perfect Art Deco interior from the 1930s is preserved in this museum. The made-to-order carpets and furnishings are supplemented by paintings by the Van Buurens, as well as Old Masters including a Bruegel, *Fall of Icarus,* one of the three versions he painted. The house is surrounded by lush formal gardens. ⊠ *Av. Leo Errera 41,* ☎ *02/343–4851.* ☞ *BF300.* ☉ *Sun. 1–6, Mon. 2–6, Tues.–Sat. by appointment for groups of up to 20. Trams 23 and 90.*

🐾 **Musée des Enfants** (Children's Museum). At this museum for 2- to 12-year-olds, the purpose may be educational—learning to handle objects and emotions—but the results are fun. Kids get to plunge their arms into sticky goo, dress up in eccentric costumes, walk through a hall of mirrors, crawl through tunnels, and take photographs with an over-size camera. ⊠ *R. du Bourgmestre 15,* ☎ *02/640–0107.* ✒ *BF200.* ⊙ *Sept.–July, Wed. and weekends 2:30–5. Trams 93 and 94.*

★ **Musée Horta.** The house where Victor Horta (1861–1947), the creator of Art Nouveau, lived and worked until 1919 is the best place to see his joyful interiors and furniture. Horta's genius lay in his ability to create a sense of opulence, light, and spaciousness where little light or space existed. Lamps hang from the ceilings like tendrils, and mirrored skylights evoke giant butterflies with multicolor wings of glass and steel. For examples of how Horta and his colleagues transformed the face of Brussels in little more than 10 years, ride down Avenue Louise to Vleurgat and walk along Rue Vilain XIII to the area surrounding the **ponds of Ixelles.** ⊠ *R. Américaine 25,* ☎ *02/537–1692.* ✒ *BF150 (weekends BF200).* ⊙ *Tues.–Sun. 2–5:30. To house: Tram 91 or 92 to Ma Campagne. To Ixelles: Tram 93 or 94.*

Dining and Lodging

The star-studded Brussels restaurant scene is a boon to visitors and natives alike. Some suggest that the European Commission chose Brussels for its headquarters because of the excellence of its restaurants. While this may not be wholly true, the top Brussels restaurants rival the best Parisian restaurants; so, alas, do the prices. Most Belgians, however, value haute cuisine as a work of art and are prepared to part with a substantial sum for a special occasion.

A number of neighborhood restaurants have risen to the challenge of making dining out affordable. The choice of dishes may be more limited, and the ingredients less costly, but an animated ambience more than makes up for it. The tab is likely to be a quarter of what a dinner would cost you in one of the grand restaurants, and the uniformly high quality puts Paris to shame. The city is also richly endowed with good and mostly inexpensive Vietnamese, Italian, and Portuguese restaurants.

You can reduce the check almost by half by choosing a set menu. Fixed-price luncheon menus are often an especially good bargain. Menus and prices are always posted outside restaurants. Don't feel that you're under an obligation to eat a three-course meal; many people order just a main course. If you don't want two full restaurant meals a day, there are plenty of snack bars for a light midday meal, and most cafés serve sandwiches and light hot meals both noon and night.

As the capital of Europe, Brussels attracts a large number of high-powered visitors—one in two visitors comes here on business—and a disproportionate number of very attractive luxury hotels have been built to accommodate them. Their prices are higher than what most tourists would like to pay, but on weekends and during July and August, when there aren't many business travelers, prices can drop to below BF5,000 for a double room.

Happily, new hotels catering to cost-conscious travelers, priced at less than BF3,000 for a double, have also been constructed over the last few years. They may be less ostentatious, but they're squeaky-clean with as much attention to your comfort as the palatial five-star hotels.

For price categories, *see* Pleasures and Pastimes at the beginning of this chapter.

$$$$ ✗ **Comme Chez Soi.** Pierre Wynants, the perfectionist owner-chef, has
★ decorated his bistro-size restaurant in sumptuous Art Nouveau style.
The superb cuisine, excellent wines, and attentive service complement
the warm decor. Wynants is ceaselessly inventive, and earlier creations
are quickly relegated to the back page of the menu. One all-time favorite, fillet of sole with a white wine mousseline and shrimp, is, however, always available. One minus: ventilation is poor and it can get
very smoky. ⊠ *Pl. Rouppe 23,* ☎ *02/512–2921. Reservations essential. Jacket and tie. AE, DC, MC, V. Closed Sun.–Mon., July, Dec. 25–
Jan. 1.*

$$$$ ✗ **La Truffe Noire.** Luigi Ciciriello's "Black Truffle" attracts a sophis-
★ ticated clientele with its modern design, well-spaced tables, and a cuisine that draws on classic Italian and modern French cooking. Carpaccio
is prepared at the table and served with long strips of truffle and
Parmesan. Entrées may include Vendé pigeon with truffles, steamed John
Dory with truffles and leeks, and leg of Pauillac lamb in pie crust. The
restaurant also has a garden. ⊠ *Bd. de la Cambre 12,* ☎ *02/640–4422.
Reservations essential. Jacket and tie. AE, DC, MC, V. No lunch Sat.
Closed Sun., Easter wk, 2nd ½ of Aug., Christmas wk.*

$$$$ ✗ **L'Ecailler du Palais Royal.** This excellent seafood-only restaurant,
just off the Grand Sablon, feels like a comfortable club; many of the
clients seem to have known each other and the staff for years. Risotto
of prawns in champagne, lobster ravioli, and the best turbot you're likely
to taste for a long time are among the delicacies. ⊠ *R. Bodenbroek
18,* ☎ *02/512–8751. Reservations essential. Jacket and tie. AE, DC,
MC, V. Closed Sun., Easter wk, Aug.*

$$$$ ✗ **Maison du Cygne.** With decor to match its classic cuisine, this
restaurant is set in a 17th-century guildhall on the Grand'Place. It's
the place to go for power dining. The paneled walls of the formal dining room upstairs are hung with Old Masters, and a small room on
the mezzanine contains two priceless Bruegels. Service is flawless in the
grand manner of old. Typical French-Belgian dishes include *cocotte
d'écrivisses et petits gris de Namur* (shrimp and crayfish), and *agneau
pavillac à Cygne* (lamb). ⊠ *R. Charles Buyls 2,* ☎ *02/511–8244. Reservations essential. Jacket and tie. AE, DC, MC, V. No lunch Sat. Closed
Sun. and 3 wks in Aug.*

$$$$ ✗ **Villa Lorraine.** Generations of American business travelers have
been introduced to the three-hour Belgian lunch at the opulent Villa,
on the edge of the Bois de la Cambre. The green terrace room is light,
elegant, and airy, and there's alfresco dining under the spreading chestnut tree. Feast on red mullet in artichoke vinaigrette, fried sweetbreads
forestière (garnished with morels, bacon, and sautéed potatoes), or quails
and duckling with peaches and green pepper. ⊠ *Chaussée de la Hulpe
28,* ☎ *02/374–3163. Jacket and tie. AE, DC, MC, V. Closed Sun. and
July.*

$$$ ✗ **Castello Banfi.** On the Grand Sablon in beige-and-brown post-
modern surroundings, you can enjoy classic French and Italian dishes
with added refinements, such as toasted pine nuts with pesto. There's
excellent carpaccio with Parmesan and celery, red mullet with ratatouille,
and unbelievable mascarpone. The quality of the ingredients (sublime
olive oil, milk-fed veal imported from France) is very high. The wine
list is strong on fine Chianti aged in wood. ⊠ *R. Bodenbroek 12,* ☎
*02/512–8794. Jacket and tie. AE, DC, MC, V. No dinner Sun. Closed
Mon. and 2nd ½ of Aug.*

$$$ ✗ **La Porte des Indes.** This is the city's foremost Indian restaurant—
the creation of Karl Steppe, a Belgian antiques dealer turned restau-
rateur, who also owns the global Blue Elephant chain. The gracious
staff wear traditional Indian attire. The plant-filled lobby, wood carvings, and soothing blue-and-white decor provide a restful backdrop.

174

Dining

Adrienne, **35**

Amadeus, **42**

Au Stekerlapatte, **32**

Au Vieux Saint Martin, **26**

Aux Armes de Bruxelles, **9**

Aux Marches de la Chapelle, **23**

Bonsoir Clara, **3**

Brasseries Georges, **49**

Castello Banfi, **27**

Chez Jean, **17**

Chez Léon de Bruxelles, **10**

Comme Chez Soi, **22**

Falstaff, **13**

Gallery, **31**

In 't Spinnekopke, **4**

La Fine Fleur, **41**

La Grande Porte, **24**

La Porte des Indes, **46**

La Quincaillerie, **45**

La Roue d'Or, **19**

La Truffe Noire, **47**

L'Ecailler du Palais Royal, **28**

Les Capucines, **33**

Les Petits Oignons, **25**

Maison du Cygne, **16**

Ogenblik, **7**

Villa Lorraine, **50**

Vincent, **6**

Lodging

Alfa Louise, **44**

Amigo, **15**

Beau-Site, **40**

Château du Lac, **51**

Clubhouse, **39**

Conrad, **37**

Four Points, **43**

Gerfaut, **12**

Hilton, **30**

Le Dixseptième, **18**

Les Tourelles, **48**

Manos Stephanie, **38**

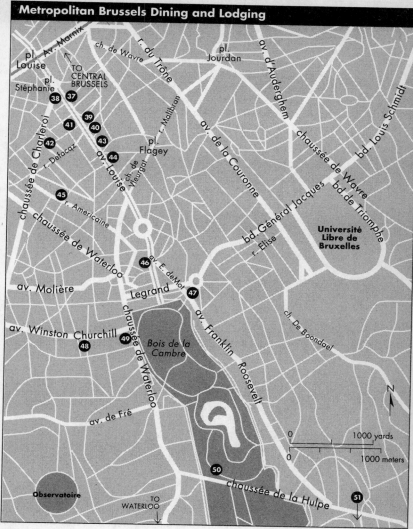

Metropolitan Brussels Dining and Lodging

pl. Louise
Av. Marnix
ch. de Wavre
r. du Trône
pl. Jourdan
av. d'Audergham
TO CENTRAL BRUSSELS
pl. Stéphanie
38
37
chaussée de Charleroi
39
41
40
42
43
r. Defacaz
44
av. Louise
r. Malibran
pl. Flagey
av. de la Couronne
ch. de Vieurgat
45
r. Americaine
chaussée de Waterloo
chaussée de Wavre
bd. Louis Schmidt
bd. de Triomphe
bd. Général Jacques
r. Elise
Université Libre de Bruxelles
46
av. E. deMot
Legrand
av. Molière
47
av. Franklin Roosevelt
ch. De Boondael
av. Winston Churchill
48
49
chaussée de Waterloo
Bois de la Cambre
N
av. de Fré
0   1000 yards
0   1000 meters
50
chaussée de la Hulpe
Observatoire
TO WATERLOO
51

Matignon, **14**
Métropole, **5**
Montgomery, **21**
Novotel, **11**
Orion, **1**
Radisson SAS Hotel, **8**
Royal Windsor Hotel, **20**
Sofitel, **34**
Stanhope, **29**

Sun, **36**
Welcome Hotel, **2**

The cuisine ranges from a mild pilaf to a spicy vindaloo. The "brass tray" offers an assortment of specialties. A vegetarian menu is also available. ☒ *Av. Louise 455,* ☎ *02/647–8651. AE, DC, MC, V. No lunch Sun.*

$$$ ✗ **Les Capucines.** This pleasant restaurant stands out amid the mediocrity of most eateries in the Place Louise shopping area. The dining room is inviting, decorated in shades of green, with huge flower arrangements. Chef Pierre Burtonboy prepares dishes such as grilled fillet of sea bream on a bed of shredded leek dressed with nut oil; lamb interleaved with goose liver, rolled and encased in pastry, with rosemary and thinly sliced potatoes; bitter chocolate mousse with crème anglaise; and iced peach soup with mint. ☒ *R. Jourdan 22,* ☎ *02/538–6924. AE, DC, MC, V. Closed Sun., Mon., Easter, and 2nd ½ of Aug.*

$$$ ✗ **Ogenblik.** This small, split-level restaurant, in a side alley off the
★ Galeries St-Hubert, has all the trappings of an old-time bistro: green-shaded lamps over marble-top tables, sawdust on the floor, and laid-back waiters. There's nothing casual about the French-style cuisine, however: chicken with sweetbreads and goose liver, millefeuille of lobster and salmon, saddle of lamb with spring vegetables. The selection of Beaujolais is particularly good. ☒ *Galerie des Princes 1,* ☎ *02/511–6151. AE, DC, MC, V. ☻ Open until midnight. Closed Sun.*

$$ ✗ **Au Stekerlapatte.** In the shadow of the Palais de Justice, this down-to-earth, efficient bistro serves Belgian specialities, such as black pudding with caramelized apples, cassoulet, sauerkraut, grilled pig's trotters, and spare ribs. ☒ *R. des Prêtres 4,* ☎ *02/512–8681. MC, V. No lunch, closed Sun.*

$$ ✗ **Au Vieux Saint Martin.** Even when neighboring restaurants on
★ Grand Sablon are empty, this one is full. A rack of glossy magazines is a thoughtful touch for lone diners, and you're equally welcome whether you order a cup of coffee or a full meal. The short menu emphasizes Brussels specialties; portions are generous. A wine importer, the owner serves unusually good wine for the price, by the glass or by the bottle. The red walls are hung with large, contemporary paintings, including works by Pierre Alechinsky, and picture windows overlook the pleasant square. A brass plaque marks the table where President Bill Clinton relaxed during a Brussels walkabout. ☒ *Grand Sablon 38,* ☎ *02/512–9292. Reservations not accepted. MC, V.*

$$ ✗ **Aux Armes de Bruxelles.** Hidden among the tourist traps of the Ilôt Sacré, this child-friendly restaurant attracts a largely local clientele with its slightly tarnished middle-class elegance and its Belgian classics: turbot waterzooi, a variety of steaks, mussels prepared every which way, and french fries, which the Belgians believe, with some justification, they prepare better than anyone else. The place is cheerful and light, and service is friendly if frequently overstretched. ☒ *R. des Bouchers 13,* ☎ *02/511–5550. AE, DC, MC, V. Closed Mon.*

$$ ✗ **Aux Marches de la Chapelle.** This very attractive restaurant, opposite
★ the Eglise de la Chapelle near the Grand Sablon, offers brasserie fare of the highest quality, including traditional cassoulet and sauerkraut. One of the Belle Epoque rooms is dominated by a splendid old bar, the other by an enormous open fireplace. ☒ *Pl. de la Chapelle 5,* ☎ *02/512–6891. AE, DC, MC, V. No lunch Sat. Closed Sun. and Aug.*

$$ ✗ **Brasseries Georges.** This brash, hugely successful brasserie was the
★ first in Brussels and is still the best. Efficient service and quality food is guaranteed. You'll find a splendid, almost gaudy display of shellfish at the entrance, an Art Deco interior with tile floor and potted palms, and fast, efficient service by waitresses in black and white. The fare includes traditional dishes, such as sauerkraut, poached cod, and potted duck, as well as more adventurous dishes such as salmon tartare and swordfish chop with a light chicory curry. Twenty-five different

wines are sold by the glass. ✉ *Av. Winston Churchill 259,* ☎ *02/347–2100. AE, DC, MC, V.*

$$ ✗ **In 't Spinnekopke.** This is where true Brussels cooking has survived and continues to flourish. The low ceilings and benches around the walls remain from its days as a coach inn during the 18th century. You can choose from among 100 artisanal beers, and many dishes are made with beer. ✉ *Pl. du Jardin aux Fleurs 1,* ☎ *02/511–8695. AE, DC, MC, V. Closed Sun.*

$$ ✗ **La Fine Fleur.** This neighborhood restaurant, a stone's throw from Avenue Louise, attracts a young, artistic clientele. Leafy plants proliferate, and French chansons set the mood. The artist owner designed the minimalist decor and serves a sort of minimalist cuisine, which includes such happy surprises as carpaccio with cèpes, beef carpaccio with truffles, and scallops with horseradish. Portions are not large. Arrive after 9 to experience the place at its busiest. ✉ *R. de la Longe Haie 51,* ☎ *02/647–6803. AE, DC, MC, V. No lunch Sat. Closed Sun., 2 wks at Easter, 2 wks in Aug.*

$$ ✗ **La Quincaillerie.** The name means "The Hardware Store," and that's precisely what this place used to be. It still looks the part, except now there are tables perched on the narrow balcony and an oyster bar downstairs. It attracts a youngish, upwardly mobile clientele. The menu consists mostly of brasserie grub, such as baked ham knuckle, but it's enlivened by honey-baked Barbary duck with lime and a glorious seafood platter. ✉ *R. du Page 45,* ☎ *02/538–2553. AE, DC, MC, V. No lunch weekends.*

$$ ✗ **La Roue d'Or.** This Art Nouveau brasserie has bright orange and yellow murals that pay humorous homage to Surrealist René Magritte. Bowler-hatted gentlemen ascend serenely to the ceiling, a blue sky inhabited by tropical birds. The good cuisine includes traditional Belgian fare, such as a generous fish waterzooi and home-made frites as well as such staples of the French brasserie repertory as lamb's tongue vinaigrette with shallots, veal kidneys with watercress cream, and foie gras. ✉ *R. des Chapeliers 26,* ☎ *02/514–2554. AE, DC, MC, V. Closed Aug.*

$$ ✗ **Les Petits Oignons.** This airy 17th-century restaurant, in the heart of the Marolles, has been furnished with plants and bright, modern paintings. It places no demands on your palate, but the ambience is enticing, and you are well looked after. Fried goose liver with caramelized onions, roast pigeon with carrots and cumin, and leg of lamb with potatoes au gratin are among the choices. ✉ *R. Notre-Seigneur 13,* ☎ *02/512–4738. AE, DC, MC, V. Closed Sun. and Aug.*

$$ ✗ **Vincent.** In a town where most of the more fashionable places now concentrate on seafood, Vincent remains unapologetically a red-meat stronghold. Sides of beef and big slabs of butter in the window announce what awaits you. You pass through the kitchen on your way to the dining room, which is decorated with hand-painted tiles. ✉ *R. des Dominicains 8–10,* ☎ *02/502–3693. AE, DC, MC, V. Closed Aug. 1–15.*

$–$$ ✗ **Amadeus.** It is not so much the food (goat cheese with honey, spare ribs, tagliatelle with salmon) as the decor that makes this converted artist's studio near the Place Stéphanie a must. Ultra-romantic, not to say kitschy, its dining rooms have an abundance of mirrors, candles, and intimate alcoves, creating a trysty, almost conspiratorial Baroque feel. ✉ *R. Veydt 13,* ☎ *02/538–3427. AE, DC, MC, V. No lunch Mon., closed mid-July–mid-Aug.*

$ ✗ **Adrienne.** The huge cold buffet draws crowds year after year at this upstairs restaurant, just around the corner from Avenue Toison d'Or. The look is rustic, with red-and-white check tablecloths; you can eat on the terrace in summer. The location is great for uptown shopping and movies, and it's also fun for kids. The Atomium branch is cheaper and of equally good quality. ⊠ R. *Capitaine Crespel 1A*, ☎ *02/511–9339; Atomium du Heysel, near Atomium*, ☎ *02/478–3000. AE, DC, MC, V. Closed Sun. evening.*

$ ✕ **Bonsoir Clara.** On downtown's trendy Rue Dansaert, this is the jewel in the crown of young restaurateur Frédéric Nicolay, who runs half a dozen fashionable cafés and eateries in the capital, including the Kasbah next door. An upbeat, refined brasserie serving excellent caramelized duck as well as fish and red-meat dishes, it's best-known for eye-catching decor, especially a back wall entirely composed of large colored squares, as if you were in a Rubik's Cube factory. ⊠ R. *Dansaert 22*, ☎ *02/502–0990. AE, MC, V. No lunch weekends.*

$ ✕ **Chez Jean.** Jean Cambien runs a reliable, unpretentious restaurant, ★ unchanged since 1931, with oak benches against the walls, backed by mirrors upon which the dishes of the day are written in whitewash. Waitresses in black and white serve poached cod, mussels cooked in white wine, chicken waterzooi (your plate is replenished as many times as you want), chicken in kriek with cherries, and other quintessentially Belgian fare. ⊠ R. *des Chapeliers 6*, ☎ *02/511–9815. AE, DC, MC, V. Closed Sun. and June.*

$ ✕ **Chez Léon de Bruxelles.** More than a century old, this cheerful ★ restaurant has over the years expanded into a row of eight old houses, while its franchises can now be found across Belgium and even in Paris. Heaped plates of mussels and other Belgian specialties, such as eels in a green sauce and fish soup, are served nonstop, accompanied by arguably the best french fries in town. ⊠ R. *des Bouchers 18*, ☎ *02/511–1415. Reservations not accepted. AE, DC, MC, V.*

$ ✕ **Falstaff.** Some things never change, and Falstaff is one of them. This ★ huge tavern, with an attractive interior that is pure Art Nouveau, fills up for lunch and, a rarity in Brussels, keeps going until 5 AM, with an ever-changing crowd, from students to pensioners. Straightforward Belgian cuisine is served, but the waiters display the kind of off-hand arrogance one would associate with Paris, not Brussels. Falstaff II (⊠ R. Henri Maus 25) has the same food but not the ambience. ⊠ R. *Henri Maus 19*, ☎ *02/511–8789. AE, DC, MC, V.*

$ ✕ **Gallery.** This Vietnamese restaurant looks like a minimalist art gallery, with contemporary black chairs and tables, artfully suspended spotlights, and temporary exhibitions of black-and-white photographs. The kitchen holds no surprises, but the food is well prepared and the helpings of dishes such as Vietnamese pancakes, hot-and-sour soup, and beef with chilis and peppers are substantial. ⊠ R. *du Grand Cerf 7*, ☎ *02/511–8035. AE, DC, MC, V. No lunch Sun. Closed 1st ½ of Aug.*

$ ✕ **La Grande Porte.** A long-time favorite in the Marolles area that makes no concession to fashion or style, this old place has a player piano and offhand but jovial waiters. It serves copious portions of popular Brussels specialties, such as *ballekes à la marollienne* (spicy meatballs) and *carbonnade à la flamande* (beef and onions stewed in beer). The later in the evening it becomes, the livelier the atmosphere and the greater the demand for the restaurant's famous onion soup. ⊠ R. *Notre-Seigneur 9*, ☎ *02/512–8998. DC. Closed Sun., no lunch Sat.*

$$$ ✕🏠 **Château du Lac.** Half an hour from the city center and a good choice ★ as a peaceful base from which to visit the capital and the provinces, this mock-Florentine castle is a former Schweppes bottling plant. In the late 1990s the hotel expanded to make room for more luxurious green and white rooms. The older light beige rooms are equally well furnished; the decor in the public rooms is contemporary, mostly green and wine red. The splendid gastronomic restaurant, Le Trèfle à Quatre, serves classic French cuisine and is itself worth a visit here, not only for its superb fish and game, but also for the views over the lake. ⊠

Av. du Lac 87, B 1332 Genval, ☎ *02/654–1122,* FAX *02/655–7444.
121 rooms. Restaurant, bar, pool, sauna, fitness, convention center. AE,
DC, MC, V.*

$ ✕🏨 **Welcome Hotel.** Among the charms of the smallest hotel in Brus-
★ sels are the young owners, Michel and Sophie Smeesters. The six
rooms, divided into economy, business, and first class and with king-
or queen-size beds, are as comfortable as those in far more expensive
establishments. This little hotel, located in the center of Brussels near
the fish market, is much in demand, so book early. There's a charming breakfast room and around the corner on the fish market, Michel
doubles as chef of the excellent seafood restaurant La Truite d'Argent
($$$), where hotel guests get a special rate. ⊠ *R. du Peuplier 5, B 1000,*
☎ *02/219–9546,* FAX *02/217–1887. 6 rooms. 2 restaurants, meeting
room, free parking. AE, DC, MC, V.*

$$$$ 🏨 **Conrad.** Opened in 1993 on the elegant Avenue Louise, this hotel
combines the classic facade of an 1865 mansion with a sleek, deluxe
American interior. Rooms come in many different shapes but are all
spacious and have three telephones, a desk, bathrobes, and in-room
checkouts. The intimate, gourmet Maison de Maître restaurant is well
respected, while Café Wiltcher's offers all-day brasserie dining. The large
piano bar is pleasantly chummy. ⊠ *Av. Louise 71, B 1050,* ☎ *02/542–
4242,* FAX *02/542–4300. 269 rooms, 15 suites. 2 restaurants, 2 bars,
exercise room, shops, convention center, parking (fee). AE, DC, MC, V.*

$$$$ 🏨 **Hilton.** One of the first high-rises in Brussels back in the 1960s, this
one outclasses most other Hiltons in Europe and is continuously being
refurbished floor by floor. The four floors of executive rooms have a
separate check-in area; there are nine floors of business rooms. The
location is great for upscale shopping, and the building has a fine
panoramic view over the capital. The first-floor restaurant, the Mai-
son du Boeuf, is one of the best in town; the ground-floor Café d'Eg-
mont stays open around the clock. ⊠ *Bd. de Waterloo 38, B 1000,* ☎
02/504–1111, FAX *02/504–2111. 430 rooms, 39 suites. 2 restaurants,
bar, sauna, exercise room, shops, convention center, parking (fee). AE,
DC, MC, V.*

$$$$ 🏨 **Montgomery.** The owners of this 1993 hotel set out to create new
standards of service for the business traveler and, for the most part,
they have succeeded. Fax machines, three telephones (with a private
line for incoming calls), good working desks, safes, triple-glazed win-
dows, and bathrobes are standard. Rooms are decorated in Chinese;
English cozy; or cool, clean colonial style. There's a library and a bar-
restaurant with a wood-burning fireplace. The small meeting rooms
are well appointed. The location is conveniently close to the European
Commission. ⊠ *Av. de Tervuren 134, B 1150,* ☎ *02/741–8511,* FAX
*02/741–8500. 61 rooms, 2 penthouses, 1 suite. Restaurant, bar, health
club, library, meeting rooms, parking (fee). AE, DC, MC, V.*

$$$$ 🏨 **Radisson SAS Hotel.** Near the northern end of the Galeries St-Hubert,
★ this hotel opened in 1990 and was an instant success. The floors are
decorated in a variety of styles—Asian (wicker furniture and Asian art),
Italian (Art Deco fixtures and furnishings), and Scandinavian (light-
wood furniture and parquet flooring). The greenery-filled atrium in-
corporates a 10-ft-high section of the 12th-century city wall. The Sea
Grill is a first-rate seafood restaurant, and Danish open-face sandwiches
are served in the atrium's café. A copious buffet breakfast is included.
There's no extra charge for children under 15. ⊠ *R. du Fossé-aux-Loups
47, B 1000,* ☎ *02/219–2828,* FAX *02/219–6262. 281 rooms. 3 restau-
rants, 2 bars, sauna, health club, business services, convention center,
parking (fee). AE, DC, MC, V.*

$$$$ 🏨 **Royal Windsor Hotel.** Near the Grand'Place and favored by visit-
ing dignitaries, this hotel celebrates its 25th birthday in 1999. All

rooms have blond-wood paneling; the bathrooms, in Portuguese marble, are among the most beautiful in Brussels. They are, however, on the small side. The lobby is businesslike, with leafy plants, comfortable sofas and chairs placed around marble-top tables, and music wafting in from the adjacent piano bar. The elegant dining room, Les Quatre Saisons, serves light, imaginative, and expensive French cuisine; the Windsor Arms is an English-style pub. ⊠ *R. Duquesnoy 5, B 1000,* ☎ *02/505–555,* FAX *02/505–5500. 266 rooms, 43 suites. Restaurant, bar, sauna, health club, dance club, convention center, parking (fee). AE, DC, MC, V.*

$$$$ 🏨 **Stanhope.** This small, exclusive hotel was created out of three adjoining town houses. All the rooms and suites have high ceilings, marble bathrooms, and luxurious furniture, but each has its own name, and no two are alike. The Linley, for example, has furniture handmade by Viscount Linley, nephew of the Queen of England. You can have English-style afternoon tea in the ground-floor salon; the gastronomic Brighton restaurant, a copy of the banqueting room of the Royal Palace, serves French specialties. The bar is open to the public. ⊠ *R. du Commerce 9, B 1000,* ☎ *02/506–9111,* FAX *02/512–1708. 25 rooms, 25 suites. Restaurant, bar, sauna, health club, meeting rooms, parking (fee). AE, DC, MC, V.*

$$$ 🏨 **Amigo.** Just a block from the Grand'Place and decorated in Spanish Renaissance style with touches of Louis XV, the Amigo looks more turn-of-the-century than 1950s, when it was built. Rooms vary in furnishings, size, and price; those on higher floors, with views over the surrounding rooftops, are more expensive. The Presidential Suite has a large terrace overlooking the Grand' Place. Bathrooms are on the small side. Amigo is known for its understated luxury. The service is excellent. ⊠ *R. d'Amigo 1–3, B 1000,* ☎ *02/547–4747,* FAX *02/513–5277. 178 rooms, 7 suites. Restaurant, bar, meeting rooms, parking (fee). AE, DC, MC, V.*

$$$ 🏨 **Métropole.** Stepping into the Métropole, you would think you were boarding the *Orient Express.* The hotel, built in 1895, has been restored to the palace it was during the Belle Epoque. The lobby sets the tone, with its enormously high coffered ceiling, chandeliers, marble, Oriental rugs, and old-fashioned wood-paneled lift. The theme is carried through in the bar, with potted palms, deep leather sofas, and Corinthian columns; in the café, which opens onto the sidewalk of Place de Brouckère; and in the Alban Chambon restaurant (named for the architect). The rooms are understated modern in varying shades of pastel (some with trompe l'oeil murals), with furniture upholstered in the same material as the bedspreads. ⊠ *Pl. de Brouckère 31, B 1000,* ☎ *02/217–2300,* FAX *02/218–0220. 410 rooms. Restaurant, bar, café, health club, convention center, airport shuttle, free parking. AE, DC, MC, V.*

$$$ 🏨 **Sofitel.** Opened in 1989, the six-floor Sofitel has a great location opposite the Hilton. There's a chic shopping arcade on the ground floor, and you reach the lobby on an escalator. Public and guest rooms have been refreshed with green and russet colors. Bathroom telephones and bathrobes are standard. The restaurant, at the back of the lobby, has been downgraded to a buffet breakfast room, but there is good room service. ⊠ *Av. de la Toison d'Or 40, B 1000,* ☎ *02/514–2200,* FAX *02/ 514–5744. 160 rooms, 11 suites. Bar, exercise room, meeting rooms. AE, DC, MC, V.*

$$ 🏨 **Alfa Louise.** Opened in 1994 on the prestigious Avenue Louise, this hotel is distinguished by its large rooms with sitting areas and office-size desks, making it an excellent choice for budget-minded business travelers. Bathrobes and room safes are additional conveniences. There's a jazz piano bar off the lobby. ⊠ *Av. Louise 212, B 1000,* ☎

02/644–2929, FAX 02/644–1878. *40 rooms. Bar, meeting rooms. AE, DC, MC, V.*

$$ 🏨 **Beau-Site.** Gleaming white and with flower boxes suspended from the windowsills, this former office building, opened as a hotel in 1993, makes a smart impression. The location (a block from the upper end of Avenue Louise) and the attentive staff are big pluses. The good-size rooms come in shapes other than the standard cube, and bathrooms have blow-dryers and bidets. The complimentary buffet breakfast includes bacon and eggs. ⊠ *R. de la Longue Haie 76, B 1000,* ☎ *02/ 640–8889,* FAX *02/640–1611. 38 rooms. AE, DC, MC, V.*

$$ 🏨 **Clubhouse.** The large, blue-carpeted lobby, which opens on a small garden and has a fire in the open hearth on chilly days, is particularly inviting. The location, on a quiet side street off the elegant Avenue Louise, is another plus. The rooms have pastel walls; salmon-pink carpeting; flower-pattern bedspreads and curtains; and a sofa, easy chair, and desk. ⊠ *R. Blanche 4, B 1000,* ☎ *02/542–5800,* FAX *02/537–0018. 81 rooms. Bar, meeting rooms, parking (fee). AE, DC, MC, V.*

$$ 🏨 **Four Points.** The concept of this Sheraton property is to offer superior rooms with limited services at moderate rates. Completed in 1991, the hotel has large rooms, each with blond-wood furniture, a reclining chair, and good work space. There is a beige-and-green atrium bar and a restaurant that serves generous breakfasts and a limited selection of specialties for lunch and dinner. The basement restaurant has a separate entrance. ⊠ *R. Paul Spaak 15, B 1000,* ☎ *02/645–6111,* FAX *02/ 646–6344. 128 rooms. 2 restaurants, bar, sauna, health club, meeting rooms, parking (fee). AE, DC, MC, V.*

$$ 🏨 **Le Dixseptième.** Opened in 1993 between the Grand'Place and
★   Gare Centrale (Central Station), this hotel occupies the stylishly restored 17th-century residence of the Spanish ambassador. Rooms surround a pleasant interior courtyard, and suites are up a splendid Louis XVI staircase. Named after Belgian artists, rooms have whitewashed walls, plain floorboards, exposed beams, suede sofas, colorful draperies, desks, blow-dryers, and second telephones. Suites have decorative fireplaces. ⊠ *R. de la Madeleine 25, B 1000,* ☎ *02/502–5744,* FAX *02/502– 6424. 12 rooms, 13 suites. Bar, kitchenettes, in-room modem lines, in-room safes. AE, DC, MC, V.*

$$ 🏨 **Manos Stéphanie.** The Louis XV furniture, marble lobby, and antiques
★   set a standard of elegance seldom encountered in a hotel in this price category. The rooms have rust-color carpets, green bedspreads, and good-size sitting areas. The hotel, opened in 1992, occupies a grand town house, so the rooms are not rigidly standardized. The atrium restaurant is enlivened by gaily striped chair coverings. ⊠ *Chaussée de Charleroi 28, B 1060,* ☎ *02/539–0250,* FAX *02/537–5729. 50 rooms, 5 suites. Restaurant, bar, meeting rooms, parking (fee). AE, DC, MC, V.*

$$ 🏨 **Novotel.** A stone's throw from the Grand'Place, this hotel was built in 1989 but with an old-look, gabled facade. Some French lodging chains mass-produce hotels that are functional but motel-like, and this one is no exception. The rooms have white walls and russet carpets; all come with a sofa that can, for 500 BF, sleep an extra person; there's no extra charge for up to two children under 16. There are 20 executive rooms. ⊠ *R. du Marché-aux-Herbes 120, B 1000,* ☎ *02/514–3333,* FAX *02/ 511–7723. 136 rooms. Restaurant, bar, no-smoking floor, meeting rooms, parking (fee). AE, DC, MC, V.*

$$ 🏨 **Les Tourelles.** This cheerful, family-run hotel is south of central Brussels but well connected by tram and street networks. The mock-medieval turreted facade and traditional wood decor suggest an antique hunting lodge, with comfortable rooms and friendly service. Try to get a back-facing room as the front looks out over a main road.

✉ *Av. Winston Churchill 135, B1180,* ☎ *02/344—9573,* FAX *02/346-4270. 22 rooms. 2 conference rooms, parking. AE, MC, V.*

$ 🖭 **Gerfaut.** In this cheerful hotel opened in 1991, the rooms—in light beige with colorful bedspreads—are of reasonable size. Rooms with three and four beds are available at modest supplements. Breakfast is served in the bright and friendly Winter Garden room. The location in Anderlecht near the Gare du Midi (South Station), though not choice, provides an opportunity to see a part of Brussels most visitors ignore. ✉ *Chaussée de Mons 115–117, B 1070,* ☎ *02/524–2044,* FAX *02/524–3044. 48 rooms. Bar, free parking. AE, DC, MC, V.*

$ 🖭 **Matignon.** Only the facade was preserved in the conversion of this Belle Epoque building to a hotel in 1993. The lobby is no more than a corridor, making room for the large café-brasserie that is part of the family-owned operation. Rooms are small but have generous beds, blow-dryers, and large-screen TVs, a welcome change from the dinky TVs you find in most other European budget hotels. Recently added rooms are decorated in salmon and with floral prints. Windows are double-glazed, vital in this busy spot across the street from the Bourse and two blocks from the Grand'Place. Advance payment is requested. ✉ *R. de la Bourse 10, B 1000,* ☎ *02/511–0888,* FAX *02/513–6927. 37 rooms. Restaurant, bar. AE, DC, MC, V.*

$ 🖭 **Orion.** This residential apartment hotel accepts guests staying for a single night, too. The whitewashed surfaces are offset by bright red details. Rooms have pull-out twin beds, and junior suites sleep four. All have fully equipped kitchenettes. Rooms on the courtyard are the quietest. ✉ *Quai au Bois-à-Brûler 51, B 1000,* ☎ *02/221–1411,* FAX *02/221–1599. 169 rooms. Kitchenettes, meeting rooms, parking (fee). AE, DC, MC, V.*

$ 🖭 **Sun.** Rooms are on the small side and the bathrooms are cramped, but the beds have firm mattresses and decor is a pleasant pastel green. The attractive breakfast room has a striking glass mural; snacks are served there during the day. The hotel is on a quiet but slightly dilapidated side street off the busy Chaussée d'Ixelles. ✉ *R. du Berger 38, B 1050,* ☎ *02/511–2119,* FAX *02/512–3271. 22 rooms with bath or shower. In-room safes, parking (fee). AE, DC, MC, V.*

Nightlife and the Arts

The Arts

A glance at the "What's On" supplement of weekly English-language newsmagazine *The Bulletin* reveals the breadth of the offerings in all categories of cultural life. Tickets for most events can be purchased by calling **Fnac Ticket Line** (☎ 070/344644).

FILM

First-run English-language and French movies predominate: The Belgian film industry is small but of high quality, with directors Jaco Van Dormael, Alain Berliner, Géard Corbiau and Stijn Coninx all achieving international acclaim. In summer, the excellent **Arenberg/Galeries** (✉ Galeries St-Hubert, ☎ 0900/29550) cinema hosts the Ecran Total (Total Cinema) festival, which screens classic Hollywood and French movies alongside new talent from around the world. The most convenient movie theater complexes are **UGC/Acropole** (✉ Av. de la Toison d'Or, ☎ 0900/29930) and **UGC/De Brouckère** (✉ Pl. de Brouckère, ☎ 0900/29930). Arthouse films show at the **Vendôme** (✉ Chaussée de Wavre 18, ☎ 0900/29909). The biggest—26 theaters—is the futuristic **Kinepolis** (✉ Av. du Centenaire 1, Heysel, ☎ 02/474–2604). The **Musée du Cinéma** (✉ R. Baron Horta 9, ☎ 02/507–8370) shows classic and silent movies (BF60 24 hours in advance; BF90 at door).

CLASSICAL MUSIC

The principal venue for classical music concerts is the Horta-designed **Palais des Beaux-Arts** (⊠ R. Ravenstein 23, ☎ 02/507–8200). Chamber music concerts and recitals are held in the more intimate **Royal Conservatory** (⊠ R. de la Régence 30, ☎ 02/507–8200). Many concerts are held in churches, especially the **Chapelle Protestante** (⊠ Pl. du Musée) and the **Eglise des Minimes** (⊠ R. des Minimes 62).

In spring, the gruelling **Queen Elisabeth Music Competition** (the penultimate round is at the Royal Conservatory, the final week at the Palais des Beaux-Arts), a prestigious competition for young pianists, violinists, and singers, takes place in Brussels. The monthlong **Ars Musica** (☎ 02/512–1717) festival of contemporary music in March and April attracts new music ensembles from around the world.

OPERA AND DANCE

The national opera house is the excellent **La Monnaie/De Munt** (⊠ Pl. de la Monnaie, ☎ 02/218–1211). This is where the 1830 revolution started: Inflamed by the aria starting "Amour sacré de la patrie" (Sacred love of your country) in Auber's *La Muette de Portici,* members of the audience rushed outside and started rioting. The brief and largely bloodless revolution against the Dutch established the Belgian nation state. Visiting opera and dance companies often perform at **Cirque Royal** (⊠ R. de l'Enseignement 81, ☎ 02/218–2015). Dance is among the liveliest arts in Belgium. Its seminal figure, Anne Teresa De Keersmaeker, is choreographer-in-residence at the opera house, but her Rosas company also performs at the **Lunatheater** (⊠ Pl. Sainctelette 20, ☎ 02/201–5959) as do the Royal Flanders Ballet and many other Belgian and international dance troupes.

THEATER

Nearly all the city's 30-odd theaters stage French-language plays; only a few present plays in Dutch. Talented amateur groups also put on occasional English-language performances, and top British companies, including the Royal Shakespeare Company, are becoming regular visitors. Avant-garde performances are often the most rewarding. Check what's on at **Rideau de Bruxelles** (⊠ Palais des Beaux-Arts, R. Ravenstein 23, ☎ 02/507–8200), **Théâtre Le Public** (⊠ R. Braemt 64–70, ☎ 0800/94444), **Théâtre National** (⊠ Pl. Rogier, ☎ 02/203–5303), and **Théâtre Varia** (⊠ R. du Sceptre 78, ☎ 02/640–8258).

Nightlife

By 11 PM, most Bruxellois have packed up and gone home. But around midnight, bars and cafés fill up again, as the night people take over; many places stay open till dawn. By and large, Belgians provide their own entertainment but, while Brussels's nightclubs are not in the same league as London's or Amsterdam's, the scene has been improving for the past few years.

BARS AND LOUNGES

There's a café on virtually every street corner, most boasting a wide selection of alcoholic drinks. Although the Belgian brewing industry is declining as the giant Interbrew firm muscles smaller companies out of the market, Belgians still consume copious quantities of beer, some of it with a 10% alcohol content. If you like Gypsy music, try the late-night **Ateliers de la Grande Ile** (⊠ R. de la Grande Ile 33).

The sidewalk outside **Au Soleil** (⊠ 86 R. du Marché-au-Charbon) teems with the hip and would-be hip, enjoying relaxed trip-hop sounds and very competitive prices. Fashionable Flemings, meanwhile, flock to the **Beurs Café** (⊠ R. Auguste Orts 20–26, near Bourse), a huge, minimalist hall with a friendly atmosphere next door to the innovative

Beursschouwburg cultural center. **Chez Moeder Lambic** (⊠ R. de Savoie 68, St-Gilles) claims to stock 600 Belgian beers and a few hundred more foreign ones. **De Ultieme Hallucinatie** (⊠ R. Royale 316) is an Art Nouveau masterpiece, with a pricey restaurant as well as its roomy tavern. **Fleur en Papier Doré** (⊠ R. des Alexiens 53) was the hangout for Surrealist René Magritte and his artist friends and their spirit lingers on. At the tiny **Java** (⊠ R. de la Grande Ile 22), the bar is shaped like a huge anaconda. On the Grand'Place, **'t Kelderke** (⊠ Grand'Place 15) is a bustling, friendly option. In the trendy Place Saint-Géry district, **Zebra** (⊠ Pl. St-Géry 35) attracts a comfortably fashionable crowd.

Brussels's sizable French-speaking black population, hailing mostly from the Republic of Congo (the former Zaïre), congregates in the area of Ixelles commune known as Matonge. **Chaussée de Wavre** is the principal street for African shops, bars, and restaurants.

There are a number of favored Anglo-expat hangouts in Brussels. **Conway's** (⊠ Av. Louise 344) is a singles bar where the staff's ice-breaking activities are the stuff of local legend. **Rick's Café Américain** (⊠ Av. Louise 344, ☎ 02/648–1451) is flashy.

Like most western European cities, Brussels has a sizable number of "Irish" bars: **The James Joyce** (⊠ R. Archimède 34, ☎ 02/230–9894), **Kitty O'Shea's** (⊠ Bd. de Charlemagne 42, ☎ 02/230–7875), and **O'Reilly's** (⊠ R. Archimède 34, ☎ 02/230–9894). Among the most popular hotel bars are those in the **Hilton**, the **Amigo**, and the **Métropole** (☞ Dining and Lodging, *above*).

CABARETS
Transvestite shows spark **Chez Flo** (⊠ R. au Beurre 25, ☎ 02/512–9496). **Do Brasil** (⊠ R. de la Caserne 88, ☎ 02/513–5028) has a Latin American beat. At **Show Point** (⊠ Pl. Stephanie 14, ☎ 02/511–5364) the draw is striptease.

DANCE CLUBS
Action starts at midnight in most clubs. Salsa addicts can indulge their habit at **Cartagena** (⊠ R. du Marché-au-Charbon 70, ☎ 02/502–5908). Electronica fans prefer **Fuse** (⊠ R. Blaes 208, ☎ 511–9789), a bunker-style techno haven with regular gay and lesbian nights. **Griffin's** (⊠ R. de l'Homme Chrétien, ☎ 02/505–5200) appeals to young adults and business travelers. **Mirano Continental** (⊠ Chaussée de Louvain 38, ☎ 02/227–3970) remains the glitzy hangout of choice for the self-styled beautiful people. **Who's Who's Land** (⊠ R. du Poincon 17, ☎ 02/512–6343) has made big waves among good-time house fans.

GAY BARS
Brussels is not nearly as advanced as Amsterdam when it comes to gay culture, but several clubs, notably **Fuse** (☞ Dance Clubs, *above*), hold regular gay and lesbian nights. **Belgica** (⊠ R. du Marché-au-Charbon 32), is a trendy meeting point at the heart of what passes for the gay quarter. **Tels Quels** (⊠ R. du Marché-au-Charbon 81, ☎ 02/512–4587) can offer up-to-date information about the capital's gay scene. For lesbians, **Le Féminin** (⊠ R. Borgval 9) or **Sapho** (⊠ R. St-Géry 1) are the best bets.

JAZZ
After World War II, Belgium was at the forefront of Europe's modern jazz movement: Of the great postwar players, harmonica maestro Toots Thielemans and vibes player Sadi are still very much alive and perform in Brussels. Other top Belgian jazz draws include guitarist Philip Catherine and the experimental ethno-jazz trio Aka Moon. Among the best jazz venues are **L'Archiduc** (⊠ R. Antoine Dansaert 6, ☎ 02/512–0652),

the **New York Café Jazz Club** (✉ Chaussée de Charleroi 5, ☎ 02/534–8509), **Sounds** (✉ R. de la Tulipe 28, ☎ 02/512–9250), and **Travers** (✉ R. Traversière 11, ☎ 02/218–4086).

Mainstream rock acts and big-league French chansonniers stop off at **Forest-National** (✉ Av. du Globe 36, ☎ 02/340–2211). **Ancienne Belgique** (✉ Bd. Anspach 110, ☎ 02/548–2424), hosts a wide range of rock, pop, alternative, and world music, as does **Le Botanique** (✉ R. Royale 236, ☎ 02/218–3732), which has a superb 10-day festival, *Les Nuits Botanique,* in September. For up-and-coming British and European alternative bands, try **VK** (✉ R. de l'Ecole 76, ☎ 02/414–2907).

Outdoor Activities and Sports

Participant Sports

GOLF

The top clubs in the area are **Keerbergen Golf Club** (✉ Vlieghavenlaan 50, Keerbergen, ☎ 015/234961), **Royal Golf Club de Belgique** (✉ Château de Ravenstein, Tervuren, ☎ 02/767–5801), and **Royal Waterloo Golf Club** (✉ Vieux Chemin de Wavre 50, Ohain, ☎ 02/633–1850). For more information, call the **Royal Belgian Golf Federation** (☎ 02/672–2389).

HEALTH AND FITNESS

Several hotels have well-equipped fitness centers open to the public. The best are at the **Europa Brussels** (✉ R. de la Loi 107, ☎ 02/230–1333), **John Harris Fitness** at the Radisson SAS Hotel (✉ R. du Fossé-aux-Loups 47, ☎ 02/219–8254), and **Sheraton** (✉ Pl. Rogier 3, ☎ 02/224–3111). Fees average BF1,000 a session. Prices are considerably lower at independent health clubs, such as **California Club** (✉ R. Lesbroussart 68, ☎ 02/640–9344) and **European Athletic City** (✉ Av. Winston Churchill 25A, ☎ 02/345–3077).

HORSEBACK RIDING

For outdoor horseback riding, try **Le Centre Equestre de la Cambre** (✉ Chausée de Waterloo 872, ☎ 02/375–3408), **Musette** (✉ Drève du Caporal 11, ☎ 02/374–2591), or **Royal Etrier Belge** (✉ Champ du Vert Chasseur 19, ☎ 02/374–3870).

JOGGING

For in-town jogging, use the **Parc de Bruxelles** (✉ R. de la Loi to the Palace); for more extensive workouts, head for the **Bois de la Cambre** (✉ Southern end of Av. Louise), a natural park that is a favorite among joggers and families with children. The park merges on the south into the beech woods of the 11,000-acre **Forêt de Soignes,** extending as far south as Genval with its lake and restaurants.

SWIMMING

Hotel swimming pools are few and far between. Among covered public pools, the best are **Calypso** (✉ Av. Wiener 60, ☎ 02/663–0090), **Longchamp** (✉ Sq. de Fré 1, ☎ 02/374–9005), and **Poseidon** (✉ Av. des Vaillants 2, ☎ 02/771–6655).

Tennis

Popular clubs include the **Royal Léopold** (✉ Av. Dupuich 42, ☎ 02/344–3666), **Royal Racing Club** (✉ Av. des Chênes 125, ☎ 02/374–4181), and **Wimbledon** (✉ Waterloosesteenweg 220, Sint-Genesius-Rode, ☎ 02/358–3523).

Spectator Sports

HORSE RACING

Going to the races is second in popularity only to soccer, and there are three major racecourses: **Boitsfort** (✉ Chaussée de la Hulpe 53, ☎ 02/

675–3015), which has an all-weather flat track; **Groenendael** (✉ Sint-Jansberglaan 4, Hoeilaart, ☎ 02/675–3015), for steeplechasing; and **Sterrebeek** (✉ Du Roy de Blicquylaan 43, Sterrebeek, ☎ 02/675–5293), for trotting and flat racing between February and June. For more information, contact the **Jockey Club de Belgique** (☎ 02/672–7248).

SOCCER

Soccer is Belgium's most popular spectator sport, and the leading club, **Anderlecht,** has many fiercely loyal fans—even despite poor showings in recent seasons and the discovery that club bosses bribed referees during a European competition in the early '80s. Their home pitch is Parc Astrid (✉ Av. Theo Verbeeck 2, ☎ 02/522–1539). Major international games are played at the **Stade Roi Baudouin** (✉ Av. du Marathon 135, ☎ 02/479–3654). For information and tickets, contact the **Maison du Football** (✉ Av. Houba de Strooper 145, ☎ 02/477–1211).

Shopping

The Belgians started producing high-quality luxury goods in the Middle Ages, and this is what they are skilled at. This is not a country where you pick up amazing bargains. Value added tax (TVA) further inflates prices, but visitors from outside the European Union can obtain refunds.

Shopping Districts

The stylish, upmarket shopping area for clothing and accessories comprises the upper end of **Avenue Louise** and includes **Avenue de la Toison d'Or,** which branches off at a right angle; **Boulevard de Waterloo,** on the other side of the street; **Galerie Louise,** which links the two avenues; and **Galerie de la Toison d'Or,** another gallery two blocks away. The **City 2** mall on Place Rogier and the pedestrian mall, **Rue Neuve,** are fun and inexpensive shopping areas (but not recommended for women alone after dark). There are galleries scattered across Brussels, but low rents have made **Boulevard Barthélémy** the in place for avant-garde art. The **Windows** complex (✉ Bd. Barthélémy 13), houses several good galleries. On the **Place du Grand-Sablon** and adjoining streets and alleys you'll find antiques dealers and smart art galleries. The **Galeries St-Hubert** is a rather stately shopping arcade lined with upscale shops selling men's and women's clothing, books, and interior design products. In the trendy **Rue Antoine Dansaert** and **Place du Nouveau Marché aux Grains,** near the Bourse, are a number of boutiques carrying fashions by young designers and interior design and art shops.

Department Stores

The best Belgian department store is **Inno** (✉ R. Neuve 111, ☎ 02/211–2111; ✉ Av. Louise 12, ☎ 02/513–8494; ✉ Chaussée de Waterloo 699, ☎ 02/345–3890). Others, such as **C&A** and **Marks & Spencer,** are clustered at the Place de la Monnaie end of Rue Neuve, a tawdry street that is now undergoing a much-needed face-lift.

Street Markets

Bruxellois with an eye for fresh farm produce and low prices do most of their food shopping at the animated open-air markets in almost every borough. Among the best are those in **Boitsfort** in front of the Maison Communal on Sunday morning; on **Place du Châtelain,** Wednesday afternoon; and on **Place Ste-Catherine,** all day, Monday through Saturday. In addition to fruits, vegetables, meat, and fish, most markets include traders with specialized products, such as wide selections of cheese and wild mushrooms. The most exotic market is the Sunday morning **Marché du Midi,** where the large North African community gathers to buy and sell foods, spices, and plants, transforming the area next to the railway station into a vast bazaar.

In the Grand'Place there's a **Flower Market,** daily, except Monday, and a **Bird Market,** Sunday morning. You need to get to the flea market, **Vieux Marché** (⊠ Pl. du Jeu de Balle) early. It's open daily 7–2. The **Antiques and Book Market** (⊠ Pl. du Grand-Sablon), Saturday 9–6 and Sunday 9–2, is frequented by established dealers.

Specialty Stores

BEER

400 bières artisanales (⊠ Chaussé de Wavre 175, ☎ 02/511–3742), a little off the beaten track, should be visited by anyone with a serious interest in Belgian beer. The owner is friendly and knowledgeable and his selection of ales is well-judged and continually surprising. Don't forget to buy the glass that goes with your *dubbel* or *tripel.*

BOOKS

The **Galerie Bortier** (⊠ R. de la Madeleine–R. St-Jean) is a small, attractive arcade devoted entirely to rare and secondhand books. It was designed by the architect responsible for the Galeries Saint-Hubert. **Libris** (⊠ Espace Louise, ☎ 02/511–6400) is well stocked with current French-language titles. Shops specializing in comic strip albums include those at Chaussée de Wavre Nos. 167, 179, and 198, and the **Tintin Boutique** (⊠ R. de la Colline 13, off Grand'Place). **Tropismes** (⊠ Galerie des Princes 11, ☎ 02/512–8852) carries more than 40,000 titles and will help you find out-of-print books.

English-language bookstores include **La Librairie des Etangs** (⊠ Chaussée d'Ixelles 319, Ixelles, ☎ 02/646–9051), an international bookseller; **Librairie de Rome** (⊠ Av. Louise 50b, ☎ 02/511–7937), which has a large selection of foreign newspapers and magazines; **Sterling** (⊠ R. du Fosse-aux-Loups, ☎ 02/223–6223), a friendly store run by a team whose enthusiasm for reading is infectious; and the less personal **Waterstone's** (⊠ Bd. Adolphe Max 71–75, ☎ 02/219–2708), which carries hard covers, paperbacks, and periodicals. The *International Herald Tribune* and the *Wall Street Journal* are sold by almost all newsdealers.

CHOCOLATES

Godiva (⊠ Grand'Place 22 and other locations) is the best known, with **Neuhaus** (⊠ Galerie de la Reine 25–27 and other locations) a close second. **Leonidas** (⊠ Chaussée d'Ixelles 5 and other locations) is the budget alternative, but still high quality thanks to Belgium's strict controls on chocolate. The best handmade pralines, the crème de la crème of Belgian chocolates, are made by **Pierre Marcolini** (⊠ Pl. du Grand Sablon 39, ☎ 02/511–3321), the boy wonder of the chocolate world; at **Mary** (⊠ R. Royale 73, ☎ 02/217–4500); and at **Wittamer** (⊠ Pl. du Grand Sablon 12, ☎ 02/512–3742).

CRYSTAL

The Val-St-Lambert mark is the only guarantee of handblown, hand-engraved lead crystal vases and other glass. You can buy it in many stores; the specialist is **Art et Sélection** (⊠ R. du Marché-aux-Herbes 83, ☎ 02/511–8448).

LACE AND LINEN

Manufacture Belge de Dentelle (⊠ Galerie de la Reine 6–8, ☎ 02/511–4477) and **Maison F. Rubbrecht** (⊠ Grand'Place 23, ☎ 02/512–0218) sell local handmade lace. Lace sold in the souvenir shops is likely to come from East Asia. An introductory visit to the **Musée du Costume et de la Dentelle** (⊠ R. de la Violette 6, ☎ 02/512–7709) is a good idea if you're planning to shop for lace. For Belgian linen, try **Martine Doly** (⊠ Bd. de Waterloo 27, ☎ 02/512–4515).

LEATHER GOODS

Delvaux (⊠ Galerie de la Reine 31, ☎ 02/512–7198; ⊠ Bd. de Waterloo 27, ☎ 02/513–0502) makes outstanding, classic handbags, wallets, belts, and attaché cases. Be prepared to part with a hefty sum, but the Delvaux products last and last.

Side Trips

Waterloo

Waterloo, like Stalingrad or Hiroshima, changed the course of history. There are numerous Waterloos scattered across the world, but this site 19 km (11 mi) south of Brussels is the original. As Brussels spreads south, Waterloo appears to be a prosperous suburb, complete with large, white-washed villas and smart boutiques, rather than a separate town. Home to two American international schools, it has a cosmopolitan feel to it. More than one fifth of the population is foreign, many of them American, French, and Canadian.

The Duke of Wellington spent the night of June 17, 1815, at an inn in Waterloo, where he established his headquarters. When he slept here again the following night, Napoléon had been defeated. The inn in the center of this pleasant, small town is now the **Musée Wellington** (Wellington Museum). It presents the events of the 100 days leading up to the Battle of Waterloo, maps and models of the battle itself, and military and Wellington memorabilia in well laid-out displays. ⊠ *Chaussée de Bruxelles 147,* ☎ *02/345–7806.* ⊠ *BF100.* ⊙ *Apr.–mid-Nov., daily 9:30–6:30; mid-Nov.–Mar., daily 10:30–5.*

The actual **Champ de Bataille** (Battlefield) is just south of Waterloo (signposted "Butte de Lion"). This is where Wellington's troops received the onslaught of Napoléon's army. A crucial role in the battle was played by some of the ancient, fortified farms, of which there are many in this area. The farm of Hogoumont was fought over all day; 6,000 men, out of total casualties of 48,000, were killed here. Later in the day, fierce fighting raged around the farms of La Sainte Haye and Papelotte. In the afternoon, the French cavalry attacked, in the mistaken belief that the British line was giving way. Napoléon's final attempt was to send in the armored cavalry of the Imperial Guard, but at the same time the Prussian army under Blücher arrived to engage the French from the east, and it was all over. The battlefield is best surveyed from the top of the **Butte de Lion**, a pyramid 226 steps high and crowned by a 28-ton lion, which was erected by the Dutch 10 years later.

The visitor facilities at the battlefield were below par for many years, and some of the tackiness remains, including some overpriced restaurants and a seedy wax museum. The smart **visitor center**, built several years ago, is an improvement, offering an audiovisual presentation of the battle, followed by a mood-setting film of the fighting seen through the eyes of children. You can buy souvenirs here, too—from tin soldiers and T-shirts to soft toy lions and model cannons. There are also plenty of books, some highly specialized, about the battle and the men who led the fighting. The adjacent **Battle Panorama Museum**, first unveiled in 1912, contains a vast, circular painting of the charge of the French cavalry, executed with amazing perspective and realism. ⊠ *Rte. du Lion 252–254,* ☎ *02/385–1912.* ⊠ *BF275, including Butte du Lion and Panorama.* ⊙ *Apr.–Oct., daily 9:30–5:30; Nov.–Feb., daily 10:30–4; Mar., daily 10:30–5.*

From the prevalence of souvenirs and images of Napoléon, you might think that the battle was won by the French. In fact, there were Belgian soldiers fighting on both sides. Napoléon's headquarters during his last days as emperor were in what is now the small **Musée du Cail-**

lou in Genappe, south of the battlefield. It contains the room where he spent the night before the battle, his personal effects, and objects found in the field. ⊠ *Chaussée de Bruxelles 66,* ☎ *02/384–2424.* 🖅 *BF60.* ☼ *Apr.–Sept., Tues.–Sun. 10:30–6:30; Nov.–Mar., Tues.–Sun. 1:30–5.*

DINING AND LODGING

$$$ ✕ **La Maison du Seigneur.** In a peaceful, white-washed farmhouse with a spacious terrace, Ghislaine De Becker and his son Pilou offer elegant, classical French cuisine. The menu, which changes with the seasons, includes sole with shrimp sauce and veal cooked in Porto and roast cherries. ⊠ *Chaussée de Tervuren 389,* ☎ *02/354–0750. AE, DC, MC, V. Closed Mon.–Tues., Feb., and 2nd ½ of Aug.*

$$ ✕ **L'Auberge d'Ohain.** This country inn northeast of Waterloo has an
★ elegant dining room decorated in shades of peach and champagne, and a kitchen capable of great things: tagliatelle with langoustine and salmon, roast pigeon and langoustine ravioli. The four-course *menu découverte* (tasting menu) is excellent value. ⊠ *Chaussée de Louvain 709,* ☎ *02/653–6497. AE, DC, MC, V. Closed Sun.–Mon. and 2nd ½ of July.*

$ ✕ **L'Amusoir.** Popular with resident Americans, this is an unpretentious steak house in an old white-walled building in the center of town. It serves excellent filet mignon, prepared with a variety of sauces, and hearty Belgian traditional dishes. ⊠ *Chaussée de Bruxelles 121,* ☎ *02/ 353–0336. AE.*

$$ ✕🏠 **Le 1815.** This small hotel is actually on the battlefield. Each room is named for one of the participating generals and decorated with his portrait. The style is Art Deco, but with details evocative of the period of the battle, and there is even a minigolf course modeled after the battle. The restaurant is much better than those clustered at the foot of the Butte du Lion. ⊠ *Rte. du Lion 367, B 1410,* ☎ *02/387–0060,* FAX *02/387–1292. 14 rooms. Restaurant, bar, mini-golf. AE, DC, MC, V.*

Mechelen

Mechelen (Malines in French), 28 km (17 mi) north of Brussels, is a small, peaceful gem that has preserved its medieval and Renaissance past but that is never, like Brugge, overrun by tourists. It is also an important ecclesiastical center, being the residence of the Roman Catholic Primate of Belgium. The city is the center of vegetable production, especially asparagus, whose stalks reach their height of perfection in May, and witloof, the Belgian delicacy known elsewhere as chicory or endive.

Mechelen's brief period of grandeur coincided with the reign (1507–30) of Margaret of Austria. She established her devout and cultured court in this city while she served as regent for her nephew, who later became Emperor Charles V. The philosophers Erasmus and Sir Thomas More were among her visitors, as were the painters Albrecht Dürer and Van Orley (whose portrait of Margaret hangs in the Musée d'Art Ancien in Brussels), and Josquin des Prés, the master of polyphony.

★ **Sint-Romboutskathedraal** (St. Rombout's Cathedral), completed in the 1520s, represents a magnificent achievement by three generations of the Keldermans family of architects, who were active in cathedral building throughout Flanders. The beautifully proportioned tower, 318 ft high, was intended to be the tallest in the world, but the builders ran out of money before they could reach their goal. Inside are two remarkable 40-ton carillons of 49 bells each; carillon-playing was virtually invented in Mechelen (the Russian word for carillon means "sound of Mechelen"), and student carillonneurs still come here from all over the world. The town's carillon school, the oldest in the world, celebrated its 75th anniversary in 1998. The best place to listen to the bells is in the Minderbroedersgang. The interior of the cathedral is spacious and lofty, particularly the white sandstone nave dating from the 13th century. Chief among the art treasures is Van Dyck's *Crucifixion* in the south transept. ⊠ *Grote Markt.* ☉ *Mon.–Sat. 9–4 (until 6 in summer), Sun. 1–5; check tourist office for tower tours; carillon concerts Sat. 11:30 AM, Sun. 3, Mon. 11:30 PM.*

Seldom have two parts of a single building had such vividly contrasting styles as do those of the **Stadhuis** (Town Hall). To the right is the Gothic, turreted, 14th-century *Lakenhalle* (Cloth Hall). To the left is the flamboyant palace commissioned by Charles V to accommodate the *Grote Raad* (Grand Council) of the Burgundian Netherlands. Work was abandoned in 1547 but resumed and completed in the 20th century in accordance with the Keldermans' original plans. ⊠ *Grote Markt.* ☉ *Guided tours (from tourist office), Easter–June and Sept., weekends 2; July–Aug., daily 2.*

NEED A BREAK? The smallest café in Mechelen is the **Borrel Babel** in the charming Sint-Romboutshof, behind the cathedral. Different varieties of *genever* (Dutch gin) are the potent specialty.

The **Koninklijke Manufactuur Gaspard De Wit** (Royal Tapestry Factory) is the best place to understand and distinguish between different styles of tapestry weaving, and one of the few places where this ancient and glorious art is still practiced. Tours of the workshops permit you to watch the experts making and restoring tapestries, and you can view a collection of antique and contemporary tapestries. Official opening hours are severely restricted, but see what the Tourist Office can do for you at other times. ⊠ *Schoutetstraat 7,* ☎ *015/202905.* ☒ *Guided tours, BF200.* ☉ *Guided tours, Aug.–June, Sat. 10:30.*

On the old **Haverwerf** and **Zoutwerf** wharves on the river Dijle, oats and salt, respectively, were loaded. Next to one another on the Haverwerf stand three remarkable houses. The green one, called **Het Paradijs** (Paradise), is Gothic, with a relief showing the banishment of Adam and Eve. In the middle stands the **Duivelsgevel** (Little Devils), with a 15th-century timber facade decorated with carved satyrs. The red one, **Sint Josef**, is a Baroque house from 1669. On the Zoutwerf stands the old fishmongers' guildhall from the 16th century, embellished by a magnificent golden salmon. ⊠ *Haverwerf.*

�཰ At **Planckendael,** more than 1,000 animals lead a life of near-freedom. The vast park has an adventure trail for children, a large playground, and a children's farm. The park can be reached by boat from Mechelen (Colomabrug), with departures every 30 minutes from 9 to 8:30. ⊠ *Leuvensesteenweg 582, Muizen,* ☎ *015/414249.* ☒ *BF380.* ☉ *Jan., daily 9–4:30; Feb., mid-Oct.–Dec., daily 9–4:45; early Mar., early Oct., daily 9–5:15; late Mar.–June, Sept., daily 9–5:45; July–Aug., daily 9–6:15.*

☹ **Speelgoedmuseum Mechelen** (Mechelen Toy Museum) is one of the biggest toy museums in the world. It has more than 8,000 tin soldiers standing ready to do battle on a model of Waterloo plus a vast collection of toys and games, both ancient and modern, and a play area for young and old. A fast-rotating series of exhibitions make this a ceaselessly fascinating place. ⊠ *Nekkerspoel 21,* ☎ *015/557075.* ☒ *BF170.* ☉ *Tues.–Sun. 10–5.*

DINING

$$$ ✗ **D'Hoogh.** In a grand gray-stone mansion on the Grote Markt, its
★ second-floor dining room looking over the square, this glamorous landmark presents top-quality *cuisine du marché* (whatever is fresh-

est): smoked-eel terrine with pistachios; poached goose liver in port jelly with caramelized apples; turbot and zucchini spaghetti in vinaigrette and olive oil; and, in April and May, the most wonderful asparagus imaginable. ⊠ *Grote Markt 19,* ☎ *015/217553. Reservations essential. AE, DC, MC, V. No lunch Sat., no dinner Sun. Closed Mon. and 1st 3 wks of Aug.*

$ ✕ **'t Korenveld.** This tiny, old-fashioned bistro has been primly restored and decked with pretty floral wallpaper and tile tabletops. Its cuisine is unpretentious, featuring simple fish and steaks at low prices. It adjoins the Alfa Hotel and has some tables in the hotel bar. ⊠ *Korenmarkt 20,* ☎ *015/421469. AE, MC, V. No dinner Sat. Closed Sun.–Mon. and Aug.*

Leuven

Some 26 km (16 mi) east of Brussels, Leuven (Louvain), like Oxford or Cambridge, is a place where underneath the hubbub of daily life you sense an age-old devotion to learning and scholarship. Its ancient Roman Catholic university, founded in 1425, was one of Europe's great seats of learning during the Middle Ages. One of its rectors was elected Pope Adrian VI. Erasmus taught here in the 16th century, as did the cartographer Mercator and, in the following century, Cornelius Jansen, whose teachings inspired the anti-Jesuit Jansenist movement. The city was pillaged and burned by the Germans in 1914, when 1,800 buildings, including the university library, were destroyed; in 1944 it was bombed again. In the 1960s, severe intercultural tensions caused the old bilingual university to split into a French-language and Dutch-language university. The French speakers moved their university south of the linguistic border to the new town of Louvain-la-Neuve; the Dutch-speakers remained in Leuven. Present-day **Katholieke Universiteit Leuven** has a student body of more than 25,000, including about 1,000 seminarians from many different countries.

★ Every Flemish town prides itself on its ornate, medieval **Stadhuis** (Town Hall). This one escaped the 1914 fire because it was occupied by German staff. It is the work of Leuven's own architectural master of Flamboyant Gothic, Mathieu de Layens, who finished it in 1469 after 21 years' work. In photographs it looks more like a finely chiseled reliquary than a building; it is necessary to stand back from it to fully appreciate the vertical lines in the mass of turrets, pinnacles, pendants, and niches, each with its own statue. The interior contains some fine 16th-century sculpted ceilings. ⊠ *Grote Markt.* ☺ *Guided tours from tourist office weekdays 11 and 3, weekends 3.*

NEED A BREAK?   **Gambrinus,** on the corner of the busy Grote Markt, has a terrace with a view of the Town Hall and an atmospheric interior with fin de siècle decor. ⊠ *Grote Markt 13,* ☎ *016/201238.*

Sint-Pieterskerk (Collegiate Church of St. Peter) has had a troubled architectural history. A shifting foundation led to the shortening of the tower in the 17th century and to the replacement of the spire with a cupola in the 18th. The interior, however, is remarkable for the purity of the Gothic nave. The ambulatory and choir are closed for restoration, but some treasures usually found there, including *The Last Supper,* by Leuven's 15th-century official painter Dirk Bouts, are on temporary display in the nave. ⊠ *Grote Markt.* ▣ *Church and Stedelijk Museum, BF200.* ☺ *Tues.–Sat. 10–5, Sun. 2–5; mid-Mar.–mid-Oct., also Mon. 10–5.*

The **Stedelijk Museum Vander Kelen-Mertens** (Municipal Museum) gives you an idea of how Leuven's upper crust lived 100 years ago. The building, which dates from the 16th century, was originally a college. It became the mayor's residence in the 19th century. A series of rooms in different styles reflect his taste. The art collection includes works by Albrecht Bouts (died 1549), son of Dirk, and Quentin Metsys (1466–1530), a remarkable portraitist, as well as Brabantine sculptures from the 15th and 16th centuries. ✉ *Savoyestraat 6,* ☎ *016/226906.* 💵 *BF200 for St-Pieterskerk and museum.* ⊙ *Tues.–Sat. 10–5, Sun. 2–5.*

Every Flemish city worth its salt has a *begijnhof,* a city within a city, formerly inhabited by members of a Christian sisterhood dating from the 13th century. The original members were widows of fallen Crusaders. The **Groot Begijnhof** is the largest in the country. The quiet retreat numbers 72 tiny, whitewashed houses, with religious statues in small niches, dating mostly from the 17th century, grouped around the early Gothic Church of St. John the Baptist, not far from several university colleges. The carefully restored houses are inhabited by students and university staff. ✉ *Tervuursevest; from Grote Markt take Naamsestraat to Karmelletenberg and across Schapenstraat.*

DINING

$$$ ✕ **Belle Epoque.** This grand town house, by the station, offers the most lavish dining in Leuven, served with considerable pomp in an Art Nouveau setting. Try lobster salad with apple, langoustines with caviar, or Bresse pigeon with truffle sauce. There's also a pleasant terrace. ✉ *Bondgenotenlaan 94,* ☎ *016/223389. Reservations essential. AE, DC, MC, V. Closed Sun.–Mon. and 3 wks in July–Aug.*

$ ✕ **Domus.** Tucked into a back street off the Grote Markt, this café adjoins the tiny Domus brewery, famous for its honey beer. The ambience is young and casual, the decor authentically rustic: craggy old beams, a brick fireplace, a labyrinth of separate rooms, bric-a-brac, and paisley table throws. The Burgundian menu includes traditional dishes such as black-and-white pudding with apples. ✉ *Tiensestraat 8,* ☎ *016/201449. No credit cards.*

Brussels A to Z

Arriving and Departing

BY BUS

Eurolines offers up to three daily express bus services from Amsterdam, Berlin, Frankfurt, Paris, and London. The Eurolines Coach Station is located at CCN Gare du Nord (✉ R. du Progrès 80, ☎ 02/203–0707).

From London, the **City Sprint** bus connects with the Dover–Calais Hovercraft, and the bus then takes you on to Brussels. For reservations and times, call Hoverspeed (☎ 01304/240241).

To **Waterloo,** Bus W from Brussels (Place Rouppe) runs at half-hour intervals.

BY CAR

Belgium is covered by an extensive network of four-lane highways. Brussels is 204 km (122 mi) from Amsterdam on E19; 222 km (138 mi) from Düsseldorf on E40; 219 km (133 mi) from Luxembourg City on E411; and 308 km (185 mi) from Paris.

If you piggyback on Le Shuttle through the Channel Tunnel, the distance is 213 km (128 mi) from Calais to Brussels; the route from Calais via Oostende is the fastest, even though on the Belgian side the highway stops a few kilometers short of the border. If you take the ferry to Oostende, the distance is 115 km (69 mi) to Brussels on the six-lane E40.

Brussels is surrounded by a beltway, marked RING. Exits to the city are marked CENTER. Among several large underground parking facilities, the one close to the Grand'Place is particularly convenient if you're staying in a downtown hotel.

To **Leuven,** take the motorway from Brussels toward Liège; the Leuven exit is marked.

BY PLANE

All flights arrive at and depart from **Zaventem** (☎ 02/753–2111), Brussels's National Airport. **Sabena, American, Delta, United,** and **City Bird** fly into Brussels from the United States. **Sabena, British Midland,** and **British Airways** fly to Brussels from London's Heathrow Airport; **Air UK,** from Stansted; and **British Airways,** from Gatwick. Several regional centers in the United Kingdom also have direct flights to Brussels, as do all capitals in Europe and a growing number of secondary cities. The no-frills airline **Virgin Express** offers scheduled flights between London and Brussels.

Between the Airport and Downtown: Courtesy buses serve airport hotels and a few downtown hotels: Inquire when making reservations. **Express trains** leave the airport for the Gare du Nord and Gare Centrale stations every 20 minutes (one train an hour continues to the Gare du Midi). The trip takes 20 minutes and costs BF125 one way in first class, BF85 second class. The trains operate 6 AM to midnight. **Taxis** are plentiful. A taxi to the city center takes about half an hour and costs about BF1,200. You can save 25% on the fare by buying a voucher for the return trip if you use the Autolux (☎ 02/411–1221) taxi company. Beware freelance taxi drivers who hawk their services in the arrival hall.

BY TRAIN

Eurostar (☎ in Great Britain: Rail Europe Rail Travel, 990/848–848; Connex South-Eastern, 0870/603–0405) trains from London (Waterloo) use the Channel Tunnel to cut travel time to Brussels (Gare du Midi) to 2 hours, 40 minutes. Trainsstop at Ashford (Kent) and Lille (France). At press time (fall 1998) there were 10 daily services, and a first-class, one-way ticket cost BF8,700; second class cost BF5,900 (during the week) or BF3,490 (on the weekend). A number of promotional fares are available but must be booked seven days in advance.

Brussels is linked with Paris, Amsterdam, and Liège by **Thalys** (☎ 0900/101/77) high-speed trains. The TGV links in France and Belgium mean you can go from Brussels to Paris in a stunning 85 minutes. In Holland, until new tracks have been laid, which is likely to take several years, they provide a slower but very comfortable ride of just over 3 hours.

Conventional train services from London connect with the Ramsgate–Oostende ferry, hovercraft, or catamaran, and from Oostende the train takes you to Brussels. The whole journey, using hovercraft or catamaran, takes about 6½ hours; by ferry, about 9 hours. For more information, contact **Connex South-Eastern** (☎ 44/870/603–0405) or the **British Tourist Authority** (✉ Av. Louise 306, B 1050 Brussels, ☎ 00/32/2/646–3510). **Belgian National Railways** (SNCB, ☎ 02/203–3640) is the national rail line.

There is frequent commuter train service to **Waterloo.** The trip to **Mechelen** from Brussels takes 15 minutes; to **Leuven,** 20 minutes.

Getting Around

BY METRO, TRAM, AND BUS

The metro, trams, and buses operate as part of the same system. All three are clean and efficient, and a single ticket, which can be used on all three, costs BF50. The best buy is a 10-trip ticket, which costs BF320, or a one-day card costing BF130. You need to stamp your ticket in the appropriate machine on the bus or tram; in the metro, your card is stamped as you pass through the automatic barrier. You can purchase these tickets in any metro station or at newsstands. Single tickets can be purchased on the bus or on the tram.

Detailed maps of the Brussels public transportation network are available in most metro stations and at the **Brussels tourist office** in the Grand' Place (☎ 02/513–8940). You get a map free with a Tourist Passport (also available at the tourist office), which, for BF300, allows you a one-day transport card and reductions at museums.

BY TAXI
Call **Taxis Verts** (☎ 02/349–4949) or **Taxis Oranges** (☎ 02/349–4343). You can also catch one at cab stands around town. Distances are not great, and a cab ride costs between BF250 and BF500. Tips are included in the fare.

Contacts and Resources

CAR RENTALS
Avis (☎ 02/730–6211). **Budget** (☎ 02/646–5130). **EuroDollar** (☎ 02/735–6005). **Europcar**(☎ 02/640–9400). **Hertz** (☎ 02/513–2886).

EMBASSIES
U.S. (⌧ Bd. du Régent 27, ☎ 02/508–2111). **Canadian** (⌧ Av. de Tervuren 2, ☎ 02/741–0611). **British** (⌧ R. d'Arlon 85, ☎ 02/287–6211). **Australian** (⌧ R. Guimard 6, ☎ 02/231–0516). **Irish** (⌧ R. Froissart 89, ☎ 02/230–5337). **New Zealand** (⌧ Bd. du Régent 47, ☎ 02/ 512–1040).

EMERGENCIES
Police (☎ 101). **Accident and Ambulance** (☎ 100). **Doctor** (☎ 02/479–1818). **Dentist** (☎ 02/426–1026). One **pharmacy** in each district stays open 24 hours; the roster is posted in all pharmacy windows. In an emergency call 02/479–1818.

GUIDED TOURS
ARAU (⌧ Bd. Adolphe Max 55, ☎ 02/219–3345) organizes thematic city bus tours from March through November, including "Brussels 1900: Art Nouveau" and "Brussels 1930: Art Deco." The cost is BF600 for a half-day tour. The original tours run by **Chatterbus** (⌧ R. des Thuyas 12, ☎ 02/673–1835; early June–Sept.) either visit the main sights on foot or by minibus (BF600) or follow a walking route that includes a visit to a bistro (BF250). **De Boeck Sightseeing** (⌧ R. de la Colline 8, Grand'Place, ☎ 02/513–7744) operates city tours (BF790) with multilingual cassette commentary; they also visit Antwerp, the Ardennes, Brugge, Gent, Ieper, and Waterloo. Passengers are picked up at major hotels or at the tourist office in the town hall.

Qualified guides are available for individual tours from the Tourist Information Brussels (TIB; ☎ 02/513–8940) in the town hall. Three hours costs BF3,000, and up to 20 people can share the same guide.

In Waterloo expert guides, **Les Guides 1815** (⌧ Rte. du Lion 250, ☎ 02/385–0625), can be hired to take you around the battlefield for one hour (BF1,400) and three hours (BF2,200); group tours in English (BF100 per person) are weekends at 4, July through August.

There are no regularly organized guided tours of Leuven, but you can arrange with the tourist office (☞ Visitor Information, *below*) for an English-speaking **personal guide** (BF1,200) for two hours.

TRAVEL AGENCIES
American Express (⌧ Houtweg 24, ☎ 02/245–2250). **Carlson/Wagonlit Travel** (⌧ Bd. Clovis, ☎ 02/287–8811).

VISITOR INFORMATION

Tourist Information Brussels (TIB; ⊠ Hôtel de Ville/Grand' Place, ☎ 02/513–8940). **Leuven Dienst voor Toerisme** (City Tourist Office; ⊠ Leopold Vanderkelenstraat 30, ☎ 016/211539). **Mechelen Dienst voor Toerisme** (City Tourist Office; ⊠ Stadhuis, Grote Markt 21, ☎ 015/297655). **Waterloo Office de Tourisme** (Tourist Office; ⊠ Chaussée de Bruxelles 149, ☎ 02/354–9910).

HAINAUT

Hainaut is a proud old region that was the nursery of French kings, the rich dowry of dynastic marriages, and for many years the buffer between expansionist France and quarrelsome Flanders. You'll see land scarred by the industrial revolution and ancient, fortified farms turned into centers of highly productive agriculture; cathedrals spared the ravages of war; and parks and châteaux that are reminders of the feudal world that was.

You can explore Hainaut as an excursion from Brussels or as a stopover en route to France. It is also possible to cut across from Bouillon in southwest Luxembourg through France along the scenic, winding road beside the Semois River, and begin the tour of Hainaut in Chimay.

Attention! As you drive south from Brussels through Flemish Brabant, Tournai is signposted as Doornik. This changes to Tournai as you cross the linguistic border at Enghien/Edingen.

Numbers in the margin correspond to points of interest on the Hainaut map.

Gaasbeek

1 *15 km (9 mi) west of Brussels, 29 km (18 mi) northwest of Nivelle.*

In Gaasbeek you are in Bruegel country, almost as if you had stepped inside one of his paintings of village life. The area is called Pajottenland, and you may be familiar with the landscape from Bruegel's works, many of which were painted here. From the terrace of the **Gaasbeek Château** you have a panoramic view of this landscape. The rulers of Gaasbeek once lorded it over Brussels, and the townspeople took terrible revenge and razed the castle. Restored in the 19th century, it contains outstanding 15th- and 16th-century tapestries. Rubens's will is among the documents in the castle archives. The surrounding park is popular with picnickers. ⊠ *Kasteelstraat 40,* ☎ *02/532–4372.* ▨ *BF150.* ☉ *Apr.–June and Sept.–Oct., Tues.–Thurs. and weekends 10–5; July–Aug., Sat.–Thurs. 10–5.*

En Route Beersel is just off the motorway as you head south from Brussels. It is the site of a stark 13th-century fort, the **Kastel van Beersel,** surrounded by a moat, which was part of Brussels's defenses. The interiors are empty, except for one room, a well-equipped torture chamber. ⊠ *Lotsestraat 65,* ☎ *02/331–0024.* ▨ *BF100.* ☉ *Mar.–mid-Nov., Tues.–Sun. 10–noon and 2–6; mid-Nov.–Dec. and Feb., weekends 10:30–5.*

In Attre, near Ath, stands the splendid **Château d'Attre,** built in 1752 and preserved intact. It is still inhabited, and visits are limited to the salons and drawing rooms of the ground floor. Among its treasures are paintings by Franz Snyders and Murillo. The semi-wild park surrounding the château has great charm. ☎ *068/454460.* ▨ *BF150.* ☉ *Apr.–Oct., weekends 10–noon and 2–6; July–Aug., Thurs.–Tues. 10–noon and 2–6.*

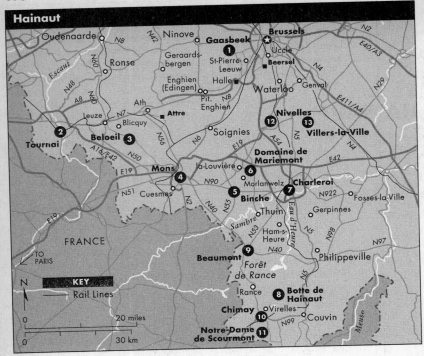

Hainaut

🐦 **Park Paradisio** is an ornithologist's dream come true. On a former monastic domain, amid old ruins, bushes, ancient trees, a river, and three lakes, more than 2,500 birds of 400 different species live in semi-liberty. Birds of prey live inside a 50-ft-high cage of 30,000 square ft, which visitors may enter. Special care is taken with birds of endangered species so that their offspring can be returned to the wild. There's also a children's farm, restaurants, and a playground. The park is near Attre. ⊠ *Domaine de Cambron, Cambron,* ☎ *068/454653.* 🎟 *BF395.* ⊙ *Apr.–Nov. 8, daily 10–6, July–Aug. until 7.*

Tournai

❷ *86 km (52 mi) southwest of Brussels, 48 km (29 mi) west of Mons, 28 km (17 mi) east of Lille (France).*

Tournai was an important center when the Roman legions were marching around these parts. Clovis, the Merovingian king who became the first Christian ruler of France, was born here in 465. At various times, Tournai has been English, French, and Austrian. Through these vicissitudes the city remained a flourishing center of art. The German bombardment in May 1940 destroyed virtually all the priceless old buildings, with the exception of a few Romanesque houses from the 12th century—unique in Western Europe—and a handful of 14th- and 15th-century Gothic buildings.

★ The **Cathédrale Notre-Dame,** with its five towers, all different, dominates the city today. Begun in 1110 and completed in 60 years, it is the most original work of religious architecture in Belgium and the beginning of a distinctive style that spread from Tournai down the river Escaut (Scheldt). You get the best general view of the cathedral from Place Paul-Emile Janson, and you need to walk around it to get the full effect of its vast proportions and the massive silhouettes of its five towers. Inside is an overpowering Renaissance screen in polychrome marble, contrasting with the Romanesque purity of the nave. The transept, almost a cathedral within the cathedral, contains what remains of 12th-century frescoes and well-restored 14th-century windows. In the chapels are paintings by Rubens (the magnificent *Purgatory*), Pourbus the Elder, and Martin de Vos. Foremost among the objects in the treasury are reliquaries in gilded copper and silver by two of the great 13th-century silversmiths and masters of Art Mosan, Nicholas de Verdun, and Hugo d'Oignies. ⊠ *Pl. Paul-Emile Janson.* ☉ *Cathedral, daily 9–noon and 2–6; Treasury, Apr.–Oct., Mon.–Sat. 10:15–11:45 and 2–5:45, Sun. and holidays 2–6:45; Nov.–Mar., Mon.–Sat. 10:15–11:45 and 2–3:45, Sun. and holidays 2–3:45.*

NEED A BREAK?	**A l'Bancloque** (⊠ R. des Chapeliers 46, ☎ 069/222149) is a classic Belgian drinking room with high, coffered ceilings and an old stone fireplace.

The 240-ft-high **Beffroi** (Belfry) on the Grand'Place is the oldest in this land of old belfries, dating from 1188. Hanging here are two bells from 1392 and a 15th-century carillon. It cannot be visited as it is undergoing restoration.

The **Pont des Trous** is a rare example of a 13th-century fortified bridge built to control river access. The bridge was blown up in 1940; it was rebuilt after the war and raised 8 ft to allow river traffic to pass through—exactly what the old bridge was built to prevent. Sightseeing boats leave from the landing stage below the bridge. ⊠ *Quai Staline.*

The **Musée de la Tapisserie** (Tapestry Museum) vividly illustrates the long and profitable tradition of tapestry-making in Tournai and displays an outstanding selection of tapestries from the Middle Ages to the present day. In the contemporary section there are demonstrations of tapestry weaving every weekday. ⊠ *Pl. Reine Astrid,* ☎ *069/234285.* ▣ *BF80.* ☉ *Wed.–Mon. 10–noon and 2–5:30.*

The bright and airy star-shape **Musée des Beaux-Arts** was designed by Victor Horta, the master Art Nouveau architect, to allow a maximum of natural light. Its exceptional collection of early Flemish art includes copies of works by native son Roger de la Pasture, better known as Rogier Van der Weyden, who is represented by a Nativity scene and the *Salve Regina* triptych; Impressionist masterpieces such as Manet's *Couple d'Argenteuil;* works by Monet and Seurat; and modern Belgian art, including a witty armadillo sculpted by master ceramist Pierre Caille. ⊠ *Enclos St-Martin,* ☎ *069/222043.* ▣ *BF120.* ☉ *Wed.–Mon. 10–noon and 2–5:30.*

☉ **Centre de Loisirs de l'Orient** is a family-oriented leisure center with boats, games, barbecues, a swimming pool, and a waterside pub. ⊠ *Chemin de Mons 8 (exit 32),* ☎ *069/222635.* ▣ *Free, except for pedal-boats and pool.* ☉ *Apr.–mid-Sept., daily 10–10.*

☉ **Archeosite** is an open-air museum and experimental archaeological center, with prehistoric dwellings with mud walls and thatched roofs reconstructed in accordance with archaeological findings. Activities include basketwork, weaving, pottery, bronze casting, and iron-ore processing. ⊠ *R. de l'Abbaye 15, Aubechies,* ☎ *069/671116.* ▣ *BF150.* ☉ *Nov.–Easter, weekends 9–5; Easter–Oct., weekdays 9–5, weekends 2–6.*

★ ❸ **Beloeil** is the magnificent, fairy-tale château of the Prince de Ligne, whose ancestors have lived here since the 14th century. The 17th-century château is partially a reconstruction from the original plans, following a fire in 1900. It contains fine furniture and tapestries, and the heirlooms include gifts from Marie Antoinette and Catherine the Great, friends of the Maréchal de Ligne; his grandson was offered, but refused, the Belgian crown. The elegant park, with a 5-km (3-mi) vista, is patterned after Versailles. ⊠ *R. du Château 11, Beloeil,* ☎ *069/689426.* ☜ *BF280 (tour of castle BF500 extra).* ☉ *Apr.–Sept., daily 10–6.*

Dining and Lodging

$$$ ✕ **Le Pressoir.** Tucked away at the end of the Marché-aux-Poteries, between the cathedral and the Beffroi, this elegant but unpretentious restaurant combines historical atmosphere (exposed brick, illuminated oil paintings) with surprising urbanity: The bar draws BCBG (*bon chic–bon genre*) clientele, and the restaurant hosts visiting VIPs. Try the roast farm pigeon with young turnips or saffron-perfumed bouillabaisse of *rouget* (red mullet). ⊠ *Marché-aux-Poteries 2,* ☎ *069/223513. AE, DC, MC, V. No dinner Sun.–Thurs. Closed Tues., Carnival wk, last 3 wks of Aug.*

$ ✕ **Bistro de la Cathédrale.** This modernized, brightly lighted storefront restaurant offers reasonable fixed-price menus and large portions of good, simple, well-prepared food: fresh oysters, salads of *crevettes grise* (tiny shrimp), and rabbit with prunes. The ambience is casual, the staff friendly. ⊠ *Vieux Marché-aux-Poteries 15,* ☎ *069/210379. AE, DC, MC, V.*

$ ✕ **Ô Pères au Quai.** On the riverside behind the columns of a 17th-century house, this friendly, value-for-money restaurant consists of one room, where meat is grilled in the large fireplace, and a pleasant garden. Fixed-price menus include an all-you-can-eat buffet of salads and cold meats and a generous supply of wine. ⊠ *Quai Notre-Dame 18,* ☎ *069/232922. AE, DC, MC, V. No lunch Sat., no dinner Mon.*

$$$ 🛏 **Le Panoramique.** As the name indicates, this hotel has sweeping views from its hilltop location a couple of miles from the center of town. Almost all of the modern rooms have been refreshed and one more floor has been added. This is more like a ski lodge than an ordinary hotel— long on comfort, short on charm. ⊠ *Pl. de la Trinité 2, B 7542 Mont Saint-Aubert,* ☎ *069/891616,* FAX *069/233323. 46 rooms. Restaurant, meeting rooms. AE, DC, MC, V.*

$$ 🛏 **Holiday Inn Garden Court.** A fully modernized chain-style business hotel, it stands at the foot of the cathedral in the center of town. Some rooms look onto the small square. ⊠ *Pl. St-Pierre, B 7500,* ☎ *069/215077,* FAX *069/215078. 59 rooms. Restaurant, café, meeting rooms. AE, DC, MC, V.*

$ 🛏 **L'Europe.** On the Grand'Place, with rooms looking out toward the Beffroi and historic architecture, this is a cheerful, comfortable hotel in an old step-gabled house. The rooms, surprisingly quiet at the back, given the central location, have been cheaply decorated but with a lavish, almost kitschy touch; most have toilets down the hall. The restaurant-tavern downstairs draws crowds of locals for stone-grilled meats. ⊠ *Grand'Place 36, B 7500,* ☎ *069/224067. 8 rooms. Restaurant. AE, MC.*

Outdoor Activities and Sports

TENNIS
Plaine de Jeux Bozière (⊠ Av. Bozière 1B, ☎ 069/223586) has basketball, volleyball, mini-soccer, and tennis.

Mons

❹ *48 km (29 mi) east of Tournai, 67 km (40 mi) south of Brussels, 72 km (43 mi) west of Namur.*

The hilly streets of Mons, lined with elegant if grimy 17th- and 18th-century brick houses, have considerable charm. At the highest point stands a remarkable **belfry,** known locally as *le château*, for it stands next to what once was the castle of the counts of Hainaut. Built in the 17th century, it's a Baroque tower, 285 ft high and crowned by an onion dome. The tower is undergoing restoration and cannot be visited, but you can hear the carillon bells ringing the hours.

Mons has had its share of misfortunes. Like most of Wallonia's cities, it was repeatedly occupied and lost by the troops of Louis XIV, of the French Revolution, and of Napoléon. It was at Mons in August 1914 that the British Expeditionary Force first battled the Germans. Many of the self-styled Old Contemptibles spoke of a vision of the "Angels of Mons" helping them hold their position longer than seemed possible. Thirty years later, further destruction was wrought by a running battle between advancing American troops and the retreating Germans.

The **Hôtel de Ville** (Town Hall) in the Grand'Place is largely the work of Matthieu de Layens, the master of the Town Hall in Leuven, which it vaguely resembles, although it is less overwhelming. Next to the door stands a forged-iron statuette of a monkey. If you touch its head with your left hand, it will bring you good luck, as it has done for believers since the Middle Ages.

NEED A
BREAK? **La Terrasse** (✉ Grand'Place 6) is an attractive café with a yellow facade that serves homemade soups and simple Belgian snacks such as cheese croquettes.

The **Collégiale Ste-Waudru** (Collegiate Church of St. Waudru), named for the wife of a Merovingian dignitary who, legend has it, founded a monastery in the 7th century around which the city developed. The church was begun in 1450 by the women of St. Waudru's Noble Chapter of Secular Canonesses. The elaborately decorated *Car d'Or* (Golden Coach), which carries the reliquary of St. Waudru on an annual procession through the streets on Trinity Sunday (eighth Sunday after Easter), stands in the nave next to doors that are opened only on special occasions. The precious objects in the treasury include what is purported to be St. Waudru's ring. ✉ *Pl. du Chapitre.* 🎫 *Treasury, BF50.* ☉ *Apr.–Oct., Tues.–Sat. 1:30–6, Sun. 1:30–5.*

The town of **Cuesmes** was once home to **Vincent van Gogh.** He came to the Borinage, the depressed area south of Mons, as a preacher in 1878 and stayed with a family of miners, the Decrucqs. It was here that he began drawing the landscape and scenes of the miners' lives. The **house** where he lived still stands. The original environment has been reconstructed; there is an exhibition of reproductions of his work and an audiovisual presentation. ✉ *R. du Pavillon 3, Cuesmes,* 🕾 *065/355611.* 🎫 *BF100.* ☉ *Tues.–Sun. 10–6.*

★ **Grand-Hornu** is a remarkable example of early industrial architecture seeking to humanize working conditions, in an area dotted with conical slag heaps—reminders of a coal-mining past. The vast, semi-ruined redbrick complex of workshops, offices, and housing, including a library, dance hall, and bathhouse, was built by Henri De Gorge in the early 19th century in neoclassical style, with arcades, pediments, and half-moon windows. It served its purpose for well over a century. Fortunately it was rescued from demolition and is now a multipurpose cultural center, with some offices rented out to companies. Further renovations and an extended cultural program are expected by 2002. ✉ *R. Ste-Louise 82, Hornu, Mons,* 🕾 *065/770712.* 🎫 *BF100.* ☉ *Mar.–Sept., Tues.–Sun. 10–6; Oct.–Feb., Tues.–Sun. 10–4.*

Dining and Lodging

$$ ✕ **Alter Ego.** This handsome, stylish brasserie with grape-shape deco-
★   rations on the ceiling offers regionally inspired cuisine: homemade *con-
fit de canard* (pressed duck), duck fillets cooked in raspberries, and
potatoes sautéed in goose fat. ⊠ *R. Nimy 6,* ☎ *065/351730. AE, DC,
MC, V. No dinner Sun. Closed Mon., mid-July–mid-Aug.*

$ ✕ **Le Sans-Soucis.** This elegant tearoom (open until 7)—with lamps on
the tables, English china, fresh flowers, and piped classical music—serves
the best light lunches in town: quiches, vegetable tarts, good salads,
and marvelous cakes. ⊠ *R. d'Havré 79,* ☎ *065/319333. Closed Sun.*

$$ ✕⌂ **Casteau Resort Hotel.** The setting is peaceful for this modern
hotel some 8 km (5 mi) northeast of Mons, which makes it a good base
for exploring the region. The rooms are pretty standard, but there are
thoughtful amenities, such as a trouser press. The restaurant menu offers some unusual items, including brioche with smoked eel and a
poached egg. ⊠ *Chaussée de Bruxelles 38, 7061 Casteau,* ☎ *065/
320400,* ℻ *065/728744. 75 rooms. Restaurant, 2 tennis courts, convention center. AE, DC, MC, V.*

$$ ✕⌂ **Château de la Cense au Bois.** This 19th-century château in a 40-
★   acre park on the outskirts of Mons has luxurious and tasteful rooms
and offers gastronomic weekends. Each room is different from the others,
but all have large beds, large bathrooms, and a view of the park. There
is no obligation to eat in the restaurant, L'Osciètre Gris ($$$; closed
Mon., no dinner Sun.), which serves ambitious French, seasonal cui-
sine. ⊠ *Rte. d'Ath 135, B 7020 Nimy,* ☎ *065/316000,* ℻ *065/361155.
10 rooms. Restaurant, bicycles. AE, DC, MC, V.*

Outdoor Activities and Sports

GOLF
There's an 18-hole public golf course west of Mons, **Golf du Mont Garni**
(⊠ R. du Mont Garni 3, Baudour, ☎ 065/622719).

TENNIS
Try the **Waux-Hall** (⊠ Av. St-Pierre 17, Mons, ☎ 065/337923) for tennis, boats, and camping.

Binche

❺ *16 km (10 mi) east of Mons, 62 km (37 mi) south of Brussels.*

Binche is the only remaining walled city in Belgium, and its center, complete with a cobbled, café-fringed square and an onion-dome town hall,
is still intact behind 25 towers and 2¼ km (1½ mi) of ramparts. However, its biggest claim to fame is that it is the carnival capital of Belgium. The carnival begins the Sunday before Ash Wednesday, when
hundreds of men dressed as "Mam'zelles" dance in the streets to the
music of fiddles, barrel organs, and drums, and 1,500 Binche dancers
form a procession. Shrove Tuesday is the big day. The dancers, or Gilles,
have celebrated the rites of spring since the 14th century. They dance
with dignity and gravity, repeating ritual gestures such as ringing cow-
bells and distributing—throwing, actually—oranges. They assemble at
dawn and go from house to house in fantastic costumes emblazoned
with red and yellow heraldic lions. In the morning they wear wax-covered
masks on which are painted green glasses, whiskers, and moustaches.
In the afternoon, their enormous hats are crowned with huge plumes
of ostrich feathers. To the rhythm of drums, the Gilles move through
the streets in a slow, shuffling dance. The day ends with fireworks, but
the Gilles continue dancing through the night. Traditionally, they drink
nothing but champagne.

The **Musée International du Carnaval et du Masque** has been installed
in the former Augustine college. It contains one of the world's finest

collections of masks and costumes, and there's an audiovisual presentation of the local carnival, in case you're in Binche at the wrong time for the real thing. ⊠ *R. du St-Moustier 10,* ☎ *064/556–6913.* ✉ *BF150.* ☉ *Apr.–Oct., Mon.–Thurs. 9–noon and 2–6, Sat. 2–6, Sun. 10–noon and 2–6; Nov.–Mar., Mon.–Thurs. 9–noon and 1–5, weekends 2–6. Closed Carnival, Nov. 1, Dec. 22–Jan. 6.*

★ The **Plan Incliné de Ronquières** is a grandiose engineering feat that did not bring about the hoped-for results. This mile-long inclined plane was designed to allow river traffic to enter huge tanks, which were winched up 225 ft to a higher level, avoiding time-consuming locks. Now a new attraction has been added in the tower overlooking the installation. To experience *Un Bateau, une Vie* (A Boat, a Life), visitors are issued infrared helmets that provide an interactive virtual-reality experience. You have the impression of following a boatman down into his barge, living the traditional as well as the modern way of life on the canal, and sharing the confidences of its people. ⊠ *N535, Ronquières, halfway between Binche and Brussels,* ☎ *065/360464.* ✉ *Virtual-reality show BF250; boat trip BF100.* ☉ *Show: June–Nov., daily 10–7 (last ticket, 5); boats May–Sept., Tues. and Thurs.–Sun. noon, 2:30, 3:30, and 5:30.*

❻ The **Domaine de Mariemont** is a 110-acre English-style park, one of the most attractive in Belgium. It is embellished with sculptures by a number of artists, including Auguste Rodin and Constantin Meunier. Only ruins remain of the château that once stood here, but there is a well-planned museum containing excellent collections of ancient and Chinese art, archaeological finds, and Tournai porcelain. The museum also has a café-restaurant and holds excellent sculpture retrospectives. ⊠ *Chaussée de Mariemont, off N59, or Exit 19 from E42, north of Binche, near Morlanwelz,* ☎ *064/212193.* ✉ *Free.* ☉ *Tues.–Fri. and most Sat. 10–12:30 and 1:30–6.*

☼ The **Musée des Sciences de Parentville** is a playful, family-oriented science museum with laboratory and interactive displays, plus a playground with scientific games. ⊠ *R. de Villers 227, Couillet,* ☎ *071/600300.* ✉ *BF150.* ☉ *Weekdays 9:30–5:30, Sun. 10–6.*

Dining

$ ✕ **L'Industrie.** This is one of the few places serving the Binche specialty, *doubles* (buckwheat pancakes filled with cheese), but order by telephone the day before. This gracefully aging restaurant is so discreet that you might miss it. It's on the corner of Grand'Place and Rue de la Hure. Head cheese, *anguilles au vert* (eels with herb sauce), and mussels are standard menu items. ⊠ *Grand'Place 4,* ☎ *064/331053. No dinner Mon., Tues. Closed Wed.*

Charleroi

❼ *20 km (12 mi) east of Binche.*

Charleroi, much larger than Binche and former capital of the "Black Country" (iron and steel manufacturing region) has been hard hit by a recession that has made steel production almost obsolete. The city has a large population of Italian origin, many of whom came to work in the mines thanks to a reciprocal, post–World War II labor agreement between Belgium and Italy. Hundreds died in the country's worst mining accident in 1956. Charleroi has a good choice of Italian restaurants, an active contemporary dance scene, and some fascinating museums. The **Musée de la Photographie,** in an old abbey, tells the story of photography from its infancy to the present day and mounts superb temporary exhibitions. ⊠ *Av. Paul Pastur 11,* ☎ *071/435810,* 🖾 *BF150.* ⊗ *Tues.–Sun. 10–6.*

Botte de Hainaut

❽ *50 km (30 mi) south from Charleroi into France.*

The boot-shape Botte de Hainaut region is rich in wooded valleys, vil-
🐾 lages, châteaux, and lakes. The **Eau-d'Heure** is a lake surrounded by
a wild, wooded 4,500-acre park with trails, as well as aquariums, an
ecological museum, and a panoramic tower. ⊠ *Boussu-lez-Walcourt,*
☎ *071/633534.* 🖾 *BF180.* ⊗ *Easter–Sept., daily 9–6.*

❾ The **Tour Salamandre** in **Beaumont** is all that remains of a major fortified castle built in the 11th century. The tower has been restored and
houses a museum of local and regional history. ⊠ *N40 or N53, Beaumont,* ☎ *071/588191.* 🖾 *BF50.* ⊗ *May–Sept., daily 9–7; Oct., Sun.
10–5.*

❿ All the way south is **Chimay,** a small town with vivid memories of the
great nation to the south. It was the home of Froissart, the 14th-
century historian whose chronicles furnished the background information
for many of Shakespeare's plays. Later, Chimay became the home of
Madame Tallien, a great beauty who was known to revolutionary
France as Notre Dame de Thermidor. She narrowly escaped the guillotine, married her protector, Citizen Tallien, and persuaded him to in-
stigate the overthrow of Robespierre. Eventually she was again married,
to François-Joseph Caraman, prince of Chimay, and ended her days
in peace and dignity as mistress of the **Château de Chimay**. The warrant for her arrest, signed by Robespierre, is preserved at the château,
along with other French memorabilia, such as the baptismal robe
worn by Napoléon's son, the king of Rome. Classical music concerts
are held in the castle on the second Saturday of every month. ⊠ *R. du
Château,* ☎ *060/212823; concerts, 060/214444.* 🖾 *BF200.* ⊗ *Guided
tours Mar.–Oct., daily 10–noon and 2–6; Nov.–Feb. by appointment.*

⓫ **Notre-Dame de Scourmont** is a Trappist monastery whose monks produce some of the best cheese and tastiest, most potent beer in Belgium.
Although the monastery is not open to the public, except for retreats,
you can purchase Chimay beer and cheese here. ⊠ *About 1⅓ km
(1 mi) south of Chimay.*

Dining and Lodging

$$ ✕🏠 **Hostellerie du Gahy.** Overlooking a large garden, this small inn
has six rooms decorated in traditional style. The ambitious cuisine fa-
vors seafood and cakes: Try lobster with vanilla flavoring in puff-pastry
or quails stuffed with foie gras. Half-board is obligatory in summer.
⊠ *R. du Gahy 2, B 6590 Momignies,* ☎ *060/511093,* 🖾 *060/512879.
6 rooms. Restaurant. AE, DC, MC, V. No dinner Sun. and Wed.
Closed Mon.*

$ ✕🏠 **Hostellerie Le Virelles.** Just north of Chimay, in the open green-
★ ery around the Etang de Virelles, this old country inn offers simple,
regional cooking in a pretty, well-weathered beam-and-copper setting.
You can have trout or *escavèche* (spicy, cold marinade of cooked fish),
or a more ambitious, multicourse menu based on regional freshwater
fish and game. Rooms, named after field flowers, are simple and cozy,
some with four-poster beds. The adjacent nature reserve is great for
long walks. ⊠ *R. du Lac 28, B 6461 Virelles,* ☎ *060/212803,* 🖾 *060/
512458. 7 rooms with bath or shower. Restaurant. AE, DC, MC, V.
No dinner Tues. Closed Wed.*

Outdoor Activities and Sports
ARCHERY
You can practice crossbow shooting in Beaumont at the **Arbaletriers Beaumontois** (⊠ Parc de Paridaens, ☎ 071/588255).

 HORSEBACK RIDING
Horseback riding is popular in many parts of the province, particularly in the less densely populated south. In Chimay you can arrange treks with the **Centre Equestre des Fagnes** (⊠ R. de la Fagne 20, ☎ 060/411169).

Nivelles

⑫ *34 km (21 mi) south of Brussels, 13 km (8 mi) west of Villers-la-Ville.*

★ **La Collégiale Ste-Gertrude** (St. Gertrude's Collegiate Church), the pride of Nivelles, is, in fact, a reconstruction. This old town suffered terribly from bombardment in May 1940, when more than 500 buildings were destroyed, including the original church dating from the 7th century when the Merovingian kings ruled the land. Reparations from Germany paid for the rebuilding of the church—Belgium's finest Romanesque building, whose beauty derives from its severe simplicity. The most unusual feature is the two choirs, one symbolizing the power of the Holy Roman Emperor and the other that of the Pope. The church is named for the daughter of Pepin the Old, St. Gertrude, who founded a convent in Nivelles in about 650. The crypt contains the burial vaults of St. Gertrude and her parents. For group guided visits in English, telephone for an appointment. ⊠ *Grand'Place,* ☎ *067/882245.* ☞ *BF100.* ☉ *Weekdays 9–6 (Oct.–Mar. until 5); guided tours, weekdays 2 and 3:30.*

NEED A BREAK? Locals swear by **Pâtisserie Courtain** (⊠ Bd. Fleur de Lys 14) for the Nivelles specialty, *tarte al djote,* a succulent cheese and vegetable pie, served hot.

Villers-la-Ville

⑬ *36 km (22 mi) south of Brussels, 15 km (9 mi) southwest of Ottignies/Louvain-la-Neuve, 13 km (8 mi) east of Nivelles.*

★ The **Abbaye de Villers-la-Ville** (Abbey Ruins) dates from 1147. St. Bernard is believed to have laid the foundation stone, and as usual the Cistercians had a knack for building their monasteries in spots of great natural beauty. The abbey became one of Europe's most important and wealthy. It was repeatedly expanded, but it all ended when the French Revolution reached Belgium and the abbey was burned, sacked, and relegated to being a quarry for building material. Cistercian masonry is, however, not easily destroyed, and the walls and vaults of cloister, dormitories, refectory, and chapter hall form an impressive architectural unit. Open-air concerts and drama performances are staged here every summer. ⊠ *At crossroads north of village,* ☎ *071/879555.* ☞ *BF150; guided visits (Sun. 3) BF250.* ☉ *Apr.–Oct., Mon.–Tues. noon–6, Wed.–Sun. 10–6; Nov.–Mar., Wed.–Fri. 1–5, weekends 10–5.*

Hainaut A to Z

Arriving and Departing
BY CAR
Roads leading south from Brussels pass through Flemish-speaking Brabant; thus roads are signposted to Bergen (Mons), Doornik (Tournai), and Rijsel (Lille). The E19 motorway from Brussels to Paris

passes Mons on the way. The E42 from Liège joins the E19 before Mons and branches off from it between Mons and the border to continue to Tournai and Lille. South of Charleroi, roads are mostly two-lane highways.

BY TRAIN

There is one local train an hour from Brussels to Tournai (55 minutes) and one to Mons (45 minutes). Three of the express trains to Paris also stop at Mons. There are two trains an hour to Charleroi (40 minutes).

Getting Around

Tournai, Mons, and Charleroi are linked by rail, with one train an hour taking a half hour between each stop. Excursions to destinations other than these principal cities are best made by car.

Contacts and Resources

GUIDED TOURS

City tours are organized on request by the individual tourist offices in Tournai, Mons, Charleroi, and Binche. For tours of the southern part of the province, contact the tourist office in Beaumont (☞ Visitor Information, *below*).

VISITOR INFORMATION

Province of Hainaut (⊠ R. des Clercs 31, Mons, ☎ 065/360464). **Beaumont** (⊠ Grand'Place 10, ☎ 071/588191). **Binche** (⊠ Hotel de Ville/Grand'Place, ☎ 064/336727). **Charleroi** (⊠ Av. Mascaux 100, Marcinelle, ☎ 071/866152). **Mons** (⊠ Grand'Place 22, ☎ 065/335580). **Tournai** (⊠ Vieux Marché-aux-Poteries 14, ☎ 069/222045).

FLANDERS: GENT, BRUGGE, AND THE NORTH SEA COAST

If you ask the locals to define Flanders, you will almost always start a heated argument. Politically, it is the part of Belgium that lies north of the linguistic border, except Brussels. Many Flemish people contend that Brussels, too, is Flemish, which is historically correct but politically a point of contention. However, nobody can dispute that only two provinces, to the west of Antwerp and Brussels, bear the name: East Flanders and West Flanders.

The wealth of the Flemish cities was created by the weaving trade. The sumptuous clothing so lovingly depicted in numerous paintings was all locally produced. The merchants built their magnificent houses in Flemish style, and they engaged Flemish artists to paint their portraits. Flemish architects designed the churches and town halls. All of this combined to create a remarkable homogeneity, and in that sense, Brugge and Gent are twin towns, and Kortrijk, Ieper, and the others are the closest of kin. Even today, a Fleming would, if left to his own devices, build himself a home that would not look out of place in medieval Brugge or Gent.

Brugge and Gent, the art cities of Flanders, represent the magnificent flowering of the late Middle Ages. Here, Flemish painters arrived in the 15th century and left behind some incomparable treasures—Jan van Eyck's *Adoration of the Mystic Lamb* altarpiece and Hans Memling's St. Ursula Shrine, to name but two. Long before, the region had attracted other visitors—the Vikings. It was to fend off these marauders that Baldwin of the Iron Arm, first Count of Flanders, built the original fortifications at both Brugge and Gent. The cities came to prominence as centers of the cloth trade. Flemish weavers had been renowned since Roman times, but it was in the Middle Ages, when they began using the finest wool from England, Scotland, and Ireland, that their products became truly superior. Thus, the English acquired an interest in keeping Flanders from the French. This early form of industrialization also prepared the groundwork for communal strife, pitting common weavers against patrician merchants. The destinies of the two cities diverged in the 19th century. Brugge settled into a graceful decline from which it has only roused itself in the last few decades. Gent, however, embraced the industrial revolution, becoming an important textile center once more.

The cities of Kortrijk and Ieper, to the south, recall the long history of battles fought in the region since the time of Julius Caesar. In the Hundred Years' War, Flemish pikemen unhorsed French cavalry in the Battle of the Golden Spurs; in the War of the Spanish Succession, Marlborough confronted Louis XIV on Flemish soil; and in World War I, the unspeakable No Man's Land stretched across Flanders Fields. Today, the North Sea coast continues to be irresistible to invaders, but of a more peaceful kind, drawn by fresh air, sand, and calm.

Naturally, this is seafood country: Brugge ships in fresh fish daily from its port, Zeebrugge; and the coast towns serve North Sea delicacies directly from the source, at terrace restaurants whipped by sand and salt air. Even in landlocked Gent, some 50 km (30 mi) from the coast, locals snack on whelks and winkles (sea snails) as if they were popcorn. The essentials are *mosselen* (mussels) and *paling* (eels), the latter as common a source of protein here as chicken or beef is elsewhere. Their flesh is firm, fatty, and sweet, served in long cross-sections that contain an easy-to-remove backbone. The most prevalent preparation by far is "in green," stewed in a heady mix of sorrel, tarragon, sage, mint, and parsley. The side dish? Frites, of course. You'll inevitably find sole and turbot poached, *barbue* (brill) grilled or broiled, and a limited choice of classic sauces: grilled fish with rich béarnaise or mustard sauces and poached fish with only slightly lighter sauce mousseline. When the Flemish aren't eating their fish straight or in a blanket of golden sauce, they consume it in the region's most famous dish, fish waterzooi. The citizens of Gent have a chicken version of the dish.

For two vegetable delicacies of Flanders, it's worth arranging your visit to be here in springtime: asparagus, white and tender, served either in sauce mousseline or with the traditional Flemish garnish of chopped hard-boiled egg and melted butter; and the rarer, expensive *jets de houblon* (hops sprouts)—sweet, delicate shoots of the hops plant, abundant in March and April in beer-making country.

Unlike Antwerp and Brussels, Brugge is not a conference town but its opposite: This is where city residents like to get away for romantic weekends. Brugge is happy to accommodate them with honeymoon suites and other romantic trappings. Many hotels also work hard to supply appropriately Old Flemish decor in the public areas and, when possible, in the rooms. Recent changes in fire codes left Brugge struggling between the need to install fire escapes and the desire to preserve its historic landmarks. The results are discreet but comforting in this city that often glows with a thousand wood-burning hearths. Gent, like Brugge, aims at weekend visitors but hasn't developed an industry of romantic hotels; lodgings, with few exceptions, are modern. In Gent you can, however, stay in the oldest hotel in the world, in business since the 13th century. In these historic towns, even modern hotel chains blend in with the local architecture.

Check with the tourist offices of Brugge and Gent for package arrangements that include room reservations and some restaurant meals, for a reasonable fixed price. Coast hotels aim for longer visits and often offer half-board plans; in summer, be sure to book well in advance.

Almost any time of year is fine for visiting this region, although January and February may be too chilly for sightseeing on foot. Some restaurants along the coast close for the winter months, but many people enjoy walking along the beaches when the sea air is bracing and visiting Brugge in early spring or late fall, when there are few tourists. Museums in Brugge and Oostende are closed on Tuesday; in the rest of the country the closing day is generally Monday.

Water Sports

The Belgian coast, with its prevailing breeze and wide, sandy beaches, offers splendid opportunities for sailing, swimming, windsurfing, sand yachting (skimming along the beach aboard a wheeled platform equipped with a sail), and other sports. Even horseback riding is a semi-aquatic sport here, with horses splashing along the water's edge at full stretch.

Numbers in the text correspond to numbers in the margin and on the Gent, Brugge, and the Coast and the Gent and Brugge maps.

Gent: Gateway to Flanders

55 km (33 mi) northwest of Brussels, 60 km (36 mi) southwest of Antwerp on E17.

The seat of the regional government of Flanders, Gent (known to the English as Ghent and the French as Gand) is a lively town with much to offer in politics, business, and the arts. The city developed around two 7th-century abbeys, Sint-Pieter (St. Peter) and Sint-Baafs (St. Bavo), and the 9th-century castle of Gravensteen, which dominates the river Leie. The canal joining Gent and Damme, Brugge's port, was dug in the 13th century; 100 years later, more than 5,000 men were working at the weaver's trade in Gent.

In the early Middle Ages, the wealthy burghers were loyal to the counts of Flanders, who owed allegiance to the kings of France. But the weavers were dependent for their livelihood on wool shipments from England, France's enemy in the Hundred Years' War. In 1302 the weavers took up arms against the French, defeating them in a battle that, to this day, is vividly recalled by Flemish patriots.

In 1448, the people of Gent refused to pay a salt tax imposed by Philip the Good, Duke of Burgundy. For five years their militia stood firm against Philip's troops, and when they were finally overwhelmed, 16,000 townspeople perished. Gent continued to rebel, again and again, against perceived injustices. The emperor himself, Charles V, who was born in Gent, was not immune to their wrath. He responded by razing the St. Bavo Abbey and suppressing the rights of Gent's residents. Religious fervor was added to this volatile mixture when the Calvinist iconoclasts proclaimed the city a republic in 1577, only to be overthrown by Spanish forces seven years later. In the 18th century, French armies marched on Gent on four different occasions. This did little to dampen the conflict between French and Flemish speakers in the city.

Gent was rescued from economic oblivion by a daring young man named Lieven Bauwens, who, in 1800, smuggled a spinning jenny out of Britain in a reversal of what had happened hundreds of years earlier, when Flemish weavers emigrated to England. Bauwens's exploit provided the foundation for a textile industry that employed 160,000 workers a century later.

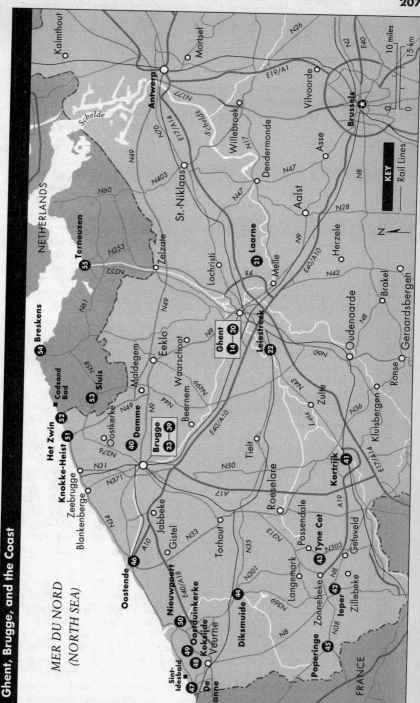

Ghent, Brugge, and the Coast

MER DU NORD
(NORTH SEA)

NETHERLANDS

FRANCE

KEY
— Rail Lines

N

Kalmhout
Mortsel
Antwerp
Vilvoorde
Brussels
Willebroek
Asse
Schelde
Dendermonde
Aalst
St-Niklaas
Herzele
Terneuzen 55
Zelzate
Laarne 21
Brakel
Breskens
Lochristi
Melle
Oudenaarde
Geraardsbergen
Cadzand Bad
Sluis 53
Eeklo
Ghent 14–20
Leiestreek 22
Ronse
Het Zwin 52
Waarschoot
Maldegem
Kluisbergen
Knokke-Heist 51
Oostkerke
Beernem
Zulte
Kortrijk 41
Zeebrugge
Damme 40
Brugge 23–39
Blankenberge
Tielt
Jabbeke
Roeselare
Oostende
Gistel
Torhout
Passendale
Tyne Cot 43
Geluveld
Nieuwpoort 46
Langemark
Oostduinkerke
Diksmuide 44
Zonnebeke
Ieper 42
Koksijde 49
Veurne
Poperinge 45
Zillebeke
Sint-Idesbald 47
De Panne

10 miles
15 km

To facilitate textile exports, a new canal was built to link Gent's inland port with the North Sea. It remains vital to modern industrial development, such as an automobile assembly plant. Today, huge car carriers sail up the canal to Gent.

Exploring Gent

A Good Walk

Start at **Sint-Michielsbrug** ⑭, taking in the view of the city's three spires, then walk north along the right side of the river Leie, on the **Graslei** ⑮, admiring the 17th-century and older buildings on this side and on the Kornelei opposite. When you reach Hooiard, follow the river along the Vleeshuistragel until you reach the Groenten Markt, then cross into Leinie Vismarkt and walk up to the medieval **Gravensteen** ⑯. Head back to Kleine Vismarkt then turn left onto **Kraanlei**, nipping into the **Museum voor Volkskunde** ⑰ and exploring the **Patershol** district behind. Cross the river via Zuivelbrugstraat, stroll across the Vrijdagmarkt onto Kammerstraat, then turn right down Belfortstraat. Passing the **Stadhuis** ⑱ on your right, head onto the Botermarkt and admire the view from the **Belfort** ⑲, then go to Sint-Baafsplein to see **Sint Baafskathedraal** ⑳ and Van Eyck's masterpiece. You'll need to take taxis from the center to the city's remaining sites: the **Lakenhalle**, the **Klein Begijnhof**, the **Museum voor Schone Kunsten**, and the **Stedelijk Museum van Actuele Kunst**.

TIMING

For Gent, you should allow a couple of hours, especially if you're stopping off to see the *Mystic Lamb*. The view from the bridge at night is stunning, and a canal-side stroll in the late evening is worth the effort. Gent is very cold between December and February.

Sights to See

⑲ **Belfort** (Belfry). The tower, 300 ft high, symbolizes the power of the guilds during the 14th century. Begun in 1314, it was not completed until 1913, when the spire with its gilded details was added, based on the original 14th-century elevation. The Belfry contained documents listing the privileges of the city, jealously guarded behind double doors with triple locks, and bells that were rung in moments of danger, until Charles V ordered them to be removed. Now a 52-bell carillon, said by experts to be the best in the world, hangs on the fifth floor, and one of the damaged old bells rests at the foot of the tower. The carillon can only be visited with a guide. ✉ *St-Baafsplein*, ☎ *09/233–3954.* ✉ *BF100, guided visits BF100.* ☯ *Guided visits Apr.–mid-Nov., daily 10–12:30 and 2–5:30; mid-Nov.–Mar., weekdays 10 min past hr, weekends afternoon only.*

★ ⑮ **Graslei.** This magnificent row of guild houses is best seen from across the river Leie. The **Vrije Schippers** (Free Bargemen), at No. 14, is a late Gothic building from 1531, when the guild dominated inland shipping. No. 11 is the **Korenmetershuis** (Grain Measurers' House), a late Baroque building from 1698. Next to it is the narrow Renaissance **Tolhuis** (Toll House), where taxes were levied on grain shipments. It stands side by side with the brooding, Romanesque **Koornstapelhuis** (Granary), which was built in the 12th century and served its original purpose for 600 years; this was where the grain claimed by the tax collectors was stored. The guild house of the **Metselaars** (Masons), finally, is a copy of a house from 1527. The original, which stands near the transept of St. Nicholas's Church, has also recently been restored. Every night in season (and Friday and Saturday nights, November through April), the Graslei and all other historic monuments are illuminated from sunset to midnight. ✉ *Graslei.*

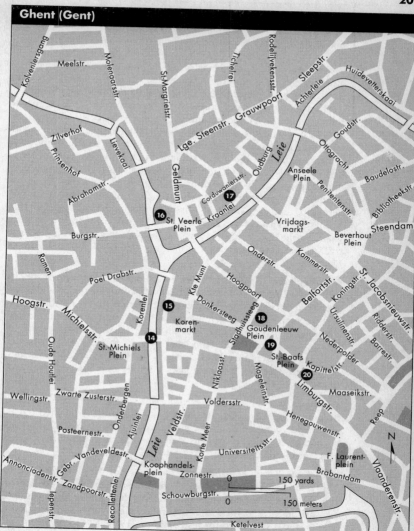

Ghent (Gent)

Belfort, **19**
Graslei, **15**
Gravensteen, **16**
Museum voor
Volkskunde, **17**
Sint-
Baafskathedraal, **20**
Sint-Michielsbrug, **14**
Stadhuis, **18**

If you're wandering around after 7, stop in at **De Tap en de Tepel** (✉ Gewad 7, closed Sun.–Tues. and Aug.), a wine and cheese house filled with flickering candles and lined with shelves of wine bottles.

⑯ Gravensteen. The castle of the counts of Flanders resembles an enormous battleship, steaming down the sedate Lieve Canal. From its windswept battlements, there's a splendid view over the rooftops of old Gent. Rebuilt several times—most recently in the 19th century to reflect what the Victorians thought a medieval castle should look like—it has little in common with the original fortress, built by Baldwin of the Iron Arm to discourage marauding Norsemen. Its purpose, too, changed from protection to oppression as the conflict deepened between feudal lords and unruly townspeople. One of the rooms contains a gruesome display of torture instruments, and there is an *oubliette* (secret dungeon) deep below the floor of another room. It was here, too, that the Continent's first spinning mule was installed after being spirited away from England; soon the castle's chambers were invaded by the clattering of looms, and Gent became a textile center to rival Manchester. ✉ *St-Veerleplein,* ☎ *09/225–9306.* 💶 *BF200.* ☼ *Daily 9–6 (Oct.–Mar. until 5).*

Klein Begijnhof (Small Beguine House). Founded southeast of the city center in 1234 by Countess Joanna of Constantinople, it is the best preserved of Gent's three beguinages. It is protected by a wall and portal. The small houses, each identified by a statue of a saint and surrounding a spacious green, are still occupied by a small number of Beguines, leading the life stipulated by their founder 750 years ago. They are the last of their kind. You may walk through the Klein Begijnhof (quietly, please), but the houses cannot be visited. ✉ *Lange Violettenstraat 71.*

Kraanlei. Two Baroque houses along this waterfront have elaborately decorated facades. The panels of No. 79 represent the five senses, crowned by a figure of a flute player, while those at No. 77 illustrate six acts of mercy. The house used to be an inn; hospitality to travelers was considered the seventh act of mercy. ✉ *Kraanlei.*

Lakenhalle (Cloth Hall). Built as the center for the cloth trade in the 15th century, the structure was still unfinished when the trade collapsed. It now serves as the entrance to the Belfort. Its vaulted cellar was used as a prison for 150 years and is currently a not very good restaurant. The facade is scheduled for restoration in 1999. ✉ *St-Baafsplein.*

Museum voor Schone Kunsten (Fine Arts Museum). The neoclassical museum in Citadel Park is one of Belgium's finest; it contains paintings and sculptures from the Middle Ages to the early 20th century. Its collections include two outstanding paintings by Hieronymus Bosch, *Saint Jerome* and *The Bearing of the Cross;* in the latter, Christ is shown surrounded by grotesque faces of unmitigated cruelty. There is also a fine selection of works from the flowering of Belgian art around the turn of the century. ✉ *Nicolaas de Liemaeckereplein 3,* ☎ *09/222–1703.* 💶 *BF100.* ☼ *Tues.–Sun. 9:30–5.*

⑰ Museum voor Volkskunde (Folklore Museum). The museum; the **Kraanlei** waterfront, on which it stands; and **Patershol**, the quarter behind it, form an attractive ensemble. The museum consists of a score of small, 16th-century almshouses, surrounding a garden, that have been reconstructed to offer an idea of life in Gent 100 years ago: One room is a grocer's shop, another a tavern, a third a weaver's workshop, and there are several ordinary rooms. ✉ *Kraanlei 65,* ☎ *09/223–1336.* 💶 *BF80.* ☼ *Tues.–Sun. 10–12.30 and 1:30–4:30.*

Patershol. The quarter used to house many of the textile workers from the Gravensteen and eventually turned into a badly neglected slum. Now crammed with smart cafés and restaurants, the district is the in place for young, well-off couples and families who have converted the small houses for their use. ⊠ *Bounded by Kraanlei, Lange Steenstraat, and Geldmunt.*

NEED A
BREAK?

Het Waterhuis aan de Bierkant (⊠ Groenmarkt 7), which overlooks the canal and has a pleasant outside terrace, offers over 100 beers, each lovingly if eccentrically described on the menu. Simple, inexpensive snacks include a good selection of cheeses.

★ ⓴ **Sint Baafskathedraal** (St. Bavo's Cathedral). This church, begun in the 13th century but finished in the 16th in the ornate Brabantine Gothic style, contains one of the greatest treasures in Christendom, *The Adoration of the Mystic Lamb.* Now in the De Villa Chapel, to the left of the entrance, the masterpiece is a stupendous polyptych by Jan van Eyck, completed in 1432. It has a history as tumultuous as that of Gent itself. When the iconoclasts smashed St. Bavo's stained-glass windows and other treasures, the painting was hidden in the tower. Napoléon had it carried off to Paris. Joseph II of Austria found the panels of Adam and Eve prurient because theirs were the first naturalistically depicted human bodies in Western art. They disappeared and remained lost for 100 years. The other side panels were sold and hung in a Berlin museum. In 1920 the masterpiece was again complete, but 14 years later a thief removed the panels on the lower left side. He returned the St. John the Baptist panel, but apparently died while waiting for a ransom for the panel of the Righteous Judges. Most people believe the panel is hidden somewhere in Gent, possibly even in the cathedral. The whole altarpiece was sent to France for safekeeping during World War II, but the Germans located and stole it. American troops eventually discovered it in an abandoned salt mine in Austria.

The central panel is based on the Book of Revelations: "And I looked, and, lo, a Lamb stood on the mount Sion, and with him an hundred forty and four thousand, having his Father's name written in their foreheads." There are not quite that many people in the painting, but it does depict 248 figures and 42 different types of flowers, each botanically correct. But statistics do not even suggest its grandeur. It uses a miniaturist technique to express the universal; realism to portray spirituality; and the blood of the sacrificial lamb mixes with the fountain of life to redeem the world. To the medieval viewer, it was an artistic *Summa Theologica,* a summation of all things revealed about the relationship between God and the world. An old tradition identifies the horseman in the foreground of the panel, to the immediate left, as Hubert van Eyck, Jan's brother, while the fourth figure from the left is believed to be Jan himself. It is now thought by art historians that Hubert, once believed to be co-creator of the luminous oil panels, was merely the carver of the imposing wooden frame of the altarpiece. As for the paintings themselves, Jan used brushes so delicate that the finest consisted of a single boar's bristle. The work was completed on May 6, 1432.

Originally dedicated to St. John, the cathedral became the site for the veneration of St. Bavo, Gent's own saint, after Charles V had the old Abbey of St. Bavo razed. The Order of the Golden Fleece, instituted in Brugge by Philip the Good in 1430, was convened here in 1559 by Philip II of Spain. It is still in existence, currently presided over by King Juan Carlos of Spain as grand master. The coats of arms of the 51 knights who first belonged to the Order still hang in the south transept. The

cathedral's remarkably ornate pulpit is carved in white Italian marble
and black Danish oak. In one of the radiating chapels hangs a Rubens
masterpiece, *Saint Bavo's Entry into the Monastery.* ✉ *St-Baafsplein.*
🎫 *Cathedral free; De Villa Chapel BF60.* 🕙 *Cathedral daily 8:30–6;
chapel Apr.–Oct., Mon.–Sat. 9:30–noon and 2–6, Sun. 1–6; Nov.–
Mar., Mon.–Sat. 10:30–noon and 2:30–4, Sun. 2–5. No visits to
cathedral or chapel during services.*

★ ⑭ **Sint-Michielsbrug** (St. Michael's Bridge). The best way to begin a tour
of Gent is to view the three medieval towers from this bridge. The closest is the tower of **Sint-Niklaaskerk** (St. Nicholas's Church), the parish
church of Gent's merchants. Its sober style is sometimes called Scheldt
Gothic, for it traveled down the river Scheldt from Tournai, where it
originated. Next comes the ☞ **Belfort.** In the background stands the
honey-color sandstone tower of ☞ **Sint-Baafskathedraal.**

🐌 **Schoolmuseum Michel Thiery** (Michel Thiery School Museum). In St.
Peter's Abbey, the museum is an original institution, with different sections focusing on geography and various sciences, but the greatest attraction is a sound-and-light show featuring a large-scale model of Gent
as it was 400 years ago. ✉ *St-Pietersplein 14,* ☎ *09/222–8050.* 🎫
BF100. 🕙 *Mon.–Thurs. and Sat. 9–12:15 and 1:30–5:15, Fri. 9–12:15.*

⑱ **Stadhuis** (Town Hall). The building is an early example of what rais-
ing taxes can do to a city. In 1516, Antwerp's Domien de Waghemakere
and Mechelen's Rombout Keldermans, two prominent architects, were
called in to build a town hall that would put all others to shame. But
before the building could be completed, Emperor Charles V imposed
new taxes that drained the city's resources. When work resumed in 1580,
during the short-lived Protestant Republic, it was completed in a
stricter and more economical style. Among its features are the tower
on the corner of Hoogpoort and Botermarkt, the balcony expressly built
for announcements and proclamations and, above all, the lacelike
tracery that embellishes its facade. The building is not open to the public, but you can arrange a tour through the Gidsenbond van Gent (☞
below). ✉ *Botermarkt,* ☎ *09/233–0772.*

Stedelijk Museum van Actuele Kunst (Museum of Contemporary Art,
or Smak). As well as the permanent displays—hyperrealism, Pop Art,
and works by artists of the CoBrA group from Copenhagen, Brussels,
and Amsterdam—the museum, one of Belgium's most innovative,
avant-garde spaces, holds frequent temporary shows with an emphasis on installations and performance art. The museum occupies a former casino opposite the Fine Arts Museum; renovations scheduled to
finish in May 1999 may be accompanied by a price increase. ✉ *Citadel-
park,* ☎ *09/221–1703.* 🎫 *BF100.* 🕙 *Tues.–Sun. 9:30–5.*

Dining and Lodging

$$$ ✕ **Waterzooi.** In the shadow of the Castle of the Counts, this tiny restau-
rant is named for Gent's contribution to Belgian gastronomy, a creamy
fish and vegetable stew. Specialties include turbot with three pepper
sauces and lobster ravioli with tarragon. ✉ *St-Veerleplein 2,* ☎ *09/
225–0563. Reservations essential. Jacket and tie. AE, DC, MC, V. Closed
Wed., Sun., and 1st 3 wks in Aug.*

$$ ✕ **Buikske Vol.** Probably the best among the nouveau-chic of Patershol's trendy eateries, this restaurant likes to surprise diners with un-
usual combinations, such as fillet of Angus beef with onion confit, or
crisp sweetbreads with rabbit. ✉ *Kraanlei 17,* ☎ *09/225–1880. AE,
MC, V. No lunch Sat., no dinner Wed. Closed Sun., Easter wk, and
1st ½ of Aug.*

$$ ✕ **Het Coorenmetershuis.** One flight up from the Graslei, in an ancient
★ guild house, this venturesome little restaurant serves well-executed
contemporary dishes, such as fillet of lamb with lentils, sole in Riesling wine, and John Dory with a parsley coulis. ⊠ *Graslei 12,* ☎ *09/223–4971. Reservations essential. AE, DC, MC, V. Closed Wed.,
Sun., and July 15–Aug. 15.*

$ ✕ **'t Kattenhuis Grill.** A feline theme dominates the stained-glass windows and primitive-style pictures and paintings that decorate this cozy,
family-run restaurant, popular with locals. It specializes in char-grilled
kebabs, served with generous portions of baked potatoes and salad.
Starters include garlic-drenched stuffed mushrooms and scampi with
cream and tomato sauce. ⊠ *Hertogstraat 9, No credit cards.*

$ ✕ **Taverne Keizershof.** Touristy taverns are much the same all over Belgium, but this one is popular with locals as well, always a good sign.
The daily plates are large portions of good, solid food, and all-day snacks
include toasted sandwiches and spaghetti. ⊠ *Vrijdagmarkt 47,* ☎ *09/223–4446. MC, V. Closed Sun.*

$$$–$$$$ ▣ **Sofitel Gent Belfort.** The Gent outpost of this comfortable, top-of-the-line French hotel chain, decorated in Art Nouveau style with warm
brown-and-beige house colors, is in the heart of the old city. ⊠ *Hoogpoort 63, B 9000,* ☎ *09/233–3331,* 🆋 *09/233–1102. 127 rooms.
Restaurant, bar, health club, convention center, parking (fee). AE, DC,
MC, V.*

$$$ ▣ **Novotel Gent Centrum.** Though part of a cookie-cutter, look-alike
hotel chain, this modern lodging is in the center of the tourist and shopping area and compresses a sprawl of business-class luxuries—lounges,
garden, swimming pool—into a small urban space. Some windows open
onto an inner courtyard, with its pool and greenery, and some take in
the city monuments. The decor is modern with warm and lively colors. ⊠ *Goudenleeuwplein 5, B 9000,* ☎ *09/224–2230,* 🆋 *09/224–3295. 117 rooms. Restaurant, bar, pool. AE, DC, MC, V.*

$$ ▣ **Gravensteen.** This handsome 19th-century mansion with a superb
canal-front location a few steps from the Castle of the Counts has been
restored to its original Second Empire style. The historic atmosphere
of the grand public spaces compensates, perhaps, for the small but personalized rooms. ⊠ *Jan Breydelstraat 35, B 9000,* ☎ *09/225–1150,*
🆋 *09/225–1850. 37 rooms. Bar, breakfast room, lounge, parking
(fee). AE, DC, MC, V.*

$$ ▣ **Sint Jorishof.** Napoléon stayed here. So did Emperor Charles V and
Mary of Burgundy, for this is one of the oldest hotels in the world. Needless to say, the step-gabled old inn has been much tinkered with over
the centuries, but a great deal of the Gothic spirit has been preserved,
especially in the reception area and restaurant, which serves classic French
fare. Rooms are less atmospheric. ⊠ *Botermarkt 2, B 9000,* ☎ *09/224–2424,* 🆋 *09/224–2640. 28 rooms with bath (some in annex across
street). Restaurant, meeting rooms, parking (fee). AE, DC, MC, V.*

$ ▣ **Erasmus.** From the flagstone and wood-beam library-lounge to the
★ stone mantels in the bedrooms, every inch of this noble 16th-century
home has been scrubbed, polished, and decked with period ornaments.
Even the tiny garden has been carefully manicured. The couple that
runs the hotel does everything from answering the bell pull at night to
serving breakfast in the parlor. ⊠ *Poel 25, B 9000,* ☎ *09/224–2195,*
🆋 *09/233–4241. 11 rooms with bath. Lobby lounge. AE, DC, MC,
V. Closed mid-Dec.–mid-Jan.*

Nightlife and the Arts

THE ARTS

Cultural life in Gent is lively and varied, and it's worthwhile checking
The Bulletin's "What's On" section under the heading "Other Towns."

Many events take place in the **Kunstencentrum Vooruit** (Vooruit Arts Center; ✉ St-Pietersnieuwstraat 23, ☎ 09/267–2828), which offers a top-quality program of dance, theater, and jazz, plus rock and contemporary classical concerts. **Gele Zaal** (✉ Nonnemeerstraat 26, ☎ 09/235–3702) hosts largely avant-garde jazz and classical music as well as a range of ethnic music. **De Vlaamse Opera** (Flemish Opera House; ✉ Schouwburgstraat 3, ☎ 09/225–2425), which shares its name and frequently excellent productions with a sister company in Antwerp, has a splendid ceiling and chandelier.

NIGHTLIFE

As in most Belgian towns, nightlife in Gent is a laid-back affair, although the student presence gives it a slight edge. A few cabarets and night-clubs exist, but the Gentenaars much prefer their pubs and cafés. **Backstage** (✉ St-Pietersnieuwstraat 128, ☎ 09/233–3535), a café-restaurant near the Vooruit center, presents occasional classical and jazz concerts. For clubbing, try **Democrazy** (✉ Reynaertstraat 125, ☎ 09/227–5196). **Lazy River Jazz Café** (✉ Stadhuissteeg 5, ☎ 09/223–2301) is a friendly, intimate place beloved of locals and students. **Pakhuis** (✉ Schuurkenstraat 4, ☎ 09/223–5555) is a bustling brasserie/tavern off the Korenmarkt, with trendy modern decor and, incongruously, a giant Greek statue.

Outdoor Activities and Sports

Gent has an extensive sports and recreation center only minutes from the city, the 250-acre **Blaarmeersen** (✉ Zuiderlaan 5, ☎ 09/221–1414). It is equipped with outdoor and indoor tennis courts, squash courts, a roller-skating track, jogging and cycling tracks, and facilities for windsurfing, sailing, canoeing, and camping.

Shopping

Langemunt and **Veldstraat** are the major shopping streets. **Voldersstraat** is where the smartest fashion boutiques are located. There are also several exclusive shopping galleries, where boutiques are interspersed with cafés and restaurants, such as the **Bourdon Arcade** (Gouden Leeuwplein) and **Braempoort** (between Brabantdam and Vlaanderenstraat).

The largest market is on the attractive and historic **Vrijdagmarkt,** held Friday from 7 to 1 and Saturday from 1 to 6. This is where leaders have rallied the people of Gent from the Middle Ages to the present day. You can take home a supply of "Gentse Mokken," syrup-saturated biscuits available from any pastry shop.

Laarne

㉑ *13 km (8 mi) east of Gent.*

Laarne Castle, one of the best-preserved medieval strongholds in the country, was built in the 14th century to protect Gent's eastern approaches and was converted to peaceful use in the 17th. Inside are fine examples of Brussels tapestry weaving and an outstanding collection of silver from the 15th to the 18th century. ✉ R4, Exit 5, Heusden–Laarne, ☎ 09/230–9155. 💰 BF150. 🕐 Easter–June and Sept.–Oct., Sun. 2–5; July–Aug., Tues.–Thurs. and weekends 2–5:30.

Leiestreek

㉒ *Just southwest of Gent.*

The Leiestreek (Leie Region) is a charmingly bucolic area that has attracted many painters. The fact that they are not widely known abroad makes it even more pleasant to discover their work in its original setting. The best way to enjoy the banks of the Leie is by rented motor-boat or bike. **Sint-Martens-Latem,** with its 15th-century wooden wind-mill, was home to Gustave van de Woestyne, an artist who worked during the early years of the 20th century. He was followed, after World War I, by Constant Permeke and the Expressionists. In the village of **Deurle,** the house and studio of the Gent painter Gust De Smet has been turned into the **Museum Dhondt-Dhaenens.** It contains a major collection of Expressionist paintings, including works by Permeke, Van den Berghe, and Albert Servaes. ⊠ *Take N466 south from Exit 13 off E40 north from Gent,* ☎ *09/282–5123.* 🖼 *BF70.* ⊙ *Feb.–early Dec., Wed.–Fri. 2–6, weekends 10–noon and 2–6.*

In the village of **Deinze,** beside an attractive Gothic church next to the river, you'll find the **Museum van Deinze en Leiestreek,** with works by Luminist pioneer Emile Claus, as well as by the Latem group of painters. ⊠ *Lucien Matthyslaan 3–5,* ☎ *09/381–9670.* 🖼 *BF60.* ⊙ *Weekdays except Tues. 2–5:30, weekends 10–noon and 2–5.*

Brugge: A Medieval Wonder

96 km (58 mi) northwest of Brussels, 45 km (27 mi) west of Gent, 28 km (17 mi) east of Oostende.

Brugge belongs to the world. Few other places have so well preserved their ancient heritage. Visitors flock here in numbers that occasionally seem overwhelming, but there are always quiet corners in this city offering refuge, where time appears to have stood still. The city may be better known by its French name, Bruges, but you'll score points with the locals by using the correct Flemish, Brugge (pronounced Bruhg-guh).

Brugge is where Flemish painting began. In fact, painting with oil was invented by Van Eyck in the 1420s, and the technique was taken to Italy by his pupil Petrus Christus. The art of the so-called Flemish Primitives represented a revolution in realism, portraiture, and perspective; it brings their era alive in astonishing detail. Jan van Eyck was named court painter to Philip the Good, Duke of Burgundy, who married Isabella of Portugal in a ceremony of incredible luxury in Brugge's Prinsenhof in 1429.

Linked with the estuary of the Zwin on the North Sea by a navigable waterway, Brugge was one of the most active members of the Hanseatic League during the 13th century. It exported Flemish cloth and imported fish from Scandinavia, furs from Russia, wine from Gascony, and silk from Venice. Italian merchants from Lombardy, Tuscany, and Venice set themselves up in Brugge, and the town established Europe's first stock exchange.

In 1301, the French queen Jeanne of Navarre was annoyed by the finery flaunted by the women of Brugge. "I thought I alone was queen," she said, "and here I am surrounded by hundreds more." The men of Brugge, in return, were annoyed at being requested to pay for the French royal couple's lavish reception. One fine morning in May 1302, they fell upon and massacred the French garrison and then went on with the men of Gent and Ieper to defeat the French chevaliers in the epic Battle of the Golden Spurs.

The last Burgundian feast in Brugge was the wedding of Duke Charles the Bold to Margaret of York, sister of England's Edward IV, in 1468. At the end of the century adversity struck. Flemish weavers had emigrated across the Channel and taught their trade to the English, who became formidable competitors. Even worse, the Zwin had begun to silt up, and the people of Brugge did not have the will or the funds to

Brugge

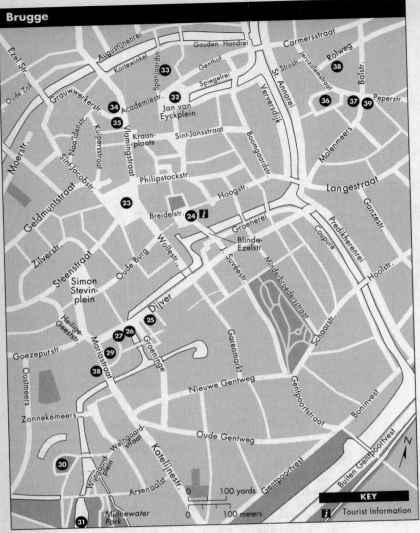

Begijnhof, **30**

Brangwyn
Museum, **26**

Burg, **24**

Groeninge
Museum, **25**

Gruuthuse
Museum, **27**

Huize ter Beurze, **34**

Jan Van Eyckplein, **32**

Jeruzalemkerk, **37**

Kantcentrum, **39**

Markt, **23**

Memling
Museum, **28**

Minnewater, **31**

Museum voor
Volkskunde, **38**

Onze-Lieve-
Vrouwekerk, **29**

Saaihalle, **35**

Sint-Anna, **36**

Spanjaardstraat, **33**

build the canal that might have saved their industry. Instead, trade and fortune switched to Antwerp.

Today the principal industry in Brugge is tourism. In the 19th century, British travelers on their way to view the battlefield of Waterloo rediscovered Brugge and spread its fame as a perfectly preserved medieval town. Its beauty is famous, but much of the city was redesigned in the 19th century by British architects keen to spread the Gothic revival. Only two of the original timber medieval houses remain. A novel by Georges Rodenbach, *Bruges-la-Morte* (Brugge, the Dead), brought more visitors but created an image that has been difficult to throw off. The administrative center of West Flanders, the city incorporates within its limits the new port of Zeebrugge and fields fiercely competitive soccer teams.

Exploring Brugge

A Good Walk

Begin at the **Markt** ㉓, the old market square. From its southeast corner, follow Breidelstraat to the city's main square, the **Burg** ㉔. In a corner of the square stands the small **Heilig Bloed Basiliek,** a basilica from the 12th century. Also on the Burg is the 14th-century **Stadhuis.** The Town Hall is linked with the graceful **Oude Griffie** by a bridge arching over the narrow Blinde Ezelstraat. Follow Blinde Ezelstraat south across one of the **Reien** (canals) and turn right on Dijver, following it along the canal to the **Groeninge Museum** ㉕. The canal makes a sharp turn to the left here; across the canal is the **Brangwyn Museum** ㉖; next door is the **Gruuthuse Museum** ㉗, the house of a 15th-century nobleman. Continue along Dijver and turn left on Mariastraat to the **Memling Museum** ㉘ on the right. Across the street is the **Onze-Lieve-Vrouwekerk** ㉙. Continue on Mariastraat to Weinggaardstraat on the right. Follow it across the canal to the **Begijnhof** ㉚. The canal flows into the **Minnewater** ㉛. At the other end of the center of the city, north of the Markt, lies **Jan Van Eyckplein** ㉜. Follow **Spanjaard-straat** ㉝ north from the square, turn left at the canal on Kortewinkel and left again on Vlamingstraat. Walk south to the **Huize ter Buerze** ㉞ and the **Saaihalle** ㉟, just across the narrow Grauwwerkerstraat from the Huize ter Buerze. From here, you can follow Academiestraat back through Jan Van Eyckplein to Genthof, across the canal; follow the canal south to Sint-Anna-Kerkstraat and turn left into the **Sint-Anna** ㊱ quarter. Next, follow Jeruzalemstraat to the **Jeruzalemkerk** ㊲. Backtrack on Jeruzalemstraat to Rolweg, and the reconstructed interiors of the **Museum voor Volkskunde** ㊳. Return down Jeruzalemstraat to Peperstraat to see the laces at the **Kantcentrum** ㊴.

TIMING

For Brugge, you're likely to need three hours. It's worth getting up at the crack of dawn to do the walkable sights and then go into the museums as the crowds start to hit the Burg. You might also visit the Groeninge first thing and postpone your stroll to the early evening. The weather can be raw in deep winter.

Sights toSee

★ ㉚   **Begijnhof** (Beguinage). This serene cluster of small, whitewashed houses surrounding a pleasant green has been an oasis of peace for 750 years. It is at its best in spring, when daffodils bloom and sunlight, dappled by high poplars, falls over the lawns. The Begijnhof was founded in 1245 by Margaret, Countess of Constantinople, to bring together the Beguines, many of them widows of Crusaders. The congregation flourished for 600 years. The Beguines have been replaced by Benedictine sisters, and you may join them, discreetly, for vespers in their small church of St. Elizabeth. Although most of the present-day houses are from the 16th and 17th centuries, they have maintained the architectural style of the houses that preceded them. One house has been set aside as a small museum. Visitors are asked to respect the silence. ⊠ *Monasterium de Wijngaard, Oude Begijnhof,* ☎ *050/330011.* ☜ *Free; house visit, BF60.* ⊙ *Apr.–Sept., daily 10–noon and 1:45–5:30; Oct.–Nov. and Mar., daily 10:30–noon and 1:45–5; Dec.–Feb., Wed.–Thurs. and weekends 2:45–4:45, Fri. 1:45–6.*

㉖ Brangwyn Museum. On the first floor of an 18th-century house that also contains an outstanding collection of lace, a craft long and lovingly practiced in Brugge, the Brangwyn display comprises hundreds of brooding drawings and paintings by Frank Brangwyn (1867–1956). His father was a Welsh architect who, like a number of other British romantics, settled in Brugge, and the son stayed on to paint many an homage to the city. ⊠ *Dijver 16,* ☎ *050/448711.* ☜ *BF80; combination ticket (includes the Gruuthuse, Memling, and Groeninge museums;* ☞ *below), BF450.* ⊙ *Apr.–Sept., daily 9:30–5; Oct.–Dec. and Feb.–Mar., Wed.–Mon. 9:30–12:30 and 2–5.*

★ **㉔ Burg.** This is an enchanted square, never more so than when discreetly floodlit after dark. The Burg derives its name from the fortress built by Baldwin of the Iron Arm, which is long since gone. So is, alas, the Carolingian Cathedral of St. Donaas, built around 900 and wantonly destroyed by French Republicans in 1799; the cathedral's site is now a small park. ⊠ *Hoogstraat and Breidelstraat.*

★ **㉕ Groeninge Museum.** This is one of the world's important art galleries. In the very first room hangs Jan van Eyck's wonderfully realistic *Madonna with Canon Van der Paele.* Van Eyck achieved texture and depth through multiple layers of oil and varnish, and his technique has withstood the ravages of more than five centuries. All the Flemish Primitives and their successors—Petrus Christus, Hugo Van der Goes, Hans Memling, Hieronymus Bosch, Rogier Van der Weyden, Gerard David, Pieter Bruegel (both Elder and Younger), Pieter Pourbus—are represented. The survey of Belgian art continues through the romantics and realists to Surrealists and contemporary artists. The Groeninge is set back from the street in a diminutive park behind a medieval gate. Although it is blessedly small, such are its riches that it warrants a half day or more. ⊠ *Dijver 12,* ☎ *050/448711.* ☜ *BF200; combination ticket (includes the Gruuthuse, Memling, and Brangwyn museums;* ☞ *above and below), BF450.* ⊙ *Apr.–Sept., daily 9:30–5; Oct.–Mar., Wed.–Mon. 9:30–12:30 and 2–5.*

NEED A BREAK?
The attractive **Taverne Groeninge** (⊠ Dijver 13) is decorated with works by Frank Brangwyn.

㉗ Gruuthuse Museum. This was the home of Lodewijk Van Gruuthuse, a prominent and powerful nobleman of the Netherlands in Burgundian times. He financed Edward IV's campaign to regain the throne of England in 1461. Room 6 is an attractive Gothic interior with a 15th-century mantelpiece and stained-glass windows. ⊠ *Dijver 17,* ☎ *050/ 448711.* ☜ *BF130; combination ticket (includes the Groeninge, Memling, and Brangwyn museums;* ☞ *above and below), BF450.* ⊙ *Apr.– Sept., daily 9:30–5; Oct.–Mar., Wed.–Mon. 9:30–12:30 and 2–5.*

Heilig Bloed Basiliek (Basilica of the Holy Blood). The Lower Chapel of this church has kept its pure, austere 12th-century Romanesque character, with massive pillars supporting a low, vaulted roof. The baptismal scene carved on the tympanum is original. An almost ridiculously elaborate Gothic external stairway leads to the Upper Chapel, which was twice destroyed—by Protestant iconoclasts in the 16th century and by French Republicans in the 18th—but both times rebuilt. The last reconstruction is not to everyone's taste. A phial thought to contain a few drops of the blood of Christ was brought from Jerusalem to Brugge in 1149 by Derick of Alsace. It is exposed here every Friday, and on Ascension Day it is carried through the streets in the magnificent Procession of the Holy Blood, a major pageant that combines religious and historical elements. There is a small **museum** next to the basilica containing the 17th-century reliquary. ✉ *Burg.* 🎫 *BF40.* ⏲ *Apr.–Sept., daily 9:30–11:50 and 2–5:50; Oct.–Mar., daily 10–noon and 2–4 (closed Wed. pm).*

NEED A BREAK? **Opus 4** is reached through the shopping gallery Ten Steeghere, which starts next to the basilica. Overlooking a pleasant stretch of canal, it's a good place for a quiet beer, snack, or cake.

34 **Huize ter Buerze** (House of Purses). Built in 1453 and recently carefully restored, this was where money was exchanged. The name lives on as the modern Beurs, or Bourse. ✉ *Intersection of Academiestraat and Vlamingstraat.*

32 **Jan Van Eyckplein.** This colorful square with a statue of the painter lies at the center of Hanseatic Brugge. It includes the old **Tolhuis** (Customs House), built in 1477, where vehicles on their way to market had to stop; and **Poortersloge**, a late Gothic building with a slender spire, owned by the guild of porters and used as a meeting place for the burghers. The rampant bear that occupies one niche represents the legendary bear speared by Baldwin of the Iron Arm; it became the symbol of the city. ✉ *Intersection of Spinolarei, Academiestraat, Genthof, Spiegelrei, and Spanjaardstraat.*

37 **Jeruzalemkerk** (Jerusalem Church). The striking church, which dates from the late 15th century, was built by two pilgrims returning from the Holy Land, copying the Church of the Holy Sepulchre in Jerusalem, as it was then. It is still privately owned. The black marble mausoleum of the pilgrims Anselm Adornes and his wife occupies a central position. ✉ *Jeruzalemstraat 3.* 🎫 *Free.* ⏲ *Weekdays 10–noon and 2–6, Sat. 10–noon and 2–5.*

39 **Kantcentrum** (Lace Center). This foundation that aims to maintain the quality and authenticity of the ancient craft includes a lace museum in the Jerusalem almshouses in Balstraat as well as a school where youngsters are taught the intricate art of the bobbins. ✉ *Peperstraat 3,* ☎ *050/330072.* 🎫 *BF60.* ⏲ *Weekdays 10–noon and 2–6, Sat. 10–noon and 2–5.*

23 **Markt** (Market Square). Used as a marketplace since 958, the square has as its focus a statue of the city's medieval heroes, Jan Breydel and Pieter De Coninck, who led the commoners of Flanders to their short-lived victory over the aristocrats of France. The west and north sides of the market square are lined with old guild houses. Most of them shelter restaurants of unremarkable quality that spill out onto the sidewalk. On the east side stand the provincial government house and the post office, an excellent pastiche of Burgundian Gothic. On the south side of the Markt stands the **Belfort** (Belfry), rising to a height of 270 ft. It commands the city and the surrounding countryside with more puissance than grace. The octagonal lantern that crowns the tower, added in the 15th century, contains the 47 bells of the remarkable Brugge carillon. ✉ *Intersection of St-Jacobstraat, St-Amandstraat, Steenstraat, Breidelstraat, Philipstockstraat, Wollestraat, and Vlamingstraat.* 🎫 *BF100.* ⏲ *Apr.–Sept., daily 9:30–5; Oct.–Mar., daily 9:30–12:30 and*

1:30–5. Carillon concerts: June 15–Sept., Mon., Wed., Sat. 9 PM–10 PM, Sun. 2:15–3; Oct.–June 14, Wed. and weekends 2:15–3.

★ ㉘ **Memling Museum.** The collection contains just six works, but they are of breathtaking quality and among the greatest—and certainly the most spiritual—of Flemish Primitives. Hans Memling (ca.1440–1494) was born in Germany but spent the greater part of his life in Brugge. In *The Altarpiece of St. John the Baptist and St. John the Evangelist,* two leading personages of the Burgundian court are believed to be portrayed: Mary of Burgundy (buried in the Onze-Lieve-Vrouwekerk; ☞ *below*) as St. Catherine, and Margaret of York as St. Barbara. The "paintings within the painting" give details of the lives of the two saints. The miniature paintings that adorn the St. Ursula Shrine are marvels of fine detail and poignancy; Memling's work gives recognizable iconographic details about cities, such as Brugge, Cologne, Basel, and Rome. The Memling Museum is inside the medieval **Sint-Janshospitaal**, which was founded in the 12th century and remained in use until the early 20th: The building underwent major renovation in 1998. The middle ward, the oldest of three, was built in the 13th century in Romanesque style. There is a fascinating painting from the 18th century that shows patients arriving by sedan chair and being fed and ministered to by sisters and clerics. ⊠ *Mariastraat 38,* ☎ *050/448711.* 🎟 *BF140; combination ticket (includes Gruuthuse, Groeninge, and Brangwyn museums;* ☞ *above) BF450.* ☉ *Apr.–Sept., daily 9:30–5; Oct.–Mar., Wed.–Mon. 9:30–12:30 and 2–5.*

㉛ **Minnewater.** Romantically but incorrectly termed "the Lake of Love," this man-made lake was created in the 13th century to expand the city harbor; it often accommodated more than 100 ships. The swans of Minnewater evoke an etymological legend or perhaps a historical truth: In 1488, six years after his wife's death, Maximilian of Austria was imprisoned by the people of Brugge, and his advisor, Pieter Lanchals, was decapitated. Because the name *Lanchals* is very close to the Dutch word for "long neck," when Maximilian was freed, he ordered Brugge to expiate its crime by keeping swans in the canals of the city in perpetuity. Maximilian went on to become emperor; his grandson was Charles V. ⊠ *Just south of Begijnhof.*

NEED A
BREAK?

Straffe Hendrik, on the delightful Walplein, is a brewery pub, part of the Henri Maes brewery, which you can tour. "Straffe" means strong, and this beer, at 9%, certainly lives up to its billing.

㊳ **Museum voor Volkskunde** (Folklore Museum). Housed in a row of white-washed almshouses, it was originally built for retired shoemakers. It now contains various reconstructed interiors: a grocery shop, a living room, a tavern. ⊠ *Rolweg 40,* ☎ *050/330044.* 🎟 *BF80.* ☉ *Daily 9:30–5; Oct.–Mar., closed Tues.*

㉙ **Onze-Lieve-Vrouwekerk** (Church of Our Lady). The tower is 400 ft high, which makes it the highest brick construction in the world. While brick can be built high, it cannot be sculpted like stone; hence the tower's somewhat severe look. The church's most precious treasure is the small *Virgin and Child,* an early work by Michelangelo, who sold it to a merchant from Brugge when the original client failed to pay. Carved in white marble, it sits in a black marble niche in an altar at the end of the south aisle. The choir contains two mausoleums: that of Mary of Burgundy, who died in 1482 at the age of 25 after a fall from her horse; and that of her father, Charles the Bold, killed in 1477 while laying siege to Nancy in France. Mary was as well loved in Brugge as her husband, Maximilian of Austria, was disliked. Her finely chiseled effigy captures her beauty. ⊠ *Gruuthusestraat.* ☉ *Apr.–Sept., daily 10–11:30 and 2:30–5 (Sat. until 4); Oct.–Mar., 10–11:30 and 2:30–4:30 (Sat. until 4). Closed Sun.* AM *except to worshipers.*

Oude Griffie (Former Recorder's House). The 16th-century structure, a mixture of Gothic and Flemish Renaissance elements, is still used as part of the law courts and is not open for visitors. Squeezed into the corner next to the Oude Griffie is the tiny **Museum van het Brugse Vrije** (Museum of the Brugge County Council), a remnant of the 15th-century Brugse Vrije county hall. Its principal treasure is the courtroom with its huge oak and black-marble chimney piece. A large bas-relief depicts a robust, nearly life-size Charles V, carved in dark oak and marble by Lancelot Blondeel while the emperor was still a young man. ⊠ *Burg.* ☜ *BF100 (joint ticket with Stadhuis;* ☞ *below).* ☉ *Apr.–Sept., Tues.–Sun. 9:30–12:30 and 1:15–5; Oct.–Mar., 9:30–12:30 and 2–5.*

★ **Reien** (canals). With their old humpbacked stone bridges, the canals give Brugge its character, opening up the perspective and imposing their calm. The view from the **Meebrug** is especially good. Farther along the **Groenereit** and the **Godshuizen De Pelikaan** canals are almshouses dating from the early 18th century. There are several such charitable buildings in the city, tiny houses built by the guilds for the poor, some still serving their original purpose. **Steenhouwersdijk** overlooks the brick rear gables that were part of the original county hall. Just beyond the Vismarkt (Fish Market), where fresh seafood from Zeebrugge is sold Tuesday through Saturday, is the little **Huidenvettersplein** (Tanners' Square), with its 17th-century guild house. Next to it, from the **Rozenhoedkaai** canal, the view of the heart of the city includes the pinnacles of the town hall and basilica and the belfry: the essence of Brugge.

③⑤ **Saaihalle** (Serge Hall). The houses of the Venetian and Florentine merchants have disappeared, but the Genoese trading house still stands, The original crenellated curtain wall has been replaced by a bell-shape gable. ⊠ *South corner of Vlamingstraat and Grauwwerkersstraat.*

NEED A BREAK? **Vlissinghe** (⊠ Blekersstraat) is the oldest pub in Brugge; people have been enjoying the beer here since 1552, and it hasn't changed much. You can also relax among the rosebushes in the courtyard.

③⑥ **Sint-Anna** (St. Anne Quarter). The neighborhood illustrates how yesteryear's poverty becomes today's picturesque sights. The small houses that now look so tidy were the homes of the 19th century's truly needy. By way of contrast, the 17th-century **Sint-Annakerk** (St. Anne's Church) is filled with riches, sculpted wood, and copper as well as enormous paintings. The tourist office warns that, due to staff shortages, there is no guarantee of finding the church open. ⊠ *Sint-Annaplein.* ☜ *Free.*

③③ **Spanjaardstraat.** The street leads up to the quay where goods from Spain were unloaded. The house at No. 9 was where St. Ignatius of Loyola stayed when he came to Flanders on holidays from his studies in Paris. Directly ahead are the three arches of the **Augustijnenbrug.** Dating from 1391, it's the oldest bridge in Brugge. On the other side of the canal, **Augustijnenrei** is one of the loveliest quays.

Stadhuis (Town Hall). This jewel of Gothic architecture with strong vertical lines was built of white sandstone at the end of the 14th century. It marked the transition of power from the nobility to the city aldermen and served as the model for all the other town halls that adorn every self-respecting Flemish town. The statues that originally embel-

lished the facade were smashed by the French Republicans and have
been replaced by modern replicas. Inside, a staircase ascends to the Gothic
Hall, which has a marvelous double-vaulted timber roof. Its 19th-century
frescoes relate a romantic version of the history of Brugge. ⊠ *Burg.*
🕮 *BF100 (includes Museum van het Brugse Vrije; ☞ Oude Griffie,
above).* ⊙ *Apr.–Sept., daily 9:30–5; Oct.–Mar., daily 9:30–12:30 and
2–5.*

Dining and Lodging

$$$$ ✕ **De Karmeliet.** In a lovely 18th-century house with a graceful En-
★ glish garden, this culinary landmark offers such delicacies as Bresse pigeon in truffle juice and cod carpaccio with asparagus. The wine cave
lives up to the kitchen's standard, which is stratospheric; the ambience
is genteel, the service flexible and pleasant. ⊠ *Langestraat 19,* ☎ *050/
338259. Reservations essential. AE, DC, MC, V. No dinner Sun.
Closed Mon.*

$$$$ ✕ **De Witte Poorte.** Under low brick vaults and stone arches, with rear
★ windows looking onto a lush little garden, this formal restaurant offers rich, contemporary French cooking, with an emphasis on seafood.
Specialties include monkfish in Riesling wine and saffron, langoustine
waterzooi, langoustine tails with vinaigrette and truffle juice, and a superb dessert cart. ⊠ *Jan Van Eyckplein 6,* ☎ *050/330883. AE, DC,
MC, V. Closed Sun.–Mon.*

$$$$ ✕ **Den Gouden Harynk.** Few of his colleagues can claim the natural
flair of chef Philippe Serruys. Holding forth in a small, unpretentious,
antiques-filled dining room just south of the Dijver, he serves international cuisine with an artist's gift, not only for presentation but also
for planning, pacing, and inspired combinations. The menu offers langoustines brushed with a light curry blend or *foie d'oie* (goose liver)
on a bed of rhubarb with pink peppercorns. ⊠ *Groeninge 25,* ☎ *050/
337637. AE, DC, MC, V. Closed Sun.–Mon., Christmas, Easter and
last 2 wks of July.*

$$$ ✕ **De Waterput.** This small, whitewashed farmhouse, in the middle of
★ the polder-land, has a superb restaurant presided over by a most orig-
inal chef, Willy Bataillie. There's no menu, because he uses only those
products that are freshest and the best on any given day. A meal might
include home-smoked wild salmon, John Dory with chives, wild duck
with small onions, or crepes suzette. ⊠ *Rondsaartstraat 1, Oostkerke,
9 km (5 mi) north of Brugge,* ☎ *050/599256. Reservations advised.
DC, V. Closed Tues.-Thurs., mid-Dec.–mid-Jan.*

$$$ ✕ **'t Bourgoensche Cruyce.** In one of the most medieval-looking build-
ings in Brugge (though its weathered timbers and sharp-raked roofs
were rebuilt at the turn of the century), this restaurant also has one of
the most romantic canal-side settings: Dining-room windows shed
warm light over the water, the reflections tinted by the salmon- and
copper-colored decor. The cuisine is equally appealing, including turbot and asparagus *en papillote* with ginger; roasted lobster with thyme,
bay leaf, and sweet garlic; and pigeon with sauteed spinach and potato
galette (round, flat cake), tender scallops, and wild mushrooms. ⊠
Wollestraat 41, ☎ *050/337926. AE, MC, V.*

$$ ✕ **Breydel–De Coninck.** Directly en route between the Markt and the
Burg, this no-frills restaurant is known to everyone in Brugge, but it's
not spoken of for fear it will be invaded by tourists. The place is fa-
mous for the freshness of its mussels and other seafood. Austere pink
tablecloths and plain banquettes leave the focus on the basics, and while
there are token offerings of eel and steak, nothing could be more basic
than a huge crock heaped high with shiny, blue-black shells. ⊠ *Brei-
delstraat 24,* ☎ *050/339746. AE, MC, V. Closed Wed. and June.*

$$ ✕ **De Visscherie.** Overlooking the Vismarkt, this restaurant, which has
★ a striking modern sculpture hanging from its balcony of a fisherman
with a large fish, is impossible to miss. The menu features imaginative
fish dishes, including langoustines with foie gras and a variety of tur-
bot preparations. ⊠ *Vismarkt 8,* ☎ *050/330212. AE, MC, V. Closed
Tues., mid-Nov.–mid-Dec.*

$$ ✕ **'t Paardje.** Off the beaten track, this little family-owned restaurant
concentrates all efforts on a few specialties: Mussels, eel, and steak are
prepared in a variety of sauces. Its terra-cotta and lace decor is cozy,
clean, and unpretentious, and its cooking dependably good. ⊠ *Langestraat 20,* ☎ *050/334009. MC, V. No dinner Mon. or Tues..*

$–$$ ✕ **Sint-Joris.** Among the dozen or so competitive brasseries crowded
along the Markt, this low-key spot maintains a more civilized profile
than its neighbors do. Flowers, linens, candles, a roaring fire, and a
comfortable clutter of ceramics and copper warm the dining room, and
you'll find a choice of either sheltered or open terrace. The cooking is
a cut above average, as well, and regional dishes are exceptionally well
prepared: fish-based waterzooi, eel in green sauce, and mussels. ⊠ *Markt
29,* ☎ *050/333062. AE, DC, MC, V.*

$–$$ ✕ **Steakhouse De Tassche.** Though you may feel far removed from the
romance of old Brugge, you'll be compensated by the attention, commitment to detail, and overall sincerity of this restaurant. A wide range
of simple dishes, from steak and fries to grilled sole, are served in a
setting of pink damask and copper. The cooking comes from the heart:
Even the fries are hand-cut, and the chef cruises the dining room like
a true gastronome. ⊠ *Oude Burg 11,* ☎ *050/330319. MC, V. Closed
Tues.*

$ ✕ **Staminee De Garre.** Tucked in an alley off the well-worn Breidel-
★ straat, this tiny two-tier coffeehouse is a brick-and-beam oasis, offering Mozart and magazines along with plunger coffee and 136 beers.
There are simple cold platters and grilled sandwiches, attractively
served, and traditional nibbles of cheese with the heartier beers. ⊠ *Off
Breidelstraat,* ☎ *050/341029. No credit cards.*

$ ✕ **Taverna Curiosa.** The cross-vaulted crypt makes a comfortable, at-
mospheric hideaway from tourist traffic. It's an ideal place for conversation, a light meal, and one of the myriad beers offered, many of
them local. Snacks include omelettes, sandwiches, and *visschotel*
(smoked fish plates), as well as pancakes and ice cream. ⊠ *Vlamingstraat
22,* ☎ *050/342334. AE, DC, MC, V. Closed Mon., July.*

$ ✕ **Tom Pouce.** Despite its somewhat stuffy and slightly faded air—heavy
velour drapes, splashy carpet, cracked crockery, noisy open service bar—
this old, friendly, urban tearoom dominates the Burg every afternoon.
Tourists, shoppers, and loyal retirees dig into traditional Belgian food,
warm apple strudel, airy waffles, and the tour de force: hot *pan-
nekoeken,* pancakes that are light, eggy, and vanilla-perfumed, with a
pat of butter and a sprinkle of dark brown sugar. There are lunch plates
as well. ⊠ *Burg 17,* ☎ *050/330336. AE, DC, MC, V. Dec. 25 and Jan. 1.*

$$$–$$$$ ✕🏠 **Die Swaene.** Lavishly decorated in every period excess, this fam-
★ ily-run hotel, which has won various accolades, including romantic hotel
of the year and best urban sanctuary, tries harder. Its location—facing
one of the prettier canals in the heart of the tourist center—enhances
the romance of the swagged tulle, crystal, and any number of marble
nymphs inside. Its most popular room is a relatively subdued converted
Flemish kitchen with a stone fireplace and a carved four-poster. The
romantic, candlelit French restaurant ($$$$) serves such specialties as
goose liver with caramelized apples, grilled turbot, and lobster-and-
spinach lasagna. ⊠ *Steenhouwersdijk 1, B 8000,* ☎ *50/342798,* FAX
*050/336674. 24 rooms. Restaurant, bar, swimming pool, sauna. AE,
DC, MC, V.*

$$–$$$ ✕⛩ **De Castillion.** This hotel is named for a bishop whose residence it was in the 18th century. Some of the guest rooms have cherry-wood period furniture; others are furnished in a modern style. The restaurant's offerings include filet mignon of venison in a Pomerol stock, duck's liver, and a fricassee of monkfish and wild salmon. The fixed-price menus are great value for the money. Predinner drinks and postprandial coffee are served in the handsome Art Deco salon, which is decorated in shades of blue and green. ✉ *Heilige Geetstraat 1, B 8000,* ☎ *050/ 343001,* FAX *050/339475. 18 rooms with bath, 2 suites. Restaurant, sauna, meeting rooms. AE, DC, MC, V.*

$$$$ ⛩ **De Tuileriëen.** This stately 15th-century mansion was converted
★   into a sumptuous hotel in 1988 and furnished with genuinely patrician taste: discreet antique reproductions, weathered marble, and warm mixed-print fabrics in shades of celadon, slate, and cream. The firelighted bar is filled with cozy tartan wingbacks, and the breakfast room has a massive mantel and a coffered ceiling. Despite its aristocratic air, this is a welcoming stop. Caveat: Canal views entail traffic noise; courtyard rooms are quieter. ✉ *Dyver 7, B 8000,* ☎ *050/ 343691,* FAX *050/430400. 26 rooms, 7 suites. Bar, indoor pool, sauna, massage, parking (fee). AE, DC, MC, V.*

$$$$ ⛩ **Holiday Inn Crowne Plaza.** There was inevitable skepticism when Holiday Inn got permission to build a hotel right on the Burg in the heart of the city, but the critics have been confounded: The new red-brick hotel, with a red-tile roof and modern steel gables, fits in remarkably well with its surroundings. Rooms are large, modern, and decorated in muted colors; the best ones have steps leading up to them and dark-wood ceiling beams, giving you the feeling of being under the eaves. On display in the basement are remnants of the old ramparts and artifacts found during construction. Children up to 18 sharing their parents' room stay free. ✉ *Burg 10, B 8000,* ☎ *050/345834,* FAX *050/ 345615. 89 rooms, 7 suites. Restaurant, bar, pool, sauna, health club, convention center, parking (fee). AE, DC, MC, V.*

$$$ ⛩ **Bryghia.** Restored in 1965 and renovated in 1997, this 15th-century landmark (once a German/Austrian trade center) has seamless modern decor, with beechwood cabinetry and soft pastel florals. The management works hard on details of comfort, offering in-room teakettles, flowers, valet parking, and mosquito repellent when the canal waters run slow. ✉ *Oosterlingenplein 4, B 8000,* ☎ *050/338059. 18 rooms. Breakfast room. AE, DC, MC, V.*

$$$ ⛩ **Oud Huis Amsterdam.** Packaged like a fine gift, this snug, central
★   retreat occupies two noble 17th-century houses, combining the grace of another era with the polish and luxury of a new first-class property. Antique details—tooled Cordoba leather wallpaper, rough-hewn rafters, and Delft tiles—have been preserved, and services, such as international newspapers and umbrellas, have been added. Owner Philip Traen has even mounted ancestral art in an Old Master vein. Rooms with canal views also overlook a busy street; back rooms with roofline views are calmer. ✉ *Spiegelrei 3, B 8000,* ☎ *50/341810,* FAX *050/338391. 34 rooms, 2 suites. Bar. AE, DC, MC, V.*

$$–$$$ ⛩ **Pandhotel.** This frequently redecorated, family-run hotel was built as a private mansion in the 1830s and renovated as a hotel in 1979. A member of the Romantik chain, it mixes a jewel-box neoclassical decor with modern touches—dark ceramic baths, a skylighted breakfast room. Junior suites are all decorated with Ralph Lauren fabrics. The hotel offers competitively priced two- and three-night packages. ✉ *Pandreitje 16, B 8000,* ☎ *50/340666,* FAX *050/340556. 24 rooms. Breakfast room, bar. AE, DC, MC, V.*

$$–$$$ ⛩ **Wilgenhof.** Halfway between Brugge and Damme, and a stone's throw from the canal, this bucolic mansion-on-the-polder is a good base for excursions in either direction and to the coast, which is just 12 km (7 mi) away. Rooms are pleasant but fairly basic. ⊠ *Polderstraat 151, B 8310 St. Kruis,* ☎ *050/362744,* FAX *050/362821. 6 rooms. Breakfast room. AE, DC, MC, V.*

$$ ★ 🏨 **Egmond.** Gracefully situated in the lush Minnewater park, this manorlike inn offers garden views from every room, as well as the occasional skylight, parquet floor, 18th-century fireplace, or dormer-sloped ceiling. Breakfast is served in an oak-beam hall with a Delft-tile fireplace. With the park in front and the quiet Beguinage behind, you may feel pleasantly isolated from the bustle of the center, though it's only 10 minutes' walk. ⊠ *Minnewater 15, B 8000,* ☎ *50/341445,* FAX *050/342940. 9 rooms. Breakfast room. No credit cards.*

$$ 🏨 **Europ.** Run by an enthusiastic and friendly couple, this mid-price hotel focuses less on historic atmosphere than on basic comforts and a personal touch: Good big beds with Swiss-flex construction are in every room, and the Continental breakfast buffet is generous. All rooms have recently been refreshed. The hotel was first built in a 1789 house, with a modern wing added in 1970, but the current decor is spare and contemporary in both parts. ⊠ *Augustijnenrei 18, B 8000,* ☎ *050/337975,* FAX *050/345266. 31 rooms, 28 with bath. Bar. DC, MC.*

$$ 🏨 **Ter Brughe.** A renovation of this 16th-century step-gabled house, in 1989, created a slick, modern, efficient hotel in which the decor might seem generic (beige and bamboo) but for the heavy beams, tempera murals, and leaded-glass windows. The oldest part of the building is the vaulted cellar. Originally built as a warehouse, it now serves as the breakfast room and opens directly onto the canal. ⊠ *Oost-Gistelhof 2, B 8000,* ☎ *050/340324,* FAX *050/338873. 24 rooms. AE, DC, MC, V.*

$ ★ 🏨 **De Pauw.** Homey and warmly furnished, from the fresh flowers and doilies to the bronzed baby booties in the breakfast parlor, this is a welcoming little inn passed on from mother to daughter. Every room has a name instead of a number, needlepoint cushions, and old framed prints. (Two rooms with shower down the hall are super values.) Breakfast, which includes six kinds of bread, plus cold cuts and cheese, is served on pretty china. ⊠ *St-Gilliskerkhof 8, B 8000,* ☎ *050/337118. 8 rooms, 6 with bath. Breakfast room. AE, DC, MC, V.*

$ 🏨 **Fevery.** The living quarters of the family seem to spill over into the lounge area of this friendly, comfortable hotel; the magazines and knickknacks make you feel like family guests. There's even a baby monitor so parents can relax with a drink downstairs after putting a child to bed. ⊠ *Collaert Mansionstraat 3, B 8000,* ☎ *050/331269,* FAX *050/ 331791. 11 rooms. Bar. AE, DC, MC, V.*

$ 🏨 **Jacobs.** The plush and crystal in the public rooms may look posh, but the staff is young and friendly, and the breakfast tables are garnished with plastic waste buckets. There are inexpensive rooms with bathrooms outside, as well as full-facility doubles with homey decor. ⊠ *Baliestraat 1, B 8000,* ☎ *050/339831. 25 rooms, 23 with bath. Breakfast room, bar. AE, MC, DC, V.*

Nightlife and the Arts

The Arts

The monthly *Agenda Brugge* (at the tourist office) gives details of all events in the city. Also check listings in *The Bulletin.*

The **Stadsschouwburg** (City Theater; ⊠ Vlamingstraat 38, ☎ 050/ 443060), which presents classical music, dance, and theater, is a stop-off point for most of the major Flemish companies.

Nightlife

Among the nicest hotel bars are **Academie** (⊠ Wijngaardstraat 7–9, ☎ 050/332266), **De Medici** (⊠ Potterierei 15, ☎ 050/339833), and **The Meeting** (⊠ Spiegelrei 3) at the Oud Huis Amsterdam.

Brugge is not the liveliest city at night, but there are several options. The **Cactus Club** (⊠ St-Jakobstraat 36, ☎ 050/332014) is Brugge's major venue for pop, rock, folk, and blues acts. Discos, mostly catering to a clientele not much older than 20, are clustered around Eiermarkt, back of the Markt: **Ambiorix** (⊠ Eiermarkt 11 bis, ☎ 050/337400), **Coolcat** (⊠ Eiermarkt 11, ☎ 050/340527), and **The Pick** (⊠ Eiermarkt 12, ☎ 050/337638). At 't Zand are **Graffiti** (⊠ 't Zand 9, ☎ 050/336909) and **Ma Rica Rokk** (⊠ 't Zand 8, ☎ 050/338358). **Villa Romana** (⊠ Kraanplein 1, ☎ 050/343453) attracts an older crowd.

Outdoor Activities and Sports

Check out the city's **Sports Service** (⊠ Walweinstraat 20, ☎ 050/448322).

Running

The green city wall is pleasant for jogging. For a more extensive workout, try the Tillegembos Provincial Domain in St-Michiels.

Swimming

Try the Olympic-size pool at the new **Provinciaal Olympisch Zwembad** (⊠ Olympia Park, Doornstraat, St-Andries, ☎ 050/390200). There's also a sauna and solarium.

Tennis

At the **Bryghia Tennis Club** (⊠ Boogschutterslaan 37, St-Kruis, ☎ 050/353406) indoor courts cost BF240 per person for one hour, outdoor courts BF200 per person per hour.

Shopping

Brugge has many trendy boutiques and shops, especially along **Steenstraat** and **Vlamingstraat,** both of which branch off from the Markt. **Ter Steeghere** mall, which links the Burg with Wollestraat, deftly integrates a modern development into the historic center. The largest and most pleasant mall is the **Zilverpand** off Zilverstraat, where 50-odd shops cluster in Flemish gable houses around a courtyard with sidewalk cafés.

Street Markets

The Burg is the setting for the **Wednesday Market** (weekly except July and August) with flowers, vegetables, and fruit. The biggest is the **Saturday Market** on 't Zand. The **Fish Market** is held, appropriately, on the Vismarkt, daily except Sunday and Monday. All three are morning events, from 8 to approximately 12:30. On weekend afternoons (March through October) there's a **Flea Market** along the Dijver.

Specialty Stores

Brugge has many art and antiques dealers. **Guyart** (⊠ Fort Lapin 37, ☎ 050/332159) is both an art gallery and a tavern. **Papyrus** (⊠ Walplein 41, ☎ 050/336687) specializes in silverware. **'t Leerhuis** (⊠ Groeninge 35, ☎ 050/330302) deals in contemporary art.

Brugge has been a center for lace-making since the 15th century, and such intricate variations on the art as the rose pattern and the fairy stitch, which requires more than 300 bobbins, were developed here. You can find pieces costing a few hundred francs in a great many souvenir shops. Handmade lace in intricate patterns, however, takes a very long time to produce, and this is reflected in the price. For work of this type, you should be prepared to part with BF10,000 or more. The best shop for the serious lace-lover is in the Sint-Anne Quarter, just behind the church: **'t Apostelientje** (✉ Balstraat 11, ☎ 050/337860), which is also a museum (admission free).

Damme

❹⓪ *7 km (4 mi) north of Brugge.*

Damme lies in the midst of peaceful polder landscape. You can go here by miniature paddle steamer, the *Lamme Goedzak,* on a canal lined with tall and slender poplars, all slightly bent by the prevailing breeze. Damme owes its place in history to a tidal wave in 1134 that opened up an inlet of the sea, from the Zwin to the neighborhood of Brugge, whose people were quick to build a canal to link up with it. Damme became an important port that held exclusive rights to import such varied commodities as wine from Bordeaux and herring from Sweden. The "Maritime Law of Damme" became the standard for Hanseatic merchants. Damme is believed to have been the home of the legendary Till Eulenspiegel, whose merry pranks, detailed in Charles de Coster's novel, were often directed at the Spanish occupying force.

It was in Damme's **Onze-Lieve-Vrouwekerk** (Church of Our Lady) that Charles the Bold and Margaret of York were married. On the facade of the **Stadhuis** (Town Hall) you can see their effigies, the noble duke presenting the wedding ring to his fiancée.

The **Boudewijnpark en Dolphinarium** offers 30-odd family attractions, including dolphin and ice shows. ✉ *A. De Baeckestraat 12, St-Michiels, 2 km (1 mi) south of Damme,* ☎ *050/383838.* *BF510 for all attractions; BF180 Dolphinarium only.* *Park: Easter–May, daily noon–6; May–Aug., daily 10–6; Sept., Wed. and weekends noon–6. Dolphinarium: daily, shows at 11 and 4, more during peak season.*

"Flanders Fields": The Historic Battlefields

The highways south from Brugge and Gent point in the direction of "Flanders Fields," where decisive battles have been waged since the time of Julius Caesar. Here, longbowmen fought cavalry in heraldic colors, and here, the horrors of World War I were played out. "Flanders Fields" evoke both the pastoral peace of fields ready for harvest, dotted with crimson poppies, and the terrible war that shattered it; Simon Schama has called it "the blood-polluted source of all our sorrows." The provinces of West and East Flanders form the original, big-sky "platte land," the flat land that haunted singer Jacques Brel's imagination. It seems to induce a touch of wistfulness, and considering the many battles waged around here, this is understandable. The historic sites are testimony to the unique spirit of the Belgian people who, centuries ago, thought nothing of taking on the might of France or Spain.

Kortrijk

❹① *51 km (31 mi) south of Brugge, 45 km (27 mi) southwest of Gent, 90 km (54 mi) southwest of Brussels.*

Kortrijk (Courtrai in French) was the flax capital of Europe in the Middle Ages and the uncontested producer of damask during the Renaissance. Today it is a center of carpet and furniture-fabric production, with shops and restaurants that attract well-to-do customers from the entire region.

The Battle of the Golden Spurs (which the French call the Battle of Courtrai) was fought immediately outside the city walls, close to the present

Groeningelaan. On July 11, 1302, poorly armed weavers and crafts-men from Brugge, Gent, and Ieper took on the flower of French no-bility. The battle had actually been going well for the French infantrymen, but they were brushed aside by the mounted knights, who were spoiling for a fight. A hidden canal, the Groeninge, was the Flemings' greatest ally; many of the knights plunged into it, to be speared by the Flemish pikemen. After the battle, 700 pairs of golden spurs were removed from the bodies and triumphantly hung in the Church of Our Lady in Kortrijk as a votive offering. This story has a sequel: 80 years later the French returned, defeated the Flemings, burned the city, and retrieved their spurs. The **Groeningeabdij Museum** depicts the history of Kortrijk and the Battle of the Golden Spurs and has displays of locally produced damask and silver. ⊠ *Houtmarkt,* ☎ *056/257892.* 🎫 *Free.* ☉ *Tues.–Sun. 10–noon and 2–5.*

The **Broeltoren,** on either side of the river Leie, are what remain of the medieval fortifications. A 45-ft-high neo-Gothic monument was erected in 1902 on the spot where the Battle of the Golden Spurs was fought in 1302, and it is commemorated on the weekend closest to July 11 with a parade or a tournament. These are curiously low-key affairs, given the importance of the battle in the annals of Flemish nationalism, although Flanders as a whole is gearing up for a huge celebration of the 700th anniversary in 2002.

The **Begijnhof** (Beguinage), with its cobbled streets and whitewashed houses, is an oasis of calm in this busy city and among the most beautiful beguinages in Europe. The Begijnhof is open to the public, and there's a museum. The adjoining **Onze-Lieve-Vrouwekerk,** the church where the Golden Spurs once hung, contains a beautiful alabaster figure of St. Catherine from 1380, standing in the Chapel of the Counts of Flanders. ⊠ *Begijnhof: Begijnhofstraat.* ☉ *Tues.–Thurs. and weekends 2–5 and by appointment. Church: Begijnhofstraat and Groeningestraat,* ☎ *056/244800.* ☉ *Mar.–Sept., 8:30–noon and 2–7; Oct.–Apr. 8:30–noon and 2–4:30.*

NEED A BREAK?	The elegant **Tea Room D'haene** (⊠ Sint-Maartenskerkstraat 4–1) serves very good pancakes, waffles, and pastries throughout the day, and pleasant light lunches.

The **Nationaal Vlas-, Kant- en Linnenmuseum** (National Flax, Lace, and Linen Museum), in an old farmhouse, tells the story of flax-growing and lace- and linen-making in a series of lifelike tableaux, peopled with wax models of Flemish historical celebrities. The river Leie, which passes through Kortrijk on its way to Gent, was known as the Golden River in the Middle Ages because of the fields of flax on its banks. ⊠ *Etienne Sabbelaan 4,* ☎ *056/210138.* 🎫 *Flax wing, BF100; linen wing, BF100; joint ticket, BF170.* ☉ *Mar.–Nov., Mon. 1:30–6, Tues.–Fri. 9–12:30 and 1:30–6, weekends 2–6; lace and linen sections closed Dec.–Apr.*

Dining and Lodging

$ ✕ **Restaurant Beethoven.** This intimate restaurant specializes in a variety of grilled meats. The chicken with saffron sauce is also popular, and there's a daily special that's generously served and competitively priced. ⊠ *Onze-Lieve-Vrouwestraat 8,* ☎ *056/225542. No credit cards. No dinner Wed. Closed Mon.*

$$$$ ✕🏨 **Gastronomisch Dorp Eddy Vandekerckhove.** Just south of Kort-
★   rijk, Eddy's "gastronomic village" is a gourmet's heaven. On the menu are such delicacies as new potatoes with langoustines and caviar, lobster and sea scallops with braised chicory and onion marmalade, and thinly sliced venison with *trompettes de la mort* (a kind of black mushroom) and celeriac mousse. The large, luxurious rooms overlook fields

on one side and an exotic botanical garden and pond on the other. ⊠ *Sint Anna 5, B 8500,* ☎ *056/224756,* ℻ *056/227170. 7 rooms. Restaurant. AE, DC, MC, V. No dinner Sun. Closed Mon., 2 wks in Nov.*

$$$ ⌕ **Damier.** This is a grand little hotel, impeccably renovated and in a
★ superb location, right on Grote Markt. From its lavish café, with florid plasterwork and chandeliers, to its Laura Ashley rooms, to its beeswaxed oak wainscoting and Persian carpets, it exudes grace and seamless style; there are no musty corners or creaky halls hiding behind the decor. The hotel dates from the French Revolution, but its comforts are thoroughly modern. ⊠ *Grote Markt 41, B 8500,* ☎ *056/221547,* ℻ *056/228631. 49 rooms. Restaurant, bar, café, sauna. AE, DC, MC, V.*

Ieper

➍➋ *32 km (19 mi) west of Kortrijk, 52 km (31 mi) south of Brugge, 125 km (75 mi) west of Brussels, 91 km (85 mi) northeast of Calais.*

This is Ypres of World War I fame and shame, "Wipers" to the Tommies in the trenches, Ieper to the locals. The city was wiped off the face of the earth during the war. Today's Ieper is a painstaking reconstruction, which was not completed until after World War II.

In Flanders Fields Museum, formerly the Ypres Salient Museum, has been transformed into an overwhelmingly powerful interactive display that should keep the memory of those who died alive well into the 21st century. Each visitor receives a "smart card" with details of a soldier or civilian and follows that person's fortunes throughout the war. The museum is housed on the second floor of the magnificent Lakenhall (Cloth Hall), a copy of a building that had stood here since 1304. ⊠ *Grote Markt,* ☎ *057/200724.* ▦ *BF250.* ⊙ *Apr.–mid-Sept. 10–6; Oct.–Mar., Tues.–Sun. 10–5.*

St. George's, a small Anglican church, contains an abundance of war memorabilia; the adjoining **Pilgrims' Hall** was built for those who visit Ieper looking for a relative's grave. ⊠ *Elverdingsestraat 1,* ☎ *057/ 215685.*

★ East of town, the **Menenpoort** (Menin Gate) is among the most moving of war memorials. After World War I, the British built the vast arch in memory of the 300,000 soldiers who perished nearby. Every night at 8, traffic is stopped at the gate as buglers sound the Last Post. The practice was interrupted during World War II, but it was resumed the night Polish troops liberated the town, September 6, 1944. ⊠ *Menenstraat.*

Kasteelhof 't Hooge is one of the few places where bomb craters can still be seen. A new museum, **Hooge Crater 1914–18,** has been installed in the old chapel. Items on display include bombs, grenades, rifles, and uniforms. ⊠ *Meenseweg 467, Zillebeke,* ☎ *057/468446.* ▦ *BF80.* ⊙ *Feb.–mid-Dec. 10–7.*

Follow the signs via Canadalaan and Sanctuary Wood to **Hill 62,** where, in addition to photographs, weapons, and assorted objects salvaged from the field of battle, the owner has preserved some of the original trenches and tunnels on his land. You'll need to wear boots to inspect them. ⊠ *Canadalaan, Zillebeke,* ☎ *057/466373.* ▦ *BF120.* ⊙ *Apr.–Sept. daily 9:30–8, Oct.–Mar. 9:30–6.*

Dining and Lodging

$ ✕ **Old Tom.** Here you'll find unfussy but appetizing Flemish standards such as beef stew with beer and chicken waterzooi. ⊠ *Grote Markt 8,* ☎ *057/201541. AE, MC, V. Closed Fri.*

$ ✕ **'t Ganzeke.** This large, popular eatery acquits itself well with giant kebabs and steaks, satisfying but unspectacular meals. ⊠ *Vandepeereboomplein 5,* ☎ *057/200009. MC, V. Closed Mon.*

$$$ ✕⌂ **Hostellerie Mont Kemmel** (Kemmelberg). This luxurious hotel and restaurant sit atop Flanders's highest mountain, altitude 475 ft. There's a panoramic view over "Flanders Fields" from the well-appointed rooms, and chef Solange Bentin cooks up sophisticated specialties, such as nettle-braised frogs' legs and squab with a spice crust and port sauce. ⊠ *Berg 4, B 8958 Kemmel, 7 km/4 mi south of Ieper on N331,* ☎ *057/444145,* FAX *057/444089. 16 rooms. Restaurant, bar, golf privileges, tennis court, meeting rooms. AE, DC, MC, V. No dinner Sun. Closed Mon., mid-Jan.–Feb., 1st wk of July.*

$$ ⌂ **Regina.** Directly on Ieper's Grote Markt in a sturdy neo-Gothic brick building, this is a fresh, comfortable hotel, its generous spaces full of light, its rooms up to date. Everything has been upgraded except the windows; traffic noise is the only drawback. ⊠ *Grote Markt 45, B 8900,* ☎ *057/219006. 17 rooms. Restaurant, bar. AE, DC, MC, V.*

Tyne Cot

43 *8 km (5 mi) northeast of Ypres.*

Some 44 million shells were fired over this stretch of the Western Front in the two world wars, and a fair number failed to explode. Flemish farmers still turn up about 200 every month, and the bomb disposal experts have to be called in. The poison-gas canisters cause special concern. **Tyne Cot,** near Passendale, a British cemetery with 12,000 graves, is the best known of more than 170 military cemeteries in the area. It is awe-inspiring, more austere than many other British cemeteries that dot the countryside, some as small and lovingly tended as a country graveyard. ⊠ *From Ieper via Zonnebeke to N303.*

Diksmuide

44 *20 km (12 mi) north of Ieper on N369.*

Here you can visit the so-called **Dodengang** (Death Walk), a network of trenches west of the town, where Belgian troops faced their German adversaries for four years. ⊠ *IJzerdijk 65,* ☎ *051/505344.* 🎫 *Free.* ☉ *Apr.–Sept., daily 10–noon and 1–5:30.*

Like Ieper, Diksmuide has been completely rebuilt in its original style. The **IJzertoren,** a tower 275 ft high, has been erected in honor of the defenders. To many Flemish people it represents their struggle for autonomy. ⊠ *2 km (1 mi) southwest of Diksmuide.*

The monument in the German war cemetery of **Praetbos-Vlasdo** conveys a touching message. It is a sculpture of two grieving parents by the great German artist Käthe Kollwitz, whose son was among the many young men who fell here. ⊠ *4 km (2 ½ mi) northeast of Diksmuide.*

Poperinge

45 *11 km (7 mi) west of Ieper on N38.*

In this town, you'll find one of the rare positive interludes of the war they called "great": **Talbot House,** founded by an Anglican priest, "Tubby" Clayton. It provided an opportunity for soldiers to get together, just south of the front line, regardless of rank, for mutual support and comradeship. Photographs and art by soldier artists are displayed, and the attic chapel can be visited. Talbot House became known also on the opposite side of the front as a symbol of peace. Today it provides free accommodations for young volunteers who help maintain the war cemeteries. ⊠ *Gasthuisstraat 43, Poperinge,* ☎ *057/ 333228.* 🎫 *BF50.* ⊘ *Daily 9−noon and 2−5.*

Dining

$$$ ✕ **D'Hommelkeete.** A low-slung Flemish farmhouse, where the rustic and the modern coexist, this is, according to experts, the best place to experience the elusive and expensive delicacy called *jets de houblon* (hop shoots). It is only available for three weeks in spring, so call ahead. Braised sea scallops with morel sauce, warm goose liver with Calvados, and venison *noisettes* (nuggets) are also recommended. ⊠ *Hoge Noenweg 3, Poperinge,* ☎ *057/334365. AE, DC, MC, V. No dinner Sun. and Wed. Closed Mon. and 1st ½ of Aug.*

The North Sea Coast

From De Panne in the southwest to Knokke in the northeast is only 65 km (39 mi), but it's a considerable distance in terms of taste, from middle to upper class. There's a total of 20 resorts so close together that it's difficult to know where one ends and the next begins. Currents can be tricky, and you should swim only at beaches supervised by lifeguards. A green flag means bathing is safe; yellow, bathing is risky but guards are on duty; red, bathing is prohibited. Do not ignore warnings. Many resorts also offer good public outdoor pools.

You can walk for miles along the dike, flanked by modern apartment houses where flats are rented by the week or month. For many Belgians, an apartment by the sea is the equivalent of a summer house. All along the coast, parents help their kids fly kites, youngsters ride pedal cars, horseback riders thunder by along the water's edge, lovers walk arm in arm, dogs chase sticks, children dig in the sand, and sun worshipers laze in deck chairs protected from the North Sea breezes by canvas windbreaks. The coast, with those prevailing breezes, offers splendid sailing opportunities. Good yacht harbors include Blankenberge, Nieuwpoort, Oostende, and Zeebrugge.

Belgians flock to the shore over the weekend year-round. Quite a few profess to like it best in the off-season, when you can walk along the beach in the pale winter sun, filling your lungs with bracing sea air, and then warm up in a cozy tavern with a plate of steaming mussels.

Oostende

46 *115 km (69 mi) northwest of Brussels, 28 km (17 mi) west of Brugge, 98 km (59 mi) northeast of Calais.*

Oostende (Ostend in English, Ostende in French) leads a double life, as a transportation and fishing center on the one hand, and as a somewhat old-fashioned, slightly naughty resort on the other. It is the largest town and the oldest settlement on the coast, with a history going back to the 10th century. It was a pirates' hideout for centuries, and it was from here that Crusaders set sail for the Holy Land. In the early 17th century, Oostende, which backed the Protestant cause, withstood a Spanish siege for three years.

One of Continental Europe's first railways was built between Oostende and Mechelen in 1838, eventually resulting in regular mail packet services to Dover, England, beginning in 1846. Oostende also drew its share of royalty: Queen Victoria herself came here for the sea air, and Leopold II built himself a sumptuous villa on the beach.

On the fashionable **Albert I Promenade** shops and tearooms compete for attention with the view of the wide beach and the sea. At one end stands the **Casino** (Kursaal), which, in addition to gambling facilities, has a vast concert hall and exhibition space. The gaming rooms contain murals by Surrealist Paul Delvaux. ⊠ *Oosthelling,* ☎ *059/705111 or 059/707618 (reservations for shows).* ☼ *Gaming rooms, 3 PM–dawn.*

The **Visserskaai** (Fishermen's Wharf) is filled with an almost uninterrupted row of fish restaurants across from stalls where women hawk seafood in all its forms. ⊠ *Albert 1 Promenade, end opposite from Casino.*

NEED A BREAK? **James Café** (⊠ James Ensorgalerij), in a small, refined shopping precinct named after the city's most famous resident, is renowned for its shrimp croquettes.

James Ensorhuis (James Ensor House) is an introduction to the strange and hallucinatory world of the painter James Ensor (1860–1949), who has only lately been recognized as one of the great artists of the early 20th century. Using violent colors to express his frequently macabre or satirical themes, he depicted a fantastic carnival world peopled by masks and skeletons. The displays in this house, which was his home and studio, include many of the objects found in his work, especially the masks, and copies of his major paintings. ⊠ *Vlaanderenstraat 27,* ☎ *059/805335.* 🔲 *BF50.* ☼ *June–Sept., Wed.–Mon. 10–noon and 2–5; Oct.–May, weekends 2–5.*

A number of paintings and drawings by James Ensor, as well as works by Expressionists such as Permeke and Brusselmans, can be seen in the **Museum voor Schone Kunsten** (Fine Arts Museum). ⊠ *Wapenplein,* ☎ *059/805335.* 🔲 *BF50.* ☼ *Wed.–Mon. 10–noon and 2–5.*

Oostende also has a good modern art museum, the **Museum voor Moderne Kunst** (PMMK), where contemporary artists are well represented by Pierre Alechinsky, Roger Raveel, and Paul Van Hoeydonck (whose statuette, *The Fallen Astronaut,* was deposited on the moon by the *Apollo XV* crew), and others. The admission fee is increased for special exhibitions. ⊠ *Romestraat 11,* ☎ *059/508118.* 🔲 *BF100–300.* ☼ *Tues.–Sun. 10–6.*

☝ **Mercator,** the three-masted training ship of the Belgian merchant marine, is now moored close to the city center. Decks, fittings, and the spartan quarters have been kept intact, and there's a museum of mementoes brought home from the ship's exotic voyages. ⊠ *Vindictivelaan,* ☎ *059/705654.* 🔲 *BF100.* ☼ *Apr.–June and Sept., daily 10–1 and 2–6; July–Aug., daily 9–6; Oct.–Mar., weekends 11–1 and 2–5.*

Provinciaal Museum Constant Permeke, the home of Belgium's outstanding Expressionist painter and sculptor (1886–1952), is filled with 150 of his paintings and virtually all his sculptures. Many of his paintings are somber, in shades of green and brown, drawn from the lives of peasants and fishermen. ⊠ *Gistelsesteenweg 341, Jabbeke (between Oostende and Brugge),* ☎ *050/811288.* 🔲 *BF100.* ☼ *Tues.–Sun. 10–12:30 and 1–6 (until 5 in winter).*

Dining and Lodging

$$$ ✕ **Villa Maritza.** Bearing the name of an Austro-Hungarian countess who caught Leopold II's fancy, this 100-year-old villa, furnished in Renaissance Flemish style and restored in 1998, serves a seafood cuisine based on the finest ingredients: monkfish roasted with thyme, fennel, and anise; lobster carpaccio with garlic; and duck's liver served sweet-and-sour with sherry. ⊠ *Albert I Promenade 76,* ☎ *059/508808. Reservations essential. Jacket and tie. AE, DC, MC, V. No dinner Sun. Sept.–June. Closed Mon. and 2nd ½ of June.*

$$ ✕ **Lusitania.** This is arguably the best among the several restaurants that crowd the Visserskaai, and a little more expensive than its rivals. They all serve variations on the same seafood theme: salad of tiny, sweet shrimps, fish soup, grilled langoustines, and sole prepared in a variety of ways, including one that features béchamel sauce, shrimps, and mussels. ✉ *Visserskaai 35,* ☎ *059/701765. AE, DC, MC, V. Closed Fri.*

$ ✕ **Mosselbeurs.** Mussels are the focus at this cheap and cheery restaurant not far from the station. The mustard-color exterior walls are studded with enormous mock-mussel shells, while inside, the black-and-white check floor and tidy decor suggest a maritime theme. The meaty mollusks are served in a wide variety of ways. ✉ *Dwarsstraat 10,* ☎ *059/ 807310. AE, DC, MC, V. Closed lunch Tues. and Wed.*

$$$$ ✕🏨 **Oostendse Compagnie/Le Vigneron.** This palatial villa, once a royal
★ residence, is right on the beach, with ocean views from the dining room with its splendid terrace and from the large bedrooms. The restaurant has had its ups and downs in recent years, but it's now firmly on an upward trajectory. Among its specialties are eels with Chinese cabbage, honey, and dim sum; beef fillet with Perigord truffles and a shallot salad; turbot in fennel cream sauce with caviar; and langoustines with green apple, pasta, and lime. ✉ *Koningstraat 79, B 8400,* ☎ *059/704816,* FAX *059/805316. 13 rooms. Restaurant, beach, parking. AE, DC, MC, V. No dinner Sun. Closed Mon., 1st 2 wks of Mar., Oct.*

$$$ 🏨 **Andromeda.** So close to the Casino that you can practically hear the rolling of the dice, this luxury hotel has rooms in restful colors that match the sea, making up for the spectacular ugliness of its facade. Junior suites come with balconies overlooking the beach. ✉ *Albert 1 Promenade 60, B 8400,* ☎ *059/806611,* FAX *059/806629. 90 rooms. Restaurant, bar, indoor pool, sauna, health club, meeting rooms, private parking. AE, DC, MC, V.*

$–$$ 🏨 **Old Flanders.** In a handsome brick building opposite the cathedral, this hotel offers family atmosphere, comfortable if nondescript rooms, and a generous breakfast buffet. ✉ *Jozef II Straat 49, B 8400,* ☎ *059/ 806603,* FAX *059/801695. 15 rooms. Bar, breakfast room. AE, DC, MC, V.*

Nightlife and the Arts

THE ARTS

Check *The Bulletin*'s *What's On* section under "Other Towns" for cultural activities. There are frequent retrospectives at Oostende's museums. Concerts of all kinds, from classical to rock, pop, and jazz, draw crowds from far away to the **Oostende Casino**'s 1,700-seat hall (☎ 059/ 707618). Flemish singing superstar Helmut Lotti, the best-selling artist in the country's history, is a frequent performer.

NIGHTLIFE

The closure rate among seasonal nightspots is high; make sure the place you select is still in business. The best bet along the coast is generally the local casino, where gambling underwrites the nightclub entertainment.

The **Bar Baccara** (✉ Oosthelling, ☎ 059/705111), which is run by the Casino, is the classiest nightspot in Oostende (entrance costs 150 BF). Young male visitors from across the Channel who arrive bent on a bender head straight for the dowdy **Langestraat,** where there's a wide choice of snack bars, beer joints, pizza houses, topless bars, and disco-clubs.

Outdoor Activities and Sports

GOLF

There is an 18-hole golf course at **De Haan** (☎ 059/233238), 12 km (7 mi) east of Oostende.

HORSE RACING

In Oostende the **Wellington Hippodrome** (☎ 059/806055) is a top track for flat racing and trotting. Flat racing is July and August, Monday, Thursday, weekends, and bank holidays; trotting races are May through September, Friday at 6:45 PM.

WINDSURFING

Windsurfing is extremely popular and special areas have been set aside for it along many beaches. In Oostende, there's a water sports center (✉ Vicognedijk 30, ☎ 059/321564 in the afternoon) on the Spuikom waterway (also used for oystering).

De Panne

❹⁷ *31 km (19 mi) southwest of Oostende, 55 km (33 mi) southwest of Brugge, 143 km (86 mi) west of Brussels, 63 km (38 mi) northeast of Calais.*

De Panne is a family-friendly resort with the widest beach on the coast and sand dunes protected from developers. On the beach you can see sand yachts looking like sailboats on wheels, zipping along at up to 120 kph (72 mph). Riding horses along the beach and on trails through the dunes is also very popular. The royal family resided here during World War I because De Panne was part of the narrow band of Belgium that the Germans never occupied. The dunes west of the resort are a nature reserve, **Westhoek,** where you can roam around on your own; guided walks are organized in season. ✉ *Dynastielaan,* ☎ *058/421818.*

☾ **Meli Park** is a large family park with a circus, a playground, action-oriented attractions, a nature park with animals and exotic birds, and a dream park where fairy-tale scenes are enacted. ✉ *De Pannelaan 68, Adinkerke,* ☎ *058/420202.* ☞ *BF595.* ☉ *Apr.–1st wk of Sept., daily 10–6 (July and Aug. until 7); rest of Sept., Wed. and weekends 10:30–6.*

Outdoor Activities and Sports

The best places for sand yachting are De Panne and Oostduinkerke (☞ *below*), where the beach is up to 820 ft wide and the facilities are excellent.

Koksijde

★ ❹⁸ *5 km (3 mi) southeast of De Panne on N35.*

Koksijde and Sint-Idesbald are small resorts, separated by just a few kilometers, that offer more than beach life. Koksijde has the highest dune on the coast, the **Hoge Blekker,** 108 ft high. Nearby are the ruins of the Cistercian **Duinenabdij** (Abbey of the Dunes) with an archaeological museum. ✉ *Koninklijke Prinslaan 8,* ☎ *058/511933.* ☞ *BF100.* ☉ *June 15–Sept. 15, daily 10–6; Sept. 16–Dec. and Feb.–June 14, daily 9–noon and 1:30–5.*

The architecture of the strikingly modern **Onze-Lieve-Vrouw ter Duinenkerk** (Our Lady of Sorrows of the Dunes Church), north of the Abbey, suggests both the dunes and the sea. ✉ *Jaak Van Buggenhoutlaan.*

Many art lovers head for Sint-Idesbald to discover the **Paul Delvaux Museum.** It is dedicated to the painter, famous for his surrealist mix of nudes, skeletons, and trains, who died in 1994 at the age of nearly 100. A pleasant outdoor restaurant is attached to the museum. ✉ *Paul Delvauxlaan 42,* ☎ *058/521229.* ☞ *BF250.* ☉ *Apr.–June and Sept., Tues.–Sun. 10:30–5:30; July–Aug., daily 10:30–5:30; Oct.–Dec., Fri.–Sun. 10:30–5:30.*

Oostduinkerke

49 *4 km (2 ½ mi) east of Koksijde.*

At this town there are still some horseback shrimp fishers. At low tide, the sturdy horses, half immersed, trawl heavy nets along the shoreline. If you miss seeing them in action, you can study their unusual approach to fishing in the **Nationaal Visserijmuseum** (National Fisheries Museum), which contains interesting models of fishing boats over the past millennium. ⊠ *Pastoor Schmitzstraat 4,* ☎ *058/512468.* 🖾 *BF80.* ☉ *Apr.– Oct., Tues.–Sun., 10–noon and 2–6; July–Aug., daily 10–noon and 2–6.*

| NEED A BREAK? | **In De Peerdevisscher** (⊠ Pastoor Schmitzstraat 6; closed Oct.–Apr.), a traditional *estaminet* (old-style public house) converted into café and snack bar, continues the marine theme of the fisheries museum. |

Nieuwpoort

50 *5 km (3 mi) northeast of Oostduinkerke; Exit 3 from E 40.*

This is the country's premier yachting center, with some 3,000 leisure craft moored in the estuary. Nieuwpoort was once the home of a sizable fishing fleet; although the coastal fishing industry has largely been edged out by modern super-trawlers, amateur fishermen can participate in daylong sea fishing trips aboard the *Sportvisser* (☎ 058/235600) for BF1,200 per person. There's also a lively fish market and good wharfside seafood shops and restaurants. A monument to King Albert marks the spot where, in October 1914, the monarch gave the command to open the sluices of the river IJzer, inundating the polder and permanently halting the German advance.

Dining and Lodging

$$ ✕ **De Braise.** Run by the parents of Le Fox's chef, who ran Le Fox (☞ *below*) when it was a simple tavern, this is the Buyens family's return to their roots: an old-fashioned regional restaurant, offering updated local cooking in a homey setting. Though the menu reads like a thousand others in the region—turbot poached or grilled, sauce hollandaise/dijonnaise, sole meunière—the portions are generous, the preparation superb, and the service sophisticated. ⊠ *Bortierplein 1,* ☎ *058/422309. AE, DC, MC, V. Closed Mon., Tues. in off-season, 2nd ½ of Jan., Oct.*

$$$ ✕🖾 **Hostellerie Le Fox.** Chef Stephane Buyens took over his parents'
★ tavern and fashioned a prestigious, welcoming gastronomic retreat. Creating dishes such as brie, truffles, and roquette salad with honey; and turbot in an aromatic mix of 10 oils, herbs, and beet juice, he has drawn a loyal following. Guests stay in graciously furnished rooms (some have windows angled toward the waterfront) and work as many meals into the weekend as they can. The dining room is cozy, the ambience down to earth and the wine list innovative. ⊠ *Walckierstraat 2, B 8620,* ☎ *058/412855. 14 rooms. Restaurant, bar. AE, DC, MC, V. No lunch Tues. Closed Mon., 2nd ½ of Jan., Oct.*

$$ 🖾 **Sparrenhof.** This is a self-contained oasis, cut off from the beachfront scene but only 500 ft from the water. Its pretty pool is cloistered in a garden; many rooms face the greenery. The original building, which has seven guest rooms, dates from the 1950s. The new wing is flashy and modern. The restaurant is open year-round and has a woodburning fireplace and poolside tables. ⊠ *Koninginnelaan 26, B-8660,* ☎ *058/411328,* 🖾 *058/420819. 25 rooms. Restaurant, bar, pool, parking. AE, DC, MC, V.*

Knokke-Heist

⑤ *33 km (20 mi) northeast of Oostende, 17 km (10 mi) north of Brugge, 108 km (65 mi) northwest of Brussels.*

Knokke-Heist (which includes five resorts—Knokke, Heist, Alberstrand, Het Zoute, and Duinbergen) is to young Belgians of ample means the place go to show off the latest fashions or with your newest flame. But those who inhabit the old-money villas of Het Zoute, just inland from the beach, would not dream of letting the world know about their chauffeurs and butlers. Along the Kustlaan, on the leeward side of the dike, you'll find a branch of virtually every fashionable shop in Brussels, all of them open Sunday. The Casino has an enormous chandelier of Venetian crystal, and some of the world's top entertainers come here to perform. Gaming, however, is for members only.

NEED A
BREAK?
The Albertplein (Albert Square), widely known as the *Place M'as-tu-vu* (Did-you-see-me Square), is a gathering place for the chic-at-heart. The newest and most fashionable tearoom-restaurant is **Le Carré** (✉ Albertplein 16, ☎ 050/611222), perfect for people-watching.

★ **⑤** **Het Zwin** is a remarkable 375-acre nature reserve and bird sanctuary, preserved thanks to the efforts of naturalist Count Léon Lippens in the early 20th century. Saltwater washes into the soil at certain times, making for some unusual flora and fauna. The best times to visit are in spring for the bird migrations and from mid-July for the flowers, especially the native *Zwinneblomme*, or sea lavender. Rubber boots are a must, binoculars can be rented. From the top of the dike there's a splendid view of the dunes and inlets. Storks nest in the aviary, which also holds a large variety of aquatic birds and birds of prey. A former royal villa, the Châlet du Zwin, is now an attractive restaurant. ✉ *Graaf Léon Lippensstraat 8,* ☎ *050/607086.* ▨ *BF165.* ☼ *Daily 9–7 (Oct.–Mar. until 5).*

Dining and Lodging

$$$$ ✕ **Ter Dijken.** Discretion and charm are the bywords at this restaurant, known for its terrace adjoining a magnificent garden. Langoustines with chives au gratin, croquettes of hand-peeled shrimp, and baked potato with caviar are among the favorites here. ✉ *Kalvekeetdijk 137, Knokke,* ☎ *050/608023. Reservations essential. AE, DC, MC, V. Closed Mon.– Tues., Jan.*

✕ **New Alpina.** Despite token efforts at elegance, with pink linens and multiple stemware, this is a seafood diner at heart, where a friendly husband-and-wife team have served North Sea classics since 1970. Fresh skate, turbot, sole, and shrimp are served with simple sauces; the multicourse, fixed-priced "Gourmet Menu" is a seafood feast. It's just off the beach, by the tourist office. ✉ *Lichttorenplein 12, Knokke,* ☎ *050/ 608985. MC, V. No dinner Mon. Closed Tues.*

$$$$ ▥ **La Réserve.** This vast country club of a hotel, complete with a saltwater treatment center and a man-made lake, was built as a private mansion in 1964. It was expanded, under various managements, into the enormous complex it is today. Flowers and antique-like details do little to warm the airport-style public spaces, but guest rooms are bright and lovely, in soothing sponge-painted pastels. You can buy in as far as you like, from a simple bed-and-breakfast arrangement to a full-out thalassa-treatment package. It's across from the Casino, three minutes from the beach. The restaurant is good and getting better. ✉ *Elizabetlaan 158–160, B 8300 Albertstrand,* ☎ *050/610606,* ▣ *050/ 603706. 112 rooms. Restaurant, bar, saltwater pool, beauty salon, massage, mineral baths, sauna, 4 tennis courts, windsurfing. AE, DC, MC, V.*

$$$ 🔲 **Katelijne.** This charming, whitewashed brick auberge, built in the 1930s in traditional Flemish style, seems out of place amid the boutiques and snaking traffic of the beachfront. It offers an atmospheric retreat, with fireplace, Oriental runners, fringed plush furniture, and darkened timbers. The rooms are equally cozy and dated, though the marble-travertine baths are deluxe (rooms are being refurbished in 1999). There's a garden and terrace, and a welcoming copper-decked restaurant with an emphasis on fish dishes. ⊠ *Kustlaan 166, B 8060 Knokke-Le Zoute,* ☎ *050/601216,* FAX *050/615190. 14 rooms with bath. Restaurant, bar. AE, DC, MC, V.*

Nightlife and the Arts

The **Casino** (⊠ Zeedijk 507, ☎ 050/630500) offers gala nights with international stars, theater, movies, ballet, exhibitions, and two discos, **Number 1** (entrance on Zeedijk) and **Dubbel's** (entrance on Canada Square). Another favorite is the **Gallery Club** (⊠ Canada Square 22, ☎ 050/608133).

Outdoor Activities and Sports

There are two 18-hole golf courses at Knokke-Heist's **Royal Zoute Golf Club** (⊠ Caddiespad 14, ☎ 050/601227).

Dutch Flanders

The Het Zwin nature preserve continues on the Dutch side of the border. Zeeuwsch-Vlaanderen, part of the Dutch province of Zeeland, stretches 60-odd km (about 36 mi) to the mouth of the Scheldt, north of Antwerp. When Belgium declared its independence in 1830, this Protestant province stayed with the Dutch, mostly for religious reasons. The best-known town is **Sluis,** reached from Knokke on N376 (N58 in the Netherlands). This small town shared the wealth of Brugge, for it was on the waterway that linked Brugge with the sea. Many Belgians come here to shop and bank.

The beach proper begins with **Cadzand Bad,** which has several good hotels. From **Breskens,** you can take a car ferry to Vlissingen on Walcheren. Zeeuwsch-Vlaanderen is well suited for a holiday with children precisely because the resorts are uncrowded, with wide and quiet beaches. N252 south, from the port city of **Terneuzen,** links up with R4 to Gent. There's a second car-ferry service east of Terneuzen, from Kloosterzande on N60 to Kruiningen on Walcheren. Going south on N60 you link up with N49 in Belgium, 26 km (16 mi) from Antwerp.

Flanders A to Z

Arriving and Departing

BY CAR

Brugge is 5 km (3 mi) north of the E40 motorway, which links Brussels with Gent and Oostende. It is 126 km (76 mi) from the Le Shuttle terminus at Calais.

From Brussels, **Gent** is reached via the E40, which continues to Brugge and the coast. Traffic can be bumper-to-bumper on summer weekends. Gent is 292 km (175 mi) from Paris on the E15/E17.

Kortrijk is reached from Brussels by the E40, branching off on the E17 from Gent (which continues to Lille and Paris), or the A17 from Brugge. The easiest way to reach **Ieper** is via the A19 from Kortrijk, which peters out north of the city; highway N38 continues to Poperinge, where you're close to the French highway linking Lille with Dunkirk and Calais.

The six-lane E40 from Brussels passes both Gent and Brugge en route to **Oostende.** On summer weekends, a better alternative is the N9 from Gent via Brugge; for **Knokke,** you branch off on N49. A back road to the resorts southwest of Oostende is N43 from Gent to Deinze, and then N35 to the coast. From Calais, the E40 has been completed on the French side, but a few kilometers of two-lane road remain before linking up with the rest of the E40 to Oostende and Brussels.

BY TRAIN

There are two trains to **Brugge** per hour from Brussels (50 minutes) and three trains an hour from Gent (25 minutes) and from Oostende (15 minutes). For **train information** in Brugge, call 050/382382.

Non-stop trains to **Gent** depart on the hour, and 27 minutes past the hour, from Brussels (28 minutes). For **train information** call 02/203–3640 or 09/221–4444.

Oostende is the terminus of the Cologne–Brussels–Oostende railway line, which connects with ferry service to Ramsgate and the boat train to London. A train departs every hour from Brussels (1 hour, 10 minutes), from Gent (40 minutes), and from Brugge (15 minutes). For **train information** in Oostende call 059/701517.

There's local, hourly train service from Gent to **De Panne** (1 hour, 10 minutes), and direct service every hour from Brussels to **Knokke** (1 hour, 15 minutes) via Gent and Brugge.

A train runs every hour from Brussels to **Kortrijk** (1 hour, 10 minutes). There are also several trains a day from Lille (35 minutes), where the *Eurostar* from London stops (change stations from Lille Europe to Lille Flandres). To get to **Ieper** by train you have to change in Kortrijk to an infrequent local service (30 minutes); it also goes to **Poperinge** (40 minutes).

Getting Around

BY BICYCLE

A bike is perfect for getting around **Brugge** and its environs. Bikes can be rented at the **railway station** (BF150 per day with a valid train ticket), at **De Ketting** (⊠ Gentpoortstraat 23, ☎ 050/344196; 150 BF for the day), **Eric Popelier** (⊠ Hallestraat 14, around the corner from the Belfry, ☎ 050/343262; BF150 for four hours, BF250 for the day), or at **Koffiebontje** (⊠ Hallestraat 4, ☎ 050/338027; BF150 for four hours, BF250 for the day). Several hotels provide bikes free of charge for their guests.

In **Gent** you can rent bikes at the train station at a reduced rate. In the **battlefield** region and along the **coast** you can also rent bikes at railway stations.

BY BOAT

Motorboats for trips around the **Gent** waterways and/or down the river Leie can be rented from **Minerva** (☎ 09/221–8451), at BF1600 for a two-hour cruise. Boats take four to five people and no license is required. The embarkation and landing stage is at Coupure, on the corner of Lindenlei.

BY BUS

In **Brugge** the **De Lijn** bus company runs most buses every 20 minutes, including Sunday; minibuses are designed to penetrate the narrow streets.

BY CAR

Access for cars and coaches into **Brugge**'s old city is severely restricted. There are huge car parks at the railway station and near the exits from the ring road. To visit the **battlefields,** driving is definitely the best solution, because the various World War I sights are located in different directions from Ieper. The **coastal road,** N34, is very busy in summer. Allow ample time for driving between resorts.

BY TAXI

Brugge has large taxi stands at the railway station and at the Markt. In **Gent** there are taxi stands at the railway station and at major squares.

BY TRAM

If you arrive in **Gent** by train, take Tram 1, 11, or 12 (fare: BF50) for the city center.

Along the **coast** there's a tram service—a happily preserved relic of another era—all the way from Knokke to De Panne. The trams are modern, and it's a pleasant ride, but don't expect uninterrupted views of the sea; the tram tracks are on the leeward side of the dike. The service runs every 15 minutes from Easter through September. Tickets cost from BF50 depending on distance.

ON FOOT

The center of **Brugge** is best seen on foot. The winding streets may confuse your sense of direction, but if you look up, there's always the Belfry to guide you back to the Markt. Sturdy footwear is recommended. Key sights are illuminated after sunset, giving the old city an enchanted air.

In **Gent,** as most of the sights are within a radius of half a mile from the Stadhuis, by far the best way to see them is on foot.

Contacts and Resources

CAR RENTAL

For car rental to visit battlefields and the coast from Brugge, try **Europcar** (⊠ Spoorwegstraat 106, ☎ 050/385312).

GUIDED TOURS

By Bicycle. The **Back Road Bike Co.** (☎ 050/343045) organizes tours covering six villages near **Brugge.** Mountain bikes are supplied, and the guided four-hour rides take only back roads.

By Boat. In **Brugge,** independent motor launches depart from five jetties along the Dijver and Katelijnestraat as soon as they are reasonably full (every 15 minutes or so) daily from March to November and depending on the weather in December and February. The trips take just over half an hour and cost BF175.

Sightseeing boats depart from the landing stages at Graslei and Korenlei for 35-minute trips on the **Gent** waterways, Easter through October (BF150).

On the **coast, Seastar** (⊠ Havengeul 17, Nieuwpoort, ☎ 058/232425) operates regular sailings between Oostende and Nieuwpoort in July and August with departures in both directions. The trip along the coast takes 1½ hours and costs BF450.

River excursions on board the **_Jean Bart III_** (☎ 058/232329) on the IJzer, through the polder from Nieuwpoort to Diksmuide and back, are operated daily at 2 PM in July and August; call in the morning at other times. The cost is BF 250.

By Bus. Quasimodo (☎ 050/370470) runs all-day minibus tours from Brugge featuring a drive along the coast (Wed. and Fri. in season; BF1,300) with English-language commentary, or to the "Fields of Flanders" (Sun., Tues., Thurs.; BF1,400).

By Carriage. Horse-drawn carriages wait in Sint-Baafsplein in **Gent.** A half-hour trip for up to four people is BF800 and gives you a general idea of the town center. **Brugge** has carriages on the Markt (BF 900). You may have to wait for more than an hour for a short ride with inadequate commentary and then be asked for "something for the horse." Kids love it, however.

By Taxi. In **Gent** you can arrange for a taxi with an English-speaking driver (☎ 09/223–2323).

Personal Guides. In **Brugge** you can book an English-speaking guide through the **tourist office** (☎ 050/448686). Guides charge a minimum of BF1,500 for two hours, BF750 per extra hour. In July and August, groups are consolidated at the tourist office every day at 3; the cost per person is BF200 (children free).

Your **Gent** experience can be much enhanced by a personal guide. Call **Gidsenbond van Gent** (Association of Gent Guides; ☎ 09/233–0772) weekdays between 9 and 12:30. The charge is BF1,500 for the first two hours, BF750 per additional hour.

OUTDOOR ACTIVITIES AND SPORTS

For information about sports federations throughout the region, contact **BLOSO** (Flemish Sports Association; ⊠ R. des Colonies 31, Brussels, ☎ 02/510–3411). For information on water sports, contact **Vlaamse Vereniging voor Watersport** (⊠ Beatrijslaan 25, Antwerp, ☎ 03/219–6967).

VISITOR INFORMATION

For Western Flanders as a whole: **Westtoerisme** (⊠ Kasteel Tillegem, Brugge, ☎ 050/380296). **Brugge: Toerisme Brugge** (Brugge Tourist Office; ⊠ Burg 11, ☎ 050/448686). City Tourist Information Services (Dienst voor Toerisme): **De Panne** (⊠ Zeelaan 21, ☎ 058/421818). **Diksmuide** (⊠ Grote Markt 28, ☎ 051/519146). **Gent** (⊠ Predikherenlei 2, ☎ 09/225–3641; ⊠ Town Hall, under belfry, ☎ 09/266–5232). **Ieper** (⊠ Stadhuis, Grote Markt 34, ☎ 057/200724). **Knokke-Heist** (⊠ Zeedijk 660 ☎ 050/630380). **Kortrijk** (⊠ St-Michielsplein 2, ☎ 056/239371). **Nieuwpoort** (⊠ Marktplein 7, ☎ 058/224444). **Oostende** (⊠ Monacoplein 2, ☎ 059/701199). **Poperinge** (⊠ Stadhuis, Markt 1, ☎ 057/334081).

ANTWERP

In its heyday, Antwerp (Antwerpen in Flemish, Anvers in French) played second fiddle only to Paris. Thanks to artists such as Rubens, Van Dyck, and Jordaens, it was one of Europe's leading art centers. Its printing presses produced missals for the farthest reaches of the Spanish empire. It became, and has remained, the diamond capital of the world. Its civic pride was such that the Antwerpen *Sinjoren* (patricians) considered themselves a cut above just about everybody else. They still do.

The Flemish word Antwerpen is very close to the word *handwerpen,* which means "hand throwing," and that, according to legend, is exactly what the Roman soldier Silvius Brabo did to the giant Druon Antigon. The giant would collect a toll from boatmen on the river and cut off the hands of those who refused, until Silvius confronted him, cut off the giant's own hand, and flung it into the river Scheldt. That's why there are severed hands on Antwerp's coat of arms.

Great prosperity came to Antwerp during the reign of Emperor Charles V. Born in Gent and raised in Mechelen, he made Antwerp the principal port of his vast domain. It became the most important commercial center in the 16th century, as well as a center of the new craft of printing. The Golden Age came to an end with the abdication of Charles V in 1555. He was succeeded by Philip II of Spain, whose ardent Roman Catholicism brought him into immediate conflict with the Protestants of the Netherlands. In 1566, when Calvinist iconoclasts destroyed paintings and sculptures in churches and monasteries, Philip II responded by sending in Spanish troops. In what became known as the Spanish Fury, they sacked the town and killed thousands of citizens.

The decline of Antwerp had already begun when its most illustrious painters, Rubens, Jordaens, and Van Dyck, reached the peak of their fame. The Treaty of Munster in 1648, which concluded the Thirty Years' War, also sealed Antwerp's fate, for the river Scheldt was closed to shipping—not to be opened again until 1863, when a treaty obliged the Dutch, who controlled the estuary, to reopen it.

The huge and splendid railway station, built at the turn of the century, remains a fitting monument to Antwerp's second age of prosperity, during which it hosted universal expositions in 1885 and 1894. In World War I, Antwerp held off German invaders long enough for the Belgian army to regroup south of the IJzer. In World War II, the Germans trained many V-1 flying bombs and V-2 rockets on the city, where Allied troops were debarking for the final push.

Antwerp today is Europe's second-largest port and has much of the zest often associated with a harbor town. The city has traditionally taken pride in being open to influences from abroad and in welcoming newcomers. Yet in recent elections, a large number of votes have been cast for Vlaams Blok, a party with extreme right-wing tendencies.

Antwerp is known as the City of the Madonnas. On almost every street corner in the old section, you'll see a high niche with a protective statuette of the Virgin. People tend to think that because Belgium is linguistically split it is also religiously divided. This emphatically is not so. In fact, the Roman Catholic faith appears to be stronger and more unquestioning in Flanders than in Wallonia, where the anti-clericalism of fellow French-speakers has struck a responsive chord.

Rubens is ever-present in Antwerp, and a genial presence it is. His house, his church, the homes of his benefactors, friends, and disciples are all over the old city. His wife also seems ever-present, for she frequently posed as his model for his portraits of the Virgin Mary. Rubens and his fellow Antwerper Van Dyck both dabbled in diplomacy and were knighted by the English monarch. Jacob Jordaens, less widely known, stayed close to Antwerp all his life; long regarded as an also-ran, he has only recently been recognized for his artistic genius.

In addition to being home to the Old Masters, Antwerp is also on the cutting edge in art. The sharpest designers and most far-out artists are here, rather than in the capital, and the galleries and modern art museum celebrate contemporary concepts.

Exploring Antwerp

The area that surrounds the magnificent railway station is in the commercial center of the city, but not representative of its character. Hop on the subway to Groenplaats and walk past the cathedral and then into the Grote Markt. This is where Antwerp begins. Although you can "do" Antwerp in a day, you would do much better with two days, allowing time to sample some of the great restaurants and the lively nightlife and to properly explore the rich collections of the Royal Museum of Fine Arts and other museums. Antwerp is also a good base for excursions throughout the province of the same name and neighboring Limburg. Antwerp can be visited year-round, but avoid Monday, when the museums are closed, for they are an integral part of enjoying this city. An excursion to the province of Limburg is best made in spring or summer; it is at its very best at apple-blossom time.

Numbers in the text correspond to numbers in the margin and on the Antwerp map.

A Good Walk

From the **Grote Markt** ① walk down Suikerrui toward the river, stopping en route at the **Etnografisch Museum** ②. At the end of the street, turn right to the waterfront fortress, the **Steen** ③. Walk up the block-long Repenstraat to the step-gabled **Vleeshuis** ④. Proceed along Oude Beurs and its continuation, Wolstraat, turning left on Minderbroedersrui and then right on Keizerstraat, to **Rockoxhuis** ⑤, the Renaissance home of Rubens's benefactor. Retrace your steps along Wolstraat to the church of **Sint-Carolus Borromeus** ⑥ on the attractive Hendrik Conscienceplein. Walk down Wijngaardstraat in the direction of the Grote Markt, going around the cathedral to its entrance on Handschoenmarkt. The Gothic **Onze-Lieve-Vrouwekathedraal** ⑦ contains some of Rubens's greatest paintings. A few steps to the left from the front of the cathedral, and you're in Koornmarkt. At No. 16 begins the **Vlaeykensgang** ⑧, an old cobblestone lane. It merges into Pelgrimstraat. Turn right, then right again on Reyndersstraat, past the Baroque house of the painter Jacob Jordaens; then right on Hoogstraat and right again on Heilige Geeststraat, and you're at the **Plantin-Moretus Museum** ⑨, the printer's stately home and workshops. Cross the Vrijdagmarkt, and walk along Steenhouwersvest and Lombardenvest to Korte Gasthuisstraat, where you turn right and proceed to **Museum Mayer Van den Bergh** ⑩ with its outstanding Bruegels. By way of Huidevettersstraat and Meir, the main shopping area, you arrive at Wapper and **Rubenshuis** ⑪, the painter's home. Farther along Meir and its continuation, Leys and De Keyserlei, you arrive at the Diamond District, turning right on Appelmansstraat for **Diamondland** ⑫ and the Diamond Museum. Just to the south of Diamondland on Lange Herentalsestraat is the **Provinciaal Diamantmuseum** ⑬. North of Diamondland, De Keyserlei takes you east to Central Station and, beyond it, the **Zoo** ⑭ You can take a cab or tram to the southwestern side of the center and the **Koninklijk Museum voor Schone Kunsten** ⑮, with its stellar collection of Flemish art.

TIMING

Walking this route, with short stops at the museums, will take you four to five hours. Time permitting, you would be well advised to break at the Rubenshuis and see the Diamond District and the zoo the following day.

Sights to See

Centraalstation (Central Station). Next to the ☞ Zoo, the neo-Baroque railway terminal was built at the turn of the century during the reign of Leopold II of Belgium, a monarch not given to understatement. The magnificent exterior and splendid, vaulted ticket-office hall and staircases call out for hissing steam engines, peremptory conductors, scurrying porters, and languid ladies wrapped in boas. Alas, today most departures and arrivals are humble commuter trains. ✉ *Koningin Astridplein.*

Diamond District. The diamond trade has its own quarter in Antwerp, where the skills of cutting and polishing the gems have been handed

Antwerp

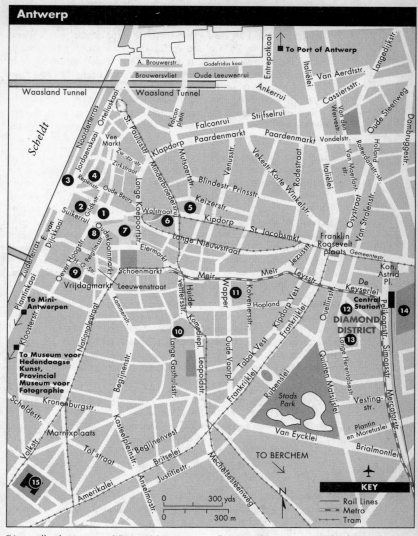

To Port of Antwerp

A. Brouwerstr.
Godefridus kaai
Brouwersvliet
Oude Leeuwenrui

Waasland Tunnel
Waasland Tunnel

Scheldt

Vee Markt

Falcon plein
Falconrui
Stijfselrui
Ankerrui

Paardenmarkt
Paardenmarkt
Vondelstr.

Klapdorp

Blindestr. Prinsstr.
Keizerstr.
Wolstraat
Kipdorp
St. Jacobsmkt.

Lange Nieuwstraat

Franklin Roosevelt plaats
Gemeentestr.

Eiermarkt

Schoenmarkt
Meir
Meir
Leysstr.

Vrijdagmarkt
Leeuwenstraat
Wapper

Kon. Astrid Pl.

De Keyserlei
Central Station

DIAMOND DISTRICT

Hopland

To Mini-Antwerpen

To Museum voor Hedendaagse Kunst, Provincial Museum voor Fotographie

Kronenburgstr.

Stads Park

Marnixplaats

TO BERCHEM

Van Eycklei

Vestingstr.

Plantin en Moretuslei

Brialmontlei

Amerikalei

Mechelsesteenweg

N

0   300 yds
0   300 m

KEY
— Rail Lines
≡ Metro
··· Tram

Diamondland, **12**	Museum Mayer Van den Bergh, **10**
Etnografisch Museum, **2**	Onze-Lieve-Vrouwekathedraal, **7**
Grote Markt, **1**	Plantin-Moretus Museum, **9**
Koninklijk Museum voor Schone Kunsten, **15**	Provinciaal Diamantmuseum, **13**
	Rockoxhuis, **5**
	Rubenshuis, **11**
	Sint-Carolus Borromeus, **6**
Vlaeykensgang, **8**
Vleeshuis, **4**
Zoo, **14**

down for generations by a tightly knit community. Multimillion-dollar deals are agreed upon with a handshake, and the industry has created its own Diamond High Council to establish strict quality control and high standards. Some 70% of the world's uncut diamonds pass through Antwerp. Twenty-five million carats are cut and traded here every year, more than anywhere else in the world. The district occupies a few nondescript city blocks west of Central Station. Shop signs in Hebrew, and the distinctive clothing and ringlets worn by many Hasidic men, are the only clues that this area is any different from the rest of Antwerp. Below the elevated railway tracks, a long row of stalls and shops gleams with jewelry and gems.

Diamond-cutting began in Brugge but moved to Antwerp in the 16th century, along with most other wealth-creating activities. Antwerp's preoccupation with beauty and money helped the diamond trade flourish. Today the industry employs some 18,000 people, divided among 6,000 independent firms. In addition to cutters, grinders, and polishers, there are about 3,000 traders, of whom two-thirds are Jewish and one-fifth Indian, with a heavy sprinkling of Lebanese and Armenians. Nearly all come from long-established diamond families. Some of Antwerp's Jews managed to flee Belgium during World War II, but many more perished in the concentration camps. ⊠ *Bounded by De Keyserlei, Pelikaanstraat, Herentalsestraat, and Lange Kievitstraat.*

⑫ **Diamondland.** A spectacular showroom, Diamondland was created to enable visitors to see some of the bustling activity. Because security is of the essence in this business, outsiders were not previously allowed to watch any of the activity inside. Diamondland has three floors of slide shows and films, showcases of rough and polished diamonds, and several diamond cutters at work. ⊠ *Appelmansstraat 33A,* ☎ *03/234–3612.* ☉ *Mon.–Sat. 9–5:30.*

❷ **Etnografisch Museum** (Ethnographic Museum). This fascinating museum explores the art, myths, and rites of the native peoples of Africa, the Americas, Asia, and the South Seas. Among its 30,000 masks, tools, weapons, sculptures, and other objects are several unique pieces, some of them described in *La Musée Imaginaire,* André Malraux's compilation of the world's most important art and artifacts. ⊠ *Suikerrui 19,* ☎ *03/220–8600.* ☑ *BF100.* ☉ *Tues.–Sun. 10–5.*

❶ **Grote Markt.** The heart of the Old Town, the Grote Markt is dominated by a huge fountain splashing water over much of the square. It is crowned by the figure of the legendary Silvius Brabo, who has been about to fling the hand of the giant Druon Antigon into the river Scheldt for the past 100 years. Another famous monster slayer, St. George, is perched on top of a 16th-century guild house at Grote Markt 5, while the dragon appears to be falling off the pediment. The triangular square is lined on two sides by guild houses and on the third by the Renaissance **Stadhuis** (Town Hall). Antwerp's Town Hall was built in the 1560s during the city's Golden Age, when Paris and Antwerp were the only European cities with more than 100,000 inhabitants. In its facade, the fanciful fretwork of the late Gothic style has given way to the discipline and order of the Renaissance; the public rooms are suitably impressive, though the heavy hand of 19th-century restoration work is much in evidence. ⊠ *Grote Markt,* ☎ *03/220–8211.* ☑ *BF30.* ☉ *Mon.–Wed. and Fri. 8–6, Sat. 8–4; guided tours weekdays at 11, 2, and 3, Sat. at 2 and 3.*

⑮ **Koninklijk Museum voor Schone Kunsten** (Royal Museum of Fine Arts). A must for the student of Flemish art, the collection here is studded with masterworks from Bruegel to Ensor. In 1999, there's a blockbuster retrospective of more than 80 works by Van Dyck, culled from the world's top galleries. The paintings here, recovered from the French after the fall of Napoléon, form the nucleus of a collection of 2,500 works of art. Room H is devoted to Jacob Jordaens; Room J, mostly monumental Rubens; and Room M, Bruegel. The collection of Flemish Primitives includes works by Van Eyck, Memling, Roger van der Weyden, Joachim Patinier, and Quinten Metsys. On the ground floor there's a representative survey of Belgian art of the past 150 years—Emile Claus, Rik Wouters, Permeke, Magritte, Delvaux, and especially James Ensor. ⊠ *Leopold de Waelplaats 2,* ☎ *03/238–7809.* 🖾 *250BF.* ☉ *Tues.–Sun. 10–5, Wed. until 9, closed May 21. Take Tram 8.*

☺ **Mini-Antwerpen.** The name says it all. Most, if not all, of Antwerp can be found here, scaled down to kid size. The tour ends with a mini-sound-and-sights show recounting the history of the city. ⊠ *Hangar 15, Cockerillkaai,* ☎ *03/237–0329.* 🖾 *BF190.* ☉ *Weekdays 10–5, weekends 10–6.*

★ ⑩ **Museum Mayer Van den Bergh.** Bruegel's arguably greatest and most enigmatic painting, *Dulle Griet,* is the showpiece here. Often referred to in English as "Mad Meg," it portrays an irate woman wearing helmet and breastplate—a sword in one hand, and food and cooking utensils in the other—striding across a field strewn with the ravages and insanity of war. There is no consensus on how to read this painting. Some consider it one of the most powerful antiwar statements ever made. Others claim that it denounces the Inquisition. Either way, nothing could be further from the Bruegelian villages than this nightmare world. In 1894, Mayer van den Bergh bought *Dulle Griet* for BF488. Today it is priceless. There's one more set of Bruegels in the collection, his witty, miniature illustrations of *Twelve Proverbs,* based on popular Flemish sayings.

Mayer van den Bergh was a passionate art connoisseur who amassed a private collection of almost 4,000 works in the 19th century. The collection includes treasures such as a life-size polychrome statue from about 1300 of St. John resting his head on Christ's chest. It is, however, the two Bruegel paintings that make this small museum a must. Closed for renovations in late 1998, the museum reopens in April 1999. ⊠ *Lange Gasthuisstraat 19,* ☎ *03/232–4237.* 🖾 *BF100.* ☉ *Tues.–Sun. 10–5.*

NEED A BREAK?

De Foyer (⊠ Komedieplaats 18) occupies the ornate rotunda of the 150-year-old Bourla Theater. The decor alone is worth a visit, but the café serves buffet lunch and light snacks and is open from noon to midnight. It's popular with locals, especially on Sunday, when the buffet breakfast is booked weeks in advance.

Museum voor Hedendaagse Kunst (MuHKA; Museum of Contemporary Art). This museum shows contemporary painting, installations, video art, and experimental architecture, including works by the mysterious Flemish theater director/choreographer and artist Jan Fabre, whose sculptures and installations, often based on or involving insects, have established him as one of the country's leading artists. The museum is in a renovated grain silo in the trendy Waalse Kaai district. ⊠ *Leuvenstraat 32,* ☎ *03/238–5960.* 🖾 *BF150.* ☉ *Tues.–Sun. 10–5. Bus 23.*

★ ❼ **Onze-Lieve-Vrouwekathedraal** (Cathedral of Our Lady). A miracle of soaring Gothic lightness, the Onze-Lieve-Vrouwekathedraal is landmarked by its 404-ft-high north spire—now restored to its original gleaming white and serving as a beacon that can be seen from far away. Work started in 1352 and continued in fits and starts until 1584. Despite this, it is a totally homogeneous monument, thanks to a succession of remarkable architects, including Peter Appelmans, Herman and Domien de Waghemakere, and Rombout Keldermans the Younger. The tower holds a 47-bell carillon (played Friday 11:30–12:30, Sunday from 3 PM–4 PM, and Monday in summer 8 PM–9 PM).

The cathedral's art treasures were twice vandalized, first by Calvinists in 1566 and again by the French revolutionary army at the end of the 18th century. The French even broke up the floor so that their horses would not slip on it. The masterpieces were either sold at auction or carried off to Paris. Some, but by no means all, have subsequently been returned. Other works, either donated or purchased, make up an outstanding collection of 17th-century religious art, including four Rubens altarpieces, glowing with his marvelous red, allegedly fortified by pigeon's blood. The panels of *The Descent from the Cross* triptych— Mary's visit to Elizabeth (with the painter's wife as Mary) and the presentation of Jesus in the temple—are among the most delicate and tender biblical scenes ever painted. *The Assumption of the Virgin Mary,* painted for the high altar, shows the Virgin being carried upward by massed ranks of cherubs toward the angel waiting to crown her Queen of the Angels. *The Assumption* is skillfully displayed so that the rays of the sun illuminate it exactly at noon. ⊠ *Handschoenmarkt,* ☎ *03/231–3033.* ☞ *BF70.* ⊙ *Weekdays 10–5, Sat. 10–3, Sun. 1–4.*

★ ❾ **Plantin-Moretus Museum.** This was the home and printing plant of an extraordinary publishing dynasty. For three centuries, beginning in 1576, the family printed innumerable bibles, breviaries, and missals; Christophe Plantin's greatest technical achievement was the *Biblia Regia* (in Room 16): eight large volumes containing the Bible in Latin, Greek, Hebrew, Syriac, and Aramaic, complete with notes, glossaries, and grammars.

The first three rooms were the family quarters, furnished in 16th-century luxury and containing several portraits by Rubens. Others remain as they were when occupied by accountants, editors, and proofreaders, while many contain Bibles and religious manuscripts dating back to the 9th century, including one owned by King Wenceslas of Bohemia. The workshops are filled with Plantin's 16 printing presses. Two typefaces designed here, Plantin and Garamond, are still in use. The presses are in working order—you can even purchase a copy of Plantin's sonnet, *Le Bonheur de ce monde (An ode to contentment),* in any of seven European languages, printed on an original press. ⊠ *Vrijdagmarkt 22,* ☎ *03/233–0294.* ☞ *BF100.* ⊙ *Tues.–Sun. 10–5.*

Port of Antwerp. Although the Port of Antwerp is 88 km (53 mi) from the sea, it is Europe's second-largest port (after Rotterdam). Giant locks facilitate navigation up the river Scheldt; the largest measures 550 yards by 75 yards. Every year, 100 million tons of goods are shipped here, serving a vast area stretching across half of Europe. Surprisingly, in the midst of all this hustle and bustle is a fishing village, Lillo, nestled among the enormous refineries, the tankers, and the buildings of the chemical industries. In Lillo, life continues as of old. ⊠ *Scheldelaan, on the banks of the river 20 km (12 mi) from town.*

⓭ **Provinciaal Diamantmuseum** (Provincial Diamond Museum). This museum relates the history of the diamond trade in maps, models, and videos, and there's a complete 19th-century diamond workshop. Exceptional jewelry is displayed in the treasure room. ⊠ *Lange Herentalsestraat 31–33,* ☎ *03/202–4890.* ☞ *Free, except during exhibitions.* ⊙ *Daily 10–5; demonstrations Sat. 2–5.*

NEED A
BREAK? **Pakhuis** (⊠ Vlaamse Kaai 76), a crowded former warehouse, is dominated by a series of shiny vats, used to brew the café's three beers; the Antwerp Blond in particular is vastly superior to even Belgium's mass-

produced brews. The building's conversion is slightly sterile, but the ales, well-prepared snacks, and professional service can't be faulted.

Provinciaal Museum voor Fotografie (Provincial Photography Museum). This collection celebrates the likes of Cartier-Bresson, William Klein, and Man Ray. There's also a display tracing the history of photography, from the "miragioscope" of the early 19th century to a James Bond camera disguised as a gun. This is among the world's leading photography museums. ✉ *Waalse Kaai 47,* ☎ *03/242–9300.* 🖃 *Free; temporary shows, BF150.* ☉ *Tues.–Sun. 10–5.*

⑤ Rockoxhuis. This was the splendid Renaissance home of Rubens's friend and patron Nicolaas Rockox, seven times mayor of Antwerp. A humanist and art collector, Rockox moved here in 1603. The collection includes two of his protégé's works. One is *Madonna and Child,* a delicate portrait of his first wife, Isabella, and their son, Nicolaas; the other is a sketch for the *Crucifixion.* The collection also includes works by Van Dyck, Frans Snijders, Joachim Patinier, Jordaens, and David Teniers the Younger. The setting is important. Rather than being displayed on museum walls, the paintings are shown in the context of an upper-class Baroque home, furnished in the style of the period. A documentary video describes Antwerp at that time. ✉ *Keizerstraat 10–12,* ☎ *03/231–4710.* 🖃 *Free.* ☉ *Tues.–Sun. 10–5.*

★ ⑪ Rubenshuis (Rubens House). A fabulous picture of the painter as patrician is presented here at Rubens's own house. Only the elaborate portico and temple, designed by Rubens in Italian Baroque style, were still standing three centuries after the house was built. Most of what we see is a reconstruction (completed in 1946), but from the master's own design. This was Rubens at the pinnacle of his fame. During this time he was appointed court painter to Archduke Albrecht and, with his wife, was sent on a diplomatic mission to Madrid, where he also painted some 40 portraits. He conducted delicate peace negotiations in London on behalf of Philip IV of Spain. While in London he painted the ceiling of the Whitehall Banqueting Hall and was knighted by Charles I of Great Britain. The most evocative room in Rubens House is the huge studio. Drawings by Rubens and his pupils, as well as old prints, often re-create this room. In Rubens's day, visitors could view completed paintings and watch from the mezzanine while Rubens and his students worked. Rubens completed about 2,500 paintings, nearly all characterized by the energy and exuberance that were his hallmark. A few Rubens paintings hang in the house, including a touching sketch in the studio of an Annunciation and a self-portrait in the dining room. Unfortunately, his young widow promptly sold off some 300 pieces after his death in 1640. ✉ *Wapper 9,* ☎ *03/232–4747.* 🖃 *BF100.* ☉ *Tues.–Sun. 10–5.*

⑥ Sint-Carolus Borromeus (St. Charles Borromeo). A noted Jesuit church, Sint-Carolus Borromeus also bears the imprint of Rubens. The front and tower are generally attributed to him, and his hand can certainly be seen in the clustered cherubim above the entrance. The church's facade suggests a richly decorated high altar, inviting the observer into the church. The interior was once magnificent, but most of Rubens's frescoes were destroyed by fire, and other works were carted off to Vienna when the Austrians banned the Jesuits in the 18th century. The square is one of the most attractive in Antwerp, flanked by the harmonious Renaissance buildings of the Jesuit convent, now occupied by the City Library. ✉ *Hendrik Conscienceplein 12,* ☎ *03/233–8433.* 🖃 *Free.* ☉ *Mon. 2–4 and Wed.–Fri. 10–noon and 2–4, Sat. 10–noon and 3–6:30, Sun. 9:30–12:30.*

NEED A
BREAK?

Its name, **Het Elfde Gebod** (✉ Torfbrug 10), means the 11th Command-
ment, and it's crammed with plaster saints and angels salvaged from old
churches. The food and drink are straightforward but hearty, and you
can sit on the terrace.

❸ Steen. The Steen is over 1,000 years old and looks it. A 9th-century
fortress, it was built to protect the western frontier of the Holy Roman
Empire. It was partially rebuilt 700 years later by Emperor Charles V.
You can distinguish the darker, medieval masonry extending midway
up the walls from the lighter upper level of 16th-century work. The
Steen was used as a prison for centuries. Opposite the entrance is a
cross where those sentenced to death said their final prayers. It now
houses the **National Scheepvaartmuseum** (National Maritime Museum), with a large collection of models, figureheads, instruments, prints,
and maps.

The Steen is the only survivor of the original waterfront. Many houses
were torn down in the 19th century to make room for the wide,
straight quays that today are practically deserted, the port having
moved north of the city. The **Noorderterras**, a promenade starting at
the Steen, is a popular place for a Sunday stroll along the Scheldt, which
here is 550 yards wide. "God gave us the river," say Antwerpers, "and
the river gave us all the rest." ✉ *Steenplein,* ☎ *03/232–0850.* ▨ *BF100.*
☉ *Tues.–Sun. 10–4:45.*

★ **❽ Vlaeykensgang.** A quiet cobblestone lane in the center of Antwerp, the
Vlaeykensgang seems untouched by time. The mood and style of the
16th century are perfectly preserved here. There is no better place to
linger on a Monday night when the carillon concert is pealing from
the cathedral. The alley ends in Pelgrimsstraat, where there is a great
view of the cathedral spire. **Jordaenshuis,** nearby, was the home of Jacob
Jordaens (1593–1678), the painter many saw as the successor of
Rubens. It's a gem adorned with many Baroque touches—and with its
very attractive courtyard rivals the Rubenshuis. ✉ *Reyndersstraat 6,*
☎ *03/233–3033.* ▨ *Free.* ☉ *Wed.–Sun. 10–5.*

NEED A
BREAK?

De Groote Witte Arend (✉ Reyndersstraat 18), in another secret courtyard near the Jordaens house, is in a former convent. The background
music tends to be Vivaldi or Telemann, the atmosphere is genteel without
being snobby, and it has a good selection of draft beers and tasty sandwiches.

❹ Vleeshuis (Butchers' Hall). Still one of the tallest buildings in the Old
City, it was completed in 1503. The designer was Herman de Waghemakere, member of a family of architects who did much to embellish
their native city. The walls were built of alternating bands of brick and
sandstone, creating an oddly pleasing layered effect. The ground floor
was originally used as a meat market, while the upper floors were occupied by a banquet hall and council chambers. Today, most of the space
is crammed with miscellaneous antiquities of local origin. ✉
Vleeshouwersstraat 38–40, ☎ *03/233–6404.* ▨ *BF100.* ☉ *Tues.–Sun.*
10–4:45.

Vleeshouwersstraat. The Vleeshuis (☞ *above*) is the most prominent
landmark of the residential neighborhood that has newly arisen in this
historic district. Many ancient buildings remain, among them **De
Spieghel** (The Mirror) off Oude Beurs at Spanjepandsteeg. Originally
built for the archers' guild, it was bought in 1506 by Pieter Gillis, a
leading humanist. At the beginning of his most famous work, Sir
Thomas More describes a visit to Antwerp. He is walking back from

Mass in the cathedral with Gillis when they encounter a traveler, who recounts his adventures on an island named Utopia. Erasmus, another friend of Gillis's, had the first edition of *Utopia* printed in Leuven. ✉ *Bounded by Oude Beurs, Kuipersstraat, Jordaenskaai, Doornikstraat, and Veemarkt.*

🄬 **Zoo.** The Antwerp Zoo houses its residents in style. Giraffes, ostriches, and African antelopes inhabit an Egyptian temple; a Moorish villa is home to the rhinoceroses; and a thriving okapi family grazes around an Indian temple. In part, this reflects the public's taste when the zoo was created 150 years ago. Today animals are allowed maximum space, and much research is devoted to endangered species. The zoo also has dolphin tanks, an aquarium, and a house for nocturnal animals. ✉ *Koningin Astridplein 26,* ☎ *03/202–4540.* 🖃 *BF450.* ☉ *Oct.–Mar., daily 9–4:45; Apr.–June and Sept, daily 9–5:45; July–Aug., daily 9–6:15.*

OFF THE BEATEN PATH	In **Berchem,** the 19th-century entrepreneur Baron Edouard Osy and his sister, Josephine Cogels, bought an old castle, demolished it, and built some refreshingly eccentric houses reflecting the eclectic tastes of that era. There are houses in Renaissance, Greek classical, and Venetian styles, but most of all, there are beautiful Art Nouveau buildings, especially at the southern end of Cogels Osylei and Waterloostraat. Berchem is southeast of the city center, the first stop on the line to Brussels. This is where international trains stop, rather than going into and backing out of Centraal Station. **Openluchtmuseum Middelheim** (Middelheim Open Air Sculpture Museum) provides an excellent survey of three-dimensional art, from Rodin to the present. There are more than 300 sculptures in this very attractive setting, including ones by Henry Moore, Alexander Calder, and Zadkine. There is also a new pavilion that houses smaller or more fragile sculptures. Middelheim is just south of the city, above the tunnel for the expressway to Brussels. ✉ *Middelheimlaan 61,* ☎ *03/827–1534.* 🖃 *Free, except during special exhibitions.* ☉ *Tues.–Sun. 10–sunset (5 PM in midwinter; 9 PM in summer).*

Dining

Antwerp remains remarkably conservative in its culinary tastes, focusing with understandable devotion on fish—presented with few frills in even the finest restaurants, often poached or steamed, and reasonably priced. From the chilled whelks and periwinkles (marine snails) picked out of their shells with pins, to piles of tender little *crevettes grises* (small shrimp), to the steamy white flesh of the mammoth turbot, the scent of salt air and fresh brine is never far from your table. The ubiquitous mussels and eels, showcased in mid-priced restaurants throughout the city center, provide a heavier, heartier version of local fish cuisine. Bought live from wholesalers, the seafood is irreproachably fresh.

For dining price categories, *see* Dining *in* Pleasures and Pastimes at the beginning of this chapter.

$$$$ ✗ **'t Fornuis.** In the heart of old Antwerp, this cozy restaurant, deco-
★ rated in traditional Flemish style, serves some of the best food in the city. Ever-creative, chef Johan Segers likes to change his menu at regular intervals, but roasted sweetbreads with a wild truffle sauce are a permanent fixture. ✉ *Reyndersstraat 24,* ☎ *03/233–6270. Reservations essential. Jacket and tie. AE, DC, MC, V. Closed weekends, last 3 wks in Aug., Dec. 25–Jan. 1.*

$$$ ✕ **De Matelote.** In a house on a narrow street, this tiny bi-level restaurant has a mezzanine that is reached by a winding staircase. Chef Didier Garnich turns out such delicious creations as langoustines in a light curry sauce, sea scallops cooked with a stock of mushrooms and sorrel, and grilled asparagus with fresh morels and poached egg. The crème brûlée is outstanding. Local gourmets consider this the best seafood restaurant in town. ⊠ *Haarstraat 9,* ☎ *03/231–3207. Reservations essential. AE, DC, MC, V. Closed Sun., July.*

$$ ✕ **Cirque Belge.** A replica of the Atomium, a facsimile of the *Manneken Pis,* portraits of famous Belgians, and paintings of national products from beer to Rizla papers: This is a nation's ironic revenge for decades of Belgian-bashing, a knowingly kitschy extravaganza that extends even to the well-executed, locally inspired cuisine and the huge range of beers. Try fish soup, rabbit in beer, or fried beef in shallots and marvel at this crash course in Belgitude. ⊠ *Ernest Van Dijckkaai 13–14,* ☎ *03/232–9439. No credit cards.*

$$ ✕ **Het Nieuwe Palinghuis.** An Antwerp landmark, it has dark wood, pottery, and a comfortable relaxed air. Its seafood specialties are well prepared and handsomely priced. The name means The New Eelhouse, and the sweet-fleshed fish, prepared in a variety of ways, are the house specialty, along with grilled turbot, grilled scallops, and sole in lobster sauce. ⊠ *St-Jansvliet 14,* ☎ *03/231–7445. AE, DC, MC, V. Closed Mon.–Tues. and June.*

$$ ✕ **Hungry Henrietta.** Father and son run this Antwerp institution next to Sint-Jacobskerk, the church where Rubens is buried. It's a stylish, spacious place and you can dine in the garden. Fillet of salmon with endive, quail salad, and leg of lamb are on the menu. ⊠ *St-Jacobsstraat 17,* ☎ *03/232–2928. AE, DC, MC, V. Closed weekends and Aug.*

$$ ✕ **In de Schaduw van de Kathedraal.** Cozier and more traditional than the wave of contemporary restaurants dominating the scene, it has a comfortable little dining room facing the cathedral square. In warm weather, you can dine on the terrace, in the shadow of the cathedral. Try the nutmeg-perfumed gratin of endive and crevettes grises, or steamed sole with scampi in fresh basil. ⊠ *Handschoenmarkt 17,* ☎ *03/232–4014. AE, DC, MC, V. Closed June–Sept., Tues.; Oct.–May, Mon.–Tues.*

$$ ✕ **Neuze Neuze.** Five tiny houses have been cobbled together to cre-
★   ate this handsome, split-level restaurant with plenty of nooks and crannies on different levels, whitewashed walls, dark brown beams, and a blazing fireplace. Warm smoked salmon with endive and a white beer sauce, scallops with rhubarb preserve, and goose liver meunière with caramelized pineapple are some of the dishes executed with flair. Service is excellent and the genial patron, Domien Sels, is ever-present. ⊠ *Wijngaardstraat 19,* ☎ *03/232–5783. AE, DC, MC, V. Closed Sat. lunch, Sun., 2 wks in July and 2 wks in Jan.*

$$ ✕ **Sir Anthony Van Dijck.** Once a top gourmet restaurant, this dining
★   spot now serves brasserie fare such as salad liègeoise, duck à l'orange, and tuna steak. The menu is changed every month. Under high, massive beams supported by stone pillars, diners sit surrounded by flowers and carved wood, at tables overlooking an interior courtyard. There are two seatings a night. ⊠ *Vlaeykensgang, Oude Koornmarkt 16,* ☎ *03/231–6170. AE, DC, MC, V. Closed Sun., Aug. 2–30.*

$ ✕ **Kiekekot.** Antwerp students satisfy their craving for spit-roasted chicken and fries at this no-frills "chicken coop," which offers a juicy, golden half-chicken for under BF200. ⊠ *Grote Markt 35,* ☎ *03/232–1502.* ⊙ *6 PM–4 AM (Fri.–Sat. till 6 AM, Sat.–Sun. from 12:30 PM). MC, V. Closed Tues.*

$ ✕ **'t Brantyser.** This old café, with dark rafters, brick, and stucco, on two open levels, offers more than just drinks and the usual snacks: The tavern fare is supplemented by a good range of salads and affordable specials. ⊠ *Hendrik Conscienceplein 7,* ☎ *03/233–1833. MC, V.*

$ ✕ **'t Hofke.** This restaurant is worth visiting for its location alone—it's in the Vlaeykensgang alley, where time seems to have stood still. The cozy dining room has the look and feel of a private home, and the menu includes a large selection of salads and omelettes, as well as more substantial fare. ⊠ *Vlaeykensgang, Oude Koornmarkt 16,* ☎ *03/ 233–8606. AE, MC, V. Closed Mon.*

$ ✕ **Zout'n'Peper.** Among the best of Antwerp's many trendy eateries, it has warm, African-influenced decor and jazz and funk music. The top-value fixed price menu offers a three-course meal with an aperitif and a generous carafe of wine. Tasty fish soup, grilled salmon, steak Diabolo, and excellent desserts are among the high points. ⊠ *Wijngaardstraat 5,* ☎ *03/231–7373. MC, V. No lunch. Closed Wed.*

$ ✕ **Zuiderterras.** A stark, glass-and-black-metal construction, this riverside café and restaurant was designed by avant-garde architect bOb (his spelling) Van Reeth during the city's stint as Cultural Capital of Europe in 1993. Here you can have a light meal and enjoy seeing the river traffic on one side and, on the other, a view of the cathedral and the Old Town. ⊠ *Ernest Van Dijckkaai 37,* ☎ *03/234–1275. Reservations not accepted. AE, MC, V.*

Lodging

For lodging price categories, *see* Lodging in Pleasures and Pastimes at the beginning of this chapter.

$$$$ ▦ **Antwerp Hilton.** Antwerp's newest luxury hotel, a five-story complex opened in 1993, incorporates the former fin de siècle Grand Bazaar department store and a gigantic ballroom seating 1,000. Rooms have mahogany doors, three telephones, safes, and executive desks. Afternoon tea is served in the marble-floored lobby, and lunch and dinner are offered in the Het Vijfde Seizoen restaurant. ⊠ *Groenplaats, B 2000,* ☎ *03/204–1212,* FAX *03/204–1213. 189 rooms, 18 suites. 2 restaurants, bar, no-smoking floors, sauna, health club, convention center, shops, parking (fee). AE, DC, MC, V.*

$$$ ▦ **Classic Hotel Villa Mozart.** This small, modern hotel in an old building is in a pedestrian zone next to the cathedral. The interior is modern, with the emphasis on business-class comforts: air-conditioning, electronic security. The rooms are slightly cramped—due, in part, to the generous beds—but many look out toward the cathedral. ⊠ *Handschoenmarkt 3–7, B 2000,* ☎ *03/231–3031,* FAX *03/231–5685. 25 rooms. Restaurant, bar. AE, DC, MC, V.*

$$$ ▦ **Firean.** This Art Deco gem, built in 1929, was restored in 1986, not
★ only to its original architectural style but also to the welcoming gracefulness of its era. It offers sweet relief to travelers numbed by the uniformity of chain hotels. Its location—a residential neighborhood south of the center but on the route into town from the Brussels expressway—reinforces the tranquillity inside, expressed by fresh flowers, rich fabrics, and a tasteful mix of antiques and reproductions. The service is that of a family-owned and -operated establishment. Breakfast eggs come in floral-print cozies, and jazz piano is discreetly piped into public areas. The rooms themselves are quiet sanctuaries. A tram to the Old Town stops outside the door. ⊠ *Karel Oomsstraat 6, B 2018,* ☎ *03/237–0260,* FAX *03/238–1168. 9 rooms, 6 in annex next door. Bar, breakfast room. AE, DC, MC, V. Closed last week of July, 1st ½ of Aug., Dec. 24–1st weekend after Jan. 6.*

$$ ▦ **Prinse.** Set well back from an Old Town street, this 400-year-old landmark with an interior courtyard opened as a hotel in 1990. It was once the home of 16th-century poet Anna Bijns. A member of the Re-

lais du Silence (Quiet Inns) group, the hotel has a modern look, with
black leather chairs, soft blue curtains, and tile bathrooms. Exposed
beams give top-floor rooms more character. ⊠ *Keizerstraat 63, B
2000,* ☎ *03/226–4050,* FAX *03/225–1148. 35 rooms. Breakfast room.
AE, DC, MC, V.*

$ ⊞ **Pension Cammerpoorte.** Owned by the managers of the nearby
Cammerpoorte Hotel, this small pension is run with considerable enthusiasm by its proud proprietor. Substantial breakfasts are served in
a tidy brick-and-lace café downstairs. The cheerful, sizeable rooms—
on landings reached by a narrow staircase—are full of bright pastels
and offer basic kitchen facilities; some can comfortably accommodate
a family of four. ⊠ *Steenhouwersvest 55, B 2000,* ☎ *03/231–2836,*
FAX *03/226–2968. 9 rooms with shower. Breakfast room. AE, DC,
MC, V.*

$ ⊞ **Rubenshof.** Once a cardinal's residence, this hotel shows remnants
of its former glory with a mixture of turn-of-the-century styles. The
hotel is owned by a friendly Dutch couple, and the location is close to
the Fine Arts Museum. ⊠ *Amerikalei 115-117, B 2000,* ☎ *03/237–
0789,* FAX *03/248–2594. 24 rooms, 3 with bath. Breakfast room, free
parking. AE, DC, MC, V.*

$ ⊞ **Scoutel.** This hotel, owned by the Boy Scouts and Girl Guides but
open to all ages, is in a modern building five minutes' walk from Central Station. The double and triple rooms are simple but adequate; all
have toilets and showers. Rates are lower for people under 25, and most
of the guests *are* young people. Breakfast and sheets are included;
towels can be rented. Guests are provided with front-door keys. ⊠
Stoomstraat 3, B 2000, ☎ *03/226–4606,* FAX *03/232–6392. 24 rooms
with shower. Breakfast room, 6 meeting rooms. No credit cards.*

Nightlife and the Arts

The Arts

Check *The Bulletin* (☞ Nightlife and the Arts *in* Brussels, *above*) for
details on arts events in Antwerp.

DANCE

Antwerp is home to a host of innovative and exciting ballet and dance
troupes, and its school is internationally renowned. The major ballet
company is the **Koninklijk Ballet van Vlaanderen** (Royal Flanders Ballet; ⊠ 't Eilandje, ☎ 03/234–3438), whose productions tour regularly
across the Benelux. The companies of other leading Belgian choreog-
raphers, including Anne Teresa De Keersmaeker, Wim Vandekeybus,
and Alain Platel, frequently perform at **deSingel** (⊠ Desguinlei 25, ☎
03/248–2424).

OPERA AND CONCERTS

The opera is **Koninklijke Vlaamse Opera** (Royal Flanders Opera; ⊠
Van Ertboornstraat 8, ☎ 03/233–6685), which has a sister company
in Gent. The **Koninklijk Philharmonisch Orkest van Vlaanderen** (Royal
Flanders Philharmonic) most frequently performs at **deSingel** (⊠ Desguinlei 25, ☎ 03/248–2424), the city's flagship cultural venue. Another venue for classical music is the **Koningin Elisabethzaal** (⊠
Koningin Astridplein 23, ☎ 03/233–8444). Visiting rock stars perform
at the **Sportpaleis** (⊠ Schijnpoortweg 113, ☎ 03/326–1010), although
Antwerp is inexplicably not on the regular gig circuit.

THEATER

The flagship of the more than two dozen theaters in Antwerp is the
Bourla Theater (⊠ Komedieplaats 18, ☎ 03/231–0750), a marvelously
restored 150-year-old theater, which is now the home of the **Koninklijke Nederlands Schouwburg** (Royal Dutch-speaking Theater). Two

other important theater venues are **deSingel** (⊠ Desguinlei 25, ☎ 03/248–2424) and **Monty** (⊠ Montignystraat 3–5). The **Poppenschouwburg Van Campen** (Van Campen Puppet Theater; ⊠ Lange Nieuwstraat 3, ☎ 03/237–3716) presents traditional puppet performances in Flemish dialect between September and May.

Nightlife

BARS

There are 2,500 taverns in Antwerp—one per 200 inhabitants. Many are in the Old Town. **Bar Tabac** (⊠ Waalse Kaai 43, ☎ no phone) is a studiously seedy mock-Gallic truckers' café. **Beveren** (⊠ Vlasmarkt 2, ☎ 03/231–2225) is boisterous and old-fashioned. The most famous bar is probably the **Bierhuis Kulminator** (⊠ Vleminckveld 32–34, ☎ 03/232–4538), which stocks, cools, and pours 550 different kinds of beer, including EKU-28, known as the strongest beer on earth; some of the beers are 30 years old. In **Blauwe Steen** (⊠ Ernest van Dijckkaai 34, ☎ 03/231–6710), you can listen to street musicians performing Antwerp music while you sip beer. **Kafe Marque** (⊠ Grote Pieter Potstraat 3, ☎ 233–2428) is a small, bright bar that stocks a bizarre range of American and Asian beers and has an unpretentious alternative/New Wave disco downstairs. In the riverfront Waalse Kaai district, try the laid-back, Mediterranean-inspired **Le Routier** (⊠ Waalse Kaai 33, ☎ 03/257—1599). **Pelgrom** (⊠ Pelgrimsstraat 15, ☎ 03/234–0809) is in a 16th-century tavern.

DANCE CLUBS

For mainstream sounds, try **Beach Club Antwerp** (⊠ Groenplaats 36, ☎ 03/227—0527). **Café d'Anvers** (⊠ Verversrui 15, ☎ 03/226–3870), in the red-light district, is the city's flagship house and techno venue, attracting ravers from across Europe to its friendly dance floors. **Café Local** (⊠ Waalse Kaai 25, ☎ 03/238–5004) in the trendy riverfront area south of the center, imaginatively recreates pre-Castro Cuba, although the music is uninspired chart dance. If you're prepared to venture south of the Waalse Kaai area, **Zillion** (⊠ Jan van Gentstraat 4, ☎ 03/248–1516), is the biggest, flashiest nightclub in town.

GAY BARS

The clubbing capital of Belgium, Antwerp has a more upfront gay scene than most Belgian cities; Van Schoonhovenstraat, near the Centraal Station, is clustered with gay bars, and there are plenty dotted around the city center. Start at the **Gay and Lesbian Centre** (⊠ Dambruggestraat 204, ☎ 03/233–1071), which offers a "gay map" of Antwerp detailing clubs, bars, restaurants, saunas, and clinics. For lesbians, there are **Lady's Pub** (⊠ Waalse Kaai 56, ☎ 03/238–5490) and **Shakespeare** (⊠ Oude Koornmarkt 24, ☎ 03/231–5058). **'t Catshuis** (⊠ Grote Pieter Potstraat 18, ☎ 03/234–0369) is one of the newer hangouts for gay men.

JAZZ CLUBS

There isn't live music every night in these clubs, so check beforehand. Try **De Hopper** (⊠ Leopold De Waelstraat 2, ☎ 03/248–4933), which offers music occasionally and in a rather formal environment; **deSingel** (⊠ Desguinlei 25; ☎ 03/248–2424), or **Swingcafé** (⊠ Suikerrui 13, ☎ 03/233–1478).

Outdoor Activities and Sports

Golf

The **Brasschaat Open Golf Club Center** (⊠ Miksebaan 248, Brasschaat, ☎ 03/653–1084), 15 km (9 mi) from the city center.

Skating

The most popular skating rink is **Antarctica** (⊠ Moerelei 119, Wilrijk, ☎ 03/828–9928).

Tennis

The eight courts at **Het Rooi** (⊠ Berchemstadionstraat 73, ☎ 03/239–6610) are each available for BF170 per hour. Rates at **Beerschot** (⊠ Stadionstraat, ☎ 03/248–7189) are BF300 an hour each for the 10 outdoor and 4 indoor courts.

Shopping

That Antwerp is a young, style-conscious city is reflected in the city's smart, trendy shops and boutiques. Dedicated followers of fashion regard Antwerp as a trend-setter second only to Milan. Credit for this development goes to the so-called Antwerp Six and in equal measure to the remarkable designer who trained them, Linda Loppa. Ready-to-wear by Ann Demeulemeester, Dirk Bikkembergs, Dries Van Noten, and others command high prices in Antwerp, but in the shopping area just south of Groenplaats, prices are less astronomical.

Shopping Streets

The elegant **Meir,** together with its extension to the east, **De Keyserlei,** and at the opposite end, **Huidevettersstraat,** is where you will find high-street standbys and long-established names. Shopping galleries branch off from all three streets—**Century Center** and **Antwerp Tower** from De Keyserlei, **Patio** from Meir, and **Nieuwe Gaanderij** from Huidevettersstraat.

Many boutiques cater to more avant-garde tastes. The best-known area is **De Wilde Zee,** consisting of Groendalstraat, Lombardenstraat, Wiegstraat, and Korte Gasthuisstraat; the nearby Scuttershofstraat is currently in vogue. Another pedestrian area for general shopping is **Hoogstraat,** between Grote Markt and Sint-Jansvliet, with its appendix, **Grote Pieter Potstraat.** Here you find good secondhand bookshops and all kinds of bric-a-brac.

Street Markets

There's an antiques market on **Lijnwaadmarkt** (Easter–Oct., Sat. 9–5), just north of the cathedral. The **Rubensmarkt** (Rubens Market, Aug. 15 annually) is held on the Grote Markt, with vendors in 17th-century costumes hawking everything under the sun. Antwerp's most popular and animated market is **Vogelmarkt** (the bird market, Sun. 9–1). Public auction sales of furniture and other secondhand goods are held on **Vrijdagmarkt** (Wed. and Fri. 9–noon). On Oudevaartplaats (a block south from Rubenshuis on Wapper), the **market** also includes flowers and plants, fruit and vegetables, and lots of pets.

Specialty Stores

CLOTHING

The success of the Antwerp Six in the early '90s put Belgium on the fashion map, and Antwerp in particular is a haven for cutting-edge women's and men's ready-to-wear fashions. Ann Demeulemeester, Martin Margiela (the so-called seventh member of the Antwerp Six, who now works for Hermès), and rising star Raf Simons are represented at **Louis** (⊠ Lombardenstraat 2, ☎ 03/232–9872). Other leading fashion boutiques are Dries Van Noten's magnificent **Modepaleis** (⊠ Nationalestraat 16, ☎ 03/233–9437) and **Closing Date** (⊠ Korte Gasthuisstraat 15, ☎ 03/232–8722). At press time, Van Noten had been given planning permission for a new fashion center in an old station building in the Zuid district.

DIAMONDS

Diamonds are tax-free and available at good prices to both individual customers and the many dealers who come to Antwerp for them. (Note: Tax-free does not mean duty-free when you return home.) If you are not an expert, you can rely on the advice given by the staff at **Diamondland** (⊠ Appelmansstraat 33A, ☎ 03/234–3612). The quality of the stones is guaranteed by a Diamond High Council certificate.

Antwerp A to Z

Arriving and Departing

BY CAR

Antwerp is surrounded by a ring road from which expressways shoot off like spokes in a wheel. The city is 48 km (29 mi) north of Brussels on the E19; 60 km (36 mi) northwest of Gent on the E17; 119 km (71 mi) northwest of Liège on the A13.

BY PLANE

Deurne Airport (☎ 03/218–1211), 5½ km (3 mi) southeast of the city center, has several flights a day from London. **Brussels National Airport** (Zaventem) is linked with Antwerp by frequent bus service (hourly 7 AM–11 PM). The trip takes 50 minutes.

BY TRAIN

Four to five trains an hour link Antwerp with Brussels; the trip takes about 45 minutes. The train ride north to Rotterdam takes an hour. **International Thalys trains** between Paris and Amsterdam stop at Berchem Station south of the city center rather than entering the downtown Centraal Station (⊠ Koningin Astridplein, ☎ 03/204–2040).

Getting Around

BY BUS

De Lijn bus lines mostly begin outside Central Station in the Koningin Astridplein. Longer-distance buses start from the Franklin Rooseveltplaats.

BY TAXI

There are **taxi stands** in front of Central Station and at other principal points. It is often easier to call for one: **Antwerp Taxi** (☎ 03/238–3838) or **Metropole Taxi** (☎ 03/231–3131).

BY TRAM AND SUBWAY

You can travel by tram all over central Antwerp. Some operate underground as the pre-Metro system. The **most useful subway line** for visitors links Central Station (Metro: Diamant) with the left bank via the Groenplaats (for the cathedral and Grote Markt). A BF40 ticket is good for one hour on all forms of public transport; BF105 buys unlimited travel for one day. Tickets are available at De Lijn offices, the tourist office, and at the Diamant, Opera/Frankrijklei, and Groenplaats Metro stops.

Contacts and Resources

B&B RESERVATION AGENCIES

The **City Tourist Office** (⊠ Grote Markt 15, ☎ 03/232–0103, FAX 03/231–1937) has a list of the 20 best bed-and-breakfast accommodations, complete with photographs.

CAR RENTALS

Avis (⊠ Plantin en Moretuslei 62, ☎ 03/218–9496). **Budget** (⊠ Ankerrui 20, ☎ 03/232–3500). **Hertz** (⊠ Deurne Airport, ☎ 03/233–2992).

EMERGENCIES

Police (☎ 101). **Ambulance** (☎ 100). **Emergency Rooms:** Middelheim (⊠ Lindendreef 1, ☎ 03/280–3111); Stuivenberg (⊠ Lange

Beeldekensstraat 267, ☎ 03/217–7111). The name of the **pharmacy**
on night and weekend duty is displayed in all pharmacy windows.

GUIDED TOURS

Flandria (☎ 03/231–3100) operates 90-minute boat trips (🎫 BF250)
on the river Scheldt, departing from the Steenplein pontoon, next to
the Steen (May–Sept., Tues. and Thurs.–Sun. 1 and 2:30; Oct., weekends 1 and 2:30). The company also offers boat tours of the port (2½
hours, 🎫 BF 400), which leave from Quay 13 near Londonstraat, (May–
Aug., Tues. and Thurs.–Sun. 2:30; 2nd ½ of Apr. and Sept.–Oct.,
weekends 2:30.

Touristram (☎ 03/480–9388) operates 50-minute tram tours with
cassette commentary in the Old Town and old harbor area. Tickets (🎫
BF125) are sold on the tram. Departure is from Groenplaats (Apr.–
Dec., daily, every hour on the hour, 11–5; Feb.–Mar., weekends 11–5).

Qualified **personal guides** are available through the City Tourist Office (☞ Visitor Information, *below*), which requires two days' notice.
The rates are BF1,500 for two hours and BF750 for each additional
hour.

TRAVEL AGENCIES

Huybrechts (✉ Carnotstraat 39–41, ☎ 03/231–9900). **VTB** (✉ St-
Jacobsmarkt 45, ☎ 03/220–3232).

VISITOR INFORMATION

The **Toerisme Stad Antwerpen** (Antwerp City Tourist Office; ✉ Grote
Markt 15, ☎ 03/232–0103, FAX 03/231–1937) will assist with hotel
reservations. The **Toeristische Federatie Provincie Antwerpen** (Antwerp
Provincial Tourist Office; ✉ Karel Oomsstraat 11, ☎ 03/216–2810)
will help plan trips throughout the province.

NORTHEAST BELGIUM

The northeast quarter of Belgium, composed of the provinces of
Antwerp and Limburg, is not so frequently visited by travelers from
abroad but is much loved by Belgians. It stretches from the sandy moors
of Kempen (La Campine to French-speakers) in the north to the fer-
tile plains of Haspengouw (La Hesbaye), with its prosperous-looking
farms, orchards, and undulating fields. On the east, it borders the narrow Dutch corridor stretching south to Maastricht.

Until fairly recently, Limburg's economy was linked to its coalfields.
Today the explosive growth of small businesses has restored the
province to a degree of prosperity. The economy also benefits from the
Albert Canal, which leaves the Meuse just north of Liège to follow a
course parallel to the river and then veers off across the country to carry
the heavy Liège traffic to Antwerp. Thanks to the canal, Genk is a center for the automotive and petrochemical industries. In spite of the presence of industry both light and heavy, this is a green and pleasant land.

*Numbers in the margin correspond to points of interest on the North-
east Belgium map.*

Kalmthout

🔟 *18 km (11 mi) north of Antwerp on N11/N122 via Kapellen.*

The **Kalmthoutse Heide** (heath) is a vast area of pines, sand dunes, and
ponds, with flourishing bird life. The heath is crossed by marked paths.
The **Arboretum** contains more than 6,000 trees in a 25-acre park,
where you can wander freely across the lawns. It's a peaceful oasis with

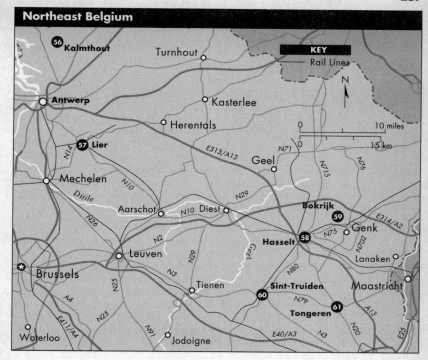

Northeast Belgium

a varied range of colors every season, the presence of wildflowers providing a special accent. ✉ *Heuvel 2,* ☎ *03/666–6741.* ⌑ *BF150.* ◷ *Mar. 15–Nov. 15, daily 10–5.*

Lier

★ ⑤⑦ *17 km (10 mi) southeast of Antwerp on N10, 45 km (27 mi) northeast of Brussels on E19/N14 via Mechelen.*

The small town of Lier may seem a sleepy riverside settlement, but it has long attracted poets and painters and has even known its moment of glory. It was here in 1496 that Philip the Handsome of Burgundy married Joanna the Mad of Aragon and Castile, daughter of King Ferdinand and Queen Isabella of Spain. From that union sprang Emperor Charles V and his brother and successor as Holy Roman Emperor, the equally remarkable Ferdinand I of Austria.

The **Sint-Gummaruskerk** (St. Gommaire's Church), where Philip and Joanna were wed, is yet another product of the De Waghemakere–Keldermans partnership, which worked so well in building the cathedral in Antwerp. It is well endowed with stained-glass windows from the 15th and 16th centuries. Those in the choir were the gift of Maximilian of Austria (father of Philip the Handsome), who visited in 1516 and is depicted in one of the windows, along with his wife, Mary of Burgundy. ✉ *Follow Rechtestraat to Kerkstraat.*

The Kleine Nete flows straight through the heart of town; the Grote Nete and a canal encircle the center. Along the riverside, willows bend over the water. Across the river stands the **Zimmertoren,** a 14th-century tower renamed for Louis Zimmer, who designed its astronomical clock with 11 faces in 1930. His studio, where 57 dials show the movements of the moon, the tides, the zodiac, and other cosmic

phenomena, is inside the tower. ⊠ *Zimmerplein 18,* ☎ *03/491–1395.*
🖃 *BF50.* ⊘ *Apr.–Oct. daily 9–noon and 1–6; Nov.–Mar., daily 9–
noon and 1–5.*

NEED A
BREAK?

Van Ouytsels Koffiehoekje (⊠ Rechtestraat 27, ☎ 03/480–2917) still
roasts its own coffee. Don't pass up the delicious syrup-filled biscuits,
Lierse Vlaaikens, which are the local specialty.

The **Begijnhof** (Béguinage) differs from most other Beguine communities in that its small houses line narrow streets rather than being
grouped around a common. A Renaissance portico stands at the entrance, and on it a statue of St. Begge, who gave his name to this congregation and who probably derived his own from the fact that he was
un begue (a stammerer). Beguines were members of ascetic or phi-
lanthropic communities of women, not under vows, founded in the
Netherlands in the 13th century. ⊠ *Begijnhofstraat.*

Dining

$$ ✕ **'t Suyckeren Schip.** Just across from the church, this restaurant of-
fers *cuisine bourgeoise* (French country): steaks with a variety of
sauces, and five different preparations of sole. The setting has an in-
formal, comfortable, brick-and-beams look. Sunday crowds come after
church. ⊠ *Rechtestraat 49,* ☎ *03/489–0140. AE, DC, MC, V.*

$–$$ ✕ **De Fortuin.** At this romantic restaurant and tavern, the tavern is less
expensive. Shrimp croquettes are a specialty, and the service is friendly.
In summer you can eat on the terrace overlooking the river. ⊠ *Felix
Timmermansplein 7,* ☎ *03/480–2951. AE, DC, MC, V. Closed Mon.*

Hasselt

⑤⑧ *77 km (46 mi) southeast of Antwerp, 82 km (49 mi) east of Brussels,
42 km (25 mi) northwest of Liège.*

Limburg has the youngest population in Belgium, and it is the province
where the rate of development is fastest. This is particularly noticeable
in Hasselt, a town with busy shopping streets, innovative museums,
and lively music. Its cathedral has the most striking gargoyles in Belgium.

The **Nationaal Jenevermuseum** perpetuates Hasselt's slightly raffish
distinction of having had gin distilling as its major industry. The museum dates from 1803 and is one of the country's oldest surviving distilleries. *Jenever* means "gin" in Dutch, and a tour of the installations,
which include changing exhibits such as vintage gin advertisement
posters, ends at the paneled tasting room. You can taste gin of various ages, flavors, and proofs from two dozen Belgian distilleries. ⊠
Witte Nonnenstraat 19, ☎ *011/241144.* 🖃 *BF90.* ⊘ *Tues.–Fri. 10–
5, weekends 2–6.*

The **Stadsmuseum Stellingwerf-Waerdenhof** (Municipal Museum) is
a strikingly modern space with white walls, red balconies, and large
mirrors, installed in two beautifully converted mansions. Its collection
consists of dramatically arranged Art Nouveau ceramics, church silverware (including the world's oldest monstrance, from 1286), and exhibits illustrating the history of the region. ⊠ *Maastrichterstraat 85,*
☎ *011/241070.* 🖃 *BF90.* ⊘ *Tues.–Fri. 10–5, weekends 2–6.*

The third of Hasselt's unusual museums is the **Modemuseum** (Fashion
Museum), in a 17th-century hospital building. The collection illustrates
the development of fashion trends over the past two centuries. Today's
fashion photographers, stylists, and designers of accessories are also

represented. ⊠ *Gasthuisstraat 11,* ☎ *011/239621.* 🖂 *BF90.* ☉ *Tues.–Fri. 10–5, weekends 2–6.*

NEED A BREAK? **'t Stokerijke** (⊠ Hemelrijk 3) is the place to continue your education in Dutch gin—the owner is an expert. This is a convivial and attractive place, just behind the cathedral.

The **Japanse Tuin** (Japanese Garden) is an exquisite gift from the Japanese city of Itami, Hasselt's twin city. The 6-acre park is one of great beauty and subtlety, with rocks, ponds, cherry trees, and 1,000 irises. There's also a Japanese teahouse. ⊠ *Gouverneur Verwilghensingel (on the ring),* ☎ *011/235200.* 🖂 *BF100.* ☉ *Apr.–Oct., Tues.–Fri. 10–5, weekends 2–6.*

★ 59 The **Bokrijk** is arguably the best and certainly the largest (1,360 acres) open-air museum and nature reserve in Europe. The museum, over 90 acres in size, has more than 100 carefully restored buildings forming four small villages. There's also a small 16th-century urban area. The farm buildings have been transplanted from Limburg and other Flemish provinces. Each building has its own custodian, many of whom are gold mines of local folklore. The interiors are filled with old peasant furniture and utensils. There's a chapel, a windmill, a forge, and an inn, where you can enjoy traditional fare—spicy sausages, smoked ham, rich cheeses, and red Rodenbach beer. A full complement of artisans work in original costumes. In the large playground are a children's village, chutes, pony rides, and other attractions. The sports center has tennis courts, miniature golf, and a soccer field. The nature reserve shows the unspoiled Kempen country of heather and pine, sand and broom, with marshes and ponds frequented by waterfowl. ⊠ *Domein Bokrijk, 6 km (4 mi) northeast of Hasselt, near Genk,* ☎ *011/224575.* 🖂 *Open-air museum BF250 (Apr.–June and Sept., Sun. and holidays; July–Aug., daily), when 33 farmsteads are open and at least 10 craftsmen are on duty; BF200 on "green days" (Apr.–June and Sept., Mon.–Sat.), when 22 farmsteads are open and at least 5 craftsmen are on duty; BF100 on "blue days" (Oct., daily), when just a few cottages are open. Nature reserve free.* ☉ *Museum Apr.–Oct., daily 10–sunset; cottages close at 6 (5 in Oct.).*

Dining and Lodging

$ ✕ **De Egge.** This charming restaurant offers the best efforts of a young couple who believe in their excellent taste: The decor is pretty and discreet, with whitewashed brick and café curtains, and the cooking is imaginative and beautifully executed. Try monkfish on a bed of leeks, or goat cheese brushed with honey and fresh thyme and served hot on a bed of julienne of apple, endive, and *mâche* (lamb's lettuce). ⊠ *Walputstraat 23,* ☎ *011/224951. AE, DC, MC, V. Closed Wed.*

$ ✕ **Majestic.** This big tavern on the Grote Markt with leaded glass, high ceilings, and a grand, historic feel draws locals for drinks, cards, snacks, and light meals such as sandwiches, trout, steak, or an inexpensive menu of the day. ⊠ *Grote Markt,* ☎ *011/223330. AE, DC, MC, V.*

$$$$ ✕🖾 **Scholteshof.** Owner-chef Roger Souvereyns created a mecca for ★ many a Belgian and foreign gourmet on his 18th-century farm 7 km (4 mi) west of Hasselt. He keeps adding new touches, such as a beautiful fountain in the interior courtyard, where you can enjoy cocktails. There's also a sculpture-filled English garden and an extensive herb garden. A meal in the candlelit dining room is a romantic and relaxing experience; the imaginative menu includes pumpkin soup with langoustines, carpaccio with a ball of caviar on green tomato jelly, sweetbreads roasted with rosemary, and grilled turbot with rhubarb mousse.

Eating here may be a once-in-a-lifetime experience: The checks are staggeringly high. Rooms are spacious and furnished with magnificent antiques. ⊠ *Kermtstraat 130, B 3512 Stevoort,* ☎ *011/250202,* FAX *011/254328. 11 rooms, 7 suites. Reservations essential. Jacket and tie. AE, DC, MC, V. Closed Wed., 2 wks in Jan., 2 wks in July.*

$$ ✗🍽 **Holiday Inn Hasselt.** Completed in 1990, this has become Hasselt's hotel of choice. Centrally located, it has been built to the chain's global standards. The design is post–Art Deco and the house color a light oyster gray. ⊠ *Kattegatstraat 1, B 3500,* ☎ *011/242200,* FAX *011/223935. 107 rooms. Restaurant, bar, pool. AE, DC, MC, V.*

Outdoor Activities and Sports
GOLF

There are excellent facilities at the **Vlaams-Japanese Golf & Business Club** (⊠ Vissenbroekstraat 15, ☎ 011/263482). Although the 18-hole course is for members only, the nine-hole training course is open to the public.

Sint-Truiden

⑥ *17 km (10 mi) southwest of Hasselt, 94 km (56 mi) southeast of Antwerp, 63 km (38 mi) east of Brussels, 35 km (21 mi) northwest of Liège.*

All around Sint-Truiden (St-Trond in French, St. Trudo in English) thousands upon thousands of trees are in bloom in the spring, for this is the center of Haspengouw, Flanders's fruit-growing district. The town developed around the abbey founded by St. Trudo in the 7th century. The **Begijnhof,** dating from 1258, has a well-restored church, from the end of the 13th century. It is now the **Provinciaal Museum voor Religieuze Kunst** (Provincial Museum of Religious Art) and is known for its 38 frescoes, executed over four centuries. ⊠ *Begijnhof, off Speelhoflaan,* ☎ *011/691188.* 🎟 *Free.* ☾ *Apr.–Oct., Tues.–Fri. 10–noon and 1:30–5, weekends 1:30–5.*

At the **Festraets Studio,** also in the Begijnhof, you can see the astronomical compensation clock, constructed by Camille Festraets out of 20,000 mechanical parts. It is more than 6 ft tall and weighs more than 4 tons. ⊠ *Begijnhof 24,* ☎ *011/688752.* 🎟 *BF60.* ☾ *Visits Apr.–Oct., Tues.–Sun. at 1:45, 2:45, 3:45, and 4:45.*

Lace-making has been revived in Sint-Truiden over the past few decades with a great deal of originality. The results can be seen at the **Kantmuseum** (Lace Museum) in the school of the Ursuline Sisters. ⊠ *Naamsestraat 5,* ☎ *011/682356.* 🎟 *BF30.* ☾ *Sun. and holidays 2–5.*

Sint-Gangulfskerk (St. Gangulphe's Church) is worth the small detour. One of the few remaining Romanesque basilicas from the 11th century, it has been carefully restored. ⊠ *Diesterstraat.*

The **Sint-Leonarduskerk** (St. Leonard's Church) in Zoutleeuw, west of Sint-Truiden, dates from the 13th century and seems out of proportion to the town's current size. The church's great treasure is a tall paschal candlestick incorporating a Crucifixion scene, made by Renier van Thienen in 1453 and considered one of the finest brasswork pieces in Belgium. ⊠ *12 km (7mi) northwest of St-Truiden; take N3 and turn right after 8 km (5mi).* ☾ *Easter–Sept., Mon.–Sat. 9:30–noon and 1:30–6, Sun. 1:30–5; Oct.–Easter, Sun. 1:30–4.*

Dining
$$$ ✗ **De Fakkels.** The ambitious restaurant offers well-executed French cooking: *pot-au-feu de St-Pierre aux raviolis de langoustines* (stew with lobster ravioli) or sweetbreads on a bed of zucchini and mushrooms. The setting is a romantically decorated 1930s house with fabric-

covered walls in cream tones. ⊠ *Stationstraat 33,* ☎ *011/687634. AE, DC, MC, V. No dinner Sun. Closed Mon., last wk of Jan., 2nd ½ of Aug.*

$ ✕ **Century.** A classic old tavern/restaurant on the Grote Markt, with oak, green-velvet banquettes, and great windows framing the market scene, this simple spot is as comfortable for a drink as for a meal. Typical "snacks" include half a roasted chicken with fries and salad, omelettes, steaks, sole, and sandwiches. ⊠ *Grote Markt 5,* ☎ *011/ 688341. AE, DC, MC, V.*

Tongeren

⓺₁ *20 km (12 mi) east of Sint-Truiden, 20 km (12 mi) southeast of Hasselt, 87 km (52 mi) east of Brussels, 19 km (11 mi) northwest of Liège.*

Tongeren (Tongres in French) started life as a Roman army encampment. It is one of Belgium's two oldest cities (the other being Tournai), and is visibly proud of the fact. This is where Ambiorix scored a famous but short-lived victory over Julius Caesar's legions in 54 BC. The Roman city was considerably larger than the present one; over the centuries, it was repeatedly sacked and burned. By the end of the 13th century, the city had retreated within its present limits and enjoyed the occasionally burdensome protection of the prince bishops of Liège. The Moerenpoort gate and sections of the ramparts remain from that period.

★ The elaborate **Onze-Lieve-Vrouwebasiliek** (Basilica of Our Lady) is one of the most beautiful medieval monuments in the world. The original church was built on Roman foundations in the 4th century and was the first stone cathedral north of the Alps. After it was destroyed during a siege in 1213, construction of the Basilica began, taking three centuries to complete. The 12th-century Romanesque cloister of the original church is still intact. The Chapter House contains the Treasury, also known as the **Basilica Museum Tongeren.** This is the richest collection of religious art in the country, including a 6th-century ivory diptych of St. Paul, a Merovingian gold buckle from the same century, and a truly magnificent head of Christ sculpted in wood in the 11th century. The central nave, up to the pulpit, the choir, and the south transept, dates from 1240. The candlesticks and lectern, from 1372, are the work of Jehan de Dinant, one of the outstanding artists of metalworking who flourished in the cities of the Meuse valley. The basilica has excellent acoustics and is often used for symphony concerts. ⊠ *Grote Markt. Basilica Museum:* ☎ *012/390255.* ⊡ *BF80.* ⊙ *May–Sept., Mon. 1:30–5, Tues.–Sun. 10–noon and 1:30–5; Oct.– Apr., by appointment.*

NEED A BREAK? **De Pelgrim** (⊠ Brouwerstraat 9) is a charming old-fashioned tavern, open late, that serves light and simple meals such as *omelette paysanne* (country omelette) and cheese croquettes.

Gallo-Romeins Museum (Gallo-Roman Museum) is a breath of fresh air in the museum world, as different from dusty collections of ancient bric-a-brac as you can imagine. Opened in 1994, it displays objects in the same way they were found, allowing visitors to discover them in much the same way as they were discovered by archaeologists. The subterranean amphitheater uses visual and sound effects conceived by Stijn Coninx (director of the cult film *Daens*). The symbol of the exposition is a 12-facet ball—several such objects have been found, and nobody knows what they represent or were used for. There's also an audiovisual space and a cafeteria. ⊠ *Kielenstraat 15,* ☎ *012/233914.* ⊡ *BF200.* ⊙ *Mon. noon–5; Tues.–Fri. 9–5, weekends 10–6.*

Dining and Lodging

$$$$ ✕ **Clos St. Denis.** This enormous 17th-century farmhouse with at-
★   tached barns is an elegant country inn, and one of Belgium's top
restaurants. Chef Christian Denis serves extravagant fare: lobster
tartare with chives; gratin of oysters in champagne and caviar; ravioli
of *foie d'oie* (goose liver) in truffle cream. There's choucroute with suck-
ling pig and mustard as well. Four dining rooms outdo each other for
period luxury—burnished parquet, Persian runners, chinoiserie. ✉
Grimmertingenstraat 24, Vliermaal-Kortessem, ☎ *012/236096. Reservations essential. AE, DC, MC, V.*

$$ 🏨 **Ambiotel.** This cozy hotel in the historic center of Tongeren is right
next to the cathedral. The beige-painted rooms are small and functional.
Toilets are communal. ✉ *Vleemarkt 2, B 3700,* ☎ *012/262590,* FAX
*012/261542. 22 rooms with bath or shower. AE, DC, MC, V. Restau-
rant, bar, meeting room, garden, free parking.*

Northeast Belgium A to Z

Arriving and Departing

BY CAR

Lier is a short drive from Antwerp on the N10 or from Brussels on the
E19/N14 via Mechelen. **Hasselt** is a straight drive, almost as the crow
flies, from Antwerp on the A13/E313 motorway (which continues to
Liège); from Brussels, take the E40/A2 via Leuven to Exit 26, then the
E313 for the last few miles. **Sint-Truiden** is reached from Hasselt on
the N80 and **Tongeren** on the N20 (they are linked by the N79); from
Brussels take the E40 to Exit 25 for the N3 to Sint-Truiden, to Exit 29
for the N69 to Tongeren.

BY TRAIN

There are hourly trains from Antwerp to Lier (15 minutes), Hasselt (1
hour, 5 minutes), and Tongeren (1 hour, 40 minutes). There is also an
hourly train from Brussels (Midi, Centrale, and Nord) taking 55 min-
utes to Sint-Truiden, 1 hour and 10 minutes to Hasselt.

Getting Around

If you're not driving, consider the humble bike. Hasselt, Sint-Truiden,
and Tongeren are equidistant from one another, each leg of the trian-
gle about 20 km (12 mi). Local tourist offices can supply maps and in-
formation on bicycle trails. Two of the most popular trails are the
Trudofietsroute, 54 km (32 mi) long, based on the travels of St. Trudo,
and the Tongria route in Tongeren, 45 km (27 mi) long.

Contacts and Resources

EMERGENCIES

Police: ☎ 101. **Ambulance:** ☎ 100. The address of the on-duty **late-
night pharmacy** is posted in all pharmacy windows.

GUIDED TOURS

At Lanaken, near the Dutch border east of Hasselt, you can rent a **horse
and wagon** through the local tourist office (☎ 089/722467) and set
off for a one-day excursion along a route mapped out for you, from
May through October.

The Lanaken tourist office also takes bookings for a wide variety of
boat trips on the Meuse and the South-Willems and Albert canals.
Stiphout Boat Trips (☎ 089/722467 runs a candle-light dinner cruise
(🎫 BF190–BF1,490; ☉ Apr.–mid-Sept.).

OUTDOOR ACTIVITIES AND SPORTS

For general information on sports facilities and opportunities, contact
the **Sportdienst** (✉ Universiteitslaan 1, Hasselt, ☎ 011/237250).

VISITOR INFORMATION
Provincial Tourist Office, **Limburg** (✉ Universiteitslaan 1, Hasselt, ☎ 011/237450). City Tourist Offices: **Hasselt** (✉ Lombaardstraat 3, ☎ 011/239540); **Sint-Truiden** (✉ Grote Markt 68, ☎ 011/701818); **Ton-geren** (✉ Stadhuisplein 9, ☎ 012/390255).

WALLONIA: FROM THE MEUSE TO THE ARDENNES

Rushing streams between steep rocks, high moorland and dense forests, feudal mountaintop castles and hamlets with cottages of rough-hewn stone, Romanesque churches and prosperous fortified farms, rustic inns serving trout from the rivers and wild boar from the woods: This is Wallonia, an amazing variety of scenic and historic treasures combined with the pleasures of good food and wine served in atmospheric surroundings.

Wallonia, the southern part of Belgium, consists, west to east, of the provinces of Hainaut, Namur, and Liège and, to the southeast, Belgian Luxembourg. While the northern part of the country is flat, Wallonia is hilly, even mountainous, attracting nature-lovers who enjoy walking, biking, and canoeing. Southerners all speak French; one in three also understands Walloon, a dialect descended from demotic Latin. The linguistic frontier corresponds roughly to the northern boundary of the Roman empire, and "Walas" was the name given to the Romanized Celts of the region. Today, the economy of rust-belt Wallonia has been overtaken by that of hi-tech Flanders. The coal mines are a thing of the past, and the steel industry is fighting a tenacious battle to remain competitive. The Walloons are highly conscious of their culture and linguistic heritage and take pride in their separate identity within the framework of the nation.

Eating in the Ardennes is one of the most straightforward pleasures Belgium has to offer. The territory is chockablock with atmospheric gray-stone inns. The cuisine is redolent of forest and farm, with ham, sausage, trout, and game to the fore. The region's charcuterie is among the best in central Europe. Ardennes sausage, neat and plump, is made with a blend of veal and pork and is smoked over smoldering oak; its flavor is a wholesome compromise between simple American summer sausage and the milder Italian salamis. The real charcuterie star is *jambon d'Ardennes,* ham that is salt-cured and delicately smoked so that its meat—as succulent as its Parma and Westphalian competitors—slices up thin, moist, and tender, more like a superior roast beef than ham. Restaurants offer generous platters of it, garnished with crisp little gherkins and pickled onions or, if you're lucky, a savory onion marmalade. Trout makes a slightly lighter meal, though once poached in a pool of butter and heaped with toasted almonds, it may be as rich as red-meat alternatives. One pleasant low-fat alternative, though not always available, is *truite au bleu* (blue trout). Plunged freshly killed into a boiling vinegar stock, the trout turns steely blue and retains its delicate flavor.

Hotel rooms in this region tend to be low-priced, even if there's an outstanding restaurant downstairs. They usually fill up on weekends and during high season, June through August. If you prefer to eat somewhere other than in the hotel you've booked, clear it with the management: You're often expected (and sometimes obliged) to eat in their restaurant. Many hotels offer *demi-pension* (half-board) arrangements, as well as "gastronomic weekends," which include two or three lavish meals with two nights' lodging. Also available, and especially popular with families, are a wide variety of farmhouse accommodations and B&Bs.

To acquire the Wallonia habit, start by leaving the highway, stopping off in a city, or driving around the countryside—and arriving at your final destination a few hours or a couple of days late! Wallonia is at its best April through June and September through October. The Ardennes are very popular with Belgian and Dutch vacationers, especially during the school holiday season.

The Outdoors

This is one of the great attractions of Wallonia. Hiking on the high moors is an undemanding activity that attracts even the most sedentary. You need to be in somewhat better shape to shoot the rapids in a kayak, but you can pick your river in accordance with skill and the number of watery thrills and spills you think you can handle. Mountain bikes are readily available for hire, and in winter there's generally enough snow for a handful of ski lifts to stay open for a few hopeful weeks. Even from a car, you can discover the real Wallonia along rural routes. You crest a hill, and there's an unexpected vista of miles and miles of woods and lakes and fields; you turn a corner and find yourself in a village where every house has slate walls and roof. You roll down the window and the fresh air is so incredible you have to stop.

Numbers in the margin correspond to numbers on the Meuse and the Ardennes map.

The Meuse Valley

The Meuse River comes rushing out of France, foaming through narrow ravines. In Dinant it is joined by the Lesse and flows, serene and beautiful, toward Namur, watched over by ancient citadels. At Namur comes the confluence with the Sambre, tainted from its exposure to the industries of Charleroi. Here, the river becomes broad and powerful, and gradually the pleasure craft are replaced by an endless procession of tugboats and barges, before the Meuse reaches the sea in Holland under a different name, the Maas.

From the name of the river is derived the adjective "Mosan," used to describe an indigenous style of metalworking of extraordinary plasticity. It reached its finest flowering during the 12th and 13th centuries with masters such as Renier de Huy, Nicolas de Verdun, and Hugo d'Oignies. They worked with brass, copper, and silver to achieve artistic levels equal to those of the Flemish painters two centuries later.

Roman legions commanded by Julius Caesar marched up the Meuse valley 2,000 years ago and made it one of the principal routes to Cologne. Later, it served a similar purpose for Charlemagne, linking his Frankish and German lands. Little wonder that massive forts were built on the rocks dominating the invasion routes. Even so, the French came through here under Louis XIV and again under Napoléon. The Dutch, who ruled here for little more than a decade after Waterloo, expanded these fortifications. A century later, the Germans broke through here, pushing west and south in World Wars I and II.

Han-sur-Lesse

 123 km (74 mi) southeast of Brussels, 64 km (38 mi) southeast of Namur, 77 km (46 mi) southwest of Liège.

Han-sur-Lesse owes its fame to the magnificent **Grottes de Han** (Han Caves), which were rediscovered in the mid-19th century. The caves had provided refuge for threatened tribes since neolithic times. To

The Meuse and the Ardennes

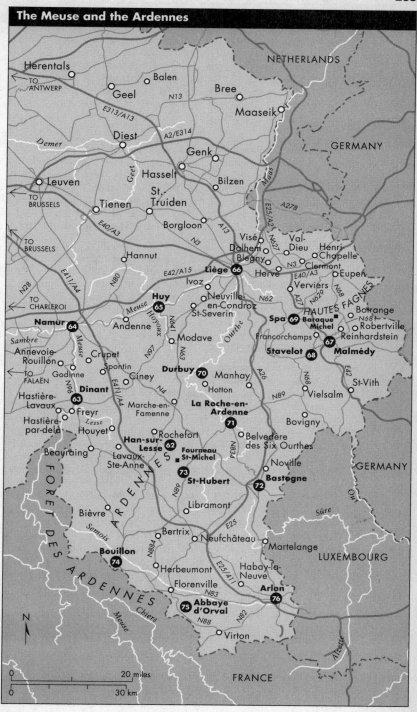

NETHERLANDS

GERMANY

Herentals

TO ANTWERP

Balen

Geel

Bree

Diest

Maaseik

E313/A13

N13

Leuven

Genk

TO BRUSSELS

Hasselt

Bilzen

Tienen

St. Truiden

A2/E314

Geet

Demer

Borgloon

Visé
Dalhem
Blegny

Val-Dieu

Henri Chapelle

TO BRUSSELS

Hannut

N3

A13

Liège **66**

Herve

Clermont

Eupen

E40/A3

N28

TO CHARLEROI

E42/A15

Ivoz

Neuville-en-Condroz

Verviers

N62

HAUTES FAGNES

Botrange

Huy **65**

St-Severin

Namur **64**

Andenne

Modave

Spa **69**

Baraque Michel

N68

Robertville

Reinhardstein

Sambre

Annevoie-Rouillon

Crupet

Spontin

Ciney

Durbuy **70**

Manhay

Francorchamps

Stavelot **68**

67

Malmédy

TO FALAËN

Godinne

Dinant **63**

Freyr

N4

Hotton

Marche-en-Famenne

La Roche-en-Ardenne **71**

A26

Vielsalm

St-Vith

Hastière-Lavaux

Hastière-par-dela

Houyet

Rochefort

Belvédère des Six Ourthes

Bovigny

Beauraing

Han-sur-Lesse **62**

Lavaux-Ste-Anne

Fourneau St-Michel

Noville

GERMANY

FORÊT DES ARDENNES

Bièvre

73

St-Hubert

Bastogne **72**

Libramont

Bertrix

Neufchâteau

Martelange

Sûre

LUXEMBOURG

Bouillon **74**

Herbeumont

Habay-la-Neuve

Arlon **76**

Florenville

Abbaye d'Orval **75**

Chiers

Virton

FRANCE

N

0 — 20 miles

0 — 30 km

tour them, board an ancient tram in the center of town that carries you to the mouth of the caves. There, multilingual guides take over and lead groups on foot through 3 km (2 mi) of dimly lit chambers, with occasional glimpses of the underground river Lesse, past giant stalagmites into the vast cavern called the Dome, 475 ft high, where a single torchbearer dramatically descends the steeply sloping cave wall. The final part of the journey is by boat on the underground river. The trip takes about 90 minutes. ⊠ R. J.-Lamotte 2, ☎ 084/377213. ☜ BF350. ☼ Apr.–Nov., daily 10–4:30, May–June until 5, July–Aug. until 6.

The **Réserve d'Animaux Sauvages** (Wildlife Reserve) is part of the domain of Han. The 625-acre park is filled with animals native to the region, such as wild boars, brown bears, bisons, wolves, and lynx. A panoramic coach takes you through the park, where you can observe the animals in their natural habitat. The trip takes an hour and 15 minutes. ⊠ R. J. Lamotte 2, ☎ 084/377212. ☜ BF250. ☼ Mar. 11.30–1; Apr. and Sept.–Nov., daily 10–4:30; May–June, daily 10–5; July–Aug., daily 10–6.

Château de Lavaux-Ste-Anne is a superb, moat-encircled castle from the 12th century, rebuilt in the 16th century and modified in the 18th. The towers and dungeon are medieval, the interior court Renaissance. The castle also houses a small hunting and nature museum with a fine ornithology section and an impressive restaurant (☞ Dining and Lodging, below). ⊠ R. du Château 10, Lavaux-Ste-Anne, ☎ 084/388362. ☜ BF190. ☼ Mar.–Oct., daily 9–6, July–Aug. until 7; Nov.–Feb., daily 9–noon and 12:30–5.

Dining and Lodging

$$$$ ✕☰ **Château de Lavaux-Ste-Anne.** The owner decided to plant an
★   herb garden in the courtyard and then opened a restaurant in this castle. It rapidly became a great success, as the chef progressed from self-taught amateur to virtuoso. The stripped-down decor is offset by a vast hunting painting, and *la patronne* handles the service as if to the manner born. Try rabbit consommé with truffles, pikeperch cooked in sauerkraut and wild juniper, or veal kidney in wine served with lamb's lettuce. The smallish rooms ($$) are in an annex called Maison Lemonnier. ⊠ R. du Château 10, B 5580 Lavaux-Ste-Anne, ☎ restaurant 084/388883; hotel 084/387217, ℻ restaurant 084/388895; hotel 084/387220. 8 rooms. Restaurant, horseback riding. AE, DC, MC, V. Hotel and restaurant closed Mon.–Tues., mid-Dec.–mid-Jan., 1 wk May–June, 1 wk Aug.–Sept.

$ ✕☰ **Les Ardennes.** This is an acceptable roadhouse stopover for families visiting the caves, but most rooms are musty, with spongy beds and old bath fixtures; those overlooking the garden are more pleasant. Guests are required to eat in the hotel, which is no great punishment: There's honest regional cooking ($$) with some French fuss, friendly and competent service, and an unusually well-chosen wine list. The hotel has a second, more luxurious neighboring establishment with 14 rooms ($$), called Ardennes II, at the same telephone and fax. ⊠ R. des Grottes 2, B 5580 Han-sur-Lesse, ☎ 084/377220, ℻ 084/378062. 26 rooms. Restaurant, bar, outdoor café. AE, DC, MC, V. Closed Wed. mid-Nov.– Jan.; closed mid-Feb.–mid-Mar.

Dinant

❻❸ 40 km (24 mi) northwest of Han-sur-Lesse, 29 km (17 mi) south of Namur, 93 km (56 mi) southeast of Brussels, 80 km (48 mi) southwest of Liège.

The drive toward Dinant is filled with stunning views from the road of towering rock formations across the river. Freyr, on the left bank, is considered the best rock-climbing center in Wallonia. The **Château de Freyr** is an impressive Renaissance building with beautiful interiors decorated with 17th-century woodwork and furniture, including a restored child coach. Louis XIV visited here during the siege of Dinant in 1675. Its park has been laid out in accordance with the design principles of Le Nôtre, the French landscape architect. ⊠ *Domaine de Freyr, Waulsort,* ☎ *082/222200.* ▨ *BF220.* ☉ *July–Aug., weekends, and holidays 2–6.*

Just before Dinant, the needle-shape **Rocher Bayard** looms on the right bank. Legend has it that Bayard, the steed of the four Aymon brothers, who were the implacable foes of Charlemagne, split the rock with his hoof. The passage was widened by the troops of Louis XIV as they advanced on the city.

Dinant has a most scenic but strategic location, which has led to its involvement in an interminable series of wars. The 13th-century collegiate church of **Notre-Dame** huddles under the citadel. Its bulbous blue bell tower is a 17th-century addition.

Cable cars take you up to the **Citadel,** which is not as old as you might think—the ancient fortification was razed in 1818 by the Dutch, who replaced it with a new fort just before they were ousted. The view is splendid, and there is an arms museum, where cannons and cannonballs add to the military atmosphere. The French word *dinanderie,* meaning the art of brass- and copper-working, is derived from Dinant, where it was developed in the 12th century and spread downstream to Namur and Huy. The copperware sold today in the town's souvenir shops is not, alas, of the same quality. The **Dinanderie Museum,** also in the citadel, has a unique collection of weather vanes and all manner of household utensils. ⊠ *Le Prieuré 25,* ☎ *082/223670.* ▨ *BF195, including cable car.* ☉ *Apr.–Oct., daily 10–6; Nov.–Mar., daily 10–4:30.*

But for Dinant, who knows what jazz would be like? This is the birthplace of Adolphe Sax (1814–94), inventor of the saxophone and other musical instruments. He died penniless, but today his image adorns the BF200 note—at least until 2002, when the Belgian franc is replaced by the euro.

NEED A BREAK? | Visit the **Patisserie Solbrun** (⊠ 30 R. Adolphe Sax) to savor Dinant's specialties: *flamiches* (cheese, egg, and butter tarts), to be eaten piping hot; and the hard, spicy *couques,* made of pastry and honey in many fanciful shapes. Although the town's streets are lined with cafés, this one has the advantage of a great river view.

☯ **Mont-Fat,** 400 ft above Dinant, offers the combination of a guided tour of prehistoric caves and a chairlift ride to an amusement area. ⊠ *R. en Rhée 15,* ☎ *082/222783.* ▨ *BF160.* ☉ *Apr.–Aug., daily 10:30–7; Sept.– Nov. 18, weekends 11–6.*

La Merveilleuse, a cave whose many stalactites are remarkably white, is on the left bank, about 490 yards from the bridge, on the road toward Philippeville. A visit takes about 50 minutes. ⊠ *Rte. de Philippeville 142,* ☎ *082/222210.* ▨ *BF180.* ☉ *Mar.–May and Sept.–Nov., daily 11–5; June–Aug., daily 10–6.*

Shooting the rapids of the river **Lesse** in a kayak can be a great adventure. This is one of the liveliest tributaries of the Meuse, which it joins just south of Dinant. The starting point is **Houyet.** The 21-km

(13-mi) ride takes you through two rapids and past the eagle's-nest Walzin Castle to Anseremme on the Meuse. Train service to the starting point is available from Anseremme, which you can reach by bus from Dinant.

The moated **Château de Spontin,** east of the Meuse, is typical of the province's treasures. Built in 1200, it has a 16th-century roof and a Renaissance brick superstructure. The drawbridge can still be operated, and there are secret staircases and lookouts. You can also spend a gastronomic weekend in one of the five suites ($$$). ⊠ *Chaussée de Dinant 8,* ☎ *083/699055.* ⊠ *BF150.* ⊙ *Daily 11–4.*

In nearby **Crupet** stands a massive, river-encircled square dungeon from the 12th century. Also in the area is **Purnode,** with its family-owned brewery, the **Brasserie du Bocq,** which has produced excellent beers since 1858. ⊠ *R. de la Brasserie 4, Purnode,* ☎ *082/699214.* ⊠ *BF50.* ⊙ *Easter–Oct., Sun. at 2, 3, 4, and 5.*

At **Falaën,** west of the Meuse, you can rent pedal-powered "gang cars" for self-propelled trips on disused railway tracks along the scenic Molignée Valley. ⊠ *Les Draisines de la Molignée, R. de la Gare 82, Falaën,* ☎ *082/699079.* ⊠ *BF600 (1 hr)–BF800 (2 hrs).* ⊙ *Daily 10–6.*

Dining and Lodging

$$$ ✕ **Le Jardin de Fiorine.** This ambitious restaurant in a restored graystone mansion has a pretty garden behind. Specialties include lobster and sweetbread salad, sweetbread with asparagus, sole fillets with apples and truffle, and roast pigeon with corn cakes. ⊠ *R. Georges Cousot 3,* ☎ *082/227474. AE, DC, MC, V. No dinner Sun. Closed Wed., 2 wks Feb. and 2 wks July.*

$$$ ✕ **Le Vivier d'Oies.** This country inn is in a lovely stone farmhouse with a modern stone-and-glass wing. The ambience is urbane, and the cuisine above reproach: goose liver sautéed with caramelized pears, crayfish with artichoke hearts and a spring asparagus menu. ⊠ *R. Etat 7, Dorinne, northeast of Dinant, about 3 km (2 mi) east of Yvoir,* ☎ *083/ 699571,* 𝔽𝔸𝕏 *083/699036. AE, DC, MC, V. No dinner Tues. Closed Wed., 2 wks June–July, 2 wks Sept.–Oct.*

$$ ✕ **Thermidor.** The decor may be on the stodgy side, but the cooking here is all it should be: traditional French cuisine, sauces made fresh on the spot, a few experiments in new combinations. Try the grilled salmon steak with fresh-whisked mustard sauce or chicken breast with a drizzle of vanilla butter. ⊠ *R. Station 3,* ☎ *082/223135. AE, MC, V. No dinner Mon. Closed Tues.*

$ ✕🍽 **Auberge de Bouvignes.** This 1830 roadhouse just north of Dinant combines beautifully restored architecture—beams, stonework, whitewashed brick—with an elegant decor and superb cooking ($$$$). Its wine caves are blasted into the solid stone bluff behind, and its rustic bedrooms overlook the Meuse. Lobster dishes of all kinds are a specialty, including lobster ragout with asparagus, morels, and fresh pasta; or there may be Bresse pigeon with braised endive and truffles. ⊠ *R. Fétis 112, 5500 Bouvignes,* ☎ *082/611600,* 𝔽𝔸𝕏 *082/613093. 5 rooms with bath, 1 with shower. Restaurant. AE, DC, MC, V.*

$ ✕🍽 **Le Mosan.** In Anseremme, just upstream from Dinant, this welcoming old roadside hotel sits right on the riverbank. It's very well kept, with fresh, light decor in pretty pastels—worth the mild inconvenience of bathrooms down the hall. Downstairs, the traditional restaurant offers trout and steak to enjoy either on the glassed-in porch or in the charming dining room. ⊠ *R. Dufrenne 2, B 5500 Anseremme-Dinant,* ☎ *082/222450,* 𝔽𝔸𝕏 *082/224679. 8 rooms without bath. Restaurant. AE, DC, MC, V.*

En Route Between Dinant and Namur, the **Château et Jardins d'Annevoie** (Chateau and Gardens of Annevoie) present a happy blend of 18th-century French landscaping and romantic Italian garden design, remarkable for its use of natural waterfalls, fountains, and ponds to animate the gardens with their flowerbeds, lawns, statues, and grottoes. The water displays function without mechanical aids and have remained in working order for more than two centuries. The château blends perfectly with the gardens; the furniture, paneling, and family portraits all contribute to an ambience of elegant refinement. ⊠ *Rte. des Jardins 47,* ☎ *082/611555.* ▦ *BF180.* ⊙ *Apr.–Oct., daily 9:30–6:30.*

Namur

★ ⑭ *29 km (17 mi) north of Dinant, 64 km (38 mi) southeast of Brussels, 61 km (37 mi) southwest of Liège.*

Namur, at the confluence of the Meuse and the Sambre, takes pride in its beautifully preserved center, whose appealing streets are lined with 17th-century pink-brick houses and, here and there, a rich Baroque church, all under the shadow of the Citadel, perched on the promontory overlooking the city. It is the seat of the body governing the affairs of the semiautonomous Walloon Region, chosen as a compromise acceptable to Charleroi and Liège, both of which are twice as large. Much of the center of Namur is a pedestrian zone, with cafés, art galleries, and boutiques. This is a university town, and the student population helps to liven up what passes for nightlife around the Rue St-Loup. The 18th-century theater, in old Namur, has been beautifully renovated. In the very center is the quiet Place du Marché-aux-Légumes, with the Eglise de Saint-Jean Baptiste.

NEED A BREAK? The **Le XVIIIe** (⊠ Pl. du Marché-aux-Légumes) is in an old building, so named for its 18th-century stucco ceiling. The specialty is pancakes with generous fillings.

The **Institut des Soeurs de Notre-Dame** contains the Trésor Hugo d'Oignies, a collection of the finest crosses, reliquaries, and other religious artifacts made by Brother Hugo d'Oignies for the monastery in nearby Oignies at the beginning of the 13th century. Because of the remarkable finesse with which he worked the silver and enamel inlays, often depicting miniature hunting scenes, Hugo d'Oignies has been recognized as one of the masters of Art Mosan. ⊠ *R. Billiart 17,* ☎ *081/230342.* ▦ *BF50.* ⊙ *Tues.–Sat. 10–noon and 2–5, Sun. 2–5.*

The **Musée Archéologique** (Archaeological Museum) contains Roman and Merovingian antiquities from the Namur region, including a collection of jewelry from the 1st to the 7th centuries with some magnificent specimens. It is installed in the handsome, 16th-century Butchers' Hall on the waterfront. ⊠ *R. du Pont,* ☎ *081/231631.* ▦ *BF80.* ⊙ *Tues.–Fri. 10–5, weekends 10:30–5.*

The **Musée Félicien Rops** (Félicien Rops Museum) honors an artist who was considered totally scandalous in his lifetime. Rops, a friend and illustrator of Baudelaire and other allegedly decadent French writers, was a master printmaker. A Surrealist before his time, he created works that were, by turns, satirical and erotic. ⊠ *R. Fumal 12,* ☎ *081/220110.* ▦ *BF100.* ⊙ *Nov.–Easter, Tues.–Sun. 10–5; Easter–June and Sept., Tues.–Sun. 10–6; July–Aug., daily 10–6.*

The **Citadelle** (Citadel) commands fabulous views in all directions: Namur was besieged again and again for centuries on end. The 15th-century bastions were further fortified by the Spanish and, much later, the Dutch, who constructed their Fort d'Orange on the same site. Today you can reach the Citadel by car up the hairpin curves of a mile-long road called the Marvelous Route, or you can enjoy a scenic ride by cable car. ⊠ *Rte. Merveilleuse 8,* ☎ *081/226829.* 🎟 *BF210; cable car temporarily out of service.* ⊘ *Easter–May, weekends 11–5; June–Sept., daily 11–5.*

There are several museums at the Citadel, including the **Musée Provincial de la Forêt** (Provincial Forestry Museum). Housed in an old hunting lodge, it gives an overview of the region's flora and fauna. ⊠ *Rte. Merveilleuse 71,* ☎ *081/743894.* 🎟 *BF50.* ⊘ *Apr.–Oct., Sat.–Thurs. 9–noon and 2–5.*

Ⓒ The **Reine Fabiola** center, on the Citadel grounds, includes a large playground with miniature golf, go-carts, and electric cars. ⊠ *Rond Point Thonar 1,* ☎ *081/738413.* 🎟 *BF100.* ⊘ *1st ½ of May and Sept.–mid-Oct., Wed. 1–6, weekends 11–6; mid-May–Aug., Thurs.–Tues. 11–6, Wed. 1–6.*

Dining and Lodging

$$$ ✕ **Biétrumé Picar.** Noted chef Charles Jeandrain is based in Les Plantes,
★ a Namur suburb, and the verdant surroundings inspire him to ever-greater heights. The handsome dining room is tiled with flagstones from Jura, and the terrace, with its picturesque view, is ideal in summer. The menu includes a creamy bouillon with green asparagus and turbot, sautéed langoustines with tomato and leek base, and rhubarb fricassee with caramelized peaches. ⊠ *Tienne Macquet 16,* ☎ *081/230739. Jacket and tie. AE, DC, MC, V. No dinner Sun. (except July–Aug.). Closed Mon.*

$$ ✕ **Le Temps des Cerises.** On a narrow street in old Namur, chockablock
★ with little restaurants, this retro café serves rich, hearty fare—fish soup with *rouille* (garlic and red-pepper sauce), kidneys in garlic and juniper sauce—in artful and generous portions and often using local produce. The setting is charmingly Old Belgium, with lace café curtains, vintage postcards, knickknacks, and furniture and paneling painted a glossy cherry red. ⊠ *R. des Brasseurs 22,* ☎ *081/225326. MC, V. No lunch Sat. Closed Sun.*

$ ✕ **Brasserie Henry.** In an attractive, high-ceiling building in old Namur, this is the place for traditional brasserie dishes—sauerkraut, steamed cod, and cassoulet. The restaurant is open until midnight. A children's menu is available. ⊠ *Pl. Saint-Aubain 3,* ☎ *081/220204. AE, DC, MC, V.*

$–$$$$ ✕▥ **Les Tanneurs.** This exquisite hotel is the creation of Christian Bou-
★ vier, who defied promoters prepared to demolish a row of ancient buildings in the heart of Namur. The interiors have been renovated with remarkable taste, using material such as oak and marble, and decorated with beautiful fabrics and delightful pictures. Each room is different, ranging from simple, inexpensive ones to a duplex deluxe. There are two restaurants: **L'Espièglerie** ($$$, no lunch Sat., closed Sun. and mid-July–mid-Aug.), serving delicacies such as quail stuffed with sweetbreads, and roast duck with figs; and **Grill des Tanneurs** ($), one flight up, which serves brasserie fare. ⊠ *R. des Tanneries 13, 5000,* ☎ *081/231999,* FAX *081/261432. 24 rooms. 2 restaurants, bar, sauna. AE, DC, MC, V.*

$ ✕▥ **Ferme du Quartier.** Just outside Namur, near the Bouge exit from the highway, this delightfully restored old stone farmhouse stands in a silent country oasis. Interiors are modern, in natural materials, with some brick-vaulted ceilings and beams. The locals dine in its simple, traditional restaurant on steaks, rabbit in mustard sauce, grilled salmon, or *pintadeau* (guinea fowl) in beer. Rooms in the converted barn are smaller and even quieter than those in the main house. ⊠ *Pl. Ste-Marguerite 4, 5004 Bouge-Namur,* ☎ *081/211105,* 𝔽𝔸𝕏 *081/215918. 14 rooms with bath or shower. Restaurant, bar. AE, DC, MC, V. No dinner Sun. Closed July, last wk of Dec.*

$$ 🏨 **Beauregard.** Built into a wing of the Namur Casino, this is a polished, fashionable business hotel, with vivid color schemes (lime, salmon, teal) and sleek decor. Rooms with wide views of the river cost slightly more. A breakfast buffet is served in a vast hall overlooking the river. ⊠ *Av. Baron de Moreau 1, 5000,* ☎ *081/230028,* 𝔽𝔸𝕏 *081/ 241209. 47 rooms. Restaurant, bar, breakfast room, casino. AE, DC, MC, V.*

$$ 🏨 **Château de Namur.** This is primarily a hotel school, located in a grand mansion built in 1930, that sits at the top of the Citadel's bluff, high above the city. Much of the mansion's former grandeur is subjugated to its current role as a teaching vehicle. Public spaces are sparse and underfurnished, but the rooms, most of which are freshly decorated, are comfortable, and the views are spectacular. Ask for a corner room, with double views. In the dining room, students practice serving rough-edged but ambitious French cooking. ⊠ *Av. de l'Ermitage 1, 5000,* ☎ *081/729900,* 𝔽𝔸𝕏 *081/729999. 39 rooms. Restaurant, bar, tennis court, convention center. AE, DC, MC, V.*

$$ 🏨 **Novotel.** This French chain hotel is on the river before you reach Namur coming from Dinant, in the heart of the strawberry-growing region. Worldwide standardization makes rooms, public areas, and restaurant rather impersonal. Still, riverside walks start at the door, and the staff will make all sorts of excursion arrangements. ⊠ *Chaussée de Dinant 1149, 5001 Wepion-Namur,* ☎ *081/460811,* 𝔽𝔸𝕏 *081/461990. 110 rooms. Restaurant, bar, indoor and outdoor pools, sauna, health club, meeting rooms. AE, DC, MC, V.*

En Route For a beautiful detour on the way to Huy, leave the N90 at Andenne and drive south via Ohey to Havelange. You are now in the heart of the fertile plateau of the **Condroz**. Continue on the N97 to Pont-de-Bonne and **Modave**. There, overlooking the Hoyoux, clearest and coldest of the rivers of the Ardennes, stands the 17th-century **Château des Comtes de Marchin**, with its restored moat. Its elegant rooms have stucco polychrome ceilings. The hydraulic machinery that brought water from the river to the cliff top was copied in France to bring water from the Seine to the Palace of Versailles. ☎ *085/411369.* 🎫 *BF150.* ☉ *Apr.–mid-Nov., daily 9–6.*

Huy

⑥⑤ *32 km (19 mi) east of Namur, 83 km (50 mi) southeast of Brussels 33 km (20 mi) southwest of Liège.*

Huy (pronounced "we"), where the Hoyoux joins the Meuse, is an ancient place; its city privileges of 1066 are the oldest that have been preserved in Europe. The first stone of the Gothic **Eglise Collégiale de Notre-Dame** (Collegiate Church of Our Lady) was laid in 1311. It has a rose window, the so-called Rondia, 30 ft in diameter. Its treasury contains several magnificent reliquaries, two of them attributed to Godefroid de Huy, who followed in the footsteps of Renier, also a native of Huy and a master of the Mosan style. ⊠ *R. de Cloître.* 🎫 *BF50.* ☉ *Mon.–Thurs. and Sat. 9–noon and 2–5, Sun. 2–5 except during services.*

The town's **Grand'Place** is dominated by a remarkable copper fountain, the **Bassinia**, a bronze cistern decorated with saints that dates from 1406. In the 18th century, the Austrians topped it with their double eagle.

From the square you can wander through winding alleys to the old Franciscan monastery, which is now the **Musée Communal,** a mine of local folklore and history with an exceptional Art Mosan oak carving of Christ. ✉ *R. Vankeerberghen 20,* ☎ *085/232435.* ▦ *BF100.* ☉ *Apr.–Oct., daily 2–6.*

For a great view of the town and the surrounding countryside, take a mile-long ride on the cable car from the left bank of the Meuse across the river to the cliff-top **Citadelle,** part of the defenses built by the Dutch in the early 19th century. During World War II, the Germans used it as a prison for resistance members and hostages. It now contains a **Musée de la Résistance** (Resistance Museum) composed of photographs, documents, and scale models. ✉ *Chaussée Napoléon,* ☎ *085/215334.* ▦ *BF120.* ☉ *Apr.–June and Sept., weekdays 10–5, weekends 10–6; July–Aug., daily 10–8; cable car July–Aug., daily.*

© **Plaine de Jeux Mont Mosan** (Mont Mosan Recreation Park) is a large playground on the heights above Huy, complete with games, an inflatable village, a sea lion show, clowns, and miniature golf, to name a few. It's at the end of the cable car line that also stops at the Citadel. ✉ *Plaine de la Sarte,* ☎ *085/232996.* ▦ *BF130.* ☉ *Mar. 20–Oct., daily 10–8.*

Dining and Lodging

$ ✕▦ **Le Fort.** Tucked under the Citadel, across from the arching bridge over the Meuse, this is the simplest of roadhouses, but its rooms have been carefully decorated and maintained and the owners pamper you in the unpretentious tavern downstairs. There's a brief, standard menu with trout, sole, or chicken, each with frites and salad, at reasonable prices. ✉ *Chaussée Napoléon 5-6, B 4500,* ☎ *085/212403,* 𝔽𝔸𝕏 *085/ 231842. 34 rooms, 25 with bath. Restaurant, bar. AE, DC, MC, V.*

$$ ▦ **Le Sirius.** The newest, most expensive hotel in Huy is modern and businesslike, providing comfort and efficiency rather than charm. It overlooks the river, although the view is not the most beautiful. ✉ *Quai de Compiègne 47, 4500,* ☎ *085/212400,* 𝔽𝔸𝕏 *085/212401. 26 rooms. Bar, parking. AE, DC, MC, V.*

Liège and Environs

The people of Liège are the most francophile among the francophones: Many Belgians feel that visiting Liège, gateway to the Ardennes, is almost like going abroad. The Liégeois, for their part, see little reason for going to Brussels; if they hanker for bright lights, they head for Paris. It was no accident that writer Georges Simenon could so easily transplant the cafés and streets of the Liège of his boyhood to Maigret's Paris.

The history of Liège differs fundamentally from that of the rest of the country. For 8 of its 10 centuries it was an independent principality of the Holy Roman Empire, from the time Bishop Notger transformed his bishopric into a temporal domain at the end of the 10th century. His successors had to devote as much time to the defense of the realm— much larger than the present province—as to pastoral concerns. The power of the autocratic prince-bishops was also hotly contested by the increasingly independent-minded cities. The end was brought about by the French Revolution, which many Liegeois joined with enthusiasm. The ancient Cathedral of St. Lambert was razed, and the principality became a French *département* in 1815, after Napoléon.

In the 19th century, after Belgian independence in 1830, the country saw an upsurge in industrial activity. The first European locomotive was built in Liège and the Bessemer steel production method was developed here; it is to the burning furnaces that Liège owes its nickname, *la cité ardente* (the Fiery City). Drawing on a centuries-old tradition of weapons manufacturing, the Fabrique Nationale started to build precision firearms, and Val-St-Lambert began to produce glassware that has gained wide renown. In August 1914 the forts of Liège kept the German invasion force at bay long enough for the Belgian and French troops to regroup; in 1944–1945, more than a thousand V1 and V2 missiles exploded in the city.

Now modern apartment blocks blot views of the river, but the secret courtyards, narrow medieval lanes, and steep streets are well worth a visit. The Liegeois are famed for their laid-back, some say maddeningly slow, friendly manner and sardonic sense of humor: Belgium's eccentric custard-pie-thrower Noel Godin, who splattered Bill Gates in 1998, was born here. Today a dilapidated, worn-out look has settled over some areas. The long years of crisis in the steel industry have taken their toll and the impact on the city's finances has been disastrous.

Liège

66 *33 km (20 mi) northwest of Huy, 97 km (58 mi) east of Brussels, 122 km (73 mi) southwest of Cologne.*

The bustling city of Liège—Luik to the Flemish and Dutch, Lüttich to the Germans—is quietly romantic. Surrounded by hills, it sits deep in the Meuse Valley at the confluence of the Meuse and Ourthe rivers. Here the Meuse is slate-gray, and pleasure craft play second fiddle to coal barges and tankers. Among the not always obvious charms of Liège are the *cafés chantant* (singing cafés), where everyone is welcome to burst into song.

Place de la Cathédrale is a pleasant square with flowerbeds in the center, lined with sidewalk cafés on two sides, and flanked by the north wall of the Gothic **Cathédrale St-Paul** (St. Paul's Cathedral). Inside, you'll see some handsome statues by Jean Delcour, including one of St. Paul; other graceful works by this 18th-century sculptor dot the old city. The cathedral's most prized possessions are in the Treasury, especially the *Reliquaire de Charles le Téméraire* (Reliquary of Charles the Bold), with gold and enamel figures of St. George and the bold duke himself on his knees; curiously, their faces are identical. This reliquary was presented to Liège by Charles the Bold in 1471 in penance for having had the city razed three years earlier. 🎫 *BF50.* ☉ *Daily (except during services) 10–11:45 and 2–4, Sun. 2–4. Ring bell next to cloister door.*

NEED A
BREAK?

Le Panier Fleuri (✉ Pont d'Avroy 20) is right out of the Belle Epoque. A cozy, crimson-wall tavern, it serves beer, spirits, and a small selection of traditional Belgian snacks. The decor is more exciting than the food.

Vinâve-d'Ile, a charming and animated triangular square with a fountain by Delcour, adjoins Place de la Cathédrale. The **Eglise Saint-Denis** (Church of St. Denis) is one of the oldest in Liège, founded by Bishop Notger. It has a handsome reredos portraying the Suffering of Christ. ✉ *Pl. St-Denis, via R. de la Cathédrale,* ☎ *04/223–5756.* ☉ *Mon.–Sat. 9–noon and 1:30–5, Sun. 9AM–10AM.*

Place St-Lambert is a true eyesore. What should be the city's most prestigious square has, in fact, been a hole in the ground for more than 20 years. It's as though the destruction of Cathédrale St-Lambert during the French Revolution cast a spell on the site. Works are in progress and the square is surrounded by cranes. On the other side of the square stands the enormous **Palais des Princes-Evêques** (Palace of the Prince-Bishops), rebuilt at different stages since Notger's days. The present facade dates from 1734. The colonnaded 16th-century courtyard has remained unchanged. Each column is decorated with stone carvings of staggering variety. The palace is now used for government offices and law courts, which explains the presence of police and metal detectors. ⊠ *R. de Bruxelles, R. Léopold, R. Joffre, R. du General Jacques, and R. Souv Pont.*

Place du Marché is as old as the city itself. For centuries, this was where the city's commercial and political life was concentrated. A number of the old buildings surrounding it were among the 23,000 houses destroyed by German bombs. In the center stands the **Perron**, a large fountain sculpted by Jean Delcour, a symbol of municipal liberty. ⊠ *R. du General Jacques, R. des Mineurs, En Feronstree.*

NEED A BREAK? The **Café à Pilori** (⊠ Pl. du Marché 5) is a dark, low-ceilinged tavern, with a large fireplace and a beam ceiling. It serves light lunches and an appetizing amber-color home brew, La Rousse.

La Batte is the animated riverfront of the old city. On Sunday from 9 to 2, it becomes a mile-long street market where you can buy anything, from bric-a-brac and foodstuffs to songbirds, pets, clothing, books, records, and toys. Visitors from neighboring Holland and Germany descend regularly on Liège to join the locals at the Sunday market, but it's not so much the merchandise that makes it attractive as the good-natured ambience. ⊠ *Quai de la Batte, Quai de la Goffe, Quai de Maestricht.*

The **Ilôt St-Georges** is an interesting example of urban archaeology. Twelve dilapidated buildings were taken apart, brick by brick, and put together again to form an appealing architectural whole. Here, too, is the **Musée de l'Art Wallon**, containing works by Walloon artists from the 17th century to the present day, including Surrealists René Magritte and Paul Delvaux. ⊠ *En Féronstrée 86,* ☎ *04/221–9231.* 🎫 *BF50.* ⊙ *Tues.–Sat. 1–6, Sun. 11–4:30.*

The **Maison du Jazz** (Jazz House) is a documentation center, where you can study the history of jazz and listen to CDs. ⊠ *R. Ste-Marie 11,* ☎ *04/254–4600.* ⊙ *Tues.–Thurs. 11–5; weekends 10–2.*

The **Musée d'Armes** (Arms Museum) is a handsome 18th-century riverside mansion in the neoclassical style, opulently furnished. Napoléon slept here, at different times, with Josephine and Marie-Louise, and there's a portrait of him as First Consul by Ingres. Since the Middle Ages, Liège has been famous for its arms manufacturing, and the collection reflects this with many rare and beautifully executed pieces. ⊠ *Quai de Maestricht 8,* ☎ *04/221–9416.* 🎫 *BF50.* ⊙ *Mon.–Sat. 10–1 and 2–5, Sun. 10–1.*

Musée Curtius, a patrician mansion built for the arms manufacturer Jean Curtin in the 16th century, contains 100,000 art and ornamental objects. One is a masterpiece, Bishop Notger's *Evangelistery,* an exquisite 10th-century manuscript of the Gospels. On the ornamental cover is an ivory relief, carved in the year 1000, showing the bishop praying to Christ the King. The house, also home to a glass museum, is made of limestone and brick. ⊠ *Quai de Maestricht 13,* ☎ *04/221–9404.* 🎫 *BF50.* ⊙ *Mon.–Sat. 10–1 and 2–5, Sun. 10–1.*

Le Musée d'Ansembourg is a sumptuous mansion, once the home of the 18th-century merchant and banker Michel Willems, after whom the building is named. It was converted into a decorative and fine arts museum in 1903. The sculptures, tapestries, marble fireplaces, painted ceilings, and ceramics evoke Willems's opulent lifestyle. ⊠ *En Féronstrée 114,* ☎ *04/221–9402.* 🎫 *BF50.* ⊙ *Tues.–Sun. 1–6.*

A la Bonne Franquette (✉ En Féronstrée 152) is a no-frills neighborhood eatery where you can enjoy a meal or snack.

★ The **Eglise St-Barthélemy** (St. Bartholomew's Church) contains Liège's greatest treasure, the Baptismal Font of Renier de Huy, which dates from between 1107 and 1118. This brass masterpiece of Art Mosan, weighing half a ton, is decorated with figures of the five biblical baptismal scenes in high relief. The scenes are of an extraordinary suppleness, and the font rests on 10 oxen, which are also varied and interesting. It is well displayed and well lit. During the French Revolution the font was hidden by the faithful, but the cover has disappeared. The church, consecrated in 1015, is one of the rare Romanesque churches to escape transformation into the Gothic style, retaining its sober austerity. The nave has, however, been retouched in baroque fashion. ✉ *Pl. St-Barthélemy,* ☎ *04/223–4998.* ⌑ *BF80.* ◷ *Mon.–Sat. 10–noon and 2–5 except during services, Sun. 2–5.*

Impasses were the narrow mews where servants had their tiny houses in the days of the prince-bishops. Prominent citizens lived along En Hors-Château. As late as the 1970s, it was believed that the best approach to urban redevelopment was to tear down these houses. Luckily, common sense prevailed and many small houses along these tiny streets have been restored to mint condition. The **Impasse de la Vignette** and its neighbor **Impasse de la Couronne** are fine examples. Here, as in many other places around Liège, you find a number of potales (wall chapels), devoted mostly to the Virgin or to St. Roch, who was venerated as the protector against disease epidemics. ✉ *Off En Hors Château.*

The **Montagne de Bueren** is a stairway with 373 steps ascending from Hors-Château toward the Citadel. The stairway is not much more than 100 years old, but it evokes the memory of Vincent van Bueren, a leader of the resistance against Charles the Bold. In 1468 he climbed the hill with 600 men, intending to ambush the duke and kill him. Betrayed by their Liégeois accents, they lost their lives and the city was pillaged and burned. Charles was loved in Burgundy, but he never had a good press in Liège. At the foot of the stairs, you can turn left through the cobbled **Impasse des Ursulines**, which leads to the small and peaceful Beguinage. Next to it stand old buildings rescued from demolition elsewhere in Liège, including a 17th-century post house. Continuing uphill, you come to a gate in the wall on the left. Push through it, and you're in a large and verdant hillside park. ✉ *Hors-Chateau.*

The **Musée d'Art Religieux et d'Art Mosan** (Museum of Religious and Mosan Art) contains many fine pieces, including an 11th-century *Sedes Sapientiae* (Seat of Wisdom), a stiff and stern-faced, seated Virgin, reflecting a more austere age. ✉ *R. Mère Dieu 11,* ☎ *04/221–4225.* ⌑ *BF50.* ◷ *Tues.–Sat. 1–6, Sun. 11–4:30.*

The **Musée de la Vie Wallonne** (Museum of Walloon Life), in an old Franciscan convent, has carefully reconstructed interiors that give a vivid and varied idea of life in old Wallonia, from coal mines to farm kitchens to the workshops of many different crafts. It even includes a court of law, complete with a guillotine. One gallery is populated by the irreverent marionette *Tchantchès* and his band, who represent the Liège spirit. ✉ *Cour des Mineurs,* ☎ *04/223–6094.* ⌑ *BF80.* ◷ *Tues.–Sat. 10–5, Sun. 10–4.*

Outremeuse (Across the Meuse) is a sort of alternative Liège, the self-styled *Republique libre d'Outremeuse* (Free Republic). Its inhabitants continue to speak Wallon, an ancient tongue of Latin origin, and main-

tain old traditions. It was the home of two celebrities, Georges Simenon
and Tchantchès. Simenon left Liège as early as he could, and only one
of his more than 400 books, *Le Pendu de Saint-Pholien,* is set in the
city; nevertheless the tourist office arranges occasional Simenon walks
for his fans. Tchantchès is strictly a local character, a marionette who
impersonates the "true Liegeois"—caustic, irreverent, and funny. His
home is the **Musée Tchantchès.** ✉ *R. Surlet 56,* ☎ *04/342–7575.* 💰
BF40. ☼ *Tues., Thurs. 2–4, closed in July.*

The **Maison de la Métallurgie** (House of Metallurgy) is consecrated to
the industrial glory that was Liège's. It is a 19th-century steel mill, south
of Outremeuse, converted into a museum of industrial archaeology, including a 17th-century Walloon forge. ✉ *Bd. Raymond Poincaré 17,*
☎ *04/342–6563.* 💰 *BF100.* ☼ *Weekdays 9–5, Sat. 9–noon, Sun. 2–6.*

The **Musée d'Art Moderne et Contemporain** (Museum of Modern and
Contemporary Art) provides a useful survey of French and Belgian art
since the 1850s. Almost all the big names are represented in the collection of 700-odd paintings. The museum stands in an attractive park
west of Outremeuse, much favored by the Liégeois for a stroll far away
from the traffic. ✉ *Parc de la Boverie 3,* ☎ *04/343–0403.* 💰 *BF50.*
☼ *Tues.–Sat. 1–6, Sun. 11–4:30.*

The **Eglise St-Jacques** (St. James's Church) is a mini-cathedral a few
blocks south of Liège's center. The grimy exterior belies a wonderful
interior in which marble, stained glass, and polished wood achieve outstanding visual harmony. The glory of the church is the Gothic vault,
decorated in intricate patterns of vivid blue and gold and containing
myriad sculpted figures. ✉ *Pl. St-Jacques,* ☎ *04/222–1441.* ☼ *Weekdays 8–noon, Sat. 4–6.*

The **Cristalleries du Val St-Lambert,** at Seraing, on the Meuse south of
Liège, are among Europe's great glassworks. You can see glassblowers and engravers at work, walk through well-restored factory buildings from the 19th century, see an exhibition of museum and
contemporary glassware, and visit the shop. ✉ *R. du Val 245, Seraing,*
☎ *04/337–0960.* 💰 *BF200.* ☼ *Daily 9–5.*

The **Préhistosite de Ramioul** is a reconstruction of the world of prehistoric humans. Different hypothetical dwellings give an idea of their
technical aptitude, and visitors can try their hand at making pots and
polishing stones. The museum is next to the cave of Ramioul, where
a new lighting system has brought out the beauty of the rock formations. Guided visits explain the use of the cave by humans and its animal life. ✉ *R. de la Grotte 128, Ivoz-Ramet, near Seraing,* ☎ *04/
275–4975.* 💰 *BF290.* ☼ *Apr.–Oct., weekdays 2–5, weekends 2–6,
one guided visit per day, starting at 2.*

Fort de Loncin has remained as it was at 5:15 PM on August 16, 1914,
when a German shell scored a direct hit, killing most of the garrison.
✉ *R. des Héros 15 bis, northeast of Liège,* ☎ *04/246–4425.* 💰
BF100. ☼ *Wed.–Sun. 10–4; guided tours Apr.–Sept., 1st and 3rd Sun.
of month at 2.*

Fort de Battice brings memories of World War II. It held out against
the Germans for 12 days in May 1940, while the German tanks rolled
on into France. ✉ *Rte. d'Aubel, Battice, east of Liège,* ☎ *087/679470.*
💰 *BF100.* ☼ *Guided tours late Mar.–Nov., daily at 1:30.*

Cimetière Américain des Ardennes (American Cemetery) is one of two
American war cemeteries and the final resting place for 5,327 soldiers
of the U.S. First Army who fell in the Ardennes, at the Siegfried Line
and around Aachen. The memorial, decorated with an immense Amer-

ican eagle, contains a nondenominational chapel. ☒ *Rte. du Condroz 164, Neuville-en-Condroz, southwest of Liège,* ☎ *04/371–4287.* 🎟 *Free.* ☉ *Nov.–Mar., daily 9–5; Apr.–Oct., daily 9–6.*

The **Cimetière de Henri-Chapelle** is the burial site of 7,989 American soldiers who fell in the Battle of the Bulge during the last winter of World War II. The crosses and stelae are arranged in arcs converging on the central monument, which also contains a small museum. From here, there is a great view over the plateau of Herve. Ceremonies are held here and at Neuville-en-Condroz on American Memorial Day in late May. ☒ *Rte. du Mémorial Américain, Hombourg,* ☎ *087/687173.* ☉ *Apr.–Sept., daily 8–6, Oct.–Mar., daily 8–5.*

The highlight of a visit to the **Complexe Touristique de Blegny** is a trip down the former Blegny Coal Mine, which produced 1,000 tons of coal a day at its peak. The wealth of Liège was based on coal, which was mined from the Middle Ages until 1980. An audiovisual presentation illustrates this history, and former miners lead tours of the surface and underground facilities. A complete visit takes 3½ hours. ☒ *R. Lambert Marlet 23,* ☎ *04/387–4333.* 🎟 *BF290.* ☉ *Early Apr.–mid-Sept., daily 10–4:30; Mar. and mid-Sept.–Nov., weekends 10–4:30.*

🐾 The **Wegimont Domaine,** an area of 50 acres surrounding a château, offers sporting facilities, fishing, rowing, swimming in a heated outdoor pool, miniature golf, and signposted nature walks. ☒ *Soumagne, east of Liège,* ☎ *04/377–1020.* 🎟 *BF100.* ☉ *May–Aug., daily 9–8.*

Dining and Lodging

$$$ ✕ **Au Vieux Liège.** The cuisine here is as interesting as the remarkable
★ riverside building housing the restaurant: The Maison Havart, a sprawling, ramshackle cross-timbered beauty dating from the 16th century. Duckling prepared with Armagnac and lightly smoked sweetbreads with a spicy rosemary sauce are among the delicacies. Interiors, all creaking parquet and glossy wood beams, have been furnished in Old Master luxury—Delft tiles, brass, pewter, Oriental runners. ☒ *Quai de la Goffe 41,* ☎ *04/223–7748. Reservations essential. Jacket and tie. AE, DC, MC, V. No dinner Wed. Closed Sun., Easter wk, mid-July–mid-Aug.*

$$$ ✕ **Chez Max.** There's never a dull moment at this wonderful, elegant brasserie, run by the charismatic Alain Struvay. The cuisine is enlivened by a variety of lobster specialties, such as lobster and langoustines au gratin, turbot in champagne sauce, very tender, lightly smoked salmon—and more than 100 brands of whiskey. There is a spectacular *banc d'écailler* (oyster and seafood display). ☒ *Pl. de la République Française 12,* ☎ *04/223–7748. AE, DC, MC, V. No lunch Sat. Closed Sun.*

$–$$ ✕ **Robert Lesenne.** Here's another celebrity chef who is buying up nearby cafés and spreading his name throughout a neighborhood. The fixed-price menu, with a choice of over 30 appetizers, entrées, and desserts, offers remarkable value. Many are standards given a new twist; sweetbreads are wrapped in crisp bacon and there is a stew of langoustine and frogs' legs. The handsome restaurant is soberly decorated in soft shades, offset by striking pictures. ☒ *R. de la Boucherie 9,* ☎ *04/222–0793. Reservations essential. AE, DC, MC, V. No lunch Sat. Closed Sun., 2nd ½ of July.*

$ ✕ **Brasserie Florian.** This unpretentious restaurant, with inoffensive pastel decor and a mural of Liège life on one wall, specializes in fish and seafood. ☒ *Quai sur Meuse 16,* ☎ *04/232–1880. AE, DC, MC, V. No dinner Sun.*

$ ✕ **Café Lequet.** Once the choice of the Simenon family, this rundown, wood-paneled, riverside restaurant still serves honest, home-style cooking: chicken with endives, veal fricassee, mussels with fries. ⊠ *Quai sur Meuse 17,* ☎ *04/222–2134. No credit cards. No dinner Sun.*

$$$ ⌨ **Bedford.** Opened in 1994, this hotel on the banks of the Meuse is just a few blocks from major museums and the old city. The bright, air-conditioned rooms have leather armchairs and marble bathrooms with blow-dryers. The brasserie-style restaurant is in the oldest part of the hotel, which dates from the 17th century. ⊠ *Quai St-Léonard 36, B 4000,* ☎ *04/228–8111,* FAX *04/227–4575. 149 rooms. Restaurant, bar, meeting rooms. AE, DC, MC, V.*

$$$ ⌨ **Holiday Inn.** Next to the Palais des Congrès, this is the hotel of choice for European Congress delegates and businesspeople. The lobby and guest rooms have recently been refurbished, and the riverfront location is very pleasant. ⊠ *Esplanade de l'Europe 2, B 4020,* ☎ *04/342–6020,* FAX *04/343–4810. 219 rooms. Bar, no-smoking rooms, indoor pool, health club, sauna, convention center, parking (fee). AE, DC, MC, V.*

$ ⌨ **Comfort Inn l'Univers.** A cut above most train-station hotels, this landmark has been kept up to date with double windows, sharp room decor (beige and burgundy), and a modernized brasserie-bar downstairs. ⊠ *R. des Guillemins 116, B 4000,* ☎ *04/254–5555,* FAX *04/254–5500. 49 rooms. Bar. AE, DC, MC, V.*

$ ⌨ **Simenon.** Named for Liège's most famous native son and located
★ in his old neighborhood east of the river, this splendid Belle Epoque house has been converted into a theme hotel: Each room is named for one of the author's novels. Excellent homemade ice-cream is served in the tearoom. ⊠ *Bd. de l'Est 16, B 4020,* ☎ *04/342–8690,* FAX *04/344–2669. 11 rooms. Lobby lounge, tearoom. AE, DC, MC, V.*

Nightlife and the Arts

Check times at **Infor-Spectacles** (⊠ En Féronstrée 92, ☎ 04/222–1111). You can also buy tickets there. For all sorts of events in Liège, look under "Other Towns" in *The Bulletin*'s *What's On* section.

THE ARTS

Music and Opera. Liège has an excellent opera company, the **Opéra Royal de Wallonie** (⊠ Théâtre Royal , R. des Dominicains, ☎ 04/221–4720), considered the country's most innovative. The city's symphony orchestra, **l'Orchestre Philharmonique de Liège,** has recorded prizewinning discs and tours internationally with a largely contemporary repertoire. The **Wallonia Chamber Orchestra** and other ensembles participate in the annual Festival de la Wallonie (in Liège, Sept., ☎ 04/222–1111), with concerts also in Spa and Stavelot. The **Stavelot Music Festival** (☎ 080/862450) is held every August, with concerts in the old abbey.

Puppet Theater. On Wednesday at 2:30 and Sunday morning at 10:30, you can see puppet theater featuring the irrepressible Tchantchès at the **Théâtre Royal Ex-Impérial de Roture** (⊠ R. Surlet 56, ☎ 04/342–7575) and the theater of the **Musée de la Vie Wallonne** (⊠ Cour des Mineurs, ☎ 04/223–6094). The **Théâtre Al Botroule** (⊠ R. Hocheporte 3, ☎ 04/223–0576) has puppet shows for adults (Sat. at 8:30) and for children (Sat. and Wed. at 3).

Theater. The most interesting theater performances in French or Walloon are generally at the **Théâtre de la Place** (⊠ Pl. de l'Yser, ☎ 04/342–0000). It's worth checking out what's on at **Les Chiroux** (⊠ Pl. des Carmes, ☎ 04/223–1960). The **Festival du Théâtre de Spa** (☎ 087/771700) is a showcase for young and talented actors and directors. Programs and information about the three-week August season are available starting in early June.

NIGHTLIFE

Cafés and Discos. The Liegeois have an amazing ability to stay up until all hours, and nightlife is booming on both sides of the Meuse. The

Carré quarter, on the left bank, is favored by students and those who go to a show first and out afterward. Two *cafés chantant,* which are very typical of this city, should be tried: **Les Caves de Porto** (⌧ En Féron-strée 144, ☎ 04/223–2325; closed Tues. and Thurs.) and **Les Olivettes** (⌧ R. Pied-du-Pont des Arches 6, ☎ 04/222–0708). You can finish the evening quietly in an ambience of Liège folklore at the **Café Tchantchès** (⌧ R. Grande-Beche, ☎ 04/343–3931), a true Liège institution. Try **La Chapelle** (⌧ R. Chapelle-des-Clercs 3, ☎ 04/223–2685) for trendy contemporary dance music. **La Notte** (⌧ R. St-Paul 10 has live jazz on Tuesday. A café with traditional ambience is **La Taverne St-Paul** (⌧ R. St-Paul 8, ☎ 04/223–7217) near the cathedral.

Jazz. The cobbled, narrow-laned Roture quarter in Outremeuse is where people go for a full night's entertainment. There's hardly a house without a café, club, ethnic restaurant or jazz hangout. **Cirque Divers** (⌧ En Roture 13, ☎ 04/341–0244) offers literary happenings, film events, dance, and classical concerts. **Le Lion s'envoile** (⌧ En Roture 11, ☎ 04/342–9317) has jazz Wednesday night.

Outdoor Activities and Sports

BOATING

There's a yacht harbor along Boulevard Frère Orban in Liège, and water sports are popular upstream from the Pont Albert I.

GOLF

There are two 18-hole courses in the Liège area: the **International Gomzé Golf Club** (⌧ Sur Counachamps 8, Gomzé-Andoumont, ☎ 04/360–9207) and the **Royal Golf Club du Sart Tilman** (⌧ Rte. du Condroz 541, Angleur, ☎ 04/336–2021).

SWIMMING AND SKATING

The **Palais des Sports de Coronmeuse** in Liège (⌧ Quai de Wallonie 7, ☎ 04/227–1324) provides facilities for swimming in a heated outdoor pool in summer and skating in winter.

Shopping

In Liège, the **Carré** is almost exclusively a pedestrian area, with boutiques, cafés, and restaurants. The most important shopping arcades are **Galerie du Pont d'Avroy** (⌧ off R. du Pont d'Avroy), **Galerie Nagelmackers** (⌧ between Pl. de la Cathédrale and R. Tournant St-Paul), and the **Passage Lemonnier** (⌧ between Vinâve d'Ile and R. de l'Université).

Glassware from Val St-Lambert can be found in a number of shops and most advantageously at the factory shop (⌧ R. du Val 245, Seraing, ☎ 04/337–0960). **Firearms,** an age-old Liège specialty, are still handmade to order by some gun shops, notably Lebeau-Courally (⌧ R. St-Gilles 386, ☎ 04/252–4843). Keep in mind that only a licensed arms importer may carry arms into the United States.

En Route Traveling from Liège to Malmédy, the Hautes Fagnes are the big attraction. You leave the E40 motorway to Aachen at the exit for **Eupen,** where all the signs are in German, although you haven't crossed the border; this small town is the capital of Belgium's third (and by far the smallest) language group. From Eupen, you drive through dense woods that open up into the **Hautes Fagnes** (High Fens), a national park of almost 10,500 acres. Here the vistas open over vast tracts of moor, with bushes and copses harboring rich and varied vegetation and bird life. The marshland is waterlogged, and wooden walkways have been laid out across the area. You're well advised not to stray from them, and to be exceedingly careful with matches during dry spells. Paths are clearly marked. **Baraque Michel** is the starting point for paths across the moors. At the à **Botrange** nature center, you can get a professional introduction to the flora and fauna of the High Fens. Parts of the area can only be visited with a guide, especially the peat bogs and the feeding areas of the *capercaillies* (large and very rare woodland grouse). You can book an individual guide in advance, and you can also rent boots and bikes. ⊠ *Robertville,* ☎ *080/445781.* 🎟 *BF100.* ☉ *Daily 10–6. Closed Dec. 25 and Jan. 1.*

Schloss Reinhardstein, the loftiest and possibly the best-preserved medieval fortress in the country, is reached by a mile-long hike through the High Fens. It sits on a spur of rock overlooking the river Warche and has been in the hands of such illustrious families as the Metternichs, ancestors of Prince Metternich, the architect of the Congress of Vienna in 1815. The Hall of Knights and the Chapel are gems. ⊠ *Robertville,* ☎ *080/446868.* 🎟 *BF200.* ☉ *Tours mid-June–mid-Sept., Sun. at 2:15, 3:15, 4:15, and 5:15; July–Aug., also Tues., Thurs., and Sat. at 3:30.*

Malmédy

❻❼ *57 km (34 mi) southeast of Liège, 156 km (94 mi) southeast of Brussels, 16 km (10 mi) southeast of Spa.*

Malmédy and its neighbor, Stavelot, formed a separate, peaceful principality, ruled by abbots, for 11 centuries before the French Revolution. The Congress of Vienna, redrawing the borders of Europe, handed it to Germany, and it was not reunited with Belgium until 1925. In a scene straight out of *Catch 22,* the center of Malmédy was destroyed by American bombers in 1944 after the town had been liberated. Still, there's enough left of the old town, where street signs are often in French and Walloon, for an interesting walk. The town's carnival, beginning on the Saturday before Lent, is among the merriest in Belgium. To learn more about it, visit the **Musée du Carnaval.** ⊠ *Pl. de Rome 11, 3rd floor (no elevator),* ☎ *080/337058.* 🎟 *BF100.* ☉ *July–Aug., Wed.– Mon. 3–6; Sept.–June, weekends 2:30–5:30.*

NEED A BREAK?
Le Floreal (⊠ Pl. Albert I 8) serves breakfast, lunch, dinner, and snacks, such as the local ham, *jambon d'Ardennes.*

Dining and Lodging

$$$–$$$$ ✕🏠 **Hostellerie Trôs Marets.** Up the hill on the road toward Eupen, this inn offers a splendid view over the wooded valley. In fall, the fog hangs low over the nearby High Fens; in winter, cross-country skiing beckons. The main building contains the restaurant and rustic, cozy rooms. A modern annex has suites (furnished in contemporary English style, with fireplaces) and a large indoor pool. The restaurant serves up such specialties as duck's liver with caramelized apples, asparagus in truffle vinaigrette, grilled duckling with honey, and Herve cheese soufflé with Liège liqueur. Half-board is good value. ⊠ *Rte. des Trôs Marets 2, B 4960 Béverçé, 3 km (2 mi) north on N68 from Malmédy,* ☎ *080/337917,* 🖷 *080/337910. 7 rooms, 4 suites. Restaurant, covered pool. AE, DC, MC, V. Closed mid-Nov.–Dec. 23.*

$$ ✕🏠 **Ferme Libert.** This landmark is beautifully located on the edge of
★ the forest, a few miles north of town on the Eupen road. The architecture is traditional rustic, and the large dining room overlooks the valley. The menu is long on meat of all kinds, including ostrich, bison, and springbok. The ambience is similar to that of an Alpine resort, with skiing in winter (at least for a few weeks), bracing walks the rest of the year. Half-board is required on weekends. ⊠ *Chaussée de Béverçé– Village 26, B 4960 Béverçé,* ☎ *080/330247,* 🖷 *080/339885. 18 rooms with bath, 22 with shower. Restaurant. AE, MC, V.*

Outdoor Activities and Sports

The **Worriken Sports Center** (✉ R. Worriken 9, Bütgenbach, ☎ 080/
446961) offers horseback riding in the Hautes Fagnes region.

Stavelot

68 *15 km (9 mi) southwest of Malmédy, 59 km (37 mi) southeast of
Liège, 158 km (95 mi) southeast of Brussels.*

Although Stavelot is practically a twin town of Malmédy, its traditions
differ. Here Carnival is celebrated on the fourth Sunday in Lent and is
animated by about 2,000 *Blancs-Moussis* (White Monks), dressed in
white with long capes and long bright red noses, who swoop and rush
through the streets. The Blancs-Moussis commemorate the monks of
Stavelot, who in 1499 were forbidden to participate in Carnival but
got around it by celebrating Laetare Sunday (three weeks before Easter).
Stavelot, too, was badly damaged in the Battle of the Bulge, but some
picturesque old streets survive, particularly Rue Haute, off Place Saint-
Remacle. The square is named for St. Remacle, who founded a local
abbey in 647. His reliquary, now in the **Eglise St-Sébastien,** is one of
the wonders of Art Mosan. Dating from the 13th century, it is 6½ ft
long and decorated with statuettes, of the apostles on the sides and of
Christ and the Virgin on the ends. ✉ R. de l'Eglise 7, ☎ 080/862284.
🎫 BF50. ⊙ July–Aug., daily 9–noon and 2–5; rest of yr by appointment.

Only a Romanesque tower remains of the original buildings that
formed the **Ancienne Abbaye** (Old Abbey). The present buildings date
from the 18th century, and the refectory has become a concert hall.
The old stable has been converted into the **Musée d'Art Religieux Ré-
gional** (Regional Museum of Religious Art), and the vaulted cellars of
the abbey have been put to somewhat anachronistic use, housing the
Musée du Circuit de Spa-Francorchamps (Museum of the Spa-
Francorchamps Racecourse), which displays Formula I racing cars, sports
cars, and motorcycles illustrating the history of motor racing since 1907.
✉ Stavelot, ☎ 080/862706. 🎫 BF150; valid also for Museum of Religious Art. ⊙ Daily 10–12:30 and 2–5:30 (Nov.–Mar. until 4:30).

En Route The road from Stavelot runs through attractive landscape. The shortest—via Francorchamps—uses, in part, the former Grand Prix racing
circuit. An alternative, even more rewarding route, is via **Coo;** kayak
trips down the Amblève River start at the bottom of the waterfalls. Chair-
lifts take you up to **Telecoo,** a plateau where there's a splendid view
of the Amblève River valley, an extensive amusement park, and a 200-
acre Ardennes wildlife park (☎ 080/684265).

Dining and Lodging

$$ ✕🏨 **Le Val d'Amblève.** A member of the Romantik Hotels chain, the
★ hotel has a fresh ambience. Rooms face a lawn with century-old trees.
The restaurant ($$$) menu includes brill with asparagus and quail salad
with croutons and bacon. ✉ Rte. de Malmédy 7, 4970, ☎ 080/862353,
📠 080/864121. 13 rooms. Restaurant. AE, DC, MC, V. No dinner
Thurs. Closed Mon., 3 wks in Jan.

$$ ✕🏨 **Hôtel d'Orange.** A former post house, this friendly hotel has been
in the same family since 1789. The charming rooms are in Laura Ash-
ley style and there's a range of fixed-price menus, including one for
kids. Quail, ever popular in these parts, chicken à l'estragon (with tar-
ragon), and lamb are staples on the menu. ✉ Devant les Capucins 8,
4970, ☎ 080/862005, 📠 080/864292. 16 rooms with bath or shower.
Restaurant. AE, DC, MC, V. Closed in winter except weekends and
holidays.

Outdoor Activities and Sports

Virtually all the rivers of the Ardennes are great for canoeing, and the meandering Amblève is one of the best. Single or double kayaks can be rented at **Cookayak** (✉ Stavelot, ☎ 080/684265) for a 9-km (5-mi) ride from Coo to Cheneux (about 1½ hrs) or a 23-km (14-mi) ride to Lorcé (about 3½ hrs). Bus service back to the starting point is provided.

Spa

⑟   *18 km (11 mi) north of Stavelot, 38 km (23 mi) southeast of Liège, 139 km (83 mi) southeast of Brussels.*

The spa from which all others have derived their name: The Romans came here to take the waters, and they were followed over the centuries by crowned heads, such as Marguerite de Valois, Christina of Sweden, and Peter the Great. Less welcome was Kaiser Wilhelm II, who established his general headquarters in Spa in 1918. By then Spa was already past its prime. During the 18th and 19th centuries, Spa had been the watering place of international high society, and many gracious houses remain from that period. The pleasures of "taking the cure" in beautiful surroundings were heightened in those days by high-stakes gambling, playing *pharaon* or *biribi* for rubles, ducats, piastres, or francs. Gambling in today's casino is more sedate. The **Casino** dates from 1763, making it the oldest in the world, but the present building is from the beginning of the 20th century. Gaming rooms and the lobby are in Louis XVI style, a far cry from Las Vegas.

With its slightly geriatric air, Spa gives an impression of pleasantly faded elegance. The two best-known water sources in the center of town—locally known as *pouhons*—are the **Pouhon Pierre-le-Grant** and **Pouhon Prince-de-Condé,** which can be visited by tourists as well as *curistes* (people taking the cure). The price for a glass straight from the source is a modest BF7. ✉ *Town center,* ☎ *087/795353.* ⊙ *Baths: Easter–Oct., daily 10–noon and 2–5:30; Nov.–Easter, weekdays 1:30–5, weekends 10–noon and 1:30–5.*

The **Grottes de Remouchamps,** once inhabited by primitive hunters, are beautifully lit underground caves where you can take the "longest subterranean boat ride in the world." ✉ *Rte. de Louveigné,* ☎ *04/360–9070.* ▦ *BF300.* ⊙ *Feb.–Nov., daily 9–6.*

The **Grotte de Comblain-au-Pont** was reopened in 1994 with modern lighting, allowing visitors to discover the caves on their own. There's an abandoned underground quarry and a 10-km (6-mi) signposted walk so that you can fully appreciate the geological and botanical riches of the region. ✉ *R. du Grand Pré 25, Comblain-au-Pont,* ☎ *04/369–4133.* ▦ *BF330.* ⊙ *Apr.–mid-Nov., daily 10–5.*

Dining and Lodging

$$
★   ✕ **L'Art de Vivre.** Jean-François Douffet's fresh approach contrasts pleasantly with the old-fashioned gentility of his competitors. Sautéed goose liver accompanied by a potato pancake, pikeperch with deep-fried basil leaves, roast pigeon with a balsamic vinegar sauce, and ice cream with figs are among his creations. ✉ *Av. Reine Astrid 53,* ☎ *087/770444. AE, DC, MC, V. Closed Tues., Wed. (except July).*

$$
★   ✕ **La Brasserie du Grand Maur.** This graceful 200-year-old city mansion houses a lovely restaurant with a loyal clientele. Tartare of salmon, lamb infused with tomato and thyme, and duck's breast with raspberries and red currants are special favorites. The setting, all polished wood, linens, and antiques, enhances the meal. ✉ *R. Xhrouet 41,* ☎ *087/773616. AE, DC, MC, V. Closed Mon.–Tues., 3 wks Dec.–Jan., 2 wks in June.*

$–$$ ✕ **Old Inn.** A simple, slightly touristy lunch stop on the main street across from the baths, this beamed and wainscoted restaurant serves inexpensive regional dishes (ham, game), as well as mussels and crepes. It's one step up from a tavern, with pink linens covered by paper mats with ads for local businesses. ⊠ R. Royale 23–25, ☎ 087/773943. AE, DC, MC, V. Closed Wed.

$$ ▣ **Cardinal.** Offering a real taste of old Spa, this grand urban resort
★ hotel opened in 1924—and was completely renovated in 1948. Its period decor and interior architecture are completely intact and as fresh as new. Have tea in the muraled salon, hot chocolate in the beautiful all-oak café, or dinner in the swanky chandeliered dining hall. Most rooms have smooth gold oak paneling. ⊠ Pl. Royale 21–27, B 4900, ☎ 087/771064, ⅢⅩ 087/771964. 29 rooms. Restaurant, bar, tearoom. AE, DC, MC, V.

Outdoor Activities and Sports

Motor-sport fans know **Francorchamps** (near Spa) as one of the world's top racing circuits, but the Belgian Government's decision to ban tobacco advertising prompted Formula I to abandon the race; the August 1998 event was the last in its history. There are several other motorcycle and automobile races throughout the year, including a 24-hour rally. Contact Intercommunale du Circuit de Spa-Francorchamps (⊠ Rte. du Circuit 55, Francorchamps, ☎ 087/275138) for information.

Belgian Luxembourg

The Belgian province of Luxembourg is almost twice as large as the independent Grand Duchy of Luxembourg. Luxembourg made common cause with Belgium against the Dutch in 1830, but while Belgium gained its freedom, the Grand Duchy was divided by decree of the major European powers, with the western part going to Belgium and the rest, as a sort of consolation prize, handed to the unpopular William I of the Netherlands. It remained under Dutch domination for another 50-odd years. Luxembourg is the largest and, with just 200,000 inhabitants, by far the most sparsely populated province of Belgium. Here you can fill your lungs with fresh mountain air. It's a land of forests and dairy farms, slate-gray houses and fortresses perched on high rocks, swift streams and flowering meadows.

Durbuy

★ ⑳ 40 km (24 mi) southwest of Spa, 51 km (31 mi) south of Liège, 119 km (71 mi) southeast of Brussels.

Durbuy had just 400 inhabitants until 1978, when it unwillingly merged with surrounding parishes and became 20 times bigger. Before that, nothing much had changed since 1331, when Durbuy received its city charter from John the Blind of Luxembourg. Wander around the narrow streets and soak up the atmosphere of a remarkably homogeneous and well-preserved architecture, including the 16th-century, half-timbered grange where peasants brought the part of the harvest due the lord of the manor.

Eight kilometers (five miles) southeast of Durbuy is **Wéris,** one of the country's most beautiful villages, with half-timbered houses and a great fortified farm surround an 11th-century Romanesque church. A number of megaliths bear witness to an older culture.

Dining and Lodging

$ ✕ **Le Moulin.** The mill dates from the 13th century, the cuisine from the 20th, and the seasoning comes from Provence: thyme, garlic, and saffron. Loin of lamb, duckling breast with honey and sherry, and seafood

couscous are among the offerings. ⊠ *Pl. aux Foires 17,* ☎ *086/212970.*
AE, MC, V.

$$ ✕🖼 **Le Sanglier des Ardennes.** Dominating the center of town, this
inn–cum–luxury restaurant has a stone fireplace, beams, and public
spaces punctuated by glass cases with perfume, leather, and French
scarves for sale. Rooms are classic pastel-modern, and the bathrooms
are large. The restaurant ($$$$) offers grand French cooking with some
regional touches. Back windows overlook the Ourthe River. ⊠ *R.
Comte d'Ursel 99, B 6940 Durbuy,* ☎ *086/213262.* FAX *086/212465.
41 rooms. Restaurant, bar, outdoor café. AE, DC, MC, V. Closed Thurs.,
Jan.*

La Roche-en-Ardenne

★ **71** *29 km (17 mi) south of Durbuy, 77 km (46 mi) south of Liège, 127
km (76 mi) southeast of Brussels.*

La Roche-en-Ardenne is marvelously situated and full of tourists.
They're here for a good reason: The surroundings are the very essence
of the Ardennes. The main attraction is a trip out of town to admire
the view, and the principal part is played by the river Ourthe, a me-
andering stream that splashes through a landscape of great beauty. Fol-
low N834 south and turn left on N843 to **Nisramont,** which has an
excellent view. Cross the river and go left on N860 to Nadrin, and left
again on N869 to the **Belvedère des Six Ourthes,** thus named because
it has six different views of the meandering river. A 120-step climb to
the top of the observation tower will reward you with a magnificent
view of wooded hills and valleys. You can return on the pretty N860,
following the banks of the Ourthe toward La Roche.

The **château,** whose ruins dominate the small town, dates from the 9th
century. Subsequently it was expanded by a long series of occupants,
until the Austrians decided to partially dismantle it in the 18th cen-
tury. *Pl. du Marché,* ☎ *061/212711.* 🎟 *BF70.* ☉ *Apr.–June and Sept.,
daily 10–noon and 2–5; July–Aug., daily 10–7; Oct.–Mar., weekends
10–noon and 2–4.*

La Roche-en-Ardenne suffered badly during the Battle of the Bulge,
when some 70,000 shells hit the town. The **Musée de la Bataille des
Ardennes** (Museum of the Battle of the Ardennes) displays uniforms,
vehicles, weapons, and personal belongings found on the battleground.
⊠ *R. Châmont 5,* ☎ *084/411725.* 🎟 *BF180.* ☉ *Daily 10–6.*

Dining and Lodging

$$ ✕ **La Huchette.** Though a bit out of place in this hardy forest resort,
this elegant and welcoming restaurant serves good, classic French
cooking—delicate *quenelles* (dumplings) of pike in lobster broth,
salmon tournedos in tarragon, pigeon with red cabbage—in a decidedly nonrustic setting of pink, brass, and terra-cotta. ⊠ *R. de l'Eglise
6,* ☎ *084/411333. AE, MC, V. No dinner Tues. Closed Wed.*

$$ ✕🖼 **Hostellerie Linchet.** At the best address in an otherwise touristy
town, this new hotel has large rooms that overlook the Ourthe valley.
The restaurant ($$$) offers splendid views and a traditional cuisine that
includes such dishes as stuffed crayfish, poached trout in Alsatian
white wine, and fillet of venison with truffle sauce; there's alfresco dining in season. ⊠ *Rte. de Houffalize 11, B 6980,* ☎ *084/411223,* FAX
*084/412410. 13 rooms. Restaurant. AE, MC, V. Hotel and restaurant
closed Wed.–Thurs. Mar., 3 wks June–July.*

$$ ✕🖼 **Les Genets.** Even the rooms are pretty in this romantic old sprawl
of a mountain inn, with stenciled wallpaper and a homey mix of plaid,
paisley, and chintz. Picture windows take in valley views on two sides.

The restaurant offers gastronomic menus (grilled and smoked trout salad with hazelnut vinaigrette, pigeon in juniper). ⊠ *Corniche de Deister 2, B 6980,* ☎ *084/411877,* ℻ *084/411893. 8 rooms, 7 with bath. Restaurant, bar, garden, terrace. AE, DC, MC, V. Closed 3 wks June–July, 1st ½ of Jan.*

$ ✕🏨 **Du Midi.** This tiny old cliffside hotel is worth a visit for the food, which is the Real Thing: straightforward regional specialties, simply and stylishly served. In season wild game is superbly cooked (tenderloin of young boar in old port) and served with *gratin Dauphinois* (scalloped potatoes) and poached pear; there's also air-dried Ardennes ham with candied onions. The setting is local—oak, green plush, brass lamps, spinning-wheel chandeliers—though not old. The hotel is renovated, and all the rooms have bath or shower. ⊠ *R. Beausaint 6, 6980,* ☎ *084/411138,* ℻ *084/412238. 8 rooms with bath or shower. Restaurant. AE, DC, MC, V. Closed 2nd ½ of Jan.*

Bastogne

⑫ *34 km (20 mi) south of La Roche-en-Ardenne, 88 km (53 mi) south of Liège, 148 km (89 mi) southeast of Brussels.*

Bastogne is where General MacAuliffe delivered World War II's most famous response to a surrender request: "Nuts!" Although a number of Ardennes towns were destroyed during the Battle of the Bulge, Bastogne was the epicenter. The town was surrounded by Germans but held by the American 101st Airborne Division. The weather was miserable, making it impossible for supplies to be flown in to the Americans. On December 22, 1944, the Germans asked the U.S. forces to surrender. They didn't. On December 26 the skies cleared and supplies were flown in, but it took another month before the last German stronghold was destroyed. To this day, a Sherman tank occupies a place of honor in the center of town.

The **Colline du Mardasson** (Mardasson Hill Memorial) honors the Americans lost in the battle. The names of all U.S. Army units are inscribed on the wall, with a simple phrase: "The Belgian People Remembers Its American Liberators." Mosaics by Fernand Léger decorate the crypt's Protestant, Catholic, and Jewish chapels. The **Bastogne Historical Center,** next to the memorial monument, is built in the shape of a five-point star. The ebb and flow of the battle are shown in multivision in the amphitheater, and there are also showings of a remarkable new film, including footage shot during the battle. The collections include authentic uniforms, arms, and wartime memorabilia. ⊠ *N84, 3 km (2 mi) east of Bastogne,* ☎ *061/211413.* 🎫 *BF245.* ☉ *Sept.–Apr., daily 10–4; May–June, daily 9:30–5; July–Aug., daily 9–6.*

Dining and Lodging

$ ✕ **Wagon-Restaurant Léo.** Originally a tiny chrome railroad diner, this local institution has spilled over across the street into the new, chicly refurbished Bistro Léo. The restaurant serves huge platters of basic Belgian standards—mussels, trout in riesling, *filet Américain* (steak tartare), frites; in the bistro, cold ham plates, quiche, and homemade lasagna are the fare. ⊠ *R. du Vivier 8,* ☎ *061/216510. MC, V.*

$$ ✕🏨 **La Ferme au Pont.** On a country road between Bastogne and La
★ Roche, this calm, idyllic farmhouse inn is surrounded by forests, with the Ourthe rushing just behind it. Dating from 1747, with whitewashed brick, flower boxes on every sill, and a dining room with views of landscaped grounds, the inn offers good, simple French cooking—grilled ham and smoked trout—and comfortable rooms decked with ivy-print fabrics. ⊠ *Rte. N834, 16 km (10 mi) north of Bastogne,*

*near Ortho, B 6983, ☎ 084/433161, ℻ 084/333269. 6 rooms, 3
with bath. AE, DC, MC, V.*

$$ ⊞ **Melba.** A couple of minutes from Place MacAuliffe, this is a mod-
ern if somewhat anonymous hotel, with access for persons with dis-
abilities. A large buffet breakfast is included, supplied from the patisserie
of the same name. ⊠ *Av. Mathieu 49-51, B 6600, ☎ 061/217778, ℻
061/215568. 24 rooms with bath. Breakfast room, meeting rooms. AE,
MC, V.*

$ ⊞ **Du Sud.** Airy and solid in its new, postwar form, this straightfor-
ward little hotel kept its local atmosphere—oak details, game tro-
phies, tile floors—and offers simple comforts. Back rooms are quietest.
⊠ *R. de Marche 39, 6600, ☎ 061/211114. ℻ 061/217908 13 rooms
with shower. Café, garden. MC, V.*

St-Hubert

🕖 *28 km (17 mi) west of Bastogne, 25 km (15 mi) south of La Roche-
en-Ardenne, 137 km (82 mi) southeast of Brussels.*

St-Hubert bears the name of the patron saint of hunters. According to
legend, Hubert, hunting in these woods on Good Friday in 683, saw
his quarry, a stag, turn its head toward him; its antlers held a crucifix.
Hubert lowered his bow and went on to become a bishop and a saint.
On the first Sunday in September, the old **Basilica** has a special Mass
that includes music played with hunting horns, followed by a histori-
cal procession; and on November 3, St. Hubert's Feast Day, there's a
blessing of the animals in the Basilica. The Basilica is stunningly beau-
tiful, with a late Gothic interior of noble proportions and luminosity.
⊠ *Pl. de l'Abbaye, ☎ 061/612388. ▨ BF25. ⊙ Daily 9–6.*

Fourneau St-Michel has two interesting museums. One is an **Industrial
Museum** that includes a preserved 18th-century ironworks complex
and shows ironworking techniques up to the 19th century. The other
is an open-air **Museum of Rural Life**, with 25 structures, including
thatched cottages, tobacco sheds, a chapel, and a school. ⊠ *Rte. de
Nassagne, 7 km (4 mi) north of St-Hubert, ☎ 084/210890. ▨ BF100
per museum. ⊙ Mar.–Dec. (Rural Life until mid-Nov.), daily 9–5 (in
July–Aug. until 6).*

♻ The **Euro Space Center** shows off the latest technology in a futuristic
setting, with models (some full-scale) of the *Discovery* space shuttle,
Mir space station, and the *Ariane* satellite launcher. There's an educa-
tional program as well. ⊠ *R. Devant-les-Hêtres 1, Transinne, east of
St. Hubert, ☎ 061/656465. ▨ BF395. ⊙ Apr.–Nov., daily 10:30–6.*

Dining

$ ⊞ **Borquin.** In the shadow of the handsome Basilica, this small, friendly
hotel comprises a few reasonably comfortable rooms. The unabashedly
kitschy restaurant serves honest, home-style cooking. ⊠ *Pl. de l'Ab-
baye, 6870, ☎ 061/611456, ℻ 061/612018. 9 rooms, 7 with bath.
Restaurant. AE, DC, MC, V. Closed Wed. and 2nd ½ of Aug.*

Bouillon

🕗 *56 km (34 mi) southwest of St-Hubert, 81 km (49 mi) southwest of
La Roche-en-Ardenne, 161 km (97 mi) southeast of Brussels.*

In Bouillon, the Semois River curls around a promontory crowned by
one of Europe's most impressive castles. This tiny town was capital of
a duchy almost equally small, which managed to remain independent
for 800 years. Its most famous native son, Godefroid de Bouillon, sold
it to the Bishop of Liège in 1096 to improve his cash flow, before de-
parting on the first crusade and becoming Defender of the Holy Sepul-

chre. Bouillon owed its independence to the **Château Fort,** an impressive example of medieval military architecture. Successive modifications have done little to alter the personality of this feudal stronghold, with its towers, drawbridge, guardroom, torture chamber, dungeon, and enormous walls. There's an outstanding view from the top of the Tour d'Autriche. Visits by torchlight are organized nightly (except Monday and Thursday) in July and August. In season, the town is packed with tourists. ⊠ *On hill above city,* ☎ *061/466257.* ⊑ *BF150.* ☉ *Mar.–June and Sept.–Nov., daily 10–5; July–Aug., daily 9:30–7; Dec. and Feb., weekdays 1–5, weekends 10–5.*

The **Musée Ducal** is installed in an 18th-century mansion in front of the château. Its collections illustrate the history of the Crusades; another section is devoted to the printing press that published Voltaire, Diderot, and other writers when they could not publish in France. ⊠ *R. du Petit 1–3,* ☎ *061/466956.* ⊑ *BF120.* ☉ *Apr.–June and Sept.–Oct., daily 10–6; July–Aug., daily 9:30–6.*

★ ㊄ The **Abbaye d'Orval** was once one of Europe's richest and most famous monasteries. Founded by Italian Benedictines in 1070, it flourished for 700 years before being twice destroyed by French troops. The grandeur and nobility of the medieval and 18th-century ruins are remarkable. The tomb of Wenceslas, first Duke of Luxembourg, is in the choir of the abbey church, and outside it is the spring where Mathilde, Duchess of Lorraine, once dropped her wedding band, only to have it miraculously returned by a trout. The monastery was finally reconsecrated as a Trappist abbey in 1948. The monks are known not only for their spirituality but also for the excellence of their bread, cheese, and potent Trappist beer. ⊠ *Villers-devant-Orval,* ☎ *061/311060.* ⊑ *BF100.* ☉ *Mar.–May, daily 9:30–12:30 and 1:30–6; June, daily 9:30–12:30 and 1:30–6:30, Sept.–Feb., daily 10:30–12:30 and 1:30–5:30.*

Dining and Lodging

$$$$ ✕▥ **Auberge du Moulin Hideux.** Nestled in a valley amid leafy woods, this inn is synonymous with gracious living. The fountain is illuminated at night, swans glide in the small pond, and breakfast is served on the flower-bedecked terrace. The cuisine is traditional but updated with a lighter touch; woodcock mousse, black and white *boudins* (blood sausage) with truffles, and fabulous game in season are among the highlights. The rooms have been decorated with great taste by the owner. Interestingly, the name means the "Hideous Mill," a play on words from the fact that there used to be two mills, *il y a deux.* ⊠ *Rte. de Dohan 1, B 6831 Noirefontaine, 4 km (2½ mi) north of Bouillon,* ☎ *061/467015,* ℻ *061/467281. 10 rooms, 3 suites. Restaurant, bar, bicycles, pool. AE, DC, MC, V. Closed Dec.–mid-Mar.*

$$ ✕▥ **Au Gastronome.** This auberge, once a roadside café, is one of Bel-
★ gium's top restaurants ($$$$). The chef explores the usual stellar routes of haute cuisine, without losing any of its freshness. A local delicacy is suckling pig, roasted in its crisp skin, its juices blending with those of its stuffing of green pepper and lime. The setting is a little stuffy, but rooms upstairs are pleasantly old-fashioned, in shades of pink and cream, with floral prints. All overlook the garden. ⊠ *R. de Bouillon 2, B 6850 Paliseul, 15 km (9 mi) north of Bouillon,* ☎ *061/533064,* ℻ *061/533891. 9 rooms. Restaurant, pool, garden. AE, DC, MC, V. No dinner Sun. Closed Mon., Jan.–early Feb., last wk June–1st wk July.*

$ ✕▥ **Auberge d'Alsace.** In the center of Bouillon, with the river Semois across the street and the château towering behind, is this ambitious little hotel-restaurant. Having had the interior rebuilt from the ground up, the proprietress has lavished the rooms with flashy materials—brass, lacquer, lace, and the occasional baldachin. Striking a similar tenuous balance between store-bought chic and Old Ardennes, the restaurant downstairs offers good cooking: monkfish with kiwi, curried shrimp, home-smoked trout and *civet de marcassin* (stew of preserved young boar). ⊠ *Faubourg de France 1–3, B 6830,* ☎ *061/466588,* 🖷 *061/ 468321. 36 rooms, two suites. Restaurant, café, outdoor café. AE, MC, V.*

$$ 🖬 **De la Poste.** This is the most historic and atmospheric hotel in town, but not consistently the most comfortable. Since Napoléon III, Emile Zola, and Victor Hugo stayed at this 1730 stagecoach stop, its original rooms have been left virtually unchanged, balancing burnished oak and antiques with aged fixtures and small baths. The annex, built in 1990, offers modern comfort. Downstairs, the grandeur remains intact, with a charming mix of Victorian antiques and rustic brocante. The restaurant stretches along the riverfront; the menu features French classics. ⊠ *Pl. St-Arnould 1, B 6830 Bouillon,* ☎ *061/465151,* 🖷 *061/ 465165. 77 rooms, 68 with bath or shower. Restaurant, bar, outdoor café. AE, DC, MC, V.*

Arlon

❼⓰   *55 km (33 mi) east of Bouillon, 187 km (112 mi) southeast of Brussels, 29 km (17 mi) west of Luxembourg.*

Arlon, like Tongeren to the north and Tournai to the west, has a Roman past, which is vividly present in the **Musée Luxembourgeois.** The museum contains a number of Roman tombstones from the first 300 years AD, sculpted with reliefs of mythical figures as well as scenes from daily life. The best-known and most vivid is *The Voyagers.* There is also a section of Merovingian objects and jewelry. ⊠ *R. des Martyrs 13,* ☎ *063/226192.* 🖭 *BF100.* ☉ *Mid-Apr.–mid-Sept., Tues.–Sat. 9–noon and 1:30–6, Sun. 2–6.*

Dining and Lodging

$ ✕ **Le Clos St-Donat.** This downtown upstairs restaurant, decorated in pastel colors offset by showy copper, is a relaxing place to stop. The menu scales no heights: spring chicken with raisin sauce, blanquette of veal. Value-for-money fixed-price menus are available. ⊠ *Pl. Didier 31,* ☎ *063/234384. AE, MC, V. No lunch Sat., no dinner Sun. Closed 1st ½ of Sept.*

$$$ ✕🖬 **Château du Pont-d'Oye.** Close to the French border in Habay-la-Neuve, this graceful château stands on the edge of the forest, surrounded by ponds and ancient linden trees. The architectural splendor extends to the rooms and to the restaurant, where a distinguished clientele enjoys seafood coulis, quail stuffed with wild mushrooms. Book very early. ⊠ *R. du Pont d'Oye 1, B 6720 Habay-la-Neuve, 8 km (5 mi) north of Arlon,* ☎ *063/422148,* 🖷 *063/423588. 18 rooms. Restaurant. AE, DC, MC, V. No dinner Sun. Closed Mon., 2nd ½ of Feb., last wk in Aug.*

Wallonia: From the Meuse to the Ardennes A to Z

Arriving and Departing

BY CAR

In the **Meuse Valley,** Han-sur-Lesse is close to the E411 highway, which links Brussels with Luxembourg and runs south and east. Namur is close to the intersection of the E411 with the E42, which links Liège with Charleroi, Mons, and Paris, as well as with Tournai, Lille, and Calais.

Liège is almost halfway to Cologne from Brussels on the E40. The city is also linked with Paris by the E42, which merges with E19 from Brussels near Mons, and Antwerp by the E313, and with Maastricht and the Dutch highway system by E25, which continues south to join the E411 to Luxembourg.

The main arteries to and through the **Belgian Luxembourg** region are the E411 highway from Brussels, which can get very busy during school holidays, and the E25 from Liège, generally less traveled, which joins the E411 not far from the border with the Grand Duchy. When the E411 is busy, the N4 highway from Namur to Bastogne is often a good alternative. The N63 highway from Liège links up with the N4 at Marche-en-Famenne, and the N89 connects La Roche-en-Ardenne with Bouillon via Saint-Hubert. On this network of highways you are never more than a few miles from your destination.

BY TRAIN

Two trains an hour link Brussels with **Namur** (1 hour from Brussels's Gare du Midi, 50 minutes from the Gare du Nord). They connect with a local service to Dinant (25 minutes). For **train information** in Namur, call ☎ 081/223675.

Two trains run every hour from Brussels to **Liège** (1 hour by express train from Brussels Nord, 1 hour and 10 minutes from Brussels Midi; local trains are 10 minutes slower). Thalys high-speed trains cut 15 minutes off travel time from Brussels Midi. All express trains from Oostende to Cologne stop at Liège, as do international trains from Copenhagen and Hamburg to Paris. Liège's station is the **Gare des Guillemins** ☎ 04/252–9850).

Local trains from Brussels to Luxembourg stop in **Belgian Luxembourg** at Jemelle (near Rochefort) and Libramont (halfway between St-Hubert and Bouillon). Trains run every hour; the trip to Jemelle takes 1 hour and 5 minutes; to Libramont, 2 hours. The trains connect with local bus services.

Getting Around

BY BUS

From train stations in Liège, Verviers, Eupen, and Trois-Ponts there is bus service to other localities. In Liège, a single trip on a bus in the inner city costs BF36, and eight-trip cards sell for BF200.

BY CAR

The most convenient way of getting around the Meuse Valley, the Liège region, and Belgian Luxembourg is by car. Public transportation services are scant. The E411 highway cuts through the region. Elsewhere, you travel chiefly on pleasant, two-lane roads through lovely scenery.

BY TAXI

Taxis are plentiful in Liège. They can be picked up at cab stands in the principal squares or summoned by phone (☎ 04/367–6600).

BY TRAIN

Local train services exist from Liège via Verviers to Eupen, and to Trois-Ponts (near Stavelot).

Contacts and Resources

CAR RENTAL

Avis (✉ Bd. d'Avroy 238, Liège, ☎ 04/252–5500; ✉ Av. des Combattants 31, Namur, ☎ 081/735906). **Europcar** (✉ Sq. Léopold 20, Namur, ☎ 081/313256). **Hertz** (✉ Bd. d'Avroy 60, Liège, ☎ 04/222–4273).

GUIDED TOURS

By Boat. Boat tours, ranging from short excursions to all-day trips, are available in both Dinant and Namur: **Bateau Ansiaux** (✉ R. du Vélodrome 15, Dinant, ☎ 082/222325); **Bateau Bayard** (✉ Quai de Meuse 1, Dinant, ☎ 082/223042). With some advance planning, you could probably arrange to sail the entire length of the Meuse from France to the Netherlands by sightseeing boats: **Bateau Val Mosan** (✉ Quai de Namur 1, Huy, ☎ 025/212915).

From Liège, there are one-day sightseeing boat excursions to Maastricht in the Netherlands on Friday during July and August. A visit to the Blegny Coal Mine and museum is included. Departures are from the Passerelle on the right bank of the Meuse. For reservations call ☎ 04/387–4333.

On Foot. Guided walks are available April through September in **Mozet** (☎ 085/842155) on the third Sunday of each month, and in **Chardeneux** (☎ 086/344407) on the first Sunday of each month. In **Namur,** walking tours of the old city and the Citadelle, plus tours with a theme, such as local painters or gardens in the city, take place every day during July and August, starting at the Information Center (✉ Sq. Léopold, ☎ 081/246449). The price, per person, is BF140.

You can hire an English-speaking guide from the **Liège** City Tourist Office (☞ Visitor Information, *below*). Rates are BF1,600 for two hours, BF2,350 for three hours. If your French is up to it, you're welcome to join a guided walking tour with French commentary, starting from the city tourist office, July and August, Wednesday through Sunday, at 2, for BF140.

OUTDOOR ACTIVITIES AND SPORTS

Biking. In the **Meuse Valley** you can rent mountain bikes at **Bill's Bike Evasion** (✉ Chaussée de Namur 14, Profondeville, ☎ 081/414155), **Kayaks Ansiaux** (✉ R. du Vélodrome 15, Anseremme-Dinant, ☎ 082/222325), and **Kayaks Lesse & Lhomme** (✉ Le Plan d'Eau, Han-sur-Lesse, ☎ 082/224397).

Biking in **Belgian Luxembourg** requires strong legs. Mountain bikes can be rented from **Ardenne Adventures** and **Ferme de Palogne** (☞ Canoeing, *below*) and **Moulin de la Falize** (☎ 061/466200), a multisport facility with a swimming pool, bowling alleys, a sauna, and a fitness room.

Canoeing, Kayaking, Rafting. In the **Meuse Valley** region, the Lesse is one of the liveliest tributaries to the Meuse, great for kayaking. You can choose between the upper Lesse, where Lessive is the starting point, and the 21-km (13-mi) ride from Hoyet, through two rapids and past the high cliffs holding Walzin Castle, to Anseremme on the Meuse, just south of Dinant. Most of the kayak-rental companies also have mountain bikes (☞ Biking, *above*); others include **Kayaks Libert** (✉ Quai de Meuse 1, Dinant, ☎ 082/226186) and **Lesse Kayaks** (✉ Pl. de l'Eglise 2, Anseremme, ☎ 082/224397). The season runs from April through October. Rentals start at around BF800.

In **Belgian Luxembourg** the rapid rivers of the Ardennes are ideal for all three sports. Equipment can be rented by day or by distance, generally with return transportation to the point of departure. For the river Ourthe, try **Ardenne Adventures** (✉ La Roche-en-Ardenne, ☎ 084/411900; kayaks Apr.–Oct., rafting Nov.–Mar.) or **Ferme de Palogne** (✉ Vieuxville, ☎ 086/212412). For the Semois River, go to **Récréalle** (✉ Alle-sur-Semois, ☎ 061/500381), which also functions as a general sports center with facilities for table-tennis, minigolf, bowling, fishing, and volleyball, or **Saty Rapids** (✉ Bouillon, ☎ 061/466200).

Fishing. In the **Meuse Valley,** fishing is permitted on several stretches of the Meuse and on some livelier tributaries, where it is mostly of the sitting-on-the-bank kind. Licenses can be purchased at local post offices (✉ R. St-Martin, Dinant; ✉ Av. Bovesse, Namur-Jambes).

Horseback riding. In the **Meuse Valley** region several stables organize treks with overnight accommodations. Horses can be rented for about BF500 per hour. Contact the Provincial Tourist Office (☞ *below*) for a list of more than 20 stables. In **Belgian Luxembourg Centre Equestre de Mont-le-Soie** (✉ Grand-Halleux, ☎ 080/216443) offers both instruction and guided trail rides.

Rock Climbing. The sheer cliffs along the **Meuse** are excellent. Many hopeful mountaineers learn the skills here for more dramatic exploits. Contact **Club Alpin Belge** (✉ Av. Albert I 129, Namur, ☎ 081/224084).

Sailing. In the **Meuse** region sailing is extremely popular, with yacht harbors at Namur, Profondeville, Dinant, and Waulsort. Contact **Royal Nautique Club de Sambre et Meuse** (✉ Chemin des Pruniers 11, Wepion, ☎ 081/461130).

VISITOR INFORMATION
For the entire region of **Wallonia:** Office de Promotion du Tourisme (✉ R. du Marché-aux-Herbes 63, Brussels, ☎ 02/504–0200). **Province of Belgian Luxembourg:** Tourist Office (✉ Quai de l'Ourthe 9, La Roche-en-Ardenne, ☎ 084/411011). **Province of Liège:** Tourist Office (✉ Bd. de la Sauvenière 77, ☎ 04/222–4210). **Province of Namur:** Tourist Office (✉ Parc Industriel, R. Pieds d'Alouette 18, Naninne-Namur, ☎ 081/408010).

City tourist offices: **Arlon** (✉ R. des Faubourgs 2, ☎ 063/216360); **Bastogne** (✉ Pl. MacAuliffe 24, ☎ 061/212711); **Bouillon** (✉ Bureau du Château-Fort, ☎ 061/466257; during high season, ✉ Porte de France, ☎ 061/466289); **Dinant** (✉ R. Grande 37, ☎ 082/222870); **Durbuy** (✉ R. Comte d'Ursel, ☎ 086/212428); **Eupen** (✉ Marktpl. 7, ☎ 087/553450); **Huy** (✉ Quai de Namur 1, ☎ 085/212915); **La Roche-en-Ardenne** (✉ Syndicat d'Initiative, Pl. du Marché 15, ☎ 084/411342); **Liège** (✉ En Féronstrée 92, ☎ 04/221–9221); **Malmédy** (✉ Pl. du Châtelet 10, ☎ 080/330250); **Namur** (✉ Sq. de l'Europe Unie, ☎ 081/246449); **Spa** (✉ R. Royale 41, ☎ 087/795353); **St-Hubert** (✉ R. St-Gilles, ☎ 061/613010); **Stavelot** (✉ Ancienne Abbaye, ☎ 080/862706).

BELGIUM A TO Z

Arriving and Departing

From North America by Plane
All intercontinental and most international flights arrive at **Brussels National Airport,** in Zaventem. The airport is linked with Antwerp by coach service and with all other Belgian cities by rail.

Sabena (☎ 02/723–2323), the Belgian national carrier, flies to Brussels from New York, Boston, and Chicago; **City Bird,** a new, ultra-budget airline (☎ 02/752–5252), from Los Angeles, San Francisco, Las Vegas, Miami and Orlando; **American Airlines** (☎ 02/508–7700), from Chicago; **Delta** (☎ 02/730–8200), from New York and Atlanta; **United** (☎ 02/646–5588), from Washington, D.C.

Sample flying times are as follows: 6 hours, 50 minutes from New York to Brussels; and seven hours from Boston to Brussels. Return flights are about an hour longer.

From the United Kingdom
BY BUS
City Sprint, operated by Hoverspeed (☎ 01304/240241), offers bus service to Dover, Hovercraft service to Calais, and another bus connection to Brussels or Antwerp. Both trips take about seven hours. **Eurolines**

(☎ 0900/143219) has daily and overnight services, using the ferry to
Oostende. The trip takes about 10½ hours.

BY CAR

For information about using the Channel Tunnel, *see* Driving *in* the
Gold Guide.

The main ferry route to Belgium is from Ramsgate or Dover to Oostende. Unless you're traveling in the dead of winter, and sometimes even
then, it's essential to book well in advance (☞ By Ferry, *below*). Rates
vary according to the length of your vehicle, the time of your crossing, and whether you travel in peak, shoulder, or low season.

Both the **Automobile Association** (✉ Fanum House, Basingstoke,
Hants. RG21 2EA, ☎ 01345/500600) and the **Royal Automobile Club**
(✉ 1 Forest Rd., Feltham, Middlesex, TW13 4RR, ☎ 0181/917–2500)
operate on-the-spot breakdown and repair services across Belgium. Both
companies will also transport cars and passengers back to Britain in
case of serious breakdowns. AA has 5-day, 12-day, and 31-day coverage; RAC offers 10-day and 31-day coverage.

BY FERRY

The principal route across the English Channel to Belgium is Ramsgate to Oostende, operated by **Sally Line** (✉ ☎ 01843/853896). The
crossing by ferry takes four hours, with two sailings each way on
weekdays, and one each way on weekends.

Hoverspeed (✉ ☎ 059/559955) operates the Seacat catamaran services between Oostende and Dover; taking around two hours, there
are between five and seven daily sailings each way. The Belgium–England ferry services have undergone considerable upheaval in recent
years, so it pays to check that the operator you select for your holiday
is still in business before you sail.

BY PLANE

British Airways (☎ 02/725–3000) flies to Brussels from London
(Heathrow and Gatwick); **British Midland** (☎ 02/772–9400), **Sabena**
(☎ 02/723–2323), and **Virgin Express** (☎ 0044/171/744–0004) from
London (Heathrow). Other U.K. cities with direct or nonstop flights
to Brussels include Birmingham, Manchester, Newcastle, Leeds, Bristol, Edinburgh, and Glasgow. Flying time from London to Brussels is
40 minutes; Brussels to London is 45 minutes.

BY TRAIN

For details on the Eurostar and Thalys high-speed trains, *see* Rail
Travel *in* the Gold Guide.

Car Rentals

Major firms in Brussels include **Alamo** (☎ 02/753–2060), **Astral**(☎
02/734–3090), **Avis** (☎ 02/726–9488), **Budget** (☎ 02/646–5130), **Eurodollar** (☎ 02/725–6066), **Europcar** (☎ 02/348–9212), and **Hertz** (☎
02/726–4950).

Guided Tours

General-Interest Tours

Listed below is a sample of the tours and packages that concentrate
on Belgium. For tours that cover the Benelux region, *see* Tour Operators *in* The Gold Guide.

FROM THE U.K.

Shearing Holidays (✉ Miry La., Wigan, Lancashire WN3 4AG, ☎
01942/824824) features a five-day city break centered in Brugge with

excursions to Brussels and other places of interest. **Time Off Ltd.** (⊠ 1 Elmfield Park, Bromley, Kent, BR1 1CV, ☎ 0990/846363) has packages from two to seven nights to Brussels and Brugge.

Special-Interest Tours

FROM THE U.K.

The Belgium Travel Service (⊠ Bridge House, 55–59 High Rd., Broxbourne, Herts. EN10 7DT, ☎ 01992/456166) specializes in inclusive holidays to the major cities, and it also organizes tailor-made individual tours to several destinations in Belgium. **Holts' Tours** (⊠ 15 Market St., Sandwich, Kent CT13 9DA, ☎ 01304/612248) organizes tours of World War I battlefields in France and Belgium, with an emphasis on the Ieper battlefield. Waterloo and Battle of the Bulge tours are also available.

Package Deals for Independent Travelers

American Airlines Fly Away Vacations (☎ 800/832–8383) offers independent packages for as long as you like for visits to Brussels, Brugge, and Antwerp. **Northwest WorldVacations** (☎ 800/225–2225) provides visitors to Brussels with preferred hotel and car-rental rates and tour options for a minimum of two nights. **Travel Bound** (⊠ 599 Broadway, Penthouse, New York, NY 10012, ☎ 212/334–1350 or 800/456–8656) offers tailor-made packages for independent travelers. **United Vacations** (⊠ 106 Calvert St., Harrison, NY 10528, ☎ 800/678–0949) will customize your itinerary in Belgium.

Languages

Belgium is bisected by a linguistic border, with Dutch spoken to the north and French to the south of it. Written Flemish is indistinguishable from Dutch, but spoken Flemish may include dialect variations. Some French-speakers have Walloon, a separate German-influenced tongue, as a second language. German, spoken by 200,000 people at the eastern end of the country, is Belgium's third official language. Brussels is officially bilingual (Dutch/French).

Language is a sensitive subject in Belgium. You are advised to use English rather than French in Flanders, even though both are widely understood. You will have no problem finding English-speakers in Brussels. In Wallonia you may have to muster some French, but in tourist centers you will be able to find people who speak some English.

Mail

Postal Rates

An airmail letter or postcard to the United States costs BF34 for up to 20 grams, BF60 for up to 50 grams. Letters (up to 20 grams) and postcards to the United Kingdom cost BF17; up to 50 grams, BF41. Airmail letters must have an "A PRIOR" sticker.

Money and Expenses

Currency

The monetary unit in Belgium is the Belgian franc. There are bills of 100, 200, 500, 1,000, 2,000, and 10,000 francs, and coins of 1, 5, 20, and 50 francs. From January 1, 1999, the European single currency (euro) will also be in use electronically across the Benelux (the actual currency will not come into circulation until January 1, 2002; one euro will be worth around BF40. At press time (winter 1999), one dollar was worth about BF35; one pound sterling, BF57; one Canadian dollar, BF23; one Australian dollar, BF22; one New Zealand dollar, BF19; and one Irish punt, BF51.

What It Will Cost

Inflation is low, currently at less than 2%. Brussels, with its influx of business travelers and officials on EU business, has some very expensive hotels and restaurants, but enterprising hoteliers and restaurateurs offer similar quality at much lower prices. Value Added Tax (TVA) is always included in the price quoted for accommodations and meals. It ranges from 6% on basic items to 21% (☞ Shopping, *below*).

SAMPLE COSTS

A cup of coffee in a café will cost you BF45–BF60; a glass of beer, BF40–BF85 for a 25cl pils, BF80–BF120 for a Trappist or specialty beer; a glass of wine, about BF100. Train travel averages BF7 per mile, the average bus/metro/tram ride costs BF50, theater tickets are about BF500, and movie tickets cost about BF250.

Outdoor Activities and Sports

Two organizations provide information on all sports facilities in the country: **BLOSO** (⊠ R. des Colonies 31, ☎ 02/510–3411), for Flemish speakers, and **ADEPS** (⊠ Bd. Léopold II 44, ☎ 02/413–2800), for French speakers.

Cycling

The flat land of Flanders is ideal for this sport, but it can get windy at times. The steep hills of the Ardennes are for athletes. You can rent bikes cheaply at many railway stations, but they aren't state-of-the-art models. Specialized rental shops exist in most tourist centers.

Golf

Until recently, golf was strictly a rich man's sport in Belgium—there are no public courses in the country—but it is becoming more popular, with courses near all major cities. For locations, contact the **Fédération Royale Belge de Golf** (Royal Belgian Golf Federation; ⊠ Chaussée de La Hulpe 110, 1000 Brussels, ☎ 02/672–2389).

Mountaineering

The Ardennes may not be the Alps, but the many cliffs, especially along the Meuse River valley, provide excellent opportunities for rock-face climbing. For information, call the **Club Alpin Belge** (⊠ Av. Albert I 129, Namur, ☎ 081/224085).

Tennis

There are tennis courts aplenty, but book early because this is a very popular sport. Your hotel concierge will generally help. For more information, contact the **Fédération Royale Belge de Tennis** (Royal Belgian Tennis Federation; ⊠ Galerie Porte Louise 203, 1050 Brussels, ☎ 02/513–2920).

Water Sports

All along the coast, as well as on lakes and man-made bodies of water, you'll see large numbers of people windsurfing. For information on this and other water sports, contact the **Vlaamse Watersportvereiningen** (Flemish Water Sport Association; ⊠ Beatrijslaan 25, Antwerp, ☎ 03/219–6967).

Shopping

Good-quality lace is available in several shops in Brussels (but not in souvenir shops); even so, you may wish to wait until you've seen what is available in Brugge before making your choice. Similarly, if you're interested in fashion, wait until you've checked out the avant-garde boutiques in Antwerp. If your visit includes Liège, go first to the Val St-

Lambert factory shop before buying crystal elsewhere. Chocolate is best bought as close to departure as possible. Some of the leading brands (Godiva, Neuhaus) are available in the airport shop at the airport.

Many shops advertise that goods are available tax-free. There's a simpler option than those mentioned in the Gold Guide, but it requires trust. At the time of purchase by credit card, you pay the price without TVA and you also sign, with your card, a guarantee in the amount of the sales tax. You are given two invoices: One is your record and the other must be stamped by customs when you leave Belgium (or the last EU country on your itinerary). You must return the stamped invoice to the store within three months, or you forfeit the guarantee.

Student and Youth Travel

The youth information service in Brussels is **Infor-Jeunes** (☎ 070/233444), and there's also an English-language **Help Line** (☎ 02/648–4014), which provides both practical information and crisis intervention. **Acotra** (✉ R. de la Madeleine 51, ☎ 02/512–7078) will help in finding inexpensive accommodations.

Youth hostels are inexpensive and numerous. For information on facilities in Wallonia, write to **Les Auberges de la Jeunesse** (Belgian Youth Hostels; ✉ R. de la Sablonnière 28, 1000 Brussels, ☎ 02/219–5676); for Flanders, **Vlaamse Jeugdherbergcentrale** (Flemish Youth Hostel Center; ✉ Van Stralenstraat 40, 2060 Antwerp, ☎ 03/232–7218).

Telephones

Local Calls
Pay phones work with Telecards, available in a number of denominations, starting at BF200. These cards can be purchased at any post office and at many newsstands. Most phone booths that accept Telecards have a list indicating where cards can be bought. Public phones in Brussels metro stations are still coin-operated, taking 5- and 20-franc coins. A local call costs between BF10 and BF20.

International Calls
The least expensive way to call is to buy a high-denomination Telecard and make a direct call from a phone booth; a five-minute call to the United States at peak time will cost about BF750. Most hotel rooms are equipped with direct-call telephones, but nearly all add a service charge that can be substantial. It's better to ask beforehand what service charges are applied.

To call collect or by credit card, to the United States, dial 0800/10010 for **AT&T**; 0800/10012 for **MCI**; or 0800/1014 for **US Sprint**; to the United Kingdom, dial 0800/10044 for **BT Direct.** Similar services now exist for most countries; consult the phone book under "Communications internationales manuelles."

Tipping

A service charge is included in restaurant and hotel bills, and tips are also included in the amount shown on the meter in taxis. Additional tipping is unnecessary unless you wish to say thank you for good service. Hotel porters generally get a gratuity of BF100 for carrying bags to your room. Tip doormen BF50 for getting you a cab. Porters in railway stations ask a fixed per-suitcase price of BF60. In movie theaters, ushers expect a BF10 tip when you present the ticket. Washroom attendants get a BF10 tip. Hairdressers usually receive 10%–20%.

Transportation

By Bus

Intercity bus travel is not well developed in Belgium. You can, however, reach a number of localities surrounding each city by the local bus company.

By Car

Belgium has a magnificent network of motorways and, in contrast with the railroads, not all are spokes from the Brussels hub. You can, for instance, drive along fast, four-lane highways from Antwerp to Gent, or Liège to Tournai or Brugge to Kortrijk, without passing through the capital. There are no tolls, and most highways are illuminated at night.

You must carry a warning triangle, to be placed well behind the car in case of a breakdown. There are emergency telephones at intervals along the motorways. The speed limit is 120 kph (74 mph) on motorways, 90 kph (56 mph) on secondary roads, and 50 kph (31 mph) in built-up areas. At intersections, always check traffic from the right even if you're on a thoroughfare; Belgian drivers can be reckless in insisting on "priority on the right, and your insurance will be liable in any such accident. Gas costs about the same as in other European countries, which means quite a bit more than in the United States (almost a dollar a liter).

By Plane

There is no domestic air service.

By Train

The **Société Nationale des Chemins de Fer Belge** (✉ SNCB/Belgian National Railways, R. de France 85, 1070 Brussels, ☎ 02/203–3640) provides frequent train service—first and second class—from Brussels to all major cities in the country. Very few are more than an hour away. This means that you can, if you wish, see most of the country on day trips while remaining based in Brussels and traveling on reduced-price, same-day return tickets. Tickets are sold only at railway stations.

RAIL PASSES

Tourrail Tickets allow unlimited travel on the Belgian network for any five days during a one-month period. The price is BF2,995 first class and BF1,995 second class. A **Go-Pass,** available at BF1,360 for persons between 12 and 26, is good for 10 one-way trips in a six-month period; it is not individual and can be used by a group traveling together. Rail passes can be bought in any Belgian railway station.

Visitor Information

The **main national tourist office** (✉ R. Marché-aux-Herbes 63, ☎ 02/504–0390) for Belgium (except Brussels) is near the Grand'Place in Brussels.

4 Luxembourg

Tiny Luxembourg, nestled between Germany, France, and Belgium, has been a pawn of world powers for much of its 1,000 years. Today it looms large as a world financial powerhouse and one of Europe's most scenic countries. Come here for rambles through medieval villages and hilltop castles, strolls along riverbanks and through deep forests, and hearty meals in country inns. From sophisticated Luxembourg City, with its ancient fortifications and modern skyscrapers, to the Ardennes plateau, site of the World War II Battle of the Bulge, to the wineries along the Moselle, Luxembourg is 999 square miles of beauty, history, and good times.

By Nancy
Coons

Updated by
Jennifer
Abramsohn

THE CAPITAL OF LUXEMBOURG greets visitors with an awe-inspiring view: Up and down the length of the Alzette River stretches a panorama of medieval stonework—jutting fortification walls, slit-windowed towers, ancient church spires, massive gates—as detailed and complete as a 17th-century engraving come to life. Then you abruptly enter the 20th century. The Boulevard Royal, little more than five blocks long, glitters with glass-and-concrete office buildings, each containing a world-class bank and untold anonymous, well-sheltered fortunes.

Luxembourg, once sovereign to lands that stretched from the Meuse to the Rhine, was reduced over the centuries to being a pawn in the power struggles between its many conquerors. Until recently little more than a cluster of meager farms and failing mines, Luxembourg today enjoys newfound political clout and the highest per capita income in the world.

The Grand Duchy of Luxembourg, one of the smallest countries in the United Nations, measures only 2,597 square km (999 square mi). Less than the size of Rhode Island, it has a population of 420,000. It is dwarfed by its neighbors—Germany, Belgium, and France—yet from its history of invasion, occupation, and siege, you would think those square miles were filled with solid gold. In fact, it was Luxembourg's fortresses carved out of bedrock, its very defenses against centuries of attack, that rendered it all the more desirable.

It started in 963, when Charlemagne's descendant Sigefroid, a beneficiary of the disintegration of Central Europe that followed Charlemagne's death, chose a small gooseneck, carved by the Alzette, to develop as a fortress and the capital of his considerable domain. Thanks to his aggressions and the ambitions of his heirs, Luxembourg grew continuously until, by the 14th century, its count, Henry IV, was powerful and important enough to serve as Henry VII, king of the German nations and Holy Roman Emperor. During that epoch, Luxembourg contributed no fewer than five kings and emperors, including Henry VII's son, the flamboyant John the Blind (Jean l'Aveugle), who, despite leading his armies to slaughter in the Battle of Crécy (1346), remains a national hero.

After John the Blind's death, Luxembourg commanded the greatest territory it would ever rule—from the Meuse to Metz and the Moselle—and its rulers, Charles IV, Wenceslas I and II, and Sigismund, carried the name of the House of Luxembourg to European renown. If Luxembourg had a golden age, this was it, but it was short-lived. Plague, the decay of feudalism, marital and financial intrigues among leaders who rarely, if ever, set foot in Luxembourg—all these factors finally left the duchy vulnerable, and Philip the Good, Duke of Burgundy, took it by storm in 1443.

From that point on, Luxembourg lost its significance as a geographical mass and took on importance as a fortress. It was controlled from 1443 to 1506 by Burgundy, from 1506 to 1714 by Spain (with a brief period, 1684–97, under Louis XIV of France), and from 1714 to 1795 by Austria; Napoléon took it from the Habsburgs in 1795. Each, in taking the fortress, had to penetrate miles of outworks whose battlements filled the countryside. After having penetrated the outer defenses, the aggressors then faced a citadel perched on sheer stone cliffs, from which weapons pointed at them and within which the soldiers outnumbered the citizens. To take it by frontal attack was out of the question; the solution, usually, was siege and starvation.

Having been torn and ravaged for 400 years by its conquerors' games of tug-of-war, Luxembourg continued to provoke squabbles well into the 19th century. The Congress of Vienna gave a territorially reduced Luxembourg independence of a sort. The Grand Duke of Luxembourg was also King of Holland when Belgium rebelled against Dutch rule in 1830. Only the presence of a Prussian garrison kept Luxembourg in the Dutch camp. Nine years later, Luxembourg was again partitioned, with the western half becoming a Belgian province. William II became the first and last Dutch Grand Duke to achieve popular acclaim; he created a parliament and laid the foundations for modern Luxembourg. In 1867 Luxembourg was declared an independent and neutral state by the Treaty of London, and its battlements were dismantled, stone by stone. What remains of its walls, while impressive, is only a reminder of what was once one of the great strongholds of Europe.

The Grand Duchy's neutrality was violated by the Germans in 1914. When World War I ended, the people of Luxembourg gave their confidence, by popular vote, to Grand Duchess Charlotte, who remained a much-loved head of state for 45 years until abdicating in favor of her son, Jean, in 1964. Grand Duke Jean is married to Grand Duchess Joséphine-Charlotte, the daughter of Belgium's King Leopold and his Swedish-born Queen Astrid. Their large family has remained untouched by the types of scandals that have marred the reputations of other royal houses.

In the late 19th century, breakthroughs in both farming and mining technology turned the country around. A new, efficient technique for purifying iron ore created an indispensable by-product, fertilizer, which started a boom that put Luxembourg on 20th-century maps. A steel industry was created and, with it, more jobs than there were local workers. Thousands of workers came from Italy, and later Portugal, to take up residence in Luxembourg. Even today, about 20% of the workforce lives outside Luxembourg and crosses the border daily going to and from work.

Most recently, Luxembourg has become one of the world's top financial centers, with 225 banks from throughout the world established in the Grand Duchy. The broadcasting and communications satellite industries are also important to the national economy.

Hitler was convinced that Luxembourg was part of the greater Germanic culture. Suppressing *Lëtzebuergsch* (Luxembourgish, the local language) and changing French names into German, he launched a campaign to persuade Luxembourgers to *Heim ins Reich*—come home to the fatherland as ethnic Germans. Yet a visit to any war museum will show that the Luxembourgers weren't having any of it, and that the majority has yet to forget that the German invasions left Luxembourg hideously scarred and that thousands of its men were conscripted during the German occupation and sent as so much cannon fodder to the Russian front.

The experiences of two world wars convinced Luxembourg that neutrality does not work. Native son Robert Schuman was one of the founding fathers of the Common Market that eventually became the European Union, with Luxembourg a charter member. The European Court of Justice and other European institutions are located in Luxembourg. The Grand Duchy is fiercely opposed to any suggestions that it would save money if all such bodies were headquartered in Brussels. It is most unlikely to happen during the lifetime of the present European Commission, whose president is the former, long-serving prime minister of Luxembourg, Jacques Santer.

Soldiers from Luxembourg serve with young men from France, Germany, and Belgium in the European Army. Small it may be, but the army is a powerful symbol of the unity that has replaced old enmities. The men from Luxembourg can communicate with their European brothers more easily than the others, because they are fluent in both French and German. French is the official language of the Grand Duchy, and the teaching of German is mandatory in the schools. Luxembourgers' own language, *Lëtzebuergsch,* descended from the language of the Rhineland Franks, has the added advantage of being understood by virtually no one else, be they occupiers, business partners, or tourists. This is the language in which the national motto is expressed: *Mir wölle bleiwe wat mir sin,* "We want to stay what we are." Today that means being a powerful, viable grand duchy in the heart of modern Europe.

Pleasures and Pastimes

Archaeology

The adventure of discovering a world of the past can be enjoyed to the fullest in old Luxembourg City, which has been declared a World Heritage Site by UNESCO. Walks have been laid out that let you explore the city's 1,000-year history, and an exciting vertical museum allows you to contemplate the evolution of human habitation on this rock.

Castles

Luxembourg City was not the only place that knew how to defend itself. There are more than 50 feudal castles in this small country, of all sizes, ages, styles, and states of repair. You come around a bend in a road, or crest a hill, and in front of you looms a feudal stronghold, dominating the surrounding landscape with its squat towers, slender turrets, and massive walls.

Dining

"French quality, German quantity"—that's an apt and common description of Luxembourg cuisine. Local posted menus tend toward *cuisine bourgeoise*—veal with cream and mushrooms, beef entrecôte with peppercorn sauce, veal *cordon bleu* (stuffed with ham and cheese)—all served in generous portions, with heaps of *frites* (french fries) on the side. Yet this tiny country has its own earthy cuisine, fresh off the farm: *judd mat gardebounen* (smoked pork shoulder with broad beans), *jambon d'Ardennes* (smoked ham served cold with pickled onions), *choucroute* (sauerkraut), batter-fried whiting, and spicy *gromperekichelcher* (fried potato patties). More upscale additions to the national specialties are *écrevisses* (crayfish), cooked with local wine, and all manner of trout.

Luxembourg has more star-studded French *gastronomique* restaurants per capita than any other European country. Many restaurants—including some of the top ones—offer a moderately priced luncheon menu. Ethnic restaurants present less expensive alternatives, and, given the sizable population of people of Italian descent, pasta and pizza have almost acquired the status of a national cuisine. Fast-food eateries are also present in force, especially in the capital.

Lunch takes place mostly between noon and 2. Dinner, except in the fanciest restaurants, tends to be earlier than the European norm, generally between 7 and 9.

CATEGORY	COST*
$$$$	over Flux 3,000
$$$	Flux 1,500–3,000
$$	Flux 750–1,500
$	under Flux 750

per person for a three-course meal including service and tax and excluding beverages

Lodging

Hotels in Luxembourg are tidy and straightforward, rarely reaching the peaks of luxury, but equally rarely representing tremendous bargains. Most hotels in Luxembourg City are relatively modern and vary from the international style, mainly near the airport, to family-run establishments in town. Many of these, often filled with business travelers on weekdays, offer reduced rates on weekends. Outside the capital, hotels are often in picturesque buildings.

The **Office National du Tourisme** (✉ ONT, B.P. 1001, L-1010 Luxembourg, ☎ 4008–0820, FAX 404748) will make hotel reservations free of charge. Such bookings must be confirmed by the traveler. The ONT offices at the airport and railway station will make reservations for travelers arriving without one.

Inexpensive youth hostels are plentiful; many are set in ancient fortresses and castles. Most are linked by marked trails of 10–20 mi. For information, contact **Centrale des Auberges Luxembourgeoises** (✉ 2, R. du Fort Olisy, L-2261 Luxembourg, ☎ 225588). The Grand Duchy is probably the best-organized country in Europe for camping. It has some 120 sites, all with full amenities. Listings are published annually by the **National Tourist Office** (✉ ONT, B.P. 1001, L-1010 Luxembourg).

CATEGORY	COST*
$$$$	over Flux 8,000
$$$	Flux 5,000–8,000
$$	Flux 2,500–5,000
$	under Flux 2,500

for two persons sharing a double room, including service and tax

Wines and Spirits

Luxembourg takes pride in its Moselle wines. The vineyards stretch along the hills lining the Moselle River, taking maximum advantage of the region's muted sunlight. The best wines include a crisp Riesling or Auxerrois, a dry Pinot Gris or a rounder Pinot Blanc, and the rare, rosé-like Pinot Noir. More commonplace varieties, often served in pitchers or by the glass, are Rivaner and Elbling. Luxembourg's Moselle wines lend themselves well to the French aperitif *kir,* a glass of white wine tinted pale pink with a touch of cassis, a version of which is made in the castle village of Beaufort. Be sure to try the local liqueur, eaux de vie, made from the fruity essence of *quetsch* (a little blue plum), *mirabelle* (halfway between a plum and a yellow cherry), kirsch, or—for the hard core—grain, the last best mixed in a mug of strong coffee. Moselle wines, both sparkling and regular, can be tasted and purchased in gift packs from most of the wineries. Artisanale distilleries also sell their eaux-de-vie along the Moselle highway.

Exploring Luxembourg

The Old Town of Luxembourg is of necessity small; there's not much space within the walls of a fortress built on a rock. This makes it eminently walkable, and there's an elevator to transfer you down to the level of the surrounding part of town. Short distances make it possible, too, to visit the rest of the country within the space of a few pleasant days.

One attractive region of Luxembourg goes by the nickname "Little Switzerland." In a way, that appellation could apply to the Grand Duchy as a whole. Whether you are walking, driving, or riding a bike, the pleasure of being surrounded by an attractive and well-tended countryside is ever present, from the vineyards along the Moselle to the steep hills and deep woods to the north.

Great Itineraries

Numbers in the text correspond to numbers in the margin and on the Luxembourg City and Luxembourg Ardennes maps.

IF YOU HAVE 2 DAYS

On the first day, take in the classic sights of 🗺 **Luxembourg City** ①–㉕, with visits to the French-built Citadelle du Saint-Esprit, the Bock, the maze of underground defense passages known as the Casemates, and the Cathédrale Notre-Dame with its royal crypt. The interactive Musée de la Ville de Luxembourg, which traces Luxembourg's 1,000-year history, the Palais Grand-Ducal, the art treasures of the Musée National d'Histoire et d'Art, the Grund district along the Alzette, the Vallée de la Petrusse, the banking street, Boulevard Royal, and the main pedestrian shopping street, Grand-Rue, are also worth visits.

On the second day, allow ample time for the Wenzel Walk through space and time. It leads from the Bock down into the valley, past ancient gates and ruins, over 18th-century military installations, and along the Alzette, with audiovisual presentations along the way. Use the afternoon to re-enter the 20th century at Kirchberg, a plateau to the east of the old city that is home to the European Union institutions, including the European Court of Justice. Here, too, are modern bank palaces of architectural and artistic interest.

IF YOU HAVE 3 DAYS

Follow the itinerary above, and on the third day, drive north to the Luxembourg Ardennes via **Diekirch** ㉖, whose Museum of Military History brings alive the Battle of the Bulge, then on to **Vianden** ㉗, home of one of the most spectacularly dramatic castles you're ever likely to see.

Continue north to **Clervaux** ㉘, where there's another sprawling castle, now the permanent home of *The Family of Man* photo exhibition.

IF YOU HAVE 5 DAYS
Follow the itinerary above and stay overnight in 🏨 **Clervaux** ㉘. Turning south, stop in tiny **Esch-sur-Sûre** ㉙, circled by the river and dense forests, and continue on to **Bourscheid** ㉚ with its romantic castle ruins overlooking three valleys. Past Diekirch, head for **Larochette** ㉛ and its striking, step-gabled castle. At Reuland, you enter the Müllerthal and are now in the very pretty countryside known as **Petite Suisse** ㉜. Stop over at 🏨 **Echternach** ㉝. On the fifth day, visit this town on the river Sûre, which is the home of the unique and ancient dancing procession at Whitsun (Pentecost). Travel south along the Sûre River, which here forms the border with Germany until it meets the Moselle. The vineyards have been cultivated since Roman times and cover every slope. Pretty little **Ehnen** ㉞, a well-preserved village, is a good place for a stop to see the wine museum. Heading back toward Luxembourg City from Remich, stop at **Hamm** ㉟ to visit the American Military Cemetery, where General George Patton is buried with 5,000 comrades-at-arms who fell during the liberation of Luxembourg.

When to Tour Luxembourg

April through October is a good time to visit the Grand Duchy, with spring and early fall being the best. Outside the capital, many museums and other attractions open at Easter and stay open through October. Landlocked Luxembourg is far enough from the sea so that winters are a bit colder and summers a bit warmer than in neighboring Belgium. A number of the best restaurants should note that them are closed most of August.

LUXEMBOURG CITY

391 km (243 mi) southeast of Amsterdam, 219 km (136 mi) southeast of Brussels, 29 km (18 mi) east of Arlon.

The capital, perched on a bluff at the confluence of the Pétrusse and Alzette rivers, goes by the same name as the country—*Lëtzebuerg* in Luxembourgish. When Luxembourgers themselves refer to visiting the capital, they merely say they are going *en ville* (to the city). Ranging from southern European blue-collar workers to international bankers and European civil servants, half of Luxembourg's modest population of 80,000 are foreigners. This has given the city a cosmopolitan sheen and enriched it with a variety of ethnic restaurants, but the Luxembourgers themselves remain essentially homebodies, who go home for lunch if they can and see no point in hanging about in town after dark.

Exploring Luxembourg City

In Luxembourg-Ville (Luxembourg City), at leisure, you can explore the fortifications, the old cobbled streets, the parks, the cathedral, and the museums and, after shopping, relax in a shaded terrace café, listening to street musicians or a brass band. The city is small enough to be done in a day if you are pressed for time. But if you have a bit more time, you may find quiet little Luxembourg a romantic base for day trips and a lovely place at night, with its illuminated monuments and walls and its inviting public squares.

A Good Walk

Start at the **Pont Viaduc** ①, spanning the Pétrusse valley, for a view of the ledges on which the city was built. The **Monument National de la Solidarité** ②, at the north end of the bridge, commemorates Luxembourg's World War II victims. East of the monument stands the 17th-century fortress, the **Citadelle du St-Esprit** ③. To the northwest, along the city wall, lies **Place de la Constitution** ④ and the entrance to the **Casemates de la Pétrusse** ⑤, the tunnels carved into the fortifications. A block north of the Place on rue des Capucins and two blocks east on rue Notre-Dame stands the late-Gothic **Cathédrale Notre-Dame** ⑥. East of the cathedral, the outstanding **Musée d'Histoire de la Ville de Luxembourg** ⑦ traces the city's history. The town's three main squares align diagonally from southeast to northwest: First comes elegant **Place Clairefontaine** ⑧, then the market square, **Place Guillaume** ⑨, and finally, the welcoming **Place d'Armes** ⑩. On the southeast corner of the Place d'Armes stands the **Cercle/Palais Municipal** ⑪, the home of the tourist office. The **Maquette de la Forteresse** ⑫, behind the Cercle, is a scale model of the fortifications of the city. Once the residence of the dukes, the **Palais Grand-Ducal** ⑬, east of Place d'Armes, now hosts state occasions. Behind the palace is the square known as **Marché-aux-Poissons** ⑭, the oldest part of town. On the square, inside a row of 16th-century houses, is the collection of the **Musée National d'Histoire et d'Art** ⑮. Northeast of the museum is the **Porte des Trois Tours** ⑯, part of the original battlements. The old **Eglise St-Michel** ⑰ stands next to the city wall overlooking the Grund. The promontory on which Luxembourg's original castle was built, **Le Bock** ⑱, with an entrance to the casemates, a fascinating museum, and some ruins, looms above the Alzette valley on the eastern side of the city. Return south to Place du St-Esprit, where you can take an elevator down to the **Grund** ⑲ district, in the river valley below the Bock. Here, the excellent, interactive **Musée d'Histoire Naturelle** ⑳ explores the secrets of the natural world. North on the riverside rue Munster is the Baroque **Eglise St-Jean Baptiste** ㉑. In the other direction, past the confluence of the Alzette and the Petrusse, the parklands of the **Vallée de la Pétrusse** ㉒ spread westward. Walk up narrow switchbacks from the valley or take the elevator to Place du Saint-Esprit and cut across on Boulevard Roosevelt to **Boulevard Royal** ㉓, Luxembourg's Wall Street. Perpendicular to Royal is **Grand-Rue** ㉔, Luxembourg's pedestrian-only shopping street. Northeast of the center, across the Pont Grande Duchesse Charlotte above the Pfaffenthal district, lies the **Plateau Kirchberg** ㉕, a moonscape of modern architecture housing banks and European Union institutions.

Sights to See

★ ⑱ **Le Bock.** Luxembourg's raison d'être juts dramatically out over the Alzette river valley. This cliff served as the principal approach to the town, as far back as Celtic and Roman times, until bridges were constructed. The name comes from the Celtic *büück*, meaning the promontory supporting a castle. Over its farthest point looms the ruined tower of the castle of Sigefroid himself. He founded the fortress Lucilinburhuc in 963; it was expanded, over the centuries, from this dominant point, and finally razed in 1875.

Vertiginous views from here take in the **Plateau du Rham** across the way, on the right, and, before it, the massive towers of **Duke Wenceslas's fortifications**, which in 1390 extended the protected area. The block-like **casernes** (barracks) were built in the 17th century by the French and function today as a hospice for the elderly. Below them, at the bottom of the valley, is the 17th-century **Neumünster Abbey**, which, from 1869 to 1984, served as a prison.

Here also is one access point for the city's underground defensive labyrinth (☞ Casemates de la Pétrusse, *below*), the **Casemates du Bock**, dug into the rock below the city in 1745. At the entrance, the

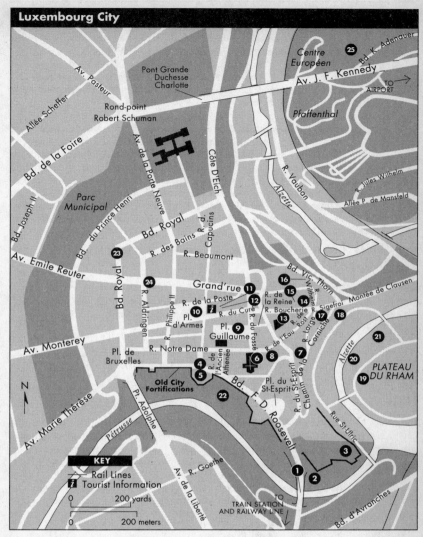

Luxembourg City

Le Bock, **18**
Boulevard Royal, **23**
Casemates de la
Pétrusse, **5**
Cathédrale
Notre-Dame, **6**
Cercle/
Palais Municipal, **11**
Citadelle du St-Esprit, **3**

Eglise St-Jean
Baptiste, **21**
Eglise Saint-Michel, **17**
Grand-Rue, **24**
Grund, **19**
Maquette de la
Forteresse, **12**
Marché-aux-
Poissons, **14**

Monument National
de la Solidarité, **2**
Musée d'Histoire
Naturelle, **20**
Musée d'Histoire de la
Ville de Luxembourg, **7**
Musée National
d'Histoire et d'Art, **15**
Palais Grand-Ducal, **13**

Place d'Armes, **10**
Place Clairefontaine, **8**
Place de la
Constitution, **4**
Place Guillaume, **9**
Plateau Kirchberg, **25**
Pont Viaduc, **1**
Porte des Trois Tours, **16**
Vallée de la Pétrusse, **22**

Archaeological Crypt provides an excellent introduction, with an audiovisual presentation depicting Luxembourg history from the 10th to
the 15th centuries. ⊠ *Monteé de Clausen.* 🎫 *Crypt and casemates Flux
70.* 🕙 *Mar.–Oct., daily 10–5.*

NEED A   On the Corniche, stop at the shady outdoor tables of the **Breedewée**
BREAK?   (⊠ R. Large 9, ☎ 222696) for a drink or a light, French-accented plat
              du jour.

㉓ Boulevard Royal. Luxembourg's mini–Wall Street was once the main
moat of the fortress. Lined with as many of the 225 foreign financial
institutions as could squeeze onto the five-block street, Boulevard
Royal is the symbol of a financial center where the securities trading
operation has a higher turnover than that of the New York Stock Exchange. The pinstripe suits can get some relief from their labors through
gazing at Niki de St. Phalle's large and brightly colored statue, *La Tem-
pérance,* which adorns their street. ⊠ *Between Pl. de Bruxelles and
Côte d'Eich.*

❺ Casemates de la Pétrusse (military tunnels). At the height of her power
and influence, Luxembourg was protected by three rings of defenses
comprising 53 forts and strongholds. During the many phases of the
fortress's construction, the rock itself was hollowed out to form a hon-
eycomb of passages running for nearly 24 km (15 mi) below the town.
Ten gates controlled admittance through the walls, and the town was,
in effect, 440 acres of solid fort. The Casemates served not only defensive purposes but were also used for storage and as a place of refuge
when the city was under attack. Two sections (☞ Casemates du Bock,
above) of the passages, containing former barracks, cavernous slaugh-
terhouses, bakeries, and a deep well, are open to the public. ⊠ *Pl. de
la Constitution.* 🎫 *Flux 70.* 🕙 *Easter, Whitsun (Pentecost, 7th Sun.
after Easter), and July–Sept., daily 11–4.*

❻ Cathédrale Notre-Dame. In late-Gothic style, the cathedral has a fine
portal sculpted by Daniel Muller of Freiburg and an attractive Baroque
organ gallery. During the fortnight of national pilgrimage starting on
the third Sunday after Easter, large numbers of Luxembourgers flock
to their cathedral. The closing ceremony, attended by the royal family, is an event no politician can afford to miss, regardless of party and
persuasion. The crypt, down a broad staircase, contains the tomb of
John the Blind, the gallant 14th-century King of Bohemia and Count
of Luxembourg, who fell at the Battle of Crécy in France during the
Hundred Years' War. Here, too, are the tombs of the grand-ducal dynasty. ⊠ *R. Notre-Dame.* 🕙 *Easter–Oct., weekdays 10–5, Sat. 8–6,
Sun. 10–6; Nov.–Easter, weekdays 10–11:30 and 2–5, Sat. 8–11 and
2–5, Sun. 10–5.*

⓫ Cercle/Palais Municipal (Municipal Building). With its bas-relief of the
Countess Ermesinde granting Luxembourg its charter of freedom in
1244, the municipal building is also the home of the tourist office. ⊠
East end, Pl. d'Armes.

❸ Citadelle du St-Esprit (Citadel of the Holy Spirit). Built by Vauban, the
brilliant French military engineer, in the 17th century on the site of a
former monastery, it has typically wedge-shape fortifications. The
"prow" affords wraparound views: the three spires of the cathedral,
the curve of the Alzette, and the incongruous white tower of the European Parliament secretariat. ⊠ *R. du St-Esprit.*

㉑ Eglise St-Jean Baptiste (Neumünster) (Church of St. John the Baptist).
Once the place of worship of the Benedictines of Neumünster Abbey,
who were expelled when the French Revolution hit Luxembourg, the

Baroque church contains many treasures. One of its most important is a Black Madonna, whose protection against pestilence was prayed for over many centuries. The church passage along the river provides splendid views of the side of the cliff and the towering fortifications across the Alzette. It leads to a former abbey courtyard, the **Tutesall**—where convicts once worked sewing bags—today a stylish exhibition venue. Another building, the former men's prison, is being converted into a cultural center. ⊠ *R. Münster.*

NEED A BREAK? **Scott's Pub** (⊠ Bisserwée 4, ☎ 475352), at the bottom of the valley, is a gathering place for the English-speaking, where outdoor tables line the picturesque Alzette. It's the place to have a pint of bitter or sample the Anglo-American cuisine.

⑰ Eglise St-Michel (St. Michael's Church). This church was built in 1320. ⊠ *R. Sigefroi at R. Large.*

㉔ Grand-Rue. On Luxembourg's pedestrian-only shopping street the same brands vie for your attention as in New York; but then, investment bankers have pockets here as deep as anywhere else. Pastry shops and sidewalk cafés add the middle-class touch so deeply typical of Luxembourg. There are pooper-scooper automats for the poodles, and the occasional street musician will, as likely as not, be playing a Bach partita. ⊠ *Between Bd. Royal and Côte d'Eich.*

★ **⑲ Grund.** Once considered dank and squalid, the district is now in vogue. You'll find chic restaurants, exclusive clubs, and skylighted, renovated town houses among the tumbledown laborers' homes. ⊠ *Alzette River Valley: R. Munster, R. de Trèves, Bisserwée.*

⑫ Maquette de la Forteresse (Scale Model of the Fortress). This relief model is a copy of one (now in Paris) made of the fortress-city for Napoléon in 1804, when the fortified complex was at the peak of its glory. The model shows how the fortress was constructed. ⊠ *R. du Curé,* ☎ *222809.* ☐ *Flux 60.* ☉ *Easter–mid-Oct., Mon.–Sat. 10–12 and 2–6.*

⑭ Marché-aux-Poissons (Fish Market). The oldest part of town, the site of the old fish market, was originally the crossing point of two Roman roads. ⊠ *Junction of rues de la Boucherie, du Rost, and Wiltheim.*

❷ Monument National de la Solidarité (National Monument of Unity). Commemorating Luxembourg's World War II victims, the stark granite-and-steel monument suggests the prisons and concentration camps where they suffered. The walls of the small chapel, containing a symbolic tombstone, are made entirely of stained glass. It was as a direct result of its war experiences that Luxembourg abandoned traditional neutrality for international cooperation. ⊠ *Bd. F. D. Roosevelt at Citadelle du St-Esprit.*

⑳ Musée d'Histoire Naturelle (Museum of Natural History). Housed in a converted women's prison, the museum has thought-provoking interactive exhibits and dioramas. ⊠ *R. Munster 23,* ☎ *462–2321.* ☐ *Flux 100.* ☉ *Tues.–Thurs. 2–6, Fri.–Sun. 10–6.*

★ **❼ Musée d'Histoire de la Ville de Luxembourg** (Luxembourg City Historical Museum). Partially underground, the multimedia, interactive museum, opened in 1996, traces the development of the city over 1,000 years. Its lowest five levels show the town's preserved ancient stonework. From a glass-wall elevator, you can enjoy a wonderful view of the ravine from the upper floors. ⊠ *R. du St-Esprit,* ☎ *229–0501.* ☐ *Flux 200.* ☉ *Tues.–Sun. 10–6, Thurs. 10–8.*

⑮ **Musée National d'Histoire et d'Art** (National Museum of History and Art). Set in an attractive row of 16th-century houses, the museum has some outstanding paintings by the expressionist Joseph Kutter, probably Luxembourg's greatest artist. The art gallery includes a fine Cranach and two Turner watercolors of the Luxembourg fortress. The museum also hosts the spectacular Bentinck-Thyssen collection of 15th- to 19th-century art, including works by Bruegel, Rembrandt, Canaletto, and other masters. ☒ *Marché-aux-Poissons,* ☎ *479–3301.* ▭ *Flux 100.* ☉ *Tues.–Sun. 10–5.*

....

NEED A
BREAK?

The **Welle Man** (☒ R. Wiltheim 12, ☎ 471783), on the street that runs alongside the National Museum, is the quintessential Luxembourgish museum bar. Sit on the tiny terrace and enjoy the magnificent view. Sip a glass of local white Elbling or Rivaner wine, or try a kir, made from black-currant liqueur and white wine.

....

⑬ **Palais Grand-Ducal** (Grand-Ducal Palace). The city's finest building dates from the 16th century. Its elaborate facade shows a distinct Spanish-Moorish influence. Formerly home to the Grand Ducal family, it is now used for business and entertaining. Official receptions are held in the festive hall on the second floor, and foreign envoys are received in the Hall of Kings. Its extensive art collection was dispersed during World War II but was returned afterward. ☒ *R. du Marché-aux-Herbes.* ▭ *Flux 200; tickets sold only at the City Tourist Office (early booking recommended).* ☉ *July 15–Aug. 29, Mon.–Tues. and Thurs.–Sat.; guided tours only (in English at 4). Opening and tour hours may change; check with City Tourist Office.*

⑩ **Place d'Armes.** Once the innermost heart of the fortified city, the square today, lined with symmetrical plane trees and strung with colored lights, is the most welcoming corner of town. In fine weather its cafés and benches are full of both locals and visitors. The bandstand has concerts every summer evening by visiting bands. Every second and fourth Saturday, a *brocante* (antiques/flea) market fills the square. ☒ *R. de la Poste; Av. de la Porte Neuve; Rues des Capucins, Génistre, du Curé, de Chimay, and Philippe II; and Av. Monterey*

⑧ **Place Clairefontaine.** The sloping, elegant square has a graceful statue of Grand Duchess Charlotte and imposing 18th-century ministerial offices. ☒ *Rues Notre-Dame, du Fosse, de l'Eau, de la Congrégation.*

④ **Place de la Constitution.** The square is marked by the gilt *Gëlle Fra* (Golden Woman), on top of a tall column. This World War I memorial was destroyed by the Nazis in 1940 and rebuilt, with original pieces incorporated, in 1984. ☒ *Bd. F. D. Roosevelt and R. Chimay.*

⑨ **Place Guillaume.** The square is known locally as the Knuedler, a name derived from the girdle worn by Franciscan monks who once had a monastery on the site. On market days (Wednesday and Saturday mornings) it is a mass of retail fruit and vegetable stands, vivid flower vendors, cheese and fish specialists, and a few remaining farmers who bring in their personal crops of potatoes, apples, cabbage, and radishes—as well as homemade jam, sauerkraut, and goat cheese. That's Grand Duke William II on the bronze horse; he reigned from 1840 to 1849, while Luxembourg was flush with new independence. The Hotel de Ville (Town Hall), its stairs flanked by two bronze lions, was inaugurated in 1844. ☒ *Off R. du Fossé at R. de la Reine*

㉕ **Plateau Kirchberg.** A number of banks, needing more space than that available on Boulevard Royal (☞ *above*), have put up huge edifices on Kirchberg, across the Alzette northeast of the center. Gottfried Boehm's glass-and-aluminum Deutsche Bank encloses a giant atrium, frequently used for art exhibitions, and Richard Meier's sober Hypobank is the perfect foil for an explosively dynamic sculpture by Frank Stella. The banks are cheek by jowl with the modernistic buildings of the European Union institutions, often accompanied by contemporary sculpture—the European Court of Justice, with pieces by Henry Moore and Lucien Wercollier; the Jean Monnet Building, with a replica of Carl-Fredrik Reuterswärd's *Non-Violence*; the European Center, where the Council of Ministers meets; and others, whose presence in Luxembourg are visible reminders of the disproportionately important role played by this tiny country in the politics of the European Union. ⊠ *Bd. Konrad Adenauer, Niedergrünewald, Pl. de l'Europe.*

❶ Pont Viaduc. From the bridge also known as the Passerelle (footbridge), which spans the Pétrusse valley, you'll have a first glimpse of the rocky ledges—partly natural, partly man-made—on which the city was founded. The Pétrusse, more a brook than a river, is now contained by concrete, but the valley has been made into a singularly beautiful park. ⊠ *Between Av. de la Gare and Bd. F. D. Roosevelt.*

⓰ Porte des Trois Tours (Gate of the Three Towers). These three turrets, remains of the fortress, are among the city's most romantic sights. The oldest of the towers was built around 1050. During the French Revolution, the guillotine was set up here. From here you can clearly see the source of Luxembourg's strength as a fortress: the Bock (☞ Le Bock, *above*). ⊠ *Foot of R. Wiltheim at Bd. J. Ulveling.*

㉒ Vallée de la Pétrusse (Petrusse Valley). Full of willows, cherry trees, and bluffs, the broad park lies in the canyon of the Pétrusse river. Near the high Viaduc (☞ Pont Viaduc, *above*), you'll see the **Chapelle Saint-Quirin** built into the rocks. The cave is said to have been carved by the Celts; it is known to have housed a chapel since at least the 4th century. ⊠ *Between R. de la Semois and R. St-Quirin.*

Dining

In the capital, as in the rest of the Grand Duchy, workers drop everything at noon and, jamming the streets, rush home to a leisurely hot meal, then rush back at 2, jamming the streets once more. Most restaurants offer a relatively speedy plat du jour for those who don't commute twice a day. Evening meals at home tend to be a cold supper of ham, sausage, dark bread, and cheese; the occasional meal out is usually a celebration, enjoyed at length. The Sunday noon meal is the most important of the week. Most Luxembourg restaurants are closed on Sunday, but country restaurants—some of the best and most enjoyable in the country, and never very far away—are booked with three-generation families, who spend the afternoon eating and drinking before an afternoon stroll, after which the men retire to the local pub.

Luxembourg City has a wide variety of restaurants, offering everything from top French cuisine to simple local specialties; you'll also find an assortment of international choices and a plethora of pizzerias. It's easy to find a fixed-price menu or plat du jour by wandering from restaurant to restaurant, but beware: The best places are often booked up at weekday lunchtime; if you know where you want to eat, phone ahead. Dress is casual unless indicated otherwise.

$$$$ ✕ **Clairefontaine.** Airy, bright, and ultrachic, this dining spot on the
★ city's most attractive square attracts government ministers and visiting dignitaries as well as genuine gourmets. Chef-owner Tony Tintinger's inspirations include a showcase of foie gras specialties, innovative fish dishes (soufflé of langoustines flavored with aniseed), and game novelties (tournedos of doe with wild mushrooms). ⊠ *Pl. de Clairefontaine 9,*

☎ 462211. *Reservations essential. Jacket and tie. AE, DC, MC, V. No lunch Sat. Closed Sun., 1 wk in May, 2 wks in Aug., 1st wk in Nov.*

$$$$ × **L'Agath.** Franky Steichen is the rising star in Luxembourg gastron-
★   omy. His restaurant, on the edge of a park, is in Howald, well south
       of the city center. This does not stop the faithful from trekking to his
       place to enjoy sautéed langoustines with crisp potato pancakes, smoked
       salmon crepes au gratin, and herb-encrusted fillet of lamb. The dessert
       trolley offers a dozen different sorbets. ⊠ *Rte. de Thionville 274,* ☎
       *488687. Reservations essential. AE, DC, MC, V. No dinner Sun.
       Closed Mon. and mid-July–early Aug.*

$$$$ × **St-Michel.** In a 16th-century building behind the Ducal Palace,
       warmly lighted and intimate, this gastronomic-astronomic restaurant
       is rich in historical atmosphere. It is owned by an inventive German
       chef, Joerg Glauben, who has introduced expense-account diners to
       his lobster salad with green asparagus tips, pigeon stuffed with foie gras
       and accompanied by rhubarb compote, and sumptuous desserts. The
       staff is young, skilled, and down to earth, and the ambience is gen-
       uinely welcoming. ⊠ *R. de l'Eau 32,* ☎ *223215. Reservations essen-
       tial. Jacket and tie. AE, DC, MC, V. Closed weekends and 3 wks in
       Aug.*

$$$ × **Bouzonviller.** The modern, airy dining room is a pleasure in itself
      with a magnificent view over the Alzette valley. Over the years, Chris-
      tian Bouzonviller has built up a following among serious gourmets with
      dishes such as sea scallops in lemon butter, loin of veal with eggplant
      pissaladière (flaky tart filled with onions, anchovies, olives, and egg-
      plant), and original desserts, including a chocolate fondant glacé with
      grapefruit sauce. ⊠ *R. Albert-Unden 138,* ☎ *472259. Reservations
      essential. Jacket and tie. MC, V. Closed weekends and 3 wks in Aug.*

$$$ × **Jan Schneidewind.** Changing art exhibits, chosen by chef-owner Jan
      Schneidewind, decorate the exposed-brick walls in this cozy but ele-
      gant two-story restaurant. The menu focuses on fish and seafood pre-
      pared in an ambitious, French-influenced style, such as herb-encrusted
      king crab in fowl juices, or sole with an asparagus and morel stew. Don't
      miss the simple but stunning salmon mousse if it's on the seasonally
      changing menu. ⊠ *R. du Curé 20,* ☎ *222618. AE, DC, MC, V. No
      lunch Sat. Closed Mon., 3 wks in Sept. or Feb.*

$$$ × **La Lorraine.** Strategically located on the Place d'Armes, this restau-
      rant in landlocked Luxembourg specializes in outstanding seafood. The
      display of coast-fresh fish and shellfish, in a shop attached to the
      restaurant, is so attractive it draws photographers. A three-course
      menu terroire, made up of local dishes, can be had in the new brick-
      wall brasserie in back. ⊠ *Pl. d'Armes 7,* ☎ *471436. AE, DC, MC, V.
      No lunch Sat. Closed Sun. and 2nd ½ of Aug.*

$$ × **Ancre d'Or.** This tidy, friendly brasserie, just off Place Guillaume,
     serves a wide variety of traditional Luxembourgish specialties. Try the
     judd mat gardebounen (smoked pork with broad beans) or *treipen* (blood
     pudding), as well as lighter fare. The apple tart (Luxembourgish style,
     with custard base) is homemade. Portions are generous, service is
     friendly, and the clientele is local. ⊠ *R. du Fossé 23,* ☎ *472973. MC,
     V. Closed Sun.*

$$ × **Bacchus.** This Italian pizzeria attracts an upscale, downtown set, as
     much for its location in the historic center and its slick peach-and-brass
     decor as for its food, which is straightforward and reasonably priced.
     Wood-fired pizza and classic pastas are dependable choices. Reserve
     for a seat in the tranquil courtyard. ⊠ *R. Marché-aux-Herbes 32,* ☎
     471397. AE, DC, MC, V.

$$ × **Kamakura.** If heavy Western cuisine palls, take the elevator down
     from Saint-Esprit to the Grund and try this elegant Japanese restau-
     rant. A number of fixed-price menus offer a variety of delicate, nouvelle-

Dining

Ancre d'Or, **15**
Bacchus, **16**
Bouzonviller, **2**
Clairefontaine, **18**
Ems, **24**
Jan Schneidewind, **11**
Kamakura, **17**
L'Agath, **26**
La Lorraine, **10**
La Table du Pain, **8**
Mousel's Cantine, **13**
Oberweis, **12**
St-Michel, **14**
Times, **9**

Lodging

Auberge le
Châtelet, **22**
Carlton, **23**
Cottage, **25**
Cravat, **19**
Hotel InterContinental,
4
Italia, **21**
La Cascade, **20**
Le Royal, **6**
Parc Belair, **7**
Romantik
Hotel/Grunwald, **3**
Sieweburen, **1**
Sofitel and Novotel, **5**

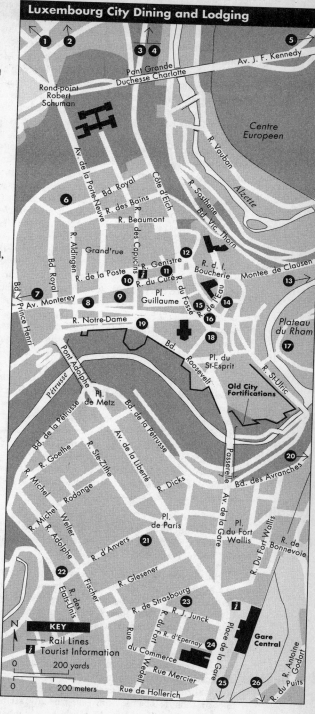

Luxembourg City Dining and Lodging

accented dishes, artfully presented and graciously served. A la carte specialties, considerably more expensive, include impeccably fresh sashimi and light tempura vegetables. ⊠ *R. Munster 2–4,* ☎ *470604. AE, DC, MC, V. Closed Sat. lunch and Sun.*

$$ ✕ **Mousel's Cantine.** Directly adjoining the great Mousel brewery, this comfortable, wood-paneled café serves up heaping platters of local specialties—braised and grilled ham, sausage, broad beans, and fried potatoes—to be washed down with crockery steins of creamy *Gezwickelte Béier* (unfiltered beer). The front café is brighter, but the tiny fluorescent-lighted dining room has windows into the brewery. ⊠ *Montée de Clausen 46,* ☎ *470198. MC, V. Closed Sun.*

$$ ✕ **Times.** On a pedestrian street of art galleries and boutiques, you'll
★ also find this restaurant, offering excellent food at reasonable prices. Its narrow dining room is lined with Canadian cherry wood and is often filled with artists and journalists. The cuisine favors ambitious creations, such as monkfish medallions with cider and caramelized apples. A meal-size appetizer, not to be missed, is the *gromperkichelcher,* crisp potato pancakes topped with smoked salmon and crème fraîche, on salad. ⊠ *R. Louvigny 8,* ☎ *222722. MC, V. Closed Sun.*

$ ✕ **Ems.** Across the street from the train station, this lively establishment with vinyl booths draws a loyal, local crowd. Many come for its vast portions of mussels in a rich wine-and-garlic broth (available September through March), accompanied by french fries and a bottle of sharp, cold, and inexpensive Auxerrois or Rivaner. ⊠ *Pl. de la Gare 30,* ☎ *487799. AE, DC, MC, V. No lunch Sat.*

$ ✕ **Oberweis.** Luxembourg's most famous patisserie also serves light lunches in its upstairs tearoom. You select your meal at the counter (quiche lorraine, spinach pie, and the like), and it is served at your table. Beer and wine are available. ⊠ *Grand'Rue 19–20,* ☎ *470703. Reservations not accepted. AE, DC, MC, V. Closed Sun.*

$ ✕ **La Table du Pain.** This working boulangerie-patisserie is decorated
★ like a French country farmhouse, with pine tables to seat 2 or 20, and rustic sideboards and cupboards lining the walls. Copious soups, salads, and sandwiches, as well as warm dishes, can be ordered from a waiter. Don't forget to buy a loaf of Luxembourg's best bread, or one of the almost-too-pretty-to-eat cakes or pastries. The locally made jams, jellies, and wines on display are also for sale. ⊠ *Av. Monterey 19,* ☎ *241608. No credit cards. Closed after 7 PM.*

Lodging

Hotels in the city center are generally preferable to those clustered around the train station. There are also large, modern hotels near the airport and on the Plateau Kirchberg.

$$$$ ▦ **Hotel Inter-Continental.** Rising above the outskirts of Luxembourg like a 20th-century château-fort, this modern, 19-story deluxe hotel opened in 1985 and competes directly with Le Royal (☞ *below*) downtown. Its rooms are gracious, with comfortable, wide beds. The restaurant, Les Continents, attracts locals for its upscale French cooking. ⊠ *R. Jean Engling, L-1013 Dommeldange,* ☎ *43781,* ℻ *436095. 337 rooms. 2 restaurants, bar, café, indoor pool, sauna, health club, convention center, parking (fee). AE, DC, MC, V.*

$$$$ ▦ **Le Royal.** This is the prestige place to stay, with its glass-and-marble
★ lobby, surmounted by an enormous modern chandelier, and smaller lobbies on each floor. The rooms, surprisingly, are no more than standard modern. However, this is the kind of hotel where cellular phones are not allowed in the restaurants and where the gift shop sells "Les must de Cartier." The piano bar is popular, as is the brasserie–breakfast room Le Jardin, especially when the fountain terrace is open. ⊠ *Bd. Royal*

12, L 2449, ☎ *2416161,* FAX *225948. 180 rooms. 2 restaurants, bar, indoor pool, barbershop, beauty salon, sauna, tennis court, exercise room, bicycles, parking (fee). AE, DC, MC, V.*

$$$$ ⌧ **Sofitel and Novotel.** Sofitel and Novotel ($$$) are joined properties, both owned by the Accor group. Previously under joint management, the two separated in 1998. The Sofitel, built in 1993, is more spacious than the Novotel, although both share amenities. The Novotel is a good choice if you're doing serious business with the Kirchberg institutions. ✉ *Centre Européen, L 2015,* ☎ *Sofitel, 437761; Novotel, 4298481,* FAX *Sofitel, 425091; Novotel, 438658. Sofitel: 100 rooms, 4 suites; Novotel: 260 rooms. Restaurant, bar, indoor pool, sauna, conference center. AE, DC, MC, V.*

$$$ ⌧ **Cravat.** This charming Luxembourg relic—moderately grand, modestly glamorous—straddles the valley and the Old Town in the best location in the city. Though corridors have a dated, institutional air, the rooms are fresh and welcoming in a variety of tastefully retro styles. The art deco coffee shop has been freshened up but still draws fur-hatted ladies to tea. The prime minister and his cabinet can be found in the hotel tavern most Friday afternoons. ✉ *Bd. F. D. Roosevelt 29, L 2450,* ☎ *221975,* FAX *226711. 60 rooms. Restaurant, 2 bars. AE, DC, MC, V.*

$$$
★ ⌧ **Parc Belair.** Privately owned and family run, this hotel is a few blocks from the city center. It stands on the edge of the Parc de Merl, next to an attractive playground. Rooms are a warm beige; those facing the park are the quietest. The complex includes a separate restaurant with an outdoor café. A copious buffet breakfast is included. ✉ *Av. du X Septembre 109, L 2551,* ☎ *442323,* FAX *444484. 45 rooms. Restaurant, playground, meeting rooms, parking (fee). AE, DC, MC, V.*

$$ ⌧ **Auberge le Châtelet.** At the edge of a quiet residential area but within easy reach of the station and the Old Town, this pleasant hotel (formerly the Auberge du Coin) has stone and terra-cotta floors, double windows, Oriental rugs, and tropical plants. Rooms are freshly furnished in knotty pine with new tile baths. There's a restaurant serving traditional Luxembourg cuisine, and a comfortable oak-and-stone bar. The nine rooms in the adjoining annex cost slightly less. ✉ *Bd. de la Pétrusse 2, L 2320,* ☎ *402101,* FAX *403666. 40 rooms. Restaurant, bar. AE, DC, MC, V.*

$$ ⌧ **Italia.** This former private apartment house, converted into a hotel, has lost some old-world charm in the renovation. Nevertheless, the rooms are solid, clean and newly furnished, all with private tile bathrooms. The restaurant downstairs is one of the city's best Italian eateries. ✉ *R. d'Anvers 15–17, L 1113,* ☎ *486626,* FAX *480807. 20 rooms. Restaurant, bar. AE, DC, MC, V.*

$$
★ ⌧ **La Cascade.** This turn-of-the-century villa has been converted into a hotel of considerable charm and elegance. There's a good French Provençale restaurant and a lovely terrace overlooking the Alzette River. A bus stops outside to take you to the center, just over a mile away. ✉ *R. de Pulvermuhl 2, L 2356,* ☎ *428736,* FAX *4287–8888. 8 rooms. Restaurant, bar, free parking. AE, DC, MC, V.*

$$ ⌧ **Romantik Hotel/Grunewald.** A member of the Romantik group, the Grunewald is just outside the city and at the high end of its price category. The old-fashioned lounge is crammed with wing chairs, knickknacks, and old prints; rooms have Oriental rugs, rich fabrics, and Louis XV–style furniture. Rooms overlooking the attractive garden are worth booking ahead; street-side windows are triple-glazed. There's a terrace for alfresco breakfasts. The pricey restaurant (closed Sun.) serves rich, classic French cuisine. ✉ *Rte. d'Echternach 10–14, L 1453 Dommeldange,* ☎ *431882,* FAX *420646. 26 rooms. Restaurant, meeting rooms. AE, DC, MC, V.*

$$ ⊞ **Sieweburen.** At the northwestern end of the city is this attractively rustic hotel, opened in 1991; the clean, large rooms have natural-wood beds. There are woods in the back and a playground in front. The brasserie-style tavern, older than the rest of the property, is hugely popular, especially when the terrace is open. ⊠ *R. des Septfontaines 36, L 2634,* ☎ *442356,* ℻ *442353. 14 rooms. Restaurant, bar, playground, free parking. MC, V.*

$ ⊞ **Carlton.** This vast hotel near the station, built in 1918, has a quiet inner court and is buffered from the Rue de Strasbourg scene by a row of stores. The quarters are roomy and quiet, and a generous breakfast is included in the room price. The beveled glass, oak parquet, and terrazzo floors are original. Each room has antique beds, floral-print comforters, and a sink; wooden floors, despite creaks, are white-glove clean. No rooms have toilets; there are two bathrooms per floor. Six rooms have private showers. ⊠ *R. de Strasbourg 9, L 2561,* ☎ *484802,* ℻ *299664. 50 rooms without bath. Bar. No credit cards.*

$ ⊞ **Cottage.** Modern budget hotels are few and far between. The one closest to the city (a 15-minute train ride away) is the motel-style but pleasant Cottage. ⊠ *R. Auguste Liesch, L-3474 Dudelange,* ☎ *520591,* ℻ *520576. 45 rooms with bath. Restaurant, bar, free parking. AE, DC, MC, V.*

Nightlife and the Arts

Luxembourg City hosts a disproportionate number of arts events for its size. Watch for posters on kiosks, and check the tourist office on the Place d'Armes, where tickets to many of them are sold. Tickets to performances at the **Municipal Theater** (⊠ Rond-Point Robert Schuman, ☎ 470895) are sold at its box office. The *Luxembourg News,* an English-language weekly translating local news from the city dailies, offers up-to-date events listings; it is sold at bookstores and magazine stands. *Luxembourg Weekly* and *Rendez-vous Lëtzebuerg,* both available at the tourist office, also carry listings.

The Arts

CLASSICAL MUSIC

Luxembourg is home to the **Orchestre Philharmonique du Luxembourg,** which performs a series of weekly concerts, usually on Thursday night in the Municipal Theater and Friday night at the new Conservatoire de Musique (⊠ R. Charles Martel 33, ☎ 4796–2950). Watch for posters announcing "Concerts du Midi" (⊠ Villa Louvigny, in central municipal park): They may feature Philharmonic Orchestra members as soloists or other professional chamber groups, and they are free.

FILM

The best films in any language usually come to **Cine Utopia** (⊠ Av. de la Faiencerie 16, ☎ 472109), where reservations are accepted by phone. At the huge cinema complex, **Utopolis** (⊠ Av. J.F. Kennedy 45, ☎ 429595), opened on the Plateau Kirchberg in 1998, 10 theaters show everything from art-house films to blockbusters, most in the original language, but there are no reservations; arrive early on weekends.

THEATER

Good traveling plays in French and German pass through the municipal theater, the **Théâtre Municipal de la Ville de Luxembourg** (⊠ Rond-Point Robert Schuman, ☎ 4796–2710).

VISUAL ARTS

In addition to a number of art galleries, Luxembourg now has a permanent space for modern and contemporary art exhibits: the **Casino**

Luxembourg (✉ R. Notre-Dame 41, ☎ 225045), where Liszt played his last public concert, converted in 1995 into an exemplary exhibition venue.

Nightlife

BARS AND CAFÉS

Am Häffchen (✉ Bisserwée 9, ☎ 221702) serves drinks and meals in an intimate, retro setting, complete with bookshelves, a terrace, and a piano bar. **Bonaparte** (✉ Bisserwée 9, ☎ 221702) has the ancient rock face as its back wall and serves up pasta and pizza as well as drinks. **Café des Artistes** (✉ Montée du Grund, ☎ 461327) is an old, welcoming café with great ambience and a mostly middle-age clientele, where sing-along evenings make the chandeliers ring. **Chiggeri** (✉ R. du Nord 13–15, ☎ 228236), which draws a sophisticated international crowd (the owner is a literary editor), has a wide choice of beers and wines, plus midnight snacks. Downstairs, **Club 5** (✉ 5 R. Chimay, ☎ 461763) is a warm and eclectic bar; upstairs it's a brasserie with an outdoor roof garden and a specialization in carpaccio. **Interview** (✉ R. Aldringen 21, ☎ 473665) draws a very young, stylish crowd (mostly students from the European School) to a setting of Warhol-esque urban decay. **Lentzen Eck** (✉ R. de la Boucherie 2, ☎ 462050) offers a traditional old-Luxembourg setting, plus a good list of the local liqueur, eaux-de-vie.

DISCOS

Barbarella (✉ R. du J. Junck 36, ☎ 491350) is a tiny boîte that plays variations on pop and dance music for its varied clientele. **Didjeridoo** (✉ R. de Bouillon 41, ☎ 440049) in Hollerich, on the highway to Esch-sur-Alzette, is Luxembourg's largest disco. **Pulp** (✉ Bd. d'Avranches 36, ☎ 496940) is the current weekend hot spot.

GAY BARS

Café Big Moon (✉ R. Vauban 14, ☎ 431746). **Café du Nord** (✉ Av. Emile Reuter 30, ☎ 453284). **Chez Gusty** (✉ Côte d'Eich 101, ☎ 431223).

JAZZ CLUBS

Melusina (✉ R. de la Tour Jacob 145, ☎ 435922) is basically a disco (pop and techno on weekends) but also draws top local musicians and touring guests for occasional jazz concerts.

Outdoor Activities and Sports

Biking

In Luxembourg City, you can rent bicycles for forays throughout the Grand Duchy from **Vélo en Ville** (✉ R. Bisserné 8, ☎ 4796–2383), in the Grund.

Golf

The **Golf Club Grand-Ducal** (☎ 34090) at Senningerberg, about 7 km (4 mi) east of the city, has narrow fairways surrounded by dense woods; it is open only to members of other private clubs. The **Kikuoka Country Club Chant Val** (☎ 356135) is at Canach, about 10 km (6 mi) east of Luxembourg City.

Shopping

As Luxembourg has only partially and recently abandoned its rural roots, its citizens are for the most part unsentimental about the traditional blue-and-gray crockery and burnished pewter that once furnished every home; nowadays, they prefer their local Villeroy & Boch vitro-porcelain in jazzy, modern designs. All three types can be found in most home-furnishings and gift shops. For souvenirs, there are lovely photography books on Luxembourg's historic sites, as well as reproduced engravings of the city in all its fortified glory. *Taaken,* miniature cast-iron firebacks with bas-relief scenes of Luxembourg, are made by the Fonderie de Mersch and are available in gift and souvenir shops.

Because Luxembourg City is home to a large population of bankers and well-paid Eurocrats, as well as its own newly wealthy, it has an unusually high number of luxury and designer shops for such a tiny city. Clerks, however, are not always overwhelmingly friendly.

Shopping Districts

The best of high-end shopping is on the **Grand'Rue** and streets radiating out from it; shops along **Avenue de la Gare** and **Avenue de la Liberté,** both forking north from the train station, offer more affordable goods.

Department Stores

C & A (⊠ Pl. Guillaume, and R. de la Gare 15) is the Continent's answer to Macy's or Marks & Spencer—your basic department store, with added flair. The interconnected shopping plazas **Centre Brasseur** (⊠ Grand'Rue 36–38) and **Centre Neuberg** (⊠ Grand' Rue 30) have a mix of independent stores selling housewares, clothing, and specialty foods.

Specialty Shops

CHINA

Villeroy & Boch porcelain has been manufactured in Luxembourg since 1767. The factory outlet (⊠ R. de Rollingergrund 330, Bus 2, ☎ 4682–1278), on the northwest edge of town, offers good reductions on virtually flawless goods, and rock-bottom bargains on pieces with slightly visible flaws, but will not ship your purchases. The glossy main shop (⊠ R. du Fossé 2, between Grand'Rue and Pl. Guillaume, ☎ 463343) has a wide selection of quality, full-price goods and will ship.

CHOCOLATES

Namur (⊠ R. des Capucines 27, ☎ 223408) and **Oberweis** (⊠ Grand'Rue 19, ☎ 470703) are the city's finest patisseries, both with a mean sideline in *knippercher,* Luxembourg chocolates.

PRINTS

Galerie Kutter (⊠ R. des Bains 17, ☎ 223571) offers good framed prints and stationery taken from the works of Luxembourg watercolorist Sosthène Weiss, who painted Cezanne-like scenes of Luxembourg's Old Town.

Street Markets

An **antiques fair** takes over the Place d'Armes every second and fourth Saturday. The annual **Braderie,** a massive, citywide sidewalk sale, slashes prices on the last weekend in August or the first weekend in September. The main **farmers' market** is held in Place Guillaume every Wednesday and Saturday morning.

Side Trip

The signposted **Valley of the Seven Châteaux** can be visited on a circle tour west of **Mersch,** 17 km (10 mi) north of the capital, cutting west to **Redange,** south to **Hollenfels, Marienthal,** and **Ansembourg** (which has an old castle in the heights and a new one in the valley below), then working west to **Septfontaines** and south to **Koerich.** The castles, in various stages of repair and representing a broad historical spectrum, have not been restored for visitors, but they loom above forests and over valleys much as they did in Luxembourg's grander days. Follow the road signs marked "Vallée des Sept Châteaux": This rather obscure and never-direct itinerary takes you through farmlands, woods, and—just outside Koerich, at **Goeblange**—to the foundations of two 4th-century **Roman villas,** their underground heating and plumbing systems exposed; the rough cobbles leading into the woods are original, too.

Luxembourg City A to Z

Arriving and Departing

BY CAR

The proper motorway exits for Luxembourg City are poorly indicated; if you're arriving from France, watch for "Belgique/Brussels–Liège/Luxembourg aeroport" with "centre-ville" in fine italics; from Belgium, exit for Strassen and turn left on the route d'Arlon. From Germany, the motorway empties directly into the center.

BY PLANE

Findel Airport, 6 km (4 mi) east of the city center, serves the entire country.

Between the Airport and Downtown: Luxair buses leave the airport hourly from 6 AM to 10 PM, heading nonstop for the train station. Tickets cost Flux 120. Luxembourg City Bus 9 leaves the airport at regular intervals for the main bus depot at the train station. Tickets are Flux 40. A taxi ride airport to city center costs about Flux 600.

BY TRAIN

Luxembourg has frequent train service from Brussels (under three hours) and Paris (Gare de l'Est, four hours). From Amsterdam, you travel via Brussels (six hours). Most connections from Germany channel through Koblenz. The train services of the Luxembourg National Railways (mainly one north–south and one east–west route) are supplemented by a bus network reaching virtually every locality.

Getting Around

BY BUS

Luxembourg City has a highly efficient bus service covering town and outlying areas. Get tickets and details about services at the information counter in the underground crossroads below the Centre Aldringen, where buses arrive and depart from quais across from the post office. A 10-ride ticket costs Flux 300. Buses for other towns throughout the country leave from the train station (Gare Centrale, ⊠ intersection of Av. de la Gare, R. de Strasbourg, and Av. de la Liberté, ☎ 492424).

BY CAR

A car is a liability in this small, walkable city. It's best (and least expensive) to deposit your vehicle in a central parking area, either Parking Glacis, near the Grande-Duchesse Charlotte bridge, or Parking Knuedler, under Place Guillaume.

BY TAXI

You can **call for a cab** (☎ 482233 or 480058) or pick one up at stands by the central post office and the train station.

Contacts and Resources

CAR RENTALS

Avis (⊠ Pl. de la Gare 2, ☎ 489595). **Budget** (⊠ Findel Airport, ☎ 437575). **Europcar/InterRent** (⊠ Rte. de Thionville 84, ☎ 404228; ⊠ Findel Airport, ☎ 434588). **Hertz** (⊠ Findel Airport, ☎ 434645). **Rent-a-Car** (⊠ Rte. de Longwy 191, ☎ 440861).

GUIDED TOURS

Segatos Tourisme (⊠ R. Kalchesbrück 7, ☎ 422288, ext. 1) offers two-hour tours (Flux 450) in English every afternoon from mid-April through October. Leaving from Platform 5 of the bus station (next to the railway station) or from the war memorial in Place de la Constitution, they visit the historic sights of the center, the area housing various branches of the European Union, and some of the villas on the city outskirts. On weekends from May to September half-day trips take in Vianden and other Ardennes castle towns and the Little Switzerland region.

From March through mid-November, guided **minitrain tours** (☎ 422–2881; Flux 230) of the Old Town and the Pétrusse valley start from Place de la Constitution.

You can rent a **self-guided city walking tour** with headphones and cassette (Flux 190) at the bus booth on Place de la Constitution.

The **Vauban Walk** is a self-guided military history tour starting at the Bock that leads through the Pfaffenthal to Les Trois Glands (the Three Acorns), 18th-century Austrian fortifications.

The **Wenzel Walk** allows visitors to experience 1,000 years of history in 100 minutes, though you are well advised to take your time. It is named for Wenceslas II, Duke of Luxembourg and Holy Roman Emperor (no relation to the "good king" of the Christmas carol), who played an important part in fortifying the city. The walk starts at the Bock and leads down into the valley, over medieval bridges, through ancient gates, and past ancient ruins and exact reconstructions (always labeled as such). Two audiovisual presentations are included along the way. The walk also takes in French military architecture of the 17th century and a stroll along the Alzette River, which played an important role in the city's defense system. Good walking shoes and a reasonably sound constitution are required. The walk is signposted, with full explanations at each sight. A descriptive leaflet is available from the City Tourist Office in Place d'Armes, which also can provide a guide (Flux 1,600 regardless of the size of the group).

VISITOR INFORMATION

Luxembourg National Tourist Office (ONT) (⊠ Railway Station, ☎ 4282–8220; ⊠ Findel Airport, ☎ 4282–8221).

The **Luxembourg City Tourist Office** has pamphlets and brochures and general information about the city. ⊠ Pl. d'Armes, ☎ 222809. ☉ Apr.–mid-Oct., Mon.–Sat. 9–7, Sun. 10–6; mid-Oct.–Mar., daily 9–6.

THE LUXEMBOURG ARDENNES AND THE MOSELLE

Vast, rolling green hills and dense fir forests alternate in Luxembourg's northern highlands, the southeast corner of the rocky, wooded Ardennes plateau. Higher and harsher than the Duchy's southern Bon Pays (Good Country), with bitter winters and barren soil, it is relatively isolated and inaccessible; indeed, even in the 1940s, no one expected the Germans to attempt an attack across such rough and uneven terrain. They did, of course, twice. The second led to one of the most vicious conflicts in World War II, the Battle of the Ardennes, or the Battle of the Bulge. Throughout its history, the region has been the hunting grounds of kings and emperors, Celts, Romans, and Gauls; shaggy deer and great, bristling wild boar still occasionally charge across a forest road. Castles punctuate its hills and valleys, and rocky rivers and streams pour off its slopes, making this an attractive vacation area for northern Europeans seeking wilderness and medieval history.

The Mullerthal—or, as some insist on calling it, Petite Suisse (Little Switzerland)—northeast of the capital, presents a more smiling face. It's a hilly area of leafy woods, rushing brooks, and old farms, ideal for hiking along its multitude of marked trails or for a picnic. South of it begins the Moselle valley, where you can see Germany on the other side of the river. This land has been cultivated since time immemorial. Roman antiquities still surface from time to time. The south-facing hills are covered with vineyards producing the fruity white wines for which Luxembourg is famous. Many of the valley's small towns and villages remain attractively old-fashioned.

Numbers in the margin correspond to points of interest on the Luxembourg Ardennes map.

Diekirch

 33 km (20½ mi) north of Luxembourg City.

Diekirch preserves memories of Roman culture, early Christianity, and the brutalities of World War II. This small, easygoing city, with a pleasant pedestrian shopping area, has several points of interest. In the center of pedestrian zone, the **Eglise St-Laurent** (St. Lawrence's Church; ✉ Pl. Bech), a small, ancient Romanesque church, has portions dating from the 5th century. It was first built over the foundations of a Roman temple, the older parts functioning as a cemetery. In 1961, that lower section was uncovered and with it about 30 Merovingian sarcophagi, many of them containing intact skeletons. Since 1978, the cemetery has been restored and open to the public. Some of the ancient foundations of the church can be seen through a grate in the nave; you may enter the crypt by an exterior door on the right of the building. At the **Musée Municipal** (Municipal Museum), in the basement of the primary school, there are two more sarcophagi and remains found under the church, along with well-preserved Roman mosaics from the 4th century, found two blocks away. Diekirch is riddled with remains of Roman culture, though most of its treasures were carried away by invading Franks. There is a plan to move the contents of the municipal museum into the basement of the National Museum of Military History (☞ *below*) by 2000. ✉ *Pl. Guillaume.* ⬛ *Flux 50.* ☉ *Easter– Oct., Fri.–Wed. 10–noon and 2–6.*

In the **Musée National d'Histoire Militaire** (National Museum of Military History), 10 life-size, authentically equipped dioramas depict personal aspects of the hardships of the Battle of the Bulge. Unlike the museum at Bastogne, this thoughtful, neutral effort sidesteps discussions of strategies and fronts; it brings out individual details instead, from yellowed letters and K rations to propaganda flyers—both German and American—scattered to demoralize already homesick soldiers at Christmastime. All paraphernalia are authentic period pieces. The staff often welcomes veterans personally. Other exhibits illustrate Luxembourg military history since the end of the Napoléonic Wars. The museum may soon house the Roman treasures of the Municipal Museum (☞ *above*), as well. ✉ *Bamertal 10,* ☎ *808908.* ⬛ *Flux 200.* ☉ *Easter–Oct., daily 10–6; Nov.–Easter, daily 2–6.*

The **Diewelselter,** an impressive dolmen (stone altar) attributed to the Celts, stands south of Diekirch, overlooking the town. No one is sure who piled the great stones that form this ancient arch—or how they did it.

Dining and Lodging

$$$$ ✕⬛ **Hiertz.** This small hotel-restaurant looks stark and uninviting from the outside, but inside, the tired old dining room has, after 30

320

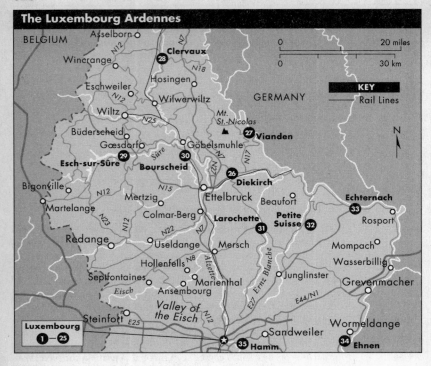

The Luxembourg Ardennes

years, finally been transformed into a jewel of a place. Sit in the hotel's pretty terraced garden for summer aperitifs and after-dinner coffee; for dinner, try carpaccio of langoustines with caviar, or turbot flavored with vanilla and raspberry vinegar. The hotel plays second fiddle to the food and is in a lower price category ($$), but rooms are comfortable; ask for one of the three back rooms facing the garden. ⊠ R. Clairefontaine 1, L-9201, ☎ 803562, FAX 808869. 9 rooms. Restaurant. AE, DC, MC, V. No dinner Mon. Closed Tues., 2nd ½ of Aug., three weeks over Christmas and New Year's.

Outdoor Activities and Sports

BICYCLING

Bikes can be rented at **Camping de la Sûre** (☎ 809425) and in summer at local train stations.

Vianden

★ ㉗ *11 km (7 mi) northeast of Diekirch, 44 km (27½ mi) north of Luxembourg City.*

In Vianden you come face to face with one of Europe's most dramatic sights: Driving around the last bend, you suddenly see a full-length view of its spectacular **castle** rearing up on a hill over the village, replete with conical spires, crenelation, step gables, and massive bulwarks. Its dramatic position enhances the tiny village's medieval air, with its steep, narrow main street and shuttered houses crouched at the feet of the feudal lord. The castle was built on Roman foundations in the 9th century, but its most spectacular portions date from the 11th, 12th, and 15th centuries. Down the hill, by the banks of the river Our, a **chairlift** carries visitors up for a remarkable view of the valley. *Castle:* ☎ 849291. ⊠ Flux 180. ⊙ Mar. and Oct., daily 10–5; Apr.–Sept., daily

10–6; Nov.–Feb., daily 10–4. Chairlift: ⊠ *Flux 180.* ☉ *Easter–mid-Oct., daily 10–6.*

The 13th-century Gothic **Eglise Trinitaire** (Trinitarian Church; ⊠ Grand'Rue) once functioned as a Trinitarian monastery; its ancient cloisters have been restored to sparkling modernity. The **Musée Victor Hugo,** closed for renovation until 2000, displays letters and memorabilia from the French writer's sojourn here in 1871. ⊠ *R. de la Gare 37,* ☎ *84257.* ⊠ *Flux 45.* ☉ *May–Oct., weekdays 9:30–noon and 2–6; Nov.–Apr. weekdays; phone ahead for exact times.*

☙ The **Musée de la Poupée et du Jouet** (Doll and Toy Museum) displays a collection of 500 dolls and toys, including antiques dating from the 16th century. ⊠ *Grand'Rue 96,* ☎ *84591.* ⊠ *Flux 100.* ☉ *Easter–Oct., Tues.–Sun. 11–5.*

Dining and Lodging

$$ ✕⊞ **Oranienburg.** In the same family since 1880, this once-traditional
★ lodging has gone deluxe, decorating its rooms and restaurant in lush, new fabrics and modern, built-in fixtures. Only the café and stairwell retain the old-Vianden atmosphere, with game trophies and burnished oak. The restaurant, Le Châtelain, now contemporary and posh as well, attracts nonguests for its ambitious French cooking and its views toward the village and castle. The hotel café is much more modestly priced. ⊠ *Grand'Rue 126, L-9411,* ☎ *834153,* ℻ *834333. 25 rooms. Restaurant. AE, DC, MC, V. Restaurant closed except for hotel guests Mon. and Tues., 2 wks in Nov.; hotel and restaurant closed Jan.–mid-Mar.*

$ ✕⊞ **Aal Veinen.** Dark, cozy, and casual, this 1683 inn serves simple food—*bouchée à la reine* (chicken à la king) with frites, omelettes, cold sausage plates—and a wide selection of grilled meats, cooked in full view of the dining area over a sizzling wood fire. (If you've given up on pork chops, this is the place to get reacquainted.) Rooms upstairs are rustically furnished and tidy, with exposed beams, stucco, and oak armoires. ⊠ *Grand'Rue 114, L-9401,* ☎ *834368,* ℻ *834084. 8 rooms. Restaurant, bar. MC, V.*

$ ✕⊞ **Heintz.** Expanded from its origins as a Trinitarian monastery, this atmospheric hotel has been in the family for four generations. During the war, owner Grandma Hansen worked with the Resistance, hiding hams, cash, and Luxembourgers with equal aplomb. The public spaces are rich with history, from the cross-vaulted oak café to the hallways filled with local antiques; rooms are simple and up-to-date. The oldest rooms, on the first floor, have antique oak furniture and original doors, but baths are down the hall; the best rooms are upstairs, with balconies over the garden and fountain. The restaurant offers French classics—grilled beef with béarnaise sauce, salmon in chives, and authentic German apple strudel with vanilla sauce. ⊠ *Grand'Rue 55, L-9410,* ☎ *834155,* ℻ *834559. 28 rooms, 2 without bath. Restaurant. AE, DC, MC, V. Restaurant closed Wed. (except mid-July–mid-Aug.), hotel and restaurant closed Nov.–Mar.*

Clervaux

★ ㉘ *31 km (19 mi) northwest of Vianden, 62 km (38½ mi) north of Luxembourg City.*

Clervaux, a forest village surrounded by deep-cleft hills, draws vacationers to hike, hunt, listen to Gregorian plainchant, and view *The Family of Man* photo exhibit in the sprawling **castle.** It was from this castle that Philip de Lannoi set forth in 1621 to make his fortune in America; one of his descendants was Franklin Delano Roosevelt (whose middle name is the anglicized version of de Lannoi). The old castle, virtually reduced to rubble in the Battle of the Bulge, has been completely restored. Two floors in the right wing of the castle house the noted exhibition of photo portraits of *The Family of Man*—considered by some to be the greatest photographic exhibition of all time—assembled by the photographer Edward J. Steichen, a Luxembourg native. ⊠ *100 m (100 yds) above center of town,* ☎ *5224241.* ▣ *Flux 150.* ☉ *Mar.– Dec., Tues.–Sun. 10–6.*

Clervaux is also home to the striking **Benedictine Abbey of Saints Maurice and Maur,** built in 1910 in the style of the Abbey of Cluny, and perched high above town. Mass at 10:30 AM and vespers at 6:30 PM are celebrated with Gregorian plainchant. There's also an exhibition on the monastic life.

Dining and Lodging

$–$$ ▣ **Koener/International.** These two hotels, owned by brothers and adjoining a shared indoor pool, offer sleek modern details; rooms on the International side are somewhat more attractive (and more expensive: $$), with dark-green and brass decor. Neither half, aside from some rooms with forest views, has much Ardennes atmosphere, but both offer full comfort. *Koener:* ⊠ *Grand'Rue 14, L-9701,* ☎ *921002,* ⒻⒶⓍ *920826. International:* ⊠ *Grand'Rue 10, L-9701,* ☎ *929391,* ⒻⒶⓍ *920492. 53/ 41 rooms. Restaurant, café, piano bar, indoor pool, sauna. AE, DC, MC, V. Koener closed mid-Jan.–mid-Mar.*

$ ▣ **Le Commerce.** Directly below the castle and slightly apart from the hotel-packed center, this spacious hotel has been in the family for two generations and shows their pride: It combines slick, spare modernity— tile, stucco, polished oak—with homey old details (fringed lamps, heavy upholstery), and there's an open fireplace in the restaurant. Some rooms have balconies over the river and hills. ⊠ *R. de Marnach 2, L-9709,* ☎ *921032,* ⒻⒶⓍ *929108. 54 rooms. Restaurant, bar, café. MC, V. Restaurant and hotel closed mid-Nov.–mid-Mar.*

The Arts

Wiltz, halfway between Clervaux and Esch-sur-Sûre, sponsors a popular **theater and music festival** in July, with performances and concerts in the outdoor amphitheater. Call or write ahead for ticket and schedule information (⊠ Syndicat d'Initiative, L-9516 Wiltz, ☎ 957441).

Outdoor Activities and Sports

There's an 18-hole golf course (☎ 929395) at **Eselborn,** 3 km (2 mi) northeast of Clervaux, with the inexpensive, 10-room Hôtel du Golf (☎ 929395) right by the course.

Esch-sur-Sûre

㉙ *27 km (17mi) southwest of Clervaux, 43 km (27 mi) northwest of Luxembourg City.*

Pretty little Esch-sur-Sûre is reached from Clervaux via Wilwerwiltz and Wiltz. Completely circled by densely forested hills, this miniature gooseneck on the river Sûre was once a stronghold, and its ruined **fortress-castle** still towers over the town (unrestored, but open to the public). Legend has it that an Esch Crusader brought home a Turk's head and hung it outside the castle gate and that it reappears to this day to warn of disaster; some claim to have seen it before the German invasion in 1940. The old **textile factory** (⊠ Rte. de Lutzhausen, ☎ 8993311) has been converted into a museum.

Dining and Lodging

$$ ✕▣ **Beau-Site.** At the edge of the village and overlooking the river, the hotel-restaurant has been updated with new woodwork and fresh tile.

The rooms are modern, some with flower boxes and river views. The restaurant offers grilled meats and cream-sauce standards at prices slightly higher than average—but the portions are staggering, and the kitchen cuts no corners. ⊠ R. de Kaundorf 2, L-9650 Esch-sur-Sûre, ☎ 899021, FAX 899024. 18 rooms. Restaurant. DC, V. Closed Feb.

Shopping

In Esch-sur-Sûre, you can buy fine candles at the old Käerzefabrik (Candle Factory).

En Route Children who finally tire of pouring imaginary boiling oil and shooting flaming arrows from Ardennes castles and who balk at another uphill forest hike can find adventure swimming or windsurfing at **Lac de la Haute Sûre,** accessible on the south shore at Insenborn and on the north shore below Liefrange.

Bourscheid

★ ③⓪ 26 km (16 mi) east of Esch-sur-Sûre, 36 km (22 mi) north of Luxembourg City.

Following the green Sûre valley toward Goebelsmühle—along a quiet, winding road that is one of the most picturesque in the Grand Duchy—look for signs for Bourscheid Moulin-Plage, where you'll see the romantic ruins of **Bourscheid Castle.** It looms 500 ft above the Sûre River, with commanding views of three valleys. Restorations have made this rambling hodgepodge of towers and walls more accessible; the views are magnificent and there's a snack bar. ⊠ Near N25, ☎ 90570. 🎫 Flux 80. ☉ Apr., daily 11–5; May, June, and Sept., daily 10–6; July–Aug., daily 10–7; Oct., daily 11–4; Nov.–Mar. weekends and holidays, 11–4.

Larochette

★ ③① 22 km (14 mi) southeast of Bourscheid, via Lipperscheid and Diekirch; 23 km (14 mi) northeast of Luxembourg City.

Larochette has a striking step-gabled **castle** that looks out over the town. The castle is privately owned and occupied, but adjoining ruins from an earlier incarnation (with evocative views over the small houses below) may be visited. ⊠ Near N25. 🎫 Flux 50. ☉ Easter–Oct., daily 10–6.

Petite Suisse

③② 36 km (22 mi) southeast of Bourscheid, 25 km (15 mi) northeast of Luxembourg City.

At Reuland is the entrance to the Müllerthal, also known as Ernz Noire Valley, and Petite Suisse, an area of dense fir and beech forests, with high limestone bluffs and twisting brooks. Auberges are sprinkled along the roadside, with terrace tables and welcoming cafés.

At the top of the Ernz Noire valley, a short detour leads to **Beaufort,** where, just west of the village, a splendid ruin, the **Château de Beaufort,** only partially restored to its 15th-century form, rises over green grounds full of sheep and forests laced with walking trails. You can step into guard towers with archers' slits, look down wells, visit the kitchen fireplace, cross a drawbridge, and ogle torture equipment, including a rack, in a dungeon. At the ticket counter, you can buy (or drink) samples of the local kirsch and cassis. ⊠ CR128, west of village, ☎ 86002. 🎫 Flux 60. ☉ Late Mar.–Oct., daily 9–6.

Shopping

At Beaufort, you can pick up a bottle of the house-label kirsch or cassis.

En Route   On the return from Beaufort, you can peer down the crevices at Wer-schrumsluff and Zickzackschluff, climb vantage points for vast panoramas of the landscape and the winding river Sûre at Perekop and Bildscheslay, and squeeze between the cliffs at the Gorge du Loup (Wolf's Throat) before arriving at Echternach.

Echternach

㉝ *58 km (36 mi) southeast of Clervaux, 35 km (22 mi) northeast of Luxembourg City.*

Echternach dates from the 7th century and is the home of the only religious dancing procession remaining in the Western world. You wouldn't guess this at first glance, for modern Echternach has been all but adopted by German visitors from across the Sûre, who fill its hotels, restaurants, and monuments every weekend. This ancient town was founded in 698 by Saint Willibrord, who came from Northumberland in England to establish a Benedictine abbey, which thrived until 1795. His remains are enshrined in the crypt of the **Basilica.** The early medieval basilica was destroyed in December 1944 and rebuilt in a modern style. The relics of the saint are contained in a neoclassical marble sarcophagus. Behind the elaborate carvings, you glimpse the simple tooled-stone sarcophagus cut in the 7th century. A few token traces of the original 7th-century chapel, founded by the saint himself, have been left exposed under heavy, modern repairs. On a hill just behind the basilica, a church, **Sts Pierre et Paul,** stands on the remains of a Roman castellum and shows, in its spare architecture, signs of Merovingian, Romanesque, and Gothic influence. Every spring, the two churches host one of Luxembourg's most important arts events: the Echternach Festival of Classical Music.

On Whit Tuesday (eighth Tuesday after Easter), Echternach is transported to the Middle Ages: More than 10,000 pilgrims (most of them young people) from throughout the region come to town to join in—and tourists come to watch—the famous **Springprozession,** a dancing procession down the streets of the town, the marchers bouncing from one foot to the other, to the tune of a polkalike march. Their chanted prayer: "Holy Willibrord, founder of churches, light of the blind, destroyer of idols, pray for us." This unique pilgrimage has been repeated every year since the 15th century.

NEED A   Just below Sts Peter and Paul's Church, have coffee and a generous
BREAK?   piece of cake at the **Café-Tea Room Zimmer** and pick up something for
           later in the adjoining bakery-confectionery, perhaps the Echternach specialty, *Macarrons Moux.*

In the Middle Ages, Echternach was known throughout the Western world for another specialty, the exquisite *illuminations* (miniature illustrations) that accompanied the hand-copied texts produced by the abbey's scriptorium. The original abbey is long gone, but the magnificent quadrant of abbey buildings from the 18th century remains, noble of line and classical in scale. Examples of the artwork produced in the abbey can be viewed in the **Musée de l'Abbaye** (Abbey Museum) in the abbey basement. The books displayed here are painstakingly executed reproductions of the originals, down to their gem-studded covers. The originals are now in various museums abroad. Even so, the exhibition provides an interesting introduction to the art of illumination in the Middle Ages. ⊠ *Parvis de la Basilique 11.* ☎ *Flux 80.* ☼ *Apr.–Oct., daily 10–noon and 2–6; Nov.–Mar., weekends 2–5.*

Echternach's cobbled **Place du Marché,** in the old town center, offers a charming mix of Gothic arcades and restored medieval houses, festooned with wrought-iron signs and sculpted drain spouts; the arched and turreted 13th-century **Hôtel de Ville** (Town Hall) is its centerpiece.

Dining and Lodging

$$$$ ✕ **La Bergerie.** One of the best restaurants in the country, La Bergerie
★ is in Geyershof, off the road to Luxembourg City. The 19th-century farmhouse nestles in an idyllic setting of forest and fields, with windows and a garden-terrace making the most of the expanse of greenery. The graceful, simple dining room features the cooking of owner-chef Claude Phal and his son Thierry, whose specialties include classics (simple foie gras; steamed turbot in champagne sauce) and sophisticated experiments (lobster fricassee with whiskey; scallops with truffles). The strawberry gratin in orange butter uses fruit from the garden; all baked goods are made in the full-scale pastry kitchen. It's a family effort, with wife, son, and daughter-in-law running the restaurant and their offshoot hotel (☞ La Bergerie, *below*) in Echternach, 7 km (4 mi) away, with free shuttle service. ⊠ *Geyershaff,* ☎ *790464. Reservations essential. AE, DC, MC, V. No dinner Sun. Closed Mon. and mid-Jan.– Feb.*

$ ✕🏠 **Commerce.** Tucked back from Place du Marché, amid quiet side streets, and with an idyllic garden behind it, this simple hotel has been kept in top running order. Although rooms have fixtures of varying vintage, all have fresh decor. The restaurant and café are atmospheric, with oak wainscoting, beams, and pink linens; standard dishes (trout, bouchée à la reine) are moderately priced and well prepared. ⊠ *Pl. du Marché 16, L-6460,* ☎ *720301,* ᶠᴬˣ *728790. 44 rooms. Restaurant, café. AE, MC, V. Closed mid-Nov.–mid-Feb.; closed weekdays mid-Feb.–Easter.*

$$ 🏠 **La Bergerie.** Managed by the owners of the La Bergerie restaurant
★ (☞ *above*) outside town, this 1988 addition to the downtown hotel scene is one of a kind: a small mansion, enclosed in a shady garden, completely converted to creamy, modern luxury, with glistening tile baths, opulent fabrics and cabinetry, and all the comforts—except a restaurant, which requires a pleasant shuttle ride into the countryside. Breakfast is served beside a large bay window overlooking the garden and fountain, or on the terrace; croissants come from the restaurant's pastry kitchen. ⊠ *R. de Luxembourg 47, L-6450,* ☎ *7285041,* ᶠᴬˣ *728508. 15 rooms with bath. Breakfast room, sauna. AE, DC, MC, V. Closed Jan.–mid-Feb.*

The Arts

CLASSICAL MUSIC

The **Echternach Festival** of classical music is one of the most important arts events in Luxembourg, bringing in world-class artists and ensembles and showcasing them in the basilica and the smaller Saints Peter and Paul's Church. It takes place on weekends for a month during May and June; tickets sell out quickly; write ahead to Lux-Festival (⊠ B.P. 30, L-6401 Echternach, ☎ 729940).

Outdoor Activities and Sports

BICYCLING

Rent bikes from **Mototek** (⊠ R. Ermesinde 17, ☎ 726475).

En Route   Leaving Echternach, follow signs for Wasserbillig/Trier and head south along the Sûre and the German border. You'll pass several small schnapps or eaux-de-vie distilleries, and their orchards. At Wasserbillig cut through town toward Grevenmacher; at the other end, you will come to the **Moselle River,** whose waters nourish Luxembourg's vineyards, cultivated since Roman times. The vines cover every exposed

slope in sight, and the farther south you drive, the more romantic the
scenery becomes. Graceful little **Wormeldange** is a key wine center; cut
inland and follow signs up into Wormeldange-Haute (Upper Wormeldange) for sweeping views over the Moselle.

Grevenmacher

*37 km (23 mi) south of Echternach, 32 km (20 mi) east of Luxem-
bourg City.*

The **Jardin des Papillons** (Butterfly Garden) seethes with fluttering
wildlife, from butterflies to birds to tropical insects, all enclosed in an
attractive greenhouse. ⊠ *Rte. du Vin,* ☎ *758539.* ⌦ *Flux 180.* ☉ *Apr.–
mid-Oct., daily 9:30–5.*

NEED A
BREAK?

Stop at Wormeldange's enormous pink-stucco **Caves Cooperatives** to
sample the local product. In a tidy adjoining pub, you can taste five
wines served on a wrought-iron, vine-shape rack. There's local grape
juice, too, for the designated driver.

Ehnen

*52 km (32 mi) south of Echternach, 21 km (13 mi) east of Luxem-
bourg City.*

Tiny Ehnen, just down the road from Wormeldange, seems frozen in
time, with its narrow old streets, carved-wood doors, and unusual circular church. It's a popular excursion goal for city dwellers who want
to contemplate the river and sample the grape. Ehnen is home to a **Musée
du Vin** (Wine Museum), set in a typical group of Luxembourgish farm
buildings, with pink stucco and cobbled courts. Its rooms are full of
tools, equipment, and photographs of the wine-making industry, and
a demonstration vineyard is planted with samples of each of the local
varietals. There are labels in English. ☎ *760026.* ⌦ *Flux 80.* ☉ *Apr.–
Oct., Tues.–Sun. 9:30–11:30 and 2–5; Nov.–Apr. by appointment.*

Musée Folklorique A Possen is a 17th-century stone wine maker's house,
restored and furnished, in the small wine village, **Bech-Kleinmacher.**
Its extraordinarily atmospheric displays include a "black kitchen," with
a ham-smoking chimney, and a cozy bedroom with a four-poster bed
and homespun linens; there are museum displays on the wine industry, and a toy collection as well. There's also a **Waistuff** (wine *stube*),
where you can taste the local wine and sample dark bread smeared with
pungent *kachkeis,* Luxembourg's favorite cheese spread. ⊠ *R. Sandt
16,* ☎ *697353.* ⌦ *Flux 120.* ☉ *May–Oct., Tues.–Sun. 2–7; Nov.–
Apr., Fri.–Sun. 2–7.*

Dining and Lodging

$ ✕⊟ **Simmer.** This Moselle institution, built in 1863 and maintained
★ in a welcoming Victorian-rustic style, is the preferred riverfront retreat
of the royal family and political luminaries, though its ambience remains comfortable and homey. Incorporating portions of a 1610 house
and the founder's butcher shop, it was taken over by the current family in 1955 and built into an elegant hotel-restaurant. The details they
added include a 17th-century fireplace in the dining room and carved
oak grotesques paneling the salon. Rooms are spacious and solid, with
dated glamour (brocade, gilt, crystal) and some antiques; in front,
there are balconies, and in back small suites. Specialties in the restau-
rant ($$$) include braised *brochet* (pike) in cream and *sandre* (pike perch)
in local Auxerrois; in summer, you can dine on the full-length, open-
front porch. It's next door to the wine museum. ⊠ *Rte. du Vin 117,*

L-5416 Ehnen, ☎ *760030,* 🖷 *760306. 15 rooms. Restaurant, bar. AE, MC, V. Closed Tues. and Feb.*

Hamm/Sandweiler

③⑤   *16 km (10 mi) west of Ehnen, 5 km (3 mi) east of Luxembourg City.*

At Hamm you'll find the **American Military Cemetery,** where General George Patton chose to be buried with his men. More than 5,000 soldiers of the Third Army were buried here, having died on Luxembourg soil; there are also 117 graves of unknown soldiers. Each grave is marked with either a Star of David or a simple cross, but they are not separated by race, rank, religion, or origin—except for the 22 pairs of brothers, who lie side by side. Only Patton's cross, identical to the others, stands by itself.

From the American Military Cemetery parking lot, a small road, about 1 km (½ mi) long, leads to Sandweiler, and across an intersection to the **German Military Cemetery,** which shelters more than twice as many war dead. Blunt stone crosses identify multiple burial sites, some marked with names and serial numbers, others marked simply *Ein Deutscher Soldat* (a German soldier).

Dining

$$$$ ✕ **Lea Linster.** As the first woman to win France's top culinary award,
★   the Paul Bocuse d'Or, Lea Linster has earned international attention and keeps her modest farmhouse—once her mother's rustic café—full of prominent guests. Have a glass of champagne in the shady garden out back (cows may wander nearby), and then relax in the elegant dining room and enjoy her prizewinning dishes: salmon-stuffed zucchini flower with cardamom sauce, rack of lamb in a crisp potato crust, and carmelized pears with rosemary-lime ice cream. The wine list is weighted toward the high end, as are prices. ✉ *Rte. de Luxembourg 17, Frisange, 12 km (7 mi) south of Luxembourg City,* ☎ *668411. Reservations essential. AE, DC, MC, V. Closed Mon.–Tues.*

$$$ ✕ **A la Table des Guilloux.** Pierrick Guilloux was responsible for the
★   Saint-Michel restaurant in Luxembourg City, in its heyday one of Europe's finest, before "retiring" to the countryside to run this great little restaurant in a converted farmhouse. Here he cooks what he pleases, mostly dishes based on the traditions of his native Brittany. Trust his recommendations; few regret it. ✉ *R. de la Résistance 17–19, Schouweiler, 13 km (8 mi) southwest of Luxembourg City,* ☎ *370008. No credit cards. Closed Mon.–Tues.*

Nightlife

The small treatment spa Mondorf-les-Bains, on the French border southeast of Luxembourg City, offers **Casino 2000** (✉ R. Th. Flamang, ☎ 661–0101), with full gaming facilities. Jacket and tie are required to play roulette and blackjack, but not for the slot machines.

The Ardennes and the Moselle A to Z

Arriving and Departing

BY BUS

Luxembourg buses connect throughout the Grand Duchy, both from Luxembourg City and from exterior towns. If you're staying outside the city, invest in the thick timetable (available at Aldringen Center in Luxembourg City), which has complete listings of connections.

BY CAR

Driving is by far the most efficient and satisfying way to explore this region, and roads are well kept, though slow and winding. From Luxembourg City, follow signs for Ettelbruck (via route E 420/RN 7). An alternative—and very attractive—route is E27 toward Echternach, turning left almost immediately on the road to Larochette, and thence to Diekirch. The Moselle area is even closer to Luxembourg City, with no point more distant than a 40-minute drive.

BY TRAIN

Small rail lines out of Luxembourg City can carry you to Ettelbruck, Bourscheid, Clervaux, and Wiltz in the Ardennes, and to Wasserbillig on the Moselle, but other sites in these areas remain out of reach by train. Ask at the tourism office (☞ Visitor Information, *below*) about one-price transit passes that offer unlimited rides on both buses and trains for a single price and a set time period.

Contacts and Resources

GUIDED TOURS

Segatos Tourisme (⊠ R. Kalchesbrück 7, L-2012 Luxembourg City, ☎ 4222881) offers coach tours for groups of 10 or more into the Ardennes or the Moselle area. Tickets can be purchased at the Place de la Constitution war memorial.

To view the Moselle by cruise boat, contact **Entente Touristique** (⊠ Rte. du Vin 10, L-6701 Grevenmacher, ☎ 758275); its graceful little ship, M.S. *Princess Marie-Astrid* stops at Wasserbillig, Grevenmacher, Remich, Bech-Kleinmacher, and Schengen, and at Wormeldange and Stadtbredimus on demand. Meals are served en route. It runs Easter through September, twice a day between 11 and 6. Call ahead for specific departure times.

Most of the wine houses along the Moselle offer guided tours and tastings. Contact **Bernard-Massard** (⊠ R. du Pont 8, L-6773 Grevenmacher, ☎ 750545), **St-Martin** (⊠ L-5570 Remich, ☎ 699091), and **St-Rémy** (⊠ L-5501 Remich, ☎ 69084).

VISITOR INFORMATION

Syndicat d'Initiative (tourist offices) are located at Clervaux (⊠ Château, ☎ 920072), Diekirch (⊠ Esplanade 1, ☎ 803023), Echternach (⊠ Porte Saint-Willibrord [Basilica], ☎ 720230), Remich (⊠ Gare Routière, ☎ 698488, summer only), and Vianden (⊠ Maison Victor Hugo, ☎ 84257).

LUXEMBOURG A TO Z

Arriving and Departing

From North America by Plane

AIRPORTS AND AIRLINES

Most of the main international airlines offer connections—usually with **Luxair** (☎ 4798–5050) allowing you to fly to London, Amsterdam, or Brussels and then connect into Luxembourg as a final destination at little or no additional cost: **British Airways** (☎ 438647 in Luxembourg or 800/247–9297 in the U.S.), **Delta/Sabena** (☎ 432–4241 in Luxembourg or 800/955–2000 in the U.S.), **Northwest/KLM** (☎ 424842 in Luxembourg or 800/374–7747 in the U.S.). All flights land at **Findel Airport,** 6 km (4 mi) east of the city center.

FLYING TIME

New York–Brussels, 8 hours, plus Brussels–Luxembourg, 45 minutes.

From the United Kingdom

BY PLANE

Luxair (☎ in Luxembourg, reservations, 4798–4242; information, 4798–5050; in the U.K., 0181/745–4254), the Luxembourg airline that connects to all major airports in Europe, has regular flights to London Heathrow, London Stansted, and Manchester. **British Airways** (☎ in Luxembourg, 438647; in the U.K., 0141/222–2345) also has regular flights to and from Luxembourg.

Flying time from London to Luxembourg is 1 hour and 15 minutes.

BY CAR AND FERRY

The entire Benelux region is easily accessible in a day from London and the southeast. Nearly all ferries from Britain to the Continent take cars, as does the Channel Tunnel train. Several companies operate sailings direct to the Belgian ports of Oostende and Zeebrugge. Sailings are most frequent from the south coast ports; in summer **Hoverspeed Ltd.** (☎ 0990/595–522, 0990/240–241) offers about 5 services daily from Dover to Oostende and up to 12 sailings a day Dover to Calais. The quickest (but most expensive) ferry crossing is from Dover to Calais via Hoverspeed's Hovercraft link: After a mere 35-minute crossing you continue by car or rail south from Calais to Lille and cut across Belgium, via Mons, Charleroi, and Namur, to reach Luxembourg. If weather and ridership permit, you'll make it from the south coast to Luxembourg in five hours. You also can take a standard ferry from Dover to Calais with **P&O Stena Line** (☎ 0990/980–980).

Fares vary considerably according to season, journey time, number of passengers, and length of vehicle. However, the approximate cost of crossing the Channel by ferry on one of the short sea routes in high summer, with an average vehicle of 4¼ m (14 ft) and two adult passengers, works out to about £130 one way. By traveling off-peak, early in the morning or late evening, or in June and September, you can reduce costs.

BY TRAIN

☞ The Channel Tunnel *in* the Gold Guide.

Car Rentals

Luxembourg has among the lowest car-rental rates in Europe, as well as easy pickup at the airport and at the train station in Luxembourg City (☞ Luxembourg City A to Z, *above*).

Customs and Duties

On Arrival

Americans and other non-EU members are allowed to bring in no more than 200 cigarettes, 50 cigars, 1 liter of spirits, 2 liters of wine or sparkling wine, 50 grams of perfume, and .25 liters of toilet water. **EU members** may bring in 800 cigarettes; 200 cigars; 10 liters of spirits; 90 liters of wine, of which 60 liters of sparkling wine; 50 grams of perfume; and .25 liters of toilet water.

On Departure

U.S. citizens may take home $400 worth of foreign merchandise as gifts or for personal use without having to pay duty, provided they have been out of the country for more than 48 hours and provided they have not claimed a similar exemption within the previous 30 days. Every member of a family is entitled to the same exemption, regardless of age, and the exemptions can be pooled. For the next $1,000 worth of goods, inspectors will assess a flat 10% duty, based on the price actually paid, so it is a good idea to keep your receipts. Included in the $400 allowance for travelers over the age of 21 are 1 liter of alcohol, 100 cigars, and 200 cigarettes. Any amount in excess of those limits will be taxed at the port of entry, and it may be additionally taxed in the traveler's home state; be sure to ask, as you may be charged late penalties if you don't pay on arrival. You may not take home meats, fruits, plants, soil, or other agricultural items.

Canadian citizens may take home 50 cigars, 200 cigarettes, and 40 ounces of liquor. Be sure to carry receipts for your purchases abroad, as any totaling more than $300 will be taxed.

British citizens may take home the same quantity of goods they were allowed to carry into Luxembourg (listed above). Because of strict rabies control, no pets or animals may be brought into the United Kingdom.

Guided Tours

General-Interest Tours

See Tour Operators *in* The Gold Guide: Smart Travel Tips A to Z for tours that cover the Benelux region. A sampling of tours and packages that concentrate on Luxembourg is listed below. For additional resources, contact your travel agent or the tourist office of Luxembourg.

FROM THE U.S.
Olson Travelworld (⊠ 1145 Clark St., Stevens Point, WI 54481, ☎ 715/345–0505 or 800/421–2255) tailors excursions in Luxembourg for groups.

FROM THE U.K.
Travel Scene (⊠ 11–15 St. Anne's Rd., Harrow, Middlesex HA11AS, ☎ 0181/427–4445) has packages of various lengths and price ranges, by air or rail, to Luxembourg.

Package Deals for Independent Travelers

The **Centre des Auberges de Jeunesse Luxembourgeoises** (⊠ R. du Fort Olisy 2; B.P. 374, L-2013 Luxembourg, ☎ 225588), Luxembourg's youth hostel association, offers do-it-yourself city, hiking, and cycling packages (mountain-bike rental included). **Travel Bound** (⊠ 599 Broadway, Penthouse, New York, NY 10012, ☎ 212/334–1350 or 800/456–8656) tailors air-hotel-car packages to Luxembourg, through travel agents only.

Language

Luxembourg is a linguistic melting pot. Although its citizens speak Lëtzeburgesch (Luxembourgish), a language descended from an ancient dialect of the Moselle Franks, they are educated in German and French, completing higher studies in French. The current generation also learns English and is, for the most part, easily conversant. The language used for government documents is French, but many are translated into German as well; a simple church service will often include German, French, Luxembourgish, and a trace of Latin. Within the travel industry, most Luxembourgers you'll meet will speak some English with you, but they'll talk *about* you in Luxembourgish.

Mail

Postal Rates

Airmail postcards and letters weighing less than 20 grams cost Flux 25 to the United States. Letters and postcards to the United Kingdom cost Flux 16.

Receiving Mail

Mail can be sent care of **American Express** (⊠ Av. de la Porte-Neuve 34, L-2227 Luxembourg). This service is free for holders of American Express cards or traveler's checks.

Money Matters

The Luxembourg franc (abbreviated Flux) is equal to the Belgian franc and used interchangeably with it within Luxembourg. Notes come in denominations of 100, 1,000, and 5,000 francs. Coins are issued in denominations of 1, 5, 20, and 50 francs; you will rarely be required to use the 50-centime piece. Be careful not to mix up French 10-franc pieces with Belgian and Luxembourgian 20-franc coins; the French coin is three times as valuable. At press time, rates of exchange averaged Flux 36 to the U.S. dollar, Flux 60 to the pound sterling, and Flux 27 to the Canadian dollar. Rates fluctuate daily, so be sure to check at the time you leave.

Costs

As Luxembourg continues to prosper, the cost of living increases annually, but hotel and restaurant prices tend to be up no more than 5% over last year's. Because of Luxembourg's low VAT (Value Added Tax), perfume, gasoline, cigarettes, and liquor continue to be notably cheaper here than in neighboring countries; you'll find combination gas station/liquor stores clustered at every border crossing. High-octane, unleaded gas costs about Flux 26 a liter; in Belgium, you'll pay 8 or 9 francs more.

SAMPLE COSTS

Cup of coffee, Flux 55; glass of beer, Flux 45; movie ticket, Flux 250; taxi ride, 4¾ km (3 mi), Flux 600 (10% higher nights, 25% higher Sunday).

Taxes

VAT is 15%, except for hotels and restaurants, where it is 3%. The airport tax (payable with the purchase of your ticket) is Flux 120. Purchases of goods for export (to non-EU countries only) may qualify for a refund; ask the shop to fill out a refund form. You must have the form stamped by customs officers on leaving the European Union. A minimum purchase of Flux 3,000 is required before you're eligible for a refund.

National Holidays

January 1; February 15, 1999, March 6, 2000 (Carnival); April 5, 1999, April 24, 2000 (Easter Monday); May 1 (May Day); May 13, 1999, June 1, 2000 (Ascension); May 24, 1999, June 12, 2000 (Pentecost Monday); June 23 (National Day); August 15 (Assumption); November 1 (All Saints' Day); December 25–26 (Christmas). Note: When a holiday falls on a Sunday, the following Monday is automatically a national holiday.

Opening and Closing Times

Banks are generally open weekdays 8:30–4:30, though some close for lunch (noon–2). In Luxembourg City, an automatic exchange machine in the Rue de la Reine accepts banknotes of most foreign currencies. **Museum** opening hours vary, so check individual listings. Most are closed Monday, and in the countryside some also close for lunch (noon–2). **Shops** and department stores are generally open Monday 2–6 and Tuesday–Saturday 9–6. Some close for lunch (noon–2). A few small family businesses are open Sunday 8–noon.

Outdoor Activities and Sports

Biking

Biking is a very popular sport in the Grand Duchy. Good routes include Ettelbruck–Vianden and Luxembourg City–Echternach. The

Luxembourg National Tourist Office—as well as those of Luxembourg City, Diekirch, and Mersch—all publish booklets and maps suggesting cycling tours within Luxembourg. Also contact the **Fédération du Sport Cycliste Luxembourgeois** (✉ B.P. 1074, L-1010 Luxembourg, ☎ 292317).

Boating and Water Sports

The Wiltz and the Clerve rivers offer challenging waters for small craft or canoes, but the Our, with its wooded gorges, is the wildest; the Sûre is most rewarding, for its length and for the thrills it offers. For further information, write to the **Fédération Luxembourgeoise de Canoë et de Kayak** (✉ R. de Pulvermuhle 6, L 2356 Luxembourg). People windsurf and sail on Lac de la Haute Sûre.

Camping

Visitors from all over Europe, especially the Netherlands, descend on Luxembourg's campgrounds every summer, making them sociable, crowded places, often near forests and riverbanks. Write for the pamphlet "Camping/Grand-Duché de Luxembourg," available through the national tourist office (☞ Visitor Information, *below*). The **Fédération Luxembourgeoise de Camping et de Caravaning** (✉ ☎ 544871) also publishes camping information.

Fishing

If you're in search of trout, grayling, perch, or dace—as well as relaxation—apply for a government fishing permit from the **Administration des Eaux et Forêts** (✉ B.P. 411, L-2014 Luxembourg, ☎ 405310) and a local permit from the owner of the waterfront, which in many cases is your hotel.

Hiking and Walking

Luxembourg is full of well-developed forest trails, often on state lands with parking provided. The book *171 Circuits Auto-pedestres,* which contains maps of walking itineraries, is available in bookshops for Flux 895. Trails will be full of strollers late Sunday afternoon, the traditional time for such outings.

Telephoning

Country Code

The country code for Luxembourg is 352.

International Calls

To dial direct internationally, start with the country code (001 for the United States, 0044 for the United Kingdom), and then dial the local number. A **Telekaart,** available with 50 or 150 time units, works in specially equipped booths, usually in post offices, where they are sold. To make an international call without direct access, you must first dial 0010.

The cheapest way to make an international call is to dial direct from a public phone; in a post office, you may be required to make a deposit before the call. To reach an **AT&T** long-distance operator, dial 0800–0111; for **MCI,** 0800–0112; for **Sprint,** 0800–0115.

Local Calls

Public phones aren't always easy to find, especially outside Luxembourg City. The best bet is at post offices and in cafés. A local call costs Flux 10. No area codes are necessary within the Grand Duchy.

Operators and Information

For international **information,** dial 016; for local information, 017.

Tipping

In Luxembourg, service charges of 15% are included in restaurant bills; for a modest meal, most people leave the small change. At a grander restaurant, you will be expected to leave a larger tip—up to 10% extra when a large staff is involved. For porters, a tip of Flux 50 per bag is adequate. Cab drivers expect a tip of about 10%.

Transportation: Getting Around

By Bus

The Luxembourg bus system carries passengers to points throughout the Grand Duchy; most buses leave from the Luxembourg City train station (Gare Centrale, junction Av. de la Gare, R. de Strasbourg, Av. de la Liberté, ☎ 492424). You can buy an *horaire* (bus schedule) to plan complex itineraries, or consult the tourist office. The **Oeko-Billjee,** a special day ticket (Flux 180), allows you to travel anywhere in the country by bus (including city buses) or rail, from the time you first use it until 8 AM the next day. They're available in Luxembourg City at the **Centre Aldringen** (⊠ Av. Monterey 8A, corner of R. Aldringen), the underground bus station in front of the central post office, or at any train station.

By Car

The best way to see Luxembourg, outside of Luxembourg City, is by car. Castles and attractive villages are scattered around and connected by pleasant, well-maintained country roads. *Priorité à droite* (yield to the right) applies here and should be strictly observed; drivers may shoot out from side streets without glancing to their left. Speed limits are 50 kph (31 mph) in built-up areas, 90 kph (55 mph) on national highways, and 120 kph (75 mph) on expressways.

By Train

Train travel within the Grand Duchy is limited; a north–south line connects Luxembourg City with Clervaux in the north and Bettembourg in the south, and another line carries you to Grevenmacher and Wasserbillig, along the Moselle. For additional information, write or call the **Chemins de Fer Luxembourgeois** (⊠ CFL, Pl. de la Gare 9, B.P. 1803, L-1018 Luxembourg, ☎ 49901).

Visitor Information

Luxembourg National Tourist Office (⊠ R. d'Anvers 77, L-1010, ☎ 4282821).

5 Portraits of the Netherlands, Belgium, and Luxembourg

The Netherlands, Belgium, and Luxembourg: A Chronology

Les Moules Sont Arrivées!

Battle Scars from the Bulge

Books and Films

THE NETHERLANDS, BELGIUM, AND LUXEMBOURG: A CHRONOLOGY

55 BC   Julius Caesar's legions extend Roman control to the Meuse and Waal rivers.

ca. AD 300   Inundation of the Frisian plain causes Rome to abandon it.

ca. 400   Roman rule retreats before invading Frisians in the north and Franks in the south.

481–511   Under their king, Clovis, the Frankish Merovingians extend their rule north.

ca. 700   Christianity is extended to the Netherlands by Saints Willibrord and Boniface.

800   Charlemagne, king of the Franks, is crowned emperor of the Romans by the pope. His domains extend from the marches of Denmark to Spain.

843   The Treaty of Verdun divides Charlemagne's empire into three. Luxembourg and the Netherlands are included in the middle kingdom of Lotharingia; Belgium is divided at the Scheldt River between France and Lotharingia. Viking attacks begin along the coast.

862   Baldwin Iron-Arm establishes himself as first count of Flanders, but rule of the Lotharingian lands is constantly disputed.

963   Siegfried, count of Ardennes, purchases an old Roman castle named Lucilinburhuc along the Alzette river. His descendants are named counts of Luxembourg.

1196–1247   Reign of Countess Ermesinde of Luxembourg, who enlarges and unifies the county, grants privileges to its cities, and founds the ruling house of Luxembourg-Limburg.

ca. 1200   With the rise of towns, the collection of duchies and counties that constitutes the Low Countries gains economic power.

1302   The men of Flanders revolt against French attempts at annexation and defeat Philip the Fair's army at the Battle of the Golden Spurs, near Kortrijk. Flanders remains a desirable prize.

1308   Henry VII of Luxembourg is elected Holy Roman Emperor; he grants the rule of the county of Luxembourg to his son, John the Blind (d. 1346).

1354   John's son, Charles, also Holy Roman emperor, raises the status of Luxembourg to a duchy.

1361   Philip the Bold, son of John II of France, establishes the great duchy of Burgundy, which, by Philip's marriage in 1369 to Marguerite, heiress of the count of Flanders, grows to include Flanders, Artois, Limburg, and Brabant.

1419–67   Philip's grandson Philip the Good extends Burgundian rule over Holland, Zeeland, and Hainaut and presides over the golden age of the Flemish Renaissance. Painters include the van Eycks, Hans Memling, and Rogier van der Weyden.

1443   Philip gains Luxembourg.

1464   Philip calls the deputies of the states—nobles, merchants, and churchmen—to meet together, thus beginning the States-General, the Dutch representative assembly.

1477 The death of Philip's son Charles leaves his granddaughter Mary of Burgundy as heiress. Mary marries the Hapsburg heir, Maximilian of Austria; their son Philip marries Juana, heiress to the throne of Spain.

1500 Birth in Ghent of Charles, son of Philip and Juana, who inherits the collective titles and holdings of Burgundy, Spain, and Austria as Charles V, Holy Roman Emperor.

ca. 1520–40 Protestantism spreads through the Netherlands.

1549 By the Pragmatic Sanction, Charles declares that the 17 provinces constituting the Netherlands will be inherited intact by his son Philip.

1555 Charles V abdicates, dividing his empire between his brother Ferdinand and his son Philip, who inherits Spain and the Netherlands. A devout Catholic, Philip moves to suppress Protestantism in the Netherlands.

1566 Revolt in Antwerp against Spanish rule provokes ruthless suppression by the Spanish governor, the duke of Alva.

1568 Beginning of 80 years of warfare between the 17 provinces and Spain.

1572 The "Sea Beggars" under William of Orange take to the natural Dutch element, water, and harass the Spanish.

1579 The Spanish succeed in dividing the Catholic south from the Protestant north with the Treaty of Arras. The seven Protestant provinces in the north—Holland, Friesland, Gelderland, Groningen, Overijssel, Utrecht, and Zeeland—declare themselves the United Provinces, under the hereditary *stadtholder* (city elder), William the Silent of Orange.

1585 Antwerp falls to the Spanish, and the division of the Netherlands between north and south is effectively completed; the Dutch close the Scheldt to navigation, depriving Antwerp of its egress to the sea and leading to its rapid decline.

1602 With the founding of the Dutch East India Company, the United Provinces emerges as a major trading nation and a cultural force. Rembrandt, Vermeer, and Hals chronicle an era of wealth, while in Belgium, Rubens and Van Dyck epitomize Flemish Baroque.

1609 The Twelve Years' Truce temporarily ends fighting between the United Provinces and Spain.

1624 The Dutch land on Manhattan and found New Amsterdam.

1648 By the Treaty of Westphalia, the Spanish finally recognize the independence of the United Provinces. What will become Belgium remains under Spanish control but is a battleground between the ambitions of France and a declining Spain.

1652–54 First Anglo-Dutch War, over trading rivalries.

1653–72 The Dutch fail to elect a new stadtholder and are ruled as a republic under the grand pensionary Johan de Witt.

1667 By the terms of the Peace of Breda, which ends the second Anglo-Dutch War, the Netherlands exchanges New Netherland, renamed New York, for England's Suriname.

1672 William III of Orange, great-grandson of William the Silent, is named stadtholder; de Witt is murdered.

1678 By the Treaty of Nijmegen William ends yet another war with France.

1689 William III is named joint ruler of England with his wife, Mary Stuart.

1697 The Treaty of Ryswick ends the War of the League of Augsburg against France, instigated by William.

1701–17 The War of the Spanish Succession ends with the Treaty of Utrecht, which transfers the Spanish Netherlands (including Luxembourg) to Austria. Depleted of men and money, the Netherlands declines in the 18th century.

1785–87 Revolt of the Patriot Party in the Netherlands, which temporarily drives out the stadtholder William V; he is restored with the help of his brother-in-law, Frederick William of Prussia.

1789–90 Inspired by events in France, the Brabançonne revolution succeeds in overthrowing Austrian rule in Belgium, but divisions between conservatives and liberals allow the Austrians to regain their territory.

1795 In the Netherlands, the Patriots eject the stadtholder and establish the Batavian Republic; the French defeat the Austrians and annex the Belgian provinces and Luxembourg.

1806–10 Napoléon establishes the Kingdom of Holland, ruled by his brother Louis Bonaparte, but finally annexes the Netherlands to France.

1815 Napoléon defeated at Waterloo, near Brussels. By the terms of the congress of Vienna, the Netherlands and Belgium are reunited under William I, but the union proves an unhappy one. Luxembourg is divided between William and Prussia.

1830 Again inspired by a revolution in France, the Belgians rise against William I and declare their independence.

1831 With the guarantees of the great powers, the Belgians draw up a constitution and elect as king Leopold of Saxe-Coburg (an uncle to soon-to-be-Queen Victoria of England).

1839 The Netherlands finally recognizes Belgium as an independent, neutral state. Luxembourg is again divided, with 60% going to Belgium while the rest remains a duchy, with William I of the Netherlands as grand duke.

1840 Faced by mounting popular opposition, William I abdicates in favor of his more liberal son, William II, who enacts reforms.

1865 Leopold II succeeds his father as king of the Belgians; begins reign as empire builder in Africa and rebuilder of Brussels at home. By the terms of an international agreement, the Prussian garrisons withdraw and Luxembourg's independence and neutrality are guaranteed.

1885 The establishment of the Congo Free State brings Belgium into the ranks of colonial powers.

1890 King William III of the Netherlands is succeeded by his daughter Wilhelmina; because Luxembourg bars female succession, the grand duchy passes to the house of Nassau-Weilburg.

1903 Birth of Georges Simenon (d. 1989), creator of Inspector Maigret and Belgium's most widely read author.

1908 Congo Free State annexed to Belgium.

1909 Albert succeeds Leopold II of Belgium; leads Belgian resistance from exile during World War I.

1914 In violation of the terms of the 1839 treaty, Germany invades and conquers Belgium at the outset of World War I. Luxembourg is also occupied; the Netherlands remains neutral.

1919 The Franco-Belgian alliance ends Belgian neutrality and signals the dominance of the French-speaking Walloons. Universal male suffrage is granted; in the Netherlands, where this had been enacted in 1917, women are now given the right to vote. In Luxembourg, a plebiscite confirms the continuation of the grand duchy under Grand Duchess Charlotte.

1934 Leopold III succeeds Albert on Belgian throne.

1940 May 10: Nazi Germany launches blitzkrieg attacks on Belgium, the Netherlands, and Luxembourg. The Dutch army surrenders May 14, the Belgians May 28. Grand Duchess Charlotte and Queen Wilhelmina flee; King Leopold III remains in Belgium, where he is eventually imprisoned. The Nazi occupation leaves lasting imprints on all three countries.

1942 Dutch Indonesia falls to the Japanese.

1944 Luxembourg City is liberated.

1947 The Marshall Plan helps rebuild devastated areas. Belgium, Netherlands, and Luxembourg form customs union.

1948 Queen Wilhelmina abdicates in favor of her daughter Juliana; the first of a series of Socialist governments initiates a Dutch welfare state. Women gain the vote in Belgium.

1949 The Netherlands and Luxembourg join NATO; the Dutch recognize Indonesian independence after much fighting.

1951 Amid controversy over his wartime role and continued ethnic dissension, King Leopold III of Belgium abdicates in favor of his son, Baudouin.

1957 Belgium, Netherlands, Luxembourg are charter members of the European Economic Community (EEC).

1960 A 50-year treaty establishes the Benelux Economic Union. The Belgian Congo gains independence.

1964 Grand Duchess Charlotte of Luxembourg abdicates in favor of her son, Jean.

1967 Already the center of the EEC, Brussels becomes host to NATO.

1975 Suriname wins its independence from the Netherlands.

1981 Queen Juliana of the Netherlands abdicates in favor of her daughter, Beatrix.

1993 King Baudouin of Belgium dies and is succeeded by his brother, Albert II.

1994 Belgium becomes a confederation with Flanders, Wallonia, and Brussels as semi-autonomous regions.

1995 Jacques Santer, Prime Minister of Luxembourg, is elected President of the European Commission.

1996 More than 300,000 people participate in a silent march in Brussels to demand improved child protection and access for victims in the "Julie and Melissa" tragedy to the judicial process.

—Anita Guerrini

LES MOULES SONT ARRIVÉES!

DAMP AND COLD mist the leaded-glass windows, but inside the café glows a scene worthy of a Flemish Master. The burnished wooden banquettes are Rembrandt's; the lace curtain, Vermeer's. Hals would have painted the diner, a lone bearded man in rumpled black leather and heavy, worn wool, his thick fingers clasping a broad-stemmed bowl of mahogany-brown beer. Before him lies a spread of crockery and mollusks, a still-life in themselves: The two-quart pot is heaped high with blue-black mussels, their shells flecked with bits of onion and celery, the broth beneath them steaming; beside them a bowl piled high with yellow *frites* (french fries), crisp and glistening; in the corner, a saucer of slabs of floury-gold cracked-wheat bread. The man works studiously, absorbed in a timeless ritual: Fish out the shell from the broth with fingers inured to the heat by years of practice. Pluck out the plump flesh with a fork and, while chewing the morsel, chuck the shell aside on a crockery plate. Sometimes he sets down the fork and uses the empty shell as pincers to draw out the meat of the next shell. As the meal progresses, the pile in the pot shrinks and the heap of empty shells grows. As the beer follows the mussels, its strong tonic paints the man's cheeks until two ruby patches radiate above his beard. The painting's caption: "Man eating moules."

It is the central image of the Flemish lowlands—the Netherlands, Flanders, even leaking into landlocked Wallonie and Luxembourg.

But this warmly lit interior scene wouldn't be as striking without its harsh exterior foil: Mussels, like the Dutch and the Flemish, are creatures of the sea; they flourish in cold, inky waters along rock-crusted shores, clustered and stacked like blue-black crystals in muddy tidal pools. They're a product of caustic sea winds and briny, chilly damp, and their bite tastes like salt air itself.

Most of the mussels consumed in the Benelux region come from the North Sea,

above all in the Waddenzee, off the northern coast of the Netherlands. Captured by the billions in great nets along the bottom of specially protected, fenced-off nursery beds, they are sorted by weight and auctioned to wholesalers in Zeeland, who return them to shallow tidal waters to recover from the trip, to mature, and to purge themselves of sandy mud. From there, they are harvested en masse and shipped live across Europe.

The cultivation of mussels dates from Roman times, though legend credits an Irish shipwreck victim who settled in La Rochelle, on the west coast of France; he is said to have noticed great colonies of the mollusks clinging to posts he planted to hold fishing nets. By placing posts closer together and arranging branches between them, he was able to create an ideal breeding ground and, in essence, mass-produce the delicacy. (The French, predictably enough, prefer their own, smaller mussels from the coasts of Brittany and Normandy, insisting that North Sea mussels are fleshy, dull, and vulgarly oversized.)

Scrubbed with stiff brushes under running water, soaked with salt to draw out the sand, and often fed flour to plump and purge them, mussels are served throughout the region in dozens of ways. The building block for French or Walloon recipes: simmering them *à la marinière*, in a savory stock of white wine, shallots, parsley, and butter. It's difficult to improve on this classic method, which brings out the best in mussels' musky sea essence—but chefs have been trying for centuries. Another common version is *à la crème*, the marinière stock thickened with flour-based white sauce and a generous portion of heavy cream. Flemish mussels, on the other hand, are nearly always served in a simple, savory vegetable stock, with bits of celery, leek, and onions creeping into the shells. The Dutch have been known to pickle them, or even to fry them in batter. Those who don't want to get their fingers messy may order their mussels *meunière*, removed from the shells in the kitchen and baked in a pool of garlicky butter. Regardless of the preparation, the Belgians and the Dutch wash their mussels down with beer, the Luxembourgers with an icy bottle of one of the coarser Moselle wines—an Elbling or a Rivaner.

Mussels rations are anything but stingy here, and on your first venture you may be appalled by the size of the lidded pot put before you. It's the shells that create the volume, and once you've plucked out the tender flesh, thrown away the shells, and sipped the broth and succulent strays from a colossal soup spoon, you'll soon find yourself at the bottom of the pot. Don't worry: Many restaurants will whisk it away and come back with Round Two—another mountain of the steamy blue creatures, another pool of savory broth. It's called *moules à volonté* (all you can eat), so gird yourself for a feast: The locals have been doing it for 2,000 years.

—Nancy Coons

BATTLE SCARS FROM THE BULGE

THE FIRST THING the sleepy American soldiers noticed was light—pinpoints of light blinking to the east, distinct in the pitch-black of an early midwinter morning. A second, or seconds, later (depending on their distance from the German frontier), there followed the roar of a thousand exploding shells, the pounding percussion of heavy artillery. Rockets and mortars screamed overhead while at five well-spaced points German foot soldiers poured through gaps in the sparsely protected front line, their way lit by searchlights that bounced off the clouds, flooding the land with eerie, artificial "moonlight."

It was 5:30 AM on December 16, 1944, along the eastern border of Belgium and Luxembourg. The Allied armed forces—having landed at Normandy in June and southern France in August and pressed steadily inland; having pushed the German armies back to the old Siegfried line and liberated France, Belgium, and Luxembourg by September; and having fought viciously, died in droves, and been hungry, filthy, and sleepless for weeks at a time—were reveling in the role of heroes in the relatively calm days before Christmas. That morning they were caught with their pants down in one of the most massive and successful surprise attacks in World War II. It was Hitler's last, desperate effort to regain western Europe, and it was one of the greatest failures of Allied intelligence in the war.

In September 1944, when Hitler first announced secret plans for an all-out attack on the western front, his army could scarcely have been in more desperate straits. More than 3½ million German men had died over the preceding five years, and massive Allied bombing raids were leveling German cities day by day. Not only had the enemy driven the Wehrmacht out of France, Belgium, and Luxembourg, but Italy was being lost in bitter fighting as well, and Russia had penetrated west to Warsaw and Bucharest. The Third Reich was in danger of being choked off from all sides, and Hitler—though not his more prudent command-

ers—saw no option but to strike out offensively. His goal: to take the all-important port at Antwerp, from where the River Schelde flowed from Belgium through the Netherlands and into the North Sea. By closing in on Antwerp, they would not only cut off the most likely source of new supplies, but also surround and capture some 1 million remaining Allied forces. His strategy: to surprise the Allies by attacking through the improbably rough, virtually impassable forest terrain of the Ardennes in southeastern Belgium and northern Luxembourg. He intended to overwhelm them with massive artillery fire, press on to take the strategic bridges of the River Meuse, reinforce with a second wave, and close out defenders with strong flanks at the north and south. Antwerp could be reached in a week, he insisted, and the Allies would be crippled by winter fog, snow, and mud.

For the task of inspiring a bitter, warweary army to what seemed even then to be a suicidal mission, Hitler named the aristocratic Gerd von Rundstedt commander in chief in the West. And, in a decision that was to set the tone for one of the most vicious and bloody conflicts in the war, in charge of the Sixth Panzer Army he placed Joseph "Sepp" Dietrich, an early Nazi loyalist and SS commander, chief executioner in the 1934 Nazi Party purge (the Night of the Long Knives), notorious for ordering the execution of more than 4,000 prisoners taken over three days at the Russian front. His kindred spirit: SS Lt. Col. Joachim Peiper, in charge of the SS Panzer Division called Leibstandarte Adolf Hitler and also notorious for brutal executions in Russia. It was Dietrich who passed on Hitler's inspirational message that this was "the decisive hour of the German people," that the attacking army was to create a "wave of terror and fright" without "humane inhibitions."

While the Germans were building up staggering quantities of materiel along the Siegfried line—tanks, artillery, rafts, and pontoons—and moving in men from all corners of the shrinking Reich, the Allied command remained remarkably unperceptive. Reconnaissance pilots flew over unwonted activity near Bitburg, Trier, and Koblenz—trains, truck convoys, heaps of equipment along the roads. Messages were intercepted and deciphered, some asking for increased forces, some for more detailed information on Ardennes and Meuse terrain. Yet Generals Bradley, Eisenhower, Middleton, and Patton continued to misinterpret, anticipating instead a predictable counterattack around Aachen and Cologne, well north of the Ardennes. (Hitler, in fact, counted on this interpretation, strutting a visible buildup of forces in the north while secretly preparing to attack elsewhere.) On December 12, an optimistic Allied intelligence summary described the vulnerability and "deathly weakness" of German forces in the area.

ON THE EVENING of December 15, the German soldiers—until then as unaware of the plan as the Allies—were finally told what morning would bring. The message from von Rundstedt: "We gamble everything . . . to achieve things beyond human possibilities for our Fatherland and our Führer!" Some, convinced the cause was lost, faced the news of further carnage with dismay; others saw a final opportunity to avenge the civilian death toll in German cities. Members of the SS, the greatest believers in the Nazi effort and thus the least restrained by the niceties of the Geneva Convention, welcomed the "holy task" with a blood lust that was to be more than sated in the weeks to come.

That night, across the border in Luxembourg, German-born film star Marlene Dietrich performed for American soldiers and went to bed early.

They attacked at 5:30 AM with a thoroughness and a ruthlessness that impressed soldiers even through their bewilderment. The assault crippled communications, and word moved as slowly as in the era before telegraph. Twenty miles from one prong of the attack, Gen. Omar Bradley had breakfast at the Hotel Alfa in Luxembourg City and, blithely unaware of the change in situation, headed toward Paris for a meeting with Eisenhower, who had just that day been promoted to five-star General of the Army. Neither heard of the conflict until late afternoon; neither be-

lieved, at first sketchy report, that it was anything more than a flash in the pan.

It was. From the first wave of "artillery-prepared" assaults—meaning systems stunned by a barrage of shells, followed by a surge of infantry attacks—to the sharp, startled, and for the most part instinctive defense of the Allies, the offensive was to escalate quickly into a battle of staggering scale, the Americans surprising the Germans in their tenacity, the Germans surprising the Americans with their almost maniacal dedication.

Over a month and a half, the two sides bludgeoned each other, struggling through harsh terrain and winter muck, reducing medieval castles to smoking rubble, and razing villages that had been liberated only months before. The ferocious tone of the fight was set early on: On December 17, SS officers of Lieutenant Colonel Peiper ordered the execution of 130 American prisoners outside Malmédy. The victims were left where they fell, periodically kicked for signs of life, and shot again. A few who survived, hiding the steam of their breath, crawled away when night fell and told their story, and the massacre at Malmédy became a rallying point for the bitter Allies. Prisoners of war were murdered on both sides, and at times the gunfights took on a guerrilla aspect, with those in danger of capture, fearing execution, dissolving into the dense forest to go it alone.

And not only soldiers were killed. On December 18, in and near Stavelot, Peiper's SS troops ordered whole families of civilians from their cellars—women, children, elderly men—and shot them methodically; the toll reached 138. On December 24, SS security men assembled all the men of Bande, screened out those over 32, stripped them of watches and rosaries, and executed them one by one. The sole survivor, before he slugged his way free and dashed for the forest, noticed that his would-be executioner was weeping.

And on December 23, Americans wrought their own kind of horror in Malmédy when Army Air Corps Marauders, headed for the German railroad center of Zulpich, mistakenly emptied 86 bombs on the village center, killing as many of its own troops as innocent citizens. As the people dug out from the rubble on December 24, another misguided swarm of American bombers dropped an even more lethal load, leveling what was left of the center. On December 25, four more planes mistook Malmédy for St. Vith and dropped 64 more bombs. Civilian victims—refugees and residents alike—were laid in rows in the school playground.

IT WASN'T A VERY MERRY Christmas anywhere in the Ardennes that year. Sleepless, shell-shocked, often out of touch, soldiers from both sides huddled in icy pillboxes and snowy foxholes. Propaganda flyers fluttered down, carefully phrased in the recipients' mother tongue. For the Americans, the not-so-inspirational message admonished them: "Why are you here? What are you doing, fighting somebody else's war? You will die and your wife, your mother, your daughters will be left alone. Merry Christmas!" For the Germans, the American pamphlets simply assured them they were losing the war, and that they'd long since lost the battle.

That wasn't altogether clear until well into January. By the time the carnage slowed and the tide turned, the Germans had pressed deep into Belgium, the central thrust "bulging" west to within miles of the Meuse and Dinant. Though Hitler grudgingly ordered retreat from the farthest point of the Bulge on January 8, the Germans fought through January 28, as they were driven all the way back to the Siegfried line.

Some 19,000 American soldiers died, and at least as many Germans. Hundreds of Belgian and Luxembourg citizens died as well, and survivors came back to find their villages flattened, their churches gaping shells, their castles—having survived assault for centuries—reduced to heaps of ancient stone. In Luxembourg, the towns of Diekirch, Clervaux, Vianden, and Echternach were prime battle zones, charred and crumbled. In Belgium, St. Vith, Houffalize, and myriad Ardennes resort towns like La Roche were wasted by artillery "preparation" and the gun-and-grenade battles

that ensued. And Bastogne, surrounded, besieged, and pounded by artillery for days, lost what was left of its town center in the concentrated bombing Hitler ordered for Christmas Eve.

Today, throughout the Ardennes region, the faces of monuments and main streets are incongruously new and shiny, their resourceful owners having taken charred, roofless, windowless shells and made the best of the worst by installing new plumbing, modern wiring, efficient windows, central heat. Yet there are scars, visible and invisible. Behind the caulked shrapnel holes, which pock foundations and farmhouse walls here and there, lurk bitter memories that weren't altogether appeased at Nuremburg. And the ugliness of the conflict, distorted by a new generation, occasionally rears its head: On the stone memorial at the crossroads outside Malmédy, where the names of the victims of the massacre have been carved, someone has spray-painted a swastika.

The cultural chasm between the two sides of the battle seems embodied in the two military cemeteries outside Luxembourg City. The American plot at Hamm is a blaze of white-marbl e glory, its 5,000 graves radiating in graceful arcs under open sun, its well-tended grass worn by the shoes of visitors. The German plot, just down the road at Sandweiler, lies apart, heavily shaded and concealed from view, with a few hundred low, dark-stone crosses marking the graves of some 5,000 men. Yet another 5,000, gathered in battle by the U.S. Army Burial Service and dumped unceremoniously in mass graves, were transferred here and buried under one heavy cross, as many as possible identified in fine print crowded on a broad bronze plaque. Those graves are tended today by busloads of German schoolchildren, who visit in the name of a concept long overdue: *Versöhnung über den Gräbern—Arbeit für den Frieden* (Reconcilation over the graves—work for peace).

—Nancy Coons

BOOKS

Netherlands

A visit to the Netherlands is greatly enhanced by a knowledge of the nation's history and a familiarity with its rich art heritage. Books of particular value and interest include *Amsterdam: The Life of a City,* by Geoffrey Cotterell (Little, Brown; 1972), a comprehensive history of the city; *Diary of Anne Frank* (in a new, improved translation from Penguin), the diary of a young Jewish girl that details the experience of living in hiding in Amsterdam during World War II; and *Images of a Golden Past,* by Christopher Brown (Abbeville, 1984), a guide to Dutch genre painting of the 17th century.

Some worthwhile histories include *The Dutch Revolt,* by Geoffrey Parker (Peregrine/Penguin, 1977), a history of the development of the Dutch nation; *The Dutch Seaborne Empire 1600–1800,* by C.R. Boxer (Penguin, 1965), which traces the development of the great Dutch trading companies in the 17th and 18th centuries; and *The Embarrassment of Riches,* by Simon Schama (Alfred A. Knopf, 1987/University of California Press, 1988), an outstanding interpretation of Dutch culture in its Golden Age. *Evolution of the Dutch Nation,* by Bernard H.M. Vlekke (Roy, 1945), is a comprehensive history of the Netherlands. *The UnDutchables: An Observation of the Netherlands; Its Culture and Its Inhabitants,* by Colin White and Laurie Boucke (White-Boucke, 1992), is a humorous portrait of the Dutch.

In addition, Janwillem Van de Wetering's mystery novels (Ballantine), set in Amsterdam, can make for good light reading on the plane.

Belgium

Barbara Tuchman's *A Distant Mirror* (Knopf, 1978) describing 14th-century European affairs, gives valuable insights, illuminated by memorable vignettes, into the conflicts between Flemish towns and the Crown of France. *The Guns of August* (Bantam, 1982) applies Tuchman's narrative technique to the events, largely in Bel-

gium, of the first month of World War I. John Keegan's *The Face of Battle* (Viking Penguin, 1983) includes a brilliant analysis of the Battle of Waterloo. Leon Wolff's *In Flanders Fields* (Greenwood, 1984) is a classic account of the catastrophic campaign of 1917, while John Toland's *No Man's Land* (Ballantine, 1985) covers the events on the Western Front in 1918.

William Wharton's *A Midnight Clear* (Ballantine, 1983) is a fictional account of the Ardennes battle as seen by American GIs. *Outrageous Fortune* (1984) by Roger Keyes is a sympathetic account of the role played by Leopold III up to 1940. Hugo Claus's *The Sorrow of Belgium* (Pantheon, 1990) an outstanding novel of life during the occupation, has been translated into many languages from the original Dutch.

Two 19th-century novels well worth dipping into are Georges Rodenbach's *Bruges-la-Morte,* (Dufour, 1986) which was contemporaneous with the rediscovery of Brugge, and Charles de Coster's picaresque *La legende d'Ulenspiegel,* which captures the spirit of Belgian defiance of outside authority. Both have been translated into English.

Maurice Maeterlinck, Marguerite Yourcenar, and Georges Simenon were all Belgian writers working in French. So was Jacques Brel, many of whose songs also contain outstanding poetry. Hergé set many of the *Tintin* cartoon adventures in foreign lands, but Tintin himself remained always the quintessential *bon petit Belge.*

Luxembourg

The Grand Duchy of Luxembourg: The Evolution of a Nationhood by James Newcomer (University Press of America, Lanham, MD, 1984) is an extensive, fairly readable history of the Grand Duchy's early woes. *A Time for Trumpets* by Charles B. MacDonald (William Morrow and Company, 1985) gives a blow-by-blow account of the Ardennes offensive, as does *The Battle of the Bulge* by Roland Gaul (two volumes, Schiffer Military Books, 1995).

FILMS

The Netherlands

A number of Dutch movies have been nominated for and/or won Oscars for best foreign film in recent years. Among them is *Karakter* (1997), set in the early 20th century and directed by Mike van Diem, which examines the relationship between a son and his cruel father while depicting social changes taking place in Rotterdam. Feminist director Marleen Gorris's *Antonia's Line* (1995) humorously and gently tells the story of an independent-minded woman who returns to her Dutch village with her daughter after World War II and ends up taking care of everyone. In the powerful, rather grim *The Assault* (1986), director Fons Rademakers explores lives torn apart—even 40 years later—by the horrors of the Nazi occupation. *Soldier of Orange* (1977), crafted by veteran director Paul Verhoeven, focuses on a similar theme in a character study showing the effects of the occupation on a group of Dutch students.

Belgium

Movies that give a sense of aspects of life in Belgium include the award-winning *Ma Vie en Rose* (*My Life in Pink*; 1997), directed by Alain Berliner, which concerns the threats to comfortable bourgeois culture posed by a little boy who truly believes he will turn into a girl. *La Promesse* (*The Promise*; 1996), a thought-provoking film directed by Jean-Pierre Dardenne and Luc Dardenne, examines the lives of a group of immigrants surviving (or not) on the edge of Belgian society and a boy who becomes involved with them. In the blackly comic *Toto the Hero* (1991) director Jaco Van Dormael transforms an old man's recollections into a somewhat suspect universal portrait of modern man.

VOCABULARY

Dutch Vocabulary

English	Dutch	Pronunciation
Basics		
Yes/no	Ja, nee	yah, nay
Please	Alstublieft	**ahls**-too-bleeft
Thank you	Dank u	**dahnk** oo
You're welcome	Niets te danken	neets teh **dahn**-ken
Excuse me, sorry	Pardon	pahr-**don**
Good morning	Goede morgen	**hoh**-deh **mor**-ghen
Good evening	Goede avond	**hoh**-deh **ahv**-unt
Goodbye	Dag!	dah
Numbers		
one	een	ehn
two	twee	tveh
three	drie	dree
four	vier	veer
five	vijf	vehf
six	zes	zehss
seven	zeven	**zeh**-vehn
eight	acht	ahkht
nine	negen	**neh**-ghen
ten	tien	teen
Days of the Week		
Sunday	zondag	**zohn**-dagh
Monday	maandag	**mahn**-dagh
Tuesday	dinsdag	**dinns**-dagh
Wednesday	woensdag	**voons**-dagh
Thursday	donderdag	**don**-der-dagh
Friday	vrijdag	**vreh**-dagh
Saturday	zaterdag	**zah**-ter-dagh
Useful Phrases		
Do you speak English?	Spreekt U Engels?	sprehkt oo **ehn**-gls
I don't speak Dutch	Ik spreek geen Nederlands	ihk sprehk **ghen** **Ned**-er-lahnds
I don't understand	Ik begrijp het niet	ihk be-**ghrehp** het neet
I don't know	Ik weet niet	ihk **veht** ut neet
I'm American/English	Ik ben Amerikaans/Engels	ihk ben Am-er-ee-**kahns**/Ehn-gls
Where is . . . the train station? the post office? the hospital?	Waar is . . . het station? het postkantoor? het ziekenhuis?	vahr iss heht stah-**syohn** het **pohst**-kahn-tohr het **zeek**-uhn-haus

Where are the restrooms?	waar is de WC?	**vahr** iss de **veh**-seh
Left/right	links/rechts	leenks/rehts
How much is this?	Hoeveel kost dit?	hoo-**vehl** kohst deet
It's expensive/ cheap	Het is te duur/ goedkoop	het ees teh **dour**/ **hood**-kohp
I am ill/sick	Ik ben ziek	ihk behn zeek
I want to call a doctor	Ik wil een docter bellen	ihk veel ehn **dohk**-ter **behl**-len
Help!	Help!	help
Stop!	Stoppen!	**stop**-pen

Dining Out

Bill/check	de rekening	de **rehk**-en-eeng
Bread	brood	brohd
Butter	boter	**boh**-ter
Fork	vork	fork
I'd like to order	Ik wil graag bestellen	Ihk veel khrah behs-**tell**-en
Knife	een mes	ehn mehs
Menu	menu/kaart	men-**oo**/kahrt
Napkin	en servet	ehn ser-**veht**
Pepper	peper	**peh**-per
Please give me . . .	mag ik [een] . . .	mahkh ihk [ehn] . . .
Salt	zout	zoot
Spoon	een lepel	ehn **leh**-pehl
Sugar	suiker	**sigh**-kur

French Vocabulary

English	French	Pronunciation

Basics

Yes/no	Oui/non	wee/no
Please	S'il vous plaît	seel voo play
Thank you	Merci	mare-**see**
You're welcome	De rien	deh ree-**en**
Excuse me, sorry	Pardon	pahr-**doan**
Good morning/ afternoon	Bonjour	bone-**joor**
Good evening	Bonsoir	bone-**swar**
Goodbye	Au revoir	o ruh-**vwar**

Numbers

one	un	un
two	deux	dew
three	trois	twa
four	quatre	**cat**-ruh
five	cinq	sank
six	six	seess
seven	sept	set
eight	huit	wheat
nine	neuf	nuf
ten	dix	deess

Days of the Week

Sunday	dimanche	dee-**mahnsh**
Monday	lundi	lewn-**dee**
Tuesday	mardi	mar-**dee**
Wednesday	mercredi	mare-kruh-**dee**
Thursday	jeudi	juh-**dee**
Friday	vendredi	van-dra-**dee**
Saturday	samedi	sam-**dee**

Useful Phrases

Do you speak English?	Parlez-vous anglais?	**par**-lay vooz ahng-**glay**
I don't speak French	Je ne parle pas français	jeh nuh parl pah fraun-**say**
I don't understand	Je ne comprends pas	jeh nuh kohm-prahn **pah**
I don't know	Je ne sais pas	jeh nuh say **pah**
I'm American/ British	Je suis américain/ anglais	jeh sweez a-may-ree-**can**/ahng-**glay**
Where is . . . the train station? the post office? the hospital?	Où est . . . la gare? la poste? l'hôpital?	oo ay la gar la post low-pee-**tahl**
Where are the restrooms?	Où sont les toilettes?	oo son lay twah-**let**
Left/right	A gauche/à droite	a goash/a drwat
How much is it? It's expensive/ cheap	C'est combien? C'est cher/pas cher	say comb-bee-**en** say sher/pa sher
I am ill/sick	Je suis malade	jeh swee ma-**lahd**
Call a doctor	Appelez un docteur	a-pe-lay un dohk-**tore**
Help!	Au secours!	o say-**koor**
Stop!	Arrêtez!	a-ruh-**tay**

Dining Out

Bill/check	l'addition	la-dee-see-**own**
Bread	du pain	due pan
Butter	du beurre	due bur
Fork	une fourchette	ewn four-**shet**
I'd like . . .	Je voudrais . . .	jeh voo-**dray**
Knife	un couteau	un koo-**toe**
Menu	la carte	la cart
Napkin	une serviette	ewn sair-vee-**et**
Pepper	du poivre	due **pwah**-vruh
Salt	du sel	dew sell
Spoon	une cuillère	ewn kwee-**air**
Sugar	du sucre	due **sook**-ruh

INDEX

Nederlands
  Architectuurinstituut, *88*
Nederlands Filmmuseum, *37*
Nederlands Keramiekmuseum
  Het Princessehof, *131*
Nederlands Openlucht
  Museum, *128*
Nederlands
  Scheepvaartmuseum, *40*
Netherlands, *4–6, 9–10, 24,
  26.* ☞ Amsterdam; Border
  Provinces; Folkloric
  Holland;"Green Heart" of
  Netherlands; Metropolitan
  Holland; Northern
  Provinces
books on, 344
business hours, 147
car rentals, 145
climate, xxxii
costs, 147
currency, 147
customs and duties, 145
dining, 26–27
guided tours, 145–146
*itinerary recommendations,
  28–30*
languages, xxiii, 146
lodging, 27, 146
mail, 146–147
outdoor activities, 147–148
student and youth travel, 148
telephones, 148–149
timing the visit, xxxii, 30
tipping, 149
*transportation, 144–145,
  149–150*
visitor information, xxxi, 150
Netherlands American
  Cemetery and Memorial,
  116
newMetropolis Science &
  Technology Center, *40*
Nieuwe Kerk (Amsterdam),
  45
Nieuwe Kerk (Delft), *85*
Nieuwpoort, Bel., *235*
Nijmegen, Neth., *129*
Nivelles, Bel., *203*
Noordbrabants Museum, *109*
Noordwijk, Neth., *64*
Noordwijk Space Expo, *78*
Northeast Belgium, *256*
*dining/lodging, 258, 259,
  260–261, 262*
outdoor activities, 262
transportation, 262
visitor information, 263
Northern Provinces, Neth., *6,
  130–131*
*dining/lodging, 133–134, 135,
  137, 138, 140*
emergencies, 143
festivals, 137
guided tours, 143
nightlife, 134, 141
*outdoor activities, 134–135,
  141*
shopping, 135, 141

transportation, 141–143
visitor information, 143
North Sea Coast, Bel.,
  231–237
arts/nightlife, 233, 237
*dining/lodging, 232–233, 235,
  236–237*
guided tours, 238–239
*outdoor activities, 233–234,
  237, 239*
transportation, 237–239
visitor information, 240
North Sea Jazz Festival, *83*
Notre-Dame church (Dinant),
  267
Notre-Dame de Scourmont,
  202

O
Oceade, *169*
Oisterwijk, Neth., *108–109*
Omniversum, *80*
Onze Lieve Vrouwe Abdij,
  104
Onze-Lieve-Vrouwebasiliek
  (Maastricht), *112*
Onze-Lieve-Vrouwebasiliek
  (Tongeren), *260*
Onze-Lieve-
  Vrouwekathedraal
  (Antwerp), *245–246*
Onze-Lieve-Vrouwekerk
  (Brugge), *220–221*
Onze-Lieve-Vrouwekerk
  (Damme), *227*
Onze-Lieve-Vrouweplein
  (Kortrijk), *228*
Onze-Lieve-Vrouweplein
  (Maastricht), *112–113*
Onze-Lieve-Vrouw ter
  Duinenkerk, *234*
Oostduinkerke, Bel., *235*
Oostende, Bel., *231–234*
Openluchtmuseum
  Middelheim, *249*
Opera
Amsterdam, 56
Antwerp, 252
Brussels, 183
Liège, 278
*metropolitan Holland, 83,
  96*
Oude Griffie, *221*
Oude Kerk (Amsterdam), *41*
Oude Kerk (Delft), *85*
Oudeschild, Neth., *70*
Oudheidskamer, *70*
Outdoor activities. ☞ *Under
  countries, cities and
  areas*

P
Package deals for travelers,
  xxix
Belgium, 293
Luxembourg, 330
Netherlands, 146
Packing for the trip, *xxv–xxvi*

Palace of Charles of Lorraine,
  168
Palace Het Loo, *120–121*
Palaces. ☞ Castles and
  palaces
Palais de Justice, *167*
Palais des Beaux-Arts
  (Brussels), *168–169*
Palais des Princes-Evèques,
  273–274
Palais du Roi, *167*
Palais Grand-Ducal, *308*
Parachuting, *72*
Parc de Bruxelles, *167*
Park Paradisio, *196*
Passports and visas, *xxvi*
Patton, George, *327*
Paul Delvaux Museum, *234*
Petite Suisse, Lux., *323–324*
Photographers, tips for, *xiv*
Pieterskerk (Leiden), *77*
Pilgrims' Hall, *229*
Plackendael Animal Farm,
  190
Plaine de Jeux Mont Mosan
  playground, *272*
Planetariums, *135*
Plane travel, *xii–xiii*
Amsterdam, 64–65
Antwerp, 255
Belgium, 292
border provinces (Neth.), 118
Brussels, 193
children, flying with, xvi–xvii
cutting costs, xx–xxi
luggage, rules on, xxv
Luxembourg, 317, 328–329
Netherlands, 144, 149
Plan Incliné de Ronquières,
  201
Plantin-Moretus Museum, *246*
Poperinge, *230–231*
Porcelain, shopping for, *28,
  87, 316*
Portugees Israelitische
  Synagogue, *41*
Pottery factories, *135–136*
Praetbos-Vlasdo war
  cemetery, *230*
Préhistosite de Ramioul,
  276
Price charts (dining/lodging)
Belgium, 155
Luxembourg, 301
Netherlands, 27
Prinsenhoftuin, *139*
Prins Hendrik Maritime
  Museum, *87*
Print shops, *316*
Provinciaal Diamantmuseum,
  246
Provinciaal Museum Constant
  Permeke, *232*
Provinciaal Museum voor
  Fotographie, *247*
Provinciaal Museum voor
  Religieuze Kunst, *260*
Puppet shows, *56, 278*
Purnode, Bel., *268*

NOTES

NOTES

NOTES

NOTES

NOTES

NOTES

With guidebooks for every kind of travel—from weekend getaways to island hopping to adventures abroad—it's easy to understand why smart travelers go with **Fodor's**.

At bookstores everywhere.
www.fodors.com

Smart travelers go with **Fodor's**™

Fodor's Travel Publications

Available at bookstores everywhere. For descriptions of all our titles and a key to Fodor's guidebook series, visit http://www.fodors.com/books/

Gold Guides

U.S.

Alaska	Florida	New Orleans	Santa Fe, Taos, Albuquerque
Arizona	Hawai'i	New York City	Seattle & Vancouver
Boston	Las Vegas, Reno, Tahoe	Oregon	The South
California		Pacific North Coast	U.S. & British Virgin Islands
Cape Cod, Martha's Vineyard, Nantucket	Los Angeles	Philadelphia & the Pennsylvania Dutch Country	USA
The Carolinas & Georgia	Maine, Vermont, New Hampshire		Virginia & Maryland
	Maui & Lāna'i	The Rockies	Washington, D.C.
Chicago	Miami & the Keys	San Diego	
Colorado	New England	San Francisco	

Foreign

Australia	Europe	Montréal & Québec City	Scotland
Austria	Florence, Tuscany & Umbria	Moscow, St. Petersburg, Kiev	Singapore
The Bahamas			South Africa
Belize & Guatemala	France	The Netherlands, Belgium & Luxembourg	South America
Bermuda	Germany		Southeast Asia
Canada	Great Britain	New Zealand	Spain
Cancún, Cozumel, Yucatán Peninsula	Greece	Norway	Sweden
	Hong Kong	Nova Scotia, New Brunswick, Prince Edward Island	Switzerland
Caribbean	India		Thailand
China	Ireland		Toronto
Costa Rica	Israel	Paris	Turkey
Cuba	Italy	Portugal	Vienna & the Danube Valley
The Czech Republic & Slovakia	Japan	Provence & the Riviera	
	London		Vietnam
Denmark	Madrid & Barcelona	Scandinavia	
Eastern & Central Europe	Mexico		

Special-Interest Guides

Adventures to Imagine	Fodor's How to Pack	Kodak Guide to Shooting Great Travel Pictures	Rock & Roll Traveler USA
Alaska Ports of Call	Great American Learning Vacations		Sunday in San Francisco
Ballpark Vacations		National Parks and Seashores of the East	
The Best Cruises	Great American Sports & Adventure Vacations		Walt Disney World for Adults
Caribbean Ports of Call		National Parks of the West	
	Great American Vacations		Weekends in New York
The Complete Guide to America's National Parks		Nights to Imagine	
	Great American Vacations for Travelers with Disabilities	Orlando Like a Pro	Wendy Perrin's Secrets Every Smart Traveler Should Know
Europe Ports of Call		Rock & Roll Traveler Great Britain and Ireland	
Family Adventures	Halliday's New Orleans Food Explorer		
Fodor's Gay Guide to the USA			Worlds to Imagine
	Healthy Escapes		

Fodor's Special Series

Fodor's Best Bed & Breakfasts
America
California
The Mid-Atlantic
New England
The Pacific Northwest
The South
The Southwest
The Upper Great Lakes

Compass American Guides
Alaska
Arizona
Boston
Chicago
Coastal California
Colorado
Florida
Hawai'i
Hollywood
Idaho
Las Vegas
Maine
Manhattan
Minnesota
Montana
New Mexico
New Orleans
Oregon
Pacific Northwest
San Francisco
Santa Fe
South Carolina
South Dakota
Southwest
Texas
Underwater Wonders
of the National Parks
Utah
Virginia
Washington
Wine Country
Wisconsin
Wyoming

Citypacks
Amsterdam
Atlanta
Berlin
Boston
Chicago
Florence
Hong Kong
London
Los Angeles
Miami
Montréal
New York City
Paris

Prague
Rome
San Francisco
Sydney
Tokyo
Toronto
Venice
Washington, D.C.

Exploring Guides
Australia
Boston &
New England
Britain
California
Canada
Caribbean
China
Costa Rica
Cuba
Egypt
Florence & Tuscany
Florida
France
Germany
Greek Islands
Hawai'i
India
Ireland
Israel
Italy
Japan
London
Mexico
Moscow &
St. Petersburg
New York City
Paris
Portugal
Prague
Provence
Rome
San Francisco
Scotland
Singapore & Malaysia
South Africa
Spain
Thailand
Turkey
Venice
Vietnam

Flashmaps
Boston
New York
San Francisco
Washington, D.C.

Fodor's Cityguides
Boston
New York
San Francisco

Fodor's Gay Guides
Amsterdam
Los Angeles & Southern California
New York City
Pacific Northwest
San Francisco and
the Bay Area
South Florida
USA

Karen Brown Guides
Austria
California
England B&Bs
England, Wales & Scotland
France B&Bs
France Inns
Germany
Ireland
Italy B&Bs
Italy Inns
Portugal
Spain
Switzerland

Pocket Guides
Acapulco
Aruba
Atlanta
Barbados
Beijing
Berlin
Budapest
Dublin
Honolulu
Jamaica
London
Mexico City
New York City
Paris
Prague
Puerto Rico
Rome
San Francisco
Savannah & Charleston
Shanghai
Sydney
Washington, D.C.

Languages for Travelers (Cassette & Phrasebook)
French
German
Italian
Spanish

Mobil Travel Guides
America's Best
Hotels & Restaurants
Arizona

California and the West
Florida
Great Lakes
Major Cities
Mid-Atlantic
Northeast
Northwest and
Great Plains
Southeast
Southern California
Southwest and
South Central

Rivages Guides
Bed and Breakfasts
of Character and
Charm in France
Hotels and Country
Inns of Character and
Charm in France
Hotels and Country
Inns of Character and
Charm in Italy
Hotels of Character
and Charm in Paris
Hotels of Character
and Charm in Portugal
Hotels of Character
and Charm in Spain
Wines & Vineyards
of Character and
Charm in France

Short Escapes
Britain
France
Near New York City
New England

Fodor's Sports
Golf Digest's
Places to Play (USA)
Golf Digest's
Places to Play
in the Southeast
Golf Digest's
Places to Play
in the Southwest
Skiing USA
USA Today
The Complete Four
Sport Stadium Guide

Fodor's upCLOSE Guides
California
Europe
France
Great Britain
Ireland
Italy
London
Los Angeles
Mexico
New York City
Paris
San Francisco

WHEREVER YOU TRAVEL, *H*ELP IS NEVER FAR AWAY.

From planning your trip to providing travel assistance along the way, American Express® Travel Service Offices are always there to help you do more.

The Netherlands, Belgium & Luxembourg

Amsterdam
American Express Travel Service
Van Baerlestraat 39
(31)(20) 6738550

Amsterdam
American Express Travel Service
Damrak 66
(31)(20) 5048777

Rotterdam
American Express Travel Service
92 Meent
(31)(10) 2803040

Brussels
American Express Travel Service
Retail Travel Call Center
100 Boulevard du Souverain
(32)(2) 6762727

do more AMERICAN EXPRESS

Travel
www.americanexpress.com/travel

Listings are valid as of March 1999.
Not all services available at all locations. © 1999 American Express.